Drugs and Drug Use in Society

A Critical Reader

edited by

ROSS COOMBER

PRINCIPAL LECTURER IN SOCIOLOGY
UNIVERSITY OF GREENWICH

Greenwich University Press

First published in 1994 by
Greenwich University Press
Unit 42
Dartford Trade Park
Hawley Road
Dartford
Kent DA1 1PF
United Kingdom

A CIP catalogue record for this book is available from the British Library

ISBN 1 874529 30 2

Designed and produced for Greenwich University Press by
Angela Allwright, Kirsten Brown, Helen Leather and Susan Smith.

Printed in Great Britain by The Bath Press, Avon.

Contents

Preface   ix

Prominent Drugs and Their Effects   1

1.   Crack in Liverpool   2
    RUSSELL NEWCOMBE AND LYN MATTHEWS

2.   What Drugs do to Users   5
    RICHARD MILLER

3.   The Effects of Drugs   24
    MICHAEL GOSSOP

The Nature of Addiction - Not a *Simple* Issue   37

4.   Is Alcoholism a Disease?   38
    NICK HEATHER AND IAN ROBERTSON

5.   Drug Dependence: Myth or Motive?   44
    JOHN FALK

6.   Excessive Gambling   58
    JIM ORFORD

7.   Dependence and Society   73
    ROBIN ROOM

Keeping Control of Drugs and Drug Users   84

8.   The Dynamics of Narcotics Control   85
    DAVID MUSTO

9.   The Drug Takers 1920-1970   90
    PHILIP BEAN

10.   The Punishment Illusion: Your Money *and* Your Life   117
    N. DORN, K. MURJI AND N. SOUTH

Treatment and Rehabilitation   135

11.   Developing Treatment Policies - Care Versus Control   137
    GERRY STIMSON AND EDNA OPPENHEIMER

12.   Aids and British Drug Policy: History Repeats Itself ... ?   154
    VIRGINIA BERRIDGE

13.   The Smoking Option   171
    JOHN MARKS, ANDREW PALOMBELLA AND RUSSELL NEWCOMBE

Drugs Education   175

14.   Looking for Effective Drug Education Programmes: Fifteen Years'
    Exploration of the Effects of Different Drug Education Programmes   177
    WILLY F.M. DE HAES

15. Drug Education to School Children:Does it Really Work?   185
    HARITH SWADI AND HARRY ZEITLIN

16. Willy Whizz   194
    S.S.H.A.

17. Paranoia and the Don't Care Bears   195
    LIFELINE

18. High in the 'E' Stand   199
    LIFELINE

Moral Panics, Drugs and Drug Use   200

19. The Sociology of Moral Panics: Toward a New Synthesis   201
    NACHMAN BEN-YEHUDA

20. A Siamese Cat in the Council Flat   221
    MAREK KOHN

21. The Media Press the Panic Button   239
    ALEX CORINA

The Problem Today   243

22. Beyond Opiates ... and into the '90s   244
    MARK GILMAN

23. Where Does All the Snow Go? - The Prevalence and
    Pattern of Cocaine and Crack Use in Britain   249
    HARRY SHAPIRO

Drugs and Crime   264

24. Drugs Crime and Violence   265
    ROBERT POWER

25. Summary Thoughts About Drugs and Violence   271
    JAMES J. COLLINS

26. Drugs and Predatory Crime   281
    JAN M. CHAIKEN AND MARCIA R. CHAIKEN

The War on Drugs - Can It Be Won?   311

27. Can a War on Drugs Succeed?   313
    GERRY STIMSON

28. International Law Enforcement: The Futile Quest for
    Control of Coca and Cocaine at the Source   319
    STEVEN WISOTSKY

29. Full Tilt Towards a No-Win 'Vietnam' War on Drugs   330
    TIM MALYON

The Legalisation of Drugs?   338

30. Narcotics: the problem and the solution   340
    E.J. MISHAN

31.   Against the Legalization of Drugs   360
JAMES Q. WILSON

32.   The Ethics of Addiction   373
THOMAS S. SZASZ

Drugs in Sport: Moral Dilemmas   383

33.   Drugs in Sport: Rhetoric or Pragmatism   384
ROSS COOMBER

34.   A Question of Drugs   396
ELLIS CASHMORE

Preface

Presenting a set of readings around (primarily illicit) drugs and their use is a difficult task. Obviously, the texts chosen must be included to the exclusion of others and attempts to be comprehensive are precluded by space, time and cost. I therefore made the decision to compile a set of texts which would provide the reader with access to perspectives which differ from those conventionally presented by the media, politicians and many high-profile education campaigns and programmes. Any understanding of drugs and their use in British or other Western societies is usefully enhanced by recourse to a range of inter-disciplinary approaches and to cross-cultural evidence about drug effects, addictive states and how the problem is perceived elsewhere, and these have been used where appropriate and/or available. There has been no attempt to provide a definitive set of readings in the given topic areas, but the extracts and articles raise useful and interesting points. In many cases however, although the perspectives given are at odds with commonly held beliefs and political rhetoric, they are nonetheless considered less than radical amongst researchers in the drugs field itself.

The Reader constitutes an attempt to dispel, counter and question assumptions about illicit drugs and drug users and many of the common misconceptions which surround them. As with Readers in other topics or disciplines, this Reader works its way through a range of relevant topic areas. Where it perhaps differs from other Readers is in its thematic style. The Reader has been compiled in such way that it is designed to build progressively upon the foundations provided by the preceding topic area(s) and in this way often has more of a feel of an edited book with writers contributing on a particular theme. In this way, it is intended that some of the later debates on the merits or drawbacks of existing and/or future policy, whether they be to do with treatment practices, education approaches or the legalisation of drugs, are more reliably informed if the earlier topics have been covered first. This is perhaps particularly true of the last two sections, *The Legalisation of Drugs Debate* and *Drugs in Sport*, the latter of which is often believed to exist as a problem separate from the problem of illicit drug use in the non-sporting world. Each topic area, however, should also be able to stand alone to a reasonable degree, allowing the 'dipping' in and out of topic areas according to personal interest.

The selections vary in their depth. This is so that the Reader is both accessible to those being introduced to the issues contained within and facilitative in raising critical questions for those who need to delve deeper. Most topic sections carry at least one text designed to introduce the reader to an advanced level of debate within that area. Complimentary to the texts, at the beginning of each section, there is a brief introduction to the issues covered, drawing the reader's attention to a number of the pertinent aspects covered and contextualising the area further. For some, a glaring omission from this Reader – given the title – will be issues relating to legal drug use in society such as cigarettes, alcohol, tranquillizers and other prescribed drugs as well as over-the-counter drugs. Each of these areas is rife with its own controversies, politics and misconceptions and the distinction between licit and illicit drugs is perhaps ultimately an unhelpful one – giving an impression of safe and unsafe, problem and non-problem drugs for use? For most, however, the word 'drugs' is synonymous with illegal drugs such as heroin, crack cocaine and ecstasy and it is in this sense that the title of this Reader is used.

The underlying theme of this Reader is to provide the opportunity to make sense of the various issues which now dominate drug policy in contemporary British and other Western societies. The assumption is made that policy on drugs and their use should be informed by a better understanding of the effects of various drugs and of the addictive state than is generally available, through either the media or political rhetoric. The position presented here is not an apologia for drugs and their use. I am no trying to deny the reality of the problems that the use of drugs may produce or to assert that they may not be dangerous, but to temper the debate somewhat with information which is not over-dramatised nor based on the type of scaremongering predictive scenarios of unstoppable epidemics, which are dragged out time and again. I think it is unproblematic to suggest that many people think that most illicit drugs are more dangerous than they actually are, and they believe that to be addicted to one of these drugs is far worse than it often is. Regrettably, some information which contextualises these issues further had to be left out. There was no room, for example, to show details such as deaths from all illicit drugs in Britain in 1991 numbered 307 (HOSB 1993) as compared to approximately 110,000 for tobacco (HEA 1991); deaths from heroin and other morphine-based substances alone in that year accounted for only 97; cocaine was reported to have killed three (HOSB 1993). Considering that it has been estimated that Britain had over 100,000 addicts at that time, the number of fatalities is perhaps much lower than we might be given to believe should be the case.

There is also growing evidence that a significant number of heroin (and other) addicts 'mature' out of their addiction, *without* the aid of drug services or treatment centres (Winick 1962, Waldorf and Biernacki 1979, Robins 1993). These studies also tell us that the addictive state need not be perceived as an inevitable slide downwards and that the drug does not necessarily 'take over' the addict. That there are addicts who 'control' their addiction, and drug users who actively prevent themselves from becoming problem users or addicts (Zinberg 1984) flies in the face of recent high-profile 'education' campaigns in the British and American media. These, however, are not the *visible* users. The most visible users are those who present with problems, either in the courts or for treatment or help of some kind. Even for many of these more visible users their real problems may be more usefully understood as emanating from the illegal context in which they use drugs not from the drugs themselves. Illegal drugs are expensive and servicing an expensive habit may cause difficulties not experienced by those who can satisfy, for example, their nicotine habit relatively cheaply. Illegal drugs are also adulterated with substances other than the drug purchased, and purity levels can vary. Both these products of black market supply produce a situation for the user which makes the drug purchased potentially unsafe and occasionally (although as we have seen not as often as is supposed), life-threatening. In this sense, ideas around drugs and addiction need to be tempered and brought back into line with what we really know not what we fear.

References

Health Education Authority, *The Smoking Epidemic: Counting the Cost in England*, HEA, London, 1991.

Home Office Statistical Bulletin. *Statistics of Drug Addicts Notified to the Home Office*, United Kingdom, 1992, Issue 15/93, 27 May, 1993.

Robins, L. N. 'Vietnam veterans' rapid recovery from heroin addiction: a fluke or normal expectation? *Addiction* 1993, 88, pp. 1041-1054.

Waldorf, D. and Biernacki, P. 'Natural Recovery from Heroin Addiction: A Review of the Incidence Literature', *Journal of Drug Issues*, Spring, 1979, pp. 281-289.

Winick, C. 'Maturing Out of Narcotic Addiction', *Bulletin on Narcotics*, January-March, 1962, pp. 1-7.

Zinberg, N.E. *Drug, Set, and Setting: The Basis for Controlled Intoxicant Use*, Yale University Press, New York, 1984.

Note on terminology

The terminology used to describe people who use drugs and the way that they use them is broad and varies between groups and over time. Official or authoritative definitions, such as drug misuser and drug misuse, drug abuser and drug abuse, often have pejorative meanings which suggest that the activity is essentially wrong, and these definitions are not neutral in their presentation. Where appropriate, I have chosen to use the terms drug use and drug user in an attempt to describe both the activity of taking drugs and a group of individuals who partake in the activity of taking drugs (whether they be addicted, occasional or controlled users) without negative connotation. The terms addiction and addict, although not intrinsically negative, have at times been attributed greater or lesser pejorative characteristics. Terms such as drug dependent and drug dependency were introduced, in part, to permit discussion on addiction in a less moralistic fashion. With the growth of different ways of describing drug use and addiction, moralistic and non-moralistic, the concept of addiction arguably now has less negative connotations than it had previously. Where appropriate, throughout this Reader I have opted to use the terms drug addict and drug addiction. All terminology used (outside of the texts) is intended to carry no judgements or moral overtones.

Publisher's note

The contents of the readings in this anthology have been reproduced as they appear in the publications from which they are taken. In the majority of cases footnotes and bibliographic material are included, the exceptions being where they are of excessive length. Photographs have not been reproduced.

Prominent Drugs and Their Effects

Any proper understanding of the range of issues relating to illicit drugs (whether it be how they impact on individuals, communities or even nations through unexpected fatalities, addiction, or crime) has to begin with an informed, and probably moderated view on the effects of those drugs. Much of what is assumed about the effects of most illicit drugs is in fact greatly exaggerated. Public conceptions of 'what drugs do to you' tend towards ideas of 'soft' drugs leading to 'hard' ones, hard ones leading to addiction and addiction leading to death, dragging family and friends into a destructive downward spiral. Perhaps the most notorious of contemporary drugs is crack cocaine, widely believed to be almost immediately addictive. Newcombe and Matthews' research on crack cocaine users in Liverpool - supporting similar findings in the USA - indicates that to *use* crack is not to be either inevitably and/or immediately enslaved by it. That there was within their sample 'occasional' as opposed to purely compulsive use, and that many had had periods of abstinence, undermines the simple messages often propagated about this drug and in fact starts to bring it back in line with what we know about other 'hard' drugs. That there is a magnification of such effects should not surprise us. It is not new to the history of drug reporting. In the 1930s in the USA the marijuana user was widely considered, due to the influence of marijuana, to be capable of, and likely to commit, the most heinous of violent and sexual crimes, a perspective that has no credence in the 1990s.

That drugs are often attributed with powers and effects beyond their capabilities and even in contradiction to their pharmacological properties is further highlighted by Miller. Here the author is concerned to demythologise some of the worst assumptions relating to what might be described as the 'hard' and thus most feared drugs. Miller aims to redress the balance of how we understand drug effects so that any decision on what to do about them is more reasonably informed.

That drug effects are neither simple nor predictable is further emphasised by Gossop. Drug effects are not best understood by considering the individual to be 'high-jacked' by the substance in question. People interrelate with drugs and the effects are in part determined by an individual's mind set (mood, expectations) and their setting (environment: such as a party; peer group pressure; isolation) and even by things such as weight and sex, as well as by pharmacology. Expectations of course can relate to the scenario expected to be played out given the context, such as a party, as well as the assumed effects that the given drug would have. That expectations play an important role can be seen by experiments which show that individuals can 'experience' drug effects even when the substance is absent and a placebo used. Gossop's emphasis thus 'serve(s) as an antidote to the more orthodox view that the effects of drugs are *intrinsic* properties of those substances' alone.

1

Class / Status.

1. Crack in Liverpool
Russell Newcombe and Lyn Matthews

The first research on crack use in the UK reveals how the drug is used by Liverpool prostitutes.

In late 1988 an outreach worker from Mersey Regional Health Authority's AIDS Prevention Unit reported that female prostitutes in Liverpool were starting to use crack, which was being sold near the area in which they operated. It was decided to survey these women about their crack use and its consequences.

Only prostitutes and drug users already in contact with the outreach worker were interviewed. Using a short questionnaire, the worker interviewed 26 people (22 female prostitutes plus four male drug users) between 23 June and 17 July 1989.

Twenty-three had tried crack. Nineteen were still using, aged on average 24 years. Although this sample was biased towards known users, the incidence of crack use among street prostitutes in Liverpool working the city's 'red light' area is estimated at 50 to 75 per cent.

Crack users were also heavily into heroin. Sixteen said they were using heroin daily and 15 were injecting on average 16 times a week each.

Clear split in use patterns

All but a few of the current crack users had been using for between 12 and 36 months. There were two clearly discernible groups:

- ten regular users had been using crack virtually every day for the last four weeks (including three males);

- nine 'occasional' users (all female) used it on between one and seven days in the last four weeks. Their main reasons for not using daily were 'being short of money' and 'not feeling like it'.

On average, occasional users had been using crack for about 18 months compared with 45 months for regular users.

The seven regular crack-using prostitutes reported selling vaginal sex an average of 18 times per week during the last month, compared with 15 times among the eight occasional users. Only one of the crack using prostitutes reported doing business without a condom (the outreach worker provides them free).

Regular users reported taking crack on average 11 times a day, compared with (on the days they used the drug) about five times a day among occasional users. Daily users reported spending on average £118 a day on crack (about four rocks), compared with £40 a day (slightly more than one rock) among occasional users. Their main methods

Russell Newcombe and Lyn Matthews: 'Crack in Liverpool', *DRUGLINK*, (September/October 1989), p.16.
© Druglink 1989.

of financing crack use were reported to be prostitution (14 respondents) and shoplifting (three respondents).

Taken together, the spending and use per day figures confirm that crack users break the 'rocks' into two to five 'one-hit' pieces, and suggest daily users use bigger doses.

Reported problems

Sixteen of the 19 crack users thought that it was either very easy or quite easy to give up using crack; none indicated it was very difficult. Only one felt addicted and two said they did not know if they were - all daily crack users. Just three wanted to give up crack.

When asked if using crack had caused any problems, just over half said no. Six regular users and three occasional users did report crack-related problems, mainly lack of money (seven), not eating properly (six), trouble sleeping (five), upsetting family (five), depression (five), and damaged lungs (four).

Only two referred to increased violence, stealing more, having sex without condom for more money, or feeling bad when crack cannot be obtained.

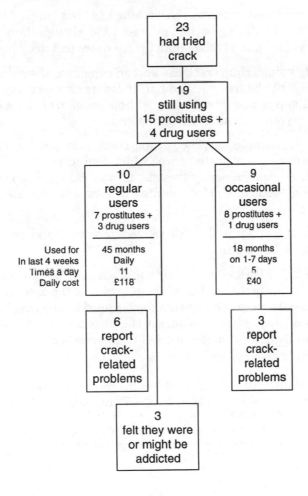

The main effect of crack use on other forms of drugtaking was reported to be a reduction in the use of heroin by six users, of whom five are daily users. Three people said using crack had led them to increase their other drug use.

Asked if there was anything that they thought was worth knowing about crack, five out of the 14 users who answered indicated general approval: "Don't knock it till you try it"; "Good buzz"; "Lovely feeling"; and "I like it!". Two each mentioned that it was expensive, bad for people, addictive. As one 28-year-old man who used crack daily put it: "If you're around people who use crack you want it, if not, you don't - you can stop using crack with no bad results at all".

A different picture of crack

This article reports the interim findings of research which has so far focused on a small number of crack users of a particular social background, so any conclusions can only be tentative and preliminary. But there is a clear disparity between the picture of crack use painted by the media and public officials and the picture provided by the findings of this study.

♦ Rather than being a new phenomenon, cocaine has been smoked in Liverpool for over a decade, with crack use dating back to at least 1986, though there is little evidence of crack use among youth groups other than opiate users and drug injectors.

♦ In this polydrug using group crack use spread rapidly to the point where more than half are now thought to be using it and half these use it every day an average of over ten times a day. Even in this group being without crack was not a disaster - they just switched back to heroin or to other drugs instead.

♦ However, half the sample had been using crack occasionally for an average of 18 months, with many periods of absteinence - which conflicts with the theory of inevitable instant addiction. A clear majority thought is was easy to stop using and only one admitted to feeling "addicted". Most wanted to continue because of the pleasurable effects.

♦ Less than half said they had crack-related problems and only a few mentioned violence or craving/withdrawals.

♦ A third said crack use had reduced their use of heroin. Combined with other findings, this implies that money problems forced them to reduce the amount of heroin they buy and/or that the rush from crack has reduced their need for the rush from injecting.[1] The HIV implications of these changes suggest the effects of crack use on injecting (and sexual) behaviour should be a major focus of future research.

Note

1. Alternatively, or additionally, "cocaine reduces the severity of opioid withdrawal and may be one reason for cocaine abuse by opioid addicts" - T. Kosten *et al*, "Cocaine abuse and opioid withdrawl", *Lancet*, 15 July 1989.

2.   What Drugs Do to Users
Richard Miller

A classic study of drug abuse provided a credo for the present book: "Plausibility is not a satisfying substitute for evidence". Common sense can muddle us through many challenges, but when stuck in a bad situation we should examine assumptions that mired us, no matter how reasonable they seem.

We assume drugs are an enemy that will destroy us, unless we destroy them. Yet even though Americans have declared war on drugs, few citizens know much about the enemy. Attacking an opponent whose capabilities are unknown or misjudged is imprudent. Let us, therefore, compile an intelligence report.

We consider drugs a monolithic entity. Most citizens make little distinction among heroin, cocaine, marijuana or LSD; neither does the law. To deal effectively with drugs, however, we must respect their differences. If we attacked "disease" in the way we fight drugs, we would make little distinction among colds, cancer, broken bones and heart attacks. All would receive the same therapy, differing only in the vigor with which it was applied. Growing numbers of citizens would be crippled or killed. Fear would stalk the land.

Let us avoid that mistake. Let us consider the characteristics of specific drugs. Although this book lacks enough pages to discuss all drugs or even all aspects of the chosen few, four notorious substances can suffice for our purposes.

Heroin

Heroin is the devil drug, synonymous with addiction and crime. Reporters, movie makers, police and politicians have shaped the public view of heroin as powerful, a swiftly addictive drug that delivers great pleasure, but at a cost of horrendous physical agony if addicts attempt to stop taking it. That picture, however, is contradicted by medical and sociological investigations.

Heroin is an opiate. Opium poppies produce sap that can be harvested, processed into opium, further refined into morphine, and then converted to heroin. Each step yields a more concentrated opiate. The form makes little difference to the human body. Body chemistry quickly converts heroin back into morphine. Tests confirm that users detect no difference between doses of morphine or heroin. Black market heroin is more common than morphine only because it is more concentrated and therefore easier to smuggle. Its market dominance is a preference of illicit suppliers, not users. All opiates, whether natural products from poppy plants or synthetic opiods from the laboratory, can be substituted for one another. Although their actions do not duplicate one another in every detail, typical opiate effects exist and have been observed repeatedly for years.

If a person injects heroin intravenously, brain tissue begins absorbing the drug 10 to 20 seconds later. Sometimes, but not always, this can produce a euphoria nicknamed the "rush", which lasts 1 or 2 minutes and is described as a bodywide sexual orgasm. Whether or not a rush occurs, a "high" lasting perhaps 4 or 5 hours is likely. The high is total satiation. To a person in a heroin high, nothing matters. Food, sex, jobs, friends, pain, frustrations and everything else no longer require attention. The high is not a particular sensation but an absence of sensation. Heroin intoxication blots out the world. "That it should be thought of as a "high" stands as mute testimony to the utter destitution of the life of the addict". Opiates have less appeal than many anti-drug zealots claim. Experimenters who give heroin and morphine injections to subjects report that hardly anyone finds the effects desirable; almost everyone expresses indifference or dislike. The high eases away, and after 6 or 7 hours the intoxication ends, often leaving a residual mental peacefulness.

These typical effects are not inevitable and depend on several factors. One is the heroin's purity. Laboratory tests confirm that consumer supplies of illicit drugs are adulterated. Some impurity is due to poor quality control, but most is probably fraud - in which dealers misbrand a cheap substitute and sell it as the high-priced real thing. Such vitiation means that a heroin user may not receive a strong enough dose to produce the desired effects, or they may be produced by an adulterant. For instance, dealers often mix quinine with heroin, and quinine can produce a rush. The method of administration also shapes effects. Heroin can be sniffed, eaten, smoked, or injected (intravenously, intramuscularly or subcutaneously). Only intravenous injection, however, is likely to create a rush.

Set and setting are two more factors crucial to a drug's effects. "Set" is a user's general personality and specific expectations about a drug. "Setting" is a person's surroundings, what other people or even background music do to the user. Set and setting guide the direction of a drug experience and can even overcome normal properties of powerful drugs. An experiment demonstrated the guidance. Some subjects who received an epinephrine (adrenalin) injection were told to expect arousal, some were told nothing, and others were misinformed about what to expect. They were then placed in the company of stooges who supposedly had also received injections, and who pretended to be affected in a particular way. Experimental subjects who lacked knowledge about what to expect from the injection imitated the behavior of the stooges, as did subjects who were misinformed. Subjects who had accurate information did not mimic the stooges. Drug users who feel a change in themselves, but who do not understand the reason for change, pick up cues from other users and imitate them. The role of such guidance can be inferred from admission statistics to the Massachusetts Mental Health Center and New York City's Bellevue Hospital. In the latter 6 months of 1967 about 10 per cent of patients suffered from bad experiences with psychedelic drugs. In the latter 6 months of 1969 only 3 such patients arrived. Similar trends were noticed by medical personnel at rock music concerts from 1973 to 1977. Researchers doubt that the number of bad psychedelic experiences had declined, but instead believe that users and their friends had achieved a better understanding of what psychedelic drugs do. The new knowledge provided a new set and setting, reducing the power of unpleasant effects; afflicted persons had enough internal strength and external support from friends to be

6

undaunted. Set and setting can even produce effects that conflict with pharmacological actions. After receiving a narcotic antagonist that chemically blocks effects of heroin, a person who then takes heroin can still have autonomic responses associated with the opiate - responses not under voluntary control by most people. Moreover, persons can feel opiate euphoria despite a narcotic antagonist's blockage of pharmacological effect. Experiments produce similar findings 'for cocaine - "cocaine actions" occurring upon presentation of environmental cues rather than upon presentation of the drug. Set and setting can do more, however, than just affect drug users' interpretation of what is happening. Barbiturates and opiates can be transformed from sedatives to stimulants, cocaine or an amphetamine from a stimulant to a sedative. Similar changes and flip-flops can occur with drugs unassociated with illicit abuse, such as atropine and digitalis.

Effects of heroin and other drugs are predictable. So is the weather. We may have expectations based on probability, but cannot have certainties based on inevitability. Even machines sometimes fail to do what is anticipated, and people are not machines. Drugs do not always do the same things to the same individuals, let alone to different persons. A drug policy based on a contrary assumption will fail.

If someone uses heroin a lot, several times a day for weeks or months, "tolerance" builds up. Higher doses are needed to produce the same level of effects. Tolerance is an oft-cited peril of illicit drugs but happens with many legal substances and causes no alarm about them. With alcohol the process is called "learning to hold your liquor", and is considered admirable. Tolerance, however, does not increase without limit. A heroin user who develops tolerance does not keep raising the dose infinitely; generally a plateau is reached at which the user feels satisfied. Consequently a user does not keep buying larger and larger amounts. The idea that dealers profit from a heroin user's need for limitless quantities is wrong. A user wants a reliable supply, not an infinite one.

Probably the most feared effect of heroin usage is addiction. People view addiction as a consequence of heroin use, a situation in which the addict will do anything to get the drug, a condition that can be broken only by undergoing terrible symptoms of heroin withdrawal. Addiction is viewed as generally permanent, leading to devastating medical problems and to a life of crime and personal degradation. This summary is widely believed but contradicted by scientific research.

If a person takes a lot of heroin frequently and for a long time, the drug may engage in a "physical resonance" with the user's body. In such a development, continued use of heroin is necessary to maintain the body's physical stability, otherwise the user feels sick. Resonance is often called "physical dependence", but that latter term is wrong - and inaccurate terms can mislead our thinking. A diabetic is physically dependent on insulin. Without it, the person gets sicker and sicker. Heroin users do not become physically dependent on their drug. Without it they get sick but soon get better and recover. Heroin users never have an organic need for the substance; that is why some drug abuse treatments can seek abstinence, because heroin users have no physical need for the drug.

To reach a state of resonance, users must work at it hard, for a long time. One obstacle they must overcome is heroin's side effects. After taking an intoxicating dose of heroin the user typically gets nauseated and often vomits. Some heroin users claim to enjoy a queasy stomach. "Yes, it's very warm, good ... My stomach would tighten and I would get that warm feeling coming up my esophagus". Another user agreed: "I get a nauseated thing, you know. The nauseating thing is actually, in the subculture, interpreted as being a desirable thing to feel". Learning the joy of nausea takes fortitude. A person unwilling to throw up several times a day will not take enough heroin to create a physical resonance, and will avoid altering the body's stability. How much heroin would be enough to cause resonance? A classic study of New York City users concluded that resonance cannot develop if someone takes the drug less than once a day. In scientific experiments using 100 per cent pure unadulterated heroin, human subjects do not lose physical stability until they have received the drug 3 times a day for 2 weeks. For 15 weeks one subject received higher doses than most addicts get, up to 200 mg daily of pure heroin, and showed no withdrawal symptoms when the drug was cut off. A month may be necessary to establish resonance on pure morphine when given 4 times a day. Those findings mean that resonance can be detected via clinical measurements, not that a user would feel distress if the drug were cut off. People can take injections of pure morphine 1 or 2 times a day for years without developing "appreciable" resonance. People taking injections 4 times a day can stop "without discomfort". Analysis of illicit heroin typically finds it so diluted that the body's physical stability could never be altered; such a consequence is pharmacologically impossible. Such a consequence can occur only if a user of illicit heroin is resourceful enough to find a supply of superior quality and reckless enough to abuse it in the way that alcoholics abuse liquor.

If those two conditions are met, a heroin user will achieve resonance and experience the "withdrawal syndrome" if heroin usage stops. The syndrome is only understood incompletely, but part of the explanation is a rebound effect. For example, heroin promotes constipation and has been used medically to treat loose bowels. A heroin user's body may adjust for the constipating action, resonating with the heroin in an effort to keep bowel movements normal. If the drug then suddenly disappears, compensating efforts still continue awhile and temporary diarrhoea may result until body chemistry rebounds to normal.

Heroin and all other opiates have the same withdrawal syndrome. Typical symptoms include sneezing, runny nose, hot and cold flashes, nausea, and diarrhoea. Opiate withdrawal symptoms mimic influenza. As with other drug effects, however, set and setting can be all important. Andrew Weil writes, "In a supportive setting, with proper suggestion, a heroin addict can withdraw without medication other than aspirin and have little more discomfort than that of a moderate cold. I saw this in San Francisco in 1968 in men with expensive daily habits". The experience is unpleasant but involves no screaming agonies and requires no medical supervision. One person kept a diary: "Now it's 16 hours since the last injection. Withdrawal symptoms are not bad, merely noticeable. The ever-present feeling of weariness just that much worse. A headache, yawning, shiverings and cold feelings, a nose that feels like a common cold, yawning again, hands a little shaky and poor in grip". A married couple addicted to heroin decided to stop. They were staying with relatives from whom they had hidden their addiction, and explained they had caught influenza. Such a charade is not unusual. People can withdraw from heroin in the privacy of their homes on a weekend. They decide heroin is troublesome, go home on Friday and emerge on Monday, cured and feeling fine. This actually happens. Few alcoholics or two-pack-a-day cigarette smokers could duplicate the feat. Breaking a heroin resonance is not only easy but safe. Withdrawal might cause serious problems if a user had an organic problem such as heart disease, but untoward consequences seldom occur. In 1916, a study found no deaths among 12,000 opiate habitués who withdrew in prison over a 12-year period of observation. The unhealthy lifestyle of most convicted criminal users, combined with prison conditions of that era, rigorously tested the safety of opiate withdrawal. (In contrast, withdrawal from substances such as alcohol or barbiturates can be fatal, regardless of medical assistance).

Physical resonance is different from heroin addiction. Resonance is only one part of the latter condition. Addiction will be discussed in detail later, but for now we can say that ending addiction is much harder than ending resonance. The ease of withdrawing from resonance is important, however, because some people believe that heroin users take the drug and accept a life of crime and debasement simply to avoid the withdrawal syndrome. People who continually use heroin will want to avoid the syndrome, but no one is likely to run the risks of illicit use simply to avoid a few days with a drippy nose and a touch of the runs. Addicts take heroin for other reasons.

Users who achieve resonance may avoid withdrawal by routinely taking a small "maintenance" dose. A maintenance dose is not strong enough to produce intoxication. No rush or high occurs. The user feels and acts normal; behavior is indistinguishable from someone who uses no opiates. Only a body fluid work-up can determine if a person is on a maintenance dose.

Job performance is normal. That fact has been documented for years. In a 1962 book Lawrence Kolb wrote,

> According to a 1919 survey, 75 per cent of addicts were gainfully employed and there were many cases where victims were people of the highest qualities, morally and intellectually, and of great value to their communities .... I have observed a number of professional and clerical workers as well as laborers who worked regularly for years despite their use of as much as 40 grains of morphine daily.

In a 1964 book Isidor Chein and associates reported, "There are many addicts we studied who continued at their jobs, with sufficient industry and deportment to satisfy their employers". Chein and associates also noted, "Work habits of the few carefully observed patients who were readdicted in the research wards at the United States Public Health Service Hospital in Lexington, were not sufficiently different from those of the other, abstinent patients to provoke comment". Around 1900, a New York Central railroad engineer was famed for making every run assigned to him during a 20-year period of morphine use. A more recent example comes from former District of Columbia police department general counsel Gerald M. Caplan, who says that around 1971 "more than

100 officers were taking heroin. How did we learn about them? Not because their performance was poor .... We took urine specimens". A study of college students grade-point averages found no significant difference between users and non-users of opiates. Physician opiate users typically have their work unimpaired. British physician addicts have been allowed to continue their medical practices and treat patients. In the United States there is the famous case of Doctor X, addicted to morphine for 62 years without noticeable impairment of physical or mental abilities. (The even more famous case of Dr William Stewart Halsted is less relevant. Halsted was a pioneer at the Johns Hopkins medical school and a top surgeon despite his morphine addiction. His case is less relevant because a brilliant person's capabilities may not be shared by the rest of us. Moreover, his teaching ability declined after he started opiates, and he occasionally disappeared for days and even weeks - behavior that few employers would tolerate from ordinary mortals).

"Normal" job productivity does not mean that a worker is unaffected by a maintenance dose of heroin or other opiates, but that such a worker performs as well as the average employee. Some experts deny that opiate users can work normally at their jobs while on maintenance doses. These denials, however, are contrary to a consensus that spans a century of observations.

Friends and even close family members may notice nothing unusual and be unaware that someone uses an opiate. "Only a few days ago I met a gentlman on Carroll avenue who has taken morphine thirteen years, in doses of from two to fifty grains daily. He was well dressed, had a healthy color, and was in every respect as respectable looking as the majority I saw on the street". That meeting occurred around 1880, when addicts could buy morphine legally. "I never knew how many individuals of this type there are until after the law made it necessary to report them to this bureau. Almost invariably they are people of importance in their communities, some of them executives in banking, business or industry". That observation was made in 1919, soon after morphine sales were forbidden. Similar observations were made in the 1960s and 1970s and 1980s, of American heroin addicts leading outwardly ordinary lives while steadily employed at middle class jobs for years.

Heroin and other opiates apparently cause no ill effects of consequence. Organic afflictions attributed to heroin more likely reflect adulterants and the users' lifestyles - including poor hygiene, such as sharing dirty hypodermic needles and using public toilet water to prepare solutions for injection. That type of behavior is particularly self-destructive, however, and (as we shall see later) has little to do with heroin.

As with job performance, some experts dissent from the consensus of opiate safety. From 1908 to 1938, opium smokers over the age of 40 in Japanese-controlled Formosa had a higher death rate than the general population. Apparently the actuarial experience of life insurance companies was consistent with the Formosa experience; around 1931 a League of Nations survey found that life insurers charged higher rates to Far Eastern opium smokers, although earlier the New York Life Insurance Company gladly issued policies to opium users because their risk was no higher than non-users. A study revealed that about 85 per cent of Formosan opium smokers used the drug as self-medication for asthma, coughs, bloody sputum, gastrointestinal illness, and gonorrhea - factors that could well affect mortality. Also, Japanese-controlled Formosa restricted opium and prosecuted tens of thousands of users; Japanese police methods may have affected mortality. A critic of heroin safety cited a finding that addicts under medical supervision in Great Britain had a higher death rate than unsupervised addicts in the United States, but the cited finding emphasized that opiates themselves appeared safe; mortality was increased by other factors such as neglect of health and nutrition. Another study noted the British addict death rate is raised by suicides. Instantaneous deaths have been observed among street users after they inject heroin intravenously, but the drug's role in such fatalities is questionable.

Despite controversy over "heroin overdose", the physical safety of opiates is widely recognized. Morphine and methadone are widely used in US medical practice, with some patients taking methadone every day for years without noticeable ill effect. The same has long been observed with persons who use opiates outside medical contexts.

Various studies reveal no psychosis caused by opiates. One study examined 200 addicts without finding a single schizophrenic. Another traced 100 addicts over a 12-year span and found just 1 schizophrenic. These are studies of people brought to the attention of authorities, through run-ins with the law or institutionalization for detoxification. If researchers cannot find heroin psychosis in that population, it probably does not exist.

Someone can be on heroin 24 hours a day, year after year, yet feel and act the same as anyone else. Methadone is an opiate, and the fact that opiate addicts can live and work normally is the basis of methadone "drug treatment" programs advocated by many government officials. Methadone patients are not cured of opiate addiction, but are merely switched from heroin (which no US physician can prescribe) to the prescription drug methadone. Opiates have "cross tolerance", meaning that methadone, heroin, morphine, and all the rest can be substituted for one another and will give a person the same effects. A maintenance dose allows addicts to function normally in society. What works with methadone will work with any opiate.

From a public health standpoint, we have no reason to fear heroin. It is far less harmful than alcohol or tobacco.

Cocaine

At first glance cocaine seems to be a chameleon drug, changing its attributes as years go by. In the early twentieth century widespread cocaine use was reported among impoverished African-Americans. By mid-century the drug was dismissed as a historical curiosity, used by hardly anyone. In the 1970s it was proclaimed the outrageously expensive drug of choice among chic rich folk, and in the 1980s it was termed a cheap "fast food drug" of urban ghettos. For decades numerous authorities insisted that cocaine was nonaddictive. In 1989, a physician told me that cocaine is the most addictive substance known. Yet, in all these years, the chemistry of cocaine never changed.

What has changed is attitudes about the drug. Such flip-flops are not unique to cocaine. Heroin was once "known" to be nonaddictive and used as a "cure" for opiate addiction. In the 1930s marijuana was feared as a drug that caused hyperactivity and violent crime. Fifty years later the weed was decried for making users lethargic and passive. The message here is not that drug actions are an impenetrable mystery - researchers know very well what they do. The message is that we can face cocaine with steadiness; Americans once had no fear of it, and its properties have not changed since then. Experience shows that, from time to time, some persons choose to promote dread about a particular drug; whenever those persons disappear from the scene, so does the panic.

Leaves of the coca plant can be processed to yield cocaine. It normally acts as a stimulant. Thus its work is just the opposite to opiates, which are soothing sedatives. A person on a heroin high wants to leave other people alone. In contrast, someone on cocaine is ready for action. Violence by cocaine users, even by hard-core criminal users, is nonetheless uncommon. Cocaine increases endurance and muscle power, gives users the impression of increased intellectual prowess, can increase a user's zest for life, and embolden a person to take risks. Such effects are documented by a century of study.

Crack, a refined derivative of cocaine, has a shorter history. Crack research only began in the 1980s, and when this book was written scientists knew little about the substance. In addition to normal cocaine effects, however, inhaling crack smoke can sometimes produce a two-minute "rush" likened to a total body sexual orgasm, followed by an afterglow of 10 or 20 minutes. As with heroin, however, the mode of administration helps determine effects - persons who sniff crack, instead of smoking it, do not report euphoria. Horror stories about "instant" crack addiction are unconfirmed by scientific research. In the early 1980s, researchers at a California clinic gave the drug to 200 volunteers. None became addicts or even turned into abusers. A study of 175 illicit crack users in Los Angeles found none with a compulsive habit; all used the drug in moderation. Monkeys allowed to smoke crack will limit their intake. Compulsive use of a drug need not grow as preparations grow in potency. A cocaine user can achieve certain effects with a particular amount of cocaine hydrochloride salt or a smaller amount of the free base of cocaine liberated from the salt. Format, admittedly, is not irrelevant; with a high potency preparation a user can achieve intense effects more easily. Yet, not all users of high potency preparations seek intense effects. Persons who use crack in moderation typically sniff it, a mode of administration that produces a low level of effects for a long time. In contrast, hedonists who desire intense experience will smoke crack, producing strong effects for a brief time. Because those hedonists want to experience the intensity for a long time, they smoke crack again whenever the effects weaken. Amount of use depends on the person, not the drug. Research on freebase cocaine is probably relevant to crack; despite different manufacturing processes the two products are similar. Freebase research shows compulsive users to have prior histories of polydrug abuse, especially amphetamines and other stimulants. Drug abusers who seek even more powerful stimulant experiences can be expected to find crack appealing; their compulsive use of crack may be due less to the drug than to well-established personalities. A 1987 survey of Canadian crack users supports that view; they used other drugs as well (marijuana, heroin, barbiturates, LSD, PCP) and in large quantities (5 or more drinks of alcohol at a time, every day). People who use a lot of crack are people who use all sorts of drugs to excess.

The pharmacological basis of cocaine's appeal is unclear. Experienced users cannot tell the difference between cocaine and a nasal anesthetic, nor can they reliably differentiate the effects of amphetamine and cocaine. At small dosage levels people feel no difference between cocaine and a placebo; effects after receiving a placebo can mimic (though not absolutely duplicate) 40 mg of cocaine; street users of cocaine have proclaimed marijuana (an active placebo) to be a satisfying substitute. A person who used cocaine daily for 55 years switched to aspirin whenever her supply ran short. Cocaine does have effects but their power may be exaggerated. Persons can sniff or smoke crack without becoming addicted and without losing social productivity. Set and setting may be more important than chemistry and may explain cocaine's fluctuating popularity. When the drug was publicized as a symbol of debonair opulence in the 1970s, it rocketed from obscurity. When it was publicized as a symbol of rebellious violence in the 1980s it became popular in urban ghettos. Cocaine use may have as much to do with social statements as with pharmacology.

Numerous afflictions have been associated with cocaine, but ailments seem related to astonishing levels of abuse, levels at which even innocuous substances such as coffee could turn nasty. Paranoia and hallucinations can occur, but they clear up quickly if cocaine usage stops. Organic brain damage is unproven. Examination of a person who used 2 grams a week for decades found no organic, mental, or social deterioration. People can *daily* use 1 gram of *crack* "without severe dysfunction". No harm has been proven among South American Indians whose blood levels of cocaine are as high as those found among users in the United States.

Some "cocaine-related" afflictions are due to a user's method of administration, not due to pharmacological effects. For instance, respiratory problems attributed to chronic cocaine smoking are found just as readily among heavy smokers of nicotine; in either case a different method of administration would avoid the lung trouble. If a user chooses to sniff cocaine powder, nasal difficulties can occur: rhinitis, nosebleeds, and in extreme cases nasal ulcers or even a perforated septum cartilage. Those difficulties can be avoided by using another means to take the drug. Another problem is the size of a lethal dose, which can change unexpectedly depending on the user's condition - a person can drop dead for a dose that gave pleasure the previous day. That seldom happens, but "seldom" also means "sometimes", and a user always takes a risk.

The above hazards are real, but in practice the damage is less than in these worst-case scenarios. Research supporting that comforting thought appears in a book endorsed by the Reagan White House and published by a legitimate scientific press, a book that can in no way be read as minimizing cocaine problems. In a passage referring to addiction, not just occasional use 2 or 3 times a year, one authority writes, "It is not uncommon for young persons to have been on cocaine for up to a year before it was noticed by their parents. In my experience a person may have snorted cocaine for up to two years or more before deterioration occurred". One could read that passage as a frightening warning, that a child might be a cocaine addict for years without a parent realizing it. Or one could read that passage as saying a person has to abuse cocaine severely, for a long time, before anything bad happens. A 1989 study found that adults need to abuse cocaine for an average of 6.6 years before experiencing a single problem.

Cocaine was studied for a century without anyone detecting resonance or physical dependence among users of the drug. Only after politicians decried cocaine in the 1980s did a handful of scientists claim that dependence develops. The claim became widely believed and merits consideration here.

Proponents of the dependence concept used innovative terminology to change attitudes toward long-observed effects of cocaine. For example, not until 1986 was a three-stage "cocaine abstinence syndrome" proclaimed. The first stage was called the "crash", likened to an alcohol hangover, in which a person who stops a cocaine binge feels exhausted and depressed. Cocaine and other stimulants work by using up energy stored in the body. At the end of a binge a person will feel like someone who has done hard physical labor for days without food or sleep. Those symptoms do not mean a person has a metabolic need for such punishment. Nor are they evidence that physical resonance has been established with cocaine, any more than a hangover is evidence of physical resonance with alcohol. If cocaine resonance existed, a user could quickly resume normal functioning by taking another dose of cocaine. But such a dose would worsen the user's condition, not restore it to normal; a maintenance dose is impossible because cocaine resonance does not exist. Although the second stage in "cocaine abstinence syndrome" was called "withdrawal", proponents of the concept admitted that "this does not mean that a classic drug abstinence syndrome formally occurs" and admitted that the second stage was "dissimilar [to] 'withdrawal' in alcohol, barbiturate, or opiate abuse". Indeed, these proponents declared, "Withdrawal has ... assumed a clinical meaning, independent of its pharmacological definition, that derives from the postdrug syndromes for which drug users seek treatment ... Strict pharmacological use of the term can cause clinical treatment errors". In other words, "cocaine withdrawal" has no pharmacological component. That is, it is not caused by the drug. The third and final "abstinence syndrome" stage was called "extinction", and describes the process by which drug-seeking behavior learned by psychological conditioning is extinguished. Once again, a pharmacological component is absent from the "cocaine abstinence syndrome".

As will be noted in a later chapter, such claims of "cocaine dependence" met immediate skepticism from scientists who research drug actions, and no consensus accepted the claims as the 1980s ended. Proponents, however, achieved a victory in 1987 when the American Psychiatric Association invented a new disease called "cocaine dependence" that did not require resonance or physical dependence for the diagnosis. An "epidemic" of "cocaine dependence" appeared overnight because the symptoms had never been classified as disease until then. Even the APA admitted this, albeit with hedging: "*Because of the broadened criteria* for Dependence included in this manual, and because of the definite increase in use in recent years, the prevalence of Cocaine Dependence is believed to be far higher" than formerly (emphasis added). The APA's action gave the term official medical and governmental recognition even though the APA itself conceded, "Continuing use of cocaine appears to be driven by persistent craving and urges for the substance rather than attempts to avoid or alleviate withdrawal symptoms". Even a prominent "cocaine dependence" proponent concurred, "This craving ... can be understood as a memory of the stimulant euphoria". Lacking a physical condition to treat, psychiatrists attempt to change a user's attitude toward cocaine.

14

Criteria that describe "cocaine dependence" are psychological and not pharmacological. The clinical condition termed "cocaine dependence" may be real, even devastating, but it is caused by a psychological process instead of a pharmacological one. Two consequences follow. First, diagnosing someone as "psychologically dependent" on cocaine is the same as saying the person likes to use cocaine a lot. Such a "diagnosis" may provide a psychiatrist with a patient but provides no insight for treatment. Second, if a pharmacological component is absent from the disease, the drug is irrelevant. Psychiatric personnel freely admit as much: "Cocaine abusers do not require a treatment program that is distinct from programs for other substance abusers". That is, despite extreme differences among opiates, cocaine, alcohol, and nicotine, the drug of abuse does not affect the disease of psychological dependence. If a drug is irrelevant to the disease, if the disease is a mental attitude about a drug, then harsh laws against the drug itself have no medical justification.

It is probably not coincidental that medical and governmental acceptance of "cocaine dependence" was followed by efforts to demonstrate a physical component that might justify harsh laws. As with "cocaine dependence", however, scientific research played a lesser role than innovative terminology. The innovative terminology, in turn, was used in a complex chain of reasoning leading to a hypothesis that a physical component exists. Proponents of the hypothesis have yet to prove its reality. Nonetheless they have affected public policy, so their proposal merits discussion here.

Cocaine, like many other drugs, affects brain chemistry. Animal studies suggest the cocaine may alter human brain tissue, but the extent and duration of such alteration in humans is uncertain. Evidence does exist that cocaine increases the dopamine level in the brain, accompanied by a decline in the number of dopamine receptors, and that their number returns to normal if cocaine usage stops. Those are facts.

These, too, are facts. Drugs operate by changing body chemistry; that is their function. Such changes, whether in the brain or elsewhere, do not mean a person has established resonance or dependence with a substance. If blood pressure declines after reducing salt intake, that does not mean a hypertensive person is physically dependent on salt. Resonance or dependence is present only if a person *sickens* temporarily or permanently when drug use *ceases*, and *recovers* upon *resuming* drug use. For example, a heroin addict functioning normally on a maintenance dose will take sick if the drug supply ends, and get well if it resumes. In contrast, someone exhausted by cocaine will not recover upon further administration of cocaine. If a drug itself sickens a person, the person is hardly dependent on it - no one has a metabolic need for illness. Nor is resonance or dependence demonstrated by continuation of symptoms after drug use stops. Someone may go blind after one drink of contaminated alcohol, but that blindness does not mean the person is physically dependent on contaminated alcohol.

Given these facts, we can now examine a hypothesis called "neuroadaptation", developed by proponents of "cocaine dependence". According to their reasoning the presence of cocaine alters brain chemistry and may alter tissue, and organic changes in the brain can affect behavior, so behavior of cocaine users demonstrates physical "neuroadaptation" of the brain to cocaine. Supposedly this "neuroadaptation" is "physiological addiction" to cocaine.

At a casual glance those statements seem straightforward, but upon analysis they degenerate into confusion. Cocaine can alter human brain chemistry and may alter tissue, but whether those alterations are damaging is uncertain. The primary example of alteration by cocaine is a decreased number of dopamine receptors as the level of dopamine increases. Rather than causing a person's behavior to change, however, such alterations may limit the amount of behavioral change. Moreover, if the number of receptors returns to normal when dopamine levels become normal, defining the shift in number as "damage" is problematic; the shift may simply be the body's compensation for fluctuations in body chemistry. Even if brain tissue alteration remained permanent, assessing effect on behavior would be difficult. People can suffer outright loss of brain tissue through surgery or cerebral hemorrhage, yet function normally. Possibly, as "neuroadaptation" proponents seem to argue, all behavior is caused by electrochemical activity in the central nervous system. But the cause-effect relationship is largely unknown. No one knows how electrochemical activity creates affection for a friend, hate for an enemy, delight for a Mozart melody, disdain for rock and roll, or even a decision to cross the street. To say that "return of the [dopamine] receptor number to normal" causes "cocaine dependence" and "cocaine withdrawal" is very bold. Still another problem arises by defining tissue change as "physiological addiction". By such definition a diabetes sufferer is addicted to insulin, an asthma sufferer is addicted to theophylline, a headache sufferer is addicted to aspirin. All these persons exhibit changes in body chemistry and tissue, accompanied by a change in behavior, after taking their drugs. Using those criteria to define addiction is a non-standard definition, and bound to cause misconceptions among people who hear the term "physiological addiction" but who are unaware of the special definition.

Although the "neuroadaptation" hypothesis involves undisputed facts, it also involves speculations and assumptions that trail off into nothingness upon scrutiny. Even the foremost proponents of "neuroadaptation" admit that no proof exists: "Neuroadaptive withdrawal state in cocaine abusers remains a not yet proven working hypothesis".

Despite lack of a pharmacological element in "cocaine dependence" and lack of proof for "neuroadaptation", the concepts dovetailed with political needs in the late 1980s and grew in popularity.

Cocaine used to be considered nonaddictive because no physical resonance, let alone dependence, was ever detected. As researchers studied addiction and improved their understanding, they began to realize that addiction can occur without physical resonance. More and more authorities now hold that cocaine can be addictive - a proposition heartily endorsed by some users. Controversy has also arisen about pharmacological tolerance, whether a cocaine user needs larger and larger doses to produce the same effects. A consensus used to exist that no tolerance develops, and indeed evidence was found that sensitizing occurs instead, that is, a person can use smaller and smaller doses to get the same effects. The old consensus is now under challenge, with some researchers claiming that tolerance does develop. These new findings are uncertain, but are consistent with the portrait of tolerance given in a later chapter where the process of addiction is examined.

If cocaine abuse is inevitable, we might be making an artificial distinction by saying ailments rarely occur without reckless usage; but abuse is not inevitable. Indeed researchers find abuse is the exception from the norm. A 1984 study concluded that 10 per cent of cocaine users might become alcoholics. A 1985 investigation found an even lower percentage of cocaine users becoming abusers, 2.5 percent. A 1984 study indicated that people can take cocaine for recreation and continue their moderation. Researchers found that most cocaine users in Canada rarely kept a supply of the drug, normally bought only 1 to 3 grams in a single purchase, made no more than 4 purchases per year, and took a dose less that once a month. A study that tracked specific New York cocaine users from 1971 to 1984 found the typical use to be intermittent rather than compulsive, a finding supported by another study that tracked specific recreational users from 1975 to 1983. A survey asked cocaine users if they had ever tried to give up the drug without success; 3.8 percent said yes. That low percentage should be compared to survey respondents who said they had tried to give up tobacco cigarettes without success, 18 percent. Very few cocaine users have an uncontrollable craving. An 11-year study concluded that most careers and lives are not wrecked if people use cocaine. One researcher summarized the findings: "People who have a stake in conventional life don't throw it all away". Such findings do not mean that cocaine abuse should be disregarded. They do mean the problem is not a fearsome crisis.

Scientific investigators find that most cocaine users do not become addicts, although some do. Reasons for the difference are unclear: "The most we can say is that in all probability whatever conditions are apt to produce amphetamine psychosis and amphetamine abuse are also apt to produce cocaine psychosis and cocaine abuse." Millions of people use amphetamines without difficulties, and we should be unsurprised if the same holds true for cocaine.

Some research does promote the idea that cocaine puts the user and society in grave peril, but close examination can make such findings less frightening. For example, in apparent contrast to the studies noted above, one scientific paper says, "Approximately 70 percent of our patients admit they were addicted after experiencing their first high". That report, however, is limited to a population of patients under medical care for cocaine abuse. One presumes the drug would affect them more than users who function normally in society. Also, the finding is based on anecdotal accounts lacking the validity of immediate clinical examination, let alone a controlled experiment; we do not know if addicts accurately remember the event they "admit". Perhaps more important is the question of whether custodial patients who are seeking release will say what they think authorities want to hear. Even the 70 percent figure is unclear; in another paper for the same symposium the investigator says the "first high of the freebased hit carries a 70-80 percent probability of addiction on the first hit." The fuzzy language disguises whether the figure refers to the first use of freebase or first high achieved, perhaps after numerous uses. Also, the population described by the investigator has changed. In the first paper he spoke of patients under medical care; in the second he applies the 70 percent figure to all freebase users. That is a big difference; hospitalized alcoholics are not the same as people who limit their alcohol use to a few weekend beers. The idea of instant addiction to cocaine is also strange. No other drug seems to have such a property, and cocaine was studied for a century before anyone noticed such a phenomenon in the

1980s. Admittedly crack cocaine is a potent variety, but a variety just the same - not a different drug. In years past "everyone knew" that a single injection of heroin caused addiction; careful scientific research disproved the notion. The same may happen with crack.

In addition to reports that cocaine users face inevitable ruin, some accounts allege grave peril to society. Some claim the drug has caused mounting number of car wrecks. A symposium paper reported telephone calls by cocaine users who desired help: "Cocaine-related automobile accidents reported by Hotline callers have nearly doubled since 1983. In 1985, nearly one-fifth of all callers said they had had at least one automobile accident ... while under the influence of cocaine or a combination of cocaine and other drugs". An accompanying chart of statistics is less ominous: in response to questioning by Hotline personnel, the number of callers who admitted car mishaps almost doubled - not the number of accidents. "Cocaine-related" car accidents includes drivers who were simultaneously drunk on alcohol, an inclusion that is bound to inflate the number of incidents. And the population generating these numbers is not a random sample of Americans, nor a random sample of cocaine users, not even a random sample of addicts, but a population of users so worried about their habit that they seek help. One would expect such persons to have dramatic problems. Despite the study's confident language, its data yields no information allowing conclusions about cocaine and automobile accidents.

Choice of language can promote fear. Hyperbole and colored adjectives are easy enough to spot; less easy are rhetorical constructions that blur reality. For example, a symposium paper that discusses cocaine smoking says, "Potentially irreversible lung damage with impairment of diffusing capacity has also been reported". Another way of phrasing that information would be, "Damage that is at least initially reversible may result, but no confirmation exists." The language in both these sentences is neutral, but the rhetorical impact is different.

Problems in the symposium papers just analyzed are not merely academic. The symposium in question was co-sponsored by the United States government, and the papers were endorsed by the Reagan White House. Such papers coat drug control policy with a scientific veneer, but lack sufficient information to reach any conclusions. In contrast, careful studies that produce reasonable conclusions are typically ignored by government officials. This contrast suggests that drug control policy may have a purpose unrelated to public health. A later chapter will ponder that possibility.

Marijuana

Marijuana is another drug that evokes strong feelings among Americans. For now, however, we shall limit our consideration to pharmacological properties. Like opiates and cocaine, marijuana comes in assorted varieties, some more potent that others. They are all the same drug, however, and produce equivalent effects if doses are adjusted for potency.

The late 1960s divided two eras in marijuana research. Although a rich store of work had been compiled by chemists and by observers of marijuana users, only 3 studies had measured effects during the drug session. And those studies, conducted in the 1930s and 1940s, failed to meet later standards of protocol - such as "double blind" administration, in which neither the scientist nor the user knew whether the administered drug was marijuana or a placebo. Almost no valid data existed, a lapse that says less about the quality of research than about general indifference toward the topic. Only in the late 1960s did researchers begin to invite users into laboratories to measure what happened. Prior to that era, marijuana laws had been passed and enforced without benefit of valid scientific data about the drug.

Andrew Weil conducted the first modern marijuana experiments, and his findings have been supported by subsequent researchers. None of the classic reports on marijuana, reviewing findings from researchers around the world, have found any physical peril for users of the drug. Weil characterizes marijuana as an "active placebo", meaning that it produces trivial physical effects and that users' psychological reactions are created entirely by set and setting rather than by pharmacological action. Earlier we noted an experiment showing that a drug user who feels sensations, but does not understand them, will mimic the behavior of nearby persons who have taken a dose. That happens with marijuana. Smokers worldwide use it for all purposes - to concentrate, stimulate, relax - a "universal drug" producing whatever effects a user wants. If marijuana is publicized as producing violent stimulation, users wanting such effects may feel them. That process may explain "reefer madness" in the 1930s. Fifty years later users sought mellowness and found it. In neither case did pharmacological properties of marijuana produce the mental states. Nor does marijuana cause psychosis.

Marijuana's pharmacological properties are so limited that an experienced user can perform any normally tasks without measurable impairment, whether or not the user is "under the influence". In a controlled experiment heavy marijuana use had no effect on productivity in "fairly demanding manual labor". Even some driving tests show the same number of errors by subjects who received a dose of marijuana and those who took no drug. Said one experimenter, "This result is puzzling because of the elaborate efforts made in this study to maximize marihuana intoxication."

Marijuana's safety can also be measured by its "therapeutic ratio", the difference between the size of dose needed for the desired effect and the size that produces poisoning. Marijuana is so safe that the therapeutic ratio has yet to be found, although it has been estimated in the thousands. Nor has the lethal dose been calculated, though extrapolation from animal experiments suggests that a person might die after eating 24 ounces all at once. Deaths from marijuana overdose are no more common than deaths from drinking too many glasses of water at one sitting.The Drug Abuse Warning Network data system, which collects information on drug-related deaths around the country, indicates marijuana's safety. The 1984 reports mention marijuana in 18 fatalities; the 1986 reports have 12 mentions. And of course a trace of marijuana residue does not mean that the drug even played a role in a particular fatality; aspirin ranked higher than marijuana in the number of mentions. Marijuana does not create physical resonance, so no withdrawal syndrome occurs. None of the major inquiries into marijuana, before or after the 1960s, detected any long-term damage from moderate use. ("Moderate use" is the only meaningful criterion in searching for damage, because "excessive use" of any substance - whether it be marijuana, coffee, or fast food burgers and fries - can cause harm).

Findings of modern researchers are supported by historical experience. Marijuana has been grown in the United States since colonial times. Marijuana, however, is also called "hemp", and had extensive industrial use in sail-powered maritime vessels. That was the primary market supplied by farmers until the twentieth century. Records from colonial times detail all sorts of drug use, but no mention of marijuana is found. Only in the 1920s did many drug-using Americans turn to marijuana, seeking an affordable substitute for the alcohol outlawed by federal Prohibition. If marijuana had any significant pharmacological action it surely would have been widely used long before then, just as opiates, alcohol, nicotine, caffeine, and cocaine were widely used.

Some people claim that marijuana is a "getaway" drug, that using it leads to more dangerous substances. The weakness of this claim is demonstrated by history, reasoning, and stark experience.

Let us first examine history. In the 1930s civic leaders, government officials, and news stories condemned marijuana as a vicious stimulant, causing users to commit heinous crimes while suffering from "reefer madness". In 1937, at the height of this panic, the federal government outlawed marijuana. In congressional hearings to establish the need for such action, Congressman John D. Dingell asked Federal Bureau of Narcotics Commissioner Harry J. Anslinger about the getaway theory:

Dingell: I am just wondering whether the marijuana addict graduates into a heroin, an opium, or a cocaine user.

Abslinger: No, sir; I have not heard of a case of that kind. I think it is an entirely different class. The marihuana addict does not go in that direction.

Whether or not Harry Anslinger knew what he was talking about, federal drug enforcement policy denied that marijuana was a gateway drug when it was outlawed. The drug was banned because supposedly it caused hyperactive insanity and brutal crime. After Congress took decisive action in response to public fear of that threat, investigators accumulated evidence that the threat was imaginary. Only after that evidence became overwhelming, after the need for banning marijuana was disproved, did the gateway claim arise. Here is the same Commissioner Anslinger in 1955. "Our great concern about the use of marihuana, that eventually if used over a long period, it does lead to heroin addiction". The pharmacological properties of marijuana did not change during the years between Anslinger's two statements. But numerous government officials had staked their reputations, and their jobs, on the premise that marijuana posed a public health threat. When the "reefer madness" theory was disproved, those government officials needed a new theory if the marijuana ban (and the longevity of their jobs) were to be maintained.

Just because they needed a new theory does not mean it was incorrect, but reasoning and experience disprove it. Traditionally, claims about gateway drugs rest on a false assumption of causality: if heroin addicts earlier used marijuana, marijuana must have led to heroin. Such arguments are venerable. In 1902 a respected scientific publisher brought out a book arguing that coffee drinking led to opium. Some people have said tobacco leads to marijuana. Charles B. Towns, a respected narcotics authority of the early twentieth century, maintaned that tobacco smoking led to opiate use. Those contentions about coffee and tobacco may sound silly today, but they were based on the same fallacy as the marijuana gateway theory. For example, persons who say marijuana leads to heroin fail to point out the even higher correlation of sniffing volatiles (such as gasoline) and later heroin use. Yet we hear no calls to ban the sale of gasoline. The earlier a criminal becomes sexually active, the younger the age at which criminal behavior begins, but that does not mean sex causes crime. Correlations do not demonstrate a cause/effect relationship.

Even if gateway theory is based on faulty reasoning, it may still be true; the universe does not operate by Aristotelian logic. Experience demonstrates, however, that marijuana does not lead to heroin. An observer of African-American ghetto residents found that 54 percent of the studied group claimed to use marijuana, but only 3 percent claimed to use heroin. In a group of drug-using criminals, 75 percent of the heroin addicts had used marijuana, but so had 68 percent of the non-addicts, a statistically insignificant difference. No progression from marijuana to other drugs has been found in Jamaica.

Despite wide use of marijuana in Amsterdam, observers have found small interest in heroin. Consider the number of American college students who have used marijuana, and then compare the number of campus heroin addicts. Actually, comparison may be impossible; a 1985 survey computed that almost 62 million Americans had tried marijuana, and 18 million were current users, but heroin usage in the sample population was so minuscule that a statistically valid total could not be generated. The British government's Wootton Report on marijuana found no progression to heroin in any country. If marijuana led to heroin, the phenomenon should be observable.

Having met defeat on the heroin front, in the 1980s gateway theorists proposed that marijuana leads to cocaine. Some even proposed that alcohol leads to cocaine. Such contentions are so recent that no consensus has emerged among researchers. If experience is any guide, however, we can be confident that the gateway theory is wrong here as well.

LSD

Not much was heard of d-lysergic acid diethylamide when this book was written in mid 1989, but the general public still feared and loathed LSD. Reasons for those emotions will be explored in a later chapter; for now we shall concentrate on what the chemical does to users.

In a way, LSD might be viewed as a stimulant, an extremely powerful stimulant. It can be used as an antidote to barbiturate poisoning. Long ago Kenneth Godfrey, a Veterans Administration psychotherapist who ran one of the last legal LSD research programs in the 1970s, told me that LSD strikes down barriers. That is the most apt summary I have found of LSD's effects. It strikes down barriers between senses, for example, allowing sounds to be seen as a shifting kaleidoscope of colors. Barriers between the conscious and unconscious mind may fall, bringing forth deep psychological concerns.

Vivid hallucinations may appear - perhaps mythological in essence, or images of ancient cultures. The hallucinations can be so vivid as to raise questions about the nature of reality; questions that go beyond the scope of this book.

As with other drugs, set and setting are important. A user who seeks self-insight may achieve it and be satisfied with a single LSD dose. A hedonist who wants to see a light show may take the drug hundreds of times. A depressed and fearful person may have a bad LSD experience, experiencing panic that deepens if nearby people become afraid as well. Several curiosity seekers with no particular expectations about the drug told me that little happened when they took it. LSD is no placebo; it is a drug of power, meriting deep respect. As powerful as it is, however, set and setting shape its effects.

Paradoxically, the powerful drug is also "exceptionally safe". The size of a lethal dose has yet to be found because no one has died from LSD. Babies have emerged unscathed from enormous doses. Massive abuse apparently causes no organic brain damage. Highly publicized reports of chromosome damage were later disproved, and infants born to LSD users show no more chromosome damage or birth defects than the general population. Psychosis lasting longer than 48 hours is rare - twice in a thousand cases for psychiatric patients, less often for normal volunteers. Results from 75,000 clincally supervised LSD, psilocybin, and mescaline experiences among nearly 10,000 persons found no subsequent suicides among normal subjects, and no more than 5 among psychiatric patients - the latter figure consistent with the rate among members of that population who did not receive a psychedelic.

Flashback is particularly feared, at least by non-users. LSD "flashback" is an unexpected repetition of a mental state achieved in an LSD session, a repetition when no psychedelic is being used. Flashback, however, is a normal experience in which a prior emotional experience is suddenly felt once again with intensity. Perhaps a song not heard for years evokes an experience associated with it; or perhaps no trigger is apparent, but memories and emotions flood over a person's consciousness and temporarily supersede present reality. Such a happenstance is a sign of normality, not mental illness. Given the occasional high emotion of some LSD experiences, an absence of flashbacks would be surprising. Someone having a flashback can normally snap out of it at will. A person is not trapped. A survey of 247 LSD users yielded only 1 report of a flashback that remained persistent while the person tried to abandon it. LSD flashbacks tend to be overreported, perhaps because the drug users are less precise about the term than clinicans are. Typical reports include remembering a psychedelic experience upon hearing music that was played at the time, or becoming drunk on alcohol and suddenly feeling afraid to die. Those are not LSD flashbacks, but such reports can inflate the statistics.

A different phenomenon is also called "flashback", but to avoid confusion let us call it "adept skill". In this situation, without using a drug someone enters an altered state of consciousness previously achieved while using a drug. An analogy would be riding a bicycle without assistance from training wheels that were formerly needed; the unassisted ride is a new one, not a replay of a past one. The phenomenon is observed with marijuana; an experienced user can slip into the desired state without help from the drug. With LSD, too, the phenomenon grows in frequency with the amount of experience an individual has with the drug. The implication is that achieving altered states of consciousness is a learned skill, an ability inherent in everyone, and that drugs simply help teach people how to do it. Once they have learned, they no longer need the drugs. From this viewpoint "adept skill" is a desirable consequence of LSD, not a hazard. Indeed, one study found that most users welcome "adept skill".

Those of us around LSD users need fear no harm from them. They cause no more traffic accidents than anyone else. Careful study fails to reveal significant psychological difference between LSD users and everyone else. LSD may be part of the lifestyle chosen by hippies and flower children, but LSD did not cause them to choose that lifestyle. Despite intense publicity, the drug has never been popular; most regular users take it in moderation; and most quit after a while (a process called "maturing out"). LSD has never raised problems of public health or social cost.

The substances mentioned in this chapter cover the range in illicit drugs of abuse - sedative, stimulants, and hallucinogens. There are none worse. Yet our examination shows them to be far less powerful and dangerous than commonly believed. Scientists who study these drugs are often unable to support claims promoted by drug war zealots; claims of instant addiction, of moral and physical degradation, of massive drug-induced psychosis stalking the land. Abuse of drugs can have bad consequences, as can abuse of anything else. We should respect these chemicals, but we need not fear them.

If illicit drugs do no harm when used in moderation, if they cause harm only when used to excess, we must face the question of why anyone would voluntarily engage in self-destructive behavior. The answer offered in the next chapter will show still more limits to the power of drugs.

3. The Effects of Drugs
Michael Gossop

In Xanadu did Kubla Khan
A stately pleasure-dome decree:
Where Alph, the sacred river, ran
Through caverns measureless to man
Down to a sunless sea.

. . . .

I would build that dome in air,
That sunny dome! those caves of ice!
And all who heard should see them there,
And all should cry, Beware! Beware!
His flashing eyes, his floating hair!
Weave a circle round him thrice,
And close your eyes with holy dread,
For he on honey-dew hath fed,
And drunk the milk of Paradise.

Opium is traditionally the drug of dreams, and these lines from Coleridge's *Kubla Khan* were inspired by opium: the rhythm of the poem reflects something of the hypnotic quality of the drug itself. There is also an intriguing allusion to opium within the poem. Coleridge had an extensive knowledge of the classics and as a lifelong opium addict he can hardly have failed to notice the references to the drug in classical literature. In the *Aeneid*, Virgil writes of *Humida mella soperiferumque papaver* (The narcotic poppy with honey-dew; Book IV, line 486).

Coleridge described how, after drinking laudanum, he fell into a drug-induced trance in which he seemed to compose two or three hundred lines of poetry. The images rose up before him as if he were the passive observer. When he awoke, he began to write them down, but was interrupted by a visitor. After returning to his writing, he found he was left with only the vaguest recollection of his original vision and could remember no more than a few scattered lines and images. Coleridge did not publish *Kubla Khan* for almost twenty years after it was written, and then only on the urging of Byron. This was probably because of his doubts about the worth of what he rather dismissively described as 'a psychological curiosity'.

The suggestion that *Kubla Khan* was inspired by opium produced intense feelings in literary circles. To some romantics, the notion that this entrancing vision could have been inspired by the drug of dreams was very appealing. Others were just as strongly offended by the idea. One recent biography, for instance, utterly rejects Coleridge's own account of how the poem was inspired, preferring instead to talk of writing poetry as 'a

Michael Gossop: *LIVING WITH DRUGS*, (Ashgate, 1993), pp. 14-29. © Michael Gossop 1993.

labour as hard and exhausting as road building'.* This same puritan reinterpretation of Coleridge's own account of the poem's origins asserts that, far from contributing to Coleridge's poetry, opium was directly responsible for extinguishing it.

In fact, both Coleridge and his puritan critics share the same misconception. Opium was not the source of his poetry nor did it lead to the death of his muse. The effects of a drug depend largely upon the psychology of the person who has taken it. Had Coleridge not experienced that particular drug-reverie of which he spoke, he might never have been inspired to write *Kubla Khan*. At the same time, the vision itself, and more particularly the translation of that experience into lines of poetry afterwards, owed more to the personality and talent of Coleridge than it did to any drug. It is patently absurd to claim that anyone can produce great poetry merely by taking drugs, though some drug takers have been convinced of the depth of their artistic vision when intoxicated.

The way in which a drug affects the person who has taken it depends as much upon the psychological characteristics of the individual (his personality, how he believes the drug will affect him, his emotional state, etc) as upon the chemical properties of the drug itself. The idea that specific drugs have fixed and predictable effects which are the same from person to person is extremely widespread, but it remains a fallacy. In the particular case of the psychoactive drugs, such effects are the exception rather than the rule.

Few people have difficulty in understanding that different people react in different ways after drinking alcohol. Thinking of other drugs, they often forget how much the psychology of the individual can influence the drug effects. The biochemistry of a drug is only one of a wide range of factors that interact to produce the final effects. These depend to a certain extent upon the basic personality structure of the person who took it. Reactions to alcohol (and to other sedative drugs such as the barbiturates), for instance, seem to depend upon whether the drinker is an introvert or an extravert. The typical extravert is sociable, likes parties, has many friends and prefers the company of others to being alone. He looks for excitement and enjoys taking chances. The typical introvert is a quiet, retiring sort of person who is reserved and reticent except with his close friends. He tends to plan ahead rather than act impulsively, is reliable, and usually rather pessimistic. Introverts seem to be comparatively resistant to the effects of alcohol, whereas extraverts succumb to its intoxicating influence much more readily. The opposite is true of stimulant drugs like amphetamine or caffeine. Introverts react more strongly to these drugs and extraverts least.

One way of demonstrating this involves giving a sedative such as a barbiturate to groups of subjects who differ in their levels of introversion/extraversion. This has been done in several experiments, and it has been found that the amount of a sedative necessary to produce a given level of sedation varies considerably between introverts and extraverts. A standard dose of the drug sufficient to sedate more than 95 per cent of the most extraverted subjects will sedate fewer than 10 per cent of the introverted subjects.

* Molly Lefebure, *Samuel Taylor Coleridge. A Bondage of Opium*. London: Gollancz, 1974.

Because of the way drugs are classified (in this case, either as stimulants or as sedatives), the way they relate to personality and behaviour is often misunderstood. It is assumed that any drug which is classified as stimulant will make the person who takes it more impulsive and excitable, whereas sedative drugs will make him quieter and less excitable - roughly speaking, that stimulants will make the user more extraverted, and sedatives will make him more introverted. In fact, the opposite is nearer to the truth. The physiological action of stimulants generally makes the user more *introverted* and sedatives make him more *extraverted*. (The physiological basis for this is quite complicated and the details need not concern us here. For the reader who is interested in this effect, a full account is given by Hans Eysenck in his book *The Biological Basis of Personality*).

In practice, the extraverting effects of sedative drugs are already well-known. Alcohol is widely used for precisely this purpose at social gatherings such as parties. At most parties, the extraverted behaviour of the guests can be directly linked to the amount of drink that has been consumed. Drunkenness is a chemical equivalent of extreme extraversion. There is, of course, a limit to this effect. In very large quantities the sedative effects of alcohol have a disruptive effect on behaviour, and finally it produces unconsciousness.

Although the introverting effects of stimulants are less well-known, these drugs have been used in psychiatry for some years, mainly in the treatment of hyperactive children. Superficially it might seem strange that stimulant drugs have been used to calm impulsive, irritable and intractable children. The paradox, however, is more apparent than real provided one reminds oneself that drugs such as the amphetamines and methylphenidate (Ritalin, an amphetamine-like stimulant) can have an introverting effect upon behaviour. Usually between 60 and 90 per cent of hyperactive children show some improvement after being given stimulants. Unfortunately, the treatment seems to be effective only for as long as the child continues to take the drugs. Many of those which show a marked improvement while on the medication fail to maintain these gains when the drug is withdrawn. In the long-term, it seems that children who have been given this form of drug treatment do no better than those who have not.

The user's beliefs about his drugs

Taking a drug is not a psychologically neutral event. Whether it is prescribed by a physician, bought over the counter of the local chemist, or obtained through illegal sources, the user will almost certainly have clear ideas about how and when it is appropriate to use the drug, and about the ways in which it is likely to affect his or her thoughts, feelings and behaviour. Even in those rare cases where users have no knowledge of the drug they have taken, they actively search for reasonable explanations about how the drug might be affecting them. These psychological and social influences are generated by the users themselves, by what they have been told by others, and by the immediate social circumstances in which the drug is taken; and these influences are powerful enough to alter a user's response to the pharmacological effects of the drug itself.

One study which demonstrates this was carried out at the University of Stockholm. The subjects who had volunteered to take part were divided into three groups. The first received a fairly large dose of one of the most common of the sleeping tablets currently being prescribed (200 mg. of pentobarbital) and were told that this would make them feel sleepy. The subjects in the second group were given the same sedative drug but the experimenter told them that he did not know what sort of effect it would have. Those in the third group were not given any drug at all, merely a capsule containing a pharmacologically inert powder, but they were given the same explanation as the first group - that this was a sleeping tablet that would make them feel tired and drowsy. As predicted, those who were given the active drug together with the information that this would make them feel sleepy, showed the greatest response. However, the direct drug effects alone were no more powerful than the experimenter's suggestions alone: both produced the same amount of drowsiness.

The physiological actions of drugs are not sufficient to produce the sort of psychological changes associated with the use of psychoactive drugs (e.g. euphoria). Before this can happen, the user must attach a psychological 'label' to the way he feels (though this labelling seldom occurs at a conscious level).

One of the best-known investigations of this labelling process was carried out by the American psychologists Stanley Schachter and Jerome Singer. In their ingenious study, the student volunteers were led to believe that they were taking part in a psychology experiment concerned with vision. The subjects were given an injection of adrenaline, a hormone produced in the central nervous system which causes a wide range of physiological changes in the body but no consistent psychological effects. One group was given an accurate description of the effects of the drug - that they might have a sensation of their heart beating faster, and experience some hand tremor and a warm and flushed feeling in the face. They were reassured that these effects would last only for a short time. Another group was given a misleading description of how the drug would affect them. They were told that it would cause numbness in the feet, itching sensations and a slight headache.

In the second part of the experiment, the subjects were asked individually to go to a waiting room to let the drug take effect before the start of the visual tests. In the waiting room was another 'subject' waiting for the visual tests. In fact, this other subject was really an actor who was part of the experiment. While the two are together in the waiting room, the actor starts to behave in a most peculiar fashion. He runs about the room playing basketball with a scrap of paper and a waste paper basket, makes paper aeroplanes which he throws around the room, and generally behaves in an exuberant and excitable manner.

The experiment was designed to investigate the ways in which emotional states (such as euphoria) are produced, and the real interest of the experimenters was to find out how the subjects behaved in the waiting room. The two groups in the experiment both received the same drug and were exposed to the same unusual behaviour of the waiting room. They differed only in one respect. The first group already knew how the drug would affect them; the second group did not. The results show that the people who had been misled about how the drug would affect them were more likely to be influenced by, and to imitate, the actor's behaviour: they too were inclined to become euphoric and excited.

The same experiment was then repeated, but with three groups. One received an injection of adrenaline plus an explanation of how it would affect them; the second group was given the drug but with no explanation of its effects; and a third was given a placebo injection. The subjects were then taken one at a time to the waiting room. This time the actor's performance was one of irritation and anger. Again, those who knew that their altered physiological state was due to the adrenaline were least affected by the actor's behaviour. Those who had been given the drug but no explanation of how it would affect them were more likely to become angry and irritable. The placebo group were less influenced by the events in the waiting room than those who had been given the drug but no description of its physiological effects, but more so than those who had received the drug plus an accurate description.

In this experiment, there are two factors at work. On the one hand, there is the physiological arousal (heart beating faster, tremor, etc) caused by the drug itself and, on the other, there are the expectations and beliefs that the person has about his state of arousal. When people do not understand why they feel the way they do, they seem to relate their feelings to the particular situation in which they find themselves. It is as if the subjects who did not know how the drug would affect them had said to themselves, 'I feel strange. My heart is racing and I am trembling. Therefore I must feel angry/happy like the other person in the experiment'. Those who already knew how the adrenaline would affect them were uninfluenced by the actor's behaviour because they could attribute their altered physiological state to the drug.

The beliefs, attitudes and expectations of the drug taker are no less important outside the laboratory. In what has since established itself as one of the classic studies of cannabis smokers, Howard Becker looked at the ways in which a person learns how to get stoned on the drug. The first time someone tries cannabis, he does not usually get high. Sometimes the user feels a little strange, but is not sure how to interpret the changes he experiences. Sometimes the effects are perceived as being physically unpleasant and the novice may actually be sick. Sometimes users may claim, rather indignantly, that they do not feel any different at all. When this happens they may decide that the whole business of smoking cannabis is simply not worthwhile; or they may be worried by their failure to experience any euphoric effects and ask others about it. In such conversations they will be made aware of specific details of their experience with the drug which they may not have noticed before, or which they had noticed but failed to identify as a part of being stoned. So the next time they try cannabis they will be better prepared to know when they are stoned.

Novices must learn the details of how if feels to be stoned, and acquire the necessary concepts to be able to identify and describe how they feel after smoking cannabis. Before that, the effects of the drug are sufficiently ambiguous for them not to know how they feel (as in the result of those experiments where the subjects did not know which drug they had taken). Inexperienced drug takers sometimes become confused and frightened by their early experiments with drugs. They may be so alarmed by the changes in their state of consciousness that they become convinced at the time that they are going insane. Yet the same alterations and distortions of consciousness which so frighten the novice may be regarded by the experienced drug taker as extremely pleasurable. Nor is there anything unique about cannabis in this respect. Drugs such as heroin also require an initial period during which the novice learns how to interpret their effects. Most people find their first experience of heroin unpleasant, and many are sick. In one study where a group of non-addicts were given either a small injection of heroin or a placebo, the placebo was reported to be more pleasurable than heroin. One can go through a whole list of drugs making the same point. Most children experimenting with their first cigarette find it a nauseous experience. Similarly, most people find their first taste of alcohol far from appealing. In order to become a regular drug user is it necessary to learn how to enjoy the effects.

After people have learnt how to experience the effects of a drug, their beliefs and expectations about that drug may lead them to react as if they were intoxicated when they had not taken a drug at all. In one study of experienced cannabis smokers, the subjects were given cigarettes containing either cannabis or a placebo preparation of cannabis material from which the active drug had been artificially removed. Although the average level of intoxication reported after smoking the placebo was lower than for cannabis, some of the subjects felt just as intoxicated on the placebo as on the active drug. The more experienced cannabis users were the most likely to get stoned on the placebo, whereas those who had had least experience with cannabis were better able to differentiate between the drug and the placebo.

The placebo effect

> Fillet of a fenny snake,
> In the cauldron boil and bake;
> Eye of newt, and toe of frog,
> Wool of bat, and tongue of dog,
> Adder's fork, and blind worm's sting,
> Lizard's leg, and howlet's wing,
> For a charm of pow'rful trouble,
> Like a hell-broth boil and bubble.
> *Macbeth*, IV.i. 12-19

Because psychological factors play such a large part in determining how people respond to drugs, it is possible for them to react as if they had taken a drug even when no such drug has been used. This is, of course, the placebo effect (i.e. those psychological and physiological changes produced by the placebo). Conventional definitions of a placebo usually emphasise that it should be a pharmacologically inert substance: starch, talc, and sugar powder are often used in making up placebos. These 'dummy' tablets may be thought of as 'pure' placebos in the sense that they have no pharmacological effects, but it is too restrictive to think of a placebo only as a completely inert preparation. 'Pure' placebos are not used very often except in controlled experiments; for most practical purposes it is the 'impure' placebo that is more important. This is any medicine or treatment which is prescribed because either the doctor, or the patient, or both, believe that it works, but which really has no specific effects upon the condition being treated. Many pharmacologically active drugs are used for their placebo effect in this way.

Placebos belong to that twilight world of medical science that has never quite been able to claim respectability. This is a pity, because the placebo effect is both interesting and important. It is important in practical terms because it is a major therapeutic influence (albeit an unacknowledged one) in many medical treatments. It is important in theoretical terms because it highlights the psychological component of the response to drugs.

All manner of extraordinary organic and inorganic substances, including almost every conceivable form of human and animal excretion, have been used as medicines at one time or another. Crocodile dung, the teeth of pigs, hooves of asses, eunuch fat, lozenges of dried vipers, powders made from precious stones, brick dust, fur, feathers, hair, human sweat, earthworms and spiders have all taken their place among the tools of the physician: by comparison, the witches' brew described in *Macbeth* seems positively benign. In these enlightened times, few physicians would place much confidence in such esoteric preparations. On the other hand, it has been suggested that as many as one-third of all prescriptions issued by British and American doctors may be for drugs which have no specific pharmacological effects upon the condition being treated (i.e. they are placebos).

To many people, the placebo carries rather derisory connotations which may, in part, be due to the idea that doctors use placebos as a harmless method of humouring demanding or difficult patients. Undoubtedly this does happen. But more often, placebos are not prescribed deliberately to deceive the patient, but with both the doctor and the patient believing them to be an effective medicine. Far from being the omniscient, detached scientists who know what 'really' has therapeutic value and who sometimes use placebos just to keep the patient quiet, many physicians unwittingly use valueless drugs because their personal experience tells them wrongly that they are 'getting results'.

In ancient Egypt, the physicians who prescribed crocodile dung did so not merely to have a cynical laugh at the patient's expense; nor is it entirely plausible to believe that they carried on using this unusual medication in the absence of any improvement by their patients. In the same way, patients have been purged, poisoned, punctured, blistered, bled, leeched, heated, frozen, sweated and shocked. Treatments which were administered so confidently have turned out to be either ineffective or dangerous, or both. One can only assume that the physicians' faith in their remedies was strong enough to establish in the patient the hope and expectation that they would lead to improvement. As a result, both the patient and the physician would interpret the symptoms more optimistically after the medicine had been taken, and in many cases there would indeed be a marked improvement in the patient's condition. Nor should the reader suppose that the problems which respond favourably to placebos are imaginary or 'only psychological'. Severe post-operative pain, chest pain associated with coronary heart disease, multiple sclerosis, diabetes, radiation sickness, stomach ulcers, toothache, sea-sickness, arthritis and the common cold are just a few of the disorders in which placebos have produced a therapeutic improvement. Across a wide range of problems, the proportion of patients who improve after receiving a placebo averages out at about 35 per cent.

Placebo responses can be more powerful than those to active drugs. The psychological response to a drug may also profoundly alter or even reverse the direct drug effects, and as with active drugs, placebos can produce unwanted side-effects. Headache, nausea, dryness of the mouth, drowsiness and tiredness have all been reported by people who have taken a placebo. In some cases there have been major toxic reactions. After being given a placebo containing sugar powder, one patient complained of extreme weakness, palpitations of the heart and nausea; another developed a widespread skin rash (which disappeared after he stopped taking the placebo). There are even cases in which people have become addicted to placebos, and in the *Journal of the American Medical Association* an editorial warned that 'When withdrawing a placebo on which a patient has become dependent it will not help him to be told that it was only a placebo.' It is difficult to imagine a more convincing illustration of the essentially psychological nature of drug dependence than an addiction to placebos.

Nor should it be imagined that an addiction to placebos is necessarily trivial. Many active drugs are used inappropriately because the user wrongly attributes the placebo effect associated with taking the drug to the drug itself. Pain-relieving (analgesic) drugs such as aspirin and paracetamol are the world's most widely used drugs. They are also the most widely misused drugs. They are seldom taken under medical supervision, and generally they are unwittingly used for the placebo effect that goes with them. For example, they are regularly taken to suppress the symptoms of the common cold, yet aspirin has no effect upon viruses or bacteria; they are also taken to help the user to get to sleep, though their sedative properties are minimal. The United States consumes more than 9,000 tons of aspirin each year (the equivalent of about 44 million tablets every day). A study of blood donors in Connecticut found that 37 per cent of the people who gave blood had recently eaten aspirin. These drugs are at least as popular in Britain which swallows a yearly supply of some 2,000 tons of analgesics (about 4,300 million tablets), and where there are more than a million people who use them regularly each day. One criterion for identifying analgesic abuse is the consumption of more than one kilo (2.2 lb) of the drug in a six-month period. On this basis, it has been estimated that there may be as many as a quarter of a million analgesic abusers in Britain. The heaviest user of such drugs that I have seen was a 42-year-old woman who was obviously dependent upon them as any junkie is upon his heroin. She was using between two and three hundred aspirin tablets per week.

This form of drug abuse is encouraged by the misconception that these tablets are not really 'drugs' at all, and that they can be used as often as one likes without ill-effects. This is not so. Some 7,000 patients each year are admitted to British hospitals for aspirin-induced gastro-intestinal bleeding (usually associated with stomach ulcers). Heavy use of these drugs can also cause kidney damage, and they are one of the most common causes of accidental death among children. Such extensive misuse of these drugs reflects a deeper need to obtain instant chemical relief from each and every one of the aches and pains that are part of living.

The placebo effect can be observed in another eternal preoccupation - the search for a reliable aphrodisiac. Papyri from ancient Egypt have been found with instructions for preparing 'erotic potions', and the Greeks too wrote at length on this subject (as in the

31

Medea of Euripides). There is even a reference to the subject in the Bible (Genesis 30: 14-16), where Leah used the mandrake to 'lie with' Jacob.

The mandrake holds a position of unrivalled importance in European witchcraft because of its magical properties. It was said, for instance, to utter such unearthly shrieks when pulled from the ground that whoever heard them might die. Early Christians thought it was created by God as an experiment before He created man in the Garden of Eden, and Machiavelli was sufficiently impressed by its erotic powers to write a comedy in its honour (*La Mandragola*). Despite all this, the mandrake has no chemical properties that would make it a useful aphrodisiac, though its major components (scopolamine, atropine and hyoscamine) could produce distortions of consciousness that might render the user more susceptible to persuasion. In this century, scopolamine has been used in interrogation procedures as a 'truth drug'.

In Western societies, the truffle and the oyster have a current reputation as aphrodisiac foods. Sadly, neither contains anything which is remotely likely to fire the passions. The constituents of the oyster are water (76-89%), carbohydrates (3.7-9.6%), mineral salts (0.9-3%), proteins (8-11%) and fat (1.2-2.5%). When subjected to this sort of chemical analysis, the truffle proved to be even less sexy: 77% water, 13.5% carbohydrates, and the remainder fat, albumen and salts. Few of the other reputed aphrodisiacs do much better. Even the humble potato was once regarded as an especially useful erotic stimulant.

The aphrodisiac effect of these foods and drugs is without any physio-chemical basis, though it is some testimony to the fact that they are not completely useless that these and other substances have been so persistently used in seductions. The reasons for this are psychological. The aphrodisiac is really a special sort of placebo. A good meal in relaxed surroundings can be a most effective means of turning the thoughts towards other sensual pleasures. This can be assisted by that least arcane of the seducer's devices - alcohol.

> Candy
> Is dandy
> But liquor
> Is quicker.
> (Ogden Nash)

However, even the effects of alcohol are indirect. It does not provoke sexual desire directly so much as remove the customary restraints on such behaviour. The would-be Lothario might do well to remember Shakespeare's warning about alcohol: 'it provokes the desire, but it takes away the performance' (*Macbeth*, IV. iii. 29-30).

Spanish fly is a quite different kinds of aphrodisiac in that its physiological effects are supposed to work directly upon the genitals. The drug is prepared from a beautiful sheen-covered beetle found in southern Europe which is dried and heated until it disintegrates into fine powder. This contains a drug called cantharidin which causes acute irritation of the gastro-intestinal system and an inflammation of the urinary tract. This provides some sort of genital stimulation which can be perceived as sexual desire. The use of Spanish fly is not to be recommended, as it carries a number of dangers.

In recent years, Vitamin E and ginseng have established themselves in some quarters as fashionable drugs. Claims about their effectiveness have been typically extravagant, and if one were to believe everything that has been said about them there would be few ills left to mankind. Vitamin E is ideally suited to the commercial exploitation of those in search of a panacea since it can be taken in enormous doses without producing any toxic effects. On the other hand, it has no beneficial effect either. It has been promoted and used for every imaginable disorder, from acne to cancer, from baldness to coronary heart disease. As a drug in search of an illness, it is the latest example of the age-old fallacy that health, happiness and sexual fulfilment are all available in tablet form. Ginseng also fulfils this need, though it is a more potent drug than Vitamin E. It has been known and used in China for thousands of years, and in traditional Chinese medicine its effects are explained in terms of harmonizing the balance of yin and yang forces in the five bodily systems. It seems to act as a mild stimulant drug, much like coffee, and it may also possess anti-inflammatory properties. Predictably, both Vitamin E and ginseng have been hailed as aphrodisiacs (few substances have not). In the end, though, there is little evidence to show the existence of any such beast as the reliable aphrodisiac. Sexual desire is too capricious to respond obediently and automatically to the demands of a drug.

Mechanisms of drug action

The significance of psychological factors in determining how someone will react to a psychoactive drug has been vastly underestimated. However, it would be just as seriously misleading to give too much weight to psychological factors. Drugs are chemical agents which are capable of producing rapid and powerful effects. A simple but valuable reminder of how drug effects are produced is shown overleaf.

The psychology of the user, the social setting in which he or she takes drugs, and the specific pharmacological properties of the drug all influence how the user finally responds to the drug. Sometimes the psychological factors are most important (as with the placebo effect); sometimes social factors are the most powerful influence; and sometimes the pharmacology of the drug plays the most important role (especially at high dose levels). The emphasis given in this chapter to the psychology of the drug taker is intended to serve as an antidote to the more orthodox view that the effects of drugs are *intrinsic* properties of those substances. It is a grave mistake to imagine that we can understand the ways in which people respond to psychoactive drugs simply as a consequence of physiological reactions to a chemical substance. Nonetheless, psychoactive drugs do have effects upon the brain and bodily systems of the drug taker, and some of these effects are very interesting in their own right.

The manner in which people take drugs can also influence the effects experienced by the user. For instance, a drug which is taken by intravenous injection will have a more rapid and more powerful impact upon the user than one which is swallowed and absorbed through the stomach. Smoking is also a very effective way of taking drugs.

Nicotine, for example, is rapidly absorbed through the lungs and reaches the brain within a few seconds. It takes only 7 seconds for nicotine in the lungs to reach the brain

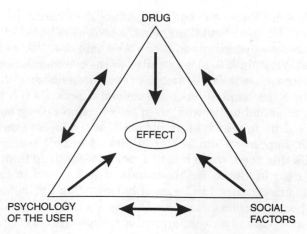

Figure 1.   A model of drug effects.

compared with 14 seconds for blood to flow from arm to brain after an intravenous injection.

The route by which a drug is taken can influence the development of dependence. In general, those who take cocaine by sniffing it appear to be at lower risk of becoming dependent than those who smoke it. Those who take tobacco as snuff do not appear to become as dependent upon the habit as cigarette smokers. Similarly, heroin smokers appear to be at lower risk of dependence than those who inject it. This lower dependence risk seems to be related to the route by which the drug is taken, though the mechanism underlying this is not known. It may be due to the user's response to the intensity or the speed of changes in drug concentrations in the bloodstream.

During the 1950s a young psychologist at McGill University in Canada was interested in the way in which particular areas of the brain affected learning. To test one of his ideas, he planned to apply an extremely small electric current to the brain of his laboratory animals. At that time, the technique of implanting electrodes in the brain was still extremely crude and unreliable, and through an accident one of the electrodes was implanted in an entirely different area of the brain to the one originally intended. As a result, the animal did not show the expected alerting response to the electrical stimulation, and many other scientists might have simply removed the animal and continued with the experiment. Dr Olds, however, was intrigued by the fact that the rat seemed to be interested in the part of the cage where it had received the electrical stimulation. After it had been given a few more tastes of the brain stimulation, the rat never left that part of the cage. It seemed as if it were waiting for more.

Later, when the experiment was systematically repeated, it was found that animals which had the opportunity of administering their own dose of electrical stimulation would press a lever repeatedly in order to obtain it. Some animals would deliver more than a hundred doses per minute; and if left to their own devices, they would maintain this pace for hour after hour. This only happened when the electrodes were located in a specific part of the brain - in what is called the limbic system. The functions of this area of the brain are not well understood, but it is known to play an important part in regulating the emotions. Olds' experiments represented a remarkable discovery. Never before had there been any suggestion that electrical stimulation of the brain could be pleasurable. And there seemed little doubt that the experimental animals enjoyed the experience. Animals that had not received any electrical stimulations for several days would jump out of the experimenter's hand into the test apparatus in their eagerness for more. On the rare occasions when this electrical stimulation has been tried with human subjects, it has produced feelings of euphoria and sexual pleasure. One female subject experienced repetitive orgasms after five to ten minutes of such stimulation. Not surprisingly, these areas of the brain rapidly became known as 'the pleasure centres'.

This research generated considerable excitement. To many people, it reawakened the ancient fear that others could take control of one's own mind. In his *Profiles of the Future*, Arthur C. Clarke spoke of the possibility that it could lead to 'the electronic possession of human robots' and commented that this research may turn out to have more far-reaching consequences than the early work of the nuclear physicists: 'the possibilities here, for good and evil, are so obvious that there is no point in exaggerating or discounting them'.

These early experiments fired the enthusiasm of some researchers who thought that stimulation of the pleasure centres could offer a neurophysiological explanation of drug taking. After a drug enters the bloodstream it is rapidly absorbed into the brain, and several proponents of this view of drug taking have suggested that many of the psychoactive drugs act directly on the pleasure centres of the brain. With repeated use these drugs were said to swamp the brain's ability to respond to other pleasurable forms of stimulation and the person's capacity to experience pleasure at all, except through the use of higher and higher doses of drugs. This account has a certain superficial plausibility, and it may contain some element of truth; but it has a number of serious weaknesses as an explanation of drug taking. It conveniently chooses to ignore those aspects of drug taking that cannot be explained in physiological terms. For instance, if psychoactive drugs stimulate the pleasure centres of the brain directly, this suggests that the drug experience should be one of unambiguous pleasure; and if the experimental studies are correct, it should be almost irresistible in its attractions. Yet many people find their first experience with drugs to be distinctly unpleasant: only later do they learn to enjoy the effects. Similarly, the vast majority of those who have used drugs on several occasions never became addicted to them; and even among drug addicts, very few people compulsively fill themselves with the maximum amount of drugs even when they have more than enough for their immediate needs, and eventually a sizeable number of addicts stop using drugs.

These features of drug taking are seldom recognized because they do not fit neatly into a physiological explanation. The reader may recall the legend of Procrustes, the robber who waylaid travellers and tied them to a bed. If they were longer than the bed he chopped off the offending limbs, and if they were too short, he stretched them until both bed and traveller were the same length.

In the middle of the 1970s, another scientific development revived flagging interest in the possible relationship between brain mechanisms and drug effects. Professor Hans Kosterlitz and his research team at Aberdeen University identified a number of chemical substances in the brain which had a remarkable biochemical similarity to morphine. The resemblance seemed so close that these substances were named endorphins, an abbreviation for endogenous (natural) morphine. Throughout the central nervous system, there are specific receptors programmed to react to these endorphins. It is too early to reach any definite conclusions about the significance of these complex neurochemicals. They are still a comparatively recent discovery, and the research programme surrounding them is now so intense that almost any statement is likely to be out of date by the time it is published.

One interesting possibility is that such chemicals are produced by the brain as a natural defence against pain. For instance, there have been several observations that endorphins are released in greater quantities during childbirth, and that this could account for the reduced sensitivity to pain at such times. It has been reported that the release of endorphins is often found after acupuncture intended to relieve pain. It has also been argued that endorphins could provide a neurochemical basis for that curious phenomenon, the placebo effect; but for the moment these comments are no more than speculative suggestions.

The existence of these chemicals and of receptors in the brain programmed to react both to them and to drugs such as heroin and cocaine, would appear to have great significance for our understanding of opiate addiction. Hans Kosterlitz has described how this recent research could provide a foundation for explaining the tolerance and withdrawal effects associated with opiate addiction. Under normal circumstances the endorphins probably maintain the balance of the nerve impulses in the brain which respond to pain and stress. The opiate drugs, however, are more toxic than their naturally occurring counterparts. As a result, the opiates overwhelm the body's natural chemicals and take over the control of these pain-inhibiting mechanisms. With repeated use, the drugs may reduce the body's sensitivity to the natural chemicals, or even reduce its capacity to produce such chemicals. The body then becomes dependent upon its outside supply of drugs in order to function normally, and when the opiates are withdrawn, the body's natural responses are inadequate.

Recent research into another brain neurochemical called *dopamine* has revived interest in the pleasure centres of the limbic system. Dopamine acts upon the mechanisms of nerve transmission in the brain and it appears to be one of the important pharmacological agents involved in the experience of pleasure.

Studies of such neurochemicals may account for at least some of the phenomena of tolerance and withdrawal in opiate addiction. It would, however, be a mistake to elevate physiological descriptions of this sort into a complete explanation of drug taking, as some have already tried to do. It would be mistaken even to assume that a description of what happens to the neurochemical systems of the body could explain all that happens to addicts as they become tolerant to opiates or during the period of withdrawal from these drugs. At most, it delineates the mechanisms upon which the symptoms of withdrawal may be based.

The Nature of Addiction - Not a *Simple* Issue

Given that the effects of drugs are less straightforward than is commonly thought, it should not be surprising to learn that an understanding of what addiction *is* is also complex. Basic formulations of addiction have often relied upon seeing it as either resulting from the compelling properties of the drug itself, acting on and making the body depend upon it or, as in the case of Alcoholics Anonymous and Narcotics Anonymous, as a 'disease' (perhaps the most common public perception) which once contracted is a disease for life, complete abstinence being the only 'cure'. Heather and Robertson seek to illustrate the weaknesses in this latter position and argue that addiction is in fact as much a learned (and thus psychological) state as it is a pathological one and as such it can be un-learned. Miller had earlier referred to therapeutic addicts, who developed resonance (physical dependence) to opiates during post-operative treatment, but who were able to withdraw from them with ease. Therapeutic addicts who respond in this way are not seen to be 'addicted' in its fullest meaning because, when the time came for ending their opiate use, a *purely* physical attachment to the drug was not sufficient to keep them wanting to use it, thus supporting the concept of addiction as having an important psychological component. More anomalies for those wishing to pursue a primarily physiological or biochemical origin to addiction are raised by Falk. Using anthropological examples of drug use he seeks to demonstrate that expected effects, including addicted states, are often primarily determined by the environment in which drug use occurs and the way the individual responds (often in a *relatively* culture bound way) to it. To this point, a purely substance or physiologically orientated perspective on what addiction *is* has been seen to be undermined by important considerations of the psychological (set) and the social (setting) environment in which it occurs. Orford takes us one step further. Should addiction be understood as only occurring where substances are involved, or is substance addiction only one component (albeit often the most visible) of a broader concept which can account for not just drug addiction but also a range of other 'addictive behaviours' such as compulsive and excessive gambling, eating, and sexual activity, amongst others? If Orford is right, then a conceptual understanding of drug addiction needs to privilege biology and/or pharmacology less, and give greater weight to the social and the psychological elements which are involved in a behaviour becoming something more than occassional and non-problematic.

The paper by Room takes us a little further again. By discussing the way that concepts like addiction are *produced,* Room questions the 'given' nature of *addiction* as something which simply exists and that we merely need to 'know' more to understand it. Rather he suggests that how we try to understand something like addiction may tell us 'as much about the structures of thought in a given social order than about the nature or reality of individual experience'.

4.   Is Alcoholism a Disease?

Nick Heather and Ian Robertson

The idea that alcoholism or problem drinking is a disease has been growing in popularity for the last 20 or 30 years, and would now be regarded as a mark of liberal and enlightened opinion. The irony is that, during this period, among those professionally involved with treating and researching alcohol problems, "the disease concept of alcoholism" has waned considerably as a credible explanatory and practical tool, and is now often regarded as deeply misleading and unhelpful. The consequence has been the emergence of a huge gap between the popular and the specialist view of the subject and a great deal of confusion. It is high time a serious attempt is made to communicate the new scientific understanding, and the evidence on which it is based, to the non-specialist.

Part of the reason for the confusion is that it is sometimes not made clear what exactly is meant by claiming alcoholism to be a disease. If all that is intended by this is that alcoholics should not be blamed and punished for their behaviour, but should be treated with compassion and care, then this is certainly not an issue. No critic of the disease concept of alcoholism suggests for one moment that we should return to a moralistic and punitive response. The trouble is, of course, that for many members of the general public, this moral attitude is the only alternative to the disease view of which they are aware.

What is essential to get across is that there does now exist an alternative model - one based on the principles of modern psychology and, in particular on the branch known as *social learning theory* - which makes it possible to deny that alcoholics are "sick" without at the same time implying that they are "bad". We will briefly describe this model later in the article.

But why is the social learning alternative necessary, and what precisely is wrong with the disease view?

The answer is that, quite apart from its general humanitarian content, the disease perspective carries with it a set of specific but erroneous assumptions about the nature of alcohol problems, which have had a profound effect on the way these problems are understood in our society. These assumptions have been strongly influenced by a stereotype of alcoholism propounded by that remarkable fellowship of men and women called Alcoholics Anonymous, and are almost daily reinforced by media representations of the subject, both factual and fictional, and by the pronouncements of celebrities who declare themselves to be "recovering alcoholics" and affiliates of AA. The efforts of AA in the field have been truly heroic, but it can be argued that its continuing influence on the public understanding of problem drinking is seriously impeding progress.

Nick Heather and Ian Robertson: 'Is Alcoholism a Disease?' *NEW SOCIETY*, 21 February, 1986, pp. 318-320. © New Society 1986. Reprinted by permission of New Statesman and Society.

The main assumptions of the disease perspective, as presented by AA, are that alcoholics possess an inborn, constitutional abnormality which prevents them from ever drinking normally; that this abnormality results in a "loss of control" over intake, and an insatiable "craving" for more which is triggered off by the smallest quantity of alcohol; that these processes are irreversible, so that the only way to arrest the disease is by lifelong and total abstention; and that, if drinking is continued, it leads invariably to further deterioration, insanity and death. Slogans such as "once an alcoholic, always and alcoholic", and "one drink, one drunk", embody this disease model. Although originally proposed by a lay fellowship, it has been enormously influential in shaping the medical response to problem drinking.

Such is the popularity of this familiar image of alcoholism that it is commonly thought to be grounded in solid scientific research. Nothing could be further from the truth. Its inadequacies became obvious from the very first introduction of proper scientific methods into the field. Indeed, historical evidence has recently been produced to show that the AA model of alcoholism derives much more from the views of the 19th century temperance campaigners than any body of contemporary scientific support.

In the first place, the evidence shows that the drinking behaviour of "alcoholics" obeys the same kind of laws and changes in response to the same kind of influences as the drinking of "non-alcoholics"; it is impossible to draw a hard and fast line between them. Moreover, a great deal of research has shown that the traditional concepts of "loss of control" and "craving" are simply unhelpful in the explanation of harmful drinking. At best these concepts are descriptively inaccurate and, at worst, tautologous - they explain nothing whatever.

Though it is true that many individuals with serious drinking difficulties are best advised, on pragmatic grounds, to solve their problem by total abstinence, the evidence clearly shows that drinking problems are not irreversible in principle. Many problem drinkers can return to harm-free patterns of drinking. Finally, longitudinal studies of drinking problems in the natural environment have found no support for the postulation of an inflexible sequence of "symptoms". Rather, people move into and out of problem-drinking status much more often than is suggested by the disease view.

Admittedly, debates about what does or does not constitute a disease can become obscure. But aside from the research evidence, there is increasing recognition among specialists that the disease perspective has many practical drawbacks for the way we respond to alcohol problems. Chief among the disadvantages for treatment is the fact that it has resulted in a restrictive concentration on the upper end of the spectrum of seriousness and dependence, ignoring the huge numbers of individuals in our society who by no means conform to the AA stereotype but who are damaging their lives in some way by their drinking.

Clearly, such individuals are unlikely to accept a treatment goal of lifelong abstinence. If they imagine this to be the only available solution, they are likely to deny having a problem in the first place. The possibility of substituting a goal of controlled or harm-free drinking has meant that problem drinkers can be helped before the maximum damage has occurred. In contrast to this, the evidence shows that AA is still a "last hope" organisation as far as many problem drinkers are concerned.

The disadvantages of the disease theory for the primary prevention of alcohol problems are perhaps even more striking. The only implication here from the disease standpoint is that, until the elusive "biochemical abnormality" (on the hunt for which millions of pounds in research funds have fruitlessly been spent) is eventually discovered, all we can do is to provide more and better treatment services. Yet the epidemiological evidence clearly shows that the number of alcohol problems to be found in a particular society is closely related to *per capita* alcohol consumption, and this in turn is related to the availability of alcohol, mainly its retail price.

This has led to the view that alcoholism is an essentially political, rather than medical, problem. Until government acts to reduce the total amount of alcohol we all consume, no improvement in alcoholism statistics can occur. Certainly, from the social learning viewpoint, alcohol problems cannot be reduced to personal characteristics of individual problem drinkers, but must be placed in the entire social and political context which gives rise to them.

In case we risk being misunderstood, we must emphasise that a rejection of the disease concept is in no way to minimise the seriousness of alcohol problems or the tragic consequences they often bring. Nor could anyone possibly dispute that excessive drinking *causes* diseases, or that the medical profession should be centrally involved in treating these diseases and, indeed, in attempting to change harmful drinking patterns. We are concerned here with a shift in perspective, rather than merely a power struggle between medical and non-medical workers.

Significantly, some of the most articulate critics of the disease perspective are themselves medically qualified psychiatrists. Their position is that the disease view - though it has resulted in some improvement in the problem drinker's lot, and in a somewhat more humane attitude from the main body of society - has now outlived its usefulness. It is time to move on to a more rational and empirically based understanding of problem drinking.

This new understanding assumes that problem drinking is a learned habitual behaviour, in the same category as compulsive gambling, some forms of over-eating, heroin or tobacco use. Indeed, some of the common features of these phenomena may be observed in a wide range of normal activities carried to excess: compulsive physical exercising, some forms of sexual behaviour, and certain types of compulsive over-working, are just three examples.

The main point is that, when people become dependent on alcohol, the behavioural patterns that develop are not uniquely attributable to the drug, ethyl alcohol. Of course, physical effects *are* important - but these have been highlighted too long at the expense of more crucial social and psychological determinants of the behaviour.

The great advantage of social psychological models of problem drinking is that they have *many* implications for treatment - which disease models do not (apart from the simple necessity of lifelong abstention from alcohol). Social learning theory is an umbrella term for a range of well-established psychological processes, ranging from classic conditioning to self-concept. In this theoretical scheme, conditioning mechanisms are not incompatible with high-level thought processes. Rather, they interact in complex ways. We will outline just a few examples of the application of social learning theory to problem drinking.

In Pavlov's classic experiments, dogs learned to salivate in response to a bell, because the bell was associated with an "unconditioned stimulus" - the smell of meat powder. Thus, the bell, a previously neutral stimulus, became a conditioned stimulus for salivation. Certain responses in humans can also become classically conditioned.

If you repeatedly drink in a certain environment, or at a certain time of day or with certain people, then these stimuli can become "cues" for the desire to drink, through a conditioning process. The main difference, in these terms, between problem drinkers and those who drink without problems is that, with problem drinkers, cues for drinking are more numerous and pervasive. There is also evidence that tolerance to alcohol, withdrawal symptoms, and craving for alcohol, are - at least partly - conditioned phenomena. This is of the greatest possible importance for the treatment of problem drinking, because it suggests that these central features of the dependence process are not irreversible and can be extinguished.

A second type of psychological process is known as instrumental learning. Behaviour which is followed by positive consequences will tend to increase, while negative consequences normally lead to a decrease in the behaviour. When applied to problem drinking, this seems at first sight nonsensical, in view of the obvious distress, injury and disruption which follows in its wake. Why do these negative consequences not lead to a decrease in consumption?

The answer lies in a fundamental law of instrumental learning - the reinforcement which follows the behaviour most closely in time will have the greatest effect on it. For problem drinkers, the immediate effect of drinking is often a reduction in the distress produced by withdrawal symptoms - or, at least, a relative decrease in that distress, compared with what is expected if no alcohol is taken. The experience of problems may not occur until hours, days or even years after the behaviour. Psychologically speaking, these consequences have weak effects because they are distant in time.

But drinking is not just a behaviour. It is also a symbol, full of meaning for drinkers and for those around them. Assuming a particular role or self-image can involve the adoption of heavy drinking as a kind of "membership badge". You have only to think of such roles as "hard-bitten journalist", "biker" or "tortured poet", to understand that drinking may be as much part of a social uniform as a studded leather jacket or a cravat. At the most obvious level, drinking for men is often a potent badge of manhood. And, increasingly, the drinks industry attempts to construct images of sexuality for female drinking.

This partly explains the epidemiological finding that most people who show some problems due to drinking in their twenties do not appear in the statistics for problem drinking 20 years later. This is because they adopt new social roles and self-images, for which heavy drinking is not an appropriate symbol. Marriage is often associated with such changes. Research shows that this is one of the more commonly cited reasons for stopping heavy drinking.

Society, in fact, has various safety nets, which tend to break up habits of youthful roistering. Obviously, however, some problem drinkers manage to slip through, and more ominous self-images and social roles await them. Heavy drinkers tend to seek each other out. They create subcultures in which excessive drinking, hangovers, and complaining spouses become part of a mythology that sustains them in a deviant behaviour pattern, and insulates them from breakdown in other areas of their lives through the bonhomie and inverted values of the pub. This is just one example of how heavy drinking can become enmeshed in an interlocking set of social roles. But many groups in society create unique "drinking cultures", where alcohol and its effects are imbued with particular significance.

Another, somewhat different, kind of role is available for the problem drinker, and is dispensed at Alcoholics Anonymous groups and many alcoholism treatment units throughout the country. It incorporates such images as "I have an incurable disease called alcoholism", and "I can never drink again". Often involved is a propensity to confessional-type disclosures and an almost ritual reciting of past misdeeds. This role has been a haven and life-saver for many problem drinkers. But it has also been unacceptable and even harmful to many others, because of its narrowness, rigidity and exclusiveness, and its tendency to promote self-fulfilling prophecies.

What does this mean in practice? By getting away from the stereotype of the "alcoholic", action falls into a public health context. From a social learning perspective, the distinction between "treatment" and "education" disappears. There could be a spectrum of "minimal" interventions, aimed at harm-free drinking. This could include self-health manuals; "alcohol education courses" for groups of homogenous individuals; or structured information and advice, given by hospital physicians, nurses, general practitioners, company doctors, welfare officers, health visitors, and social workers. The evidence is that minimal interventions can work well.

There will continue, of course, to be many problem drinkers, with more serious difficulties, who need intensive, individual help. But the main message of the new model is that drinking must be understood and treated in the social context in which it has developed and which maintains it - in the problem drinker's everyday world. It is no use whisking problem drinkers off to some residential institution miles away in the country, where they imagine they are completely cured until they return home and almost immediately relapse in the face of the powerful cues for drinking which have remained unaltered. The days of the specialised alcoholism treatment units, on which much of the British response to problem drinking has been based, are numbered. These are increasingly being replaced by the kind of comprehensive community service heralded by the reports of the DHSS Advisory Committee on Alcoholism in 1978.

Ultimately, what is needed is a radical change in norms about, and attitudes to, drinking - helped by deliberate government policies and intelligent health education campaigns. We should stop trying to ignore alcohol problems by putting the blame for them on individual alcoholics, as in the disease view. Instead, we should make them a matter of collective responsibility in which the whole of society is involved.

5. Drug Dependence: Myth or Motive?

John L Falk

FALK. J. L. Drug dependence: Myth or motive? PHARMACOL BIOCHEM BEHAV 19(3) 385-391, 1983. - The acceptability of nonmedical use for a particular drug is a function of diverse social needs. Drug dependence is due less to intrinsic effects than to the situation in which drug taking occurs. An addictive level of drug self-administration is a symptom of behavioral troubles rather than a definition of the trouble itself. The intrinsic effects of drugs do not in themselves produce either misuse or evoke specific kinds of behaviour such as sexual or aggressive activities. Drugs can, however, come to function as disciminative stimuli for socially sanctioned behavior that would not under other circumstances be tolerated. The intrinsic reinforcing potential of an agent evolves in and dominates situations in which other reinforcing opportunities are either absent or remain unavailable to an individual who is unprepared to exploit them. While certain intrinsic properties of a drug contribute to its potential as a reinforcer (e.g. rapid onset and brief duration of action), reinforcing efficacy is notoriously malleable. It is a function of historic and currently-acting factors, particularly social reinforcers. The importance of physical dependence in the maintenance of drug seeking and taking is mainly unproven and probably overrated. Situations under which important reinforcers are available only in small portions intermittently can induce various excessive activities, including an untoward concern with obtaining and using drugs. Drug dependence prevention as a species of environmental dependence can be best effected by either alterations in the intermittent reinforcement situations inducing excessive behavior or by providing opportunities and training with respect to reinforcing alternatives other than drugs.

Rudolf Virchow, the 19th century German medical microscopist and father of the discipline of pathology, insisted that a disease is not a general affliction of the body, such as a humoral imbalance, but a localized, anatomical disturbance. The pathologist was to hunt for the seat of the disease, its locus. Consonant with the search for the place where critical events occur as the first step in delineating any mechanism of action, it would be convenient to be able to specify the locus of drug dependence. Alas, it has no simple locus. It used to be regarded as a function solely of the drug agent. An innocent, upstanding individual could become dependent even from unwitting contract with an enslaving agent. In the late 19th century in this country, there was concern that drug use could have an enervating effect on indulgers, lowering society's productivity.[34] The belief that in this land of opportunity prosperity was actually attainable, when coupled with the Victorian fear that one's personal energy stores might not be equal to life's

This paper was presented at the American Psychological Association meeting in Washington, D.C., August, 1982, as the Division 28 (Psychopharmacology) Presidential; address.

tasks,[43] led to apprehension that society's progress, as well as one's personal ambitions, might be compromised by the drain on energies produced by involvement with drugs. Opiates were viewed as enslaving the individual more because they produced debilitation and passivity rather than for their drug-taking, motivational aspects. The concern was with enervation ("nervous wasting") as the key toxic consequence for a society valuing vigor and fearing the dreamy disconnection of the user. "In the largest sense, whatever the controversy over its excessive use, alcohol appeared more suited than opiates to the American experience. Alcohol represented external action, competition, manliness, and strength. Opiates appeared defeatist, introspective, unnatural".[34] In comparison with this picture, coca and cocaine "originally seemed attractive to sensitive and intelligent people seeking to maintain energy in order to work harder at socially acceptable tasks. Early users warned of its attractions to people seeking escape, but by and large saw it as a restorative".[34]

Whether a drug, then, is perceived as a social danger or help depends upon the putative behavioral effects of the drug, especially as these relate to behavior the society either encourages or finds reprehensible. But do drugs have intrinsic behavioral actions? Unless we are talking about large doses of anesthetic or convulsant agents I think that recent research in behavioral pharmacology, epidemiology, and cultural anthropology indicates that the behavioral effects of drugs are quite malleable. They do not simply release different behavioral actions such as aggression, fear, psychosis, sexual activities, euphoria or even religious revelation. As variability in the behavioral effects produced by many drugs became evident, both in their immediate effects and with respect to whether exposed individuals became dependent upon them, it was said that people responded to drugs differently depending upon what sort of persons they were. That is, personality and genetic differences were seen as the major factors accounting for behavioral differences in response to drugs. These variables, like the previous notion of the intrinsic behavioral action of drugs, are located inside the skin. While there is no reason to doubt that individual differences can affect drug response, analysis in these terms has not explained much about human drug-related behavior. These factors do not seem to account for much of the variance. There has been a long and mainly fruitless search for the "addictive personality".[29] Heavy involvement with drug-taking is certainly correlated with behavioral troubles. But the cause-effect relations are not at all clear, and there is little reason to maintain that drug overindulgence lies at the root of the troubles. Negative consequences, often thought to be attributable to drug abuse, such as unemployment and dropping out of school, are consequences which exist independently of drug use and are highly correlated with social class.[27] As Robins and her associates[39] cogently point out: "People who use heroin are highly disposed to having serious social problems even before they touch heroin. Heroin probably accounts for some of the problems they have if it is used regularly, but heroin is 'worse' than ampehtamines or barbiturates only because 'worse' people use it". We fasten on a drug such as heroin as central to a complex of social problems because it is an isolable substance, a material with all the cachet of the immediate and concrete. But crushing its use may be unproductive, for it is off the point. As society's agents, we may be behaving like the drunk who searches for his lost key under the street lamp because that's where the light is. Perhaps we are attempting to work on a complex social problem by getting at the heroin supply or blocking its effects in the user or assuming it has an isolable, reductionistic, disease-like, neurochemical basis. But drug dependence, as Laurie[30] remarks, "is a symptom and not a disease".

Let us return to the notion that drugs of abuse have intrinsic biobehavioral actions, and that these actions, working within susceptible individuals, are the processes out of which drug dependence is built. First, a study of drug usage by a large sample of young U.S. soldiers returning from Vietnam showed that while less than 1% had ever been addicted to narcotics prior to their arrival in Vietnam, about 20% became addicted there, but showed a surprisingly high remission rate after returning to the U.S.[38] Narcotic usage and addiction fell to essentially their low, pre-Vietnam levels. This result stands in marked contrast to the extremely high relapse and readdiction rate of the populations usually studied in this country: those coming to legal or medical attention. These latter groups give the impression that opiate addiction is persistent, almost to the point of irreversibility, owing to the drug's intrinsic, addictive action. The heroin available in Vietnam was inexpensive, plentiful and of high purity. The users were susceptible in that they were quite young, free of their usual societal constraints, had peer-group acceptance for usage, and were subjected to the chronic boredom and stresses of a war theatre. Yet the ready reversibility of the addiction indicates that the abuse susceptibility resided primarily in the use situation rather than in the interaction of a prone or sensitive user with a fatefully entrapping substance.

A second line of evidence on the diversity of heroin use patterns comes from the studies of Zinberg and his colleagues on nonaddictive opiate use.[52] These drug users were located through advertisements in the underground press, through universities and a variety of social service agencies, rather than because they had come to legal or medical attention owing to their use of drugs. Ninety-nine controlled-drug users were located and about half of these were opiate users. They maintained regular ties with work, school and family as well as ordinary social relationships with non-drug users. At the time of the study, the mean length of time of controlled use of the heroin users was 3.6 years, with stability of the use patterns. Drug use for these subjects occurs mainly within controlled-use groups, with solitary use being rare. For example, subjects might use heroin with friends every weekend, but more frequent use would be condemned as "junkie"-like. Addictive dependence was avoided. Long-term, moderate use patterns are possible under rather ordinary circumstances for a drug such as heroin, even though it is associated with a notable addiction liability. Apparently, the rituals and social sanctions against addiction and compulsive use within controlled use groups are sufficient to prevent the occurrence of abusive patterns. As is the case with most social drinking, repeated commerce even with a substance having strong pharmacological action and an addictive hazard by no means implies a fatefully escalating motivational destiny. Exposure to a drug is one thing, while the development and maintenance of a pattern of abuse is something else. Robins' epidemiologic study of returning Vietnam veterans and Zinberg's case studies of controlled users indicate that sustaining an addictive pattern of behavior requires not so much a strong agent and a pliant host as it does a facilitating environmental setting. This can take a variety of forms, so let us examine a third example: the stereotypical "drunken Indian".

As MacAndrew and Edgerton[32] point out in their painstaking analysis, the conventional wisdom has it that while the Indians of North America craved the white man's liquor they were intrinsically sensitive to it in a way that made them react in a most aggressive and degenerate fashion. The chronicles of traders and missionaries yield numerous accounts of mayhem and debauchery. However, these kinds of extreme reactions by Indians to alcohol were neither typical nor were they characteristic of their early contacts with the substance. How, then, did the dramatic reactions to alcohol develop which, although by no means universal, were severely disruptive? MacAndrew and Edgerton[32] indicate that "the traders recognized that alcohol was potentially the most potent trade-war in their inventory, for unlike iron skillets, hatchets, etc, (the demand for which was clearly limited), they saw that if a desire for alcohol could be created it would be insatiable. They recognized, too, that if such a desire could be made strong enough, then they, who alone could satisfy it, would be able to assume near-dictatorial control ... every conceivable form of deceit and coercion was employed in forcing liquor upon the Indians" (pp. 114-115). Still, the use of liquor was slow to develop and failed to yield a picture of intemperate craving coupled to bad behavior at that stage. Clearly, no innate sensitivity or attraction was involved.[31] But along with the liquor the traders also offered a model of violent and immoral drunken comportment. This pattern was taken over and became an excuse for doing things that ordinarily would have been subject to punishment. It was simply claimed that liquor caused an evil spirit to possess the individual. Even feigning intoxication in order to do things that would ordinarily be punishable became common, a contemporary maneuver not confined to native North Americans. There were several ways then in which the altered economic and social environment of the Indian fostered the heavy use of alcohol, provided violent and destructive models for drunken comportment and reinforced these kinds of behavior. We have no need to posit an intrinsic sensitivity and attraction to alcohol to give a plausible account of the development of problematic overindulgence.

Psychoactive drugs are complex, but they do have discernible, specific effects. The question, in behavioral terms, is whether abuse liability is built from one or more intrinsic, specific effects. The reinforcing properties of drugs have been attributed to a varied list of reputed behavioral properties. Abused drugs have been said to release tension and, on the other hand, to effect a psychic activation. Some are touted as anxiety reducers and others as euphoriants. Many are taken because they are supposed to enhance already pleasant activities, such as listening to music, sexual, or just plain social interactions. Almost any commonplace or quasi-magical behavioral effect one could desire is envisaged as having some agent, or subtle blending of agents, that will bring forth the required behavior or psychic experience. Reluctantly we must leave aside for our present purpose the question as to how or whether drugs can actually effect these wonders. We will question, however, how specific the behavioral effects of drugs are and in what sense the powerful reinforcing effects of drugs are intrinsic actions. These two, interrelated questions bear upon the sources of dependence in drug dependence.

In questioning whether a drug has a specific behavioral action, what is meant is: Does the agent either release some category of behavior, or at least strongly dispose the organism in a specific behavioral direction? As a concrete example, let us ask whether the conventional wisdom about the behavioral effects of alcohol is the case: Does it increase sexual and aggressive kinds of behavior? The common assumption is that, owing to its disinhibiting effects, carnal and pugnacious impulses, usually held in careful check, are released by alcohol. The superego is said, only half jokingly, to be soluable in alcohol. In surveying a number of South American tribal societies, MacAndrew and Edgerton[32] find some slight support for our conventional wisdom. The Abipone change from their typically calm and non-argumentative demeanor into vicious combatants with one another during a drinking party, confirming the disinhibition notion. But by far most of the evidence offers no confirmation. The warlike, head-hunting Yuruna only become withdrawn when they drink. The Camba of Bolivia studied by Heath[22] show neither aggression nor sexual license during their frequent social binge-drinking bouts. Nor does alcohol addiction occur in spite of frequent binging with their distilled product, which is undiluted 89 percent ethyl alcohol. The Aritama are a quite rigidly controlled and formal people by our standards, perfect subjects for alcohol to effect a disinhibiting release upon. But they drink "without becoming aggressive, sentimental, verbose, or amorous".[32] Examples from other societies in Mexico, Micronesia, and Japan are given by MacAndrew and Edgerton[32] in which drunken disinhibition ought to occur since they are either puritanical or repressive. But the expected drunken aggression and sexuality fails to materialize. "Indeed, the only significant change in comportment reported for any of these societies is an increased volubility or sociability" (p. 36).

Recent extensive reviews of the experimental literature on the effects of alcohol on human sexual and aggressive behavior[5,50] lead one to draw the conclusion that the conventional wisdom makes a statement about the behavioral consequences of drinking within several Western societies. The statement is that "the circumstances of drinking produce greater changes in behavior than the alcohol does".[5] So much for the much-vaunted intrinsic effect of ethanol on aggressive and sexual activities.

Perhaps alcohol is a special case. Maybe its rather nondescript chemical structure and the probable absence of specific receptors for alcohol make it an unlikely candidate for producing intrinsic, specific effects. It is worth examining another agent. There is evidence for a phencyclidine/sigma "opiate" receptor in rat cortex and hippocampus.[37] Phencyclidine (PCP), a drug with a notable abuse liability, is associated with a varied set of behavioral effects.[1,36] Its reputation for producing violence has received a good deal of attention in the mass media, particularly on televison specials. In assessing the potential of PCP for producing violence, it is necessary to consider carefully the user and the social cirumstances of its use. Violent behavior in connection with PCP use occurs upon a personal and social background and out of situational events. As Siegel[41] remarks: "Phencyclidine is not a magical drug. It does not magically produce violent, assultive, or criminal behavior". Investigation of aggressive behavior on a PCP detoxification and rehabilitation unit, compared with a heroin unit, found similar low levels of violence.[28] An ethnographic study of PCP use in four American cities revealed violence to be rather rare, appearing mainly in members of groups where fighting resolved conflicts and asserted status.[14] Physical restraint and other kinds of authoritative intervention also can trigger a reactive violence.[14,41] PCP is an hallucinogenic drug with some amphetamine-like properties. As was the case for

48

alcohol, its chemical properties and the social context of its use to a large extent determine is behavioral possibilities.

As previously pointed out, almost any conceivable, desirable behavioral effect is reputed to be produced by the intrinsic action of some agent or potion. I hope I have by now convinced you that behavioral intrinsic action in this sense has been a little oversold. But what chemistry fails to effect directly, a social group can create out of mutual conditions of reinforcement occasioned by the stimulus control of the presence of some chemical. In the technical terminology of operant conditioning, then, a drug-taking situation, as well as the bodily presence of a drug, can function as discriminative stimuli for social reinforcement. If a major component of the reinforcing effect of drugs is social, of what does this consist? Those activities functioning as reinforcers clearly will vary with the composition of the social group and its raison d'etre. But we can see how a few examples might work, realizing that they are by no means exhaustive. How we comport ourselves when under the influence of alcohol or other drugs is largely defined socially. The entire drug-taking milieu, including how one obtains the drug, as well as behavior "under the influence" defines drug-sanctioned activities. Engaging in these activities is reinforced in varied ways.

With regard to drunkenness, MacAndrew and Edgerton[32] point out that societies in which intoxication gives rise to various social transgressions are societies which indulge the transgressors, so that their bad behavior usually leads to no serious social consequences for them. Drunkenness functions as a "time out" from at least some of the rules of society. Punishment even for homicide is often mitigated if it is done after chemical indulgence. In fact, if you want to get away with it, this is the best time to do nasty things to people. There are seasonal festivals and a variety of ritual occasions during which many societies suspend certain taboos and social regulations, granting a shocking license to behavior without any pharmacological assist.[15,18] Lacking much in the way of institutionalized license-granting occasions, we make do with alcohol and other drug pretexts for deviance or rule-breaking behavior.

Drug-associated behavioral license allows the occurence of kinds of behavior that much of the time are problematic for society-at-large. Individuals find such behavior reinforcing on occasions more numerous than society could normally allow. Thus, being "under the influence" grants us aggressive and sexual indulgences. For the Bolivian Camba it does not do this. They are people, as described by Heath,[32] "virtually lacking in forms of communal expression ... Geographically dispersed nuclear families are virtually independent of each other, and kinship ties are tenuous and unstable ... Drinking parties predominate among rare social activities, and alcohol serves to facilitate rapport between individuals who are normally isolated and introverted." For the Camba, then, binging is not so much a "time-out" from social strictures as it is a "time-in" discriminative stimulus for enhancing their lives through social interaction. For many groups, the social context of drug taking is to enhance some aspect of their lives, such as the appreciation of music, attaining an ecstatic religious state, communicating with and being possessed by powerful spirits, or effecting Shamanic cures.[7, 16, 31, 49]

Thus far, drug taking has been presented as a discriminative stimulus situation occasioning essentially social reinforcers. But is drug dependence just the operation of stimulus control for the mutual provision of social reinforcers? It is certainly the case that drug dependence is sustained by much more than the drug itself, which even in the case of heroin is often quite dilute by the time it reaches the consumer. There is a network of social reinforcement when individuals continue to bring off the monetary hustles and stable connections necessary for maintaining one's reputation as a "righteous dope fiend".[45] It is a socially elite attainment and only changes into a retreatist role when an individual no longer can maintain the hustling necessary to attain drugs and becomes identified as an ineffectual "sick addict". This picture, along with material already presented, reveals the importance of non-pharmacological factors, but drugs do indeed have some specific actions. While they do not directly produce behavioral activities, the intrinsic actions of some drugs have behavioral possibilities. The manner in which intrinsic action becomes linked to behavior can illuminate the circumstances under which the linkage becomes chronic. I will try to characterize those intrinsic actions that are necessary, if not sufficient, for capturing the stream of behavior.

First, psychotropic drugs are specific stimuli. Experienced users when injected readily and reliably discriminate one drug from another, even distinguishing from among drugs of the same class.[20] Animals also can learn to make fine drug distinctions when drug injection is used to inform the animal about where to go or what to do in order to obtain a reinforcer such as food.[40] In other words, an administered drug can serve as a distinct informative stimulus with respect to the availability of some reinforcing event. The recent explosion of research in this area has told us much about how rats, pigeons and monkeys, as well as humans, categorize drugs as stimuli and is illuminating the nature of drug receptor systems every bit as quickly and informatively as traditional, isolated-tissue preparations.[51] This discriminative stimulus specificity, then, can be linked readily to reinforcing states of affairs in the environment.

Second, some psychotropic drugs, as well as being able to function as discriminative stimuli, also can function as reinforcing stimuli.[25] The conditions under which this latter function can become chronic and excessive in humans is what the problem of drug dependence is all about. What have animals revealed to us about this? For one thing, animal research and the human record agree as to which types of drugs function as reinforcers. The concordance is not complete, but it is very close.[25] It is close enough so that animal experiments can predict which new drugs have abuse liability. The reinforcing efficacy of a drug, then, is not arbitrary. The research with animals shows how special laboratory arrangements make evident the behavioral potential of drugs as reinforcers. Typically, monkeys are fitted with intravenous catheters and allowed to self-inject drug doses by pressing on a light-weight lever. Hence, drugs are attained by a simple behavior sequence and reach the animal intravenously, a route ensuring a rapid onset of action as it is uncomplicated by delays in absorption or a reluctance to overcome negative tastes. Usually there is little in the experimental situation to compete with drug self-injection, no pre-existing behavior routines strongly reinforced by agents other than drugs. These experiments show how strong some drugs can be in pre-empting the stream of behavior under conditions where other reinforcers are not engaging behavior. What social groups build drug use upon clearly is not arbitrary pharmacologically. But neither is it simply derivable from pharmacological properties.

For a drug with addiction liability to be reinforcing to the point of abuse for humans requires more than simply continued exposure to and availability of the agent. Unlike the monkey, many are exposed but comparatively few abuse. In society, our ecological situation is different than that of the laboratory-dwelling monkey. Most societies provide varied sources of reinforcement to their members who also are restrained from spending too much of their time and resources on drugs. We make abuse easy for our experimental subjects, thus maximizing the efficacy of the intrinsic properties of a drug to engage behavior, i.e., to function as a durable reinforcer. Johanson and Uhlenhuth[26] showed that for normal human volunteers the strong preference for d-amphetamine over placebo disappeared with three successive replications of the experimental series. This is an interesting experiment in several respects. Using a mood scale evaluation of how subjects felt, the drug increased vigor, elation, friendliness, arousal and positive mood, even though a rather low dose level (5-mg capsules) was employed. Further, these mood responses to d-amphetamine still occurred even in subjects whose preference had changed from taking the drug to taking placebo. The positive mood effects, which are usually assumed to be the basis of the reinforcing effect of stimulants, were not predictive of the disappearance of the drug's reinforcing efficacy. They were not sufficient for the maintenance of drug taking, probably because during the period of drug action these subjects were continuing their normal daily activities. The drug state may have been incompatible either with the customary pursuit of these activities or the usual effects of engaging in these activities. The point is that in their natural habitat these subjects showed by their preference changes that they were uninterested in continuing to savor the mood effects. They would undoubtedly be poor bets for developing stimulant abuse in spite of their continuing positive mood responses to the drug.

The environmental context, then, in which a drug occurs can alter its potential for acquiring strength as a reinforcer regardless of its pharmacological actions. Reinforcing efficacy is malleable. It is malleable by the drug becoming associated as a discriminative stimulus with various time-out and time-in activities. The social attainments and status accorded a righteous dope fiend by the peer group and those hopeful of entering it are considerable and not unlike many professional aggregations. The dynamics of stimulus-function malleability are just beginning to be mapped. For example, the same peripherally-applied, electrical shock stimulus can function either as a positive or negative reinforcer for an animal within the same experimental session.[2] It depends upon the contingency controlling the delivery of the shock and how the animal historically was introduced to the contingency. Some of the most noxious-seeming events can entrain behavior so that the events are repeatedly self-administered when available under appropriate schedules. Many drugs have noxious aspects, particularly to the drug-taking initiate. These aspects include nausea, panic, frightening hallucinations, and paranoid reactions. But they don't discourage continued commerce with a drug by the serious user. There is no rule that an efficacious reinforcer has to be pleasant in some rosy sense. The course of true reinforcers seldom runs smooth.

Recent experimental work with intravenous drug self-administration in monkeys confirms this picture of contextual malleability. Animals will work assiduously on a variable-interval schedule administering cocaine and simultaenously on a second lever where a fixed-interval schedule leads to one-minute time-out periods from the drug-attaining schedule.[44] A related duality in reinforcing function occurs for nicotine. Intravenously self-administered nicotine was found to have either pronounced reinforcing or punishing effects depending upon the availability contingency. As Goldberg and Spealman[19] state: "These findings are important because they emphasize that the behavioral effects of nicotine are neither immutable nor predictable solely on the basis of the drug's inherent pharmacological qualities".

To summarize: drug stimuli acting as discriminative stimuli can attach to a variety of socially reinforcing functions, from impassioned conversation to sexual and aggressive license. Further, any intrinsic, pharmacological reinforcing functions are altered radically by seemingly small changes in the behavioral context.

Through all this relative flux determinants, it is still possible to define a few stimulus properties of agents that are necessary, or at least greatly facilitate, the capture of behavior. As indicated in discussing the intravenous route of administration, rapid onset is an advantage in attaining a reinforcing effect. So is brief duration, as it allows a high rate of reinforcing episodes to occur. The preferred drugs of abuse are those possessing rapid onset of action coupled with brief duration of effect: consider belts of liquor, snorts of cocaine, hits of heroin, or drags on smoked substances.

Popular thinking about drug dependence all but equates it with physical dependence, a physiological need state producing a reputed zombie-like uncontrolled drive for the needed drug. The role of physical dependence in drug taking is in most respects a minor one. Drugs such as cocaine can be powerful reinforcers although they do not produce physical dependence. On reviewing the evidence on this general question, Cappell and LeBlanc[3] conclude that "it remains a strong hypothesis if not an act of faith that physical dependence plays a central role in the maintenance of the self-administration of alcohol and psychoactive drugs". In their 1981 review[4] they state: "Physical dependence seems to increase the probability of ethanol self-administration in some circumstances, but this effect is not as reliable as that for opiates. Nothing based in empirical evidence can be said about other drugs where physical dependence is concerned".

I have touched on a few ways in which intrinsic pharmacological action can engage behavior, given the right agents - but equally important - given the right circumstances. Situational circumstances can permit intrinsic action to have free play. Or circumstances can play upon the malleability of intrinsic actions changing them into either reinforcers or negative stimuli. These are ways in which a drug can come to dominate the behavioral domain.

There is another kind of environmental arrangement that produces exaggerated behavior, including overindulgence in drugs. When it comes to the oral route for taking drugs, some humans readily indulge in alcohol and a host of other agents. But the animal experimental literature was, for a long time, quite disappointing in this regard. Animals just could not be enticed to overindulge chronically by this route the way they do intravenously. Perhaps it is due to the noxious taste of most drugs, or to the slow onset of drug action by the oral route. But then again most people do not overindulge either: it takes the right environmental conditions. For animals, the conditions for producing an explosive increase in oral or intravenous drug intake turn out to be not very complex. A relatively small constraint in body weight and an intermittent schedule of access to the relevant reinforcing commodity, i.e., food, is sufficient. For example, although never deprived of water, rats receiving small food pellets on the average once per minute drank ten times as much water in three hours as they did when receiving the same number of pellets all at once and observed for three hours.[8,9] They drank about half their body weight in three hours when on the intermittent food schedule. Hence, this phenomenon has been called "schedule-induced polydipsia". This overindulgence goes on for months during each daily intermittent feeding session. It has no explanation in terms of standard physiological, nutritional or behavioral considerations.[10] Schedule-induction conditions produce many other kinds of behavioral excesses: attack, pica, hyperactivity, escape and drug intake.[11,12] They occur in a wide range of species. Under similar schedule conditions, humans show hyperactivity, overdrinking of water and increased smoking.[12] In general terms, it is not just deprivation, but temporal constraints on the episodic delivery of a valued commodity in one domain that induces excessive behavior in another domain. Of importance in the present context is the schedule-induced production and maintenance of drug overindulgence. This has been demonstrated for a number of drugs taken orally[6, 17, 33, 47]: alcohol, barbiturates, opiates, phencyclidine and amphetamine, as well as intravenously: heroin, methadone, cannabis and nicotine.[35, 42, 46] For example, alcohol was drunk excessively by a group of rats exposed continuously to an intermittent feeding schedule.[13] The alcohol solution was preferred to water and some other solutions and the chronically excessive intake resulted in severe physical dependence. Some of these agents, particularly when taken orally under normal circumstances, function only as weak reinforcers for animals. Schedule-induced drug overindulgence remains strictly a function of the current induction conditions. Even with a long history of schedule-induced alcohol drinking, with the development of physical dependence, termination of the scheduled aspect of feeding produces an immediate fall in alcohol intake to a control level.[48] Once again we have a picture of a reputedly enticing molecule failing to take over behavior in spite of chronic binging. We should not be surprised since altered circumstances revealed that heroin also had not taken over the Vietnam servicemen's behavior in a chemical-enslavement sense.

The texture of the reinforcement environments provided by both nature and society can be described as containing a host of intermittent schedules with properties sufficient for the induction of excessive behavior. These can be designated as "generator schedules". Life could be described as a scramble for commodities and activities, which are only intermittently attained: food, territory, money, sexual and social intercourse. The particuar excessive behavior induced by these natural generator schedules depends upon what behavioral opportunities are available in life's situations, and whether the individual is prepared to exploit these opportunities. Drugs offer a quick and powerful behavioral alternative when they occur in an impoverished environment upon which common generator schedules are imposed. By an impoverished environment I mean one which is poor economically or educationally or in terms of a socially reinforcing matrix. With less impoverishment, there is a greater probability that socially acceptable excessive behavior will occur in the face of generator schedules. The individual then has the personal resources to get intense about business, scientific, artistic, or harmless hobby endeavors. In terms of drug dependence alleviation, we cannot alter genetic or personal historics. Nor has prohibition of drug supplies led to signal successes. Alleviation and prevention can be approached most effectively through environmental changes: both by alteration of generator schedules and enrichment of environmental alternatives.

Perhaps it is time to make explicit reference to the title of this presentation. In what sense might drug dependence be either a myth or a motive? The development of physical dependence upon some drugs is certainly no myth, nor are the medical consequences of chronic overuse of certain agents. But as an explanation, a mechanism of action, accounting for deviant and delinquent activities, physical dependence is inadequate. Neither is the evolution of one's major interests into seeking and taking drugs merely a problem of avocation or aesthetics. It can be a symptom of a serious diversion or arrest in life's trajectory. Drug dependence is not a motive in the sense that a drug is an irresistible goody, or that its habitual use leads to a physical dependence driving further drug seeking. Pharmacologic structure does not imply motivational destiny. Yet the suppositions surrounding the notion of 'drug dependence' often give a mythic, rather than a scientific, account of the implied behavioral troubles. It is an irksome problem because the line between science and myth is not always clear. As Jacob [23, p. 11] states, "myths and scientific theories operate on the same principle. The object is always to explain visible events by invisible forces, to connect what is seen with what is assumed". But while "Scientific investigation begins by inventing a possible world, or a small piece of a possible world ... a myth ... is not just a tale from which inferences can be drawn about the world. A myth has moral content" [23, p. 12]. I'm afraid that many of our scientific notions about drug dependence are burdened with a heavy load of mythic, moral freight.

As each underclass begins to emerge in our society, as they become visible, they have attributed to them certain frightening characteristics. They are alledged to be aggresive, over-sexed and shamefully poor. This is typically the case for emerging foreign minorities, blacks, women, teenagers, and lately the aged or infirm. Each of these groups also gets some sort of substance dependence attributed to them as the mechanism of action which accounts for their ill-temper, hypersexuality, and poverty. Chinese and opium, Indians and alcohol, blacks and heroin or cocaine, teens and drugs, alcoholism in women, the homeless, and the aged. It's not that people don't have drug problems. What I question is that drugs are the major factor underlying their problems. And the problems that *are* attributed to these emerging groups are mostly not really their problems. These groups often function as wonderous screens on which to project our forbidden aggressive and sexual fantasies. They get to indulge themselves in these not-so-innocent social and chemical freedoms. It serves them right if they're underpaid. Anyhow, they got into these troubles because they abuse alcohol or some other drugs. It's comforting to fasten on this morality play and rightously combat "the problem of drug dependence".

We need to remind ourselves that drugs do not have the powers to do these things. There are reinforcers that are sweeter than drugs. It's a pity that most of them don't have the simplicity or permanence of molecular structure. The thing about drug dependence is the certainty of the effect of the drug in the context in which it's taken. It's dependable. All the more's the irony that most of this effect is situationally fabricated or socially constructed. But neither the transitory, nor certainly the illusory, has yet interfered with reinforcement efficacy in this world.

References

1. Balster, R.L. and L. D. Chait. 'The behavioral effects of phencyclidine in animals'. In: *Phencyclidine (PCP) Abuse: An Appraisal. NIDA Res. Monogr, 21,* edited by R. C. Petersen and R. C. Stillman, Washington, DC: US Gov, Printing Office, 1978, pp. 53-65.

2. Barrett. J. E. and R. D. Spealman. 'Behavior simultaneously maintained by both presentation and temination of noxious stimuli'. *J Exp Anal Behav*, 1978, 29: 375-383.

3. Cappell. H and A. E. LeBlanc. 'Tolerance to, and physical dependence on, ethanol: Why do we study them?' *Drug Alcohol Depend*, 1979, 4: 15-31.

4. Cappell. H. and A. E. LeBlanc. 'Tolerance and physical dependence: Do they play a role in alcohol and drug self-administration?' In: *Research Advances in Alcohol and Drug Problems*, vol 6, edited by Y. Israel, F. B. Glaser, H. Kalant, R. E. Popham, W. Schmidt and R. G. Smart. New York: Plenum, 1981, pp. 159-196.

5. Carpenter. J. A. and N. P. Armenti. 'Some effects of ethanol on human sexual and aggressive behavior'. In: *The Biology of Alcoholism*, edited by B. Kissin and H. Begleiter. New York: Plenum, 1972, pp. 509-543.

6. Carroll. M. E. and R. A. Meisch. 'Oral phencyclidine (PCP) self-administration in rhesus monkeys: effects of feeding condition'. *J. Pharmacol Exp Ther*, 1980, 215: 339-346.

7. Chagnon. N. A. Yanomamo: The Fierce People. New York: Holt, Rinehart and Winston, 1968.

8. Falk. J. L. 'Production of polydipsia in normal rats by an intermittent food schedule'. *Science*, 1961, 133: 195-196.

9. Falk. J. L. 'Control of schedule-induced polydipsia: type, size, and spacing of meals'. *J Exp Anal Behav*, 1967, 10: 199-206.

10. Falk. J. L. 'Conditions producing psychogenic polydipsia in animals'. *Ann NY Acad Sci*, 1969, 157: 569-593.

11. Falk. J. L. 'The nature and determinants of adjunctive behavior'. *Physiol Behav*, 1971, 6: 577-588.

12. Falk. J. L. 'The environmental generation of excessive behavior'. In: *Behavior in Excess: An Examination of the Volitional Disorders*, edited by S. J. Mule. New York: Free Press, 1981, pp. 313-337.

13. Falk. J. L. and H. H. Samson. 'Schedule-induced physical dependence on ethanol'. *Pharmacol Rev*, 1975, 27: 449-464.

14. Feldman. H. W., M. H. Agar and G. M. Beschner (eds.) *Angel Dust*. Lexington, MA: Heath, 1979.

15. Frazer. J. G. *The Golden Bough: A Study of Magic and Religion*. New York: MacMillan, 1922, (abridged edition).

16. Furtst. P. T. '"High states" in culture-historical perspective'. In: *Alternate States of Consciousness*, edited by N. E. Zinberg. New York: Free Press, 1977, pp. 53-88.

17. Gilbert. R. M. 'Schedule-induced self-administration of drugs'. In: *Contemporary Research in Behavioral Pharmacology*, edited by D. E. Blackman and D. J. Sanger. New York: Plenum, 1978, pp. 289-323.

18. Gluckman. M. *Custom and Conflict in Africa*. New York: Barnes and Noble, 1973.

19. Goldberg. S. R. and R. D. Spealman. 'Maintenance and suppression of behavior by intravenous nicotine injections in squirrel monkeys'. *Fed PRoc*, 1982, 41: 216-220.

20. Haertzen. C. A. 'Subjective effects of narcotic antagonists cyclazocine and nalorphine on the addiction research center inventory (ARCI)'. *Psychopharmacologia*, 1970, 18: 366-377.

21. Harner. M. J. (ed.). *Hallucinogens and Shamanism*. New York: Oxford University Press, 1973.

22. Heath. D. B. 'Drinking patterns of the Bolivian Camba'. *Q J Stud Alcohol*, 1958, 19: 491-508.

23. Jacob. F. *The Possible and the Actual*. New York: Pantheon, 1982.

24. Johanson. C. E. and R. L. Balster. 'A summary of the result of a drug self-administration study using substitution procedures in rhesus monkeys'. *Bull Narc*, 1978, 30: 43-54.

25. Johanson. C. E. and C. R. Schuster. 'Animal models of drug self-administration'. In: *Advances in Substance Abuse: Behavioral and Biological Research*, vol 2, edited by N. K. Mello, Greenwich. CT: JAI Press, 1981, pp. 219-297.

26. Johanson. C. E. and E. H. Uhlenhuth. 'Drug preference and mood in humans: repeated assessment of d-amphetamine'. *Pharmacol Biochem Behav*, 1981, 14: 159-163.

27. Kellam. S. G., C. H. Brown, B. R. Rubin and M. E. Ensminger. 'Paths leading to teenage psychiatric symptoms and substance use: developmental epidemiological studies in Woodlawn'. In: *Childhood Psychopathology and Development*, edited by S. B. Guze, F. J. Earls and J. E. Barrett. New York: Raven Press, 1983, pp. 17-47.

28. Khajawall. A. M., T. B. Erickson and G. M. Simpson. 'Chronic phencyclidine abuse and physical assault'. *Am J Psychiatry*, 1982, 139: 1604-1606.

29. Lang. A. R. 'Addictive personality: a viable construct?' In: *Commonalities in Substance Abuse and Habitual behavior*, edited by P. K. Levison, D. R. Gerstein and D. R. Maloff. Lexington. MA: Heath, 1983, pp. 157-235.

30. Laurie. P. *Drugs: Medical, Psychological and Social Facts*. Baltimore, MD: Penguin Books, 1967.

31. Leland. J. *Firewater Myths*. New Brunswick. NJ: Rutgers Center of Alcohol Studies, 1976.

32. MacAndrew. C. R. and B. Edgerton. *Drunken Comportment: A Social Explanation*. Chicago, Aldine, 1969.

33. Meisch. R. A. and L. J. Stark. 'Establishment of etonitazene as a reinforcer for rats by use of schedule-induced drinking'. *Pharmacol Biochem Behav*, 1977, 7: 195-203, 1977.

34. Morgan. H. W. Drugs in America: A Social History, 1800-1980. Syracuse: Syracuse University Press, 1981.

35. Oei. T. P. S., G. Singer and D. Jefferys. 'The interaction of a fixed time food delivery schedule and body weight on self-administration of narcotic analgesics'. *Psychopharmacology (Berlin)*, 1980, 67: 171-176.

36. Petersen. R. C. and R. C. Stillman. 'Phencyclidine: an overview'. In: *Phencyclidine (PCP) Abuse: An Appraisal NIDA Res Monogt 21*, edited by R. C. Petersen and R. C. Stillman. Washington DC: US Gov Printing Office, 1978, pp. 1-17.

37. Quirion. R., R. P. Hammer, Jr., M. Herkenham and C. B. Pert. 'Autoradiographic localization of the phencyclidine/sigma "opiate" receptor in rat brain'. In: *Problems of Drug Dependence, 1981, NIDA Res Monogr 41*, edited by L. S. Harris. Rockville. MD: Nat. Institute Drug Abuse, 1982, pp. 178-183.

38. Robins. L. N., J. E. Helzer and D. H. Davis. 'Narcotic use in Southeast Asia and afterward'. *Arch Gen Psychiatry*, 1975, 32: 955-961, 1975.

39. Robins. L. N., J. E. Helzer. M. Hesselbrock and E. Wish. 'Vietnam veterans three years after Vietnam: How our study changed our view of heroin'. In: *The Yearbook of Substance Use and Abuse*, edited by L. Brill and C. Winick. New York: Human Sciences Press, 1980, pp. 213-230.

40. Schuster. C. R. and R. L. Balster. 'The discriminative stimulus properties of drugs'. In: *Advances in Behavioral Pharmacology* vol 1, edited by T. Thompson and P. B. Dews. New York: Academic Press, 1977, pp. 85-138.

41. Siegel. R. K. 'Phencyclidine, criminal behavior, and the defense of diminished capacity'. In: *Phencyclidine (PCP) Abuse: An Appraisal, NIDA Res Monogr 21*, edited by R. C. Petersen and R. C. Stillman. Washington DC: US Gov Printing Office, 1978, pp. 272-288.

42. Smith. L. A. and W. J. Lang. 'Changes occurring in self-administration of nicotine by rats over a 28-day period'. *Pharmacol Biochem Behav*, 1980,13: 215-220.

43. Sontag. S. *Illness as Metaphor*. New York: Vintage Books, 1979.

44. Spealman. R. D. 'Behavior maintained by termination of a schedule of self-administered cocaine'. *Science*, 1979, 204: 1231-1233.

45. Sutter. A. G. 'The world of the righteous dope fiend'. *Issues Criminol*, 1966, 2: 177-222.

46. Takahashi. R. N. and G. Singer. 'Effects of body weight levels on cannabis self-injection'. *Pharmacol Biochem Behav*, 1980, 13: 877-881.

47. Tang. M., K. Ahrendsen and J. L. Falk. 'Barbiturate dependence and drug preference'. *Pharmacol Biochem Behav*, 1981, 14: 405-408.

48. Tang. M., C. Brown and J. L. Falk. 'Complete reversal of chronic ethanol polydipsia by schedule withdrawal'. *Pharmacol Biochem Behav*, 1982, 16: 155-158.

49. Weil. A. *The Natural Mind*. Boston: Houghton Mifflin, 1972.

50. Wilson. G. T. 'The effects of alcohol on human sexual behavior'. In: *Advances in Substance Abuse: Behavioral and Biological Research*, vol 2, edited by N. K. Mello. Greenwich. CT: JAI Press, 1981, pp. 1-40.

51. Woods. J. H., A. M. Young and S. Herling. 'Classification of narcotics on the basis of their reinforcing, discriminative and antagonist effects in rhesus monkeys'. *Fed Proc*, 1982, 41: 221-227.

52. Zinberg. N. E., W. M. Harding and M. Winkeller. 'A study of social regulatory mechanisms in controlled illicit drug users'. *J Drug Issues*, 1977, 7: 117-113.

6.   Excessive Gambling
Jim Orford

There is no doubt that the social conscience is as yet only very partially awakened to the widespread character of the gambling evil and to its grievous consequences. Like a cancer, the evil thing has spread its poisonous roots throughout the length and breadth of the land, carrying with them, where they strike, misery, poverty, weakened character, and crime. (B. Seebohm Rowntree in the Preface to Betting and Gambling: a National Evil, 1905).

For some the explanation of excessive drinking as a form of drug 'addiction', as altered pharmacological response to the ingested substance, is sufficient. It is just because such an explanation is impossible in the case of excessive gambling, that the latter constitutes such an important example of excessive appetitive behaviour. If it can be demonstrated that excessive gambling is in most respects similar to excessive drinking or drug-taking, then it follows that an adequate explanation of excessive appetites in general must account for this non-drug form of 'addiction'. The main argument of this chapter will be that the parallels between excessive gambling and excessive drinking are, in fact, many and close.

The idea that the appetite for gambling could become excessive is no more a modern invention than is the notion of alcoholic excess. As Lindner (1950) put it, 'The fact that [it] ... could assume a pathological form characterized by symptoms related to the various addictions ... seems always to have been common knowledge among common folk everywhere' (cited by Herman, 1976). An article by Clemens France in the *American Journal of Psychology* for 1902 chronicles the many nations from ancient to modern which have been accused of fostering widespread gambling of a harmful kind. Since Roman Emperors and their wives have been charged with all manner of behavioural excesses, it is not surprising to find that this author, living himself in a relatively puritanical time and place, should quote good authority to the effect that several Emperors, including Augustus, Caligula, Claudius, and Nero, were themselves 'addicted' to gambling. Even Domitian, who so effectively demonstrated his concern over excessive drinking by having half the vineyards in the Empire destroyed (Glatt, 1958), is described as 'an inveterate gambler'. Under Constantine, '.... every inhabitant of that city [Rome], down to the populace, was addicted to gambling' (Steinmetz, cited by France, p. 366).

Many societies, according to France, had found it necessary to have legal controls on gambling behaviour. In France under Henry IV, 'incalculable social affliction' resulted from gambling despite stringent anti-gambling laws, and in the reign of Louis XIV:

Jim Orford: *EXCESSIVE APPETITES: A PSYCHOLOGICAL VIEW OF ADDICTIONS*, (John Wiley & Sons Ltd, 1990), pp. 25-45. © John Wiley & Sons Ltd 1985.

> ... men ... left off tennis, billiards and other games of skill, and consequently
> became weaker and more sickly, more ignorant, less polished, more
> dissipated ... The women, who till then had commanded respect,
> accustomed men to treat them with familiarity, by spending the whole
> night with them at play ... (Steinmetz, cited by France, p. 367).

As well as illustrating a prejudice against games of chance in favour of games of skill,
a prejudice that is not infrequently betrayed by those who write on the subject of
immoderate gambling, this quotation displays the extra opprobrium which often
attaches to women when their behaviour is thought to go beyond the bounds of
moderation.

In the England of Henry VII legislation was passed prohibiting common people from
playing cards except at Christmas (France, p. 368), and Italy of the early sixteenth
century was one of a number of countries which, from time to time, legislated for total
prohibition of gambling but failed to suppress gambling behaviour (France, p.370).

Many of the descriptions of gambling which France unearthed from an earlier period
are remarkably similar to current accounts of 'compulsive gambling'. For example, a
book published in 1619 under the title, *The Nicker Nicked, or the Cheats of Gaming
Discovered*, includes the following passage about gambling house activities of the
period, which describes the phenomenon of escalation from moderation to excess that
is such a recurring theme in both historical and modern accounts of excessive appetites:

> Most gamesters begin at small game; and, by degrees, if their money or
> estates hold out, they rise to great sums; some have played first of all their
> money, then their rings, coach and horses, even their wearing clothes and
> perukes; and then such a farm; and, at last, perhaps a lordship (Ashton,
> 1898, cited by France, p. 368).

Amongst France's historical witnesses were the Englishman Cotton (1674) whose
description of gaming as, '... an enchanting witchery ... an itching disease ...' is well
known, and the Frenchman Barbeyrac. In the latter's three-volume work, *Traite du jeu*,
published in 1737, Jean Barbeyrac had this to say:

> I do not know if there is any other passion which allows less of repose and
> which one has so much difficulty in reducing ... the passion of gambling
> gives no time for breathing; it is an enemy which gives neither quarter nor
> truce; it is a persecutor, furious and indefatigable. The more one plays the
> more one wishes to play; one never leaves it, and with difficulty one resolves
> to leave off a little while from dice and cards to satisfy the needs of nature
> ... it seems that gambling had acquired the right to occupy all his
> thoughts....

The idea that *it* takes over, becomes a preoccupation, and that the wish to reduce or
leave off altogether is opposed by a stronger force that leaves the will powerless, is as
clear here as in Lillian Roth's and John Gardner's modern-day accounts of 'alcoholism'.

The Russian novelist Dostoevsky is often referred to as the most famous of all
'compulsive gamblers'. Yet he can hardly be considered typical. There have been a

number of case studies of the writer, mostly by psychoanalysts, one of the best known being that by Paul Squires published in the *Psychoanalytic Review* in 1937. He drew on about fifty sources, including Dostoevsky's own letters and his second wife's diary. Although there was mention of his 'gambling mania' and of dire financial troubles, it was his epileptic seizures and his restless, irritable, egotistical character that were to the forefront. Indeed, Squires made no mention of excessive gambling in the formal diagnosis with which he concluded:

> Our formal diagnosis runs as follows: Dostoevsky was an epileptic schizophrene, paranoid type, complicated by hysterical overlay.....

Not that an absence of reference to behavioural excess in a formal psychiatric diagnosis need imply that it was of no importance. For example, from Dostoevsky's wife's account of the year in which they married, Squires concluded that Dostoevsky was, 'Powerless in the clutches of his terrific gambling mania, which blunted his sense of moral responsibility as effectively as extreme alcohol addiction could' (p. 372). Stripped of the glamour that surrounds the life of a world renowned artist struggling with his temperament and his appetites, Dostoevsky's life story contains moments that compare with the experiences of the most obscure man or woman who has struggled with an excessive appetite for gambling. There is, for example, the irrational conviction that some stratagem or attitude to the game will bring certain gain. Writing to his first wife's sister from Wiesbaden, where he took up roulette *en route* for Paris to meet his mistress Suslova, he said:

> I really do know the secret: its terribly silly and simple and consists in restraining oneself at every moment, no matter what the phase of the game, and not becoming heated. This is the whole thing, and to lose with this is simply impossible (Minihan, 1967, p.237).

In his short novel, *The Gambler*, which he intended partly as, '... a firsthand and most detailed portrayal of roulette gambling ...' (Minihan, pp. 314-5), the hero, Aleksey Ivanovitch, describes the intense attraction of the sights and sounds of the gambling hall:

> With what trembling, with what faintness of heart I hear the croupier's cry ... With what greed I look at the gambling table along which are strewn louis d'or, friedrichs d'or, and thalers at the little columns of gold when they are scattered from the croupier's shovel into piles glowing like fire, or columns of silver a yard high lying stacked round the wheel. Even while approaching the gambling hall, two rooms away, as soon as I begin to hear the clinking of money being poured out, I almost go into convulsions (cited Minihan, p.319).

His relationship with his second wife Anna seems to have contained episodes the recounting of which would be thoroughly in place at a meeting of Gamblers Anonymous or of Gam-Anon (for family members of compulsive gamblers) in Croydon or Exeter in 1985 (see Boyd and Bolen, 1970, for descriptions of the effects of 'compulsive gambling' on some present-day marriages). They were constantly in financial difficulties and Dostoevsky was for every trying to relieve them by further gambling. His gambling was interspersed with protestations of regret and requests for forgiveness and more money with which to make good former losses. On one occasion Fyrdor and Anna travelled to Baden-Baden so that Dostoevsky could gamble. They stayed about a month, Anna spending the days waiting in their hotel room. The infuriating inconsistency in the behaviour of someone whose appetite is excessive is well portrayed in a passage in Minihan's biography which relates to a period just before the birth of Fyrdor and Anna's first daughter. The confinement had been expensive:

> Dostoevsky went a third time ... He lost, pawned his ring and begged his wife to send him the last hundred francs: '... Don't consider my request for a hundred francs mad. I'm not mad. And also don't consider it depraved; I won't act meanly, won't deceive, won't go to gamble ...' On the same evening he wrote a second letter; he had lost the money received from pawning his ring ... (Minihan, p. 332).

Finally, much later, came a turning point, an occasion, similar to those that many lesser mortals have experienced, when Dostoevsky underwent some sort of experience, impressive, difficult to describe, but associated with a radical change in the formerly-excessive appetite behaviour. It was during Anna's third pregnancy that Dostoevsky went to Wiesbaden to gamble, apparently, so Minihan would have it, at his wife's suggestion:

> Dostoevsky lost everything, and at night in despair ran in search of a Russian priest ... At midnight he wrote to his wife 'Now this fantasy has ended for ever ... Moreover, I have, as it were, been wholly reborn morally ... A great thing has happened to me. The hideous fantasy that tormented me for almost ten years has vanished ...' Actually, he underwent some sort of mystical experience. From that day Dostoevsky never gambles again in his life. 'The fantasy' had disappeared instantly and for good (Minihan, p.385).

There seems little doubt that those closest to Dostoevsky thought his gambling excessive, and possibly he thought so too from time to time. But was his gambling 'compulsive' or 'pathological'? As with drinking, so with gambling, the nature of 'true dependence', if such a thing exists, is elusive. Unnecessary controversy on this point has dogged discussions of behaviour in each of the areas considered in this book.

As is the case with *modern* commentary on the use of opiates, hallucinogens, and some other drugs, in older writings on the subject of gambling the distinction between gambling in moderation and gambling to excess is scarcely drawn at all. This is evident in the fourth revelation which Baasher (1981) mentions as part of the step-wise process towards prohibition of alcoholic drinks in the Muslim community. Here alcohol and gambling are clearly linked and total abstention from both is commanded: 'O ye who believe! Strong drink (khamr) and games of chance and idols and divining arrows are only an infamy of Satan's handiwork' (cited by Baasher, p.237). The failure to distinguish moderation and excess is also there in many of the sources cited by France in 1902 and in other writings of that period, such as those to be found in the book edited by Seebohm Rowntree at the suggestion of the York Anti-Gambling League in 1905.

The Victorian moral view of gambling is well expressed in the latter work. Although reference was made to immoderate or excessive gambling, no form or degree of gambling is free from moral taint according to this view:

> Gambling involves the denial of all system in the apportionment of property: it plunges the mind in a world of anarchy, where things come upon one and pass from one miraculously ... generates an emotional excitement that inhibits those checks which reason more or less contrives to place upon emotional extravagances. The essence of gambling consists in an abandonment of reason, an inhibition of the factors of human control. In the history of mankind, civilisation of the individual has chiefly consisted in and been measured by this increased capacity of rational control - a slow, gradual, imperfect taming of the animal instincts which made for emotional anarchy of conduct ... The practice of gambling is thus exhibited as a deliberate reversion to those passions and that mental attitude which characterise the savage or pre-human man in his conduct and his outlook (Hobson, 1905, pp. 5-6).

This view that gambling is itself undignified and appealing to the irrational and irresponsible parts of human mentality, still survives (Cornish, 1978; Herman, 1976). It offers 'something for nothing', involves 'unnecessary risk', offers gain at the expense of others' loss, and is contrary to the principle of reward for effort. Such a view was well represented in the report of the Royal Commission on Betting, Lotteries, and Gaming in 1951, and in recent publications of the Churches' Council on Gambling (e.g. 1960-1968, cited by Cornish, 1978).

Thus, although 'excessive' and 'immoderate' were adjectives often employed to qualify the term 'gambling', and hence the possibility of moderate use was acknowledged by implication, moderate and immoderate forms of gambling were not often clearly separated in the minds of writers on the subject. The idea that people can be more or less clearly separated into one group or another, or at least that we may talk and write on the subject as if they were, is a relatively recent invention. Stekel (1924) recognized gambling as one of the 'manias' - others, for example, being dipsomania, narcomania, and nymphomania - and psychoanalytic writers have recognized for some time that gambling, like sexual and other types of appetitive behaviour, could take on a compulsive form (e.g. Bergler, 1958). The creation of 'compulsive gambling' as an entity, and the possibility of 'treatment' for it, are new, however.

There are many recent accounts by psychiatrists and others of cases they have treated for 'compulsive gambling' (e.g. Barker and Miller, 1968; Goorney, 1968). The three case histories given by Barker and Miller illustrate the harm that can be associated with gambling, as well as demonstrating the range of personal reactions which this harm can evoke in the excessive gambler himself. They also hint at the possibility of inter-generational transmission of gambling problems which would provide yet another parallel with excessive drinking which does 'run in families' (Goodwin, 1976). Their Case I was a man in his early thirties, married with two children, who had recently been jailed for 18 months for obtaining money for gambling by fraud:

He had been gambling excessively on 'fruit machines' almost continuously for the past 12 years. His 'addiction' began in Rhodesia shortly after marriage. A business client invited him to a club where a 'one-armed bandit' was installed. After a few initial wins he returned to the machine every night, claiming that he gambled 'to provide a house and furniture and decent standard of living for his wife'. Within 2½ years of marriage his gambling debts exceeded £500 which were settled by a relative. On returning to England, he continued to gamble furiously and several cheques drawn for money to feed 'fruit-machines' were not honoured.

Recently he had spent all his wages (up to £15 per week) in a 'fruit-machine' in a public house every Friday night and invariably reinvested - and lost - all his winnings. Consequently his wife had to work throughout their marriage to support the family and repay his gambling debts. She vividly portrayed the situation thus: 'Over the last few years we have had a monster living with our family - a monster in the shape of a "fruit-machine". Practically every penny my husband earned went into that machine and while it consumed, we starved. He was obsessed by it. Frequently we were without food, fuel and light'. After 13 years of marriage they still lived in a rented apartment and possessed nothing but their personal effects. His wife repeatedly threatened to leave him if he did not stop gambling, and she eventually persuaded him to seek medical help (pp. 287-8).

Case II impressed Barker and Miller as a very different personality whose reaction to his gambling was in marked contrast to that of Case I. He was a 50-year-old unmarried man, living with his sister and elderly father in their old family house. He had worked with the same firm for 20 years and had had no previous financial difficulties:

He had placed a few shillings on horses and pennies on cards for years but never shown any tendency to large scale gambling. For the past 8 months he had become 'addicted' to gambling on 'one-armed bandits'. During this time he lost more than £450 and accumulated debts and IOUs amounting to £50. As soon as he saw a 'fruit-machine' he became totally immersed in gambling within seconds and spent every penny that he possessed in them. He gambled on two machines in a club and public house respectively but drank very little. His gambling followed a succession of wins on the first occasion and then he found he was unable to stop. It is significant that his wages increased considerably just before he started gambling so that for the time in his life he found he had money in excess of his needs. Finally, after spending £21 and £24 on successive nights, he became so concerned about his future that he sought psychiatric help (p. 288).

Here, then, is a man, described by Barker and Miller as '... somewhat shy, introverted ... exhibiting some obsessional traits', who seeks help after a *relatively* short and harmless gambling history. Case I, by way of contrast, is persuaded to seek treatment after a much longer and troublesome history. Interestingly, Barker and Miller described Case I as '... a co-operative and plausible man ... showing marked psychopathic traits. He had an ebullient but unstable personality ...'. The confusion between excessive appetitive behaviour and 'bad character' is a theme that recurs constantly in the literature on gambling, drinking, and other forms of excess.

Case III was similar to Case I in age, circumstances, family history of gambling, and the possession of, '... some psychopathic traits'. His particular problem, however, unlike the others, was 'the horses':

> He had gambled in 'betting shops' for more than 2 years and had lost over £1,200. Initially he ascribed his gambling mainly to boredom, but he had recently gambled to repay his debts, which exceeded £100. His usual practice was to spend all his salary (£15 to £30 per week) in a betting shop on Saturdays. He invariably reinvested his winnings on horses and returned home with nothing so that his wife and children went without food, clothes and fuel. He occasionally gambled on 'one-armed bandits' but this was not a major problem. Matters came to a head when he put his own money and the complete pay packet of a sick friend (who had asked him to collect his pay) on one horse and lost £40. This resulted in 18 months probation. His gambling has been causing serious marital difficulties and was affecting the health of his wife and his eldest son. He was referred for treatment by his doctor (pp. 288-9).

As is the case with 'alcoholism', 'compulsive gambling' implies a number of things which are not necessarily implied by simply engaging in an activity with a greater frequency or at a greater intensity than others. 'Alcoholism' is said to be more than just heavy drinking; similarly, 'compulsive gambling' is said to be more than merely heavy gambling. The first implication is that excessive gambling is one of the most important things to be said about the person concerned. It becomes a vital piece of information; it needs to be known if a person's behaviour is to be understood. It explains much, particularly any harm that a person is experiencing or problems that have befallen him or her. The status of 'compulsive gambler' may become a kind of 'master status' which may then be taken to 'explain' a variety of ills such as neglect of family, incompetence at work, financial difficulties, even marital infidelity (Herman, 1976). Like Alcoholics Anonymous, upon which it is closely modelled, Gamblers Anonymous (GA), successfully started in America in 1957, has done much to foster this view of excessive gambling. To acknowledge 'I am a compulsive gambler', is a crucial step in the GA recovery programme.

The second implication of being a 'compulsive gambler' is the supposition that there exist hallmarks - one would be inclined to call them 'symptoms' if the view is taken that 'compulsive gambling' is an illness of some kind - which make the gambling experience qualitatively different from that of the moderate or normal gambler, and sets the 'compulsive gambler' apart from him. These assumptions, that people whose gambling is excessive have much in common and that all are in marked contrast to others whose gambling is not excessive, follow easily once an apparently scientific term such as 'compulsive gambling' is used, exactly as they do in the case of drinking and 'alcoholism'. Moran (1970, 1975) is a British psychiatrist who has taken a special interest in excessive gambling, which he prefers to call 'pathological gambling'. His reasons for preferring the latter term are interesting because they touch upon one of the central facets of the psychology of excessive appetitive behaviour, namely ambivalence and conflict. Following Lewis (1936) he argues that compulsions are the behavioural aspects of obsessional states in which a person finds his own behaviour alien and tries to resist it. It is the element of resistance which in his view defines compulsion, and the term compulsive should otherwise, '... not be used no matter how strong the urge to indulge in the activity' (Moran, 1975, p.417). In his view, although ambivalence about gambling is usually present to some extent, many excessive gamblers experience enjoyment of the activity and many do not wish to stop. This betrays the existence of a common misunderstanding, namely that enjoyment and compulsion are incompatible, and it is a central matter to which this book will return in a later chapter.

Moran referred to 'the syndrome of pathological gambling' and considered that it could be recognized by the presence of any of the following:

> 1. Concern on the part of the gambler and/or family about the amount of gambling, which is considered to be excessive.
> 2. An overpowering urge to gamble so that the individual may be intermittently or continuously preoccupied with thoughts of gambling; this is usually associated with the subjective experience of tension which is found to be relieved only by further gambling.
> 3. The subjective experience of the inability to control the amount once gambling has started ...
> 4. Disturbances of economic, social and/or psychological functioning of the gambler and/or the family as a result of persistent gambling (p. 418).

It is interesting to see the close parallels that exist between this list and the list of signs and symptoms of 'alcoholism' discussed in the previous chapter. The amount of the activity itself is mentioned, although it is concern about amount rather than amount *per se* which is thought to be the criterion. So too are strength of desire and preoccupation, loss of control, and harm caused by gambling in economic, social, and psychological spheres. According to Moran the latter includes debt, loss of employment and friends, eviction, criminality, marital problems, family problems, depression, attempted suicide, and behaviour disorders in the children of compulsive gamblers. Only those aspects of 'alcoholism' which can be ascribed to alcohol being a drug (tolerance and withdrawal symptoms) are missing. Even then, Moran makes mention of tension, '... which is found to be relieved only by further gambling', and a recent article in the *British Journal of Addiction* reports that 30-50 per cent of a sample of GA members described disturbances of mood or behaviour on ceasing to bet which, if described by 'alcoholics', would be termed 'withdrawal symptoms' (Wray and Dickerson, 1981). Of those who completed a standard questionnaire (another group who responded in open-ended fashion reported almost as much disturbance) 40 per cent indicated five or more disturbances of mood or behaviour and 39 per cent listed at least one somatic disturbance. Amongst the results for individual 'symptoms', 32 per cent said they had felt anxious and 46 per cent said they had felt irritable. These percentages are remarkably similar, and in the case of irritability somewhat higher, than the comparable percentages from some studies of 'withdrawl symptoms' amongst excessive drinkers (Wray and Dickerson, 1981).

As disagreement over terms is the norm when excessive appetites are being discussed, it is no surprise to find not a little confusion in the literature on excessive gambling. This confusion, often borne of the view that someone with an excessive appetite is qualitatively different from other people, is exemplified by Bergler (1958) in his book *The Psychology of Gambling*, where he wrote, 'To avoid misunderstandings: not everyone who gambles is a gambler [*sic*]. There are millions of "harmless" gamblers who play for diversion or sociability' (p. viii). His view was that 'real' or 'pathologic' gamblers were, unlike other people, 'neurotics' with an unconscious wish to lose. Whatever one thinks of that view, he clearly recognized the possibility that gambling could constitute a very troublesome and excessive form of appetitive behaviour for some people as his list of characteristics of the 'real gambler' shows:

> Gambling is habitual
> Gambling absorbs and precludes all other interests.
> The gambler is always optimistic, never learning lessons from losing (he is, '... the last optimist ... beyond the reach of all logical objection and argument', p. 3).
> The gambler cannot stop when winning.
> The gambler may be cautious initially but eventually risks more than he can afford.
> The gambler seeks and enjoys an enigmatic 'thrill' ('pleasure-painful tension', to cite 'an observant patient' of Bergler's).

Moran would not recognize all these features as universal to 'pathological' gambling, however, since some of them, in his view, are only characteristic of certain sub-types. One of these sub-types of pathological gambling listed by Moran was 'impulsive' gambling - others being symptomatic gambling (associated with mental illness), psychopathic gambling, neurotic gambling, and subcultural gambling (arising from a social background of heavy gambling). Impulsive gambling, according to Moran, was characterized by loss of control and symptoms of craving. It is intriguing to find that these two 'symptoms' receive prominent mention in discussions of excessive gambling, as they have long been the *sine qua non* of 'alcoholism', and have come under serious attack in recent years for the way in which they have lent to the field of alcohol problems a spurious sense of precision and a medical aura (eg Pattison *et al.*, 1977).

Table 4 shows one of a number of questionnaires which are in existence, based upon these ideas of 'compulsive gambling' and particularly upon the tenets of Gamblers Anonymous, and which are designed for the self-detection of 'compulsive' or 'pathological' gambling.

The special entity or syndrome idea of excessive appetitive behaviour has come in for much the same kind of criticism when applied to gambling as it has when applied to the drinking of alcohol. Indeed, just because gambling is not a pharmacological agent, anything resembling a disease concept of excessive gambling may lack the plausibility which the disease concept of 'alcoholism' possesses. Herman (1976), for example, clearly regarded the GA tendency to define all problems as stemming from 'compulsive gambling' as an over-simplification which is functional for its members rather than being an accurate statement of cause and effect. As he said, 'This kind of "single cause"

Table 4   A typical questionnaire for self-diagnosis of compulsive gambling.

1.   Have you ever lost time from work due to gambling?
2.   Has gambling made your life unhappy?
3.   Has gambling affected your reputation?
4.   Have you ever felt remorse after gambling?
5.   Have you ever gambled to get money to pay debts or to otherwise solve financial difficulties?
6.   Did gambling ever cause a decrease in your ambition or efficiency?
7.   After losing did you feel that you must return as soon as possible and win back your losses?
8.   After a win have you had a strong urge to return and win more?
9.   Have you often gambled until your last penny was gone?
10. Have you ever borrowed to finance your gambling?
11. Have you ever sold any real or personal property to finance your gambling?
12. Are you reluctant to use 'gambling money' for normal expenditures?
13. Has gambling ever made you careless of the welfare of your family?
14. Have you ever gambled longer than you had planned?
15. Have you ever gambled to escape worry or trouble?
16. Have you ever committed, or considered committing, an illegal act to finance your gambling?
17. Has gambling ever caused you to have difficulty in sleeping?
18. Did arguments, disappointments, or frustrations ever create within you an urge to gamble?
19. Have you ever had an urge to celebrate any good fortune by a few hours of gambling?
20. Have you ever considered self-destruction as results of your gambling?

theory may not satisfy the moralist, but it may be just the ticket for the relatively uncomplicated rehabilitation of the member' (p. 101). He stated his view that there were no dividing lines betweeen moderate problem gamblers, addicted gamblers, compulsive gamblers, or pathological gamblers, and that creating a separate category of compulsive gambler' served no useful purpose. Indeed it, '... generates a set of new problems that would not otherwise exist' (p. 103).

In his very comprehensive review on gambling in Britain carried out for the Home Office Research Unit, Cornish (1978) appeared to support the division into moderate and immoderate, although he used what the present writer considers to be the most accurate expression for the latter - namely 'excessive' gambling - and fully recognized the difficulty of separating the two. He avoided defining excessive gambling in terms of supposed hallmarks or symptoms such as craving or loss of control, but rather focused upon gambling which was a social problem. As we shall see later in this book, this tactic of considering only problematic or harmful appetitive behaviour is an attractive one, but it bypasses the central questions to which this book is addressed: What is the psychological nature of excessive appetite behaviour? When and why does it occur, and under what circumstances does it disappear? Nor, as Cornish was aware, does it solve the problems of definition. He put the case for relativity as follows:

> First, the extent to which behaviour constitutes a social problem is a function not only of the behaviour itself but of its nuisance-value or its social and economic costs to the community in other ways; similar behaviours when manifested by different individuals or social groups may vary in their level of 'visibility' ...

> Secondly, an individual is more likely, or likely more rapidly, to define his behaviour as constituting a problem in some circumstances than others. The heavy gambler with plenty of money and spare time, and few other commitments, will be considerably less likely to view his behaviour with anxiety than a similar person less fortunately placed in these respects (p. 76).

This may be even more the case for gambling than for drinking, he suggests, for at least in the latter case the health hazards of drinking large quantities of alcohol impose some sort of upper limit above which relativity no longer applies.

Despite the difficulties, Cornish could at least conceive of an epidemiology of excessive gambling - the possibility of defining a case in quantitative terms, and of counting the number of those cases in a defined population. A body of epidemiological knowledge about excessive gambling does not exist to anything like the extent that it does in the case of excessive drinking, although estimates of the 'size of the problem' abound. The best that could be done in Cornish's view was to estimate the number of those 'at risk' on account of the regularity of their gambling. Based upon the results of the latest Gallup Poll (1976), Cornish estimated there to be two million regular (more often than weekly) gamblers on football pools aged 16 years or over in Britain, 1.3 million regularly engaging in off-course betting, one million in bingo gambling, 77,000 in gaming club gambling, and 24,000 in on-course betting. Employing the argument that those particularly at risk were those engaging regularly in forms of gambling which involved the possibility of continuous betting, and those who had relatively little personal disposable income (for both of which factors he found evidence), he estimated just over one million at risk of excessive off-course betting and just under one million at particular risk of excessive bingo gambling. The number of regular on-course betters and gaming club gamblers was comparatively very small, and the quite large number of regular football pools gamblers were not considered particularly at risk because of the non-continuous nature of the gambling activity involved.

Other estimates for Britain include Moody's (1972) estimate, prepared for the Churches' Council on Gambling, of the numbers of 'regular and committed' or 'thorough-going' gamblers. This estimate was 725,000 although no details were given of exactly how this figure was reached. Cornish considered this to be an example of the propaganda value for the anti-gambling lobby of maintaining estimates on the high side. The most carefully reasoned estimate is that of Dickerson (1974) based on his own close research on betting shops in the Birmingham area. He estimated 5.3 'gamblers' for each of about 15,000 betting shops in the country. 'Gamblers', according to Dickerson's definition, bet whenever there was an opportunity, stayed more than two hours in a betting shop, and bet until the end of racing. Of this group in Dickerson's study, 56 per cent thought they spent most of their own money on betting and had betting debts, 75 per cent regularly spent more than they intended, 45 per cent regularly lost all they had with them, and 36 per cent experienced some desire to cut back or to stop. He had thus identified a group who reported a high level of trouble related to their gambling and felt 'dissonance' regarding it.

A survey of gambling behaviour in the United States, carried out by the Institute for Social Research at the University of Michigan, demonstrated the extent of gambling activity but at the same time illustrated some of the difficulties and confusions involved in trying to define and enummerate 'compulsive gambling'. The survey report (Kallick *et al.*, 1979) estimated that a total of 22.4 billion dollars was ventured annually in the United States on some gambling activity or another (the equivalent figure for Britain in 1975/76 was £3.5 billion according to Cornish, 1978) and that 4.4 billion dollars, equivalent to 0.4 per cent of total personal income, was lost (or 'outlayed', i.e., amount bet minus winnings). The range of possible betting activities considered was wide, including betting with a bookmaker on various sporting events, playing commercially available 'games' such as 'jai alai', 'pickit', and 'numbers', and a whole host of ways of betting 'with friends', some of which Kallick *et al.* thought quite unusual:

> Almost one-sixth of the United States population said they bet whether some event would happen or where it would happen. For example, the hour of someone's birth, the first snowfall, whether someone would resign - or the date of that resignation - and similar events (p. 18).

When it came to estimating the extent of excessive gambling, the authors of this report adopted two strategies, both of which are unsatisfactory but for different reasons. One was to propose the concept of 'level of gambling activity'. The lowest level was not gambling at all; the next gambling only with friends or on legal, commercial games; the third level, illegal but not heavy gambling; and the highest level, illegal, heavy gambling which they defined as spending at least 50 dollars on such betting in a year. Although they demonstrated that this scale correlated with rates of divorce or separation, with proportions of subjects having children with problems, with job dissatisfaction, and with amount of time off work, this scale clearly equates and confuses 'excess' with both amount of gambling activity and with illegality.

The second, and even less sound, method was based on the common confusion, which will be discussed further in Chapter 11, between excessive appetitive behaviour and character or personality. The method consisted of assembling a 'compulsive gambling scale' from items included in eight personality inventories (of self-acceptance, risk-taking, anomic, external control orientation, etc.) which best discriminated 120 'compulsive gamblers' and an equal number of church members. The scale was then used to estimate the number of 'probable compulsive gamblers' and 'potential' compulsive gamblers' in the national survey sample. The fallacy of labelling people in this way on the basis of a scale that made no direct reference to gambling behaviour is obvious.

These difficulties and confusions not withstanding, individuals *do* seek help on account of excessive gambling and this fact is illustrated by the growth of Gamblers Anonymous in Britain. By 1975 the *Journal of Gamblers Anonymous* advertised 47 groups throughout the country, and Dickerson (1974) estimated the rate of referral to GA to be of the order of 2,000 a year with an additional 300 referrals to psychiatrists specifically on account of excessive gambling. As with 'alcoholism', referral rates of this kind are usually assumed to represent only the tip of the iceberg - those for whom excessive behaviour has become chronic and intolerable - and the 'real' prevalence of the problem is assumed to be very much greater. Rates of excessive gambling amongst clients of probation officers, and particularly amongst prisoners, are considerably greater than for the population as a whole (Cornish, p.81) - a further similarity with excessive drinking. However, it should be clear that the problems of defining and counting the incidence of 'compulsive' or 'pathological' gambling are such that very little faith can be placed in differences between reported rates from different populations. An apparently high rate amongst prisoners may reflect a truly greater than normal rate of excessive gambling, or may be a reflection of a greater involvement in gambling by members of lower socio-economic status groups from which prisoners are disproportionately drawn. Alternatively, it may be a result of the sensitivity of prison or probabtion staff to the possibility of excessive gambling, or the greater readiness of prisoners to attribute their problems to gambling. The status 'compulsive gambler' may be a less stigmatizing one than that of 'criminal' on account of the former's connotations of sickness and reduced responsibility.

It is partly this implication of reduced responsibility for behaviour which lies behind criticisms of the concept of 'compulsive gambler', as it does behind criticisms of any designation implying that excessive appetitive behaviour is the result of a condition over which a person has only limited control. In the case of gambling this debate was nicely illustrated by a leading article which appeared in *The British Medical Journal* for 13 April 1968 which followed a report in *The Times* of 2 April describing how a 'compulsive gambler' had been referred to a medical specialist and treated by the use of brain surgery. The *BMJ* leader objected to the involvement of psychiatry in such cases: 'The gambler enjoys every bit of his "compulsion" ... He may say "I cannot stop" but what he means is that he does not want to stop - the attractions are too great'. These statements go right to the heart of the dilemma presented by the phenomena of excessive appetite behaviour. How is it possible to posit a 'disease of the will' when the object of a person's so-called compulsion is an activity which constitutes for most people a source of enjoyment? The leader went on to press the distinction between true compulsions and excess behaviours like gambling and drinking:

> ... the rituals of the compulsive [i.e. the true compulsive] are uncontrollable because they arise outside consciousness. The gambler's behaviour is a source of pleasure ... the compulsive's is a burden which makes him anxious and depressed ... the excessive gambler lacks a sense of responsibility or of duty to society, but again this does not make him a psychiatric casualty. Every man in the street can imagine himself in his place....

The distinction between true compulsions and excessive behaviour is the same distinction which convinced Moran (1975) that the expression 'pathological' was preferable in the case of gambling, although it did not convince him that excessive gambling was outside the realm of psychiatry or the other helping professions. Nor did it so convince a number of readers of *The British Medical Journal* who wrote protesting about the leader, and these letters were published in subsequent issues (e.g. Carstairs, 1968; Gunn, 1968).

These and other clinicians who have been asked for help by people in distress over their own or a family member's gambling are left in no doubt that it is an over-simplification to state that all gambler's enjoy their gambling and could control their behaviour if they wished. They are as impressed by the accounts which some people give of the difficulty of controlling an activity which has become greatly excessive and damaging as have others been by the accounts of those who wish to control their drinking, drug-taking, smoking, or eating but find they cannot. Words such as 'addiction' or 'dependence', or terms such as 'compulsive gambling', seem to serve the purpose of 'explaining' or at least of describing such apparent paradoxes.

Whatever the rights and wrongs on the issue of whether excessive gambling constitutes any sort of entity or condition, and if so what such an entity should be called, it remains a fact that the availability of opportunities for gambling represents for society the same sort of behavioural control problem which alcohol presents. The control of gambling activities is as perennial a concern for national governments as has been the control of alcohol consumption.The difficulty of getting legislation right is well illustrated for gambling in recent British history by the permissive Betting and Gaming Act of 1960 and the quickly following and relatively restrictive Betting, Gaming, and Lotteries Act of 1964 and Gaming Act of 1968. There is an interesting parallel here with the reversals of the Acts of 1729, 1736, and 1751 which were aimed at the control of the sale of alcohol.

The details of the social control of a nation's gambling behaviour are as much at issue as ever. A book published by the Churches' Council on Gambling advocated, for example, the setting up of a Betting Board to complement the existing Gaming Board, totalizator rather than bookmaker betting systems, a restriction on the licensing of horse race betting facilities at other sporting events such as tennis tournaments and cricket matches, and the abolition of certain features of betting shops, such as staggered times of races from different courses and the provision of continuous commentaries direct from the racetrack (Moody, 1974). It was one of the particular arguments of that publication, which was supported by Cornish (1978), that the licensed off-course betting office, with the almost continual opportunity which it provides during racing hours for betting, listening to commentary, and then betting again on the next race, creates an atmosphere which encourages continuous or uncontrolled betting in a way that was virtually impossible before 1960 when betting was limited to on-course or unlicensed off-course betting.

In Britain the Churches' Council on Gambling has generally campaigned to reduce opportunities for gambling, whilst at the same time lending support to the modern distinction between controlled and excessive forms of gambling behaviour. The Council has defended its campaign on the grounds that a high level of gambling turnover reflects public acceptance of gambling and a climate favourable to all forms of gambling, including those that are more dangerous; that it allows more opportunities for individuals to begin gambling; and that participation in less dangerous forms of gambling may lead by generalization to participation in more dangerous forms. The parallel which this last argument suggests with hypothesis about escalating use of drugs is made the more obvious by the use of the terms 'soft' and 'hard' by the Churches' Council and other writers on gambling when writing about forms of gambling such as football pools betting and horse race gambling, respecitively.

Although there is persuasive evidence that the amount of excessive drinking in a population is directly related to the total amount of alcohol consumption in that population as a whole (Kendell, 1979), Cornish (1978), for one, doubted that the same relationship held in the case of gambling behaviour. He argued that whereas all alcoholic beverages contain the addictive ingredient alcohol, gambling activities were qualitatively different, for example in the degree to which they encouraged continuous play. His view on this would not be shared by many members of Gamblers Anonymous which advises its members to avoid even the casual playing of cards with no exchange of money, on the grounds that even such an apparently innocuous activity contains a measure of the active ingredients of tension and excitement.

The British Gaming Board has a double pronged policy for the control of gambling activities. It has argued, first, that new recruits to gambling can be limited by avoiding the artificial stimulation of demand. To this end it has succeeded in limiting the numbers and locations of gaming clubs. Secondly, it has argued for limiting the intensity of gambling by those recruited by preserving the 'essential nature' of gambling activities which are not in themselves dangerous. It has viewed Bingo, for example, as an essentially social activity and has resisted attempts to subvert this purpose by turning it into a relatively 'hard' form of gambling. Not that all bodies have shared the Gaming Board's charitable view that Bingo is a, 'neighbourly game played for modest stakes'. The Churces' Council on Gambling, for example, described it as a sterile and uncreative activity (CCG, 1960-1968, cited by Cornish, 1978).

Football pools betting is generally considered a fairly harmless form of gambling, but even in this area it is as well to remember that as recently as 1933 a Royal Commission recommended its abolition, and much more recently abolition of football pools has been advocated on the grounds that this type of betting takes place at home, thus placing young people at risk of involvement and of possible escalation to other forms of gambling.

As Cornish (1978) points out in the preface to his review, gambling occupies an equivocal position in our national life. Massive public participation, with over 80 per cent of adults taking part in one form of gambling or another, contrasts with continuing criticism of gambling on moral, social, and economic grounds, and continued awareness of the dangers of excess. Thus, gambling presents society with a problem very similar to that presented by the availability of alcohol: the problem of how to arrive at a balanced response which helps to minimize the dangers of immoderate use while at the same time detracting as little as possible from the enjoyment associated with the moderate use by the majority of citizens.

7.   Dependence and Society
Robin Room

Summary

The connections between sociocultural factors and alcohol dependence may be approached in several ways. Sociocultural factors can be treated as predictors and correlates extrinsic to dependence, viewed as a disease entity. The concept of dependence can be reexamined in terms of its presumed 'seating' - in the individual's psyche or body - and expanded to include the possibility of seating at supraindividual sociocultural levels. And the idea of dependence can be reinterpreted as 'culture-bound', that is, as depending for its existence and meaningfulness on sociocultural characteristics specific to particular times and places. The paper focuses on the latter two approaches, with particular attention to the development of sociological 'constructionist' thinking that views the concept and experiential reality of addiction or dependence as a product of particular cultural conditions rather than as a transcultural universal.

This paper is concerned with sociocultural factors in dependence, and particularly alcohol dependence. There are at least three ways in which this topic can be understood. The first way is most comprehensible for those outside the social sciences: it is simply to take dependence or addiction as a given - whether it is defined in biological, psychiatric or psychological terms, and whether it is defined as a disease or as a moral failing or as an erroneous product of social learning - and to consider psychosocial among other factors in its occurrence. The second way is to take apart the 'given,' the disease or condition or dependent variable, and to consider to what extent sociocultural factors can be part of the essence of what is to be explained. The third way is to distance ourselves from the disease or condition or dependent variable, and to shift to the question of how such conceptions as the disease concept of alcoholism or addiction arise - regarding the addiction concept, in other words, as a sociocultural creation that tells us as much about structures of thought in a given social order as about the nature of reality of individual experience. This paper will consider all three of these ways of interpreting the topic of dependence and society, but I will spend less time on the easy ground and more on the harder ground of the sociocultural construction of alcoholism and other concepts of alcohol problems.

The most usual meaning in considering sociocultural factors in dependence - the way it is usually considered in textbooks and compilations - is to consider interrelations with or the causative role of sociocultural factors in the occurrence of dependence. Kissin and Begleiter's recent edited volume on 'psychosocial factors' in 'the pathogenesis of alcoholism', for instance, includes chapters on gender, on ethnicity and nationality, on religion, on social class, on occupational factors, and on region and urbanization as factors in the occurrence of alcoholism.[1] In this perspective, the existence and nature of addiction is usually treated as a 'given' which exists outside the purview of the

British Journal of Addiction 80 (1985), pp. 133-139. © 1985 Society for the Study of Addiction to Alcohol and Other Drugs. Reprinted by permission of Carfax Publishing Company, PO Box 25, Abingdon, Oxfordshire, OX14 3UE.

sociocultural, although its prevalence is affected by sociocultural factors. It is in this spirit that textbooks of epidemiology give great importance to the triad of environment, host and agent as factors in the etiology of disease, but do not normally include within their scope discussions of the meaning, definition and nature of what is to be explained - the disease.

The second way of understanding sociocultural factors in dependence is to look at the sociocultural dimension in the 'dependence variable' - that is, within the disease or condition under study itself. As commonly used in medical discussion, in fact, the term 'etiology' subsumes this second meaning of factors intrinsic in the disease entity, along with the first meaning of extrinsic ' causal factors'. Thus theories of the etiology of a disease have included, along with the specification of 'causal' or 'risk' factors, a presumption or assertion about the seating of the disease - that is, where the disease process itself is seen as located and operating.[2] In the case of dependence, conventional discussions define the seating of the disease as being in the body or in the mind or in the soul - or in some combination. Thus, for Alcoholics Anonymous, an alcoholic is 'not only mentally and physically ill', he or she is also 'spiritually sick'.[3] Whether the conception is psychiatric or psychological or for that matter religious, the seating is usually defined as being in the individual - potentially also in the family or in a dyadic relation, in some conceptions - and the possibility of group or societal level seating is not contemplated.

In the professional literature, there has been considerable wavering back and forth over the years between a physical or a psychological or a combined 'seating'. For Norman Kerr, at the inaugural meeting of what is now the Society for the Study of Addiction, the seating was dual: while the disease of inebriety involved the drinker being driven by an ungovernable impulse' or 'pursued by a constant desire to fly to intoxicating liquors', there was also 'a physical influence in operation, a physiological neurotic effect, the tendency of which is to create an appetite for more of the intoxicating agent'.[4] The enthusiasm for degenerative genetic theories of alcoholism around the turn of the century tended to tip the scales towards physical causes and 'seating',[5] while Berridge notes that, for the leadership of the Society, the scales tipped again around 1915 "away from a purely physical emphasis towards that of 'disease of the will'".[4]

The modern era has seen a similar history of shifting back and forth on the 'seating' of dependence. In WHO Expert Committee discussions of addiction and dependence, a strong commitment to a physiological seating in the 1950s was succeeded in the mid-1960s by a shift to dual concepts of physical and psychic dependence, with psychic dependence seen as the most powerful of all the factors involved in the chronic intoxication with psychoactive drugs';[6] thus in his acceptance of the Browning Award in 1972, Nathan Eddy took the view that 'we had been wrong all those years in regarding physiological dependence as the primary phenomena'.[7] More recent formulations under WHO auspices have emphasized the interrelatedness of levels - thus the report adopting the designation 'alcohol dependence syndrome' specified that it included a 'triad' of an 'altered behavioural state', an 'altered subjective state', and an 'altered psychobiological state'[8] - or have adopted a rather metaphysical view of dependence as 'essentially located within a system' of 'phenomena' and 'relationships', taking 'account of the interaction between drug, person and environment' - a model which is contrasted with views of dependence which see it only 'in terms of what is going on within the individual, either physiologically or psychologically, or strictly in terms of behaviour alone, or in terms of the social role that the drug-user assumes'.[9] In U.S. research psychiatric circles, there is currently a strong tendency to tip the seating of alcohol dependence back to the physical level. Meanswhile, Griffith Edwards appears to be reverting, in a recent article, to a bifurcation between phenomena at the 'psycho-social' and the 'psycho-biological' levels - with the discussion of the latter level actually limited to biological dependence phenomena.[10]

In the second meaning of 'sociocultural factors in dependence', the issue can be raised whether some part of the phenomena covered by dependence concepts should rather be seen as seated at social levels, outside the individual's psyche or body[2,11]. If dependence is a concept which is invoked to explain the repeated occurrence of apparently intrinsically harmful or aversive behaviour, then it must be acknowledged that there are social mechanisms - for example, customs of 'treating', 'shouting' or 'standing rounds' - which can sustain such behaviour even in the absence of physiological or psychological dependence. Bruun's classic small-group drinking studies,[12] in which there were plenty of exhortations from one group member to another to drink up, but never a single suggestion to slow down, might thus been seen as reflecting a dependence 'seated' at group or cultural levels, rather than at psychic or physical levels. As Jellinek implied, the French concepts of 'alcoholisation' and of the 'economic origin' of alcoholism can be seen as conceptions of the seating of alcohol dependence at a societal level.[13]

If the first way of understanding sociocultural factors in dependence is to treat dependence as a clinical 'given' for which sociocultural correlates or causes are to be found, the second way thus extends the reach of sociocultural factors into the domain of the 'dependent variable' itself, pointing out and examining the sociocultural dimensions in what is to be explained. A third way of understanding sociocultural factors in dependence departs even more radically from textbook views of social epidemiology, and takes one step further back from the comfortable platonic positivism involved in most discussions of the etiology of disease. In this third view, the dependence concept itself is viewed as a sociocultural construction, located in a particular time and place and sociocultural circumstances. This third perspective goes by such terms in the social sciences as 'constructivist' and 'historical social constructionist'. It is a view which has been gaining prominence in sociology, somewhat to the puzzlement and indeed disapproval of many working in a clinical research perspective.[14] The remainder of this paper attempts a tentative synthesis of work in the tradition of this third meaning of sociocultural factors in dependence.

Let us start from some observations about dependence and addiction concepts and their intellectual and social history. Here I am paying attention not only to professional literatures but also to popular conceptions of the drunkard. I am also lumping together, without fine distinctions, the related concepts of 'alcoholism', 'alcohol dependence' and 'alcohol addiction'. In this, I have some distinguished company from among those in the mainstream of American thought in the field; Mark Keller recently offered the opinion that the 1960s WHO Committees moved 'to eliminate the word *addiction* from the expert lexicon in favour of the euphemism *dependence* for no other reason that some members felt that *addiction* was a very severe word',[15] while Donald Goodwin has waxed quite sarcastic about the efforts of WHO committees to distinguish between 'alcoholism' and 'alcohol dependence'.[16] In popular thought in the U.S., and indeed apparently in some other countries, the heart of an addiction or dependence concept - its 'pathognomic symptom', in Jellinek's famous translation of the 1950s U.S. version of the concept into scholarly terms[17] - is 'loss of control'. As is explicit in the formulation which forms the 'first step' of Alcoholics Anonymous, the loss of control is twofold; AA members must admit 'that we were powerless over alcohol - that our lives had become unmanageable'. The loss of control is not only over one's drinking behaviour, but also over one's life because of the drinking.

> With the alcoholic illness... goes annihilation of all the things worth while in life. It engulfs all whose lives touch the sufferer's. It brings misunderstanding, fierce resentment, financial insecurity, disgusted friends and employers, warped lives of blameless children, sad wives and parents.[3, p.28]

The concept is thus implicitly an explanation of perceived personal failure: the affected individual has failed to carry through on significant role expectations in his or her life; this failure is ascribed to a personal failure to control behaviour in accordance with expectations; and this loss of control is in turn ascribed to loss of control over drinking behaviour.

Over 30 years ago, Edwin Lemert pointed to the potential cultural specificity involved in rooting the concept of alcoholism in the presumption of personal self-control. Collecting a number of statements of American attitudes toward the alcoholic, he noted that the 'general theme underlying' them 'has to do with the lack of self control on the part of the drinker. This societal symbolism of the deviation as a sign of character weakness is one of the most vivid and isolating distinctions which can be made in a culture which attributes morality, success and respectability to the power of a disciplined will'. At a more general level, he proposed that

> in a given society,... in order for chronic alcohol addiction or compulsive drinking to develop, there must be strong disapproval of the consequences of drinking or of drinking itself beyond a certain point of intoxication, so that the culture induces guilt and depression over drinking and extreme drunkenness *per se* .[18]

Somewhat later, Mairi McCormick noted that, as viewed in the English novel, alcoholism first appears on the historical stage in the early 19th century: 'it seems probable that the gamma alcoholic made his appearance in society with the industrial revolution... When we look at fiction about 1830, when the industrial revolution was in full swing, we find that the same drinking may be described as existed 80 years before but that a new and more desperate kind of solitary, tragic and inexplicable drinking has come into existence beside it'.[19] Michael Russell[20] has indicated where we can see an analogous change in process today, in the shifting definition of the smoker; one result of the education and agitation about smoking in the last 30 years, he comments, has been to convert habitual smokers into unhappy and guilty ones, increasingly defined in terms of addiction.

Behind the fictional debut of the alcoholic in the early 19th century, Harry Levine has argued, lay a new concept of addiction, a 'new paradigm or model' which 'defined addiction as a central problem in drug use and diagnosed it as a disease, or disease-like. The idea that alcoholism is a progressive disease - the chief symptom of which is loss of control over drinking behaviour, and whose only remedy is abstinence from all alcoholic beverages - is now about 175 to 200 years old, but no older'.[21]

> Grounded in the optimistic *Weltanschauung* of the Enlightenment, the middle class assumed that evil need not exist - social problems were solvable or curable. However, the conditions of a 'free society', meaning individual freedom to pursue one's interests, required shifting social control to the individual level. Social order depended on self-control... In the Jacksonian era, the 1830s, Americans troubled by the disorder they perceived in their society built almshouses, penitentiaries, orphan asylums and reformatories to administer 'moral treatment' to the dependent and deviant. The idea, in all cases, was to build up the dormant or decayed powers of self-control through discipline, routine and hard work. ... Like asylum advocates, temperance supporters were interested in helping people develop and maintain control over their behavior and actions. Temperance supporters however, believed they had located, in liquor, the source of most social problems...

> In the 19th century, the concept of addiction was interpreted by people in light of their struggles with their own desires. The idea of addiction made sense not only to drunkards, who came to understand themselves as individuals with overwhelming desires they could not control, but also to great numbers of middle-class people who were struggling to keep their desires in check - desires which at times seemed irresistible (pp. 163-165).

In the context of American and British societies, then, it can be argued that both the idea of addiction and the existential experience of loss of control to which the idea refers are historical creations of a particular epoch, reflecting a particular organization of the society. In American society , in particular, the idea of a disease entity marked by a loss of control over behaviour and thus over one's life, first worked out for alcohol, has been applied in many other contexts, as both lay and professional levels. It can be seen in the proliferation of 'Anonymous' groups on the model of Alcoholics Anonymous. *Compulsive Overeater*, by Bill B., published by a major corporation in the field of treatment of alcoholism and other disorders, rigidly applies the twelve steps of AA for those who may be considered to have lost control over their eating behaviour.[22] A recent article in the 'Science ' section of the *New York Times* applies the addiction concept to sexual behaviour:

> Some types of excessive sexual activity have all the hallmarks of an addiction and can be treated in a fashion similar to other addictions, such as alcoholism and gambling, a growing number of sex therapists believe.

> People with this problem, who are now being called 'sexual addicts',
> typically use sex as a psychological narcotic. They are driven to find relief
> through sex from feelings of agitation and worthlessness. But once the
> sexual high ends they are again overwhelmed by those same feelings, and
> once again feel driven to sex. And so the cycle starts over once more. ... Sex
> becomes the all consuming focus of life, an overriding passion that is
> pursued at the cost of living a normal life, at the expense of career, family
> or marriage.[23]

According to the article, there are now hundreds of groups throughout the country
organized under such rubrics as 'Sexaholics Anonymous' and 'Sexual Addicts
Anonymous'. These examples show that the addiction conceptualizations extend in a
society like the U.S. far beyond their original realm of psychoactive drug use, to cover
behaviour which is defined as problematic and yet which is recurrent. For such
behaviours, there is a cultural expectation of self-control, and the recurrence of the
behaviour in contravention of this expectation often is viewed as prima-facie evidence
of addiction.[24]

In recent years, evidence has accumulated from the anthropological literature to
support the view of addiction concepts and loss-of-control experiences as socioculturally
specific. It has been a common observation in the literature on drinking in tribal and
village societies that alcoholism is generally rare in these societies. This has often been
taken at its face value, as one would interpret, for instance, a statement that measles
or cirrhosis mortality were rare. But recently there has been a more explicit recognition
that the rarity may reflect something else; that alcoholism as an idea and as a way of
behaving may be seen as 'culture-bound',[25] that habitual drunkenness does not become
alcoholism without a specific pattern of general cultural beliefs and norms. Thus, for
instance, Leland's careful review of the evidence on the applicability of alcohol addiction
concepts to North American Indian drinking includes a substantial questioning of
whether 'loss of control' is a meaningful concept in the context of traditional Indian
cultures. 'If controls over drinking are culturally determined, and if Indians have never
socially or culturally internalized such controls, we might be tempted to conclude that
their absence in the group should not be interpreted as *loss* of control, i.e., a symptom
of alcohol addiction'.[26] Kunitz and Levy[27] interpret the changing beliefs about alcohol
among contemporary Navahos in terms very like Levine's interpretation of the changes
in American society in the early 19th century: traditionally among the Navahos, heavy
drinking and associated health and social problems certainly occurred, but the heavy
drinkers did:

> not for the most part define themselves as sick in the same way as health
> professionals do. As the society changes, however, these behaviours
> increasingly come to be seen as maladaptive to the new world where people
> are expected to be at work on time, where no network of kin is available to
> help when a husband is out drinking; where bills must be paid and where
> all sorts of obligations the dominant society takes for granted must be
> fulfilled... In the new society that is emerging, older patterns of behaviour
> are increasingly defined as in some way deviant. The drinker's behaviour

comes to be defined as sick. He is no longer a man who drinks a lot; he is an alcoholic (pp. 254-5).

Kunitz and Levy add the strongly constructivist comment that 'the process whereby that redefinition takes place tells us more about the society which is doing the defining and undergoing the change than it does about the phenomenon known as alcoholism' (p. 257).

The concept of 'culture-bound' or 'culture-specific syndromes' exists uneasily in the interstice between transcultural psychiatry and medical anthropology, referring to diseases - particularly but not only mental diseases - that only exist in a particular cultural context.[28] Developing-country psychiatrists have called it a 'somewhat unfortunate term' as it has usually been applied, 'to denote a heterogenous group of disorders' linked only by the fact that they were encountered outside the cultural framework of European psychiatry.[29] But, as the same paper demonstrates, in a wider perspective the classical disease categories of European psychiatry can also be viewed as culture-bound. For example,

> the tendency to classify psychiatric phenomena on the basis of intrapsychic process is the result of a development strongly influenced by philosophical trends and a particular school in psychology and psychiatry. This has led to the now axiomatic 'underlying' causes even in the absence of overt manifestations... The division of mental functions into thinking and feeling has further contributed... to the establishment of a dichotomy in classificatory systems which may not be justified...Modern psychiatry has selected a few emotions like anxiety and depression to the exclusion of a whole range of other emotions like anger, greed, jealousy, hate, eroticism, etc. The excessive emphasis on two emotions appears unjustified. This emphasis is perhaps reflected in the 19 different classficatory categories for depression.

In suggesting that alcoholism can be viewed as a culture-bound syndrome, I am not of course denying the transcultural reality of the withdrawal syndrome or other physical accompaniments and sequelae of heavy or prolonged drinking - although even here different cultural patterns of drinking can shift the meaning or implications of particular symptoms.[30] Attention is directed rather to the aspects which have usually fallen under the rubric of 'psychological dependence'. In my view, looked at in a cross-cultural perspective, it is questionable whether these necessarily covary with the physical accompaniments or sequelae of heavy drinking. In such a perspective, therefore, it would be unwise to assume that the various elements described as the 'alcohol dependence syndrome' constitute a single 'psychobiological reality'[8] (p.9); rather, variations in the sociocultural construction of drinking behaviour - dependence concepts and experiences, as well as other concepts and experiences - should be made the subject of empirical investigation, along with studies of the sociocultural patterning and biological concomitants of drinking. Even in societies with many similarities, we may find significant differences in conceptualizations. Thus Raul Caetano has pointed out[31] that the recent operationalizations of the alcohol dependence syndrome differ in the U.S. and in Britain, with U.S. researchers including and British researchers excluding social consequences of drinking from the definition.

This view returns us fairly close to the position adopted by Jellinek towards the end of his life, with a view of drinking problems ('alcoholism', in his late terminology) as a 'genus' with many 'species differentiated according to the presence or absence of such features as 'psychological vulnerability', 'physiological vulnerability', 'sociocultural elements', 'economic elements', and 'type of damage incumbent upon drinking'.[32] This typology alerts us to the necessarily multidisciplinary nature of an approach to understanding and preventing alcohol problems - without a hegemony for any particular discipline's operating model. What our societies have defined as addiction and entrusted to the hands of self-help groups, professionals, or moral politics, reflects heartfelt experiences which encompass many different levels of seating. Jellinek's later typology is a long distance away from the unilinear, progressive model of a single disease entity, organized around loss of control, to which Jellinek had adhered in the late 1940s and early 1950s. Between the two conceptualizations had lain for Jellinek a rich international experience of the very different things 'alcoholism' denoted, even in the professional literatures, in different sociocultural contexts. The 100th anniversary of the Society for the Study of Addictions seems an appropriate moment to pick up the implied challenge of Jellinek's late formulation, and to add the comparative study of addiction models and other interpretations of drinking behaviour in different sociocultural contexts to the already full agenda of research on sociocultural variations in drinking behaviour and problems.

We may ask what practical difference is a comparative constructionist approach to concepts and definitions of alcohol likely to make. In the first place, it helps to liberate us from the weight of interpretations and allow us to get back to the actual presentation of alcohol problems, not only in terms of objectively verifiable symptoms but also in terms of the deeply felt experiences of men and women in a particular time and place. Secondly, it alerts us to the possibility of differentiations within a given society in the definitions of alcohol problems. The addiction concept, with its emphasis on self-control, has been especially a middle-class way of defining and looking at behaviour. This is true also of controlled drinking strategies, as the rubric of 'controlled drinking' itself implies. The concepts of drinking problems of those not in the middle class and without middle class aspirations remain to be explored.

Thirdly, it helps us to evaluate critically the applicability of new treatment fashions to a particular time and place. In the International Study of Alcohol Control Experiences, we found that there had been a remarkable and parallel growth in treatment systems in the postwar era in countries with very different political traditions and alcohol cultures; to us it seemed that 'common solutions were adopted for very different problems'.[33] Whether with respect to temperance thought, to alcohol control models, or to treatment regimes, the history of ideas about alcohol has been marked by an unusual internationalism. There are many benefits from this, but we can also observe cases in which professional enthusiasm led to the application of models in inappropriate circumstances. Getting away from the idea that there is one condition that is the same everywhere allows us to take a more critical view of the applicablitity of treatment modalities across cultures.

Lastly, the approach raises the issue of the possible contribution of attempts to alter professional or popular understandings about alcohol in the prevention of alcohol problems. As we can see from the example given by Michael Russell of the newly emergent category of unhappy and guilty smokers, dependence concepts carry a burden for those identified by them as well as offering benefits and redemption; along with defining certain patterns as deviant, they tend to locate the seating of the problem at individual rather than at societal or cultural levels. Dependence concepts also attribute great power to the psychoactive substance - again we can see this in Russell's eloquent presentation of nictonism as a dependence, for instance in his comparisons with heroin and alcohol. This attribution of power in popular understandings of dependence is why we are uneasy applying the concept of banalized substances like tea, coffee and chocolate. And it is why to talk of sexual behaviour or overeating in formal terms as an addiction is to raise the stakes on the behaviour, to turn it from the everyday to the potentially tragic or heroic.

To attribute great power to a substance, as the cultures with significant historical temperance movements have tended to do with alcohol, is a two-edged sword. As we are learning from the balanced-placebo designs and other studies of the effects of expectations on behaviour after drinking,[34] it is these socially and culturally conditioned expectations which are a large part of the explanation of alcohol's association with violence and crime. For this, we should not necessarily blame the temperance movement: it may have been strong precisely in those societies where the cultural association of drinking and violence was already deeply entrenched. While they point to no instant solution, constructivists approaches alert us to the power of ideas as well as material circumstances, and offer us a way of envisaging and considering alternatives to our present conceptualizations of alcohol and drug problems.

Acknowledgements

Revised from a paper presented at the Centennial Symposium of the Society for the Study of Addiction to Alcohol and Other Drugs, 'Addiction: A Hundred Years On', at the Royal Society, London, 25-26 October 1984. Preparation was supported by a U.S. National Alcohol Research Centre Grant (AA 05595) from the National Institute on Alcohol Abuse and Alcoholism to the Alcohol Research Group, Institute of Epidemiology and Behavioural Medicine, Medical Research Institute of San Francisco.

References

1. Kissin, B. and Begleiter, H., eds. *The Biology of Alcoholism; vol, 6: The Pathogenesis of Alcoholism: Psychosocial Factors*. New York and London, Plenum, 1983.

2. Room, R. 'The social psychology of drug dependence'. pp. 69-75 in: [Haeks, D., ed.,] *The Epidemiology of Drug Dependence: Report on a Conference: London 25-29 September, 1972*. Copenhagen, World Health Organization Regional Office for Europe, 1973.

3. Alcoholics Anonymous. New York, Works Publishing, 1939, p. 77.

4. Berridge, V. 'Editorial: The centenary issue'. *British Journal of Addiction*, 1984, 79, 1-5

5. Bynum, W.F. 'Alcoholism and degeneration in 19th Century European medicine and psychiatry'. *British Journal of Addiction*, 1984, 79, 59-70.

6. Eddy, N. B., Halback, H., Isbell, M. and Seevers, M. H. 'Drug dependence: Its significance and characteristics'. *Bulletin of the World Health Organization*, 1965, 32, 721-733.

7. Room, R. 'The Amsterdam Congress'. *Drinking and Drug Practices Surveyor*, 1973, 7, 1-6.

8. Edwards, G., Gross, M. M., Keller, M., Moser, J. and Room R., (Eds.). *Alcohol-Related Disabilities*. Geneva, World Health Organization, Offset Publication No. 32, 1977.

9. Edwards, G., Arif, A. and Hodson, R. 'Nomenclature and classification of drug- and alcohol-related problems: A WHO memorandum'. *Bulletin of the Work Health Organization*, 1981, 59, 225-242.

10. Edwards, G. 'Drinking in longitudinal perspective career and natural history'. *British Journal of Addiction*, 1984, 79, 175-183.

11. Straus, R. 'The challenge for reconceptualization'. *Journal of Studies on Alcohol*, 1979, Supplement 8, 279-288.

12. Bruun, K. *Drinking Behaviour in Small Groups*. Helsinki, Finnish Foundation for Alcohol Studies, 1959.

13. Room, R. 'The World Health Organization and alcohol control'. *British Journal of Addiction*, 1984, 79, 85-92.

14. Room, R. 'Alcohol problems and the sociological constructivist approach: Quagmire or path forward?'. Presented at the annual meeting of the Alcohol Epidemiology Section, International Council on Alcohol and Addictions, Edinburgh, June 4-8, 1984.

15. Comment by Mark Keller on p. 105 of: Gerstein, D.R. (Ed). *Toward the Prevention of Alcohol Problems: Government, Business and Community Action*. Washington, DC, National Academy Press, 1984.

16. Goodwin, D.W. 'On defining alcoholism and taking stands'. pp. 1-5 in: Cleminshaw, H. K. and Truitt, E.B., (Eds.) *Alcoholism: New Perspectives*, Akron, Ohio, University of Akron Center for Urban Studies, 1983.

17. Jellinek, E. M. 'Phases of alcohol addiction'. *Quarterly Journal of Studies on Alcohol*, 1952, 13, 673-684.

18. Lemert, E. 'Social Pathology': *A Systematic Approach to the Theory of Sociopathic Behavior*. New York, McGraw-Hill, 1951, pp. 356, 348-9.

19. McCormick, M. 'First representations of the gamma alcoholic in the English novel'. *Quarterly Journal of Studies on Alcohol*, 1969, 30, 957-980.

20. Russell, M. 'Smoking as a form of drug dependence presented at the Centennial Symposium of the Society for the Study of Addiction of Alcohol and other Drugs', 'Addiction: A Hundred Years On', at the Royal Society, London, 25 October, 1984.

21. Levine, H. G. 'The discovery of addiction: Changing conceptions of habitual drunkenness in America'. *Journal of Studies on Alcohol*, 1978, 39, 143-174.

22. B., Bill. *Compulsive Overeater: The Basic Text for Compulsive Overeaters*. Minneapolis, CompCare Publications, 1981.

23. Goleman, D. 'Some sexual behaviour viewed as an addiction'. *New York Times*, October 16, 1984, pp. 19, 21.

24. See, for example, Keller, M. 'Definition of alcoholism'. *Quarterly Journal of Studies on Alcohol*, 1960, 21, 125-134.

25. Room, R. 'Alcohol and ethnography: A case of problem deflation? (with comments and a response)'. *Current Anthropology*, 1984, 25, 169-191.

26. Leland, J. *Firewater Myths: North American Indian Drinking and Alcohol Addiction.* New Brusnwick, N. J.: Rutgers Centre of Alcohol Studies, Monograph No. 11, 1976, pp. 54-55.

27. Kunitz, S.HJ. and Levy, J. E. 'Changing ideas of alcohol use among Navaho Indians'. *Quarterly Journal of Studies on Alcohol*, 1974, 35, 243-259.

28. See discussion in Chapter 2 of: Djurfeldt G. and Lindberg, S. *Pills against Poverty: A Study of the Introduction of Western Medicine in a Tamil Village.* Lund, Sweden, Scandinavian Institute of Asian Studies Monograph No. 23, Curzon Press, 1975.

29. Wig, N.N., Setyonegoro, R. K., Shen Yucun and Sell, H. L. 'State of diagnosis and classification in the 1980s: The Third World. Prepared for an International Conference on Diagnosis and Classification of Mental Disorders and Alcohol - and Drug-Related Problems, World Health Organization', Copenhagen, 13-17 April, 1982.

30. Levy, J.E. and Kunitz, S. J. 'Economic and political factors inhibiting the use of basic research findings in Indian alcoholism programs'. *Journal of Studies on Alcohol*, 1981, Supplement 9, 60-72.

31. Caetano, R. (forthcoming). 'Two versions of dependence: The DSM-III and the alcohol dependence syndrome'. *Drug and Alcohol Dependence.*

32. Jellinek, E, M. 'Alcoholism, a genus and some of its species'. Canadian Medical Association Journal, 1960, 83, 1341-1345.

33. Makela, K., Room, R., Single, E., Sulkunen, P., Walsh, B., with 13 others. 'Alcohol, Society and the State: 1'. *A comparative Study of Alcohol Control.* Toronto, Addiction Research Foundation, 1981, p. 64.

34. See Room, R. and Collins, G. (Eds.). *Alcohol and Disinbibition: Nature and Meaning of the Link,* NIAAA Research Monograph No. 12. Washington, DC: U.S. Government Printing Office, DHHS Publication No. (ADM) 83-1246, 1983.

Keeping Control of Drugs and Drug Users

Drugs and drug users in the West have come under increasing control over the last 80 years. A plethora of punitive national laws and international conventions and agreements have brought about various restrictions on the way in which individuals can interact with various substances, through use for self-medication, use for pleasure, or in their trade. Conventional wisdom would suggest that such controls are the rational result of proper scientific and medical discretion. Drugs are dangerous; the public must be protected from them. We have seen, however, that some of the powers attributed to many illicit drugs have been exaggerated, and we should also remember that legal drugs such as alcohol and tobacco currently wreak damage way in excess of anything the illegal drugs manage to do.

Clearly then the legality/illegality of a drug may have little to do with dangers intrinsic to the drug itself. Musto in fact declares it to be essentially a political problem. The history of American drug use and its control, he argues, is centered in particular on attempts to control various (often foreign) minority groups and that their use of various substances has been used as an opportunity to act or incite against them. Bean is concerned to understand why there was a move from the British System of control to the more punitive framework (both legal and therapeutic - as we shall see later) approved in the late 1960s. Although some of the concepts Bean uses locates this piece firmly in the methodology of the 1970s, his emphasis on linking issues of control to the drug taker as opposed to the drug and to the context in which those drug takers were becoming visible, means that this piece retains much that is valuable and firmly supports the preceding piece by Musto. *Who* the drug users are, and what they are seen to represent, is probably more important a variable in assessing the nature of drug control than recourse to scientific or medical concerns over intrinsic dangers of any one drug or of the health of the population. That drug laws have symbolic content, and often little efficacy, is illustrated by Dorn et al in their analysis of recent punitive British legislation. Using the spectre of drugs and drug traffickers the Controlled Drugs (Penalties) Act 1985 and the Drug Trafficking Offences Act 1986, which overturn certain basic tenets of the British legal system, were able to be passed through Parliament relatively unopposed. Going full circle (to the initial international conventions), Britain was once more able to demonstrate solidarity with the US and its sermons to the international community by 'getting tough' on drugs, and at the same time show that it was serious about punishing wrong doers to its domestic population.

8. The Dynamics of Narcotic Control
David Musto

American concern with narcotics is more than a medical or legal problem - it is in the fullest sense a political problem. The energy that has given impetus to drug control and prohibition came from profound tensions among socio-economic groups, ethnic minorities, and generations - as well as the psychological attraction of certain drugs. The form of this control has been shaped by the gradual evolution of constitutional law and the lessening limitation of federal police powers. The bad results of drug use and the number of drug users have often been exaggerated for partisan advantage. Public demand for action against drug abuse has led to regulative decisions that lack a true regard for the reality of drug use. Relations and foreign nations, often the sources of the drugs, have been a theme in the domestic scene from the beginning of the American antinarcotic movement. Narcotics addiction has proven to be one of the most intractable medical inquiries ever faced by American clinicians and scientists. Disentangling the powerful factors which create the political issue of drug abuse may help put the problem in better perspective.

Fear of narcotics has grown with the awareness of their use. Dr Holmes in 1860 and Dr Beard in the 1870s and '80s warned that narcotics abuse was increasing. They based their attacks not only on direct observation but on the open record of import statistics. By 1900 restrictive laws on the state level had been enacted, and reformers began to look to the federal government for effective national regulation. Reform-minded leaders of the health professions agreed on the need to eliminate the nonmedical use of narcotics. Those seeking strict narcotic controls believed that either the need for money to buy drugs or a direct physiological incitement to violence led to crime and immoral behavior. Inordinate pleasure caused by drugs, moreover, was seen to provide youth with a poor foundation for character development, and a resulting loss of independence and productivity.

The most passionate support for legal prohibition of narcotics has been associated with fear of a given drug's effect on a specific minority. Certain drugs were dreaded because they seemed to undermine essential social restrictions which kept these groups under control: cocaine was supposed to enable blacks to withstand bullets which would kill normal persons and to stimulate sexual assault. Fear that smoking opium facilitated sexual contact between Chinese and white Americans was also a factor in its total prohibition. Chicanos in the Southwest were believed to be incited to violence by smoking marihuana. Heroin was linked in the 1920s with a turbulent age-group: adolescents in reckless and promiscuous urban gangs. Alcohol was associated with migrants crowding into large and corrupt cities. In each instance, use of a particular drug was attributed to an identifiable and threatening minority group.

David Musto: *THE AMERICAN DISEASE*, (Oxford, 1987), pp. 244-250. © David Musto 1987.

The occasion for legal prohibition of drugs for nonmedical purposes appears to come at a time of social crisis between the drug-linked group and the rest of American society. At the turn of this century, when the battle for political control of freed blacks reached a peak (as shown by the extent of disenfranchisement, lynchings, and the success of segregation policies), cocaine, a drug popular among whites and blacks and in the North as well as the South, was associated with expression of black hostility toward whites. Chinese and opium smoking became linked in the depressions of the late 19th century, when Chinese were low-paid competitors for employment, and this connection intensified during the bitter discrimination shown Orientals in the first decade of this century. The attack on marihuana occurred in the 1930s when Chicanos became a distinct and visible unemployed minority. Heroin, claimed to be an important factor in the "crime wave" which followed World War I, was implicated in the 1950s as part of the Communist conspiracy against the United States. A youth culture which attacked traditional values became closely connected with marihuana smoking and the use of other psychedelics. Customary use of a certain drug came to symbolize the difference between that group and the rest of society; eliminating the drug might alleviate social disharmony and preserve old order.

The belief that drug use threatened to disrupt American social structures militated against moves toward drug toleration, such as legalizing drug use for adults, or permitting wide latitude in the prescribing practice of physicians. Even if informed students of drugs such as Dr. Lawrence Kolb, Sr., in the 1920s argued that heroin does not stimulate violence, guardians of public safety did not act upon that information. The convenience of believing that heroin stimulated violence made the conviction hard to abandon. Public response to these minority-linked drugs differed radically from attitudes toward other drugs with similar potential for harm such as the barbiturates.

Narcotics are assumed to cause a large percentage of crime, but the political convenience of this allegation and the surrounding imagery suggest the fear of certain minorities, and make one suspicious of this popular assumption. During the last seventy-five years responsible officials have stated that narcotics caused between fifty and seventy-five percent of all crimes, especially in large cities like New York. Narcotics have been blamed for a variety of America's ills, from crime waves to social disharmony. Their bad effects have been given as the excuse for repressing certain minorities, as evidence for stopping legal heroin maintenance in 1919, and as evidence for starting legal heroin maintenance in 1972.

Like the speculated percentage of crimes caused by narcotic use and sales, the number of addicts estimated for the nation appears often to have been exaggerated. Peaks of overestimation have come before or at the time of the most repressive measures against narcotic use. As in 1919 when a million or more addicts and five million Parlor Reds were said to threaten the United States. Both groups were the object of severe penalties, although in retrospect both figures appear to have been enormously inflated. Still, the substantial number of addicts in the United States has presented one of the most endearingly difficult aspects of any proposed control program. The size of this population has made control of misuse in maintenance programs difficult. There has been a fair amount of diversion of drugs to the illicit market and some registration of non-addicts.

In America, control of narcotics could take only a limited number of legislative forms. The lack of broad federal police powers inhibited the restriction of drug transactions. The division of federal and state powers in effect permitted widespread and unscrupulous dissemination of untested products and unsafe drugs. When the danger of narcotics came to the attention of popular reform movements and after carefully phrased federal legislation was at last enacted in 1914, it took the Supreme Court five years to overcome the apparent obstacle of states' rights. In 1919 the court permitted the federal government almost prohibitory power for prevention of most addiction maintenance. The court's majority affirmed the reformers' belief that simple addiction maintenance was intolerable.

Nevertheless, after 1919, severe constitutional strictures continued to mold enforcement of the Harrison Act. Because all professionals (unless convicted of a violation) had to be treated equally under a revenue statute, the federal government could not discriminate against careless or unscrupulous physicians and druggists by refusing them a tax stamp or by employing some other fair form of flexible administrative punishment. This lack of legal accommodation to circumstances, the small number of agents, and a bureaucratic reward system which favored a large number of prosecutions led to harassment and intimidation as a prominent mode of regulation. Because government agents feared that precedents might prevent indictment of "dope doctors," exceptions to the no-maintenance rule were few. The mutual suspicion which grew up between agents and physicians inhibited reasonable enforcement of the law. The manner of closing the Shreveport clinic illustrates the combination of suspicion and inflexibility.

The federal narcotic authorities never forgot that theirs was a narrow path between federal and states' rights. As late as 1937 the Treasury Department chose to prohibit marihuana by a separate law because it feared an attack on the constitutionality of the Harrison Act. In spite of organized medicine's opposition in the 1920s and despite several close Supreme Court decisions, the extreme interpretation placed on the Harrison Act in 1919 continued to prevail. Why did the Supreme Court agree that a federal statute could outlaw narcotics, when the Constitution itself had to be amended to outlaw alcohol? One answer to this may be that in the case of narcotics the consensus was almost absolute; everyone appeared to agree on the evils of these drugs. For alcohol, there was no such agreement.

Foreign nations have played important roles in the American perception of its national drug problem. World War I is the watershed in national self-consciousness vis-à-vis foreign powers, dividing respectable opinion on the relative importance of domestic and international causes of narcotics used in the United States. In the prewar years the United States displayed confidence in traditional diplomatic methods and the efficacy of international treaties. Prior to the war and the immediate postwar security crisis, the usual explanation for the American drug appetite rested on characteristics of American culture - the pace of life, the effect of civilization, wealth which permitted indulgence, and inadequate state and federal laws which did not protect citizens from dangerous nostrums and incompetent health professionals.

After World War I, open official criticism of America's defects was no longer common. Whereas Hamilton Wright saw international control of narcotics as a solution to America's indigenous problem and recognized that this nation would benefit more than others from international altruism, Representative Porter in the 1920s denied any unusual appetite for narcotics in the United States, blaming our problem on the perfidy and greed of other nations. Richmond Hobson, equally as patriotic, claimed the country had an immense number of heroin addicts and consequent crime waves due to the evil influence of other nations. Hobson viewed America as surrounded by other dangerous continents - South America sent in cocaine; Europe contributed drugs like heroin and morphine; Asia was the source of crude opium and smoking opium; Africa produced hashish. Porter and Hobson sounded one theme: the American problem was caused by foreign nations. The spirit of national isolation which excluded participation in the League of Nations extended easily to international narcotic control. Americans were encouraged to condemn diplomacy as zealously as they had once sought conferences and commissions.

Projection of blame on foreign nations for domestic evils harmonized with the ascription of drug use to ethnic minorities. Both the external cause and the internal locus could be dismissed as un-American. This kind of analysis avoids the painful and awkward realization that the use of dangerous drugs may be an integral part of American society. Putting the blame on others also permits more punitive measures to be taken against certain of the culprits.

The history of American narcotic usage and control does not encourage belief in a simple solution to the long-standing problem. Reasonable regulation of drug use requires knowledge of physiological and psychological effects, an understanding of social causes of drug popularity, and an appreciation of how legal sanctions will actually effect the use and harmful results of drug ingestion. In the construction of such a policy, recognition of accidental and irrational factors in past drug legislation is essential, although no ideal program can be simply extrapolated from an historical study.

Political judgement and values have been paramount in the establishment of national drug policies. The commonsense conclusions reached by legislators, high-ranking government bureaucrats, and influential public figures, without any special or technical knowledge of drug abuse, are likely to gain acceptance from other national social and political institutions. Political judgements made in harmony with popular demands for narcotic control (or release from liquor control) have a proven longevity. Resisting instant popular demands is unusual among public officials; considerable political acumen is required to modify prevailing fear and anger into constructive programs.

As the pressure of political action reaches a climax, policy options are almost imperceptibly reduced to the few which have current political viability. The rapid crystallization of public policy in 1919-20 illustrates how quickly this last stage of policy formulation may pass. Dissidents like Rep. Volk and Dr. Bishop continued to protest, to little effect. Once the national mood had been settled, any attempt to reopen the painful question met strong resistance. The 1919 formulation defined a broad range of issues in narcotic control, and yet the battle was waged on curiously narrow lines. In the medical profession, for example, both those for and against the "disease" concept of addiction carried on their dispute over the question of whether antibodies or antitoxins were produced by morphine administration. The lack of such substances seemed to prove that addiction must be a mere habit, and that those who held out for the "disease" concept had unworthy motives. In that period of crisis over narcotic policies fifty years ago each side was unwilling to compromise and sought to sweep the adversary from the field.

Today an issue like methadone maintenance may form the model on which a consensus is reached. This might lead toward simple toleration, or to prohibition of natural and synthetic opiates for nonmedical purposes (which would include "mere addiction"). As new generations confront the narcotic question, the same old fundamental issues continue to arise. Current debates over heroin maintenance focus on such basic questions as the effect of heroin on the body and personality. One almost hears the voice of Dr. Bishop arguing that if an addict is in heroin balance he is a normal person as regards the effect of the drug, and Captain Hobson warning that heroin use gradually destroys the brain's higher centers. After more than half a century since the Harrison Act's passage one of the few statements about narcotics on which there is general agreement is that there is no treatment of hard-core addiction which leads to abstinence in more than a fraction of attempts. The lack of agreement on other crucial questions and their relative importance is almost total.

Although social and cultural influences are essential elements in the creation of the American drug problem, it is quite possible to provide a viable political response to public outcry and at the same time avoid an objective examination of critical issues: the nature of American society; the psychological vulnerability of addicts; the physiological effects of drugs; the social impact of drug use. Our society's blindness to alcohol's destructive effects is an example of how denial of reality is compatible with a politically comfortable resolution of a controversial drug problem.

We are now at a time when the credibility of previous solutions is sufficiently low so that some of the unresolved questions can be raised and again discussed. Gradually, and not necessarily as the result of formal decisions, the scientific and political alternatives regarding drug abuse may, as they have in the past, diminish. As a new workable political solution evolves the controversy tends to narrow to a few issues. Ideally, public pressure for elimination of the drug problem should not be met with fewer options. Rather the effective translation of knowledge, scientific and historical, should enable the public to avoid over-simplification, and to exert influence based on more rational understanding. But only the most determined efforts can prevent closure on drug policy by those two most powerful forces: fatigue and frustration.

9. The Drug Takers 1920-1970

Philip Bean

Having now reached the point where the broad history of control has been catalogued, the next stage is to interpret this within a sociological framework. The basic questions are, firstly, why did the system change and, secondly, what produced the impetus for change. These questions lead us to consider the types of persons who were classified as the drug takers. This issue will be the subject of this chapter. Later we can consider the role of the medical profession and then examine a number of secondary factors which were instrumental in the changes although they may not have been of primary importance.

First the type of people who were classified as the drug takers. For information about this group of people we must examine two major areas; Home Office figures and the crime statistics.

Most of the evidence about the drug takers in Britain comes from the Home Office figures. They have had an enormous influence on policy decisions; almost every Parliamentary debate on drug taking has used them to support or refute an argument, whilst a number of research workers have tried to show how they underestimate the 'true extent of drug taking'. Although they may be viewed as defective, they are still seen as "the best that is available" and still used as a sort of moral barometer.

There are a number of separate issues here. One issue centres around the arguments put forward by the labelling theorists who see deviant behaviour as simply behaviour that people so label. They would argue that until recently it would have been usual to discuss the extent of addiction in Britain by quoting and analysing the official reports - in this case the Home Office register of known addicts and the crime statistics. It would also have been usual to note that these figures ought to be treated with caution, as all such statistics contain many defects for research purposes. They are, after all, prepared by officials as book keeping records, and provide meagre information about characteristics of either the offenders or the offences which they describe. As far as the means of obtaining the information is concerned, it is well known that different kinds of behaviour in different kinds of social situations have different probabilities of becoming officially known to those agencies. However, in spite of these numerous defects, the reader was asked to 'make do' with these figures.

In the last few years the limitations of this approach have become increasingly recognised, although there is still some reluctance to abandon it entirely. As Austin Turk has remarked, "It is genuinely puzzling that scientists have been so persistent in trying to carry on research using second-hand and for their purposes virtually useless data collected by non-scientists for non-scientific purposes, and they have for so long, in Sellin's words 'permitted non-scientists to define the basic terms of their enquiry'."[1]

Philip Bean: *THE SOCIAL CONTROL OF DRUGS*, (Martin Robertson, 1974), pp. 95-129. © Philip Bean 1974. Reprinted with permission of Basil Blackwell Ltd.

Kitsuse and Cicourel have also criticized the use of official statistics, arguing that they are rates of deviant behaviour which are produced by the actions taken by persons in the social system, which define, classify and record certain behaviour as deviant. If a given form of behaviour is not interpreted as deviant by such persons it would not appear as a unit in whatever set of rates we might attempt to explain, e.g., in crimes known to the police or Court records, etc.[2]

Central to Kitsuse's and Cicourel's argument is the distinction they make between what they call the social conduct which produces a *unit* of behaviour, and the organizational activity which produces *a unit in the rate of behaviour*. The former they call the behaviour producing process, the latter the rate producing processes. So for example we may be concerned with issues about a person's drug taking (the behaviour producing process) but it would require a separate research problem to account for that person's drug taking being recorded on the Home Office figures. Or, as Turk says, "the individuals found in any category of official statistics have in other words been so classified after passing through a series of interactions with a number of people where eventually someone may affix a deviant label."

Lest anyone should doubt the value of the labelling theorists argument that the deviant is one to whom the label has been successfully applied, the following quote from the column of the British Medical Journal entitled 'Any Questions?' offers one of the clearest examples of the process in operation. One of the questions asked by a doctor to the 'Any Questions?' panel was, "What procedures, therapeutic or statutory should a G.P. follow when confronted with an addict?" The reply was that "G.P.s are seldom called upon to do more than persuade the patient to enter a suitable institution... If the patient proves completely uncooperative it may be necessary to invoke the aid of the law to apply compulsion... *Since most of the drugs concerned are included in the scope of the Dangerous Drugs Acts* 1920-1925, *it is often possible to prove an offence against these Acts for which the patient may be summoned before a Magistrate.*"![3] (Italics mine.) In other words, if the patient is co-operative the label will not be applied - if he is not, we will call him criminal.

However, whilst acknowledging a debt to the labelling theorists for drawing attention to this phenomena, the point for our purposes is to examine the *effect* official figures have had on the legal framework. By 'effect' I mean that we can accept the labelling theorists' arguments as such and notice how official figures have been classified and then show how these have been used for policy decisions.

Table II - *Number, sex and social class of addicts known to*
Home Office between 1934-1945

Year	No. of Known Addicts	Males	Females	'Professional' classes
1934	300	not known	not known	not known
1935	700	"	"	120
1936	613	313	300	147
1937	620	300	320	140
1938	519	246	273	143
1939	534	269	265	131
1940	505	251	254	90
1941	503	252	251	91
1942	524	275	249	98
1943	541	280	261	94
1944	559	285	274	93
1945	367	144	223	80

Source: Annual Reports to League of Nations for years 1934-1945

We can divide the period 1920-1970 roughly in two parts; from 1920-1945 and 1945-1970. First the period 1920-1945. Table II shows the number, sex and 'social class' of known addicts, and Table III shows the prosecutions of drug offences. There are no available figures for known addicts prior to 1934.

It will be seen from Table II that the period between 1934 and 1945 was one of steady decline in the number of known addicts. There was a slight rise in the latter half of the war followed by a decrease in 1945. It will also be seen that the male/female ratio is fairly even throughout with males being slightly more predominant. In 1945 the position changed, for no very clear reason, but whereas the numbers of males appear to fall by about 50%, there was a much smaller decrease in female addicts. The percentage of "professional classes" remained fairly steady throughout, from about 24% in 1936 to about 18% in 1940 and to about 22% in 1945. This group of "professional addicts" consists mainly of doctors, e.g., of the 143 professional addicts in 1938, 134 were medical practitioners, 5 were pharmacists, 2 were dentists and 2 veterinary surgeons.

The figures appear to justify the optimism of the Rolleston Committee as from 1935 the number of known addicts declined. The annual reports to the League of Nations in the 1930s always stated that "drug addiction is not prevalent in Great Britain" and from these figures it appears that this was so. No detailed records were kept of the drugs used during this period, but most appear to have been addicted to a single drug which in the majority of cases appears to have been morphine, e.g., in the Annual Reports for 1936, 72% were said to be addicted to morphine, 17% to heroin and 8.5% to cocaine.

Table III - *Prosecutions for offences against Dangerous Drugs Act, 1921-1945*

Year	Opium	Cannabis	Morphine	Heroin	Cocaine	Technical	Drug not known	Total
1921	184	-	6	nil	56	5	nil	251
1922	94	-	19	5	69	17	"	204
1923	167	-	44	5	68	11	"	295
1924	48	-	11	1	30	4	4	98
1925	35	-	7	2	16	8	nil	68
1926	50	-	23	2	12	7	1	95
1927	27	-	22	nil	1	10	nil	60
1928	41	-	8	"	7	6	"	62
1929	39	3	12	2	4	10	3	73
1930	16	1	21	1	3	19	4	65
1931	26	3	8	1	3	24	4	69
1932	37	6	12	1	13	12	5	86
1933	17	6	11	nil	4	11	6	55
1934	39	14	8	4	5	7	9	86
1935	13	15	10	1	4	11	7	61
1936	17	8	9	1	2	23	nil	60
1937	9	3	6	2	1	17	1	39
1938	6	18	11	4	2	14	4	59
1939	13	1	.....	not avail.	.....	25	not avail.	50
1940	14	3	.....	"	.....	29	"	54
1941	201	nil	.....	"	.....	10	"	226
1942	199	"	.....	"	.....	11	"	226
1943	147	2	.....	"	.....	13	"	189
1944	256	6	11	3	2	11	5	294
1945	206	4	7	2	1	6	4	230

Source: Annual Reports to League of Nations

The other main source of information, the record of prosecutions, is shown in Table III. Here, official figures are available from 1921-1945, except for prosecution for offences involving morphine, heroin and cocaine during 1939-1943. No reasons were given for this omission in the Annual Reports, but it may have been one further element of caution during the early war years. It should also be noted that the figures in this table relate to prosecutions rather than convictions.

The figures in Table III give a few more details about these offenders than there were for the known addicts shown in Table II. We know something about the ages and countries of origin of these offenders after 1926 when the Annual Reports were made public. Even so, the amount of information is still very limited. For example, no details are given about the areas of Britain in which the offenders for manufactured drugs occurred, or how many of those known addicts were ever prosecuted for drug offences. In other words, there is no way of linking the two tables.

It will be seen from Table III that the total number of prosecutions for all drugs fell considerably after the 1923 Act and it was not until the Second World War that they approached the pre-1920 figure. The increase in opium prosecutions during the war years has been attributed to an increase in the Chinese population in areas like Liverpool after shipping routes from the Far East had been diverted to United Kingdom ports. It had always been considered in Britain that opium offences were committed by persons of Chinese origin living in or near the large ports. An increase in prosecutions up to 1945 was therefore seen as a reflection of the increase in the Chinese population rather than an increase in the use of opium by the indigenous population. The Annual Reports for 1943 put the position clearly, if not a little complacently. "Opium smoking is essentially a habit of Eastern peoples and it is unlikely that a market can be found for the drug among Europeans in this country."

It will be seen also from Table III that prosecutions for cannabis up to 1945 were low, even during the war years. Offenders were almost always foreign coloured seamen, although there were very occasionally a few white British citizens too.

Prosecutions involving manufactured drugs also declined after 1923. Table III shows that prosecutions for cocaine in the early 1920s were easily the most numerous. By 1926, however, there were more prosecutions for morphine and this pattern continued throughout the period. There were always a very small number of prosecutions for heroine, which fits in well with what the Home Office thought was the pattern of use during that period.

In Table III "technical offences" refer to offences such as failing to keep a register and apply mainly to doctors and pharmacists. The number of these also decreased after the 1923 Act in spite of the small increase in Regulations following the 1925 and 1932 Acts. Only rarely were these offenders sent to prison, the most usually penalty being a fine of less than £10.

Because of the relatively small numbers of prosecutions per year, especially for the manufactured drugs, it is perhaps more fruitful and simpler to see the period as a whole, rather than become involved in detailed analysis with a very small number of offenders. As it is there was no information on these offenders for the period 1920 to 1925, and that which is available after 1926 is confined to age and sex with some additional facts about the offenders' occupations. Altogether there were some 3,155 persons prosecuted for drug offences between 1920 and 1945, and 2,139 during the period 1926-1945. If we concentrate on the latter group of 2,139, then in terms of sex distribution only 123, or 5.7% of these were women. About half of these were listed as nurses, doctors, dentists or chemists; the remainder were shown as being housekeepers or as having 'no occupation' which probably meant they were housewives. These women offenders were usually prosecuted for offences relating to manufactured drugs, such as morphine or heroin, but occasionally for cocaine. As far as the prosecutions for heroin and morphine were concerned, women accounted for nearly 50% of these during this period, and only rarely were they prosecuted for offences involving opium or cannabis. On the odd occasions where this occurred, they were almost always in the younger age group, i.e., 20-40, in contrast to those prosecuted for morphine and heroin offences where they were usually aged 40 or over.

Taking the figures for both sexes together, the mean age of all offenders appears to have been about 40, e.g., only 11 of the 1,139 were under the age of 20 and only 299 were under 30. The age distribution appears to have remained steady throughout, and even during the war years there was no tendency for offenders to be younger.

The data on the occupations of these offenders does not appear to have been collected in any systematic way, and it is not possible to think in terms of classifying by social class. The largest listed occupation group were 'seamen', but these included ships' officers as well as deck hands. This group was by far the largest, accounting for 1,300 or 65% of all offenders, or 75% of all male offenders. The next largest listed groups were chemists, 203 or 9% and doctors 143 or 6% - who were mainly prosecuted for 'technical offences - but there was a group of 371 persons who were listed as being in 'other occupations'.

The pattern of sentencing remains fairly similar throughout this period, the majority of drug offenders being fined. If a sentence of imprisonment was passed it was unusual for it to be more than 6 months. Even during the war years when there was an exceptionally large increase in the number of opium offenders, there were no demands for more severe penalties as was the case in 1916 or in the 1960s. Most were fined £10 or less, and in many cases £5 or less, e.g., in 1942, out of 226 offenders for that year 171 or 75% were fined £5 or less. Table IV gives a more detailed breakdown of prosecutions and convictions for 1 selected year, in this case 1936, and it can be seen from this table that 45% were fined, most of these for amounts of £10 or less, and 10 were sentenced to imprisonment, but 5 of these for less than 6 months. In this year there were 57 males and 3 females prosecuted, and 9 offenders were under 30. Their occupations were listed as Seamen 24, Medical and allied professions 30, and Others 6. The year 1936 has no special significance and was chosen only because it is the mid-point of the paired 1926-1945.

Table V gives the number, sex and origins of known addicts from 1946-1970.

Table V shows that the total number of known addicts declined from 1946 to 1953. From 1953 there was a steady increase until 1961, but then it became much more rapid until 1968 which showed the largest annual increase of all. 1970 shows a change; here the curve is beginning to level off. In fact, by 1970 there had been a decrease for the first time since 1960. The period after 1953 coincided with the increase in other types of drug taking and provided the first concrete argument for those who saw the beginnings of a changing picture. The tables also show that there were other important changes in the type of person who became a known addict, all of which fitted in with the events of the early 1950s.

Table IV - *Prosecutions and sentences for offences under the Dangerous Drugs Acts for 1936*

OFFENCE	Fined £5 or less	Fined £10 or less	Fined £11 or more	Total fined	Prob-ation	Prison 6 ms. or lesss	Prison 6 ms. or more	With-drawn	Total
Possess raw or prepared opium	2	2	-	4		2	1		7
Possess utensils for opium smoking	1	-	-	1					1
Permit or frequent premises for opium smoking	8	1	-	9					9
Possess or procure morphine	2	-	2	4	1	2	2		9
Possess heroin								1	1
Possess or procure cocaine	1			1			1		2
Possess cannabis	5	1		6		1	1		8
Fail to enter supplies in a register	4	5	5	14					14
Fail to keep drugs in a locked receptacle	2	3	1	6	2			1	9
Total	25	12	8	45	3	5	5	2	60

Source: Annual Reports to The League of Nations 1936

a) Sex. Table V shows that from 1946 to 1964 females outnumbered males, apart from the 4 years 1949-1953. After 1963 the number of male addicts increased at a much faster rate, and by 1969 were 4 times greater. For the period 1961-1970 male addicts increased by about 10 times, whereas female addicts had only doubled. After 1969 when the curve begins to level off, the number of male addicts has still continued to increase, but there has been a fall in female addicts.

b) Medical origins. Table V shows the medical origins of addicts divided into therapeutic and non-therapeutic groups. Details were not available before 1958, but in that year over 80% of all known addicts were classified as "therapeutic" in origin. This therapeutic group has remained steady throughout, and if anything has tended to decrease. The increase in known addicts therefore was entirely accounted for by the non-therapeutic group which increased from 68 in 1958 to 2533 by 1969.

Table V - *Number, sex and origins of known addicts 1946-1970*

Year	Male	Female	Therapeutic	Non-Therapeutic	Not Known	Total
1946	144	225	-	not available	-	369
1947	164	219	-	"	-	383
1948	198	197	-	"	-	395
1949	164	162	-	"	-	326
1950	158	148	-	"	-	306
1951	153	148	-	"	-	301
1952	153	144	-	"	-	297
1953	149	141	-	"	-	290
1954	148	169	-	"	-	317
1955	159	176	-	"	-	335
1956	160	170	-	"	-	330
1957	174	185	-	"	-	359
1958	197	245	349	68	25	442
1959	196	258	344	98	12	454
1960	195	242	309	122	6	437
1961	223	247	293	153	18	470
1962	262	270	312	212	8	532
1963	339	296	355	270	10	635
1964	409	344	368	378	13	753
1965	558	369	344	580	3	927
1966	886	463	351	982	16	1349
1967	1262	467	313	1385	31	1729
1968	2161	621	306	2420	56	2782
1969	2295	586	289	2533	59	2881
1970	2071	590	295	2321	45	2661

Source: Annual Reports

c) Age. Table VI gives the ages of the known addicts after 1959. In 1957 and 1958 the annual reports state that although "detailed information about age grouping is not available, the majority of addicts are over 30 years of age". The reason for not recording this information was said to be due to the small number of known addicts in the United Kingdom at that time. Table VII gives a breakdown of the ages of addicts in the 14-20 age group.

Table VI - *Ages of Known Addicts*

	1959	1960	1961	1962	1963	1964	1965	1966	1967	1968	1969	1970
Under 20	-	1	2	3	17	40	145	329	395	764	637	405
20-34	50	62	94	126	184	257	347	558	906	1530	1789	1813
35-49	92	91	95	107	47	138	134	162	142	146	174	158
50 & over	278	267	272	274	53	311	291	286	279	260	241	253
Age not known	34	16	7	22	185	7	10	14	7	82	40	32
Total	454	437	470	532	635	753	927	1349	1729	2782	2881	2661

Source: Annual Reports to the United Nations 1961-1970

Table VII - *Ages of Addicts in 14-20 Age Group*

Age	14	15	16	17	18	19	Total
1961					1	1	2
1962			1			2	3
1963			2	2	2	11	17
1964	1		1	8	11	19	40
1965		8	5	19	42	71	145
1966	1	17	26	68	111	106	329
1967		3	38	82	100	172	395
1968		10	40	141	274	299	764
1969			24	83	218	312	637
1970		1	9	49	117	229	405

Source: Annual Reports to the United Nations 1961-1970

Table VI shows that in 1959 there were no known addicts under 20, the majority being in the age group 50 and over, but there were 50, or 11.1% in the 20-34 age group. By 1960 one addict was under 20 and those in the 20-34 age group had increased to 62, from 11.1% to 14.4%. Unfortunately it is not possible to break down the age grouping further as the Home Office did not keep detailed figures until 1967. Table VI shows that the age group below 35 almost entirely accounted for the increase in known addicts; in 1961 there were only 96 or 20% under the age of 35; by 1969 there were 2426 or 84%. There was also a small increase for those aged 35-49 during this period, but a decrease for those over 50. Table VII shows a steady increase in the number of addicts under 20 from 1960-1968. However, after 1968 there appears to be a fall, and for the first time since 1963 the 1969 and 1970 figures give no new young addicts aged 14 or 15. This table would be used to support that note of "cautious optimism" sounded by the Home Office in the 1969 report as it suggests that as there are no new young addicts being recruited, those already in the under 20 group will eventually work their way out through this age group.

Table VIII - *Drugs used by known addicts in the years 1946-1970*

Year	Morphine	Heroin	Cocaine	Pethidine	Methadone
1946	Exact figs not	Exact figs not	Exact figs not	Exact figs not	Exact figs not
1947	available but	available, but	available, but	available, but	available, but
1948	% in 1935 was	in 1952 it was	1952 it was	after 1948 it	it was thought
1949	thought to be	thought 19%	thought less	was thought %	that only 2
1950	90%. By '52 it	approx. were	than 10%	varied between	persons in '49
1951	had fallen to	using heroin	using cocaine	12%-19%	and 3 in '51
1952	64% approx.				were using
1953					methadone
1954		57			
1955	179	54	6	64	21
1956	176	53	6	64	20
1957	178	66	16	92	31
1958	205	62	25	117	47
1959	204	68	30	116	60
1960	177	94	52	98	68
1961	168	132	84	105	59
1962	157	175	112	112	54
1963	172	237	171	107	55
1964	162	342	211	128	61
1965	160	521	311	102	72
1966	178	899	443	131	156
1967	158	1299	462	112	243
1968	198	2240	564	120	486
1969	345	1417	311	128	1687
1970	346	914	198	122	1820

Source: Annual Reports to United Nations 1946-1970

d) Drugs used. Finally, Table VIII shows the drugs used during this period.

Where a person has used more than one drug he has been listed under both headings. The annual totals for drugs used during each year will not therefore correspond to the numbers of known addicts. Table VIII shows that morphine was the drug most widely used up to 1957 and was by then used more often than all the others together. However, the number using heroin gradually increased after 1956 and a large increase occurred in 1960. There was a similarly large increase in those using cocaine, but this was almost entirely accounted for by the increase in heroin addicts who were also using cocaine, i.e., in 1959 18 addicts were using heroin with cocaine; in 1960 this number had increased to 44. Also in 1960 there was a corresponding decrease in those using the more 'traditional' drugs such as morphine and pethidine. The same pattern continued during the 1960s and by 1962 heroin had become the drug most widely used. However, in 1969 methadone (physeptone) become the drug most widely used and this almost certainly reflects the policy of the treatment centres of prescribing physeptone rather than heroin.

e) General. These tables show how the recorded increase in drug taking was accounted for during the 1960s by the non-therapeutic young male heroin addict group. They also show that the years 1965 to 1967 were crucial in the sense that this was the period when the percentage increase in known addicts was greatest, and it was then that a certain amount of government initiative was thought to have been lost by failing to implement quickly the recommendations of the second Brain Committee Report. Table IX shows the increase in the number of known addicts after 1956, but these are of course net increases, and stated this way mask the gross figure whilst still showing an increase. Table IX gives additional details showing how this gross increase was offset by similar increases in the large number of older addicts, mostly therapeutic in origin, who were classified in the Annual Reports as being "dropped from the Register" as a result of death or being cured. The last 2 columns list the new heroin addicts in terms of their origins. The total for column 5 is arrived at by deducting column from column 1.

Table IX - *Increase and decrease of addicts from 1956-1960*

Year	New Addicts Added to Index	New Addicts	Recidivists	No. dropped from Index	Net Increase	Therapeutic Heroin	Non-therapeutic Heroin
1956	42	39	3	37	5	17	36
1957	90	24	5	61	29	21	45
1958	104	99	5	21	83	19	43
1959	130	117	13	118	12	21	47
1960	98	88	10	115	17	22	72

Source: Annual Reports to United Nations

It can be seen from Table IX that the figures show an important increase in non-therapeutic heroin addicts after 1956 offset by an unprecedented number of addicts dropped from the Register in 1959/60. In the light of this table it is perhaps not surprising that the first Brain Committee's Report in 1960 was treated with such scepticism.

If we now examine the Criminal Statistics for drug offences (Table X), the first point to note is that like the Home Office figures these too offer a limited source of information. In the first place there are no figures for convictions for drugs such as morphine and pethidine, nor for the technical offences, after 1964. Secondly the figures for the years 1945-1954 are for prosecutions, but from 1955-1970 they are listed as convictions. In the analysis that follows I have grouped morphine, heroin, cocaine and pethidine and called them manufactured drugs, but opium, cannabis and the technical offences have been examined separately. The category listed as "not known" also includes those cases where a person is charged with possessing more than one drug. It is not clear why the annual reports included these in this category, nor why having once included them no further details were given.

Table X - *Prosecutions / Convictions for all drugs 1946-1970 under Dangerous Drugs Acts*

Year	Opium	Cannabis	Morphine	Heroin	Cocaine	Pethidine	Technical	Not Known	Total
1946	65	11	15	3	nil	-	7	2	103
1947	76	46	28	5	1	10	10	11	187
1948	78	51	16	1	4	4	9	14	177
1949	52	60	17	2	3	3	16	15	168
1950	41	86	7	1	2	9	14	9	169
1951	64	132	12	1	nil	8	9	17	243
1952	62	98	18	3	1	7	12	7	208
1953	47	88	12	1	1	6	11	13	179
1954	28	144	6	6	3	15	9	8	219
1955	17	115	8	6	1	11	5	6	169
1956	12	103	5	7	1	8	8	8	152
1957	9	51	6	2	3	7	10	2	90
1958	8	99	4	5	nil	18	10	4	148
1959	18	185	4	4	2	6	5	5	229
1960	15	235	3	7	nil	6	3	9	278
1961	15	288	8	20	4	15	2	13	365
1962	16	588	6	25	2	18	3	13	671
1963	20	663	6	30	5	16	2	4	746
1964	14	544	17	38	3	15	7	21	659 [4]
1965	13	626	-	-	-	-	-	-	767
1966	36	1119	-	-	-	-	-	-	1397 [5]
1967	58	2393	-	274	86	-	-	-	3024
1968	73	3071	-	539	111	-	-	-	4243
1969	53	4683	-	341	140	-	-	-	6095
1970	66	7520	-	281	162	-	-	-	8800

Source: Annual Reports to the United Nations 1946-1970

a) *Opium* It will be seen that the number of opium offences show a steady fall throughout this period, especially when compared with the figures for the war years. In 1960 the annual report noted that "the use of this drug is confined mainly to persons of Chinese origin." 9 of those 15 convicted were Chinese, but 5 came from Pakistan and India, and 1 from Egypt. In 1966 there had been a further increase which was thought to reflect the poly-use amongst British drug takers rather than an increase amongst the Asiatic population.

b) *Cannabis*. In direct contrast, prosecutions/convictions for cannabis up to 1951 show an irregular but important rise. Thereafter the unevenness almost certainly reflects police activity, but the trend seems to be clear, especially after 1957. In 1950 it was believed that cannabis use was increasing, but some overall account must be taken of police activity as with other drugs, because in the last few years special drug squads have been formed due to public and Parliamentary pressure.6 After 1965, however, the number of cannabis offenders increased at a rapid rate, the largest annual increase occurring in 1967 with over 100%, although the 1969 figures still showed an increase of 52%. Most of these convictions were for unlawful possession of cannabis; 4094 in 1969 or 85.2%, and 2663 in 1968 or 85.5%. The remainder were mainly for permitting premises to be used for smoking cannabis, for unlawful import and unlawful supply.7

A more detailed and comprehensive survey of cannabis offenders appears in a report by the Advisory Committee on Drug Dependence (the Wootton Report).[8] In their analysis, the Committee found that 2419 out of 2731 charged with possessing cannabis had less than 30 grams in their possession, and of these 2419 offenders, 373 or 15% were sentenced to imprisonment.9 There were 1857 persons without previous convictions for any type of offence who were convicted of possessing less than 30 grammes, but 237 or 13% were sent to prison. The Committee noted that as far as sentencing was concerned there was a notable tendency to place greater emphasis on fines and imprisonment for possession of cannabis than for other dangerous drugs, but less on probation and discharge. As far as the ages of those charged with possession were concerned, 1791 or 66% were under 25, and of those over half (990) were under the age of 20. The Report also showed the pattern of the increase in white offenders to have continued during the early 1960s, and by 1964 for the first time white persons outnumbered coloured. Three years later there were almost 3 times as many white offenders as coloured, i.e., 1,737 white and 656 coloured.

c) *Manufactured drugs*. Convictions for manufactured drugs (i.e., morphine, heroin, cocaine and pethidine) up to 1960 show a less clear picture, but the numbers are still very small. As far as is known those convicted for heroin offences were then mainly known addicts who tried to get extra drugs by false prescriptions or extra supplies from more than one doctor. From 1950 to 1955, 18 persons were convicted of 24 offences and of these 18, 15 were known heroin addicts. It was not thought that there was a substantial hidden addict population.[10] Similar details are not available for 1955-1960, but the annual reports state that offenders were still thought to be 'known addicts'. Some cases of illicit trafficking occurred, but these mainly involved drugs which were stolen in Britain as a result of breaking into chemist shops. The reports for the period note that "there was no evidence to suggest that manufactured drugs were illicitly imported into, or illicitly produced in the United Kingdom."[11] In this sense there was no evidence of organised crime on the American pattern.[12]

After 1960, convictions for heroin and cocaine steadily increased although as has already been pointed out the convictions for heroin fell in 1969 for the first time for over 10 years. This decrease was thought to be related to the policy of the treatment centres not to prescribe heroin, but it should be noted that there has been a corresponding increase in convictions for other drugs, particularly physeptone. The implication here is that convictions are related to domestic supplies, rather than to illicit imports. The Annual Report for 1969 states that "manufactured drugs seized by the police during 1969 were almost entirely of licit manufactured origin", but in July 1969 the Home Secretary reported that "the police have reported 36 persons arrested for possessing heroin not licitly manufactured in this country as well as two seizures of heroin from Hong Kong seamen." These were the first important seizures of illicit heroin ever reported and almost certainly reflect the treatment centres policy of substituting physeptone for heroin. Convictions for other manufactured drugs such as morphine and pethidine have remained low and no other details are available.

d) *Technical offences*. The number of 'technical' offences almost always involved cases of failing to keep drugs in a locked receptacle, or maintaining appropriate records. As far as can be seen, all these convictions resulted in a fine. Those convicted were always said to be "British subjects of European origin", i.e., white instead of coloured. The number of technical offences, like all other convictions, may also reflect police activity. Doctors' and pharmacists' records have been regularly inspected for 4 decades, but it is still not known what happens if an offence is discovered. Do the police employ a cautioning procedure, or is every offender immediately prosecuted? Neither is it known how strictly or regularly pharmacists' records have been inspected or how efficient the police have been in detecting offences. In 1920 when they first inspected records, there were less than 10 drugs controlled under the Act; in 1960 there were 65 and by 1970 over 100. Given the police orientation to 'crime', or as Dr Chapman suggests, dealing mainly with working class property offenders, it is reasonable to suppose that inspecting these records would be likely to be unpopular with some police authorities.[13] It might also be difficult for them to deal with persons of higher social class, who would be talking about a 'professional' and technical matter. In Canada, officers of the Central Government inspect pharmacists' records as well as manufacturers' and wholesalers', who are required at fairly frequent intervals to submit details of all transactions involving dangerous drugs. This system at least avoids some of the problems which the police seem to experience in Britain.

e) *Convictions for offences under the 1964 Drugs (Prevention of Misuse) Act*. One further group of offences not listed in the Annual Report is that involving offences under the 1964 (Prevention of Misuse) Act. Details are given in Table XI.

Table XI - *Convictions under Drugs (Prevention of Misuse) Act, 1964*

Year	Number of Convictions	
1965	958	* This figure is in respect of the
1966	1216	period 31.10.64 to 31.12.65
1967	2486	
1968	2957	
1969	3762	
1970	3885	

Source: Home Office Reports 1969 and 1970

The Report of the Advisory Committee on Amphetamines and LSD notes in paragraph 24 that the figures show "convincing evidence of the persistence of the nuisance which the Act was designed to combat." There are few details of these offenders, but it appears that 38% of the arrests in 1967 were made in the London area. The figures for 1968 show that convictions for amphetamine offenders were heavily concentrated in the younger age group with 78% being aged 25 or under. As the Advisory Committee points out, these figures do not necessarily reflect the pattern of amphetamine dependence amongst the general population, as it is the youthful drug taker who is likely to rely on illicit supplies and is likely to appear before the Courts, while his middle-aged counterpart has a better chance of obtaining supplies on medical prescription. It was noted, for example, that in a study of 498 hospital admissions for persons using amphetamines, 50% were under 25, compared with 78% under 25 who were convicted. Similarly, in 1968 there were 72 convictions for possessing LSD, 52 of which were for people in the under 25 age group.

f) *General.* Although it may be accepted that drug takers in Britain tend to be 'poly-users', it is not known how many of those convicted for drug offences have other convictions for different drugs. The annual reports and the figures for convictions under the 1964 Act do not relate these to persons, yet of the 72 convicted for LSD, 9, or 12% had convictions for previous drug offences, not necessarily for LSD. It is not known how many of the known addicts have drug convictions, either for their drug of addiction or for different drugs, but it is important to ask if some drug users are more prone to conviction for drug offences than others. Perhaps homeless drug users are more likely to be convicted than those living with their parents, not because they give away or even sell more of their prescribed drugs, but because their offences have high visibility. The main features of those tables are firstly, that the drug takers who had been labelled 'addicts' or 'criminals' are predominantly those coming from the younger age group, and secondly the vast increases in the numbers involved, the changes in the sex distribution, and the types of drugs used.

These then are some of the features of the known addicts and the drug takers who were labelled criminal deviants. We are not concerned here to establish how the labelling process operated but to point to this group as being the one about whom legal decisions were made, which in this sense is to make a fine distinction between the sociology of deviancy and the sociology of law. The Home Office figures and the Criminal Statistics produced the background to the legal norms although of course the way they were collected, and presented too for that matter, has had some influence. In the remainder of this chapter I want to link the Official Statistics with the legal process and compare the drug takers in the pre-war period with those of the post-war era.

The data presented on the drug takers during the 1930s shows that they were mainly middle aged, predominantly from the professional classes and were usually addicted to morphine. They were evenly distributed in terms of sex and were incidentally thought to be secretive in their habit and widely scattered throughout the country. They were relatively infrequently convicted for drug offences; the drug offenders themselves were predominantly Chinese seamen who smoked opium.

Compare this group with the post-war era. Up to 1960 the pattern remained as before but thereafter the majority were heroin addicts, or young amphetamine, LSD and cannabis users who tended to be convicted for drug offences and to congregate in certain selected areas - particularly Piccadilly Circus and Notting Hill. They were much younger and predominantly male. They did not come from the professional classes. In short they were in every way the antithesis of their pre-war counterparts. These factors in themselves were important enough to suggest a change in the pattern, but when these are added to the inferences that were drawn about the pre-war drug takers the link between the official statistics and the legal norms can be drawn.

My argument then is that changes in the system of control occurred as a result of the new type of known drug taker. Inevitably such an argument will be attacked on the grounds that the composition of the drug taking population was less important than the quantity of drug takers in the 1960s. Whilst sympathising with this point of view it is important to note that demands for controls occurred long before the numbers of known addicts reached the 1930s figure, and it was not until 1964 that they had overtaken the figures for 1937. With 500-600 known addicts in the 1930s, drug taking, according to the official reports, was not a problem in Great Britain.

As far back as 1950 some authorities believed that a new type of drug taker was beginning to emerge. The annual reports for that year noted that "the traffic in hemp is of much greater importance in the United Kingdom than the traffic in opium." It was thought that an increase in the number of prosecutions in 1950 was in part "a reflection of increased realisation by the police of the problems involved", but it was also believed that the traffic had spread for the first time away from the dockland areas to other parts of the country where there was a large coloured population. In 1950 there was also evidence that cannabis was being smoked by the white population in the West End of London. The first piece of information was given when a ship's steward was arrested in Southampton for possessing cannabis and said that he usually smoked it in a particular West End club. This club was subsequently raided by the police; 10 men were charged with possessing cannabis and cocaine, and a further 23 packets containing cannabis were found on the floor. All but one of those charged were between 22 and 29 years of age and, contrary to the normal experience, only one was coloured. H. B. Spear reports that the first teenage offender to come to the notice of the Home Office was arrested in 1962 for possessing cannabis. He was then 18 and said he had been smoking it since he was 16½. Over the next 8 years there was a steady increase in convictions amongst the white population. Nevertheless, by 1960 the annual report still said that most of the offenders were of African or West Indian origin.

There was some pressure to bring to the public's attention this "rapidly developing craze by the young people for doped cigarettes." In the House of Commons in 1951 the Secretary of State for the Home Department was asked if he was aware of "the public concern at the increased practice in trafficking in drugged cigarettes." A book published in 1952 entitled "Indian Hemp - A Social Menace"[14] was aimed at arousing public interest in what one reviewer in the British Medical Journal called "the possibility of an increase in the dope peddling of Indian Hemp in this country." In spite of this agitation, only a few people regarded the warnings as serious.

Many of these fears were confirmed by an earlier incident in 1949 when approximately 1,200 grains of morphine and 14 ounces of cocaine were stolen from a wholesale chemist in the Midlands.[15] Most of these drugs were subsequently sold to known addicts in the West End who were already receiving legitimate supplies. Important though this case may be, there did not appear to be any attempt by those known addicts to resell any of the drugs, nor did the person who stole them appear to sell to anyone who was not already addicted. Spear reports that "a careful examination of the background of those morphine addicts who did appear in 1950 and 1951 failed to reveal any connection with him."[16] Much more important was the second case of trafficking which occurred in 1951 when approximately 2,400 grains of morphine, 500 grains of heroin and 2 ounces of cocaine were stolen from a hospital dispensary near London. Although the full extent of this offender's activities will probably never be known, the police were able to name 14 persons who were believed to have obtained drugs from him. In contrast to the earlier case, only 2 of these had previously been recorded as known heroin addicts, although some were known to have used cannabis and cocaine. This appeared to be the first example of large scale trafficking which involved selling drugs to non-addicts; prior to this the addict population was thought to have been content to retain their drugs within their own drug taking group. It is also of interest to note that the police recovered all the stolen morphine but very little of the heroin and cocaine, suggesting that the latter drugs were now becoming more popular than morphine.

Another important change was the increase in the use of amphetamines. Evidence of widespread illicit use began to reach the Home Office by 1962, but some authorities believe that the increase occurred in the early 1950s. In fact some signs appeared as far back as 1939 when benzedrine was placed on Part I of the Poisons List under the 1933 Pharmacy and Poisons Act, due to an increase in demand. In 1954 as a result of a further increase, all amphetamines and their salts were placed on Schedule 4 of the Poisons List which meant they could then only be sold by retail chemists on a doctor's prescription. This increase in use was thought to be part of a world wide pattern, as in 1956 the W.H.O. Expert Committee on Drugs Liable to Produce Addiction reported that the abuse of amphetamines had already begun to constitute a hazard to public health in some areas.[17] Finally, in the second half of the 1950s, there was also the increase in known addicts which occurred at about the time the first Brain Committee reported but which the Brain Committee decided to ignore.

It could of course also be argued that the method of collecting the figures underestimated the extent of addiction in Britain in the 1960s. If this is so, and many research workers have attempted to give incidence and prevalence, then the same position applied in the 1930s too. In fact the method of recording in the 1930s was probably worse than for the 1960s, and where attempts were made to provide data on the extent of addiction they were made in a half hearted way. The first official estimate was in 1931 when it was reported in a discussion on drug addiction that "the Home Office know the names of 250 addicts and the number was probably not much greater." In 1934 it was thought to be about 300, but an estimate in 1935 put the number at 700.

One explanation for the lack of figures in the 1930s is that Britain was not required to provide annual statistics on the number of opiate and cocaine addicts to the League of Nations until 1937 although the Advisory Committee began to show an interest in annual returns as far back as 1930. However, after 1937 annual returns were made to the League although it is extremely doubtful if the figures have very much value, largely due to the manner in which they were collected or recorded. In 1934 a card index system was started which had a small amount of information recorded either as a result of regional medical reports following the inspection of doctors' records, or as a result of the Home Office Drugs Branch's own inspections. From 1934 it was the practice to record the names of addicts for the annual returns as long as some new information about their drug taking was available within the last 10 years. After 1944 this policy was changed and names were removed if nothing new was heard for a period of 1 year from the time they were said to be cured. The result was a large fall in the number of recorded addicts from 599 in 1944 to 367 in 1945, but there are grounds for believing that this policy was still not strictly adhered to as it was discovered that some addicts were still being recorded although nothing had been heard of them for at least 5 years. It is therefore extremely doubtful if the new index was very much more accurate than its predecessor, and it was not until 1957 that clearly defined procedures were introduced and carried out.

Apart from the Home Office itself, other officials such as the police did not appear to concern themselves with helping to produce a more accurate record system. The police had a duty to inspect retail chemists' records, but no general request was made until 1939 for them to notify the Home Office. Then a manual entitled "Notes for the guidance of police officers" asked them "to keep the Home Office informed of all persons who are having regular supplies of dangerous drugs."[18] The reason given was that "this information is of vital importance to the full control of the use of drugs in the United Kingdom." Guidance was also given as to the types of supplies which were to be reported. Even so instances still occasionally came to the notice of the Home Office in which supplies had been made regularly for several years without being reported. In the 1950s another manual was produced giving sterner and more concise instructions.

How then did the Home Office get its information at all? Mainly, it seems by drug takers reporting themselves, but their reasons for doing so remain obscure. No apparent benefits were available after they had told the Home Office as they could receive their supplies whether the Home Office knew or not. More important however, is the point that the addicts did report themselves, as this shows a trust and an affinity with government agencies which suggests a form of consensus about the addicts' position and the social control agents.

After 1945 the Home Office still had to rely on information given to them by the police as a result of inspection of records or by their other contacts with drug takers. Occasionally information was given by other agencies such as the Probation Service, but this depended on the decisions of individual Probation Officers. After 1945 and right up to 1970 some drug takers continued to report themselves, sometimes in the mistaken belief that if the Home Office knew they were receiving drugs from a doctor they were 'registered' and could not be prosecuted for having these drugs in their possession. No such registration procedure ever existed; if drugs were being received from a doctor there could be no prosecution anyway. It was not until 1968 that new regulations became operative, so that until then the method of compiling the Home Office figures was still fairly haphazard.

After 1967, when the Act introduced compulsory notification, "any medical practitioner who attends a person whom he considers, or reasonably suspects to be addicted to any drug specified in the Schedule to the Dangerous Drugs Act 1951 [is required] to furnish particulars of that person to the Chief Medical Officer, Home Office." This regulation at least provided a standard format for notification, but whether it was faithfully adhered to is another matter. Notification is still dependent on the user coming into contact with a notifying authority and that authority defining the user as a suitable case for notification.

It is interesting to compare these requirements with the Rolleston Committee's views on notification, as they had rejected it on the grounds that it was 'unnecessary'. It seems to be one of the features of giving official recognition to a new social problem that the agents of social control invariably require 'more information'. Whether this is for the sake of future decision making or a device for avoiding present decision making is as yet unclear, but it seems to be a factor which social theorists might well consider.

It is also important to note that the *numbers* of drug takers have never been the sole criteria for control. Apart from alcohol and tobacco, barbiturates are, after all, still the most widely used drugs - but the 1970 Act did not include those in spite of their addictive propensities being well known. As far back as 1950 there was evidence that barbiturates produce very serious physiological effects. "The abstinence syndrome is characteristic and dangerous ...[compared with morphine] ... barbiturate addiction is a more serious public health and medical problem because it produces greater mental, emotional and neurological impairment and because withdrawal entails real hazards". In 1968 there were 15-17 million prescriptions for barbiturates with an average of 80 tablets per prescription - or 4 times the fatal dose. The total number of barbiturates prescribed per year then is 1,360 million tablets. The number of amphetamines used by young people was never thought to be anywhere near this figure, nor were the amounts of opiates, yet amphetamines were strictly controlled in the 1960s.

The agitations for change in 1959 were not then based solely on a view that addiction was increasing but that alterations were taking place in the patterns of drug taking. Those agitating for change did so in ways similar to that of all moral entrepreneurs; they wanted 'action' and something done about a new social problem. By the mid-1960s when the numbers of known addicts had gone far beyond the totals for the 1930s there were justifications for change but, even so, changes still occurred amongst a highly selected group, i.e., the young drug takers rather than the older barbiturate addict.

It is not my intention here to involve a generation gap type argument, although such an argument would not be without its merits. Rather I am concerned to link the change in legislation and the change in the composition of drug takers with Joseph Gusfiel's notion of moral passage.[19] Gusfield's argument is similar to the point made by David Downes and Paul Rock when they state that "where hostility to the very basis of social norm is imputed to the deviant, societal reaction of a much more punitive kind is seen to be justified. Conversely contriteness on the part of the offender and co-operation with the police and welfare agencies can promote re-categorization of the deviant into a more acceptable role."[20]

Gusfield's analysis of deviant behaviour in terms of the reaction of the designators to different norm sustaining implications of an act is particularly pertinent here. He classifies behaviour into 4 types based on the symbolic character of the norm itself.

The first type is the repentant deviant. Deviation for this type is seen as a moral lapse, a fall from grace to which the deviants aspire. The repentant deviant admits the legitimacy of the norms and by so doing produces a consensus between the designator and the deviant. In other words this repentance confirms the norms.

The second type is the cynical deviant. His basic orientation is self seeking but he does not threaten the legitimacy of the normative order. His behaviour calls more for social management and repression.

The third type is the sick deviant. He neither attacks nor defends the norms as his behaviour is neutralized by being seen as uncontrolled and therefore irrelevant.

Finally there is the enemy deviant. He accepts his own behaviour as proper and derogates the public norms as being illegitimate. He refuses to internalize the public norm into his self definitions.[21]

It is the fourth type, the "enemy" deviant who particularly concerns us here, although the "sick" deviant is not without interest for our purposes. The importance of the enemy deviant is that his refusal to accept the public norms as legitimate means that when the public norms are attacked the designators need to strengthen and reinforce them. They can do this by a variety of methods, one of which is to strengthen them by legal changes, reinforced by moral sanctions.

We can illustrate Gusfield's argument by pointing to the shift in designation of the drug takers from being repentant deviants in the 1930s to being the enemy deviants of the 1960s.

To some extent the Chinese seamen convicted for opium were nearer to the cynical deviant in the sense that their behaviour was self-seeking without threatening the legitimacy of the normative order. Their behaviour was not seen as being a product of British society anyway since they had acquired the habit elsewhere. They were often transients, and according to the official reports had no interest in converting the indigenous population to drug taking. In other words they simply wanted to be left alone. To describe them as 'cynical' is perhaps inaccurate, they really constitute a fifth type of deviant, the cultural isolates, so that their behaviour was condemned but also excused on cultural grounds. Had they proselytised drug taking amongst the indigenous population, as did the West Indians with cannabis in the West End clubs, then they could easily have been transformed into enemy deviants.

The 'real' drug takers of the pre-war period, the middle-aged housewives and the group from medical and allied professions, were no threat to the value system either- though for different reasons. As members of the medical and allied professions they obviously wanted to keep their habit secret and be allowed to continue with their work. Interpretations and explanations of their addiction are an important indication of societal reaction - a point we shall return to later when we examine classificatory systems - the point here is that this group of addicts were seen as having become addicted through contact with drugs rather than contact with drug users and drug values, particularly subterranean values which were imputed to the post-war group. The housewives were seen as 'therapeutic' addicts, but both groups had their behaviour interpreted as typical of repentant deviants who were good citizens in all other respects but had unfortunately become addicted. They were pitied rather than condemned, and like all repentant deviants were seen as having fallen from grace, or having had a series of moral lapses.

This group fitted in well with Rolleston's definition of addiction and the Committee's interpretation of addictive behaviour. Rolleston saw addiction as occurring amongst people who had work which involved much nervous strain, rather than amongst groups who pursued the habit for pleasure or who were members of the 'criminal classes'. Such a view could lead to an overall impression that drug taking was not a problem and permit a complete lack of interest as far as drug taking was concerned. In this way those addicted or prosecuted could be dealt with in an unemotional way and labelled in a way which appeared to produce very little stigma. Societal reaction was then one of sympathy mixed with indifference. In this sense, where the Home Office reports stated that drug taking was not a problem, they could equally have said that the drug takers themselves were not a problem either. Their repentance confirmed the norms.

An examination of the reports and convictions confirms this view. Moral condemnation was rarely levelled at the drug taker and sentences of imprisonment were passed only in the last resort. Even during the war years when drug offences increased rapidly there were no demands either for additional punishments or for more information or even changes in the system. Societal definitions of the problem remained consistent and having once defined it in this way it is understandable that the recommendations of the Rolleston Committee were never challenged, nor was their pressure to implement the safeguards of the medical tribunals. Additional protection was seen as unnecessary for this type of repentant deviant. Protection was, however, necessary for the enemy deviant some twenty years later.

Great play was made of the lack of involvement in the illicit trafficking and the drug users in Britain were not thought to be involved in this either. For example, in 1932 the leaders of a gang of drug smugglers visited London. It was thought they had been dealing in enormous quantities on the Continent, running into thousands of kilograms of drugs, but they appeared to have come to Britain only for a holiday! Their business interests were in France, Switzerland, Germany, Turkey, the Far East and the U.S.A. In 1933 a Spaniard, named Gandarillas, was arrested in Southampton in possession of 140 lbs. of opium. He had arrived from Germany on a transatlantic liner and was hoping to transfer the opium to a contact on board, but the plan misfired, and he was left with the goods and no alternative plans for their disposal in Britain.

By the late 1950s the drug takers according to E. M. Schur still came mainly from the middle classes.[22] He reported a study of 73 patient addicts at a mental hospital from 1950-57 and noted that 74% were from middle class professions; there was no predominance of working class addicts. In his discussion with people whom he called "specialists who provided general information" they too reported a high incidence of middle class addicts. Schur concluded from these studies that age and social class of addicts were closely related, as age was dependent on which class was exposed to drugs. Where drug use began by association with other drug users, as in the U.S.A., the age and social class of the drug taker would be low. Where drug use began as a result of medical prescribing, as in Britain, the age and social class would be higher. In some respects Schur's hypothesis has been validated, but by the late 1950s he was unable to discern a trend already apparent to a number of people who opposed the first Brain Committee. Patterns were changing and producing a shift to the enemy deviant who was prepared to attack the public norm.

Jock Young in his perceptive analysis of drug taking in the 1960s has argued that drug taking is highly correlated with Bohemian Youth Culture where drug use is exalted to a paramount position ideologically and morally buttressed against the criticisms of the outside world.[23] Bohemian cultures are according to Young the major growth area as far as illegal drug use is concerned. The Delinquent Youth Culture is also an area of high drug use but Young suggests this is for different reasons. With this group drug use is not only a vehicle for the emergence of subterranean values but, because of the taboos surrounding drugs, is a method of kicking over the traces and seeking forbidden pleasures. The delinquent youth culture centres itself around the various ways available to create a world of adventure, hedonism, 'kicks' and excitement. Drugs, like delinquency, provide the avenues.

This view of drug taking as being located in two distinct youth cultures not only fits in with the changing patterns of drug taking as provided by the official figures but with another piece of research which suggests that drug takers come from two distinct groups, one middle class youngsters, who are ideologically committed to drug taking, and the other working class youngsters who are more antecedently delinquent.[24] There may, of course, be some overlapping here and the typology is crude but the point is still valid. By identifying drug taking in these areas the shift from the 1930s image is almost complete.

To be classified as an enemy it is not enough to be identified with a group, there must be an interaction between the group and the designators. This interaction can take place at varying levels although one important area is the high visibility of the deviancy. The addicts of the 1930s were secretive, and in many cases their families did not know they were addicted. The 'professional' addict, such as the medical practitioner having probably acquired his habit through contact with drugs rather than drug users, would take his drugs, and continue working as before. In the 1960s addicts were no longer secretive, nor did they continue as before.

Peter Laurie has somewhat graphically described the way in which addicts in 1967 openly advertised their dependency on drug use. He says, "It has been remarked that the most striking characteristic of the new adolescent addicts is their desire for publicity. The enquirer thinking that it is going to be difficult to meet drug users, is immediately overwhelmed by their showing off their spiritual sores like mediaeval beggars; willing to discuss their most intimate affairs at exhaustive, and soon tedious length. It has clearly no use being drug dependent in London unless one is seen to be so... It is easy enough by sleeping rough and eating irregularly, wearing dirty clothes and not bothering to shave or comb one's hair to look adequately dilapidated. 'I wear these dark glasses' said one who came to tea with me in December 'just so people know I'm a junkie. You've got to work at the image man.' And another, who refused to be photographed with her dark glasses off in case her parents could identify her, insisted on having a picture taken of her eyes - 'Them's real junkie's eyes, man' she cried, as she whipped off her shades."[25]

Other reporters have noted how easy it is to interview addicts, and few research workers have had difficulty in obtaining a 'sample'. This is not only due to the large numbers, but because there is seldom a reluctance to talk about drug taking. Schur in the late 1950s, however, found it difficult to find people who were prepared to be interviewed.

Laurie also points to the rather dramatic queue of addicts around the all-night chemists in central London as part of the need to be seen and defined as drug takers. He might also have mentioned the ease with which drug takers are caught committing offences against the Dangerous Drugs Act in Piccadilly. It is not quite as Schur suggests that victimless crimes allow both parties to arrange a mutually convenient meeting place away from the gaze of law enforcement officers, otherwise fewer drug takers would be arrested in public places. It may be as important to be defined as a drug taker as to define, both receiving status from the definition. Once visibility is established it then becomes important to establish hostility to the very basis of established norms. Unlike the 1930 drug taker, the 1960 counterpart argues that the 'system' is wrong; cannabis ought to be legalised - it is not as bad as some other drugs, such as tobacco or alcohol, and he is often unrepentant after being convicted. His values are rarely those of the Protestant Ethic which in terms of drug use becomes what one authority has called a form of "pharmacological Calvinism" or "if a drug makes you feel good it must be bad."[26] Supporters of this ethic stressed the need for individual achievement and insisted that qualifications, rewards and pleasures should be obtained by social action. Short cuts by means of drugs were 'evil' since they produced the pleasure without the corresponding effort. Drug takers of the 1960s did not appear to support these values; they sought their pleasures and wanted the short cuts. They even wasted these substances when they ought to have been kept for medical use - another anathema to the ethic supporters.

Drug takers in the 1960s use the 'junkie' argot, another feature which was absent in the 1930s. Harold Finestone has described the American negro addict, whom he calls 'the cat', in terms which apply to so many young British drug takers in the 1960s. He sees 'the cat' as one who relates to people by outsmarting them, and with a sense of superiority which stems from his aristocratic disdain for work. In contrast, the 'square' toils for regular wages, and takes orders from his superiors without complaint.[27] That few addicts work is a common experience of every Court or social work agency and in one study of a variety of drug users at 2 London Courts, only 21 out of a possible 92 were working at the time of arrest, 18 had not worked for at least 6 months and 9 others had not worked for at least 3 years.[28] In a society which stresses the Puritan Ethic, such behaviour is easily seen as attacking a fundamental value.

The drug taker in his quest for the 'kick'- and especially the kick on heroin - pursues a way of life which provides, according to Finestone, "an instantaneous intensification of the immediate moment of experience".[29] This is a further attack on conventional society by engaging in pleasure without having had the appropriate previous drudgery. Society's response is either to warn of the dangers of such immediate pleasure, or to attempt to protect the user from himself.

Finestone also notes that the drug user possesses a large, colourful and discriminating vocabulary which deals with all phases of drug experience. As one of the functions of argot according to Ulla Bondeson is to serve as a common emblem which also serves as a means of identification,[30] it defines the drug user's world from the non-user's. Finestone sees drug argot as being more concrete and earthy than the conventional world's and as such reveals an attitude of subtle ridicule towards the dignity and conventionality inherent in the common usage.

Finally, the drug user's personal appearance seems to be carefully designed to show that he is as far removed as possible from the conventional clean shaven world of suits and polished shoes, which appear to him to be personified in middle class or military values with the corresponding restriction of movement and decisions. It is easy therefore to see why the police are seen as participators in a para-military machine, attending parades, wearing military medals, addressing senior officers as 'Sir' and appearing in public in uniform looking smart and purposeful. They appear to represent the antithesis of all the drug user stands for, and for the same reasons the drug user is seen as attacking those very standards which the police must themselves accept and which they represent as "right and correct values". It may be wrong to see these two groups as totally hostile, for each may have a functional dependence on the other and each may respect the other's point of view; the police sometimes may envy the drug taker's 'freedom' and the drug taker may envy the policeman's steady job and freedom from drugs. But at one level both represent opposing value systems and the one is inimical to the other.

It may also be wrong to categorise all drug users in terms of 'the cat'; recent studies in America have shown that there are a wide variety of groups. Alan Sutter's study distinguishes between "The Mellow Dude", "The Pot head", "The Player" and "The Hustler", whilst another study of physician narcotic addicts illustrates that they have little in common with those of Sutter's study.[31] However, the point still remains that whereas the 1930 addict could be seen as a victim of circumstance, the 1960 addict is now seen as having only himself to blame. Equally it would be wrong I think to see all drug takers as having been classified as enemy deviants. Some would be cast as 'sick' although as Jock Young points out humanitarianism at this level can often be a cloak for greater control and a way of neutralizing rebellion. Occasionally the drug taker may be prepared to accept the 'sick' role, but difficulties occur if the acceptance was only temporary and designed to escape a more punitive sanction such as imprisonment. When this happens the designators assisted by members of the helping professions may be misled into thinking the role is permanent. Inevitably designators and treatment officials feel let down when there is no obvious response to long term treatment. Such a reaction will produce secondary effects, one of which is for designators to change their explanation of drug taking and see treatment "as a waste of time". A new designation is then given in terms of the drug taker being "more sick than was at first realized" or as having "more deep seated personality problems than were once apparent". Either way the effect is a redefinition of the classification which in practical terms means that other drug takers appearing at Court wanting the sick classification may find treatment avenues closed.

I have suggested in this chapter that the legislative changes which occurred in the 1960s were primarily the result of a new type of drug taker and that these changes were proposed before drug taking reached what was called "epidemic proportions". I have tried to show that the designation of the drug takers shifted with the changes in the drug takers themselves so that a redefinition of their role was inevitable. David Downes and Paul Rock have argued that where hostility to the very basis of established social arrangements is imputed to the deviant, or where the career possibilities or potential for rapid escalation are perceived as particularly threatening, societal reaction of a much more punitive kind than that measured by the objective character of the offences committed is seen as justified. Although the authors use the work of Dr. Stan Cohen on 'Mods and Rockers; to some extent the same applies to certain types of drug users, especially those in the younger age group. Downes and Rock have made an important point here as most drug taking is now seen as being hostile to the very basis of social arrangements. It is also important to note that the Early Drugs Acts imported a system of control, but the agents of social control have not been any less reluctant to deal with infringements; there is much evidence to suggest that international control has been widely accepted in Britain and readily incorporated into the value system and normative structure. In fact, judging by the Home Secretary's refusal to implement the Wootton Report as being part of a "permissive society", it would seem that drug taking has been seen to require considerable controls. Recent Press reports linking illegal Pakistani immigrants with drug trafficking - which were later denied - would also suggest that behaviour with drugs opens the way for stronger sanctions against that behaviour. Some sympathy may once have been given to illegal immigrants, but as soon as they have been linked with drug taking this rapidly evaporates. The implications here are enormous, for all deviant behaviour, political or otherwise, can then be neutralised or condemned as being excessively threatening and thus the credibility of what has been said on other matters is reduced.

And yet, this seems to be only part of the picture. We need to examine the drug takers and make links between the way in which some other control agents have contributed to the drug taking problem. I am not thinking here of the police, against whom allegations of 'planting' have been common in recent years, but rather of the medical profession who, after all, have always been the main suppliers of drugs.

References

1. Turk, A. T. *Criminality and Legal Order,* Rand McNally, 1969, p. 8.

2. Kitsuse, J. I. and Cicourel, A.V. 'A note on the use of Official Statistics', *Social Problems,* Vol 11, 1936, p. 131-138.

3. Letter to *Brit. Med. J.,* 1948, Vol 1, p. 133.

4. Details are not available for manufactured drugs for 1965 and 1966. Totals for those years were 101 and 128 respectively.

5. The method of recording was further changed classifying into Heroin, Cocaine and others. Figures for others for 1967, 1968 , 1969 and 1970 were 213, 449, 878 and 771 respectively.

6. It was announced in the House of Commons on 24.6.66 that the Drug Squad in London was to be increased to 20 officers. *Hansard* 1966, Vol. 730, p. 163.

7. In 1969, 225 persons were convicted for premises offences, 122 for unlawful import and 147 for unlawful supply with 95 for other offences. The 1968 figures were 193, 77, 87, and 51 repectively.

8. *Cannabis,* H.M.S.O., 1968, *op.cit.*

9. Ibid,Table C, pp. 26-7.

10. Hansard, 16.6.54.

11. Annual Report for 1959, para. 45.

12. In one of the few reports that give ages of offenders for this period, of the 208 prosecutions only 62 were under 30, 47 of which were for possession of cannabis. Annual Report for 1952, p. 2.

13. Chapman, D. *Sociology and the Stereotype of the Criminal*, Tavistock, 1970

14. Johnson, D. *Indian Hemp, a Social Menace,* London, 1952.

15. See also Spear, H. B. 'The Growth of Heroin Addiction in the U.K.' *British Journal of Addiction*, 1969, Vol. 64, p. 245-256, *op. cit.*

16. Ibid.

17. Leech, K. reports that amphetamines were introduced in 1897 and methylamphetamine in 1919, op. cit., p. 21. See also Kalant, O. J. The Amphetamines, Toronto University Press, 1966.

18. Similar manuals have been published in 1947 and 1957.

19. Gusfield, J. 'Moral Passage' in Crime and Delinquency, Bersani, C.A. (ed.) Macmillan, 1970.

20. Downes, D. and Rock, P. 'Social Reaction to Deviance', mimeo paper read to 4th National Conference on Research and Teaching in Criminology, Cambridge, 1970.

21. Gusfield, J. op. cit.

22. Schur, E.M. Narcotic Addiction in Britain and America, S. S.P., 1936, op. cit.

23. Young, J. The Drug Takers, Paladin, 1971, p. 143.

24. Bean, Philip 'Social Aspects of Drug Abuse' Journal of Criminal Law, Criminology and Police Science, Vol. 62 No. 1, March, 1971.

25. Laurie, P. *Drugs,* Penguin, p. 51-56.

26. Klernaw, G. 'Drugs and Social Values' *International Journal of Narcotics,* 1970, Vol. 5. No. 2, p. 317.

27. Finestone, H. 'Cats, Kicks and Colour' in Cressey, D. and Ward, D., *op. cit.,* p. 790.

28. *Op. cit.,* p. 792.

30. Bondeson, U. 'Argot Knowledge and Criminal Socialization' in *Scandinavian Studies in Criminology,* Vol. 1, Tavistock, 1965.

31. Winick, C. 'Physician narcotic Addicts' and Sutter, A. 'Worlds of Drug Use', both in Cressey, D. and Ward, D., *op. cit.*

10.   The Punishment Illusion
Your Money *and* Your Life?
Nicholas Dorn, Karim Murji and Nigel South

It is generally agreed that the powers afforded to the enforcement agencies are sweeping, and the sentences handed down by the courts are 'draconian' (Zander 1989). In Britain, persons convicted of trafficking face up to life imprisonment, plus confiscation of their assets if these are presumed to be the proceeds of trafficking.

Asset confiscation, as originally recommended by the Hodgson Committee, was intended to be a just but humane penalty. It would take away from convicted parties their ill-gained wealth, thus overcoming the perceived scandal that a person might serve a prison term and then be free to enjoy that wealth, as occurred in the notorious Operation Julie case (Hodgson *et al.* 1984:3).

It had been envisaged that the imposition of a confiscation order would be 'taken into account in reducing the length of a prison sentence' (*ibid.:* 138). In the excitable anti-trafficker climate of the 1980s, however, this aspect of the Committee's recommendations was overlooked. The Home Office, in the knowledge of the likely recommendation of the Hodgson Committee, and in spite of being concerned about Britain's growing prison population, announced that maximum terms of imprisonment for drug trafficking were to be increased, and this was subsequently confirmed by the Controlled Drugs (Penalties) Act 1985. The Association of Chief Police Officers' Broome Report applauded that move (ACPO 1985:60) although, in common with others calling for longer terms of imprisonment, it did not give any reason for doing so (cf Home Affairs Committee 1985).

The following pages put these developments in the context of the history of development of penalties in general, suggesting that trafficking legislation is very much the curate's egg of crime control.

Drug control: the story so far

As far as crime control in general is concerned, there is now a considerable literature pointing out that increasing surveillance of citizens and situations has been a historical trend from the nineteenth century to the present day (Foucault 1977; Cohen 1979; Mathiesen 1980; Marx 1988). This has involved not just the creation of a public police, with access to increasingly elaborate camera surveillance and computer databases (public and private), but also the involvement of private security firms (in shopping malls, etc.) (South 1988) and, finally, the mobilisation of every citizen in *Crimewatch* programmes. Associated with this is:

> a sharp increase in the number of registered crimes over the period in
> question (that is, not due to an increase in the detection rate, or other

Nicholas Dorn, Karim Murji and Nigel South (eds): *TRAFFICKERS: DRUG MARKETS AND LAW ENFORCEMENT*, (Routledge, 1992), pp. 176-200. © Nicholas Dorn, Karim Murji and Nigel South 1992.

variable of that kind). The increase in registered crimes could be the result of (1) a real increase in crime; (2) an increased willingness on the part of the public to report crimes to the authorities; (3) an increased readiness on the part of the police to discover crimes on their own initiative, and not through the public reporting ('direct discovery'); or, of course, a combination of any two or more of these possibilities. . . [I]t is probable that the main reason for the increase in registered conviction in the post-war period is either a real increase in crime, or an increased willingness by the public to report crimes . . . either way, the public is reporting more crime to which the social-control system has to respond in one way or another.

(Bottoms 1983: 183-4)

To Bottoms's list of possible factors causing the increase in crime, we must of course add another - the creation of new categories of crime by legislation.

Drug control provides examples of this. Throughout most of the nineteenth century there were no controls on the production, sale, import/export or possession of drugs (other than laws regulating the circumstances of sale of alcohol - Dorn 1983). Some legislation did emerge in relation to the sale of medicines containing opiates (Berridge and Edwards 1981). It was not until the First World War and thereafter that the modern structure of narcotic controls began to emerge. Regulation 40B of the Defence of the Realm Act 1914 made it an offence for anyone except doctors and similar professionals to possess cocaine, following alarm at reports that it was being taken recreationally by British troops. The Dangerous Drugs Act 1920, which was primarily motivated by the need to ratify international treaties, made it an offence to import, distribute or possess morphine, heroin and cocaine. The maximum penalty for any such offence was a £200 fine or six months' imprisonment for a first offence - a far cry from the multi-years' prison sentences to be imposed upon traffickers by the mid-1980s. In an interesting precursor of asset confiscation, the 1920 Act provided for a fine of £100 or three times the value of drugs that were imported or exported. That the legislation was not seen as effective can be judged from the fact that the Dangerous Drugs and Poisons (Amendment) Act 1923 increased the penalties to a maximum of £1,000 fine or ten years' imprisonment, but only when prosecution had the consent of the Attorney-General or Director of Public Prosecutions. Cannabis was added in the Dangerous Drugs Act 1925. Permitting premises to be used for smoking or dealing in cannabis was proscribed by the Dangerous Drugs Act 1964, and the Drugs (Prevention of Misuse) Act 1964 controlled amphetamines. LSD was controlled in 1966.

There was little change in the drug legislation until the Misuse of Drugs Act 1971 which, beside consolidating previous legislation and bringing Britain in line with post-war international conventions (Bruun *et al.* 1975), made the distinction in penalty terms between possession offences and supply offences. Modern thinking on drug control derives from debates of the 1960s which led up to the 1971 Act. Drug *users* became described as weak personalities, typically trapped in deprived environments, who had been led astray by misguided peers and unscrupulous drug pushers. They were sick or immature, and required treatment, counselling, or simply a safe space to grow as people.

Drug *dealers*, on the other hand, come to be perceived as belonging to a quite different category. One word suffices to describe them: 'bad' and, as reaction hardened, 'evil'.

It was not until the 1980s that the concept of drug 'dealing' metamorphosed into that of drug 'trafficking'. During the 1970s, most Europeans referred to drug 'pushers' or drug 'dealers'. Anyone referring to 'trafficking' would have been regarded as rather quaint, the term seeming to hark back to nineteenth-century concerns with slavery. By the end of the 1980s, however, the term 'drug trafficking' had come into common usage, in the context of increased penalties and images of violence. A similar shift in language had occurred in the 1970s in respect of street crime, as the term 'mugging' crossed the Atlantic and acted as the linchpin of a wave of police/media/public fears about violent crime by young blacks (Hall *et al.* 1978). And it is clear that 'trafficking' has similar, albeit more extreme connotations, carrying definite implications of dangerous foreigners and a need for severe punishment.

However, the increasing focus upon traffickers as objects of surveillance and control has not left drug users unaffected. Repeated panics - about amphetamines and cannabis in the 1960s, heroin and solvents up until the mid-1980s - have kept the spotlight upon drug users, especially when they are involved in small-scale supply. Whereas in earlier years such persons would have been described as 'user-dealers', today they become 'minor traffickers', and worthy of a considerable effort in bringing to court.

The development of financial penalties

As regards punishment in general, the growth of the fine was noted earlier this century as occurring across Europe.

> Imprisonment remained the central point of the whole system, but it received increasing competition from the fine... This phenomenon is not merely the result of new crimes ... but is also the consequence of a general policy of substituting the fine for imprisonment.
>
> (Rusche and Kirchheimer 1939: 166-7)

Part of the explanation for the growth of financial penalties is evidently the expansion of the money economy to incorporate the majority of citizens. There is limited scope for the use of such penalties in a society in which a sizeable proportion of citizens have no disposable income and little property that may be seized and sold. It is clear that there are certain necessary conditions to be met before a criminal justice system can begin to switch from taking away liberty to taking away the money. The fine became increasingly common in a climate of increasing European prosperity, although

> Even in England, the rise of the fine for adult indictable offenders has not been one of steady progress. The first great growth came in the late nineteenth century, but thereafter the proportionate use of the fine remained fairly static until the Second World War, during and after which there was a further increase in use. . .There have also been considerable fluctuations in the post-1945 growth of the fine, with, for example, little increase since 1970.
>
> (Bottoms 1983: 168)

The latest development of financial penalties is asset confiscation. Both fines and asset confiscation are now used, in addition to life imprisonment, for convicted drug traffickers. Asset confiscation was brought into British law by the Drug Trafficking Offences Act (DTOA) 1986. Asset confiscation means the confiscation of those assets of a person found guilty of an offence to the extent to which some or all of those assets may be suspected or shown to derive from crime (Dorn and South 1991).

Confiscation of the *proceeds* of crime generally goes wider than the *profits* of crime, since the latter phrase refers only to the difference between first, a criminal's investment in a criminal enterprise, and second, the proceeds from that enterprise. Under the DTOA, it is the whole of the proceeds (i.e. investment plus profit) that is subject to confiscation. This means, for example, that if a criminal extends his or her mortgage on the family home by £100,000 in order to finance a drug deal, and if s/he is able to sell the drugs on for £200,000, then the latter sum (and hence the house itself) is at risk, not the former sum.

In the case of a conviction for any trafficking offence, the court must make an order for confiscation of all the proceeds estimated to have been obtained not only from the offence(s) proved, but also from any other trafficking offence that the court believes may have occurred over the six years prior to when proceedings were instituted. It is not necessary for the prosecution to show that more than one offence was committed. Rather, and exceptionally in British law, the presumption is that any asset acquired over the past six years which cannot be shown by the defendant to have been obtained legitimately may be regarded as being the proceeds of trafficking, and confiscated. The burden of proof is reversed.

In these respects the DTOA follows the recommendations of the majority of the Hodgson Committee (Hodgson *et al.* 1984). However, a Note of Dissent by two members, Andrew Nicol and Clive Soley, objected to the concept that a person should have an order made against them for offences which were presumed, but not proven to have been committed.

> In our view... it is contrary to a basic principle of our criminal justice system to sentence a person for an offence that has not been proved or admitted. The other members of the Committee would empower the judge to resolve a disputed issue of whether the defendant were guilty of further wrongdoing. This is not satisfactory in our view. Defendants are entitled to have allegations of serious criminality resolved not by a judge but by jury and we fail to see why they should lose this right because they have been convicted of other, different crimes. The proposal is made apparently to save court time. Yet we do not see how this can be done without depriving the defendant of proper procedural safeguards.
>
> (Hodgson *et al.* 1984: 144)

Nicol and Soley go on to suggest that any reversal of the burden of proof would contravene the European Convention on Human Rights. Article 6 (2) of the Convention states that 'everyone charged with an offence shall be presumed innocent until proved guilty according to law' *(ibid.)*. However, a confiscation order under the DTOA does not amount to a finding of guilt in respect of presumed trafficking; it is simply a confiscation order. For example in the case of Jill (described in Chapter 2 and below), although found guilty on only one count, she was estimated by the court to have supplied several kilogrammes in the past. Accordingly, the court applied a confiscation order calculated on the basis of the street value of that larger amount.

If the convicted party does not pay the amount reckoned by the court to be the proceeds of trafficking, and if the court believes that they hold hidden assets or property outside the jurisdiction of the court, then an additional period of imprisonment is imposed by the court in place of the financial penalty. Failure to comply with a confiscation order results in additional periods in prison, according to the following scale.

£10,000 - 20,000	12 months
£20,000 - 50,000	18 months
£50,000 - 100,000	2 years
£100,000 - 250, 000	3 years
£250,000 - £1 million	5 years
Exceeding £1 million	10 years

Thus it is possible for a person to be jailed for several years for presumed but unproven offences. In such a case, one is being jailed for failing to follow the confiscation order, rather than for the presumed offence.

If the court is satisfied that a convicted party is unable to raise the whole of the sum specified in the confiscation order - for example, because they no longer have possession of part or all the money received for the drugs sold, having spent the money on living expenses and/or luxury items - the amount confiscated is whatever remains (DTOA, section 32/4(3)). In Jill's case, the court estimated that the total proceeds of the drugs she sold in small lots over an extended period amounted to £2 million. But, since her available assets amounted to only about £30,000, that was the amount of confiscation order. Jill ran her life in a business-like manner, building up savings on the scale that any other self-employed person might expect, and on conviction she lost those savings. People known to her who were convicted at the same time had apparently spent their money. The law apparently creates an incentive for traffickers to lead an extravagant lifestyle since savings are likely to be confiscated upon conviction.

During the initial years of operation of the DTOA, some police officers voiced concern that the courts were failing to follow the full requirement of the Act, especially in relation to relatively minor trafficking offences. It was felt that traffickers who do small deals over an extended period of time generate considerable cashflows. Other officers described the duty upon the court to make a confiscation order on every convicted party as onerous, both for the courts themselves and for the police. Specialist officers are tied up in preparing reports for all trafficking offenders, to be available to present to the judge in the event of conviction. Consider the situation of one offender.

The defendant does not have access to either bank or building society accounts, his living expenses being derived from his state benefit income. His rent is paid direct thus leaving a little over £10 per week for general purposes. However when one considers his admitted drugs expenditure, he requires additional income in order to satisfy it as the profit from [drug] sales despite his admissions is not sufficient for re-purchase. A breakdown of cost and retail pricing is shown [in an appendix to the officer's report]. The defendant also states that he smoked cannabis himself. If he smoked the 104 grammes he purchased that would represent 416 cigarettes, therefore over a two week period, the period he states he would buy further supplies, he would have to smoke 29 cigarettes (joints) per day, which clearly his constitution would not tolerate. The prosecution therefore assumes that the £273 with which [the defendant] purchased the cannabis together with the £48 in his possession upon arrest represents the proceeds of drug trafficking and therefore invites the Court to make a Confiscation Order.

> (from a Financial Statement prepared by an officer in a
> Drug Profit Confiscation Unit)

In this case, since the defendant had been assessed as having received £273 + £48 as proceeds of trafficking, yet had no realisable assets other than the £48 in cash, it was the latter which was taken from him. The financial cost, in terms of police investigation and court time, of making this order is not known. Some observers claim that the obligation for the courts to make a confiscation order in every case is onerous and unnecessary (cf Zander 1989). Others point out that, unless an investigation is made in every case, some traffickers who appear to have modest means but actually have substantial savings would emerge from prison (or, with minor offences, pay their fine), then to enjoy the proceeds of crime.

Escalation in imprisonment

The Misuse of Drugs Act 1971 increased the maximum penalties for what was then called drugs supply from ten to fourteen years for drugs such as heroin or cocaine. Subsequently, the Controlled Drugs (Penalties) Act 1985 increased the maximum penalty to life imprisonment.

Although the legislation does not prescribe minimum penalties, case-law from the Appeal Court has established a 'tariff' of imprisonment based on the supposed retail value of the drugs seized or presumed by the court to have been involved over a continuing period. These guidelines have an effect broadly similar to minimum penalties. Regarding the *supply* of heroin, the Lord Chief Justice, Lord Lane, thought that sentences would generally lie between three years and life: 'The sentence will largely depend on the degree of involvement, the amount of trafficking and the value of the drugs being handled' (Fortson 1988: 247). As regards *importation*, Lord Lane said, 'It is not difficult to understand why in some parts of the world, traffickers in heroin in any substantial quantity were sentenced to death and executed' (*ibid.*: 246). However, since this means of disposal is not available in Britain, a lesser scale of punishments was devised.

From the late 1980s onwards, trafficking a kilo of drugs such as heroin or cocaine (categorised as Class A, or most dangerous, under the Misuse of Drugs Act 1971) generally attracted a sentence of around ten years. Several such consignments or larger ones attracted a sentence of the order of fourteen years upwards. A few kilos of amphetamine (categorised as a medium-danger Class B drug) might attract a sentence around five years.

It is worth looking in some detail at the way the tariff is applied, since the implications for prospective traffickers are particularly clear. The basis of sentencing is

1. an appraisal by the court of the estimated money value (more properly, retail or street-level prices) of the consignment(s) of drugs
2. in some cases, especially those resting on conspiracy charges, the value taken for the purposes of sentencing will not be limited to the amount of drugs seized, but will be extended to include an amount value reckoned by the court to have been trafficked over an extended period
3. whether it appears that defendants genuinely believe (have good reason for believing) that they are handling a less dangerous drug
4. whether defendants plead guilty (in which case the sentence is reduced)
5. whether defendants are 'cooperative' in the sense that they name their contacts

From judgements handed down by the courts in Britain it appears that a combination of a guilty plea and giving information on other traffickers may result in a reduction in sentence by about one-third. In a landmark case, for example, a sentence of twelve years was reduced to eight on appeal on just such grounds (*R v. Bilinski, Criminal Law Review* 1987: 783).

Whether the defendant is considered to be an organizer, likely to benefit considerably in financial terms, or simply a courier or 'mule', unlikely to see more than a tiny fraction of the consignment's selling price, is not a major consideration in sentencing. As Jane Goodsir, director of the legal advice agency Release, has noted, 'There's not much discrimination between the sentences on simple couriers and major dealers' (Bowcott 1990b: 6; see also Carvel 1990). In spite of the keenness to catch 'big traffickers' in the organisational sense, the courts have been unable to base punishment very much upon criteria of organizational size or market dominance. If the courts were to base punishment upon such criteria, then the likely result would be to impose much lower penalties on the run-of-the-mill traffickers who get caught. However, the relatively simple sentencing guideline of weight of drugs has come into use.

As regards the money value of the consignment, one practice in calculating this is to multiply the presumed or known wholesale-level price (e.g. price for amounts of a proportion of a kilo upwards) by a factor of between three and five, and to call the result the retail value. Sometimes a more complicated approach is followed, involving a series of assumptions about the purity of the drugs (which may vary throughout a consignment), the typical weight at which the drug would be sold to users, the typical purity at customer level, and the price customers pay to their immediate suppliers. Then, the total value of the consignment is calculated as follows (Kay 1988: 815).

$$\frac{\text{Consignment weight x Consignment purity x Unit cost to customer}}{\text{Typical unit weight at customer level x Typical purity at customer level}}$$

The assumptions made about each of these variables evidently affect the estimated consignment price. Indeed, when terms in such an equation are multiplied together, relatively small changes in the assumptions made can result in quite big changes in estimated consignment 'value'. It has been shown, for example, that a kilo of heroin in Britain ' could quite easily be calculated as worth £75,000, £300,000 or £900,000' (*ibid.*: 815). The potential consequences for offenders are considerable, since length of imprisonment is related to estimated consignment value.

However, the relationship between the value of drugs such as heroin or cocaine smuggled and the prison sentence likely to be imposed is not a linear one in Britain (Harvey and Pease 1987). The judgement of the Appeal Court in the case of *Aramah* (*Criminal Law Review* 1983:271-3) laid down guidelines at a time when the maximum sentence was fourteen years. These guidelines were subsequently amended in the case of *Bilinski* in the light of the increase in maximum penalty to life imprisonment. (Fortson 1988: 246; Bucknall and Ghodse 1989).

Estimated 'value' of drugs	Sentence in years	
	Aramah (1983)	Bilinski (1987 onwards)
£1 million (many kilos)	12-14 years	14 years minimum
£100,000 (e.g. a few kilos of heroin)	7 years minimum	10 years minimum
An 'appreciable' amount (fraction of a kilo)	4 years	(no change specified)

In other words, the risk-reward ratio *decreases* as one moves to larger consignments. People who are found guilty of trafficking in fractions of a kilo (say fifty grams or so, said to be worth around £5,000) are likely to get a sentence of the order of five years. This implies one year in prison for every £1,000 in retail value of the drug. But get caught with two kilogrammes - which might be worth around £100,000 at the retail level - and the sentence would be ten years and upwards. Here the tariff is one year for every £10,000 in retail value. The audacious trafficker, shifting many kilos worth say around £1.4 million, gets fourteen years minimum. Now the tariff is of the order of one-tenth of a year for every £10,000 worth in retail value. In other words, the prison sentence incurred for the tenth kilo is actually less than that incurred for the fifth kilo; the sentence for the fifth kilo is less than for the second, and so on.

Now, if there is any relationship between the patten of crime and the system of controls in a society then the implications are fairly obvious. If one is going to traffick in heroin in Britain, then there is little point in restricting oneself to, let us say, one-quarter or half a kilo of heroin. The chances of being caught do not alter that much with increasing size of consignment (although they do with the number of consignments, due to the greater risks of a continuing operation). The implication for the calculating trafficker is rather similar to that old maxim, 'you might as well be hung for a sheep as a lamb'. One might as well traffick in as much as one can, in order to minimise the risk-reward ratio.

This is rather an odd set of inducements for a society supposedly concerned about trafficking.

THE ADMINISTRATION OF JUSTICE

Those caught face interrogation, committal for trial, remand in custody (in most cases), the court case, and sentencing, probable imprisonment and asset confiscation. In this section we examine some cases as they are processed through the criminal justice system.

We introduce the discussion of the disposal of prisoners by considering the question of remand - the power of the courts to order that persons accused be held in custody in the period up to their trial. The question of whether or not to remand a defendant in custody is quite often an issue between defence and prosecution. The defence, obviously, argues against remand, not only because being in prison for six months or so whilst the case comes to trial is an unpleasant experience and can break up families and ruin careers, but also because it makes preparation of a defence more difficult.

The prosecution generally argues for defendants to be remanded in all but the more minor trafficking cases, either because of the danger of potential witnesses being intimidated or simply because defendants may flee. This outcome can be illustrated by completing the story of the Morgans, the firm of diversifiers described in Chapters 3 and 6. The case also illustrates the way in which a carefully constructed case can fail because the prosecution themselves feel obliged to withhold some evidence. The overall result is then hardly a victory for the police.

Two that got away

In the case of the Morgans the three men charged had been granted bail against sureties of £10,000 each. By the time the case reached court, one of the threesome (given the name Garry in Chapter 6) had left the country and, rumour had it, was in Spain. We watched in court as one of the sureties, a local man, was called to the witness stand by the trial judge. As the judge remarked, 'It would appear on the face of it that you have stood surety in the sum of £10,000 and that surety is in peril, I strongly advise you to take legal advice.' The surety, presenting himself as a man let down by others, claimed that it was actually another person who had stood surety, and that he himself was simply a go-between who had helped to arrange things by telephone. Be that as it may, the score was now one defendant escaped, two to stand trial. Proceedings were adjourned whilst enquiries were made, but the missing party remained missing.

The re-convened trial then proceeded quite smoothly for the prosecution, whose star witness was the undercover officer we called Trevor in Chapter 6, who had set up this buy bust operation. However, the prosecution laboured under difficulties related to identification evidence. The second defendant, Colin, was arrested some weeks after the arrest of the other two men. His role had been to drive the car which contained the drugs and leave it in the car park before departing the scene. In court his defence enquired as to how the police could be sure of his identity having seen him only briefly. The police had to admit that he had been arrested later after being recognised by the undercover officer as someone he had met several years ago. Pressed in court, Trevor said 'I have met him on three previous occasions, with a person I've been drinking with, but if I went any further it would reveal my identity'. This is an odd expression to use whilst standing in open court before the accused, and it may be that Trevor was seeking to protect an informant who may have been present at the same time. Protecting the identities of undercover officers and of informants is a common issue in such cases.

This difficulty would have been overcome if the police had taken a photograph of the person who escaped the scene of arrest. Unaccountably, they had not. 'A balls up', according to one officer. Another officer on surveillance duty at the scene also identified Colin as having been there but, pressed by the defence, admitted that he had previously been shown a photograph of the defendant. Why did the police have a photograph of this defendant? Because they had previous dealings with him. But what would the jury make of that - would it not prejudice them against that defendant? The judge declared

> My reaction is one of great alarm and there is a danger of a grave miscarriage of justice. I do not believe that any direction from me... can possibly stop the jury coming to a conclusion based on speculation. I have come to the conclusion that the identification evidence ought not to be admitted.

Without admissible identification evidence, the case against Colin became untenable, and the judge ordered the jury to return a not guilty verdict. The score was then two free, one still on trial.

This left Dave, the third and last alleged member of the alleged gang. He was regarded by the police as a relatively minor member of the firm, but had been caught with the drugs in his car. Found guilty by the jury, he was sentenced to two years' imprisonment and ordered to pay £1,000 under an asset confiscation order.

From the point of view of the police, this result was rather disappointing, but better than nothing. It is, after all, an aspect of professionalism to be able to learn from one's mistakes, and try to do better next time.

Case study: from local bar to foreign cell

One of the by-products of the anti-trafficker push of the 1980s has been the number of women caught up in the drug enforcement effort (Carvel 1990). For some of those who have scraped by in the irregular economy for many years, the chance to make a few thousand pounds through acting as a courier or 'mule' can be hard to resist. Most of the non-British nationals in women's prisons are there for this reason (Women in Prison, personal communication). Roxanne's case provides an example, exemplifying the way in which officers try to 'work up the chain' from couriers to those who sent them.

Roxanne was born in the United States, is married and her husband is in prison. She has two children but is not eligible for welfare. She has no means of self-support. Whilst hanging around in a bar waiting for some prospect to turn up, Roxanne was approached by a man who bought drinks and then food, sounding her out about her circumstances. After meeting her on a second occasion, he suggested that she act as a courier, carrying cocaine from New York to Gatwick. She agreed. On arrival at Gatwick airport, she was stopped by a female officer who 'asked if I was carrying any drugs and first I said "no" but then I caught their eye and said "yes", because I knew I would be strip searched'.

In interrogation, after some prevarication, she described to Customs the man who sent her to Britain.

> I met him in a bar and we got into conversation. After four to six months he offered the job... I was supposed to get $7,000 and he gave me $2,300 and said the rest would be paid when I got back to the States. I have a strange feeling that the drugs were already paid for because everything happened so quick and he was so sure. I was supposed to take the Victoria line to Paddington [sic] and to phone a telephone number and to say that I was in a hotel which I was to choose and call the female and wait till she picked me up. Customs asked me if I was prepared to go through with this but I was afraid for my children so I did not. So then I was interrogated from 3.30p.m. to about 1.00 a.m. in the morning.

> On the second visit of the Customs man I was shown photographs of a number of men and I recognized the Colombian who sent me. I went to court on a Monday and was sent for remand for three and a half months in Holloway. Legal aid was the only thing because I could not afford anything else, so I had [lawyers] Mr X and a Mr Y. At one point I said, 'do you think it would be wise to cooperate?' and he said, 'you know the saying, you scratch my back and I'll scratch yours'. Then they also said that it would be dangerous, and left it up to me. I basically saw the barrister once in the whole case. I said I want this over and done with.

> (Roxanne)

In court

> I pleaded guilty and I did cooperate to some extent with the Customs and a couple of weeks ago the person who sent me was arrested in this country. I got six years and I think that I got a high sentence and that they should have given me less than six. Before I got sentenced he [the Customs officer] said 'I'll help you reduce your sentence'. I asked Mr X [a solicitor], ' if I cooperate then what will I get?' and they said five years. On another occasion they said five to eight years.

Her information brought her 'employer' to court and she agreed to testify against him.

> The guy from Customs said, 'I can help you and I can put in a good word for your first parole'. The questions I asked him were if I was going to get help with a deportation [i.e. immediate, not after parole release] and have a reduced sentence which I could serve in the United States. But I got no answers.

Roxanne says that Customs were consistently encouraging but unspecific.

> The Customs man said that 'things can be solved - I have good news for you - your Colombian friend has been arrested and we need you to go in the witness box so that we can get the credit'. I said, 'but you have no answers for me' [on deportation] and he was going to see somebody at the

Home Office, fine, but would he be honest enough? He needs me, he's been after this man for years.

A straightforward response would have been that the chances of immediate deportation were virtually nil. But such information would not have encouraged this woman in her belief that further cooperation would shortly re-unite her with her children. For convicted drug traffickers whom the enforcement agencies believe may be useful in trapping other traffickers, firm and binding agreements are certainly not the order of the day.

In such circumstances, offenders become worried that they may be putting themselves, family or friends at risk and yet may not get much in return.

> I'm gonna be worried, I am worried because I'm going to be going into the witness box. I'm doing it because I've visualised things differently and I want my conscience clear and to feel that I did my share in correcting the error that I did and anyway, I need to get out of here to see my children. I hope that they at least deport me... They should know that I am not lying. I noticed that I was being used and he said, 'Help us to get somebody else', but I was involved in this one case, not anything else.

> (Roxanne)

The case illustrates the emotional bargaining power that Customs have with some offenders, and also the practical limitations to that bargaining power in the absence of the authority to secure deportation for foreign nationals.

Case study: one who is angry

From the perspective of an outsider, Britain can seem 'a very barbaric country', in which the quality of justice available for foreigners is poor.

Carmen, a middle-class Colombian and a lawyer with her own legal firm, is serving a ten-year sentence for importation of cocaine. She maintains her innocence and has amassed documentary evidence which, she says, supports her theory of a 'fit-up' in Bogotá . Our interest here, however, will not be upon the question of guilt or innocence (this having been decided by the courts), but upon the *process* of being brought to trial and her subsequent attempts to appeal.

The case also raises a general point about the integrity of persons working for solicitors - Carmen has made a serious complaint against one solicitor. The firm and its employees may have behaved in an exemplary way, but there is undeniably scope for the kind of impropriety alleged.

Overall, the case illustrates the difficulties of conducting a defence when one does not speak the language of the country, when English classes are not available before one is convicted, when legal aid solicitors have limited resources and when one is of a 'suspect' nationality (in this case, Colombian).

The facts of the case are that Carmen, while visiting Britain together with another woman, and the latter's daughter, was arrested at Heathrow airport with just under a kilo of cocaine sewn into leather goods, transported in her baggage. Her baggage was delayed for some time, and when it eventually turned up she was challenged by a Customs officer who suggested that it was not her case. She, however, insisted that it was, and the three left the terminal and got into a taxi. Carmen was then detained by Customs and confronted with the cocaine. A legal aid solicitor, Mr First Solicitor, was called and Carmen was charged with importation. Her two travelling companions were questioned, no record was made of these interviews, and they were then released. First Solicitor and Co then represented Carmen at committal and at trial, mainly through the firm's Assistant Solicitor , who visited Carmen twice. She was remanded in police cells for three months, where she developed scabies from the dirty conditions. She was then moved to a prison and committed for trial.

At her trial, Carmen pleaded not guilty. The next day the jury retired but was unable to reach a verdict and so the judge ordered a re-trial. Why was the jury unable to agree a verdict in the first trial? In summary, the evidence was as follows.

Prosecution

Carmen was found to be importing cocaine, sewn into leather goods. She did not deny the goods were hers. She might well be a solicitor, but this in itself was not a guarantee against wrongdoing. True, she had been able to show that she was not poor since she had personal wealth in Colombia, but who was to say that this wealth was not the proceeds of past trafficking?

Defence

That there was cocaine in the leather goods was not disputed, but Carmen did not know it was there. She had been given the goods some weeks before her flight to London. Her explanation was that this man, whose amorous advances she had earlier refused, conspired with another man, whom she had sued for non-payment of a debt, to get her out of the way. The importation was not done 'knowingly' as required for a conviction.

Re-trial

At the second trial, the jury returned a guilty verdict after retiring for just over two hours. The judge handed down a sentence of ten years, based on the estimate that the 0.982 kilos of cocaine had a street value of £186,000. He also ordered a Confiscation Order under the Drug Trafficking Offences Act 1986, for £4,215 or 6 months' imprisonment in default, and recommended her for deportation at the end of her sentence. Since the sentence is over five years she is not likely to be paroled and will therefore serve at least six years.

Carmen has consistently maintained her innocence. She says that her older travelling companion was her client and had asked her to arrange an English course for her daughter. This she had done by telephoning a university in England and being advised by a Spanish-speaking member of staff that a local Academy would be suitable. She contacted the Academy, which sent her some literature. Carmen then accompanied Mrs Client and her daughter to England because Mrs Client is 'someone who can never travel. She has no experience of travel outside a small place. And she is a person who is very nervous, too much nervous, and she needs somebody to escort her when she travels.' However, she did not have any documentary evidence of this reason for her travel when she went to court.

As a solicitor herself, Carmen makes numerous criticisms of British law, of the conduct of her case, of the conditions of her imprisonment (e.g. police cells; of putting non-dangerous cases such as herself in high-security prison; of lack of language tuition therein), and of solicitors and the barrister acting for her. Her case certainly illustrates that being unable to speak the language, and being moved around the country, makes the organisation of a defence or an appeal very difficult. As she put it

> England is a very barbaric country to treat foreigners this way. The police talk very fast, your solicitors tell you to keep quiet, so you never get to exercise your defence. Then without proper instructions with barristers, you are just left feeling like a beauty queen, smiling and laughing, you don't know what is going on. This is the same for the Colombians, the Nigerians and the other Africans. My barrister said 'don't worry, it will be OK, it will be all right'.

Carmen's barrister observed in a memo to the solicitors that Carmen had been advised that sentence would be higher if she was found guilty after pleading not guilty, than if she pleaded guilty. The barrister also observed that the Court of Appeal in the case of *Bilinski* laid down a sentencing tariff of ten years and upwards for importation of Class A drugs with a street value of £100,000. The barrister advised that there were no grounds for appealing either verdict or sentence and said that legal aid would not be granted for any appeal.

Carmen has changed her solicitors several times. She first attempted to do so after Mr First Solicitor said that he had been suffering from illness and handed the case to his assistant. In 1989 Carmen made a complaint about this firm to the Solicitors Complaints Bureau, alleging that they inadequately prepared her case and that they failed to field the student as a witness at the trial. According to First Solicitor and Co, the student told them that she could not recall why Carmen was travelling with her and her mother. In direct contradiction, Carmen maintains that it was her legal advisers who recommended against calling this witness since she was another Colombian and hence unlikely to impress the Court. She says that she has a letter from the student offering to give evidence. The Solicitors Complaints Bureau, in a letter to Carmen, presented the situation as the student's unwillingness to give evidence. The Bureau also found that First Solicitor and Co did get evidence of Carmen's background and professional standing and presented it at the trial, and that there they could not be criticised on grounds of negligence.

After her sentence, Carmen was initially placed in Holloway Prison. She dismissed First Solicitor and Co and engaged the well-known London firm of Bad Reputation and Co and, at the same time (but against the advice she had been given by her barrister) initiated her own Leave to Appeal. Bad Reputation and Co's Mr Clerk (who subsequently left the firm and proved difficult to contact) attended her in Holloway to advise her about her appeal.

According to Carmen, she gave Bad Reputation's representative funds to pursue the appeal as a paying client. She has made allegations that, in the period leading up to the Leave to Appeal hearing, Bad Reputation's Mr Clerk took £2,000 or $2,000 for this purpose. Bad Reputation deny this, saying that only $250 was involved.

> [Mr Clerk] said to me, 'you have to pay me to start to work because I have to pay a barrister for advice and to pay for the work I have to do to go to court and do many papers for you... Well, for a start, you can give me £2,000 and later when we get permission for the appeal maybe you can pay more'. And I asked him, 'how much more?' And he said 'well about three to four thousand pounds more'. Because I was very desperate, because of the situation, I said, 'well, I will ring my family and get the money'.

She says that she gave Mr Clerk $250 cash that day, getting this from her money held by the prison authorities. An equivalent sterling amount is recorded in Bad Reputation's books, and there is no conflict on this point. However:

> They gave me no receipt, nothing.
> Q. Did you ask for a receipt?
> No, because I was very confused, I was in shock, I was very desperate.

She further claims to have given Mr Clerk another $400 cash at a second meeting, this money having been sent to her by her parents in the pockets of some clothes. Not having been found by the prison authorities, this amount was never held by them so there is obviously no record of it being passed over. Additionally, her family claims to have sent $1,500 cash by special delivery to Mr Clerk at Bad Reputation's. Neither of these two latter sums, $400 and $1,500, are recorded as having been received by Bad Reputation's.

Carmen pressed her complaint against Bad Reputation and Co. They put a denial in writing and said that only $250 had changed hands. Carmen was advised to 'get your family to send us at least £1,000 sterling' so that they could continue to represent her. Carmen complained to the Solicitors Complaints Bureau who replied that according to Mr Clerk and Bad Reputation's records, only $250 changed hands. No one asked about a receipt.

Clearly there is conflict of evidence here, between Carmen's version of events and Bad Reputation's. The firm and the individual may be quite blameless, but it is striking that by 1990 this particular firm had such a bad reputation amongst inmates and prison officers that little new business was coming their way from women prisoners.

Her first Leave to Appeal (against both verdict and sentence) before a single judge was rejected, the judge saying 'The jury heard your explanation and did not believe it...Ten years for this offence upon a plea of not guilty and bearing in mind the amount and value of the drugs is not excessive'. Mr Clerk then again visited her in prison and, she claims, talked about helping her with the next step of appeal, to the full Appeal Court.

> And he said, 'yes, I know that [the first appeal was turned down], I've been in the court, but don't worry. We will now make the application for the full court, don't worry, it will work in the full court'. So he *with his own hand*

131

> [her emphasis] wrote in front of me the application for the full court. I have
> it here.

That was the last time she saw him. A few months later, her second Leave to Appeal was heard by the Appeal Court, and rejected. She was not represented at this hearing, indeed a person in Bad Reputation's office appeared not to have been aware that Leave had been sought. This person, who later took over the case, wrote to Carmen saying that 'I have been trying to find out about your case but am having some problems contacting Mr Clerk'.

Around the time of her unsuccessful Leave to Appeal, Carmen was transferred to a high-security prison in the north of England, so she attempted to engage a more local firm of solicitors, Solicitor Number Three. She was seen by a partner of this firm. However, Carmen remained with Bad Reputation for a while, since in 1989 she was transferred to another prison which is nearer London. Following the failure of her complaint against Bad Reputation and Co, Carmen discharged that company and appointed Solicitor Number Four. However, she became dissatisfied with them when they asked to be put in funds to the tune of £1,000. She then attempted to change to Solicitor Number Five, a name suggested by the Colombian Consulate.

Carmen's experience of being processed through the criminal justice system is one that is shared in its essentials by many others. Had her case come to court in the early 1990s, when bilateral agreements would be in place between Britain and Colombia to allow the British courts to seize assets in Colombia, then her home and business would have been at risk as well.

WHAT ARE PENALTIES FOR?

What kind of punishments, and at what levels, are in the public interest in relation to drug trafficking?

For some observers, the upwards escalation in penalties over the past two decades has been welcome, but the scale of the problem necessitates greater efforts. These further measures are merited not simply as a response to or deterrent against any involvement with drugs trafficking and consumption, but because of what that involvement is said to represent. For former US 'Drug Czar', William Bennett

> The drug crisis is a crisis of authority - in every sense of the term 'authority'.
> - What can be done to combat this crisis of authority? Two words sum up
> my entire approach: consequences and confrontation. Those who use, sell
> and traffic in drugs must be confronted, and they must suffer the
> consequences. By consequences, I mean that those who transgress must
> make amends for their transgressions. Consequences come in many forms.
> In terms of law enforcement, they include policies such as seizure of assets,
> stiffer prison sentences, revocation of bail rights, and the death penalty for
> drug kingpins. On these points I find general agreement...
>
> We need to do more. We need to reconstitute authority. What those of us
> in Washington, in the states, and in the localities can do is to exert the

political authority necessary to make a sustained commitment to the drug war. We must build more prisons. There must be more jails.

(Bennett 1989:4)

Such pronouncements rather exaggerate the degree of consensus that there is on matters of punishment. Not all Americans, for example, favour the death penalty and, in all probability, fewer Europeans would enthuse about it. Throughout the post-war years, penalties for trafficking have soared in virtually every country of the world, yet the problem remains. Is the death penalty the answer? Are more jails? Or imprisoning more people for longer terms?

A historical anomaly

In our view, the practical merits of long prison sentences for drug trafficking have not been established. Their preventive value has not been established. They are expensive to administer. Why then have such penalties?

Part of the answer is that these are expressive penalties, having as much or more to do with the declaration of disapproval of certain acts than with any real belief that they ameliorate the drug problem. Although in Europe there is less of a sense of the need to reconstitute authority than in the United States, that desire is certainly around. It has been in those terms of symbolic confrontation through enforcement that legislation and case-law on trafficking penalties have matured.

Although prison penalties (and traffickers' counter-measures) did go up considerably in the 1970s, the mid-1980s were the time of most rapid and publicised escalation. As Grieve notes,

> Calls for the death penalty were met with the introduction of life imprisonment (Controlled Drugs Penalties Act, 1985). More severe sentences for drug trafficking alone went up from 12 years to 28 years in a four year period at the Central Criminal Court.

(Grieve 1987:163)

A massive escalation of imprisonment came to be perceived as a modest reaction - perhaps even an under-reaction, by those who favoured the ultimate sanction. Life imprisonment, in this context, presented itself as the least that society could do. Even in countries where there has been a sustained and relatively successful attempt to reduce the average prison sentence, for instance The Netherlands, prison terms for trafficking have bucked the general trend, going up whilst most other sentences have gone down (Downes 1988).

The escalation in the use of imprisonment for drug trafficking runs counter to the general trend in the twentieth century for the relative decline in the use of custody. As we indicated above, financial penalties and various forms of punishment in the community have tended to *replace* custody. In the case of trafficking, however, there has been a doubling up process at work: traffickers are nowadays much more likely to be imprisoned for a long time if caught, *and* they are subject to financial penalties that go beyond the concept of the fine to include asset confiscation.

It is time to look more closely at this anomaly. A fundamental question is being overlooked. Do exceptionally long sentences do any good, in the simple sense of restraining the drug market? This is not an abstract question of whether imprisonment up to life ought, according to some moral calculus of deterrence, to be of benefit. Rather, it is a specific question: have escalating penalties over the past few decades actually achieved their declared intention?

It has to be acknowledged that the rapid development of the scale and sophistication of drug enforcement does have its success, with more and more people apprehended and convicted for a trafficking offence, whereupon they serve long prison sentences. Yet, in spite of this, drug markets continue to expand internationally and domestically in most countries: trafficking thrives, drug availability increases, use of illicit drugs is buoyant, going through changes in fashion in regard of the substances concerned but hardly crumpling under the onslaught of enforcement.

In our view, the original intention of the Hodgson Committee in Britain, to deploy asset confiscation as a partial alternative to longer terms of imprisonment, was a good one. Unfortunately, like many proposals for reform in the criminal justice system, what was intended as an alternative became an adjunct. The virtually simultaneous passage of the DTOA and the Controlled Drugs (Penalties) Act 1985, causing the penalty of asset confiscation to be introduced alongside a further escalation of maximum prison sentences, shows an excess of gung-ho sentiments (Clutterbuck 1990) over careful analysis.

Looked at most positively, the criminal justice systems could use asset confiscation orders alongside a reduction in long prison sentences. But this potential has not been realised in relation to trafficking offences.

Treatment and Rehabilitation

Although in certain aspects of controlling drug use, the drug user and the drug market are baldly stated and acted upon in law in Britain, this is but one side of coin. The other side, often integrally linked, relates to the treatment administered to drug users and the services that are provided for them. In the last section there were suggestions that much legislation controlling drugs and drug users has in part come about for political as opposed to purely scientific or rational reasons. Historically, the tension between treatment and control is no less pronounced. At times this has been a tension between the forces of law and order - should the addict be treated or punished? - but at other times it has been a tension between drug users and those involved in their treatment and rehabilitation. This is particularly true in relation to the debate on whether drug addicts should be provided with prescribed drugs or not. Stimson and Opppenheimer guide us through some of the specific tensions produced in the new clinics, set up in the late 1960s, partially intended to resolve the supposed problem of 'over-prescribing' by general practitioners. In particular, Stimson and Oppenheimer illustrate how health care workers and doctors in the new clinics introduced new restrictive treatment which moved away from the practice of prescribing to, and, maintaining addicts in favour of detoxification and withdrawal/abstinence regimes. The problem which is highlighted amongst the detail is the desire for the clinics and those working in them to 'cure' (produce an abstinent population) as opposed to maintaining a population of drug users on drugs of dependence - even when the aim of the drug user may be stability (through maintainence doses) as opposed to abstinence. In the 1980s and 1990s this tension remains, albeit with the debate taking place in a wider forum with broader concerns.

With the emergence of HIV/AIDS in the early to mid 1980s and the finding that in some areas, such as Edinburgh, up to 50% of the drug-injecting population had contracted the virus, primarily through the sharing of needles, there was a recognition that drug users were a high-risk group for disseminating the HIV virus into the general population through sexual intercourse (in Britain the virus had to this point been considered to be largely isolated within the gay community). This new context meant that *accessing* drug users in order to modify their drug-using behaviour (primarily away from needle-sharing) became, for many services, more important than trying to impose abstinence on them. The reduction of potential harm to the general population had superceded concern to control a specific population.

The re-introduction of harm reduction into the field of drug service provision was, as Berridge shows, not entirely new, but the emergence of HIV/AIDS facilitated and justified it as a policy. The tension between treatment and control had been eased by an issue which transcended that of drugs and their use. Saving the general poulation from HIV/AIDS was more important than saving drug users from drugs. Those who had always desired service provision based on harm reduction (to drug users) were given reign to change service provision, which was more customer-orientated (the drug users wanted) and not driven by contrived medical ethics or popular moralism. In *The Smoking Option*, Marks *et al* describe one such service based in Mersey, dedicated to

135

harm reduction, not merely for the general population but for the drug users who access the service. The tension between treatment and control in Britain remains, but it is less taut in the 1990s than for many years.

11. Developing Treatment Policies - Care Versus Control

Gerry Stimson and Edna Oppenheimer

'Sir,

In your article regarding the investigation of drug addiction, I was interested to read that no addict has apparently been interviewed during the preparation of the Brain Report...... If help is expected of them in the running of these treatment centres, the authorities are making a big mistake in neglecting the wealth of information available from addicts .... As an addict with a great deal of experience of other addicts, I cannot claim that they know all the answers but they should be given the opportunity of giving what information they can. I feel that "experts" cannot have had much personal contact with addicts and, perhaps, not enough knowledge of the drug itself .... This letter has been written on behalf of the heroin and cocaine addicts in the addiction unit of St Bernard's Hospital.

> Stevie F.M. (and Yuri W., Brian W.D., Brian D., Shirley A.)
> Southall, Middlesex'
> (*The Sunday Times* 6 March 1966)

The staff of the new Clinics were uncertain of their role. There were few medical workers with extensive experience of working with addicts, and for the most part the Clinics were staffed with newcomers to this area of medical work. True, there was a wealth of experience that could have been drawn upon. There were the experiences of the general medical practitioners who had prescribed heroin and cocaine, there were the voluntary workers in the West End, and there were the addicts themselves. In the main, however, the staff had to find out for themselves what the work would entail. There were two sorts of problems to be worked out: first, the day-to-day running of the Clinic; for example, how should consultations be organized and how should prescriptions actually be written and dispensed - in other words all the administrative details that have to be arranged in any medical facility, and the additional arrangements necessitated by the peculiar clientele of the Clinics. Second were the aims of the Clinics: what would they be and how would they be implemented? As we have suggested earlier, the change in policy suggested by the Brain Committee presented two jobs for the Clinics, that of treatment and that of the control of the drug problem, and it soon became apparent that these two aims may sometimes conflict. In this chapter we look at how treatment policies developed up to the mid-1970s, a period in which the numbers of Clinic patients in England and Wales gradually rose to about 1500 (see Table 6(1)).

The clinic setting

In order to understand how policies developed in the context of Clinic work it will help to summarize the setting in which the doctors, other staff, and addicts came together.

Gerry Stimson and Edna Oppenheimer: *HEROIN ADDICTION; TREATMENT AND CONTROL IN BRITAIN*, (Tavistock Publications, 1982), pp. 93-113.

Table 6(1) *Annual average numbers of out-patients attending NHS hospitals for narcotic drug addiction in England and Wales, 1968-78*

year	out-patients London	elsewhere	total
1968*	871	220	1091
1969	918	236	1154
1970	955	200	1155
1971	830	206	1036
1972	953	299	1252
1973	1045	335	1380
1974	1125	371	1496
1975	1145	401	1546
1976	1062	391	1453
1977	1023	409	1432
1978	1023	468	1491

Note: *From May.

Sources: Central Office of Information (1979) *Prevention and Treatment of Drug Misuse in Britain*; Johnson (1975); Institute for the Study of Drug Dependence (1980).

The facilities, quality of accommodation, and staffing varied from Clinic to Clinic, but a description of University College Hospital Drug Dependency Clinic will give an idea of what they were, and are, like. The U.C.H. Clinic, situated a few minutes walk north of Tottenham Court Road, where London's West End fades away to be replaced by small businesses, workshops, and residential housing, had its own rooms in the National Temperance Hospital, with a separate street entrance for patients. Staff entered through the main hospital. Entering the Clinic from the street there were a few steps up to a waiting area, which had wooden seating on three sides. The visitor may have found six or seven waiting patients. Just opposite the street door was a cubicle for the porter, who took details of arriving patients. To the right of the entrance, and in view of the porter, were male and female toilets. Beside the porter was a corridor leading to the consulting rooms, and a door into the secretaries' office. The corridor led off to several small rooms, which were used for consultations, and a larger one, used for staff meetings. Further round the corridor there were double doors leading into the main part of the National Temperance Hospital. The busiest part of the Clinic was the secretaries' room, a large room with side windows looking out on to the street. There were several desks, telephones, filing cabinets with patients' records, and, in one corner, a kettle and cups for coffee and tea. This room was occupied by two secretaries, but was also used by social workers and doctors. The door to the waiting room was usually open, but the secretaries' room was staff territory. A patient wanting the attention of a staff member would usually wait at the doorway. In 1975, this Clinic was under the charge of a part-time consultant, helped by another senior psychiatrist, working a total of six half-day sessions a week. There were two full-time secretaries, a part-time nursing sister, two full-time social workers, and a part-time clinical psychologist. There was also a social work adviser appointed by the area Social Services Department to liaise with local services and, unusually for many Clinics, to develop a service for intermittent drug users. The Clinic opened for three half-days a week, and one evening. During 1974, a total of 328 addict patients were treated by the Clinic, of whom 102 were new referrals. In addition, and this was unusual for many clinics, twenty-eight non-opiate-using patients were seen. The effective caseload in any month would be smaller than the overall total number of patients seen in the year. Most of the patients seen were aged in their twenties and three out of four were men.

Other Clinics may have slightly different facilities. For example, St Clement's in the East End had a large room which was used as a day centre for patients; this was equipped with tables and chairs, and staff provided hot lunches. It also, like some other Clinics, had a room where patients were allowed to inject. All Clinics were, and are, run as out-patient units, with variable access to in-patient facilities. At U.C.H. detoxification took time to arrange but some patients could be admitted to a general medical ward. Patients with medical, surgical, or obstetric problems were admitted to appropriate general wards. In London and adjacent areas, specialist in-patient units are located in St Bernard's Hospital in Southall, Bexley Hospital and the Royal Bethlem Hospital in Kent, and Tooting Bec Hospital.

Staff views of treating addicts

Many doctors view treating addicts as unattractive. When the Clinics were first established there was a marked reluctance among potential recruits to accept the invitation to work in them. Treating addicts is sometimes seen as a low-status occupation within psychiatry. It is an area of medicine with few of the rewards found in other medical jobs: one doctor, writing in *World Medicine*, put a view that is probably shared by many doctors looking, as outsiders, at the addiction field:

> 'Treating drug addicts in Britain is now a full-time job. You either do it or you don't. As I have a choice, I do not because the therapeutic rewards are so small. From the acquaintance I have had with addicts in our adolescent unit, I have found heroin addicts to be dull, proletarian and not particularly gifted or intelligent.'

> (Beard 1970)

This doctor assessed work with addicts from the point of view of 'therapeutic' rewards, or success in treating addicts. But what is meant by 'treatment' in the context of the Clinics? A major aspect of Clinic treatment was the prescription of opiate drugs. Nearly all the patients who attended London Clinics received prescriptions for drugs; in the sample we followed, it was extremely unusual for a person to attend a Clinic and not receive a prescription. There was considerable variation in practice around the country. In Bristol, Crawley, and other towns away from London, some doctors refused to prescribe injectable drugs. In Birmingham, and in many London Clinics in the first years, there were some doctors who preferred to prescribe injectable methadone, and those who would attempt to get patients quickly on to oral methadone. There were also variations within Clinics, with some receiving only methadone. Other treatment was also offered in the Clinics: group therapy, individual therapy, in-patient detoxification, referral to therapeutic communities, and a wide range of social-work help.

'Treatment' is a word that conjures up the image of individual therapy, involving either curing or caring. In the context of addiction, treatment might thus be construed as helping the addicted individual to become abstinent from drugs, or helping the individual to lead as trouble-free a life as possible whilst still being addicted. But in the context of the drug Clinic treatment was often a euphemism for other goals and we have to look not just at what was done to or for patients, but also at the clinicians' motivations in so acting.

To outsiders, the fact that the Clinics are staffed by medical people and are located in hospitals might suggest that the main aim for staff is to cure people of their addiction, to help them with their problems, or, very broadly, to provide some sort of therapy. But staff to whom we spoke in 1976 talked a great deal about 'control' and 'containment' of the drug problem as a major aspect of their work. Many described their work primarily in terms of social control, or talked about 'benefits to society', seeing themselves as working 'on behalf of society' to control the drug problem. For example, a psychiatrist at one Clinic had this to say:

> 'I was a bit worried last year because I felt that there were a lot of social workers working in addiction units, who were trying to deny that we as Clinic staff should have any concern for the social control of addiction, and were trying to deny that it was one of the aims of the Clinics.'

A similar point was made in a one-page handout from another clinic, which described the impact of their work:

> 'The Clinic opened in 1967 as one of the facilities proposed as an urgent measure under the second Brain Committee Report .... The more controlled prescribing policy initiated in 1967 would seem to be a qualified success from society's viewpoint. The number of opiate addicts known to the Home Office, particularly young addicts, has only increased slowly over the past four years. There is little evidence of wide-scale illegal importation of heroin into this country and whilst the majority of addicts coming to this Clinic have criminal records, the extent of their criminal activity nowhere reaches that reported of American addicts.'

This is not to say that the staff saw their work only as social control; the people who made these statements also talked of therapy. Nevertheless, it is unusual in medicine for doctors to refer to their work as social control. Even in areas of medicine in which we can see that doctors' work is more to do with social control than treatment - for example, in issuing sickness certificates, or the detention of the mentally ill - doctors are rarely so consciously explicit about their work.

The emergence of this social control orientation can be traced to the reformulation of British policy in the second Brain Committee report of 1965. The Committee recognized that it was necessary in some circumstances to prescribe opiates to addicts, but also saw that over-prescribing could itself contribute to the increase in addiction by making supplies readily available: as the Committee put it 'if there is insufficient control it may lead to the spread of addiction - as is happening at present' (Interdepartmental Committee on Drug Addiction 1965: 7). But the dilemma was that a complete ban on heroin and cocaine, or severe restrictions on availability, might 'prevent or seriously discourage the addict from obtaining any supplies from legitimate sources' and might 'lead to the developmental of an organised illicit traffic' (Interdepartmental Committee on Drug Addiction 1965: 7). Following this analysis it was expected that Clinics should prescribe opiates in competition with, or to prevent, the development of a black market. Such a policy was often described as 'competitive prescribing' or 'keeping the Mafia out'. Let us see the implications of this policy for staff. The Clinic would be a legal source of drugs and it was hoped that this would undercut or prevent a black market. After all, if addicts could get drugs legally, the attraction of a black market should decrease. The main aim of treatment then was not necessarily individual therapy, but an attempt to affect the drug scene, mainly the supply of drugs, by the way in which individual patients were handled. Such a policy required staff to attract patients to the Clinics, to keep them there, and prescribe conservatively and accurately.

The policy of social control

How did this policy affect the doctors in the Clinics? First, they saw that their job was mainly to deal with the heroin problem, rather than deal with drug problems in general. So, with a few exceptions, they restricted their caseloads to people who were addicted to heroin or other opiates. Wary of turning on a person who was not addicted, and wishing to confine the caseload to opiate addicts, their work required an elaborate and extended process of diagnosis and acceptance. A new patient was usually expected to prove that he or she was addicted to an opiate, and a procedure developed whereby people were expected to give at least one, and usually two or three, samples of urine, which were then tested for the presence of opiates. The evidence from the specimens was checked against a detailed history of drug use, and a physical examination was conducted, which looked for signs of self-injection (the extent, site, and age of injection marks, scars, or abscesses) and for the presence of withdrawal symptoms. It was usually necessary for a patient to attend the clinic two or three times before a diagnosis was reached and a prescription decided upon (or not). The yearly numbers of new attenders at Clinics in England and Wales from 1969 to 1973 varied between 500 and 800, but not all patients were accepted (Johnson 1975: 50-1). One study, conducted in 1971, looked at new patients approaching Clinics and found that about a third of them did not receive any prescription, at least initially. Those who were not prescribed were those whose urine was found to contain no traces of opiates (Blumberg et al. 1974).

Second, as the policy required Clinic workers to control the drug problem through controlling drug supplies, much of the work in the Clinics centred around questions of how much and what should be prescribed. The task was difficult for staff. The problem was to prescribe enough drugs so that these patients did not turn to the black market for supplies, yet at the same time not to prescribe *too much* in case the patients sold their supplies and fed the black market. To do this, staff felt that they needed an effective intelligence system, to gauge what was going on 'out there', in order to make decisions about individual patients. They sought to know what drugs were available on the black market, and whether the ones being sold were legally prescribed, stolen, or illegally imported. Hence the perennial attempts by doctors to establish how many addicts there are 'out there' who do not come to the Clinics but who survive on black market supplies.

The prescribing 'tightrope' was difficult to walk. A basic problem was that there were often alternative drugs available on the black market. After the Clinics were established many other drugs became popular. In the first few months doctors made a concerted effort to reduce or eliminate the prescribing of cocaine, reasoning that it was not a drug of dependence and was, therefore, one that patients could forego. Many addicts were soon obtaining supplies of methedrine ampoules instead, an injectable amphetamine with stimulant effects, and two private doctors, Petro and Swan, switched many patients to methdrine when they were no longer allowed to prescribe heroin and cocaine. Underground newspapers campaigned against its use under the slogan 'Speed Kills' and *International Times* (9 August 1968) described it as 'one of the most dangerous drugs around at the moment'. Methedrine was eventually restricted in October 1968 when the Ministry of Health persuaded the makers, Burroughs Wellcome, to supply it only to hospitals. Ritalin, another stimulant, was popular for a short time in 1973, and from 1975 onwards illicitly manufactured amphetamine sulphate was available. Towards the end of 1968 and the beginning of 1969, just as the Clinics were beginning to drastically reduce the amount of heroin prescribed, illicitly produced heroin appeared on the black market. Until this time nearly all the heroin available in Britain had been obtained on prescription and then sold. This new, illicit heroin was imported from Hong Kong where it was manufactured from morphine or heroin obtained from the Golden Triangle in South-East Asia. It was sold by Chinese in Soho - hence its name, 'Chinese heroin'. It has continued to be available, with sporadic changes in availability, ever since. The other popular alternatives to heroin have been sleeping pills, such as Mandrax (methaqualone), and barbiturates, such as Tuinal, Secondal, Nembutal, and Sodium Amytal, all of which can be injected after they have been dissolved in water.

In the early days at the Clinics, the majority of patients, between 60 and 80 per cent, received prescriptions for heroin. The peak months for prescribing the drug, in terms of total quantities, were July and August 1968 when a total of 5889 grams of heroin were supplied to addicts. In the early years of the Clinics, doctors attempted to reduce the quantity prescribed by reducing average doses per patient and by transferring people to methadone: the total quantity of heroin prescribed had fallen to 3685 grams for July and August 1969, and in that year only 34 per cent of patients received heroin (*see also Tables 6(2)* and *6(3)*. Transfers were often achieved by a straight exchange of methadone ampoules for heroin pills, the 'rate' being one 10 mg ampoule of methadone for a 10 mg heroin pill. Methadone as a drug of choice has a peculiar history in British addiction treatment. Originally promoted in the US by Dole and Nyswander (1965) as a substitute for heroin, it was preferred by the medical profession because it 'blocked' the effects of the small doses of illicit heroin taken by American patients and because it could be taken in an oral (not injectable) form. When it was introduced in Britain it was not for its blockading effects, which do not occur with the larger doses of heroin used in Clinics here. It was introduced to addicts in injectable form because of its longer lasting effects, which meant that addicts would have to inject less frequently than with heroin. In addition, it could be dispensed in ampoule form ready for injection, thus reducing risks of infection, and did not produce the immediate, exciting 'buzz' associated with heroin. It was hoped, then, that addicts would be persuaded to accept methadone as a small step towards eventual abstinence. Taking the addicts in our sample as an example, in 1969 they were all initially prescribed heroin, but four out of five of them additionally received some form of methadone within six months of the Clinics opening.

Table 6(2) *Amounts of heroin and methadone presribed to addicts attending NHS hospitals in England and Wales (in grams)*

year	heroin	methadone ampoules	lintus and tablets
1968	16895*	**	**
1969	22778	4371*	1432*
1970	17392	11344	3488
1971	14201	11548	3742
1972	14322	14227	8227
1973	14287	19099	9072
1974	15332	21454	8295
1975	15474	20937	9563
1976	13178	17297	11682
1977	10924	14668	14022
1978	8501	14003	17498

Note: *This total is for the 6 months from July to December. **Figures not available, but totals are less than in subsequent years.

Sources: Johnson (1975); Institute for the Study of Drug dependence (1980).

By the end of 1969, nearly 50 per cent of Clinic patients in England and Wales were receiving solely methadone, and only a third were still receiving prescriptions for heroin (*see Table 6(3)*). (It is worth noting that since our sample of patients were those who were receiving heroin in 1969, they were already part of a rapidly declining proportion of Clinic patients). Since 1970, the proportion of patients receiving heroin has continued to decline, until by 1978 less than 10 per cent of them received it. It would not be exceptional for a new Clinic patient to be given heroin. Since 1970 there has been a corresponding increase in the percentage of patients being prescribed only methadone, from approximately 50 per cent at the beginning of the decade to over 70 per cent by 1978 (*see Table 6(3)*).

Interaction between staff and patients

The Clinics are an unusual medical setting in which there is a higher level of overt conflict between patients and staff than is found elsewhere in medicine, with the possible exception of Accident and Emergency departments. In most medical work settings there is the appearance of calm and order, with the views of patients often being ignored or prevented from emerging. But it is not like this in the drug Clinics. Patients' views are vociferously expressed and are difficult to ignore or suppress. Our fieldnotes written after our visits give some flavour of the atmosphere at the Clinics in 1976, and we believe are illustrative of their first few years. One of us wrote the following:

'The Clinic was teeming with people - a great deal of activity. At least twenty-seven addicts attended today and more were expected. The 'phone range continuously. The secretaries were busy writing out all the prescriptions and handing these and the notes to Dr T. to sign. Everyone seemed to be in a tremendous hurry. Constantly clients were coming up to the office door asking how much longer they had to wait.

All the addicts seem to know each other and there were little groups in the waiting room talking together.

My prospective interviewee arrived late and was in a bit of a state today. She was immediately approached by the social worker and agreed to be interviewed, but only after going to the toilet. She stayed there for a very long time. Staff were very suspicious because fixing is not allowed in the toilet.

Meanwhile M., who was hovering about listlessly at the door of the office, had been telling the staff that he wanted to get off drugs but he didn't think he could manage it at F. hospital. He wanted admission elsewhere. The secretaries suggested that he talk to the doctor about this - but not before telling him that as he is after all a junkie, why does he think he should get special treatment?

Incidentally, J., who is in our sample, turned up at the clinic. He came out of prison this morning. I gather that he wrote to Dr U. from prison asking for an early appointment. He was offered one for tomorrow. He was already very drugged because he had been to Piccadilly and scored on the way to the Clinic. He could hardly stand up. He asked for syringes from the staff nurse and there was a bit of discussion about this. The social worker warned him that if he were found with drugs and syringes today he would be in 'illegal possession' as the Clinic was not yet officially prescribing for him. He didn't seem to care and said that he wrote to Dr U. in order to avoid such a situation. He couldn't wait till tomorrow for his drugs. Finally, he was supplied with syringes and sent off with warnings to be careful.'

We noted the following observations a few days later, at a staff meeting at the same Clinic:

'Earlier in the week there had been some trouble at the Clinic when a patient had become violent. There was a discussion on how to handle such situations in future and a "post mortem" on events of this week. Apparently the hospital security man was not available, so the police were called (after the patient attacked the doctor). By the time the police came, the patient

Table 6(3) *Addict patients receiving prescriptions for different types of drugs*

year	total	heroin only	heroin plus methadone	methadone only or with drugs other than heroin	other drugs only**
		%	%	%	%
1968	-	*estimated 60-80 per cent heroin with or without methadone		-	-
1969	1466	14	20	49	17
1970	1430	13	18	51	18
1971	1555	10	15	60	15
1972	1615	9	12	67	12
1973	1815	9	12	67	12
1974	1969	8	12	66	14
1975	1951	5	11	68	16
1976	1876	4	9	70	17
1977	2018	3	8	69	20
1978	2406	3	6	71	20

Note: The numbers on which these percentages are based derive from Home Office notifications and are not directly comparable to the other tables, which are based on Department of Health returns from Clinics. The base figures refer to the UK (rather than England and Wales), include in-patients, and are as of year end (rather than annual averages). *Personal communication, Department of Health and Social Security. **Mainly opiates.

Sources: as for Table 6(1).

was calmer and with the social worker so the police left without waiting. Later, when the patient still refused to go, the police were called again but refused to come. It was decided that in future, if the police are called, the patient should be escorted out of the premises. There was some discussion about security for the staff and alarm systems but Dr U. thought that the 'phone was the best way, or simply a loud shout to alert others in the Clinic. It was suggested that, as a sanction against violence, patients could be required, if disruptive, to attend the in-patient unit and/or collect their scripts once or twice daily.'

Similar incidents were observed on a visit to another Clinic at about the same time:

'The door was locked at 5.00 pm and a couple of minutes later the doorbell rang. Somehow the staff knew (by looking out of the window?) that it was a patient who was due up for an appointment. The patient lives outside of London and comes up to the Clinic monthly for his prescription. The doorbell rang several times. Dr P. refused to allow him to be let in. The secretary had to go to the door, the door was kept on the chain. The office window was closed, and Dr P. told us to sit down - in order to keep out of sight from the street. The porter was told to lock the back door. Apparently when the patient came up he liked to stay over in London in order to score in the Dilly. Dr P. likes to get him back to where he lives as soon as possible. Last time they gave him a one-day rail warrant so that he had to return the same day; he kicked up a fuss and wouldn't leave the clinic. This time I think the secretary gave him his prescription through the door. Patient then hung around in the street for a while.

At 5.10 a friend of M.K. 'phoned saying there had been a bomb scare on the tube and that M.K. was in a taxi on the way to the Clinic. The secretary explained that it was too late as the Clinic was closed. Some doubt about whether M.K. had actually left home. The Sister spoke to the friend and said that M.K. would have to come in for an appointment to get her prescription. The Sister challenged the friend by saying that she suspected that they had both been taking too many sleeping tablets (and had overslept). She said to us it sounded like M.K. was in the background. It was agreed to leave the prescription for one day's supply at the porter's lodge.'

Finally, from the notes of the next visit to the Clinic:

'All in all quite a difficult afternoon for the staff and they had my sympathy. There was a patient who was in with his parents, arguing with staff that he should be put on injectable drugs. This person had been involved in some sort of armed robbery and had spent some time in prison. Staff told me he was suggesting that if he was not put on injectable drugs he would get a gun and shoot someone or himself. Seemed quite extraordinary to me that a bank robber should be at the Clinic with his mum and dad! He must have been there for at least an hour-and-a-half and was seen by Dr P., the Sister, and the social worker. The staff saw this [his threats] as an attempt to blackmail them and refused to put him on injectable drugs.

I was in the office and the staff mentioned that a patient was in the waiting room crying because his prescription had been reduced by one pill on a previous occasion, and how he had thought he might get it back but now realized he wouldn't. Later there was a problem between him and the secretary over his fares. The discussion over the fares went on for three-quarters of an hour, on-and-off, with the patient trying different approaches. Then a twenty-minute discussion between him and the Sister. He had been complaining that the didn't even have money for cigarettes, so the social worker gave him one from her pack, "on the NHS" as she said. The Sister, getting a bit tough with him, suggesting that if he really wanted some money he should get a job. The patient complained that he was too busy at the moment moving into ROMA (a hostel). He had been seen by Dr P. that afternoon but wanted to see him again for "two minutes"; he tried to corner Dr P. as he came into the office but Dr P. kept moving and said that he was already running an hour late. The patient asked if he could wait until the end of the Clinic to see Dr P. Dr P. said it was unlikely as he had to be at another hospital.'

Developing work routines

As is obvious from these reports, a major concern for staff in this medical setting, as in any other, was to keep sufficient order in their work-place to allow them to pursue their work in their chosen way, with minimum interruption. It is clear from other research work on encounters between doctors and patients that patient behaviour that is perceived by staff as disruptive and manipulative is met by staff strategies that aim to maintain staff dominance (Roth 1963; Stimson and Webb 1975). The drug Clinics are no exception - a wide range of staff strategies emerged that were used to keep some sense of order.

The task of prescribing drugs would be easier if the addict patients agreed with the aims of doctors. However, many do not. Addict patients know what they want and are not reluctant to convey this to staff. Furthermore, what they want is often not what the staff are prepared to give. Where staff and patients differ is in their ideas about the nature and meaning of drug use; the purpose of the Clinic, rights to prescription, and the place of therapy. The central conflict is that addict patients maintain that they have a need for the drugs they are addicted to and that it is the function of the clinic to help them by providing them with a legal and regular supply, whilst the staff see that prescribing is not a right of patients but at their discretion.

A common view among the staff we met was that 'most addicts are liars'. Indeed, in a situation where one group wants something over which another group has a monopoly, and where that second group wishes to restrict the supply, the situation is one that will generate lying on both sides. As we have observed, the upshot is that staff distrust patients, are suspicious of them, and are ever on the lookout against being conned by them. To drive this point home, staff would calculate how much a patient's prescription would be worth if sold on the street. One consultant pointed out that a patient selling a daily prescription for fifty pills of heroin would have a daily, untaxed income of around £100 (in 1976). On the other hand, patients often told staff they were using illegal drugs, hoping to persuade staff to increase the prescription of opiates. We have already seen that Clinics instituted procedures for testing urine each time the patient attended and sanctions might be imposed if illegal drugs were found to be present. In one set of case notes, the doctor referred to a 'disciplinary reduction' in dosage because illegal drugs were found in a patient's urine.

Many other procedures and rules grew up around the issue of prescriptions and the dispensing of drugs. Before the Clinics opened there were no restrictions on the quantities prescribed nor on the period the prescription was to cover. In July 1967, the Ministry of Health, following discussion with doctors working in the field, and with the Pharmaceutical Society and the NHS Chemist Contractors Committee representing dispensing chemists, circularized doctors working with addicts with guidance on precautions to prevent the misuse of prescriptions; the Memorandum in question was entitled *Treatment and Supervision of Heroin Addiction: Precautions Against Misuse of Prescriptions* (Ministry of Health 1967 and 1968). The aim was to ensure that heroin-addict patients would receive no more than one or two days' supply at a time. Since it was thought impracticable to require addicts to attend Clinics at intervals of one or two days, the measures enabled doctors to write prescriptions for longer periods, which could be dispensed daily or at other short intervals. Clinic doctors were recommended to restrict the total quantity prescribed to one week's supply (this was later extended to two weeks), with the prescription showing the amounts to be dispensed each day. For days when retail chemists or hospital pharmacies did not open, for example on Sundays and public holidays, multiple quantities were to be dispensed on preceding days. The prescription form indicated the day from which dispensing was to begin. To avoid the concentration of addicts at chemists' shops at opening times, some prescriptions were endorsed with a time, agreed between the retail chemists, before which the drugs would not be dispensed (usually 10.00 am). In general medical practice in the NHS, prescriptions are handed to patients who then take them to the retail pharmacist. Clinic doctors were advised not to give prescriptions to addict patients but to post them direct to the chemist. A new patient for whom heroin or methadone was to be prescribed should be introduced in person by a member of the hospital staff to the chemist, or, where this was not possible, the doctor should provide the patient with a letter of introduction. In the case of illness or other incapacity that prevented the patient from collecting the drugs, special alternative arrangements were to be made with the Clinic. Retail chemists were not allowed to dispense heroin to anyone other than the addict in person, unless under an arrangement with the authority of the prescribing doctor at the clinic. The chemists, for their part, were entitled to refuse to enter into arrangements to dispense heroin, or to restrict the number of such patients they received. When each daily quantity was distributed, the chemist endorsed the reverse of the prescription with the date and quantity dispensed, and entered each separate dispensation into the chemists' Dangerous Drugs Register. Heroin, along with other dangerous drugs, was to be kept under special secure conditions at the chemists' shops.

Most other rules concerning prescriptions were not formalized as they were in this Memorandum but emerged in response to problems that staff faced in dealing with patients. For example, staff thought that addicts would try to con extra drugs using the excuse that their drugs were lost or stolen. Most Clinics had a policy that there would be no variation in a prescription during the time for which it was issued. This problem was discussed at the staff meeting in one of the Clinics that we visited in 1976:

> 'Re-affirmation of policy that "no rises" or replacements for lost drugs shall be given. The doctor felt that this policy, now adopted by most Clinics, makes sense at it avoids long discussion and arguments about dosages. In fact someone at the clinic today had just received a rise .... He was told by staff not to tell anyone about this rise and said that he wouldn't.

There are two interesting points here: first, having a rule makes life easier for staff - they can refer to the rule as limiting their options, so avoiding individualized discussion with patients. Second, deviations from the rule must not be disclosed to patients - if they find out one person has had a 'rise', 'they will all want one'. The 'no tomorrows today' rule, also known as the 'no advances' rule, was part of the same policy - it prevented patients getting some of the next day's prescriptions in advance. Advances would have had to be authorized by a 'pick-up slip' presented to the chemist, allowing him or her to vary the prescription. A policy of 'no pick-up slips' backed-up the 'no tomorrows' rule. In some Clinics there were notices informing patients of these regulations, and *Figure 6(1)* reproduces a letter to patients outlining such rules.

A major consequence of a drug-control policy that put the responsibility for control in the hands of Clinic staff was that much of their time was taken up in administrative tasks concerning the issue of prescriptions. But there were many other problems that arose in Clinics that staff sought to prevent, such as buying and selling of drugs, faking urine tests, disruptions, and disrespect for staff territory. In some Clinics a staff 'bouncer' role developed - played by a person who had the respect of patients and who could keep order. It was not a fixed staff role but was adopted in different Clinics by a nurse, porter, or receptionist. The physical location of such a person in the Clinic was important. If, for example, injecting in the toilets was not allowed, the staff member had to be able to observe who entered the toilet and how long they stayed.

Figure 6(1) *Letter sent to patients by a clinic consultant in 1977.*

Dear Patient,

I understand that since I have temporarily replaced Dr. D. at this clinic, rumours have arisen that I intend to make drastic changes.

This letter is to reassure you that this is NOT so.

It is my intention to enable you to lead as normal a life as possible and so interfere with your present prescription as little as possible. However, this means not only not reducing your script but also not increasing your script.

Extras and Advances. The policy of the clinic of strict control over issuing of extras and/or advances will continue.

Requests for Extra Issues or Replacements will be refused and you must accept full responsibility for your medication and take special care of it so that it is not lost, mislaid, destroyed, stolen, mis-injected or misused. Very rarely, and only in exceptional circumstances, Mist. Methadone D.T.F. may be issued.

Requests for Advances, such as for picking up drugs a day early at short notice, put a great strain on the clinic staff and telephoning the clinic for special arrangements to be made with your chemist is very time-consuming and involves much extra work. This will have to be discontinued.

You are, therefore, asked to inform us a full week in advance if you intend to go on holiday, away for a weekend, on a course or any other reason for early issue so that an alternative chemist can dispense and arrangements made for this.

Voluntary Withdrawl. As you may know the in-patient treatment unit at J. Hospital (B Ward) is being renovated and redecorated and so will not be open until March 1977.

Whilst I believe that withdrawal from drugs is best effected by in-patient treatment, I am very willing to co-operate with any patient who voluntarily wishes to try an out-patient basis reduction of medication with a view to withdrawal.

Any patient who wishes to try to manage on a lower dosage of drugs need only mention this to the doctor and an agreed reduction will be made. I wish to assure you that should such reduction fail, that is, that you find yourself unable to cope on the reduced dosage, the doctor will change your medication and if need be increase the reduced dosage up to the amount you were receiving at the time you volunteered to reduce (but no higher).

Do not worry about failure, you can always try again.

Appointments. I am trying to arrange the appointments system on a time basis and ask your co-operation in attending on the day and time given you.

I hope, too, in the very near future to allocate patients to one particular doctor so that you see 'your own doctor' each visit. Poor time-keeping only leads to confusion in the clinic and a long wait to see the doctor. Your co-operation in respect of appointments is earnestly requested so that the clinic can function smoothly and mistakes, tensions and frustations minimised.

Finally I would be very pleased to receive constructive suggestions or criticism which you consider may help the smooth running of this clinic.

Sanctions imposed on patients who misbehaved included dosage reductions, switches from heroin to injectable methadone or oral methadone, or temporary cancellation of the prescription. Such sanctions might be imposed for failure to attend an appointment, if the patient was arrested, of if the patient did not work - as in this doctor's notes of a consultation:

> 'I made the following bargain (my offer, not his). I will supply heroin 5 x 10 mg pills daily from 14.2.75 if he can tell me of a job arranged when he comes on March 5 (with starting date) and can show me pay slips the following visit. If unemployed we shall use time for a transfer to methadone.'

Similar constraints over patient behaviour were exercised in in-patient drug units. At some, patients were asked to sign 'good behaviour' contracts; an example of these is given in *Figure 6(2)*. Addicts cannot be compulsorily detained under the Mental Health Act on the grounds of their addiction alone, but they may be 'encouraged' to stay in hospital by, as one consultant reported, the doctor's 'simple manoeuvre of refusing to supply drugs if they discharge themselves before completion of their withdrawl programme'. This coercive aspect of the doctor-addict relationship is so taken for granted that doctors do not hesitate to publicly write about this policy.

Figure 6(2) *'Good behaviour' contract for an addict in-patient admission at a London teaching hospital in 1976.*

Conditions applying to Drug Clinic patients during in-patient treatment in hospitals.

1. Visitors must be discussed with the clinic staff prior to admission. Nobody other than those agreed upon will be allowed to visit.

2. You will be expected to remain on the ward throughout your stay in the hospital.

3. You will be expected to remain dressed in pyjamas and dressing-gown while in the hospital.

4. The staff reserve the right to inspect parcels.

5. You are free to leave the hospital at any time. BUT if you leave without the agreement of the staff you will not be readmitted.

6. You are expected to use NO DRUGS other than those prescribed by the hospital staff.

I have read these conditions and accept them.

Signed   ....

Date   ....

The ability of staff to pursue such coercive strategies was enhanced by limitations on patient mobility. Clients can exert more influence over professionals when they are able to pick and choose who to consult; conversely, the power of the doctor is increased when the patient has no choice about consultation. Administrative encumbrances limit patient choice of doctor within the NHS, but patient choice was even more restricted in the Clinics. Clinics agreed among themselves not to accept patients seeking transfers from other Clinics, except in special circumstances. The Home Office notification system was used by Clinic staff to assist in preventing client movement - to check if a prospective patient was at another Clinic all that was necessary was a telephone call to the Home Office Drugs Branch. The experience of the patients in the sample of addicts we followed may be typical: in the years from 1969 to 1979, 86 per cent stayed with their original Clinic and only 14 per cent transferred to a different one.

How did staff rationalize strategies that in other medical settings would be frowned upon and that could even be seen as ethically dubious? First, addicts are well known as being difficult patients. Clinic staff felt therefore, that they were only doing what other reasonable people would do if faced with the same situation. Second, addicts, like other patients such as the mentally ill, the handicapped, or the old, are looked upon as being, in a sense, disfranchised: they might have interactive power but they have little economic or political power; they are marginal and have no effective protest. Third, staff did not see addicts as really being like other hospital patients. We found that, in their eyes, many addicts did not fit the patient role: they did not seem to want to get better (or change), they were incorrigible, they seemed to enjoy their 'illness', they behaved as though they were absolved of social obligations (in fact, staff thought that they were malingerers and should get jobs), they did not seek 'advice' or 'help' from doctors, and did not co-operate in getting 'better'. Fourth, staff could explain patient misbehaviour in terms of psychopathology: the aggravation of patients was seen as due to their 'immaturity', 'low thresholds of aggression', 'high levels of hostility', and so on; in other words it was seen as emanating in the person's psyche and not in the social situation.

Why did staff and patients endure such conflicting relationships? One solution to a difficult relationship is to terminate it; and this was certainly an option in the Clinic, but it was a limited option. From the patient's point of view, attendance would not be terminated until he or she was ready to give up drugs, or as long as the Clinic was the easiest source of their supply - the 'hassle' of the Clinic was weighed against the hassle of the black market. Clinic staff seemed to temper their termination option because it ran counter to what they saw as their broader function of social control, which could not be pursued if a patient no longer attended; therefore staff were not usually willing to terminate the relationship.

Control over the prescribing doctor

It was not only the addicts who became subject to more control, for the 1968 policy changes also introduce more governmental control over doctors. The individual GP, isolated from colleagues, was always in a potentially weak position *vis-a-vis* addicts, and the history of GP prescribing in the 1960s show how vulnerable these doctors were. The transfer of addiction treatment to the hospital system, and exclusion of the ordinary practitioner, made the activities of doctors involved much more visible, and provided them with possibilities for seeking advice and moral backing.

In a sense, the setting up of the clinics made possible increased state control over both the addicts and the doctors. While both groups may at times have been confused about the policy aims, the situation could be seen more clearly by outsiders (and is easier to see now, with hindsight). A particularly perceptive comment on the policy aims was made by Roy Jenkins, who was Labour Home Secretary under the Wilson government in 1967 when the details for the Clinics were being negotiated. He recalled the position that was adopted:

> 'Throughout, I was firmly against criminalising addiction, as I think we all were. What was wanted was other kinds of social controls, for the addicts under medical care and also - very importantly - for the doctors themselves. We thought that a chief objective had to be to institutionalise the care of addicts through the Clinic setting, in which nobody would be acting alone, but, instead, as part of a group with checks and supports for the doctors as well as more visible controls supporting the addicts.'

(Judson 1974: 91)

Practising medicine in this area became a relatively 'public' endeavour with the doctors' activities monitored by colleagues and government agencies. For example, the Clinics sent details of their patients to the Department of Health and these were then compiled to give data on the average doses prescribed at each Clinic. These data were available to Clinic consultants. The consultants met every three months at the Department of Health where they discussed their activities. There were similar meetings for social workers. Perhaps because the clinician group was small, approximately fifteen consultants and thirty junior doctors in London, the doctors were peculiarly sensitive to the comments of their colleagues. The Home Office and the Department of Health were also in a position to monitor the activities of the Clinics. It would not be accurate to think of clear-cut policy directives emanating from the government. Again, the influence was subtle. Indeed the very fact of being monitored may have exerted some influence over the doctors.

Such monitoring, though, was not unwanted or disliked by Clinic consultants; indeed, they were on friendly, first-name terms with the civil servants at the Home Office and the Department of Health. They met at conferences and seminars, they exchanged information, and were often in contact by telephone. The close involvement of these non-medical people was not seen by the doctors as a threat to their clinical freedom or professional autonomy, or as an interference in their decisions about the treatment of patients. We have seen how the primary task of the clinics was defined as the social control of addiction, and if medical work is seen as control rather than treatment then outside involvement is no danger to the position of doctors, indeed it is welcome. The doctors, then, did not see outsiders as enemies, but as allies in the fight against the 'drug problem'.

12. AIDS and British Drug Policy: History Repeats Itself . . . ?

Virginia Berridge

There appear to have been some radical changes in British drug policy since the advent of AIDS. Since the discovery of the HIV virus among British drug users at the end of 1985, the pace of policy change has been rapid. Two major reports on AIDS and Drug Misuse have followed, together with £17 million for the development of drug services. At least 100 needle exchanges offering new for used syringes are the most tangible public expression of new developments, underlining the view that the danger of the spread of AIDS from drug users into the general population is a greater threat to the nation's health than the danger of drug misuse itself. British drug policy and in particular the visible manifestation of a harm-minimisation approach in the form of needle exchanges, has attracted worldwide attention. Some commentators have as a result argued that AIDS has changed the direction of British drug policy.

> The only instance of AIDS overriding established policy objectives has been in the field of drugs . . . . The Government had abandoned its previous stance of augmenting its restrictive and punitive policies on drugs now that AIDS had come to be seen as the greater danger.[1]

Others have been more cautions. Gerry Stimson comments:

> these new ideas appear as a distinct break with earlier ones, but as with many conceptual and practical changes, the possibilities are inherent in earlier ideas and work. It is perhaps a matter of emphasis and direction, rather than abrupt rupture with the recent past.[2]

Susanne MacGregor is also more sceptical. 'Are we now entering a new fourth phase in British policy and practice regarding drugs, or are we seeing merely a modification to the third phase?'[3]

This paper aims to look at the question of the 'newness' of British drug policy post-AIDS. How far has drug policy been radically changed under the impact of AIDS? How far has AIDS been simply a vehicle whereby developments inherent in existing policy have been achieved more quickly than might otherwise have been possible? From a longer term perspective, how much is really new at all; how far do recent changes merely exemplify some very long-standing themes and tensions in British drug policy?

One historical analogy is with the debates around the impact of war on social policy. Historians have in recent years begun to look more closely at the impact of the First and Second World Wars on social and health policy in particular. They have questioned the view that war was the only catalyst for radical change. In the Second World War,

Reproduced from David K. Whynes and Philip T. Bean (eds), *POLICING AND PRESCRIBING THE BRITISH SYSTEM OF DRUG CONTROL*, (Macmillan, 1991), pp. 176-199. © David K. Whynes and Philip T. Bean 1991. Reprinted with permission of The Macmillan Press Limted.

for example, the 'national consensus for social change' appears to have been less than unanimous; and the roots of the National Health Service, established in 1948, can be found not just in wartime change, but in pre-war debates and blueprints for health care. What war did was to enable this to happen more quickly and in rather a different fashion (the nationalisation of the hospitals, for example, rather than local authority control) than might otherwise have been the case. War served, too, to lay bare the deficiencies of the existing system. The chaotic overlap of hospital services and structures pre-war was quickly rationalised in the emergency Medical Service in the war; war served to overcome vested interests and opposition to change but essential continuities with the pre-war service remained.[4] AIDS, too, fits into this paradigm. Like war, it evoked a period of political emergency reaction which was at its peak from 1986-87, but which, in the case of drugs, spilled over into 1988 with the government reaction to the Advisory Council on the Misuse of Drugs Part I report on *AIDS and Drug Misuse*. Many of the actions of central government in this period had a wartime flavour - the creation of an interdepartmental Cabinet committee chaired by William Whitelaw, Deputy Prime Minister, the 'AIDS week' on television in February 1987, when both television companies joined together on a war time model; the Commons emergency debate in November 1986.[5]

Drug policy in the 1980s: before AIDS

How far did this emergency reaction stimulate genuine new departures? To analyse this question in relation to drug policy, it is first necessary briefly to sketch in developments in the preceding years. Drug policy in Britain has been characterised historically in terms of four distinct phases. The first, in the nineteenth century, saw gradually increasing professional controls inserted into a system of open availability of opiate drugs.[6] A more stringent reaction established during the 'cocaine epidemic' of the First World War, heralded a new phase of policy.[7] The 1920 Dangerous Drugs Act marked a penal reaction to drug use; but the Rolleston Report of 1926 reasserted what became known as the 'British System' of medical prescribing of opiates, a system of medical control operating within a more penal framework of national and international controls.[8] It was not until late 1960s that a new and third phase began. The development of a drugs subculture, over-prescribing by a number of London doctors, were among the factors leading to a change in policy. The second Brain Committee report in 1965 led to changes in drug policy, in particular the limitation of the prescribing of heroin and cocaine to doctors licensed to do so by the Home Office; treatment of addiction was re-located in the 'clinics', hospital-based drug dependency units. These initially operated as prescribing centres, in the belief that 'competitive prescribing' would undercut and curtail the development of a black market in drugs. Changes in clinic policies in the 1970s, however, brought a decline in opiate prescribing and a rise in more active treatment, methods, based on short-term methadone prescribing or on no prescribing at all.[9]

In the early 1980s, drug policy again entered a new phase. What were the main changes which characterised it? Firstly, a 'new' drug problem began to emerge. At the beginning of the 1980s, the numbers of addicts notified to the Home Office underwent a sharp increase although the numbers had in fact been rising more slowly since the mid-1970s.

The 3425 addicts notified in 1975 had risen to over 12 000 by 1984. At the same time the amount of heroin seized by Customs rocketed - from under 50kg in 1980 to over 350kg in 1984. The real price of heroin in London is estimated to have fallen by 20 per cent between 1980 and 1983. The number of people involved in drug-related offences also rose steeply - from under 500 in 1975 to 2500 in 1984. Beneath this worrying surface rise in drug-related indicators there was also a realisation that the numbers of addicts or drug users was in reality far higher than the number notified to the Home Office - a multiplier of between five and ten was suggested. Customs and police between them probably at best seized only a tenth of the drugs coming into the country; a significant black market in drugs had developed. After some years of calm, Britain was clearly in the throes of a 'new drug problem'.[10]

This coincided with the emergence of drugs as a concern for politicians. Crucially however, they became not a political issue, but one of political consensus. From about 1984, the Conservative government took a direct interest in the formation of drug policy. In 1984 an interdepartmental working group of ministers and officials, the Ministerial Group on the Misuse of Drugs, was established, for the first time bringing together the 13 departments, from the Home Office and Department of Health to the Welsh Office and Overseas Development Administration, with an interest in the subject.[11] The Group is chaired by a Home Office Minister; this chairmanship, undertaken firstly by David Mellor, and then by Douglas Hogg, has proved to be far from a political liability. David Mellor during this tenureship of the office adopted a high political profile as the public exponent of the 'war on drugs'. This reawakened political interest in drugs was reflected in the Commons Select Committee System also with reports from the Social Services Committee (1984-85) and the Home Affairs Committee.[12] The latter, reporting in 1986, commented that:

> drug misuse, especially of hard drugs like heroin and cocaine, is still one of the UK's most distressing and difficult problems. Drug dealers still make princely profits and threaten us all, including our children, with a nightmare of drug addiction which has now become a reality for America.[13]

There were some signs that drugs might emerge as an issue for political division between the parties. In 1985, David Owen, leader of the Social Democratic Party, gave a lecture in which he cited research evidence linking drug use with youth unemployment, and deprivation.[14] But the incipient debate did not develop. In the 1987 general election the SDP/Liberal Alliance manifesto did not mention drugs and an election leaflet on health policy gave the subject no more than a mention. Labour's manifesto was likewise silent. Any argument was, as one commentator noted, 'about how *much* rather than *what* should be done'.[15] Some commentators have seen the 1980s as characterised by the politicisation of drug policy.[16] Drugs in fact never became a party political issue, but a Conservative issue with some degree of all-party consensus.

The public face of Conservative political interest was a policy focused on a strong penal response to drugs, on both domestic and international fronts. In 1985, the government published the first version of its strategy document for drugs, *Tackling Drug Misuse*.[17] The strategy had five main aspects, three of which were penal in orientation. Its aims were:

(a) reducing supplies from abroad;
(b) making enforcement even more effective;
(c) maintaining effective deterrents and tight domestic controls;
(d) developing prevention;
(e) improving treatment and rehabilitation.

In the same year, the Commons Home Affairs Committee in its interim report called for continued enforcement of the law; the stationing overseas of additional customs and police intelligence liaison officers; harsher penalties for trafficking offences; help for crop eradication and substitution schemes; legislation to attack and seize the profits of traffickers; and changes in banking law to impede the disposal of money derived from drug trafficking.[18] Much of this was put into effect. The Drug Trafficking Offences Act 1986 (in force since 1987) provided (with all party support) comprehensive powers for tracing, freezing and confiscating drug money, along with measures to stop the laundering of drug money. The Controlled Drugs (Penalties) Act 1985 increased the maximum penalty for drug trafficking from 14 years to life. The National Drugs Intelligence Unit was set up in Scotland Yard to provide a national link between police and Customs. The eight regional crime squads outside London developed 17 dedicated 'drugs wings'; in London, the strength of the Central Drug Squad was nearly doubled. For customs, the number of specialist drugs investigators tripled in the 1980s; nine of these were posted overseas to aid foreign law enforcement agencies. At the level of supply the British government pledged £3.4million in 1987 for a five-year crop substitution/rural development project in Pakistan and money was provided for law enforcement in Bolivia and Ecuador after a visit by David Mellor in 1986. Drug policy assumed new visibility at the level of international control. Increasingly, too, it acquired a European dimension. Britain had chaired the Pompidou Group (the Council of Europe Co-operation Group to Combat Drug Abuse and Illicit Trafficking in Drugs) since 1984. The arrival of a single European market in 1992 brought questions of drug control to the fore.

Clearly a penal reaction largely out of favour since the 1920s was back in fashion. But what was the relationship between political rhetoric and policy practice, in particular within Britain? Here the evidence about the extent and impact of the penal wing of policy was more equivocal. Research on trends in sentencing in Scotland showed that low-level drug offences were indeed receiving longer custodial sentences.[19] But mostly the operation of penal policy was the subject of hearsay rather than sustained investigation. A drop in heroin seized in 1986 was more than matched by increased seizures of cocaine; both were the result of fewer seizures of larger quantities. There was discussion of police tactics at the local level, but little by way of analysis of how policy was actually operating at that level - or indeed at the level of larger-scale distribution.[20] There was, for example, no investigation of prosecutions under the Drug Trafficking Offences Act. An economic study of the cost-effectiveness of expenditure on police and customs drug enforcement work underlined the lack of empirical data on which to base any assessment.[21] The penal response remained a powerful rhetorical symbol; what it meant in practice was rather more uncertain.

Health policy on drugs: a time of change

One aspect of policy which it did symbolise was the decline of a primarily medical response to drugs. British drug policy, as established in the 1920s, had a twin-track approach of penal control, symbolised by the lead role in policy taken by the Home Office, but also of a medical reaction, underpinned by the departmental interest of the Ministry of Health. Since the 1926 Rolleston Report British drug policy had been based on a medical response to drug addiction, symbolised in that report by its reaffirmation of the disease model of addiction and by a doctor's clinical freedom to provide maintenance doses of opiate drugs as a form of treatment. The Rolleston Committee, although arising out of Home Office concern, was established as a Health Ministry Committee, and serviced by the Ministry, in particular by its doctor-civil servant secretary, E.W. Adams. But the resultant 'British system' of medical control operated as part of a legal system based on penal sanctions and international controls as laid down in the 1912 Hague Convention and the 1919 Versailles settlement.[22] How the balance operated could vary over time.

In the 1980s, that balance did begin to drift towards a penal response. But the 'British system' had in fact been in decline well before the Conservative government introduced its package of penal measures in 1984-86. The shift in the health side of drug policy had begun in the mid-1970s. It was marked by a number of factors; a decline in medical prescribing of opiate drugs and of the clinics as centres for the treatment of drug addiction; a change in the characterisation of drug addiction; the rise of the voluntary sector and of drug treatment as part of primary health care. Perhaps most important of all, it had seen the consolidation of a new 'policy community' round drugs and the emergence (or re-emergence) of the concept of harm-minimisation as an objective of policy. It is worth looking briefly at all of these developments. The specialist model for the treatment of drug addiction within the National Health Service as exemplified by the clinic system did not long adhere to the original blueprint. Between 1971 and 1978, the amount of heroin prescribed fell by 40 per cent.[23] Increasingly injectable and oral methadone were used, following the American example; short-term treatment contracts based on withdrawal replaced longer-term prescribing. The clinics were effectively treating only addicts who were highly motivated to come off drugs. This, coupled with cuts in funding and resources, ensured that the clinics, by the early 1980s, had become what Mike Ashton called a 'backwater of our social response to drug abuse'.[24] Withdrawal from prescribing was a central feature of the medical response. This change of tactic was enshrined in the *Guidelines of Good Clinical Practice* distributed to all doctors in 1984, which emphasised the limited role prescribing had to play.[25] The weight of professional opinion against prescribing was demonstrated by the case of Dr Ann Dally, brought before the General Medical Council in 1987 for technical offences involved in prescribing in her private practice.

The 'medical model' of addiction as a disease requiring specialist treatment was disappearing in practice - and in theory as well. The older concept of addiction had given place, in official parlance at least, in the late 1960s, to the concept of dependence, enshrined in an official World Health Organisation definition.[26] But in the 1980s , this changed to the concept of the problem drug taker, paralleling similar developments in the alcohol field. The change in definitions received official sanction in the 1982 Advisory Council on the Misuse of Drugs Report on *Treatment and Rehabilitation*, which declared:

> most authorities from a range of disciplines would agree that not all individuals with drug problems suffer from a disease of drug dependence. While many drug misusers do incur medical problems through their use of drugs some do not. The majority are relatively stable individuals who have more in common with the general population than with any essentially pathological sub-group .... There is no evidence of any uniform personality characteristic or type of person who becomes either an addict or an individual with drug problems.[27]

Accompanying this change in definitions was an emphasis on a multi-disciplinary approach, based on regional and district drug problem teams and local drug advisory committees. Although medical personnel would continue to take the lead, the involvement of other agencies, local authority, police and voluntary agencies was actively sought. The voluntary agencies in particular had already been playing a more prominent role in the provision of services since the late 1970s. The Treatment and Rehabilitation report encouraged a partnership between them and the statutory services. In 1983, the Department of Health mounted a Central Funding Initiative for the development of new community-based services. Fifty-six per cent of grants were administered through health authorities; 42 per cent through the voluntary sector.[28] The aim was to displace the old hospital-based London-focused specialist treatment system. A senior Department of Health civil servant recalled:

> ... Brain had bunged clinics into London .... The most important thing was to try and get a few more services up and running .... We had to get the voluntary and hospital services working together. We had to say to generalists and generic workers that the problems of drug users are the same as others - get on and deal with this homeless person and forget he's a drug user.[29]

This approach met resistance from a variety of quarters, from some of the London clinic establishment and from some voluntary agencies, suspicious of incorporation.

But the first half of the 1980s was marked also by the formation of a new 'policy community' around drugs. Richardson and Jordan have used this concept to delineate the way in which the central policy-making machinery is divided into sub-systems in departments (organised round areas such as alcohol or drugs).[30] Close relationships can develop between these sub-systems and outside pressure groups, involving shared policy objectives and priorities. For drugs, the 1980s saw a shift from a primarily medical policy community to one which was more broadly-based, involving revisionist doctors, the voluntary agencies, researchers, and, most crucially, like-minded civil servants within the Department of Health. The change can be characterised through the changed membership of the Advisory Council on the Misuse of Drugs, the main expert advisory body on drug policy. In the 1980s, it recruited to an originally mainly medical membership, representatives of the voluntary agencies, of health education, social science research, the probation service and of general practice.[31] The increase in drug use in Liverpool and the Wirral attracted much attention; non-medical researchers and service workers there were of key importance in advocating the thesis of the 'normalisation' of drug use. But doctors also played a key role there; and it was in the Manchester area that revisionism received its clearest expression. The Regional Drug Dependence consultant introduced a 'new model service' based on satellite clinics, community drug teams and a regional training unit.[32] Developments such as these were actively encouraged by civil servants in the Department of Health.

This new policy community took the conclusions of the *Treatment and Rehabilitation* report as its bible. There were differences over questions of implementation and practice. The 1982 report's recommendations were, for example, criticised for establishing the regional drug problem team as basically the staff of a specialist service, headed by a consultant psychiatrist, rather than a genuine multi-displinary and agency partnership; and there were also differences over questions of prescribing. But another policy objective, that of the minimisation of harm from drug use, found general support. This was an aim which had long received support from within the voluntary sector of drug services and also from doctors critical of the clinic's non-prescribing policies and their consequent policy objective in the 1980s. In 1984, the ACMD's report on *Prevention* abandoned earlier divisions into primary, secondary and tertiary prevention in favour of two basic criteria: (a) reducing the risk of an individual engaging in drug misuse; (b) reducing the harm associated with drug misuse.[33] But such objectives remained difficult to enunciate publicly in relation to drug use. They certainly lacked political acceptability. When, in 1981, the Institute for the Study of Drug Dependence published a pamphlet, *Teaching About a Volatile Situation*, advocating harm-minimisation techniques (safe sniffing) for glue sniffing, there was an outcry which nearly brought an end to the Institute.[34] There was still a yawning gap between the 'political' and 'policy community' view of drugs. This gap was epitomised in the furore surrounding the government's decision to mount a mass media anti-heroin campaign in 1985-86. This essentially political decision ran counter to received research and internal policy advice which concluded that such campaigns should not be attempted and were potentially counterproductive.[35]

To sum up, 1980s drug policy pre-AIDS had a dual face - a 'political' penal policy with a high public and mass media profile; and an 'in-house' health policy based on a rhetoric of de-medicalisation and the development of community services and harm-minimisation. The relationship between policy and practice in both wings was paradoxical - and worthy of further research. For the penal response, data about its operation, let alone its effectiveness, was largely absent. And although a network of non-specialist services outside London was developed, it was notable how much this de-medicalising shift in policy was still dependent on medical support.[36] Medicine might, as Jerry Jaffe commented in his 1986 Okey Lecture, no longer sit at the top of the table, but the new system could not have moved forward if doctors and doctor civil servants had not wanted it.[37]

The impact of AIDS: the immediate response

What has been the impact of AIDS upon an area of policy already in a state of flux? Most obviously the nature of the problem presented by drug use has changed. Late in 1985 reports from Edinburgh revealed a prevalence of HIV antibody seropositivity among injecting drug misusers which was considerably higher than in the rest of the United Kingdom and also higher than in parts of Europe and the United States.[38] The issue of potential heterosexual spread was not new. The blood transfusion question and the spread of the virus among haemophiliacs had in 1983/4, raised the question of the spread of the virus into the general population.[39] But drugs made this more urgent. A Scottish Committee chaired by Dr D. McClelland, Director of the South East Scotland Regional Blood Transfusion Service, was set up to review the Scottish situation and to report on how to contain the spread of HIV infection and allay public concern. The report of this committee, published in September 1986, foreshadowed many of the more publicised statements of the later ACMD reports.[40] It enunciated harm-minimisation as a primary objective. The threat of the spread of HIV into the general population justified a response based on the minimisation of harm from drug use and on attracting drug users into contact with services.

> There is .... a serious risk that infected drug misusers will spread HIV beyond the presently recognised high risk groups and into the sexually active general population. Very extensive spread by heterosexual contacts has already occurred in a number of African countries.... There is .... an urgent need to contain the spread of HIV infection among drug misusers not only to limit the harm caused to drug misusers themselves but also to protect the health of the general public. The gravity of the problem is such that on balance the containment of the spread of the virus is a higher priority in management than the prevention of drug misuse.

Substitute prescribing and the provision of sterile injecting equipment to addicts were two major means by which these ends were to be achieved.

Members of the new policy community began to voice these objectives more openly. David Turner, coordinator of SCODA, the Standing Conference on Drug Abuse, the national coordinating body for the voluntary drug sector, commented at an AIDS conference in Newcastle in 1986, 'it is essential that no risk-reduction option is rejected out of hand because it appears to conflict with a service's stated goal of abstinence'.[41] Reports of Dutch harm-reduction strategies and needle exchange projects became more frequent. Social researchers joined in. Russell Newcombe of the Wirral Misuse of Drugs Research in Project in Liverpool, argued;

> Drug education policy-makers and practitioners should be giving serious consideration to how the reality of drug use in the '80s is best tackled. The question they should ask themselves is: would it be preferable to reduce the incidence of illicit drug use while not promoting safer forms of drug use, or would it be more realistic to give greater priority to the reduction of harm from drug use? The emerging AIDS epidemic has rapidly brought this question to the forefront of the debate. It is my view, and increasingly the

view of others who work with drug users or young people, that it is high time for harm-reduction.[42]

These objectives were, as before AIDS, shared by civil servants in the Department of Health. 'We're going to get harm minimisation much more quickly' commented one senior non-medical civil servant in the autumn of 1986.[43] Another saw it as the opportunity:

> to go out and push out a bit further. Almost fortuitously the fact we'd already shifted our policy .... was .... a fertile seed bed from which we've been able to develop .... We'd be weeping in our tea now .... The pre-existing development of community services enabled us to get harm-minimisation approaches off the ground more rapidly than if we'd been rooted in the old hospital based approach to drug misuse.[44]

The urgency of the situation enabled what had been a stumbling block to the unspoken objectives of drug policy pre-AIDS - political and media opposition to any suspicion of 'softness' on drugs - to be quietly overcome. Research was an important legitimating factor. In December 1986, Norman Fowler, Secretary of State for Social Services, announced the intention to set up a number of pilot needle exchange schemes (building on some already in operation, in Liverpool and Swindon, for example). Assessment of effectiveness in preventing the spread of the virus was an important consideration. There were doubts in the Cabinet Committee on AIDS (set up in October 1986) about the provision of syringes; and early in 1987 a project to monitor and evaluate the pilot schemes was established at Goldsmiths' College. In May 1987, the ACMD set up its own working group on AIDS and drug misuses, chaired by Ruth Runciman, a non-medical member of the Council. Of the working group's 13 members, six were non-medical. Part of the ACMD's report, ready in the Autumn of 1987, was not published by the government until March 1988, causing disquiet among some members of the working party.[45] The Report, like the McClelland Committee before it, declared the danger of the heterosexual spread of the virus to be a greater menace than the danger of drug use itself. It called for a range of harm-minimisation strategies, most notably needle-exchange and over the counter sales of syringes by pharmacists. Prescribing, too, was seen as an option to attract drug users into services. But the initial political reaction was lukewarm. Although the goal of harm-reduction was accented by Tony Newton, Minister of Health, in his statement to the Commons on 29 March 1988, only £1 million was provided for the development of services and the further results of evaluation were awaited. The response from Michael Forsyth, Scottish Health Minister, saw central funding of the two pilot schemes still in operation at an end - and a generally negative response to the particular criticisms of the Scottish situation in the ACMD Report. It seemed as though policy would founder on the rocks of political opposition. The summer of 1988 saw intense pressure from civil servants for a more positive response from ministers which brought a turn-around in the autumn, aided by research results from the Goldsmiths' group which showed that users did change to lower risk behaviours (although a disappointingly small proportion of attenders stayed on to achieve them).[46] David Mellor, the new Health Minister, announced an extra £3million for the provision of services in England. The money was specifically to enable services to expand and develop in such a way as to make contact with more drug misusers in order to offer help and advice on reducing the risk of HIV infection. Only £300 000 was allocated to Scottish services, despite the disparity in numbers of HIV positive drug users there by comparison with England. Further money followed for 1989/90 with an extra £5 million available for the development of drug services. Coming on top of pre-existing AIDS allocations, the extra funding since 1986 gave health authorities at least £17million to spend on drug services; money was being provided, too, on a recurrent basis. In Scotland the 1989/90 figure of £2.1 million for drug services was less significant than the doubling of the general AIDS allocation to £12 million. For some English projects funded by the earlier CFI, the money came just in time.

The 'normalisation' of drug policy through AIDS

What then had AIDS really meant for drug policy? At the level of policy formulation it has clearly, on the war-time model, meant the public establishment of the previous largely unspoken aims of policy. Drug policy in general and services in particular have ostensibly come out of the ghetto and the process, instigated pre-AIDS, of integration into the normal range of services, has been intensified. One of the clearest analyses of the ethos of the new approach instanced changes in assumptions about the nature of the problem; and the nature of the task is now more clearly seen, in this analysis, to be poly-drug workers rather than medical specialists. Services, too, rather than testing client's motivation with long waiting lists and abstinence-orientated treatment philosophies, must become user-friendly (including the potential provision of opiates).[47] The message of government advertising on drugs has changed, too, away from the mass shock approach to targeted harm-minimisation. A senior medical officer commented:

> AIDS may be the trigger that brings care for drug users into the mainstream for the first time ever .... The drug world can come 'in from the cold' through AIDS .... it's a golden opportunity to get it right for the first time.[48]

Drugs, so it is argued, have become a problem of public health rather than a question of individual pathology. Gerry Stimson argues:

> HIV has simplified the debate and we now see the emergence of what I will call the public health paradigm. Rather than seeing drug use as a metaphorical disease, there is now a real medical problem associated with injecting drugs. All can agree that this is a major public health problem for people who inject drugs, their sexual partners, and their children.[49]

AIDS, so it seems, has gone some way to achieving the normalisation of drug use. In declaring prescribing to be a legitimate option, it has appeared to deal with the prescribing question which had bedeviled drug policy in the 1970s and 1980s. The new 1980s policy community around drugs has been strengthened by the support of some key politicians. References to normalisation and attracting drug users to services now appear in Hansard as well as the pages of the in-house drug journals.[50] The media have been diverted away from heroin into the cocaine issue. For some members of the policy community AIDS has opened up the wider agenda of the liberalisation of drug policy. AIDS has, for some members of the drug policy community, been a type of new dawn.

A new departure for drug policy?

Policy is clearly in a state of flux and it would be unwise in the early 1990s to attempt to lay down definitive statements about either present or future directions. The rest of this paper will simply raise a number of questions about the 'new drug policy' in the light of an historical perspective. In particular it will draw attention to questions of the implementation of policy and the power relationships within policy; to the continuing war on drugs; it will question how new the 'new public health' model for drugs really is; and will speculate on the long-term impact of policy change.

The nature of the implementation of policy is important: for the rhetoric of policy and its practice can differ significantly.[51] There is relatively little information as yet on how policy is being implemented in practice within services apart from within needle-exchanges. Clearly the impact of the pre-existing local situation is important. One study of the response of Edinburgh agencies, for example, instances increased medical involvement primarily through the medium of the infectious disease specialism rather than psychiatry, which had traditionally in Scotland had little to do with drug users.[52] AIDS in some respects appears to have brought a revival of medical involvement in drug use. It has brought doctors back more centrally into drugs through the emphasis on prescribing as an option and the focus on the role of the general practitioner. There is also a new emphasis on the general health of drug users. A consultant commented:

> What's disturbing is that I have had to change positions. I hadn't seen doctors as being that important in services .... There were nineteen CDTs in X, each one autonomous and funded by the NHS, but only one headed by a doctor and the others would be headed by a community nurse, a social worker, a voluntary worker .... Now I've started arguing strongly that all drug services need a lot of doctor input .... The impact of AIDS means an urgent need for medical care .... Drug services will have to do routine health checks and be proactive in selling it.[53]

Such views were echoed at an official level. A joint Royal College of Psychiatrists and Department of Health conference in 1989 on new models of services for drug misusers highlighted 'an extreme shortage of trained psychiatrists' to guide the future development of these services. The need to cater for HIV positive drug users - potentially using methadone and AZT - led some drug services to establish specialist clinics aimed at that group. The need, underlined by the McClelland and two ACMD Reports, of contacting drug users not normally in contact with services has served to elevate the notion of treatment which has resumed its place as an unchallengeable good. The role of the voluntary sector in drug services has also been affected. Ben Pimlott's comment that the Thatcher government, with its rhetoric of voluntarism, had seen the virtual abolition of the voluntary sector, may have been exaggeration, but it did contain an element of truth.[54] The voluntary sector, in drug services as in AIDS more generally, was drawing closer to the statutory sector, and was often funded by it. Even within the voluntary sector, drug use, because of HIV, had become associated with illness. They champion the drug users' rights to treatment and to use drugs if they want because they have an illness and need a script .... The voluntary sector ends up holding a disease model.'[55] This focus on illness coincided with and complemented pre-existing tendencies in drug policy, for example the increased prominence of private addiction clinics which emphasised the old disease concept; and a revived emphasis in research into the bio-chemical and genetic basis of alcohol and drug dependence. So far as the power relationships in policy-making went, the situation had changed little from the pre-AIDS position. Without the support of influential and centrally placed doctors, the 'new departures' in policy could not have been sustained. Drug policy-making after, as before AIDS, has exemplified the influence of doctor civil servants as important in policy-making, a tradition going back to Dr E. W. Adams, a Ministry of Health civil servant and secretary of the Rolleston Committee in 1924-26.[56]

The 'war on drugs' continues

The twin-track nature of British drug policy also remains in existence post-AIDS. Penal policy still remains, albeit modified at the local level. Britain still adheres to a system of international control of drugs. The Department of Health has, through AIDS, taken a more public stance as the spokesman for certain aspects of drug policy. But the Home Office remains the lead department and the overall trend of penal policy at the international level remains as before. In June 1987, the United Nations convened an international conference on Drug Abuse and Illicit Trafficking in Vienna, followed in November by a conference on drug abuse and illicit trafficking in the western hemisphere. Tim Rathbone, chairman of the Commons All Party Committee on Drug Abuse and delegate to the later conference, commented that there was general consensus, among other aspects of drug policy, on:

> the need to maintain a hard legal and penal line on supply and to match that with more and better cures for possession and use than are presently offered within penal systems; the growing urgency of even better multinational controls, co-ordination and co-operation in tackling and reducing illegal distribution, including improved legal powers to trace, seize and confiscate the assets of drug traffickers.[57]

Increasingly, drug control is assuming a European dimension. In 1989, the Home Office signed an agreement committing the UK and Switzerland to co-operation in tracing and freezing the proceeds of drug trafficking as a direct development from the 1986 Drug Trafficking Offences Act; and negotiations were under way with other European countries. Within Britain at the local level, policies do appear to have changed, with police cooperation in the establishment of needle exchanges, police participation in local drug advisory committees, and links between police and services.[58] But the advent of cocaine as a policy issue has served to legitimate the penal response. Cocaine could potentially, too, impinge on the legitimacy of harm-minimisation as a policy. By the end of the 1980s then, penal drug policy may have been modified at the local level; but, as an overall objective, it remained firm. One senior Conservative politician in 1989 saw drug control as 'increased controlled availability at home and stronger prohibition round the edges'.

The 'new public health' approach?

The 'public health' approach to drugs engendered by AIDS had, like other aspects of policy, clear historical antecedents. One observer commented in 1988 on the parallels between the Advisory Councils part 1 report on AIDS and Drug Misuse and the Brain Committee's report on drug addiction in 1965.[59] Like the ACMD, Brain also justified change in drug policy on public health grounds - addiction was a 'socially infectious condition', a disease which 'if allowed to spread unchecked, will become a menace to the community'. And the remedies suggested by Brain - including notification and compulsory treatment - were classic public health responses. The balance required in drug policy in the 1980s between minimising the harm from drug use but not thereby promoting drug use is parallelled by Brain's attempt to graft the public health objective of preventing infection on to a system geared to individual treatment; drug workers had to prescribe opiates to undercut the black market but not so much that the market was supplied and new addicts created. There have always been tensions in drug policy, not simply between penal and medical forms of control, but between different forms of medical input. In the nineteenth century, for example, the earlier 'public health' focus on opium adulteration, on child doping or working-class industrial opiate use gave place to medical theories of addiction and disease.[60] Roy MacLeod has pointed to the focus on individual pathology rather than an environmentalist approach in late nineteenth-century discussions of inebriety.[61] Likewise Brain's public health focus in 1965 was modified in practice to a focus on active medical treatment. There has always been an implicit tension between preventive and curative approaches, in this as in other areas of health policy. There are more general parallels between drug policy in the 1960s and the 1980s which cannot be explored here. The 'public health' paradigm itself, too, has not been an unchanging absolute. Its definition and remit has changed in the twentieth century, as the nature of state intervention in social issues has itself shifted.[62] Social hygiene with its emphasis on individual responsibility for health was the reformulated public health of the 1900s; the 1970s and 1980s public health has, in its emphasis on individual life-style and on prevention, revived these earlier social hygienist concerns. Drug policy, both pre- and post-AIDS, with its emphasis on health education, on the role of the voluntary sector, on the drug user as a 'normal' individual responsible for his or her own actions and health, has epitomised some key elements of the redefinitions. Certainly the 'public health paradigm' of post-AIDS policy is nothing new.[63]

The long term impact of policy change

The question of the long-term impact of policy change should also be considered. How long will the revived 'public health paradigm' persist? It would be an unwise historian or policy scientist who attempted to predict what the long-term balance of policy might be– de- or re-medicalisation; an individualistic public health approach shifting subtly to an individualistic medicalised approach? The analogy of war and policy change with which this article began does offer some suggestive indications. The 'public health' response to alcohol in the First World War with state control of the alcohol industry and limited pub opening hours only partially survived the war.[64] The 'hard-line' emergency response to drugs at the same period was moderated in the 1920s.[65] War does lead to change – but long standing themes and tendencies also express and re-assert themselves. This article has suggested that, despite the apparent revolution in the public rhetoric of drug policy achieved by AIDS, many aspects of post-AIDS policy were already inherent in drug policy in the 1980s, most obviously the goal of harm-minimisation and the 'normalisation' of drug services. Other themes, the 'new public health' approach, for example, have an even longer history. Even harm-minimisation itself is only a re-statement in different circumstances of the principles enunciated in the Rolleston Report of 1926.[66]

> When, therefore, every effort possible in the circumstances has been made, and made unsuccessfully, to bring the patient to a condition in which he is independent of the drug, it may .... become justifiable in certain cases to order regularly the minimum dose which has been found necessary, either in order to avoid serious withdrawal symptoms, or to keep the patient in a condition in which he can lead a useful life.

Indeed the overall impression is of some long-standing tendencies – the role of medicine, the penal approach – even the revival of the nineteenth-century role of the pharmacist[67] which have not been undermined and may even have been enhanced by the impact of AIDS. Whatever the future of drug policy in the post-AIDS years, it will not escape from its history.

Notes

I am grateful to Philip Strong for comments on an earlier draft and to the Nuffield Provincial Hospitals Trust for financial support for the research on which this paper is based. My thanks are due to Ingrid James for secretarial assistance.

1. Fox, D.M., P. Day and R. Klein, 'The Power of Professionalism: AIDS in Britain, Sweden and the United States', *Daedelus*, 118 (1989), pp. 93-112.

2. Stimson, G. 'AIDS and HIV: The Challenge for British Drug Services', *British Journal of Addiction* (forthcoming).

3. MacGregor, S. 'Choices for Policy and Practice', pp. 171-200 in S. MacGregor (ed), *Drugs and British Society. Responses to a Social Problem in the 1980s* (London: Routledge, 1989).

4. For discussion of these issues, see C. Webster, *The Health Services Since the War. Vol. I: Problems of Health Care. The National Health Service before 1957* (London: HMSO, 1988).

5. Berridge, V. and P. Strong, 'AIDS Policies in the UK: a Preliminary Analysis' (forthcoming) in E. Fee and D. Fox (eds), *AIDS: Contemporary History* (Princeton University Press).

6. Berridge, V. and G. Edwards, *Opium and the People: Opiate Use in Nineteenth Century England* (London: Yale University Press, 1987).

7. Berridge, V. 'War Conditions and Narcotics Control: the Passing of Defence of the Realm Act 40B', *Journal of Social Policy*, I (1978), pp. 285-304.

8. Berridge, V. 'Drugs and Social Policy: The Establishment of Drug Control in Britain, 1900-1930', *British Journal of Addiction*, 79 (1984), pp. 17-29.

9. MacGregor, S. 'Choices for Policy and Practice', P. Bean, *The Social Control of Drugs* (London: Martin Robertson, 1974); G. Edwards, 'Some Years On: Evolutions in the "British System", in D. H. West (ed), *Problems of Drug Abuse in Britain* (Cambridge: Institute of

Criminology, 1978); H. B. Spear, 'The Growth of Heroin Addiction in the United Kingdom', *British Journal of Addiction*, 64 (1969) pp. 245-55.

10. Stimson, G. 'British Drug Policies in the 1980s: A Preliminary Analysis and Suggestions for Research', *British Journal of Addiction*, 82 (1987) pp. 477-88.

11. Home Office, *Tackling Drug Misuse: A Summary of the Government's Strategy* (London: Home Office, 1986).

12. Social Services Committee, *Fourth Report of the Social Services Committee: Misuse of Drugs with Special Reference to the Treatment and Rehabilitation of Misusers of Hard Drugs* (London: HMSO, 1985).

13. Home Affairs Committee, *First Report from the Home Affairs Committee, Session 1985-86: Misuse of Hard Drugs* (London: HMSO, 1986).

14. Owen, D. 'Need for a Scientific Strategy to Crub the Epidemic of Drug Abuse in the United Kingdom', *Lancet*, 26 October 1985, p. 958.

15. Election '87, 'What the Parties said about Drugs', *Druglink*, 2, (5) (1987) p. 7.

16. For example, G. Stimson, 'The War on Heroin: British Policy and the International Trade in Illicit Drugs', pp. 35-61 in N. Dorn and N. South (eds), *A Land fit for Heroin? Drug Policies, Prevention and Practice* (London: MacMillan, 1978).

17. Home Office, *Tackling Drug Misuse*, see note 11.

18. Home Affairs Committee, *Interim Report. Misuse of Hard Drugs* (London: HMSO 1985).

19. Haw, S. and D. Liddell, 'Drug Problems in Edinburgh District. Report of the SCODA Fieldwork Survey' (London: SCODA, 1989).

20. Dorn, N. 'The Agenda for Prevention', in V. Berridge, (ed), *Drug Research and Policy in Britain: a Review of the 1980s* (Gower/Avebury, forthcoming).

21. Wagstaff, A. and A. Maynard, *Economic Aspects of the Illicit Drug Market and Drug Enforcement Policies in the United Kingdom*, Home Office Research Studies, 95 (London: HMSO, 1988).

22. Berridge, V. 'Drugs and Social Policy, see note 8.

23. Lewis, R., R. Hartnoll, S. Bryer, E. Daviaud and M. Mitcheson, 'Scoring Smack: the Illicit Heroin Market in London, 1980-83', *British Journal of Addiction*, 80 (1985), pp. 281-90.

24. Ashton, M. 'Controlling Addiction: the Role of the Clinics', *Druglink*, 13 (1980), pp. 1-6.

25. DHSS, *Guidelines of Good Clinical Practice in the Treatment of Drug Misuse Report of the Medical Working Group on Drug Dependence* (London: DHSS 1984).

26. Edwards, G., A. Arif and R. Hodgson, 'Nomenclature and Classification of Drug and Alcohol Related Problems', Bulletin of World Health Organisation, 59 (1981), pp. 225-42.

27. DHSS, *Treatment and Rehabilitation. Report of the Advisory Council on the Misuse of Drug* (London: HMSO, 1982).

28. MacGregor, S., B. Ettorre and R. Coomber, *Summary of the First Phase of Research. An Assessment of the Central Funding Initiative on Services for the Treatment and Rehabilitation of Drug Misusers* (London: Birkbeck, 1987).

29. Department of Health civil servant, conference paper, June 1989.

30. Jordan, A. G. and J. J. Richardson, *British Politics and the Policy Process* (London: Allen & Unwin, 1987).

31. The membership of the ACMD is listed at the front of the reports on *Treatment and Rehabilitation* and *Prevention* (1984). Membership of the Working Group on AIDS and Drug Misuse is listed in the two ACMD AIDS reports. *AIDS and Drug Misuse, Parts 1 and 2* (London: HMSO, 1988 and 1989).

32. Strang, J. 'A Model Service: Turning the Generalist on to Drugs', pp. 143-69 in S. MacGregor (ed.), *Drugs and British Society*, see note 3.

33. Home Office, *Prevention. Report of the Advisory Council on the Misuse of Drugs* (London: HMSO, 1984).

34. Shapiro, H. 'Press Review July 1980-May 1981', *Druglink*, 16, pp. 6-8.

35. Dorn, N. 'Media Campaigns', *Druglink*, 1 (2) (1986), pp. 8-9.

36. Key figures were Dr John Strang, regional consultant in Manchester; Dr Dorothy Black, senior medical officer at the Department of Health; and Dr Philip Connell, chairman of the Advisory Council for the Misuse of Drugs.

37. Jaffe, J. 'Drug Addiction: The American Experience', Okey Memorial Lecture, Institute of Psychaitry, London, 1986.

38. Peutherer, J.F., E. Edmonds, P. Simmonds, J. D. Dickson, *et al.*, 'HTLV-III Antibody in Edinburgh Drug Addicts', *Lancet* 2 (1985), p. 1129; J. R. Robertson, A. B. V. Bucknall, P.D. Welsby *et al.*, 'Epidemic of AIDS Related Virus (HTLV-III/LAV) Infection among Intravenous Drug Abusers', *British Medical Journal*, 292 (1986), p. 527.

39. Berridge, V. and P. Strong, 'AIDS Policies in the UK', see note 5.

40. Scottish Home and Health Department, *HIV Infection in Scotland. Report of the Scottish Committee on HIV Infection and Intravenous Drug Misuse* (Edinburgh: SHHD, 1986).

41. Turner, D. 'AIDS and Injecting', *Druglink* 1, (3) (1986), pp. 8-9.

42. Newcombe, R. 'High Time for Harm Reduction', *Druglink* 2, (1) (1987), pp. 10-11.

43. Department of Health civil servant, observation to author, 1986.

44. Department of Health civil servant, conference paper, June 1989.

45. DHSS, *AIDS and Drug Misuse Part 1* (London: HMSO, 1988).

46. Stimson, G., L. Alldritt, K. Dolan, M. Donoghoe and R. Lart, *Injecting Equipment Exchange Schemes - Final Report* (Goldsmith's College, Monitoring research Group, 1988).

47. Stimson, G. 'AIDS and HIV: The Challenge for British Drug Services', see note 2.

48. Department of Health civil servant, conference paper, June 1989.

49. Stimson, G. 'AIDS and HIV', see note 2.

50. See speech by Chris Butler in House of Commons Debate on Drug Abuse, 9 June 1989, cols 470-4.

51. For example, an evaluation of Liverpool's 'prescribing' clinic found its actual practice little different from 'non-prescribing' Clinics. See C. Fazey, *An Evaluation of Liverpool Drug Dependency Clinic. The First Two years 1985 to 1987* (Liverpool: Research Evaluation and Data Analysis, 1988).

52. McRae, J. *AIDS, Agencies and Drug Abuse* (Norwich: Social Work Monographs, 1989).

53. Interview, drug consultant, Jan. 1989.

54. Pimlott, B. paper on Thatcher: 'The First Ten Years' conference, LSE, 1989.

55. Interview, drug consultant, Jan. 1989.

56. Berridge, V. 'Drugs and Social Policy', see note 8. Alcohol and drug policy has long been an interesting example of the relationship between medicine and the state. See R. M. MacLeod, 'The Edge of Hope: Social Policy and Chronic Alcoholism, 1870-1900', *Journal of the History of Medicine and Allied Sciences*, 22, (1967), pp. 215-45.

57. Rathbone, T. 'A Problem of Co-operation' *Druglink*, 3, (6) (1988), p. 15.

58. For example, an innovation scheme in Southwark has begun to link police referrals from the courts to helping services, in particular the Maudsley Hospital's Community Drug Team.

59. 'HIV Top Priority, says Official report', *Druglink* 3, (3) (1988), p. 6.

60. Berridge, V. and G. Edwards, *Opium and the People*, see note 6.

61. MacLeod, R. M. 'The edge of hope', see note 58.

62. Lewis, J. *What Price Community Medicine? The Philosophy, Practice and Politics of Public Health since 1919* (Brighton: Wheatsheaf, 1986).

63. For similar comments from a sociological perspective, see G. Stimson and R. Lart, 'HIV, Drugs and Public Health in England: New Words, Old Tunes' (forthcoming 1990).

64. Rose, M. 'The Success of Social Reform? The Central Control Board (Liquor Traffic) 1915-21', in M. R. D. Foot (ed.), *War and Society* (London: Joseph Elek, 1973).

65. Berridge, V. 'Drugs and Social Policy' see note 8.

66. Rolleston Report, *Report of the Departmental Committee on Morphine and Heroin Addiction* (London: HMSO, 1926).

67. In Scotland, the role of the pharmacist in the prevention of HIV spread has been important. There are parallels with the nineteenth-century role of the pharmacist in dispensing opiates and providing medical care to poor clients. See V. Berridge and G. Edwards, *Opium and the People*, note 6.

13.   The Smoking Option

John Marks, Andrew Palombella
and Russell Newcombe

For two years two Mersey drug dependency units have been prescribing smokable methadone or heroin to opiate injectors to encourage them to move away from injecting. Smokable cocaine or amphetamine are also prescribed. Smoking simulates the 'rush' from injecting and may be suitable for injectors unwilling to settle for the milder effects of taking drugs orally. Pilot research and clinical experience suggest prescribing smokables may be a viable alternative treatment for some patients.

Smokable heroin, methadone, cocaine and amphetamine cigarettes have been prescribed by Halton and Warrington drug dependency units since 1989. The aim is to help clients switch away from injecting these drugs because of the greater risks of this mode of administration - particularly HIV infection.

We adopted this innovative policy in the context of the Home Office's estimate that at least 80 per cent of opiate dependents (and probably an even higher percentage of those dependent on stimulants) are not in treatment - a reflection on the 'pulling power' of current treatment practices.

Current treatment policy is also associated with the widespread injection of adulterants and with HIV infection rates in drug addicts above 50 per cent in some areas, particularly where harm-reduction initiatives have in the past been eschewed.

There is an alternative

Injectors who may be willing to forego injecting, but not drug use, are usually given only one option: oral (swallowed) drugs. In the vast majority of drug dependency units, this means oral methadone to substitute for injectable opiates, though a few also prescribe oral amphetamine to amphetamine injectors.

However, pills and liquids are not the only alternatives to injectable drugs - most popular drugs can also be produced in sniffable or smokable forms. Indeed, for illicit drug users these two routes of administration could provide the most effective alternative to injecting for two reasons. First, many opiate injectors have indicated that they do not like the taste of oral preparations such as methadone mixture, and some say that oral preparations make them feel nauseous.

Second, most illicit drug users, whether injecting or not, take drugs by smoking or sniffing them - these are familiar, acceptable practices. The behaviours and experiences underlying these two routes of administration - chopping up powder and 'snorting', or lighting up, inhaling and tasting the smoke - are also valued by drug users.

John Marks, Andrew Palombella and Russell Newcombe: 'The Smoking Option', *DRUGLINK*, May/June 1991, pp. 10-11. © *DRUGLINK* 1991.

But smoking has a major advantage over the nasal route as an alternative to injecting. Sniffing powdered drugs onto the nasal membrane does produce the desired psychoactive effects more quickly than swallowing, but smoking produces these effects as rapidly as injecting - in seconds rather than minutes.

One of the main attractions of injecting is the 'rush' (an accelerated, intense entry into intoxication). Smoking drugs provides the closest simulation of the injecting 'rush' so could be the most effective alternative for committed drug users who nevertheless agree to try to give up injecting. If this is the case, we might expect positive changes in criminal as well as health-related behaviour.

Practicalities

We call the smokable drug prescriptions 'reefers' - packs of herbal or tobacco cigarettes which contain heroin, methadone, cocaine or amphetamine. The reefers are produced by Rankins Pharmaceuticals in Liverpool and distributed to local pharmacies. Production involves dissolving the prescribed drug in chloroform, and injecting the solution into the tobacco/herbal material in a cigarette. The chloroform evaporates in a few minutes, leaving the dissolved drug behind - a process which also stains the cigarette paper green, distinguishing the reefers from standard cigarettes and helping prevent inadvertent use.

How many reefers are prescribed and how strong they are depends on the client's needs, though current prescribing in relation to opiate users averages about 180 to 240mg of smokable opiates per day and rarely exceeds 300mg. Usually the reefers are dispensed weekly, in quantities sufficient for two to six cigarettes a day. More frequent dispensing may be required if patients prove unreliable.

It is important to note that up to two-thirds of the drug in a reefer may be lost through sidestream smoke or poor inhalation technique. With this in mind, each of our reefers contains either: 60mg or 100mg of heroin; 60mg of methadone; 40mg of cocaine; or 30mg of dexamphetamine.

For roughly equivalent prescriptions, oral methadone costs the health service £100-200 per patient per year, injectable opiates £1000-2000, and reefers £300-600.

The standard 'filling' for the cigarettes is herbal - typically Honeyrose herbal cigarettes (containing coltsfoot), or, if available, Potters Asthmatic Cigarettes (containing datura stramonium). Clients who prefer tobacco supply their own cigarettes to the pharmacist, who can then use these to prepare the prescription. It is advised that only low-tar cigarettes should be accepted for clients opting out of the standard herbal-based prescription.

Misuse of Drugs Act regulations governing the supply of drugs to addicts refer only to the drugs, not to how they are to be administered. A special licence is needed to prescribe heroin or cocaine (or dipipanone) for addiction, but doctors with this licence can prescribe these in smokable form. Any doctor can prescribe methadone or amphetamine for addiction in any suitable form - oral, injectable, or smokable.

Prescribing drugs in smokable form does not relieve doctors of their obligation to notify heroin or cocaine addicts to the Home Office.

The issues

Who to prescribe to? Most patients we prescribe smokables to are long-term opiate injectors who wish to try to stop injecting. Smokables are less likely to be prescribed to more short-term injectors as these may be weaned off injection by more conventional means. The absence of physical addiction with stimulants means prescribing these as smokables is also less likely. But newer opiate injectors and stimulant injectors are both at risk of HIV infection and other injection-related illnesses, so are not excluded from the programme altogether.

Reefers can be prescribed on their own, or combined with other prescriptions, to cater for the different needs of a wide variety of injecting clients. For those who cannot immediately give up injecting drugs, a combined injection and reefer prescription can be given, with, when appropriate, a gradual reduction in the injection component and a gradual increase in the reefer component. For those clients able to move toward stabilising on oral prescriptions, a combined oral and reefer prescription can be given, with a gradual reduction in the reefer component and a gradual increase in the oral component. Reefers are not prescribed to non-smokers.

A deeper hook? Even in smokable form, heroin is for many people easier to withdraw from than oral methadone. The half-life of methadone is much greater than heroin but the withdrawal symptoms are less severe. Some addicts find heroin's 'short, sharp' withdrawl much easier to handle than methadone's 'long-drawn out niggle'.

Passive smoking? Are you at risk of inhaling significant quantities of heroin while sitting next to an addict smoking their reefer? Even with tobacco the evidence of increased cancer risk from passive smoking is debatable - and exposure to tobacco smoke is likely to be far greater than could ever arise from the relative handful of opiate smokers.

Smoking-related disease? As we prescribe only to people who already smoke tobacco or cannabis, we consider the increased risk from opiate/stimulant reefers to be negligible - particularly compared to the risks of injecting.

Does it work? So far we have only our experience and pilot research to go on. Larger scale independent research is planned.

Halton drug dependency unit has 30 clients with long histories of intravenous drug use who are now maintained on either reefers or reefers and methadone syrup. They are monitored regularly for signs of intravenous use and urine samples are taken randomly to check that no other drugs are being used.

As previously reported,[1] between 1989 and early 1990 the percentage injecting dropped from 65 per cent to 51 per cent, a reduction which has since continued.

All clients seem to be coping well and none has returned to intravenous use. Their health has improved, relationships are now much more stable, and partners and families are relieved that worries about intravenous drug use have ceased.

Dr Russell Newcombe of Mersey RHA's Drugs and HIV Unit has conducted a small-scale pilot study comparing oral opiate medication with opiate reefers.[2] His findings suggest reefers are a viable alternative for reducing injecting behaviour. Unanalysed interviews with patients give the impression that a 'horses for courses' approach is appropriate, with some people preferring oral medication, others injectables, and others reefers.

Reference

1. Marks J. *et al*, "Prescribing smokable drugs," *Lancet*: 1990, 335(8693), p. 864.

2. Newcombe R. *Preliminary findings of the Halton smokable prescriptions study*. Unpublished, October 1990.

14. Looking for Effective Drug Education Programmes: Fifteen Years Exploration of the Effects of Different Drug Education Programmes*

Willy F.M. De Haes

Introduction

For many years people have worked on the development of drug education programmes. The aim has been to construct programmes that are effective. However, evaluation studies have repeatedly shown that the effects are often weak, that the opposite of what is expected is actually achieved and that often a mixture of positive and negative results is found.

We will show in this article that it has become more and more clear that providing information about substances is not the most important element of effective 'drug education'. If one wants to work on prevention of drug use, it is first necessary to pay attention to young people and their problems. The promotion of 'balanced thinking' about drugs and drug users is needed, in order to create an atmosphere in which 'drug use' is just one of the 'facts of life' that young people are confronted by and must deal with.

A study in Rotterdam

In the early 1970s I was involved in an evaluation study in Rotterdam (De Haes and Schuurman, 1975). We tried to find out which of three approaches to drug education was the most effective: (i) a warning approach (W); (ii) an informative approach (I); (iii) a person-oriented approach (P).

The programmes were carried out on 1035 pupils, 14-16 years old, from 50 schoolclasses distributed over four groups: one group for each approach, and a control group.

The results were surprising. I only give the (at that time) most noteworthy results.

(i) The W and I approaches showed, over a short time period (2 weeks), an increase of both correct and incorrect answers on knowledge items. Only the 'don't know' answers diminished. We concluded that honest uncertainty had become misplaced confidence.

(ii) Attitude changes on the different attitude factors were closely related to the messages contained in each of the three programmes.

*The article is partly based on the text of a lecture given at the 'Research Symposium on Addictive Behaviour', University of Dundee, March 17, 1986.

Willy F.M. De Haes: 'Looking for Effective Drug Education Programmes: Fifteen Years Exploration of the Effects of Different Drug Education Programmes', *HEALTH EDUCATION RESEARCH*, 1987, 2, No. 4, pp. 433-438. © IRL Press Limited, Oxford, England, 1987. Reprinted by permission of Oxford University Press.

(iii) As far as behaviour was concerned none of the pupils experimenting with drugs changed their behaviour, regardless of which approach was used.

(iv) Another behavioural result was that the percentage of people who first tried drugs between the baseline measurement and the long-term effect measurement (7 months later) was 3.6% for the control group, 7.3% for W, 4.6% for I and 2.6% for P.

We concluded that 'substance-oriented' drug education programmes, either purely informative or warning, have a stimulating effect on drug experimentation. We recommended that this type of drug education programme should not be encouraged.

A second conclusion was that talking about the problems young people have, as in the person-oriented approach, is effective in reducing drug experimentation, and also, as reported by the teachers involved, in reducing aggressive and attention-attracting classroom behaviour. It also stimulated a positive learning attitude. Clearly, talking about their own problems (failure to make social contacts, difficulty in first love and sexual experiences, feeling the victim of parents' divorce, etc.) leads to a feeling of being able to master a situation, to find solutions for it or to live with it. Therefore it may be expected that this approach will lead to fewer alcohol problems, less aggressive and destructive behaviour, and less interpersonal conflicts. We recommend that teacher training should encourage this type of discussion between teachers and pupils.

At the policy level the action towards these recommendations was remarkable. At both the local level (in Rotterdam) and at the national level of the ministries, the reaction was the same. Those with responsibility for health decided not to encourage substance-centred drug education programmes and to open discussions with colleagues responsible for education, to allow teachers to be trained and to implement the recommendations. On both national and local levels, people in the education system were reluctant to implement the second proposal on teacher training. They did not want to stimulate teacher - pupil discussions which were not the norm within the education system. Therefore this type of training was not at that time implemented (at least not with their encouragement and support).

The results of evaluation studies elsewhere

Many studies in the 1970s showed that programmes focusing on substances have few or no positive effects. Programmes focusing on pupils (their values, their skills, their problems, their expectations of the future) seem to show more positive results. At least it became clear that these programmes do not stimulate experimentation with drugs as much as the substance-focused programmes often do.

A review of the literature will show this point. It might further help us to find an answer to the question: what type of programmes have to be explored in the future?

Goodstadt

Goodstadt (1974) reviewed the evidence concerning the effectiveness of drug education programmes by firstly selecting studies which were methodologically rigorous enough to lead to valuable outcomes. After a detailed discussion of the results of about 20 selected studies, Goodstadt came to two main conclusions, the first:

'The majority of the evidence supports the conclusion that the drug education programs which have been evaluated have had no documented significant effect either of a positive or a negative kind: that is, there was no change as a result of the programs.' (p. 142)

The second main conclusion must be considered alongside the above:

'there is little scientific evidence from which one could confidently draw conclusions concerning the effectiveness of drug education .... it can only be concluded that the necessary evidence is not yet available, although the evidence that does exist is not encouraging.' (p. 142)

Berberian et al

A review of 27 studies by Berberian *et al.* (1976) follows the same procedure as Goodstadt; although more and different studies have been included in the study the conclusion is similar.

'Such a body of data leads to the conclusion that schools have not been able to demonstrate that they are succeeding in preventing drug abuse. A large part of this failure is due to the fact that most schools have made plans to do something about the drug abuse problem without incorporating a method for evaluating their effectiveness .... schools should recognise that the ultimate goal of drug education is drug abuse prevention or reduction and that such objectives as program popularity, gains in knowledge, or even attitude change may be irresponsible, since there is some evidence that these may be counterproductive.' (p. 395)

Hanson

Hanson (1982) also comes to the same conclusions:

'Research has demonstrated that while it is relatively easy to increase drug knowledge, it is more difficult to modify attitudes .... By far the largest number of studies have found no effects of drug education upon use. A few have found drug usage to be reduced while others have found it to be increased following drug education.'

Kinder, Pape and Walfish

In 1980, Kinder, Pape and Walfish reviewed a series of drug and alcohol education programmes aimed at students and at adult populations. Their conclusions are again very clear:

'The data reviewed indicate that drug and/or alcohol education programs have for the most part been ineffective in obtaining the goals of decreasing substance abuse or preventing future abuse. Studies of student populations have obtained contradictory results, but with repeated implications that such programs may lead to increased usage in some instances.'

Randall and Wong

A review by Randall and Wong (1976) covers more than 200 drug education programmes. But only 23 of these reported any systematic evaluation, and only 15 reported use of both pre- and post-treatment measures coupled with a control group to allow comparison of effects. They came to the following conclusion:

> 'In several programs, significant gains were made in knowledge about drugs .... However, in some studies drug education that focused on the provision of information about drugs seemed to increase the desire to experiment with drugs. It is possible to measure and report changes in attitudes about drugs so long as the measures are taken soon after the conclusion of treatment. On the other hand, not much is known about the long term behavioural consequences of drug education efforts.'

At the end of their article Randall and Wong state that 'chemicals with the capacity to alter mood are always going to be available to people'. Therefore it is unrealistic to want to eradicate drug use. People like to feel good and if drugs can help to achieve this, they will be used for that purpose.

Given these assumptions, Randall and Wong say that 'the objective of total prevention of drug use seems a little ludicrous - at least in the short run', and they formulate 'new objectives'. In eight points they outline a 'balanced approach' to the content of drug education programmes, the final point being, 'to provide the student with the decision-making skills that will enable him to make decisions regarding drug use and life goals that will lead towards long term positive outcomes for the individual'.

Based on these assumptions and objectives a 'new generation' of drug education programmes was developed, in which value clarification and the promotion of decision-making skills play an important part.

Schaps et al

In 1981 Schaps et al. published 'a review of 127 drug abuse prevention program evaluations'.

They concluded along the same lines as Randall and Wong: 'overall, the 127 programmes produced only minor effects on drug use behaviours and attitudes'. But also: 'the best of the available evaluations are tentatively encouraging about the efficacy of "new generation" prevention programmes'.

Battjes

Battjes (1985) review of drug education studies leads to the same conclusions with regard to drug education programmes. He further explores the results of programmes in which social pressures and social skills training approaches are used in relation to smoking prevention.

Although the designs and the research methodologies are sometimes weak, it becomes clear that, at least for smoking prevention, the new methods are promising.

'While much inadequate prevention research continues, research has become increasingly rigorous over the last several years. Particularly encouraging have been studies of social pressures and social skills approaches. .... While considerable evidence supports the effectiveness of these approaches in preventing smoking during early adolescence, further research is needed to confirm their effectiveness in preventing alcohol and other drug abuse, to clarify with whom these approaches are effective, and to maximize their effectiveness.'

Conclusions

The literature review seems to confirm that: (i) 'substance-oriented' drug education programmes have, in general, a negative effect or no effect at all; and (ii) programmes paying attention to young people, who they are and how they live, teaching them how to overcome day-to-day difficulties, and so forth, are effective not only in reducing drug use, but also in reducing other rebellious or attention-seeking behaviour.

Therefore, there is a need to explore the content and methods of these types of programmes. What is required initially is a point of view from which to look at the drug problem, at young people and at drug education.

A 'balanced' view of drug use behaviour

There is a need for a balanced view on the phenomenon of drug use behaviour in society.

In 1975 Helen Nowlis described such a balanced view. Her ideas are still very valuable today, and some aspects will be described below.

In relation to substances

(i) All substances have an effective dose, a toxic dose and a lethal dose.

(ii) All drugs have multiple effects and these vary from dose level to dose level, from individual to individual, from time to time and from setting to setting in the same individual.

(iii) The personal and social effects of illegal drug use are influenced by the legal status of the drug.

(iv) There are effects that depend both on special characteristics of some drugs as pharmacological substances, and on patterns of use of those substances.

In relation to young people, potential users and users

(i) Experimenting with 'new' forms of behaviour, seeking the limits of one's possibilities, and doing forbidden things is part of adolescence.

(ii) There is no specific psycho-social, educational or social-environmental factor responsible for drug use. Every user has his or her own history.

(iii) There is a clear distinction between recreational use, occasional use, regular use and heavy or compulsive use. There is no casual relationship between the first step and the following ones.

(iv) There are people who respond to problems through the use of drugs. It is tempting to see them as perverse; it is more constructive to see them as people with problems with which they cannot cope in socially acceptable ways.

In relation to the social context

(i) Recreational and occasional use can become regular use as a consequence of the reactions of parents, neighbours, teachers and health educators.

(ii) Most parents, neighbours, teachers and health educators lack balanced information about the points mentioned in the paragraphs above. As a consequence, they are afraid of any drug use, and in that way they cannot be a partner in discussions with youngsters who are using drugs.

(iii) Destructive drug use is not isolated, but is something related to other destructive behaviour such as violence and adolescent suicide.

(iv) As drug use is related to multiple background factors, it is clear that 'all youth policy is (good or bad) drug prevention policy'.

Interconnection

The above-mentioned points are grouped around three elements: the substance, the individual and the (social) context. This is not by accident. The 'epidemiological triangle' (Figure 1) is a useful tool to show the permanent interconnection of these three factors in determining drug behaviour. This same model is also the basis from which to look at treatment, at prevention and at the content of drug education programmes.

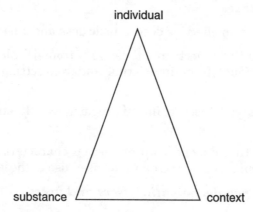

Figure 1. The epidemiological triangle.

Points of view

Discussion of drug policy, drug prevention, drug education, etc. is often hindered by the fact that people look from different positions at the same phenomena (the triangle, Figure 1), and thus see different aspects as being the most important or as 'the' cause or 'the' solution.

Four different background models can be detected in the various ways people look at the drug use phenomena.

(i) *The moral - legal model*. Drugs are prohibited by law, thus drug use is a crime, and users and sellers have to be prosecuted.

(ii) *The disease or public health model*. Drugs are harmful to the body, people using them have a kind of illness, they need medical treatment.

(iii) *The psycho-social model*. People using drugs have personality disturbances or personal problems. They need psychotherapy or help with solving their problems.

(iv) *The socio-cultural model*. People are the victims of a badly organized and unjust society. Society has to be changed: people have to be more equal and have more power over their own lives. In a 'just society' there will be no drug problems.

All four models contain some truth. Therefore it seems to be more realistic to say that only a view that takes the four points into account is a 'balanced' view.

A 'balanced view' of people in relation to drug education

The development of a programme aimed at reducing experimentation with, and use of, drugs needs to start from a realistic view of the young people it is meant for.

(i) Young people explore different aspects of the world around them; they test the values and norms of adult society. Prevention of this exploration and experimentation is not possible.

(ii) Young people, in common with adults, are not 'empty vessels' with regard to drugs. They already have knowledge, attitudes and behaviours with regard to 'riskful substances'.

(iii) Some young people are - mostly on the basis of their negative psycho-social background - in contact with 'the world of crime and illegality'. In this 'reference group' they pick up their information on drugs (see Janssen and Swierstra, 1982).

(iv) Most young people reject drugs use as a realistic alternative.

(v) Young people are very sensitive to social conformity pressures, but neither at home, nor at school do they learn to resist these pressures.

These are just a few elements that seem important when developing a drug education curriculum for schools. It is more important for people working on drug education programmes to be familiar with adolescent psychology than to know facts about drugs.

Conclusion

The literature suggests that all methods of drug education which have been tried and evaluated during the past 15 years have had no more than marginal effects on attitude and behaviour variables in relation to drug use. It seems as if one is looking for something that does not exist. It might mean that one expects too much from education as a tool to prevent drug use. It might also mean that one is aiming at the wrong goal or that one is still not using the right method.

In our 'rational society' (at least that is what we think we are) it seems so easy: 'tell them the truth, tell them the dangers and they will avoid them'. It seems to be more complex. Young people, and adults, mostly do not act in a straightforward 'rational-economic' manner on the basis of their knowledge.

However, recent literature, evaluating the results of programmes working on 'life skills' (decision making, problem solving, resistance to social pressure, self-development, etc) have shown this approach to be more promising as regards the use of dangerous substances. This seems to confirm the idea that paying attention to young people in their maturation phase is much more important than informing them about substances they might come into contact with. This does not mean that this knowledge, in some way, is not useful. It just indicates what is of prior importance.

It can be concluded that it is worthwhile to work on the development of programmes aimed at helping young people to understand themselves and the world around them while developing towards maturity. We must also aim to teach them skills and give them the tools which will enable them successfully to deal with the difficulties they are confronted with. These programmes can have many positive effects, among them less experimentation with illegal drugs. The question of whether these programmes can still be called drug education programmes does not seem relevant. Maybe the best answer is a question: do we need specific drug education programmes?

References

Battjes, R.J. (1985) 'Prevention of adolescent drug abuse'. *International Journal of Addictions*, 20, 1113-1134.

Berberian, R.M., Gross, C., Lovesoy, J. and Paparella, S. (1976) 'The effectiveness of drug education programs: a critical review'. *Health Education Monographs*, 4, 377-398.

De Haes, W.F.M. and Schuurman, J.H. (1975) 'Results of an evaluation study of three drug education methods'. *International Journal of Health Education*, 18, (Suppl.), 1-16.

Goodstadt, M.S. (1974) 'Myths and methodology in drug education. A critical review of the research evidence'. In Goodstadt, M.S. (ed.). *Research on Methods and Programs of Drug Education*. Addiction Research Foundation of Ontario, Canada. pp. 113-147.

Hanson, D.J. (1982) 'The effectiveness of alcohol and drug education'. *Journal of Alcohol and Drug Education*, 27, 1-13.

Janssen, O. and Swierstra. K.M. (1982) 'Heroinegebruikers in Nederland; een typologie van levensstijlen [Heroin users in the Netherlands: a typology of lifestyles]'. Criminologisch Instituut, University of Groningen, p. 668.

Kinder, B.N., Pape, N.E. and Walfish, S. (1980) 'Drug and alcohol education programs, a review of outcome studies'. *International Journal of Addictions*, 15, 1035-1054.

Nowlis, H. (1975) *Drugs Demystified*. The UNESCO Press, Paris. p. 92.

Randall, D. and Wong, M.R. (1976) 'Drug education to date: a review'. *Journal of Drug Education*, 6, 1-21.

Schaps, E., DiBartolo, R., Moskowitz, J., Palley, C.S. and Churgin, S. (1981) 'Review of 127 drug abuse prevention programme evaluations'. *Journal of Drug Issues*, 11, 17-43.

15.   Drug Education to School Children: Does it Really Work?

Harith Swadi and Harry Zeitlin

Summary

Despite the great efforts made by law enforcement agencies around the world, the evidence is that illicit substances are becoming more easily available. Increasing emphasis is being put on prevention by education. This review examines and evaluates some of the currently used drug education approaches and programmes. The evidence so far indicates that some programmes had limited effectiveness; most had major shortcomings, and there is little to choose between them. Certain aspects of the evaluated educational approaches have some potential. This review also discusses a possible way of combining these aspects in a school-based educational programme.

Introduction

Recently there has been a renewed interest in drug education programmes for school children. This has been shown by the public recommendation made by The Association of School Headmasters through the media that a vigorous education programme for all school children should be initiated. The Department of Health & Social Security is concerned to promote research into the effects of drug education on the prevalence and the pattern of drug use in children and adolescents. Evaluation of intervention requires the use of sound epidemiological studies on the extent and the nature of the problem, but unfortunately these are lacking in the United Kingdom. In the area of solvent abuse, for example, Woodcock[1] noted that there are no epidemiological data reliable enough for prevention programmes to be designed and implemented and therefore North American data are used in designing such programmes. He also sees the problem not confined to solvent abuse but extending across the whole range of drugs. The Institute for Study of Drug Dependence (ISDD) demonstrated this epidemiological defect when it said "The only satisfactory way of estimating the number of persons misusing drugs would be to conduct reliable large-scale representative and confidential surveys .... No such survey has ever been done".[2]

What is drug education?

The term 'Drug education' is meant to include any measure aimed at developing within the adolescent the ability, the attitude, and the free will to avoid involvement in drug taking behaviour. This essentially involves teaching or instruction of groups of children and adolescents, by all available channels. Such channels include mass media (radio, television, newspapers, youth magazines, etc), schools, and youth clubs. These 'educational' methods aim at producing measurable shift in the knowledge about, the attitude towards, and the use of drugs. Under this umbrella several approaches have

Harith Swadi and Harry Zeitlin (1987), 'Drug Education to School Children: Does it Really Work?' *BRITISH JOURNAL OF ADDICTION*, 82, pp. 741-746. Reprinted by permission of Carfax Publishing Company, PO Box 25, Abingdon, Oxfordshire, OX14 3UE.

been included. The more widely used are: adverse propaganda and mass media campaigns, factual information, the acquisition of certain social and personal skills, alternative activity programmes, and the promotion of ideas related to healthy living.

Rationale

British drug education programmes seem to be primarily based on North American ones. This means that they are likely to share the same strategies and objectives. Most programmes have been faced with severe criticism about their design, objectives, and evaluation.[3,4] However, despite the difficulty in finding a stated rationale for the use of drug education programmes, it seems to assume that:

1. Because of their lack of information on drugs, children do not know how dangerous drugs are, and therefore engage in their use.

2. The child is more likely to start experimenting under the influence of personal factors, e.g. the lack of certain skills, and environmental factors, e.g. those related to family, peer group, neighbourhood, and school.

3. The child can safely avoid substance abuse if he/she was provided with alternative sources for obtaining the desirable effects he/she would get from drugs.

From this it is further assumed that addressing these issues, leads to a measurable - and desirable - shift in the prevalence and pattern of substance abuse. In practice, however, this was not the case. There have been several attempts to evaluate the effect of various methods of education in the field of drug abuse prevention.

Mass media campaigns

The first 'educational measure' was the use of public media such as television, radio, and newspapers for mass campaigns. Following the first newspaper report in the *Denver Post*,[5] the public media showed increasing interest in solvent abuse. The phenomenon was virtually unknown in other American states until it started to be reported in other national newspapers. It is only after reporting became persistent and widespread that solvent abuse gained momentum.[6] Moreover, the use of mass media campaigns for education has been said to be counterproductive by the Special Action Office for Drug Abuse Prevention at the White House.[7] The use of such programmes was eventually severely curtailed in the U.S.A. probably in view of this. However, that office points out that the problem could have arisen from the way the information was relayed and not from the use of the media as a means of education. It concluded that the programmes exaggerated the harmful effects of drugs and created what it called a 'credibility gap' leading to polarization between the establishment on one hand and youth and the pro-drug-use culture on the other. This highlights the necessity for a distinction between 'education' and 'propaganda'. Plant *et al.*[3] raise an important point by indicating that "many initiatives which are undertaken are really propaganda and not education", and "are often mounted to demonstrate that action is being taken". They also criticize many of the so called 'mass media educational campaigns' for being "very poorly designed, ill informed, grossly alarmist, and over-sensationalized". In fact some seem to propagate the introduction to the drug abuse scene in Britain of previously unknown drugs. For example, the wide coverage recently given by the British media to the cocaine derivative 'crack' even included instructions on how to prepare a 'fix'. The Health Education Council in England and Wales warned that caution should be exercised in the use of widespread publicity. Also the Home Office has categorically stated that "National campaigns aimed specifically at reducing the incidence of drug misuse should not be attempted", and that "Media coverage of drug matters needs to be better informed". There are several other studies that came to the same conclusion.[9-13] It seems likely that "media drug campaigns may be worse than a waste of money".[14]

Drug information programmes

Another method of education is the development of school education and information programmes. Most didactic programmes of this kind aim at providing school children with factual information about drugs without overtones. Evaluation of such programmes showed that although school children acquire more knowledge about drugs, the effect on the prevalence of use of drugs were not encouraging. De Haes & Schurrman[9] compared the evaluation results of three different programmes: a school based information programme, a programme designed to tell about the 'horrors' of drug taking and a course of personal relationship skills. The results indicated that the personal relationship programme had the least negative effects and the most promising positive aspects; the 'mild horror' programme was significantly worse than the control (see table 1).

Table 1. *The Number of Children Who Said They Started Using Cannabis After Being Exposed to Three Different Drug Education Programmes*

Group	Sample number	New cannabis users
Control group	253	9 (3.6%)
Horror group	329	24 (7.3%) (significant)
Factual information	264	12 (4.6%) (not significant)
Personal relationships	189	5 (2.6%) (not significant)

The exposure of children to drug education programmes might serve to alleviate anxiety about its use and thus lead to experimenting.[15] This was confirmed by other studies[11,16] which found that there was an increased likelihood of drug taking in young people when subjected to a drug education programme. Plant et al.[3] reviewed alcohol education research and suggested that alcohol education that gives people facts about alcohol and its dangers did not seem to make any difference to their drinking behaviour. However, Moskowitz et al,[17] point out that drug education giving factual knowledge about drugs seems to give very limited results in a selected population and only when combined with other approaches. The programmes evaluated combined factual information about drugs with opportunities to develop personal skills. The results showed that drug education held some promise for 'seventh grade' (first year secondary school in U.K.)

school girls in California with respect to knowledge about drugs, cigarette smoking, and the perception of peers' attitude to drug taking. The effect was lost a year later. The programme was ineffective for males.

There is some evidence, however, to suggest that didactic education might help prevent drug users shift to a more hazardous substance.[18] This study is considered one of the best designed and carried out. About 2,700 children were randomly assigned to two groups utilizing different educational approaches and to a control group. The first approach was a didactic programme giving factual information and the second used a programme based on 'process education' (value clarification, norm setting discussion). Among others, the outcome criteria included change in the prevalence and change in the stability of the type of style or abuse. After careful analysis the results confirmed the inefficacy of the educational programme tested to affect the 'level' (prevalence and frequency) of experimentation. However, it also included that regarding the 'stability' (type of substance and style of use) of drug use "about 25% of the didactic group will be 'destabilized' by drug education in comparison with more-stable controls, whereas over 30% more controls than didactic students are likely to make extreme leaps in their drug use level once they do begin to change". In other words the didactic education programme is likely to prevent the adolescent move to abuse of potentially more harmful substances or styles of use, but that might occur at the expense of an increased use of the 'safer' forms of substances.

The evidence of the whole suggests that drug education programmes in the form of factual knowledge had yielded, at best, negligible, and sometimes counterproductive results.[1,17,19.20]

The generic approach

Many studies indicate that there is an association between drug abuse and certain risk factors related to the behaviour, personality and lifestyle of the child,[21] and between self attitudes and values and drug abuse.[22] Research results have generally concluded that adolescent drug users were more likely to have low self-esteem, tend to be alienated, have poor scholastic performance, have deficits in interpersonal skills and generally have a negative attitude towards authority.[19] The 'generic approach' of prevention aims at decreasing the extent of such factors. The approach took two directions; one that focuses on 'affective education' and one that focuses on providing the adolescent with 'Alternatives'. Evaluation of both types of programmes has given somewhat disappointing results.

'Affective Education'

'Affective Education' programmes aim at developing values, and stimulating thought, opinion making, and decision making. The Georgia State Department of Education developed a programme of 'life skills' to be delivered to the students by school teachers who had received in-service training. The programme focused on intra- and inter-personal skills, decision making, handling stress, and developing satisfying and effective interpersonal relations.[23] Evaluation showed that while there was some improvement in those aspects, it had little effect on self-reported alcohol and drug use.

The 'Alternatives Approach'

The 'Alternatives Approach' programmes aim at providing the adolescent with non-chemical means of deriving pleasure and reward, which the drug user would get from drugs.[24] Although there are several methods of application of the 'alternatives approach', none seems to be superior to another in achieving a reduction in the extent of drug use. Cook *et al.*[25] described an 'alternatives' programme that aimed at facilitating communication, self-care and self concept with the use of physical activities, creative-expressive activities and consciousness alternatives, calling it the 'Positive Alternatives Programme'. This was evaluated over a 2-year period. The results showed that there was little effect on the rate of self-reported use of drugs, but there was a significant improvement in the adolescents' attitude to drug use. However, they consider the overall time they implemented the programme for, not enough to achieve a greater impact on the rate of use. Other workers focus on 'Effective Classroom Management' as an alternative.[17] This approach, even when combined with factual drug education, gave very limited, short term results. However, it seems that most versions of the 'alternative programmes' consider addressing the area of self-esteem an important component.

Some aspects of the 'generic approach', those that originate from the 'Humanistic Education' areas such as decision making skills, and the improvement of self esteem hold limited promise with regard to altered attitude. The approach as a whole though, when implemented by itself, seems to have little effect in reducing the prevalence of drug abuse.

Comparative studies

Five models of prevention programmes were compared to each other among a student population.[26] The study included 1,575 American students of whom 299 were a control group with no intervention. The mean age was 12.73 years and just over half were girls. The programme was implemented for 'one semester' (about 18 weeks). After control for age and sex, they were allocated to one of five different prevention programmes.

1. The Humanistic Educational Model using activities designed to clarify values, stimulate thought and decision making and opinion.

2. The Peer Group Model focusing on group dynamics, problem solving and risk taking behaviour.

3. The Parent Effectiveness Model, teaching parents effective parenting styles and improving family communication.

4. A 'network' group in which prevention groups were built around common shared problems and which called upon support amongst the group members.

5. An 'advocacy' group which focused on providing information on problem solving.

The outcome variables included among others, self-reported use of alcohol and/or drugs, attitude towards drugs and alcohol, and 'responsible use' of drugs and/or alcohol. Analysing the data, they found that 'parent effectiveness and peer group models significantly surpassed control performance in prevention of alcohol, advocacy and network models were indistinguishable from control, and humanistic education performed significantly worse.' With regards to other drugs, the peer group model was the only model that surpassed the control group especially with solvent and marijuana abuse.

The NAPA study conducted in Napa, California evaluated seven prevention programmes delivered to 6,000 American students.[27] The outcome criteria included attitude, intention to use, knowledge, and self-reports or drug use among other criteria. The programmes under evaluation were different versions of the generic approach, and factual drug education. The results showed that only drug education produced some positive but short term results, and then only with 'seventh grade' (first year secondary school in U.K.) girls, clearly a result that supports the view that drug education aimed at preventing the onset of drug use is not every effective. This is more optimistic for drug education programmes, but still offers only limited effectiveness. The question arises as to why this programme was at least better than other drug education programmes. In this study, the drug education programme included in addition to factual information about drugs, opportunities to develop assertiveness, decision making and communication skills. It is not unlikely that the limited positive effect was the result of acquiring new decision making and communication skills.

In a review of 75 reports on 127 drug prevention programmes involving 10 different strategies, Schaps *et al.*[12] criticize the design, methodology, and evaluation of such programmes. The programmes that yielded some positive results were those that comprised a combination of different approaches. Indeed, some programmes were counterproductive. They recommended that "when planning prevention efforts, careful consideration should be given to the scope, intensity and duration of programme services".

Conclusion

It must be our conclusion that the available methods of drug education that aim at preventing drug abuse are at least ineffective, if not counterproductive. It is possible that the substance of such programmes is not suitable or that the methods of education are faulty. Educational programmes are less likely to be effective when they:

(a) Give incomplete, inaccurate, or incomprehensible information.

(b) Do not address the possible aetiological factors that may have a role in initiating experimenting like difficulties in problem solving and peer pressure resistance.

(c) Lack a clear and realistic objective, that is whether they aim at tackling the attitude to, the prevalence of, or the pattern of substance abuse.

(d) Concentrate on substance abuse and ignore the background against which it occurs. It should be considered as only one feature of an unhealthy way of living and be addressed as such.

(e) Use one isolated strategy. Substance abuse is very likely to have a multifactorial aetiology. Several aspects of different strategies have shown some promise. A combination of these is less likely to fail.

At the same time the methods of education are least effective if they:

(a) Use 'scare' tactics.

(b) Are delivered in such a way that they seem to be 'imposed' on the receivers.

(c) Are delivered by participants without adequate skill in dealing with adolescents.

(d) Are not an ongoing part of the school curriculum. No programme has yet managed to produce positive long-term effects.

(e) Cannot be properly evaluated.

Drug Education programmes should have a stated objective. It is ideal to aim at eradication through primary prevention. This seems to be impossible given the current social trends. However, one objective, we believe, should be common to all programmes, that is miminization of harm. If we cannot help adolescents abstain, we should try to help them modify their styles of drug use. It might even be necessary for drug education programmes to aim for only 'reasonable use' despite the ethical and sociological difficulties arising from such action. Reduction of harm may aim at a reduction in frequency, a change in type of substance towards 'safer' ones, and - appropriately now - a change in the routes of intake. This last point is particularly relevant with the current concern about the Acquired Immune Deficiency Syndrome (AIDS). Current literature points out that AIDS is very prevalent (second in order to the gay community) among drug users who use intravenous injections sharing the same 'kit'.[28] Particular effort in informing and educating drug users should be made; indeed one very suitable avenue is drug education programmes.

Another probable explanation for the failure of the present educational strategies is that each approach is insufficient in itself and that it is essential to assist young people to develop the attitude necessary to handle 'factual information'. What is clear however, is that more work is needed to explore the promise given by some of the new approaches. These focus mainly on the adolescent as an individual who has difficulties in terms of self esteem; who lacks certain personal skills; who has relationship difficulties and who has problems with resisting peer pressure. It is not sufficient for the adolescent to be more informed about drugs to avoid experimenting and subsequent regular use. Programmes that tackle the deficiencies within the adolescent and that promote a healthy, drug-free environment have more promise. A programme designed to address these issues has been developed and is currently being tested.

References

1. Woodcock, J. (1982) 'Solvent abuse from a health education perspective', *Human Toxicology*, 1, pp. 331-336.

2. ISDD (1986) *Surveys and Statistics on Drug Taking in Britain* (London, Institute for the Study of Drug Dependence).

3. Plant, M., Peck, D. & Samuel, E. (1985) 'Alcohol, Drugs and School-leavers' (London, Tavistock).

4. Dorn, N. (1981) 'Youth Culture in the U.K.: Independence and Round Drinking', *International Journal of Health Education*, 24, pp. 281-282.

5. Fluke, B. & Donato, L. (1959) 'Some glues are dangerous', *Empire Magazine* (Supplement to *Denver Post*, August 2nd).

6. Bercher, E. (1972) *Licit and Illicit Drugs: Consumers Union Report* (Boston, Little, Brown & Co.).

7. Special Action Office for Drug Abuse Prevention (1973) *The Media and Drug Abuse Messages* (Washington, D.C., The White House).

8. Home Office (1984) *Prevention: Report of the Advisory Council on the Misuse of Drugs* (London, HMSO).

9. De Haes, W. & Schurrmann, J. (1975) 'Results of an evaluation study of three drug education methods', *International Journal of Health Education*, 18 (Suppl.).

10. Dorn, N. & Thompson, A. (1981) *A Comparison of 1973 and 1974 of Mid-teenage Experimentation with Illegal Drugs in Some Schools in England* (London, Institute for the Study of Drug Dependence).

11. Kinder, B., Pape, N. & Walfish, S. (1980) 'Drugs and alcohol education programmes: a review of outcome studies', *International Journal of the Addictions*, 15, pp. 1035-54.

12. Schaps, E., Moskowitz, J., Condon, J. & Malvin, J. (1981) 'A review of 127 drug abuse prevention programme evaluations', *Journal of Drug Issues*, 11, pp. 17-43.

13. Bandy, P. & President, P. (1983) 'Recent literature on drug abuse prevention and mass media: focusing on youth, parents, women, and the elderly', *Journal of Drug Education*, 13, pp. 225-71.

14. Editorial: (1985) 'Media drug campaigns may be worse than a waste of money', *British Medical Journal*, 290, p. 416.

15. Smart, R. & Feijer, D. (1974) 'The effect of high and low fear messages about drugs', *Journal of Drug Education*, 4, pp. 225-35.

16. Tennant, F., Weaver, S. & Lewis, C. (1973) 'Outcome of Drug Education', *Paediatrics*, 52, pp. 246-50.

17. Moskowitz, J., Schaps, E., Schaeffer, G. & Malvin, J. (1984) 'Evaluation of a substance prevention programme for junior highschool students', *International Journal of the Addictions*, 19, pp. 419-30.

18. Blum, R. (1976) *Drug Education: results and recommendations* (Lexington, Ma, Lexington Books).

19. Durell, J. & Bukoski, W. (1984) 'Preventing substance abuse: the state of the art', *Public Health Reports*, pp. 23-31.

20. Wright, J. & Pearl, L. (1986) 'Knowledge and experience of young people of drug abuse 1969-1984', *British Medical Journal*, 292, pp. 179-82.

21. Nurco, D. (1979) 'Etiologic aspects of drug abuse', in: R. Dupont, A. Goldstein & J. O'Donnell (Eds) *Handbook on Drug Abuse*, pp. 315-324 (Washington, D.C., U.S. Government Printing Office).

22. Smith, G & Fogg, C. (1978) 'Psychological predictors of early use, late use, and nonuse of marijuana among teenage students', in: D. Kandel (Ed.) *Longitudinal Research on Drug Use*, pp. 101-13 (Washington, D.C., Hemisphere).

23. Dusewicz, R. & Martin, M. (1981) *Impacts of a Georgia Drug Abuse Prevention Programme* (Philadephia, Research for Better Schools Inc.).

24. Dohner, V. (1972) 'Alternatives to Drugs: a new approach to drug education', *Journal of Drug Education*, 2, pp. 3-22.

25. Cook, R., Lawrence, H., Morse, C. & Roehl, J. (1984) 'An evaluation of the alternatives approach to drug abuse prevention', *International Journal of The Addictions*, 19, pp. 767-87.

26. Sexter, J., Sullivan, A., Wepner, S. & Denmark, R. (1984) 'Substance abuse: assessment of the outcome of activities and activity clusters in school-based prevention', *International Journal of the Addictions*, 19, pp. 79-92.

27. Schaps, E., Moskowitz, J., Malvin, J. & Schaeffer, G. (1983) 'NAPA project summary: a final report on grant no. EO7DA02147, submitted to The National Institute on Drug Abuse' (Rockville, Maryland).

28. Editorial: (1986) 'AIDS: act now, don't pay later', *British Medical Journal*, 293, p. 348.

Willy Whizz
S.S.H.A

17. Paranoia and the Don't Care Bears

196

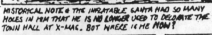

High in the 'E' Stand

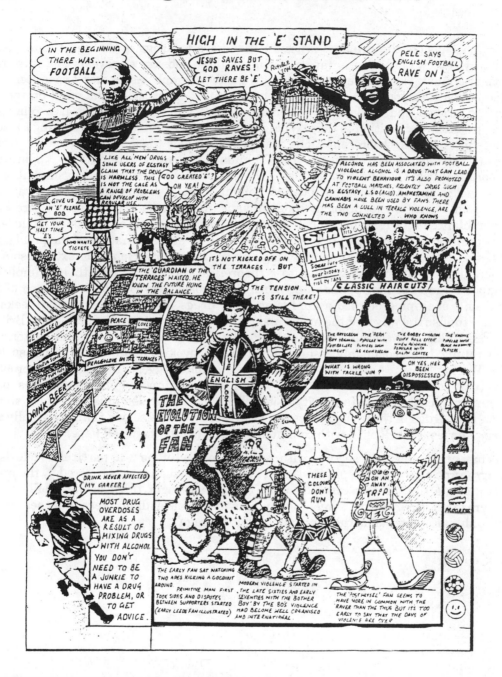

Moral Panics, Drugs and Drug Use

For most people the primary exposure they have to drugs is through the media. A cursory review of the presentation of some of these substances reveals that it is often sensationalist, exaggerated or distorts drug effects, emphasising worst case scenarios (likely death or addiction) and taken out of context. That the media often present us with distorted and misleading information in regard to illicit drugs is a relatively non-problematic position to take. What is slightly more problematic is making sense of the effects that such presentations may have and how these relate to 'moral panics' around drugs and drug users. Ben-Yehuda specifically attempts to update the theoretical basis of moral panics using the example of a particular drugs/moral panic in Israel in the early 1980s. What Ben-Yehuda usefully demonstrates is the way that representations of the 'problem' by politicians, institutions and the media bore little resemblance to the real situation: that drugs and their use may on occassion be elevated to a position of concern through the distortion of the size and nature of the problem in order to deflect attention from other high profile issues, or to lobby for extra resources or credibility. Kohn, less wedded to a theoretical framework, nonetheless implicitly supports much of Ben-Yehuda but much more colourfully relates to us some of the extreme examples of media confusion over drugs and drug users and seeks to contextualise the way that the media and politicians represented the problem in Britain in the 1980s with heroin becomining 'Public Enemy Number One' and rhetoric on controlling drugs commonly assuming metaphors invoking a military response such as the 'War on Drugs'. Again, as with Ben-Yehuda, Kohn suggests that the drugs problem usefully diverted attention from other burgeoning problems such as high unemployment and the inner-city riots. Additionally, he also illustrates how stories involving drugs in the tabloid press can be dressed up to be 'sexier' than they really are. Drug stories (embellished with commonplace mythology) help sell papers.

Corina *et al* end this section with a brief review of how a particular television programme on the philosophy and practice of harm reduction was covered by the press. They argue that in this case Granada Television sought to raise the profile of the programme prior to its screening by providing misleading press releases which 'arguably promoted a moral panic and public outrage'.

19. The Sociology of Moral Panics: Toward a New Synthesis

Nachman Ben-Yehuda

There are two alternatives theoretical perspectives developed in the sociological study of a moral panic: the moral perspective and the interest perspective. Using as illustrations a May 1982 national moral panic about drugs that occurred in Israel, this article argues that both perspectives must be used and integrated into one coherent model for a better and fuller sociological explanation of moral panics. The article provides a detailed account of the Israeli panic and an analysis clustered along two axes. One axis uses the interest perspective to analyze the <u>timing</u> of the panic by focusing on the question of why it happened when it did. The other axis uses the moral perspective to interpret the specific <u>content</u> of the panic, focusing on why the panic was about drugs.

INTRODUCTION

Moral panics

Origin of concept and explanation

The labeling approach (see, for example, Goode 1978: Schur 1971, 1979; Becker 1963) stipulates that deviance results when others apply rules and sanctions to an "offender": ".... deviant behavior is behavior that people so label" (Becker 1963, p. 9). This approach focused attention on the societal reaction to presumed acts of deviance and emphasized the role of social control agencies as amplifiers (or even manufacturers) of deviance (e.g. Wilkins 1964: Ben Yehuda 1980).

According to Becker (1963, pp. 8-9), social groups create deviance by "making the rules whose infraction constitutes deviance." These rules, however, are clearly the product of negotiations about morality among different social groups and individual actors. *Morality* refers to the set of social criteria used by actors to evaluate objects, behavior and goals as good or bad, desirable or undesirable (Lidz and Walker 1980). *Morality* is an important sociological concept because its main functions are to orient and direct social actions and to define the boundaries of cultural matrices (Ben-Yehuda 1985).

Becker (1963, Ch. 8) argued that *Moral Entrepreneurs* are actors who attempt to persuade others to adhere to particular value systems. Moral entrepreneurs start *Moral Crusades* to transform the public's attitudes toward specified issues, change legislation, and/or attempt to "deviantize" (Schur 1980) others. Thus, moral crusaders often create what Cohen's (1972) outstanding work called *Moral Panics* in which

> .... a condition, episode, person, or group of persons emerges to become defined as a threat to societal values and interests: its nature is presented in a stylized and stereotypical fashion by the mass media: the moral

Nachman Ben-Yehuda (1986): 'The Sociology of Moral Panics: Toward a New Synthesis', *THE SOCIOLOGICAL QUARTERLY*, Vol. 27, No. 4, pp. 495-513. Copyright © by JAI Press Inc.

barricades are manned by editors, bishops, politicians, and other right-thinking people: socially accredited experts pronounce their diagnoses and solutions: ways of coping are evolved, or (more often) resorted to: the condition then disappears, submerges or deteriorates and becomes more visible (p. 9).

The success of moral entrepreneurs to create a moral panic depends on several factors (e.g. Becker 1963: Eisenstadt 1984): first is their ability to mobilize power; second, the perceived threat potential in the issue for which they crusade; third, their ability to create public awareness to the specific issue; fourth, the type, quality, and amount of resistance they encounter and, last, their ability to suggest a clear and acceptable solution for the issue or the problem.

Moral panics and crusades are inevitably and intimately linked to the labeling approach because they evolve around specific subpopulations becoming deviant (Schur 1980). They are also linked to the processes through which societal control agents/agencies create or amplify deviance, as illuminated and emphasized by the labeling approach.

Two theoretical perspectives emerged in the study of moral panics and crusades. One focused on the issue of morality and capitalized on how moral panics reflected a societal moral struggle (e.g. Becker 1963: Cohen 1972). The other focused on the issue of interests, showing that moral panics use moral themes to cloak struggles between different actors or parties whose interests clash. In what might appear as cynicism, advocates of the latter approach imply that morality may be used for nonmoral issues (e.g. Dickson 1968: Galliher and Cross. 1983).[1] While these two approaches need not be mutually exclusive (Dickson 1968, p. 156), there have been no theoretical or empirical attempts to integrate the two approaches. Dickson (1968, p. 142) even used the term *alternative explanation* to describe the "interest perspective."

Using the natural history of crime approach (that is, detailing chronologically how the panic developed and died), this article argues that the two perspectives are complementary and should be used together to describe and analyze the May 1982 drug panic in Israel. The question of *content* - that is, why a moral panic about drugs occurred rather morality. The question of *timing* - that is, why the panic occurred when it did - can be answered by using the analytical category of interests. The following discussion thus uses both perspectives to provide a new integrated synthesis in the sociological analysis of moral panics.

Morality and content

Various studies have shown that moral panics can develop in or around a range of causes. Cohen (1972), who studies youthful subgroups of "Mods" and "Rockers" in Britain and categorized them as folk devils, pointed out that the specific content of a moral panic may vary, as anything from a new topic to a revival of an older one. The following examples illustrate this point. Gusfield (1963) studied alcohol consumption as a topic for a moral crusade in the United States. Zurcher et al. (1971) and Zurcher and Kirkpatrick (1976) found that public support of a specific lifestyle and a clearly defined set of values were more important to participants in antipornography moral crusades than was the actual elimination of pornography. Hills (1980. pp. 106-107) mentioned the moral crusade in Florida against homosexuals that used such symbolic, emotionally charged slogans as "save our children" to rally moral outrage. Ben-Yehuda (1980) showed how the ideology of demonic witchcraft, which served as the moral basis for the European witch craze of the fourteenth to seventeenth centuries, was fabricated by the Inquisition to justify its continued existence.

Competing moral crusaders, moral crusades, and moral panics may reflect a possible "collective search for identity" (Klapp 1969) - in such varied spheres as the political, religious, scientific, cultural, or other - and become widespread phenomena mostly in pluralistic, heterogeneous societies whose structure enables such searches. There, morality itself is the focus of continuous debate and negotiation, so that heated arguments about the nature and scope of a social system's moral boundaries always take place (e.g. Douglas 1970). "Moral" debates usually are carried out by various "moral agents" such as politicians, representatives of law enforcement agencies, lawyers, psychiatrists, social workers, media people, and religious figures.

Morality runs deeper than its "technical" or "definitional" aspects. Becker (1967) introduced the concept of "hierarchies of credibility" in which the higher one's position in the moral-social order, the more credibility one has. The analytical concept of hierarchies of credibility links morality and credibility, and introduces a stratification principle into the moral universe (Rock 1973). Thus, reactions to assumed deviance involve an explicit moralistic statement that is "deliberately organized to persuade, convert, or force others in redefining important sectors of the world" (Rock 1973, p. 100).

Moral panics make subpopulations appear deviant by "stigma contests": "partisans in collective stigma contests are widely engaged in the use of propaganda: the manipulation of political symbols for the control of public opinion" (Schur 1980, p. 135). These panics vividly illustrate clashes between different moral universes and are, therefore, linked intimately to the basic nature of various cultures. The concept of *universe maintenance* (Berger and Luckmann 1966) describes the process, stating that when two contradictory symbolic universes meet, a conflict is unavoidable: "Heretical groups posit not only a theoretical threat to the symbolic universe, but a practical one to the institutional order legitimated by the symbolic universe in question" (1966, p. 124).

As mentioned above, when the medieval Inquisition found itself without heretics to pursue, it had to find, or invent, a new type of heretic to justify the continued existence of its machinery (Ben-Yehuda 1980). The fabricated moral universe of demonic witchcraft, which the Inquisition helped into existence, was described as diametrically opposed to the positive moral universe of "true believers." Based on this negative moral universe, the Inquisition created a devastating moral panic that lasted for many years and could be said to have extended into colonial America, finding eventual and devastative expression in the Salem witch trials. In a recent work, Gusfield (1981, pp. 151-154) showed that the development of the "myth of the Killer Drunk" helps American society maintain the illusion of moral sensus about values such as sobriety, control, rationality, and even hard work. Moral panics thus have a "boundary maintenance" function of deviance (e.g. see Durkheim 1938: Erikson 1966: Lauderdale 1976: Ben-Yehuda 1985).

since moral panics take place where and when two or more moral universes clash, the "choice" of a topic for a moral panic is not just a random event. It must be related, somehow, to the nature of the clash. Examining the content of moral panics illustrates why a particular theme was "chosen" for a specified moral panic.

Interests and timing

The exact nature and topic of a moral panic - while interesting in itself - should not be the only focus for analysis. The specific political, economic, or other interests of the individual or groups involved in creating the panic also are factors in its occurrence.

This point is important, even though it was hardly emphasized in Becker's (1963) analysis of "moral entrepreneurs" and "moral crusades" and by Gusfield (1963). Schur (1979, pp. 26. 257) and Cohen (1972). They all focused on the *symbolic* value of the panics - the *moral* conflicts and threatened lifestyles. Gusfield (1963, p. 177) put it succinctly: "What is at stake is not so much the action of men, whether or not they drink, but their ideals, the moralities to which they owe their public allegiance." Making a theoretical shift to interests means analyzing the particular, political and other interests of the specific political and social actors involved instead of analyzing only depersonalized social roles.[2] A few studies in the last decade crystallized support for the idea that moral panics may have both moral reasons and "alternative" interests (Dickson 1968). Two analytically distinct types of interests can be isolated.

One type may be termed as *general political interests of system level* (e.g. Duster 1970). Morgan (1978) showed that the first antiopium crusade in U.S. history was directed against the working-class Chinese, initially brought to the United States as cheap labor. By the 1870s, the crusade had become an ideological struggle, intimately linked to a desire to remove those workers from the labor force. Morgan concluded that the first opium laws in California were a result not of a moral crusade against the drug itself, but coercive action directed against Chinese laborers who threatened the economic security of the white working class. Johnson (1975) illustrated how nineteenth-century antiopium British moral crusaders created and diffused misinformation about drugs that they equated with "evil". Hall et al. (1978) analyzed a moral panic against a perceived threat of "mugging" showing that this moral panic developed from general societal fears that "crime waves" were spreading. Hall et al's study implied that societal moral concerns and fears may cause anticipatory moral panics (preemptive policy) before anything specific happens. Bonachich's (1972) work also implied that moral crusades against ethnic minorities originated in economic interests.

Another type of interest may be termed as *middle level bureaucratic* and/or *occupational interest*. Three studies illustrate this interpretation. Galliher and Cross (1983) showed that conflicting ideas about morality in Nevada have little to do with moral value considerations and much to do with economics. State leaders of Nevada make conscious efforts to avoid any legislation that might harm state revenues gained from gambling, quick marriage and divorce, and legal prostitution in most counties. Nevada, however, also has tough antimarijuana laws, prohibits a state lottery and banned prostitution in Las Vegas. Fishman (1978) showed that media reports about a "crime wave" against the elderly in New York originated in a specific bureaucracy, which had taken little action on issues and needed to create a moral panic to justify its continued existence; official statistics indicated that there was a real decline in crimes against the elderly, contrary to the claims made by the moral crusader. Dickson (1968) indicated that initiatives in antidrug legislation in the United States could be traced to the federal Narcotics Bureau, which faced a nonsupportive environment and decreasing budget opportunities that threatened its survival. The moral crusade that the Narcotics Bureau created resulted in new legislation and in a change in societal values toward tougher penalties.

Analyzing the interests of the parties involved in a moral panic may explain why they used this clash, at a particular point in time, to reify a panic.

The Israel drug panic of 1982

In May 1982, the Israeli public learned that the rate of illicit psychoactive drug consumption among middle-class adolescents, in what were considered good (even elite) high schools, was 50%. As a result of this news, a national drug panic developed and lasted until the end of the month. The fact that the actual national average rate had been between 3-5% between 1971-1982 did not seem to have any noticeable effect on the panic.

DATA AND METHOD

Between 1979 and 1982 the author directed the central Israeli drug abuse unit, which coordinated the activities of the Israeli Interministerial and Interinstitutional Committee on Drug Abuse. The major task of the Committee (which answered directly to the Israeli government) was to institute a national drug abuse intervention policy and to coordinate all drug abuse intervention activities in the country. Almost every person in Israel who was connected with the area of drug abuse on the policy and decision making level, was on the Committee. The author was, therefore, a direct participant observer to the events described in this article. As the May 1982 panic developed, the author kept extensive notes about it. Interviews were held with twelve key figures, among them the national chief of corrections, deputy to the legal adviser to the government, police chief in charge of drug intelligence, directors of the drug abuse education activities in the Ministry of Education, and high school principals in Jerusalem and Tel Aviv. The media played a crucially important role in the drug panic - as it often does in moral panics (e.g. Cohen 1972), because it provided the information that fueled the panic. Copies of relevant printed media items that reported on the "information" leading to creating and maintaining the panic were also used as references.

ADOLESCENT DRUG ABUSE: AN HISTORICAL ACCOUNT OF A MORAL PANIC

Details of the true extent of adolescent drug abuse in Israel clearly establish that the drug panic was founded on distorted information. Public attention to drug abuse as a problem in Israel started after the Six Days War in 1967, after which Israel was flooded with volunteers from Europe and North and South America. The perception continues that many of the Western volunteers brought with them a new form of illicit psychoactive drug use - leisure time drug use (mostly of hashish). Such drug use spread throughout urban, middle-class youth and especially to the kibbutzim (Ben-Yehuda 1979). While Israel has virtually no systematic data regarding the prevalence of illicit psychoactive drug use in the general population, efforts were made to research the prevalence of illicit psychoactive drug use among adolescents. Several studies were conducted on this topic between 1971 and 1982, all of which reveal a more or less consistent picture: the percentage of young, mainly high school adolescents, who tried illicit psychoactive drugs (mostly hashish) from 1971 to 1982 remained stable at between 3-5%. The epidemiological picture is clear and consistent (Peled 1971; Peled and Schimmerling 1972; Har-Paz and Hadad 1976; Shoham, Kliger, and Chai 1974; Shoham et al. 1979, 1981; Barnea 1978; Kandel, Adler, and Sudit, 1981; Javitz and Shuval 1982; Burkof 1981; Rahav, Teichman, and Barnea 1985).[3]

BACKGROUND: PRECEDING EVENTS

One important event preceded the panic that took place in May 1982. In July 1980, the Israeli police supposedly penetrated a large drug smuggling organization in the northern part of the country. The activities of the police led to a large-scale "mopping up" operation (code named "Cleaning the Valleys") in September 1980, when about seventy people were arrested and charged with smuggling and illegally selling illicit psychoactive drugs.

In May 1982, Amos Sabag, a key state witness in the trials that followed the operation filed a statement to the Israeli Supreme Court and appeared on the Israeli television evening news denying his September 1980 testimonies and stated that he lied in court. This created much turmoil; Sabag's 1980 testimonies helped put about seventy people behind bars. The major newspapers gave Sabag extensive coverage:

> "I lied," claimed the state witness who caused the arrest of the drug dealers. He claims that operation "Cleaning the Valleys" was staged under police pressure, that he and a police agent glued accusations to various delinquents.... Amos Sabag, 26 from Tveria .... claims that he and the police agent divided the hashish into small portions and put on each portion the name of a person, as if they bought the drug from him .... Sabag claims that most of the portions were meant to frame delinquents whom the police wanted to get rid of. On September 8, 1980, all the people against whom there was "proof" were arrested .... (*Yediot Aharonot* [May 9, 1982], translated by the author).

The police denied Sabag's claims. The newspaper *Ma 'ariv* reported on May 9, 1982 that the Israeli police were angry with Sabag and that he was going to be investigated.

In early May 1982, theaters in Israel began the premiere of the German-made movie, *Christian F*. This movie is a shocking, dramatized version of a book reputed to document the true story of a 15-year-old female heroin addict in Berlin. The film contributed to an atmosphere in early May 1982 that was loaded with drug abuse issues, conducive to inciting a moral panic over "drug abuse scandals." Such a scandal, in fact, took place.

The panic begins

Discussions in the Knesset

On Wednesday, May 12, 1982, parliament member Ora Namir convened the Knesset Committee on education, which she chaired, for a discussion on drug abuse among youth. At that time, the Likud party led the governmental coalition: Namir was a member of the Ma 'arach, then the major opposition party. It seems safe to assume that Namir received a few informative "leaks" from some police officers before the May 12 committee meeting. Quite a few public officials were invited and there was a high attendance of reporters as well.

Namir opened the meeting by saying she had received some "alarming" information about drug abuse among young people. She then gave the floor to police officer Amnon Helfer, chief of detectives in the Tel Aviv police, youth branch. Helfer told the committee that, as a result of an intelligence youth survey conducted in Tel Aviv (which is the major urban, metropolitan area in Israel), the police concluded that one out of every two elite high school adolescents had tried hashish at least once; he implied that this situation probably characterized all of Israel. Zvi Ariel, head of the drug abuse unit in the national Israeli police headquarters, stated that about 22% of all schools in Tel Aviv, and about 19.5% of the youth clubs, had drug problems.

The police officers accused high school directors of not cooperating with the police. This accusation found dramatic expression in the media when, on May 13, it was repeated on the front page of *Yediot Aharonot*:

> Half of high school students experienced smoking hashish .... policemen criticized high school principals for not cooperating with the police .... Parliament member Goldstein .... attacked the teachers and claimed that high school principals run away from the subject and introduce norms of permissiveness .... Schmuel Shimoni, principal of "Tichon Hadash" in Tel Aviv, attacked the media for "overblowing" the problem .... Yoseph Mechoulam, principal of a high school in Yahud, admitted that he had a drug problem and asked for advice from the committee. Chairperson of the committee, parliament member Ora Namir accused the Ministry of Education of doing nothing about the problem .... She expressed her opinion that the increase of 10% in juvenile delinquency in 1981 was because adolescents burglarized houses and stores to finance drugs .... (translated by author).

Members of the Interministerial Committee on drug abuse were present (including the author) but were not permitted to question the data presented by the Israeli police or the methodology used to obtain it.

The session turned into an attack on high schools, high school seniors, and the Ministry of Education. A few members of the Knesset committee indicated that police efforts to curb drug abuse were hampered by "too liberal legislation." This attack clearly carried a moralistic tone. Most speakers expressed concern about an apparent "menace" of drug abuse among the elite adolescents, supposedly the future leaders of the country. Illicit psychoactive drug use was attributed to lack of morality, too much liberalism, and morally confused parents.

The accusation that high school principals did not help was interpreted to mean that the police *had* a clear and swift solution for the problem - law and order - and that principals only wanted to protect their schools' reputation (*Ha 'aretz*, May 20, p. 10). The reporters present throughout the discussion were interested in the "drug scare" and interviewed committee members after the discussion.

The panic develops

Media coverage

Namir appeared on the May 12 evening television news and told the Israel public that there was a "government" conspiracy to hide the true magnitude of drug use among Israeli youth, specifically blaming the Ministry of Education. When the interviewer questioned her data, Namir said the problem was not whether 3% or 60% of the young used drugs, but that the Ministry of Education was not doing anything about the problem.

This "conspiracy theory" was an important issue because it contrasted two opposing moral universes: a governmental secret universe, seeking to mislead innocent citizens, holding that which should not be hidden; the other nonplotting, nonsecretive, courageous, seeking to share information openly and cope with the problem directly.

On Thursday, May 12, 1983, the Israeli public was "flooded" with drug-related media items. The major daily newspapers carried front-page headlines on the supposed drug epidemic among high school seniors. A major morning radio talk show on Israel's second radio band gave the topic wide coverage including interviews with high school students. The following two or three weeks witnessed a "drug festival" in the media.

Police Versus Ministry of Education

For the most part, the Israeli police kept quiet as the panic developed. The media and the Ministry of Education, however, did not. As a result, the moral panic about illicit psychoactive drug use by elite and middle-class adolescents flourished.

On May 9, 1982, *Yediot Aharonot* openly claimed that:

> High school principals do not cooperate [with the police] in the war against drugs. A general attack on the Ministry of Education was carried out yesterday in the educational committee of the Knesset .... A principal of a prestigious high school in Tel Aviv said that there was no drug problem in his school. A secret police unit found out that at least 21 pupils in that school smoked drugs, almost regularly .... All present at the meeting said that high school principals did not cooperate with the authorities to eradicate the drug plague .... M. Turgiman, chief of Tel Aviv police, said that all the high schools in Tel Aviv that suffer from the drug plague are precisely the prestigious schools in the north .... (translated by the author).

On May 17, 1982, a spokesman for the Ministry of Education accused the police of helping to create a "drug panic":

> Every year .... the police conducts its "annual drug festival" in the educational system. The script almost repeats itself. Police detectives discover a few adolescents who use some sort of drugs, outside of school, in a city .... Later on, police officers are invited to public forums to tell the nation about the achievements of the Israeli police in capturing adolescents who use drugs .... suddenly we discover, God forbid, that we no longer deal with one city but with all of Israel .... After a few months, police officers notify [not always] the stigmatized school that the investigation was finished and then .... it is disclosed that [the problem] concerns only very few students .... The school's name, however, remains stigmatized .... This year, the police had gone too far .... The percentage of drug users in the educational system is low .... I call on the police to give us the name lists of the students who used drugs so that we would be able to treat them .... (*Ma 'ariv*, 1982, p. 3).

At the same time, there appeared in the media, police estimates that more than 100,000 high school pupils use hashish. The Ministry of Education demanded, again, to know who even some of them were - to no avail.

Meanwhile, anxious parents began to pressure the Ministry of Education to "do something" about the "terrible drug problem" in high schools, threatening to keep their children away from schools. High school students - as a category - were stigmatized without justification.

The panic continues

The Second Knesset meeting

On May 18, 1982, the Parliament Education committee held a second meeting on the youth drug abuse problem. This author met with Ora Namir before the meeting and gave her the accurate statistics, pointing out that the data used by her committee were methodologically flawed. Namir repeated her televised statements from May 12, and stated that the scientist members of the interministerial committee on drug abuse were biased and too liberal.

By this time, it was clear that "liberalism" and "lack of cooperation" had become identified with a "soft" stand on the drug issue. Members of the conservative moral universe portrayed their antagonists as conspirators, uncooperative, liberals who lack the militant spirit "needed," supposedly, to squash drug abuse, and morally confused. Adherents of the negative moral universe, according to those on the opposing moral universe, helped propagate and intensify the problem.

The May 18 session began in a very tense atmosphere. Only a handful of reporters were allowed in this time. Yehezkel Karti, then police chief of investigations, told the Committee that they should not depend upon the figures given to them only a week earlier since the "study" was, in fact, an internal intelligence report based on an intelligence survey, rather than on accepted scientific methods. (The two police officers who had presented data at the May 12 meeting were not present at the May 18, 1982 meeting).

Other members of the Committee, including some invited guests, attacked the Ministry of Education again, accusing it of doing absolutely nothing about drug abuse. They indicated that teachers, principals, and pupils had nowhere to go for help to deal with drug abuse problems. This meeting eased the tensions and put the magnitude of "the problem" in more accurate proportions but the drug panic itself did not abate.

Crystallization of Main Themes

In the following two weeks, newspapers covered the supposed "killing drugs" and the "white death" (heroin),[4] saying that illicit psychoactive drug use was a symptom of permissiveness, liberalism, and morally confused parents. Some newspapers suggested that youth drug abuse in Israel was characterized by a "silent conspiracy" that helped inflate the real magnitude of the problem and associated drug abuse with other types of morally wrong behavior.

> Drug trafficking and drug consumption in the country are no longer a peripheral phenomenon, as it used to be .... Today .... crime and corruption have become accepted norms .... Using the service of prostitutes .... contributes in no small measure to moral deterioration, part of which is using drugs .... (from Aharon Shamir, "The Death Drug." *Yediot Aharonot*, May 21, 1982, supplement 11; translated by the author).

Hed Hakriot (Haifa) associated youth drug abuse and teenagers' promiscuous sexual practices. *Yediot Aharonot* (May 23, 1982) quoted Namir as saying that "…. kids under 13 years of age sell drugs and use guns because they know that due to their age they cannot be prosecuted" (p. 4).

Between May 12 and the end of the month, items on the "youth drug abuse plague" appeared in the national and local written and electronic media. The moral panic crystallized along five distinct lines.

First, the panic focused increasingly on illicit psychoactive drug consumption among the middle-class and elite adolescents in middle-class and elite high schools. If these particular groups were morally wrong then the future of the country was in danger. The fact that much higher (and real) rates of illicit drug use existed among impoverished youth-in-distress was ignored (see note 3).

Second, strong criticisms appeared in the media about the lack of action by governmental agencies - especially the Ministry of Education - against the perceived spread of illicit psychoactive drug use. These criticisms usually expressed shock and amazement at the nature and scope of the problem among young people, frequently associating adolescent drug abuse with general societal trends such as permissiveness, desire for experience, sensation seeking, lack of parental guidance and control, and general alienation (see, for example, *Yediot Aharonot*, June 6, 1982, p. 19 and June 7, p. 11: *Ha 'areta*, May 23, 1982, "Letters," p. 9). A few blamed the police for drugs being too easily available (see, for example, *Ha 'aretz*, May 23, 1982, p. 16 Adlers' letter: Donevitz's column, p. 9).

Third, the electronic media gave advice, and the printed media provided articles on "how to find" and "what to do" if one's children used drugs. These articles gave information about the dangers and hazards associated with the abuse of various chemical substances (see, for example, *Yediot Aharonot*, June 7, 1982, p. 18. "How to Behave with a Drug Abusing Adolescent": May 24, 1982. "The Dangers of Hashish"). In one year before and after May 1982, no such items on drug abuse appeared.

Fourth, toward the end of the panic, several items appeared in the media stating that alcohol abuse among youth was the real problem and was far more dangerous than marijuana hashish abuse (see, for example, *Yediot Aharonot*, June 6, 1982, p. 5).

The fifth and last line crystallized along arguments over whether *religious* adolescents also used illicit psychoactive drugs and whether religious belief might be a "good immunization" against the illicit use of these drugs. "Drug use is prevalent among religious and traditional youth, too - this was disclosed yesterday by David Green, the head of the unit fighting drug abuse in the kibbutzim. He said that drug use became a common social phenomenon and many adolescents are curious and want to try using drugs" (*Yediot Aharonot*, June 3, 1982, p. 4): Rabbi parliament member Druckman said that the claim that religion "'does not protect against the use of drugs' has no basis in reality .... it was proven that drug use among religious youth is about 50% less than among non-religious youth .... religious education runs deeper, and is more intensive, it provides a better protection against drug abuse ...." (*Hatzophe*, June 3, 1982, p. 1). This last argument contrasts two different moral universes - secular and religious - reasons for and methods of coping with adolescent drug abuse.

The panic ends

Although both sides of the drug issue slowly lost their initial zeal and vigor, it took a national military event to end the drug panic. Tension was building up on Israel's northern border in late May and early June 1982. The Israeli invasion forces and the PLO and Syrian forces quickly overrode the moral panic about adolescent drug abuse.

DISCUSSION

The historical description makes it clear that the May 1982 Israeli drug scare was, in fact, a moral panic, as characterized by Becker, Cohen, and others. To follow Cohen's (1972) characterization, adolescent drug abuse emerged in May 1982 as a threat to societal values and interests. This threat was presented in a stylized and stereotypical fashion by the mass media by actors with high credibility and perceived morality. Actors announced diagnosis, solutions, and ways of coping. The panic then ended. The moral entrepreneurs were successful in creating the panic because they had power and were considered credible actors; the perceived threat potential in the drug issue was high; they were very successful in using the media and creating awareness to the drug problem; they encountered very little opposition, and they suggested a clear and acceptable solution for adolescent drug abuse. The nature of the panic and its historical development correspond to similar moral panics described by Cohen (1972). Dickson (1968), Ben-Yehuda (1985, pp. 23-73), Zurcher et al. (1971), Morgan (1978), Hall et al. (1978), Johnson (1975), and Fishman (1978).

This moral panic was based on distorted information, clearly aimed at sharply marking the boundaries between moral right and moral wrong. However, behind the public display about morality, there were other strong interests at work as well. The moral and interest perspectives can be used together to gain a better understanding of, insight into, and interpretation of the panic itself.

Morality, deviance, ideology, and moral panics: the question of content

Drug abuse frequently has been characterized - in many parts of the world - by moral panics. Lidz and Walker (1980, p. 252) stated that the drug crisis in the United States "was a smokescreen for the repression of political and cultural groups." Musto (1973), Goode (1972), Young (1971), Duster (1970), Conrad and Schneider (1980), Morgan (1978), Ashley (1972), Anderson (1981), Klerman (1970), Kramer (1976), and Trebach (1982) all traced antidrug campaigns to ideological moral issues. Hills (1980, p. 38) pointed out that, in the United States:

> The role and use of marijuana remain illegal .... primarily because most of the older adult public are *ideologically* opposed to total decriminalization. Use of the drug is symbolically associated in much of the public mind with many kinds of activities, lifestyles, and moral and political beliefs that these dominant groups find repugnant (for example, hedonism, sexual promiscuity, altered states of consciousness, radicalism, irreverance toward authority and so on) (emphasis in original).

Clearly, there is ample evidence that, in different time periods and in different cultures, drugs traditionally were associated with moral-ideological issues. From this perspective, "choosing" drugs as an issue around which to create a moral panic is not uniquely Israeli.

The choice of drugs as a symbol for a moral panic, while perhaps not planned cognitively, was not a random choice. There were at least two rewards for capitalizing on a "drug menace" as a societal threat.

First, "drug scares" are attractive to both the media and the masses, especially "drug scares" concerning youth. Such scares can be considered as effective ideology (Geertz 1964). According to Geertz, the function of ideology is to provide authoritative concepts capable of rendering situations meaningful and "suasive images" by which their meaning can be "sensibly grasped" and which can arouse emotions and direct mass action.[5] Drugs can be used as a "suasive image" for corrupting youth and thus destroying a country's future, inherent in widely accepted beliefs that drugs destroy young minds or that they destroy the future of the country. When used within an authoritative framework such as a parliament, the press, and ranking officials in the "hierarchy of credibility" and morality, these phrases can create, sustain, and promote an effective antidrug ideology.

The second aspect is that moral statements used in an antidrug ideology help to draw and maintain moral boundaries, especially between those who use drugs and those who do not: those who are "morally right" and those who are "morally wrong." A typical example is the argument presented toward the end of the panic as to whether orthodox

Jews somehow were not resistant or even immunized to drug abuse than were secular Jews. In the moral panic described here, one symbolic universe fabricated a negative, morally wrong, symbolic universe of drug users and campaigned successfully against those who supposedly supported this deviant, heretical symbolic universe.

The moral universe that valued the work ethic, direct coping with everyday life problems, and maximum self-control claimed moral superiority. It portrayed a negative moral universe of drug users who symbolized moral degeneracy, loss of control, inferiority, danger, lack of proper ideas, and irrationality.

The way that various organizations and the government in Israel coped with the perceived drug menace is instructive in terms of the underlying moral tones to drug abuse issues in Israel. Even the language used provides clues. AL SAM, the Israeli voluntary citizen's association against drug use, states on its letterhead that it has declared "war on drugs". In a country that has fought six wars in the last 38 years, not including antiterrorist activities, such a slogan carries heavy moral overtones.

Some governmental material on illicit psychoactive drugs published in the late 1960s and early 1970s seemed as though it was meant to create moral scares and panics deliberately by marking very strongly moral boundaries. A 1974 poster declared that ".... the number of Hashish users in Egypt is approximately five million. In the Six Day War, everyone could see the type and quality of the Egyptian soldiers. Don't delude yourself that there is no connection between these two facts ...." One from the early 1970s stated that " .... if being a man means to have a strong and stable character, those who use drugs prove the opposite: apathy, lack of initiative and ambition, indifference." Such slogans make clear and explicit moral statements by contrasting the morally desired with the morally undesired. "Drugs" become a code for corrupting the innocent, perhaps morally confused youth. Drug-abuse issues become, therefore, intimately associated with various moral and ideological issues.

In Israel, an added factor may have helped the May 1982 moral panic to flourish: the educational system in Israel is prone to various moral panics. In 1979 and again in 1981, for example, the Israeli public learned - through the media - about "terrible" problems of violence and vandalism in schools. Horowitz and Amir (1981) showed that the reports of these problems were greatly exaggerated. Eisenstad (1984) pointed out that the panics about violence and vandalism in schools probably began, and were fueled by, different groups who benefited from creating them. For example, the teacher's union was negotiating for teachers' annual salary raises and wanted to show how hard their jobs were: parents were vocally against integrating schools with students from different socio-economic status and ethnic backgrounds, and had an interest in showing that integration had disastrous outcomes. Thus, the 1982 drug moral panic could have been associated in the public's mind with perceived endemic problems.

Illicit psychoactive drug use is an almost natural topic for a moral panic. Drug abuse is an "easy enemy" (Christie and Kettil 1985; Szasz 1975): it can be used in a moral panic as a boundary maintenance vehicle in a clash between opposing moral universes. The Israeli police, however, specifically were interested in using this topic for a moral panic. The state witness who retracted his early May testimony challenged the morality, integrity - indeed, the legitimacy - of police antidrug abuse actions. Sabag's statement implied that the police deliberately used doubtful methods. The police denied Sabag's claims and had to either justify what it did, neutralize Sabag's account, or divert attention from this challenge. Choosing to focus public concern on an ultimately nonexistent drug problem was, therefore, not a random decision. Since the challenge to the police was based on the context of drug law enforcement, the proper reaction had to be within that arena. The police delivered three major messages during the drug moral panic it had helped to create: the prevalence of drug abuse is high; middle-class adolescents, in what are considered good elite high schools, are involved in this dangerous illicit drug use and thus, Israel's best young minds are in danger; the police could solve this problem if other actors would cooperate and liberalism and secrecy did not undermine their efforts.

The image projected by the police was one of being engaged in a battle with an arch-enemy that corrupted and destroyed the morality of Israel's youth and its finest minds. When such battles are waged, minor issues - the claim made by Sabag - tend to disappear. Even if the police had admitted making a mistake in the Sabag affair, the admission would have been downplayed. On the one hand was the moral universe of Israel's future and on the other hand, only a questionable character. The police successfully diverted attention from Sabag; after May 12, no one seemed to remember the state witness problem.

This analysis raises the problem of whether the May 1982 moral panic, and other panics, were fabricated or based on exaggerations or amplifications (see Wilkins 1964) of existing problems. The May 1982 panic clearly was based on an amplification of an existing problem. Similar amplifications occurred in the panics reported by Fishman (1978), Hall et al. (1978) and Horowitz and Amir (1981). Studies by Erikson (1966), Bergesen (1978), and Ben-Yehuda (1980) support the idea of fabrications.[6] The effect of fabrication or amplification depends on the specific case.

The theoretical interpretation suggested here explains why "drugs" as an issue is an almost natural choice for a moral panic. This interpretation also explains why experts such as scientists, especially members of the Interministerial Committee, were ignored or discounted: Most of them knew the facts but neither the Parliamentary Committee nor the press were interested because these facts did not explain the drug menace. In similar situations those who had accurate information that did not support the panic were hardly heard (Ben-Yehuda 1980; Gusfield 1963; Cohen 1972; Bergesen 1978).

Moral panics and specific political/economic interests: the question of timing

In the broadset sense, the May 1982 drug moral panic in Israel supports the view that these panics are the products of conflicts between members of different and competing moral universes, each trying to enforce its moral dominance over the social system. A closer look, however, reveals that a full interpretation of moral panics also must take into account various *interests* which find expression in a moral posture.

The Israeli May 1982 moral panic is an ideal event for analysis by the interest perspective. The panic had at least two parties interested in creating it: the Israeli police and Ora Namir.

The police had two types of interest in creating the panic: (1) a long-standing vested interest in pressing legislators into allocating more resources to the public fight against the "drug menace," and (2) to deflect public attention away from the Sabag incident. This second interest, from the police point of view, was the most important. Regardless of the results of this dispute, efforts to divert attention from the "state witness problem" to the "drug panic" were successful.

Namir was not only a member of the major opposition party, which at that time had some bitter arguments with then Prime Minister Menachem Begin's coalition government; she also had strong and explicit aspirations to become Minister of Education. As part of the major opposition party, Namir could not become the Minister of Education. She had a strong vested interest in attacking the Ministry of Education. The moral panic was not only an opportunity to present her moral universe to the public and contrast it with a moral universe portrayed as evil, but also to state what could and should be done regarding adolescent drug abuse. Moral boundaries thus were drawn.

The middle-level interests of two parties that had helped create the May 1982 moral panic coincided almost perfectly at that time. Drug-abuse professionals who could diffuse the panic were divided among themselves along both professional and personal lines, incapable of coordinated action and prevented from stating their views. The different parties had specific political/economic interests that led to creating and maintaining the May 1982 drug moral panic in Israel. This analysis reaffirms that moral panics may use - and abuse - moral themes for nonmoralistic purposes.

Sociology of moral panics

The moral perspective supports the term *moral panics* while the interest perspective implies that the use of the word *moral* may be inappropriate. The new synthesis presented here calls for a new awareness of both perspectives when analyzing moral panics.

It is quite clear that the sociology of moral panics sprang out of the labeling approach in deviance. Sociologists of deviance, however, have become increasingly aware that such study must be reframed within the context of total social structures, history, and politics. It thus becomes necessary to examine whether the sociology of moral panics may, in fact, relate to other, more general, areas of sociological inquiry.

The sociology of moral panics emphasizes that these panics frequently help draw the boundaries between various moral universes, in the functional sense of the argument. As such, moral panics may be linked to social movements and to a major sociological concept - societal processes of change and stability (e.g., Bonacich 1972; Cohen 1972; Gusfield 1963; Morgan 1978; Ben-Yehuda 1985).

The sociology of moral panics may be related to the sociology of social problems (see, for example, Spector and Kitsuse 1977) in two ways: (1) repeated or prolonged moral panics about specific issues may give rise to the development of a dynamic characteristic of social problems, and (2) in both areas researchers are faced with the need to cope with the problem of morality versus interests.

The panic discussed here also relates to the elusive relationship between public perception of a phenomenon and the "actual reality" of that phenomenon. This is a relevant issue: Clearly, it would be impossible to make statements about drug use among Israeli students that bear no relation to the real world and expect to be believed, unless the public were fairly uninformed about the phenomenon in question. In parallel cases of moral panics there were similar gaps between public perception of a phenomenon and the "actual reality". Such gaps, combined with the public reaction, connect the topic of moral panic to the area of mass delusions (see, for example, Goode 1984, pp. 494-493). In both cases, the public does not have a clear idea of what is "really" taking place and acts out its worst fears. The work of Fishman (1978) on the fabrication of "crime waves," Ben-Yehuda's (1980) work of the production of the imaginary crime of witchcraft, and even Orson Welles's infamous radio recitation "War of the Worlds" in 1938 all testify to this connection.

CONCLUSIONS

Theoretical formulations in the sociology of moral panics have been divided along two "alternative" interpretations: the moral perspective and the interest perspective. The May 1982 "drug scare" moral panic in Israel illustrates these two perspectives as complementary rather than competing. This new theoretical synthesis was achieved by presenting two foci for theoretical inquiry: why the moral panic happened when it did and why a specific content - drugs - was "chosen" for that panic. Combining the moral and interest perspectives in a synthesized interpretation made it possible to answer these questions.

The specific interests of the parties involved in creating the panic primarily explain its *timing*. The political and social actors involved in the May 1982 drug moral panic in Israel deliberately ignored data contradicting their views and thus achieved their specific goals. The actual *content* of the panic was explained mainly by resorting to the concepts of boundary maintenance, morality, and ideology, and secondarily to interests. Creating the moral panic provided a golden opportunity for actors adhering to one moral symbolic universe to fabricate an antagonistic moral universe, attack it, and thus redefine moral-symbolic boundaries between the morally desirable and the morally undesirable.

This particular aspect also links moral panics to the sociology of change and stability. A genuine new theoretical synthesis was achieved by applying the two previously competing perspectives to the same moral panic.

ACKNOWLEDGEMENTS

My work on this article benefitted from the comments made by four anonymous reviewers. I am indebted to Erich Goode and Stanley Cohen for their detailed and most helpful comments on previous drafts, and their warm and friendly advice and support. I am grateful to Gerald Cromer's comments, and to the editorial suggestions made by Judith A. Levy, Stanley Einstein, and Gary Albrecht.

A significantly different version of this article was presented in the section on deviance at the 1984 annual meeting of the American Sociological Association (ASA) in San

Antonio, Texas. A grant from the faculty of Social Sciences, Hebrew University, supported the research and writing of this report. I am also grateful to the Department of Sociology, SUNY-Stony Brook that provided all the necessary help needed to work on this article.

Notes

1. Spector and Kitsuse (1977) implied that we may encounter similar situations when we examine how particular patterns of behavior, or issues, emerge to be defined as "social problems." There, too, individuals or groups may use a more moral posture to cloak their interests.

2. Closer perhaps to the type of analysis presented by Banfield (1961).

3. Drug use among "youth in distress" and juvenile delinquents probably is much higher. Wolanski (1981) and Wolanski and Kfir (1982) asked counselors who work with youth in distress to fill out questionnaires regarding drug abuse by their clients. In 1981, the usage was reported as 14.2% and in 1982 as 23%, the daily estimated use in the survey was 5.5%. According to an April 1984 personal communication from Dr. M. Horowitz, then Israel's Chief of Corrections (Youth and Adults, about 50% of his clients used illicit drugs. One has to take these results, however, with great caution due to the indirect and crude measurements used.

4. For one example, see *Yediot Aharonot*, May 21, 1982 (weekend edition).

5. Geertz limits his discussion to situations in which the need for cognitive and moral reorientation is the result of the emergence of "autonomous policy;" namely, the differentiation of the political from the religious sphere. Widespread need for such reorientation, however, is the result of every process of significant institutional differentiation and change, a hallmark of modern societies characterized by continuous change, alienation, anomie, centerlessness and atomized indivualism (Lasch 1979).

6. It is possible to claim that, even in these cases, there was a high degree of amplification. I tend to disagree. Any amplification was on such a magnitude that fabrication describes the process more appropriately and accurately.

7. See Ben-Yehuda (1985, ch. 1) for a summary of this issue.

References

Anderson, Patrick, 1981, *High in America, The True Story Behind NORML and the Politics of Marijuana*, New York: The Viking Press.

Ashley, Richard, 1972, *Heroin: The Myths and the Facts*, New York: St. Martin's Press.

Banfield, Edward G, 1961, *Political Influence*, New York: The Free Press.

Barnea, Zippora, 1978, 'A Multidimensional Model of Young People's Readiness to Use Drugs'. Unpublished MA thesis, Institute of Criminology, Tel Aviv University (Hebrew).

Becker, Howard S, 1963, *Outsiders,* New York: The Free Press.

– 1967, 'Whose Side Are We On?' *Social Problems* 14(3): 239-247.

Ben-Yehuda, Nachman, 1979, *Drug Abuse in Israel - A Survey*, Jersusalem: Interministerial Committee on Drug Abuse, Ministry of Social Affairs (Hebrew).

– 1980, 'The European Witch Craze of the 14th to 17th Centuries: A Sociologist's Perspective.' *American Journal of Sociology* 86(1): 1-31.

– 1985, *Deviance and Moral Boundaries, Witchcraft, Occult, Science Fiction, Deviant Sciences and Scientists*, Chicago: The University of Chicago Press.

Berger, Peter L. and Thomas M. Luckmann, 1966, *The Social Construction of Reality*, Baltimore: Penguin Books.

Bergesen, Albert J, 1978, 'A Durkheimian Theory of 'Witch Hunts' with the Chinese Cultural Revolution of 1966-1969 as an Example', *Journal for the Scientific Study of Religion* 17(1): 10-29.

Bonacich, Edna, 1972, 'A Theory of Ethnic Antagonism: The Split Labor Market'. *American Sociological Review* 37: 547-559.

Burkof, Haim, 1981, 'Use of Drugs and Alcohol Among Youth in Ramat Hasharon - An Epidermiological Survey'. Interim Report No. 1, The Interministerial Committee on Drug Abuse, Ministry of Social Affairs, Jerusalem (Hebrew).

Christie, Nils and Bruun Kettil, 1982, *Den Gode Fiende*, Oslo: Universitetsforlaget As (Norwegian).

Cohen, Stanley, 1972, *Folk Devils and Moral Panics*, London: MacGibbon and Kee, (Republished in 1980, U.S. edition by St. Martin's Press, New York).

Conrad, Peter and Joseph W. Schneider, 1980, *Deviance and Medicalization,* St. Louis: C.V. Mosby.

Dickson, Donald T, 1968, 'Bureaucracy and Morality: An Organizational Perspective on a Moral Crusade'. *Social Problems* 16: 143-156.

Douglas, Jack, 1970, 'Deviance and Order in a Pluralistic Society'. pp. 367-401 in *Theoretical Sociology: Perspectives and Developments*, edited by J.C. McKinney and E.A. Tiryakian, New York, Appleton-Century-Crofts.

Durkheim, Emile, 1938, *The Rules of Sociological Method*, New York: The Free Press.

Duster, Troy, 1970, *The Legislation of Morality*, New York: The Free Press.

Eisenstadt, Mimi, 1984, 'The Israeli Treatment of 'Deviant Behavior' in Schools as a 'Social Problem''. MA Thesis, Institute of Criminology, Hebrew University, Jerusalem (Hebrew).

Erikson, Kai T, 1966, *Wayward Puritans*, New York: Wiley.

Fishman, Mark, 1978, 'Crime Waves as Ideology', *Social Problems* 25: 531-543.

Galliher, John, F. and John R. Cross, 1983, *Moral Legislation Without Morality*, New Brunswick, NJ: Rutgers University Press.

Geertz, Clifford, 1964, 'Ideology as a Cultural System', pp. 47-76 in *Ideology and Discontent*, edited by D. Apter, New York: The Free Press.

Goode, Erich, 1972, *Drugs in American Society*, New York: Alfred A. Knopf.

– 1978, *Deviant Behavior: The Interactions Approach*, Englewood Cliffs, NJ: Prentice-Hall.

– 1984, *Sociology*, Englewood Cliffs, NJ: Prentice-Hall.

Gusfield, Joseph R., 1963, *Symbolic Crusade: Status Politics and the American Temperance Movement*, Chicago: University Press.

– 1981, *The Culture of Public Problems: Drinking, Driving and the Symbolic Order*, Chicago: The University of Chicago Press.

Hall, Stuart, Chas Critcher, Tony Jefferson, John Clarke, and Brian Roberts, 1978, *Policing the Crisis, Mugging, the State, and Law and Order*, London: Macmillan.

Har-Paz, Haim and Moshe Hadad, 1976, 'Drug Use', pp. 58-64 in *Studies, Employment, and Leisure Time Activity Among Young People*, Tel Aviv: Department of Research and Statistics, Tel Aviv Municapality (Hebrew).

Hills, Stuart L. 1980, *Demystifying Social Deviance*, New York: McGraw-Hill.

Horowitz, Tami and Menachem Amir, 1981, 'Coping Patterns of the Educational System with the Problem of Violence'. Research Report No. 219, Publication No. 602, Jerusalem: The Szold Institute (Hebrew).

Javitz, Rachel and Judith T. Shuval, 1982, 'Vulnerability to Drugs Among Israeli Adolescents'. *Israel Journal of Psychiatry* 19(2): 97-119.

Johnson, Bruce D. 1975, 'Righteousness Before Revenue: The Forgotten Moral Crusade Against the Indo-China Opium Trade'. *Journal of Drug Issues* 5: 304-326.

Kandel, Denise B., Israel Adlerm and Myriam Sudit, 1981, 'The Epidemiology of Adolescent Drug Use in France and Israel'. *American Journal of Public Health* 71: 256-265.

Klapp, Orrin E. 1969, *Collective Search for Identity*, New York: Holt, Rinehart & Winston.

Klerman, Gerald L. 1970, 'Drugs and Social Values'. *The International Journal of the Addictions* 5(2): 313-319.

Kramer, John C. 1976, 'From Demon to Ally - How Mythology Has, and May Yet, Alter National Drug Policy'. *Journal of Drug Issues* 6(4): 390-406.

Lasch, Christopher, 1979, *The Culture of Narcissism*, New York: Warner Books.

Lauderdale, Pat, 1976, 'Deviance and Moral Boundaries', *American Sociological Review* 41: 660-664.

Lidz, Charles W. and Andrew L. Walker, 1980, *Heroin Deviance and Morality*, Beverly Hills: Sage.

Morgan, P.A. 1978, 'The Legislation of Drug Law: Economic Crisis and Social Control'. *Journal of Drug Issues* 8 (Winter): 53-62.

Musto, David, 1973, *The American Disease*, New Haven, CT: Yale University Press.

Peled, Tziona, 1971, *Attitudes of Youth in School Towards Drugs: Selective Findings from the Study of Values, Plans and Youth Behavior*, Jerusalem: The Institute for Applied Social Research (Hebrew).

Peled, Tziona, and Haviva Schimmerling, 1972, 'The Drug Culture Among Youth of Israel: The Case of High School Students'. pp. 125-152 in *Israel Studies in Criminology*, Vol. 2, edited by S. Shohan, Jerusalem: Jerusalem Academic Press.

Rahav, Giora, Meir Teichman, and Zippora Barnea, 1985, *Drugs and Alcohol Among Adolescents*, Tel Aviv: Institute of Criminology, Tel Aviv University (Hebrew).

Rock, Paul, 1973, *Deviant Behavior*, London: Hutchinson University Library.

Schur, Edwin, 1971, *Labeling Deviant Behavior*, Harper & Row.

– 1979, *Interpreting Deviance*, New York: Harper & Row.

– 1980, *The Politics of Deviance*, Englewood Cliffs, NJ: Prentice-Hall.

Shoham, Giora S., Nili Geva, P. Kliger, and T. Chai, 1974, "Drug Abuse Among Israeli Youth: Epidemiological Pilot Study." *U.N. Bulletin on Narcotics* 20(2): 9-28.

Shoham, Giora S., Giora Rahan, Y. Esformer, Joanna Blau, Nava Kaplinsky, R. Markovsky, and B. Wolf, 1979, 'Differential Patterns of Drug Involvement Among Israeli Youth'. *U.N. Bulletin on Narcotics* 30(4): 17-34.

– 1981, 'Polar Types of Reported Drug Involvement Among Israeli Youth'. *The International Journal of the Addictions* 16(17): 1161-1167.

Spector, Malcolm and John I. Kitsuse, 1977, *Constructing Social Problems*, Menlo Park, CA: Cummings.

Szasz, Thomas, 1975, *Ceremonia! Chemistry*, New York: Doubleday.

Trebach, Arnold, 1982, *The Heroin Solution*, New Haven, CT: Yale University Press.

Wilkins, Leslie T. 1964, *Social Deviance: Social Policy, Action and Research*, Englewood Cliffs, NJ: Prentice-Hall.

Wolanski, Ami, 1981, *National Survey on the Progress of Youth - 1980*, Jerusalem: Ministry of Education, Youth Branch (Hebrew).

Wolanski, Ami and David Kfir, 1982, *Characteristics, Functions and Treatment of Disconnected Youth and Those in Street Groups: Data from the Second National Survey of the Units for Progress of Youth - 1981*, Jerusalem: Ministry of Education, Youth Branch (Hebrew).

Young, Jock, 1971, *The Drugtakers*, London: MacGibbon and Kee.

Zurcher, Louis A., Jr. and George R. Kirkpatrick, 1976, *Citizens for Decency: Anti-Pornography Crusaders as Status Defense*, Austin: University of Texas Press.

Zurcher, Louis A., Jr., George R. Kirkpatrick, Robert G. Cushing, and Charles K. Bowman, 1971, 'The Anti-Pornography Campaign: A Symbolic Crusade'. *Social Problems* 19(2): 217-238.

20. A Siamese Cat in the Council Flat

Marek Kohn

'I Baked Dog In My Oven', barked the *Sun's* front-page banner for 8 January 1986. *Sun*-watchers considered it among the summits of that publication's headline excesses, though it was outshone by the celebrated effort for 13 March, 'Freddie Starr Ate My Hamster'. There was a drug angle to the dog story, in that the teenager who was sentenced to three months' detention for the crime claimed to have been suffering the after-effects of LSD taken the night before. (Freddie Starr later appeared as a reformed tabloid junkie, citing his misfortunes as a warning to readers. It was not suggested, however, that the eccentric comedian's appetite for hard drugs led to his appetite for small mammals.)[1]

The *Sun*'s rivals, however, were concerned with a drug story of a more classic kind. Daphne Guinness, of the brewing family, described the central character as 'my own Blenheim spaniel',[2] but that was all there was to the canine angle.

The *Daily Mirror*'s description was more informative. 'MARQUIS OF BLANDFORD, heir to a £66 million fortune, great nephew of Sir Winston Churchill', was how it built up its subject, in order to slam him with the banner 'YOU COMMON CRIMINAL'.[3] The words were those of the magistrate who jailed him for three months for breaking the terms of a probation order by not notifying the authorities of a change of address. This infraction came to light when the heir to Blenheim Palace was found living beneath a clothes shop on the Edgware Road in what a police officer described as a 'cocaine smoking den'.[4] Blandford had originally been sentenced for possession of heroin and kicking in a chemist's window while looking for more. 'Lord Blandford,' the magistrate said, 'through the illegal taking of drugs, you, one of the richest and most powerful men in the land, have become a common criminal.' When the original order was imposed, the bench had drawn a general lesson from the case: 'The highest in the land can fall to the lowest when drugs are taken.'

The media and the magistrates both latched on to the way in which heroin dissolved the class barriers that had survived satire, social democracy and the sixties. Those concerned with the maintenance of social order must have deplored this form of downward mobility. The tabloids dwelt with relish upon the contrast between Blenheim Palace and the surroundings in which the 'Marquis of Porridge'[5] now found himself. Readers from humbler stations in life were encouraged to take pleasure in the aristocrat's downfall, a streak of disguised malice being one of the few vestiges of the movement to transform the country's class structure which was permitted to surface in the media of the 1980s.

The attention lavished on Jamie Blandford tends to support the premise that rich people are considered more newsworthy than ordinary ones. But the heroin story of the 1980s

Marek Kohn: *NARCOMANIA: ON HEROIN*, (Faber and Faber Limited, 1987), pp. 106-132. © Marek Kohn 1987.

has a much more significant class dimension. Heroin emerged as a focus for media attention during 1984, a year in which Britain resembled a country whose forces were at war abroad. Every night the conflict between the miners and the Government dominated the news, exciting and tormenting the viewers. The casualties were negligible by the standards of war, but the struggle constantly evoked military imagery. The deadlock between the two sides and the inflexible tactics of the miners' leadership, prompted comparisons with the First World War. The media emphasis on violence and the increasingly military appearance of the police also helped to make the dispute look like a war. Above all, there was Margaret Thatcher's notorious allusions to 'the enemy within',[6] widely construed as an attempt to class the miners as enemies of the nation - enemies comparable to the Argentinians over whose military defeat she had presided two years before. The rolling shock of the year-long strike threw subterranean national anxieties into stark relief.

The social-democratic era had been founded on compromise, expediency, and the hope that these political principles would lead painlessly to equality and social justice. The electorate knew that it had ended that era when it opted for Victoriana; regulation in the home and deregulation in the marketplace. On accession to the highest office, Margaret Thatcher recited the prayer of St Francis of Assisi (incidentally introducing one of her royal affectations): 'Where there is discord may we bring harmony.' Discord was to be the keynote of her years of power. The populace had admitted the degeneracy and shallowness of the post-war consensus, but it liked the idea of everybody agreeing on the basics. Britons wanted a solution to the national malaise as well, though, and at least enough of them plucked up the nerve to opt for radicalism - in the trappings of a return to a Victorian golden age. They got riots, the decimation of the nation's industrial base, and a numbing rise in unemployment. Whatever else might be happening to the nation, it was not getting more united.

As it became clearer that the miners were being beaten, consensus discovered a profound sympathy for them. Their heroism and dignity were recognized. Another Britain was to be seen in the pit communities, a precious heritage of honourable labour and mutual solidarity, in one of the traditional industries upon which Britain's greatness was founded. Yet it was clear that this was a class struggle. However deep the sympathy for the miners might run, the issue was still divisive. The strike helped turn the tide of opinion against the Thatcher experiment, but it deepened the social divisions.

One of the many aspects of the Government's tactics which backfired upon it was the attempt to drum up support by casting the dispute as a rerun of the Falklands war. There was still too much solidarity within the working class, and respect for it from the middle classes, for a body of workers at the very heart of the labour tradition to be declared Other and treated as enemies. The Prime Minister was seen to be deliberately dividing the nation still further. With the country in such a condition, issues upon which there was general agreement were at a premium. It was the moment for heroin to make its greatest contribution to national morale.

Heroin is the consensus issue *par excellence*. Everybody is against it. Even most junkies are against it. It was clearly a problem that was increasing in magnitude as the decade wore on. It was therefore newsworthy, and gave the nation a chance to simulate going to war. Martial imagery is the norm in descriptions of the implementation of drug-control policy. The use of the word 'war' to describe drug control is routine in headlines and accompanying newspaper columns. An alternative which gives special emphasis to its moral dimension and the alien nature of the enemy is 'crusade'.[7] On the borders of America, actual skirmishing takes place. Both sides have automatic weapons, and the good guys have spy planes, counter-insurgency aircraft and attack helicopters too.[8]

There is one essential difference between the way in which illegal drugs were represented from the fifties and the seventies and the meaning given to them - especially to heroin - in the 1980s. During the earlier decades, illegal drugs were seen as the preserve of a deviant subculture, which menaces both itself and society at large. The hipsters of the fifties, lurking in their shady locales with their alien associates, evolved into a whole intercontinental youth movement proclaiming the dawn of a new age. Cult or mass movement, this was a matter for deviancy theory. When a teenage boy in the sixties grew his hair, turned against and renounced his parents, he joined the mass of the deviant movement and became the legitimate target of the relevant authorities. When a youth falls into heroin dependency in the 1980s, there is no body of people for him to join. A family torn apart by a habit remains an isolated tragedy. Heroin is no longer seen as being contained within a limited group of people. It has become universal again.

By bombing Buckingham Palace during the Second World War, the *Luftwaffe's* fliers probably raised Londoners' morale more than they damaged it. It was not, of course, that the East Enders wanted the Royal Family's home to be levelled as so many of theirs had been. It was because the highest were seen to be suffering along with the lowest. Now they had more in common than ever before. The nation was united by the menace that threatened king and loyal subjects alike. Forty years later, people would sigh wistfully for the spirit of the Blitz. It was in meagre supply, as were enemies upon whose hostile nature the nation could agree.

Reports of the Marquis of Blandford's fall were like newsreel footage of rubble in the Palace grounds. Blandford became an example of the principle that heroin was a menace to all sections of society. The sixties had swung along on shallow assertions that a touch of affluence for the workers and stardom for the odd cockney photographer would break down the class system. Something known as a 'classless accent' was taken as evidence of progress towards a 'classless society'. The discovery of fundamentalist Marxism by militant students and young workers at the end of the decade seems a most understandable reaction to such vapid substitutes for political thought. There is little left of the idea of classlessness in the papers nowadays; except for the idea of the extent of heroin's menace. That is one way of illustrating the difference between the 1960s and the 1980s.

Concealed in the baggage of the class message, and in the ambivalence with which ordinary people regard the rich and famous, is the mean pleasure taken in the spectacle of the privileged getting themselves in a state. 'The British Aristocracy Really Screws It Up' was the punchline to a sketch in the satirical *Spitting Image* television programme which featured a Blandford puppet in a parody of one of the TV anti-heroin 'advertisements'. When Olivia Channon, the twenty-two-year-old daughter of Trade and Industry Secretary Paul Channon, was found dead after an end-of-exams party at Oxford, the press enthusiastically 'peeled away the posh facade of Oxford's Hooray set to reveal a sad world of waste and decadence'.[9] As usual, the *Sun* was the least mealy-mouthed of the popular papers in its incitement to envy. 'For most undergraduates the three years at university are spent scrimping and saving in the struggle for a degree. But for the Hooray Henrys and Henriettas – upper-crust sons and daughters of rich businessmen, bankers, MPs and industrialists - it's one long binge.' Alcoholic and sexual indulgence were 'passed off as young people sowing their wild oats'. Now the new indulgence in drugs was bringing the idle rich their comeuppance. 'Wealth means worry,' the *Sun* reassured its proletarian readership, totting up Henry and Henrietta's annual bills ('College fees .... paid on the rates. Casual designer clothes .... £4,500'). No estimate was provided for drugs overheads, but Henry's lifestyle was costed at £48,385 a year. Henrietta managed on a mere £22,000.

The case demonstrated a feature of drug stories which make them so valuable for the popular press: a combination of sensation, titillation, voyeurism, and a built-in moral. The dead woman's 'secret diaries' - how many diaries are public? - were a major focus of interest, being said to reveal the 'amazing double life' of the Oxford 'Smart Set', and to 'lift the lid off the sordid world of the upper-crust drug addicts who spend fortunes feeding their habits'.[10]

The whole episode was a festival of *Schadenfreude*. Each paper was able to pick an angle to suit its own particular preferences. The *People*, the Sunday paper that had most resisted the general tabloid reorientation towards showbiz glamour, found a good traditional suburban witchcraft story in some undegraduate games played by the Channon household. Neighbour Bill Bowell described how the students set up crosses in the garden, lit candles, and 'bayed at the moon like wolves'. 'We always called the German chap Count Dracula after that,' he said.[11] The German chap must have made Fleet Street editors think Christmas had come early. Count Gottfried von Bismarck was none other than the great-great-grandson of the Iron Chancellor. Channon's exotic friend simply radiated sinister Teutonic perversion. The *Sun* printed a photograph of the prematurely-aged roué looking even more foreign in eyeliner and a Valentino turban.[12] The sheer quantity of gossip and fable amassed by the hacks unleashed among the dreaming spires made an editorial decision as to whether the Count was an evil degenerate or a wacky hedonist superfluous. On one page, both options were available. 'DRAG FUN AS A NUN' was the headline for the top half, affirming that 'nothing is sacrosanct when von Bismarck decides to have fun. He lives a bizarre life of comic debauchery - hosting the wildest parties, drinking to excess, and raising hell.' Down below was 'Blood on the Table', an account of a 'sick' party thrown by the count, where pigs' heads were suspended above the dinner, and a guest was 'absolutely sickened by the sight of blood dripping on to plates of food'.[13]

The story would have been fantasy made flesh had von Bismarck turned out to be a heroin dealer like 'The Count' that Kenneth Anger describes preying on 1920s starlets in *Hollywood Babylon*. In fact, those charged with supplying heroin to Channon were her cousin Sebastian Guinness and her friend Rosie Johnston. The papers highlighted her lifestyle by describing what killed her as a 'cocktail' of drink and heroin.[14] Although much of the newsprint devoted to the affair dwelt on the debauched amusements of rich undergraduates, there was a current of commentary which sought to portray Olivia as a secretly unhappy person. This was fuelled initially by a 'suicide note' which turned up in a dustbin, speaking of rejection in love. The post-mortem pop psychology was necessary because of the strength of media conviction that drugs imply inner problems. One common account of the origins of a habit holds that evil pushers trick ordinary kids into trying the stuff, at which point their problems start. An article informing parents how to spot if their kids are on drugs, trailing in the wake of the Olivia story, described drugs as 'an evil that can hit anyone'.[15] But the idea of drugs singling out the inadequate personality remains strong. While it is perfectly in order to attribute alcoholic excesses to a straightforward search for pleasure, drugs are deemed to be less simple. This is partly because of the strong media pressure against mentioning drugs and pleasure in the same breath. Censorship of pleasure, as though the mere scent of it will send children flocking to the pushers, produces a bizarrely distorted representation of why people take drugs. The insistence on denying the link between drugs and pleasure seems to make it difficult for some commentators to discuss drug abuse without invoking a flawed psychology.[16]

The Channon story had everything. There was even the traditional axis linking high society and low life. In this case it pivoted upon Paddington Station. There, presumably after the collector had punched her 'AWAYDAY TICKET TO HEROIN HELL', Olivia Channon would phone her pusher and, 'suitably dressed down', travel to rendezvous 'in sleazy Brixton'.[17] The light touch of derogatory racial association was continuing a tradition that began around the 1920s with the Billie Carleton case. Genealogy of a different sort was a vital ingredient in the story.

There were Royal connections. The élite circles in which the central characters moved were small. Junior Royal Lady Helen Windsor was identified as a friend of the deceased, but she was small fry. This one went to the top. 'DRUGS COUPLE TO MEET QUEEN?' wondered the *Star*, speculating on whether Rosie Johnston and Sebastian Guinness would cross the monarch's path at Her Majesty's Royal Ascot ball.[18] The idea of the Royal Family as Britain's most popular soap opera is common currency. The Channon affair crashed into the storyline like a Gothic-tinged melodrama - or simply one of those implausible disaster movies which have a habit of turning up when the ratings are flagging.

The Royal presence might bring one particular soap to mind. There was another dynasty involved, though. The Guinness story fell somewhere between American glamour-soap and Greek tragedy. Six other members of the 'doomed dynasty'[19] had met untimely deaths in the previous twenty years, one of them from a heroin overdose. The scandal surrounding the latest tragedy flushed Princess Diana's brother out on to breakfast television to appear pious. Identified as an acquaintance of the von Bismarck set, the young aristocrat denied that he had ever seen or been offered any drugs in three years at Oxford, despite having acquired the soubriquet 'Champagne Charlie' for the kind of alcohol-induced behaviour that gets proletarian youths packed off to detention centre.

'All students drink a lot,' he averred. 'I don't think there's anything wrong with that.' A touch of Gown snobbery crept into Viscount Althorp's testimony when he claimed that 'the people who take drugs are about three or four people, mostly not connected directly with the University, but affiliated colleges in Oxford and London.' Drawing on a piece of folklore usually related in connection with schoolchildren, he mentioned hearing stories about 'pushing' at college gates.[20] A few days later, the news of 'DI'S DRUG SHOCK' broke. According to the *News of the World*, Althorp had previously told Australian television viewers of his 'agony' at a party when 'someone slipped something' into his drink. This revelation of his sole drug experience, considered the reporters, was 'bound to stun the Princess of Wales, a leading campaigner against drug abuse'.[21]

It was all curiously similar to the brouhaha that enveloped Oxford in 1965 when former premier Harold Macmillan's twenty-year-old grandson Joshua died of a heroin overdose. The press descended, producing articles like the *Sunday Times's* 'Confessions of an Oxford Drug-Taker'.[22] Richard Compton-Miller, later to find fame in Fleet Street, described how he and his colleagues on the student paper *Cherwell* found 'about two hundred people taking drugs in Oxford reasonably seriously, about a thousand taking it sort of on and off, intermittently, but only about five or six people taking heroin or cocaine .... There must be about four or five people in Oxford who take cocaine and heroin now.'[23] On Althorp's evidence, the problem has actually diminished over the intervening twenty-odd years.

Once the titillation of a sensational drug story like the Channon affair has faded away, it is time for the concluding moral to be drawn. 'After Oxford, a lesson for all parents' was how the *People* introduced its how-to guide to home detection of drug abuse. 'From cossetted aristocrats to underprivileged kids, Britain's youth can be lured into the seedy world of heroin and cocaine,' it warned. 'Drug addiction respects neither riches nor rank.'[24] While the DHSS leaflets for parents are adorned with the kind of photos proudly displayed on mantelpieces, the demographic profile of addiction in the papers is definitely 'U' shaped. The twin peaks of the curve are at the top and bottom of the social scale, linking the people who live on big estates - country ones and council ones.

At the start of the 1980s heroin panic, the problem was originally painted in greys, as an expression and intensification of the plight of inner-city youth. The young had ceased to be a threat. The end of the baby boom and of the Youthquake saw to that. The traditional relationship between youth and its elders could be resumed: fear and rejection on the part of the old gave way to feelings of responsibility and protectiveness; and guilt. Youth was no longer seen as an enormous subversive gang, but as passive victims of the world their parents made for them. Above all, the political offensive launched by the Conservative administration meant that the prospect of youth growing up into a world without work weighed heavily upon the public conscience. The kids hadn't voted for it, after all. But they were in the front line.

Heroin draws much of its power to appal from its initial public appearance in the 1980s as a phenomenon connected with unemployment. It enables the issue of the dole to be kept alive. There are only so many television interviews to be done with scrap-head kids before apathy and boredom spread from the kids to the production team and the audience. News and current affairs are like the visual systems of flies and frogs. They

226

respond with surefire alacrity to movement, but are functionally blind to situations which do not change. Mass unemployment, afflicting the young disproportionately, is a fixture of the 1980s landscape. It is understood that the unemployed are particularly vulnerable to medical and psychiatric disorders, and heroin was initially identified as an addition to the list of these ills. Whether or not heroin dependency is actually caused by unemployment,[25] it is understood by the public to be associated with it. Moreover, heroin is perceived to be something which displays the characteristics of worklessness. Addicts lie about, dangerously uncoupled from the rhythms and disciplines of work. They are unproductive, but spend vast sums on their habit: this is what the idle rich and idle poor have in common. The addict is a symbol of a society at the very heart of whose problems is a decline in productivity. Around that core hovers allied anxieties about laziness and indiscipline in the national character, and about that cardinal sin of the Thatcher era, 'spending beyond one's means'. The addict is a human metaphor for the decaying nation.[26] As if this were not enough, there is the shameful possibility that the addict is also an actual result of that decay.

The economic aspect of heroin addiction also stirs a related group of anxieties. These are less to do with guilt and more to do with fear. The Victorian bourgeoisie were continually aware that the masses who had been concentrated into a proletariat to create wealth for their superiors were liable to coalesce spontaneously into a menacing concentration: the mob. In the 1980s, the mob gathered among those left over from the concentration who had remained behind, useless, in the inner cites. While youth as a whole has become an object of pity, the black youth has become a figure of terror. Heroin has never been associated with young blacks. It represents a sort of inverse violence, an incomprehensible campaign of self-directed disorder. It is, however, associated very strongly with the crime required to support a habit. The junkies can inflict plenty of damage on others in the course of their own self-destruction. Heroin not only accentuates public fears of crime, but also serves as an explanation for what in past years would have been attributed to 'mindless' anti-social tendencies.

Heroin also provides an answer to the latent question of what kind of misfortune would befall the young and workless. Inner emptiness poses that question: the emptiness of the industrial hearts of the abandoned inner cities; the unoccupied young lives. The unwelcome squatter in both turns out to be heroin. There is an alien presence in the estates; a Siamese cat in the council flat, as the singer Ian Dury put it some years ago.[27] It is a punishment visited on those who are already victims. The craving for supplies of the drug does, however, give the unemployed something to get up for in the mornings.

The new addicts, perceived as victims, are not excommunicated from family and society as their predecessors have been. Perhaps the fact that the problem is perceived to exist only among the whites helps keep them part of the family. They are treated more like kidnap victims, and everybody has a part to play in the rescue operation. Although the inner-city Skag Kids are the symbol of national decline, they are not the only young people liable to find themselves unemployed. Something had to be found to occupy idle hands, and a series of state-subsidized temporary work schemes were provided. These were a source of cheap labour, thus helping to do what the Government had signally failed to do with adult skilled and middle-class employees: to force wages down. They were heavily publicized, in an attempt to counteract the strong popular impression that the Government was unconcerned about unemployment. And they provided limited instruction in the patterns of behaviour and discipline – patterns to which earlier generations had graduated straight from school. The job creation schemes gave youngsters a course in the virtues of obedience, honesty, application and punctuality; then sent them off to the dole wanting more of the same. The ones who got hooked the most might be lucky enough to realize their desires as members of the new service class, winning little plastic stars for especial subservience in the face of pitiful wages from their employers in fast-food chains.

But McDonalds and the Youth Training Scheme were not capable of taking care of the entire problem. For one thing, there is the world of 'leisure', in which the young consumers have dangerous stretches of independence. They can hardly be blamed for their tastes. They have never known their parents' (or, more likely, their grandparents') world, in which capitalism fed mainly on the profits from production. These are the children shaped by a capitalism which now, above all, needs them as consumers. It teases and seduces them from their earliest years, teaching them to want. Its urgency demands an urgency from the consumption force: instant gratification, credit to be arranged. It trades on sensuality in everything from home furnishings to holidays in the sun. It teaches that pleasure in itself is nothing to feel guilty about. And as consumers become jaded, it devises more luxurious, more intense pleasures.

Of course, consumer capitalism needs producer capitalism to keep the consumption disciplined. Consumers must learn to abide by the rules: no stealing, and no spending beyond one's means. Wage-earning teaches such lessons and provides these disciplines. There are contradictions, particularly in capitalism's need to get consumers to borrow. It has had a difficult job destroying traditional reservations about buying on the 'never-never'. Those unfortunates for whom money is rendered invisible by a credit card, and who run up huge debts without any hope of settling them are often treated sympathetically. They are regarded as victims of a psychiatrically pathological compulsion - they are considered to be 'credit-card junkies'.[28] The similarity to drug addiction is acknowledged.

The young have been saturated in consumerism from infancy, but when they leave school and childhood, many of them are no longer channelled into the adult world of work. They see nothing morally wrong in consuming things solely for pleasure, and they feel no obligation to work for such pleasures. Drifting unshackled from workplace disciplines, the Thatcher Generation kids also drift away from respectability and legality. Yet competing traditional ideas, especially the one that says that the worth of an individual depends on them working, set up a conflict. Poverty and boredom add to the stress. All of this points in the direction of drugs, the skeleton in the cupboard of consumer capitalism.[29]

The trinklets and baubles of youth-seeking consumer capitalism have been placed on show in the name of the anti-drugs campaign. Television warnings produced in commercial format by the Scottish health authorities were nothing less than state-sponsored lifestyle marketing. Full of gaudy graphics and shiny teenagers dancing in discos, they looked for all the world like advertisements for a teen magazine or a range of make-up. The state was officially backing a formation of industries optimized for extracting money from teenagers, and recommending the products as accessories for an alternative lifestyle to drug addiction.

In the terms set by the anti-drugs campaign, the Scottish commercials were open to criticism that they missed the target. It might be the Benetton kids' idea of a good time, but it wasn't going to appeal to an alienated skid-row youth with an anti-social haircut and a taste for music that sounded like an ox being tortured in a thunderstorm. For any teenager with rebellious leanings, it was more likely to make a druggy lifestyle seem attractive in comparison. The equivalent television presentations for English and Welsh viewers are quite different. Directed by Ridley Scott, famous for the science-fiction films *Alien* and *Blade Runner,* they focus on the user. In the more celebrated of the two advertisements, a young man's initial cockiness ('I can handle it') about his heroin use declines in stages along with his health and his posture. 'I could give up tomorrow .... couldn't I? is his querulous last word. The other features a young woman whose downhill progress is symbolized by her toppling over, like a dummy. The commentary - the young woman, unlike her male counterpart, has only the punchline to herself - chronicles the colonization of the various parts of her life by heroin.

The posters and television advertisements commissioned by the Central Office of Information and the Department of Health and Social Security have sought to intensify the image of heroin's toxicity by failing to point out that most of the physical miseries associated with its use are the effects of self-neglect and dirty 'street' supplies, rather than the essential properties of the drug itself. But by comparison with the Scottish campaign and most other attempts to mobilize youth against drugs *en masse*, the efforts of the Yellowhammer advertising agency have a certain ethical superiority.

The creative people at Yellowhammer themselves would probably not see things that way. The agency was awarded the account because of its successful work in the youth market for clients such as the HMV record shop chain and the New Musical Express - in other words, because it was hip. It thus took up a special position in the construction of the discourse on drugs. The preceding couple of years had seen a groundswell of articles in the press, and broadcasts on the subject, as well as passing allusions to the phenomenon in a variety of media. This outpouring of text and speech was essentially independent of responsible authority; of state, medicine or education. It was there mainly to serve the interests of the popular press, and was loaded with sensationalism, titillation and moral indignation. By the time that the *Daily Mirror* produced its Shock Issue devoted to the subject late in 1984,[30] the commercial media had convinced the public that the nation's youth was being threatened by a plague of heroin.

The Government was thus under pressure to do something. As it happened, heroin was just the kind of enemy it had been looking for. It responded to the media campaign in kind, with a media campaign of its own that would maximize the chance that the Government would be seen to be doing something. The phoney war on drugs is being fought almost entirely with propaganda leaflets. Because of the association with unemployment, the Government can be seen to be concerned about an effect of mass idleness - without admitting either its own responsibility for the dole statistics or any casual link between being out of work and being on heroin. And it provides the perfect issue around which the Conservative Party can vaunt its image as the party of law and order. It can also use the idea of a mushrooming drug menace as a justification for the pre-existing project of strengthening and enriching the police force.

Yellowhammer, however, is not the Government. Its brief from the Government was to put together a campaign with the intention of reducing the misuse of drugs, especially heroin, among young people. The emphasis on heroin is consistent with the way that the drug issue has been presented by the media, and with the agreement between papers such as the *News of the World* and Home Office minister David Mellor that the major illicit opiate is 'Public Enemy Number One'.[31] In the event, it became Yellowhammer's exclusive target. The research they commissioned indicated that the vast majority of young people were never going to take heroin anyway. The most resistant were those who had tried 'soft drugs' but had not taken to them, and those who regarded themselves as 'discerning' cannabis users. Girls, and young people of West Indian ancestry, were also 'heroin-resistant'. Yellowhammer, commendably, interpreted their assignment strictly, and did not attempt to influence the behaviour of the great heroin-resistant masses. They also decided that posters and TV advertisements were not going to get the monkeys off addicts' backs, and so they have targeted young people 'on the cusp' of experimenting with heroin. Their scripts and copy thus display an insight into the mentality of the adolescent and the dynamics of drug dependency that is of secondary importance to campaigns with ulterior motives. Whether the two million pounds of Government money which paid for the first year of official publicity would have been better spent on providing facilities for treatment, as many voluntary bodies have argued, was not for the advertising agency to say.

The BMA is not among the bodies keen to hop aboard the bandwagon. It had criticized the priorities indicated by the 'high profile' given to a WHO-sponsored international meeting on drug abuse which was called by Britain, and held at Lancaster Gate in March 1986. In a statement made jointly with the Action on Alcohol Abuse charity, it said: 'The Government's emphasis on illicit drugs is misplaced. By lavishing attention on a relatively minor problem, the Government diverts public attention from the far greater damage and misery caused by alcohol and tobacco.'[32] It went on to estimate that 100,000 people die prematurely from smoking each year, and a further 6,500 deaths could be attributed to alcohol abuse. The most recent year's tally of deaths caused by illegal drugs was 235. Against this mortality rate, the Government was pitting £411 million a year, compared to £6 million spent on curbing alcohol and tobacco abuse. That, calculated the two organizations, worked out at £35 for each tobacco death, £344 per head for alcohol-related fatalities, and £1.7 million for each death caused by illegal drugs. But then, the Government was engaged in a weightier project than that of improving public health. The Prime Minister herself spelled it out: 'Britain - like the rest of Europe – is up against a determined effort to flood the country with hard drugs to corrupt our youth – to undermine the stability of our country.'[33]

For Mrs Thatcher, the idea of a foreign conspiracy destabilizing the country and flooding the beleaguered island has obvious political attractions – especially since so many people, asked what was responsible for the state of the nation's youth, would consider the two words 'Margaret Thatcher' sufficient answer. But heroin provides assistance in the construction of other sorts of discourses about the condition of British society. It has become a vital ingredient in lists: whenever criminal menaces or social blights are enumerated, drugs are prominent among them. It has also become an optional ingredient to be added, like monosodium glutamate, to spice up perennial tabloid stories.[34] And it is strongly defined as acting against the fundamental unit of society: the family.

The British drug panic of the 1980s largely excludes the idea of the dope fiend, in the interest of national unity. This leaves all the more vitriol for the pushers, and above them, the drug barons. (One might almost yearn for the return to the tabloids of the vanquished band of union barons, bogeys from pre-Thatcher days.) Their prey is the innocent, who are still the responsibility of their parents. One source of drug-related strife was identified by Liberal Party leader David Steel: 'Alcohol used to be a major source of family violence. Now drugs are quickly catching up. More and more children are being neglected, their parents hooked on hard drugs.'[35] It is not an especially potent argument, as the *non sequitur* caused by the association of 'hard drugs' with neglect rather than violence underlines. But the idea of addicted parents failing their children is one of the most emotive elements of the heroin discourse. It is a different kind of transgression to the alcoholic sort. A man beating up his wife and children in a drunken rage is only exceeding the limits of his authority. After all, many people would sanction his exertion of power over the family to the point of using violence against the children; and the condoning of wife-beating, though not publicly acceptable, is hardly extinct. If he goes on to develop alcohol-related diseases, this is likely to occur in middle life. As a victim he is unpromising material. His condition is self-inflicted, and he is of an age associated with responsibility and parenthood. And the drug that causes the damage is regarded primarily as a normal pleasure by much of the population. It is also legal.

Illegal drugs, on the other hand, afford the media a whole host of little victims. The search is on for Britain's youngest junkie. Reports of a five-year old glue addict in Birmingham have been trumped by the Newcastle three-year-old 'thought to be Britain's youngest victim of glue-sniffing'.[36] After the death of fourteen-year-old Jason Fitzsimmons, a senior police officer referred to the existence of thirty-five heroin addicts aged fourteen or thirteen in 'DRUGS CITY', as the *Daily Mirror* referred to Liverpool.[37] While the 'hushed' jury heard evidence which would show that the boy actually choked on his vomit after an overdose of Dalmane sleeping tablets, rather than the heroin to which his death was originally attributed, the National Association of Head Teachers 'revealed' that 'children as young as nine are becoming regular drug users'.[38] The jury returned a verdict of death through non-dependent use of drugs. 'We hope this will bring home to parents the responsibilities that they have and the constant risks that children are subjected to,' commented the foreman. The coroner's words underlined the point: 'I urge mothers and fathers to keep an eye on teenage children. Jason's death will not be in vain if we can draw lessons from it.'[39] The next day it was reported that 'teenage junkies' had turned the grave of the boy who had become their hero into a 'shrine', beside which they smoked heroin.[40] Whether these juvenile drug users had formed their image of Jason through friendship or through his representation in the press was not clarified.

A familiar story resurfaced. In the sixties, pushers were supposed to lurk outside school gates offering children ice creams or sweets laced with LSD. In 1983, the *Daily Telegraph* reported that a twelve-year-old user was 'a victim of drug pushers who waited outside Woodchurch High School, Birkenhead, offering "free gifts" to children'. Carole Wooley, an adviser to the Merseyside Drugs Council, was quoted as the source for the story. It reappeared a year later in the *Daily Express*, where she repeated the claim: 'A pusher will give them free smack three or four times, promising it will make them feel good. Then they have to start paying for it. And when they can't they turn to crime.' 'We've got the equivalent of the Black Death breaking out in the Wirral,' added the local MP Frank Field. Gifts and money may have played another part in the background to the original release of this horrifying story at that particular time. A few weeks earlier, the chairman of the Merseyside Drugs Council had appealed for funding. Subsequently a £305,000 plan to combat the heroin threat was announced.[41] Carole Wooley's claim was adopted cheerfully by the exponents of the tabloid technique of sensation through lazy generalization. Some of these journalists seem never to need to draw breath. 'Across the country, drugs are destroying lives like the plague. Kids no longer spend all of their pocket-money just on sweets and at the cinema. They are after glue, cannabis, cocaine and heroin. And when the pocket-money runs out, they'll lie, steal, prostitute themselves and even sacrifice their lives for the next fix. Pushers wait outside school gates offering heroin for £5 a go, tempting children with the dream of "chasing the dragon". They know the kids will soon be back for more. Teenage addicts are giving birth to heroin babies screaming in agony. And every day, the tragedy grows.'[42]

William Burroughs had seen it all decades before. Having fled an American drugs panic, he viewed its progress in his home country with his jaundiced junkie common sense. 'Safe in Mexico, I watched the anti-junk campaign. I read about child addicts and Senators demanding the death penalty for dope peddlers. It didn't sound right to me. Who wants kids for customers? They never have enough money and they always spill under questioning. Parents find out the kid is on junk and go to the law. I figured that either statesides peddlers have gone simpleminded or the whole child-addict setup is a routine to stir up anti-junk sentiment and pass some new laws.'[43]

The ultimate victims are infants. The *Daily Mirror* Shock Issue splashed a picture of an ordinary-looking baby splayed awkwardly on its back and labelled him 'BABY GAVIN: HEROIN ADDICT'. 'IS YOUR CHILD'S LIFE AT RISK?' it asked underneath. Adults, it seems, are immune to the 'modern Black Death'. All the big metaphors were deployed as the mighty tabloid swung into action. 'The *Daily Mirror* declares war on the drugs barons and the pushers. We want you - the ordinary people of this great nation - to help rid us of this evil epidemic.' Having ordered parents to initiate surveillance, it instructed this Home Guard of ordinary people to inform on dealers. Their finest hour was recalled by comparing major pushers to Nazi mass murderers. The courts were urged to sentence them accordingly. 'But most of all,' it concluded, 'parents, teachers, brothers, sisters and friends of victims should mobilise into a fighting crusade against this evil.

'It is, literally, a fight to the death. The death of young lives. Your kid or the kid next door.

'No one is safe unless we all act now.'

The *Daily Express* mounted a similar campaign some weeks earlier, playing heavily on the slang expression 'chasing the dragon', which has gained currency as an expression meaning 'smoking heroin'. This way of taking the drug has undoubtedly assisted its spread among youngsters whose ideas of junkies inevitably involved needles, and who have none of the strong inhibitions about heroin that kept many of the children of the 'psychedelic' era away from opiates. It has also given papers like the *Daily Mirror* and the *Daily Express* the opportunity to indulge in a little chinoiserie. Both have used an Oriental dragon graphic as an emblem of the fight against the 'deadly flood'. The *Daily Express* brought another, rather unfortunate foreign connotation - using a phrase from one of the most famous Nazi films - into its own declaration of war on the pushers with its conclusion: 'We can ensure the defeat of heroin through the triumph of the will.'[44]

The *Daily Express* was delighted to announce the recruitment of allies to its cause.[45] 'The Prince and Princess of Wales have declared war against the tide of drugs now swamping Britain,' it proclaimed. The Princess, the second part of the 'exclusive series' related, was 'now one of the most effective personalities fighting the problems of drug abuse in Britain'. She has achieved this impact in a tally of four visits, a television appearance, an endorsement and a foreword written for a National Directory of Drug Services (which totalled some seventy-seven words).

Princess Diana had made her campaign début on the BBC's *Drugwatch* programme. Hosted by the popular television personality Esther Rantzen, of the *That's Life* light entertainment consumer programme, and Nick Ross of *Crimewatch*, it combined the two shows to come up with a populist concoction of information, tragic examples, punditry and testimony. The last was crucial. In true evangelical style, the fallen were enticed into testifying. The repentant also went through their paces. Ex-addicts, put in front of TV cameras and coaxed by an alliance between the overwhelming authority of that medium and the rehabilitation agencies who imposed the disciplines which replaced their drug dependence, tend to behave in the ways expected of them. There is no deception, simply the replacement of drug users' discourse by approved ones. The programme showed training for the battle on the borders of the law as role-playing schoolchildren gave the viewers some hints on ways to refuse drugs offered, as they usually are, by friends.

This was a different kind of drug campaigning. Its brief was to police families, and especially children, rather than to sell newspapers. The mythology of the pusher had no place in this project, though the excitement of the hi-tech drug interdiction programmes was illustrated by clips from American TV. *Drugwatch* was the flagship of an anti-drug campaign whose vested interests were those of the state rather than commerce. It used the techniques of mass-audience television to build up a crusade with a benign feel to it. The emphasis was on mutual help and a sense of community, not the pseudo-militarism of the tabloids' call to arms. A sense of momentum was generated by encouraging self-help groups to make themselves known to the programme while it was being transmitted. Periodic updates geared up the bandwagon in the manner of charity 'telethons'.

The psychological sophistication of the programme was in large part imported. The semi-official anti-drugs campaign was transplanted from the USA, where Nancy Reagan had been enthroned as Patron and what her husband called the 'motivational force' of the 'Just Say No' Movement. This simple command was the key weapon in the operation aimed at preventing the spread of illicit drug use. A slogan for the 1980s indeed. In the course of promoting it, the First Lady allowed herself to be photographed sitting on the lap of the actor who played Mr T in the pyrotechnic television series, *The A-Team*: such was the motivational force of the anti-drugs movement that it could induce the wife of the spectacularly reactionary President into such close proximity to a large black man with a Mohican haircut.

Drugwatch took the 'Just Say No' concept to its bosom. It needed a home-grown equivalent to Nancy Reagan. Thus it was that the Princess of Wales walked unannounced on to the set and nervously told her interviewer: 'The drug problem is something that worries me very much. I hope families will watch together so they can talk about it openly.'

The Finale was the scrawling of the Drug Wall. Her Royal Highness inaugurated it with her signature, and was followed by a motley assortment of famous people, all just saying No. What was rather lacking at the end of it were the signatures of people likely to have some influence over the kind of young people who were actually likely to try illegal drugs. In this context, the presence of people like the chat-show host Terry Wogan, middle-of-the-road pop singers the Nolan Sisters, and entertainer Rolf Harris, may have been counterproductive. But they helped bolster the sense of unity; and it was, after all, family television.

A number of television drama programmes have tackled the drug issue. Prominent among them are those inspired or controlled by producer Phil Redmond. In the Channel 4 soap opera *Brookside*, a stereotype snivelling junkie girl arrived – and disappeared just as suddenly, taking some of her hosts' property with her. The reaction of the characters Sheila and Bobby Grant on finding the tinfoil spoon of heroin in their home was well observed: they both took particular exception to their son bringing it into the house, polluting the hearth. They did not reach for a drink, though. *Brookside* differs from its rivals *Coronation Street* and *Eastenders* in its unwillingness to indicate moments of tension by such devices, and in not focusing its characters' social life upon a pub.[46] A second heroin addict in Brookside Close, who appeared in the guise of a well-groomed professional man in the autumn of 1986, is probably the most implausible fictional addict of the whole panic. By now, it appears, the producers have put the need to educate the public about drugs second to the need for a sensation in the storyline.

Redmond, a non-drinker himself, developed the Merseyside smack-and-dole theme in a serial, *What Now?* Its characters were social-realist versions of Disney cartoons, bouncing off each other like misguided projectiles in search of a target. The watershed event in their young lives was the death of one of their number, a heroin user. 'Bloody drugs,' wailed his father, repeatedly, despite the fact that the apparent cause of death was the Ford Capri in which the youth had been doing some spur-of-the-moment racing. As if the crux of the drama were not enough, the message was reinforced down to subliminal level. One character wore a *Drugwatch* T-shirt. There were anti-heroin posters everywhere, even flashing through an action shot of a chase scene at an empty swimming pool.

By far the most effective of the anti-heroin productions from the Redmond stable has been the BBC childrens' serial *Grange Hill*, set in a school. Originally devised by Redmond, it has established a reputation for authenticity and a readiness to tackle controversial issues, as well as an enormous following among schoolchildren. It is decidedly brisk. There are none of the protracted will-she-won't-she story-lines designed to milk the ratings for all they are worth. You are liable to miss the dispatch of the teacher seen dallying with a pupil if you blink, and if you missed the very first episode of the series, you wouldn't know that the head teacher had been written out in a car crash. But the heroin story-line was carefully developed, and avoided stereotyping. It explored the psychology of the addict, his behaviour, and how others dealt with it. The alien quality of the addiction was diluted by comparisons with dependence on legal drugs. All in all, it has a strong claim to being the best of all the fictional television portrayals of heroin addiction.

Then came the 'Just Say No' Movement. Brought over as a package from America on to British soil, it hijacked the recognizable London schoolchildren and turned them into the all-dancing, all-simpering Kids From Fame. They recorded the 'Just Say No' theme song and released it as a single, with an accompanying video. Lee Macdonald, who played the addicted Zammo, was flown out along with some other cast members to see the American movement in full swing. They met a pre-teen monster rejoicing in the name of Soleil Moon Frye, apparently a local TV personality, and for the climax of the visit, were presented to Nancy Reagan. Back home, the record made the Top Ten, selling some 225,000 copies.

Genuine pop stars have proved harder to integrate into the campaigns. They are role models for youth, and members of the industry whose place as a responsible force in society has been confirmed by concerts for the Prince's Trust (its patron is said to attend wearing earplugs) and, of course, the global impact of the Live Aid charity events. It is not enough for Nancy Reagan, however. She refused to attend an anti-drugs concert at which Madonna, Ozzy Osbourne, George Michael and Aretha Franklin were billed to appear, because she considered the stars to be a 'corrupting influence'.[47] It might have been a prudent move. The 'growing army of pop stars ... warning of the grim realities of taking heroin'[48] are not the most reliable of troops. Although many allow their names to be associated with various anti-drug declarations, the benefit records and concerts have not materialized on the scale that might be expected. More publicity surrounds the fate of performers like Phil Lynott, a casualty in the war. Others fail to live up to their good intentions. 'It's up to us to play down the fashionable side of drugs. It's all very well asking teachers, doctors or even the police to remain vigilant over youngsters but they will always be seen as too authoritarian. Drugs are seen as very fashionable. So it stands to reason that rock stars should be the ones who make the most relevant statements against drug abuse.' That was Boy George's advice.

The public education campaign has infused the tabloids, helping to restructure and discipline it. But the battery of potent themes which could be brought into a drugs story remains an irresistible lure. 'A junkie mum who turned to vice to pay for heroin has made a solemn promise to Princess Diana to quit drugs and prostitution.'[49] This one had the lot: royalty, heroin, motherhood, sex - and that was all in the opening sentence. The junk story would run and run.

Notes

1. *Sun Day (News of the World* colour supplement), 6 July 1986.

2. *Daily Mirror*, 11 January 1986.

3. *Daily Mirror*, 8 January 1986.

4. *Guardian*, 11 January 1986.

5. *Daily Mirror*, 2 January 1986.

6. Thatcher used such formulations on more than on occasion, despite public outcry. A late example, 'there are, as we know, enemies of democracy both within and without', was part of the Second Carlton Lecture given at the Carlton Club on 26 November 1984.

7. There are labels: 'Thatcher's drug war' (*Guardian*, 10 August 1985). There are commands: 'Make war on pushers' (*Daily Express*, 22 September 1984). There are statements: 'Mums get the call in drug war' (*Daily Mirror*, 4 April 1986). And there are strings of alarm-signal words: 'Drug war jail crisis' (*Daily Mirror*, 27 September 1985). The use of 'crusade' is less common. 'My Crusade For The Lives Of Our Children', by Margaret Thatcher (*News of the World*, 20 October 1985), shows how her supporters strive to build an image for her which combines aggression with compassion.

8. The concept of war was extended to give the military even greater powers. The Posse Comitatus law, which prohibits US armed forces from enforcing the civilian criminal code, had to be amended to permit drug interdiction forces to make use of technologically advanced military systems such as the Sentry radar surveillance aircraft and the famous U2 spy plane (Freemantle, *The Fix*, p. 101). See also *Air International*, December 1984, and Charles Clements, *Witness to War* (London, Fontana, 1985). The latter provides a memorable account, from a target's point of view, of the use for which the A37 counter-insurgency jets sent to bomb cocaine traffickers' airstrips were built, and deployed in Latin America.

9. *Sun*, 13 June 1986. The next quotation is also from this source.

10. *News of the World*, 15 June 1986.

11. *People*, 15 June 1986.

12. *Sun*, 13 June 1986.

13. *News of the World*, 15 June 1986.

14. For example, *Sun*, 13 June 1986, *News of the World*, 15 June 1986. Subsequently Sebastian Guinness was gaoled for four months for possessing heroin and cocaine, and Rosie Johnston received a nine-month sentence after being convicted of possessing amphetamines, cannabis and cocaine and of supplying heroin to Olivia Channon.

15. *People*, 15 June 1986.

16. 'Of all the words written about the tragic death of Olivia Channon at Oxford last week, one fact beams through. She didn't like herself very much.' (Anne Robinson, *Daily Mirror*, 18 June 1986). This was a thoughtful piece with a number of insights about growing up, but the point about personality theories still stands. An article criticizing the editing process

that makes a nonsense of young people's accounts of drug-taking (glue-sniffing in this case) by removing references to its positive side appeared in the *Guardian*, 19 August 1986.

17. *News of the World*, 15 June 1986.

18. *Star*, 17 June 1986.

19. *Daily Mirror*, 12 June 1986.

20. TV-am broadcast, 17 June 1986.

21. *News of the World*, 22 June 1986.

22. *Sunday Times*, 16 May 1965.

23. Filmed interview, included in *The Rock 'n' Roll Years*, transmitted 7 July 1986 on BBC1.

24. *People*, 15 June 1986.

25. Dr David Owen, leader of the Social Democratic Party, was one who contradicted the Government's assertion that there was no causal relationship between illegal drug use and unemployment. He cited academic research in support of his claim, made in the 1985 Prime Lecture at St Thomas's Hospital in London (*Guardian*, 16 October 1985).

26. cf. Susan Sontag: 'In the Middle Ages, the leper was a social text in which corruption was made visible; an exemplum, an emblem of decay'. (*Illness As Metaphor*, London, Penguin, 1983, p. 58).

27. Then she did some smack with a Chinese chap, oh-oh, An affair began with Charlie Chan, oh-oh ...

    A song from the period of 'Chinese' heroin that began when heroin from the Golden Triangle of South-East Asia was supplied to meet the demand frustrated by the 1968 ban on prescribing. It was said to be smuggled by the Triad criminal organizations which had a presence in the British Chinese community. The Triads, incidentally, originated in seventeenth-century China as a secret nationalist movement dedicated to the overthrow of foreign rule. The foreign rulers were the Manchus.

    There's a Siamese cat in the council flat, oh-oh,
    The finest grains for my lady's veins, ooh-ooh...

    ('Plaistow Patricia', by Ian Dury and Chaz Jankel, from *New Boots and Panties*, Stiff Records, 1977. Published by Blackhill Music).

28. 'The way young people are being lured into debt is scandalous,' said the *Sun* in an editorial entitled 'Loan mania'. 'Getting into debt is really no different from getting hooked on drugs, with the money lenders acting as the pushers.' (23 June 1986).

29. cf. Christopher Lasch, the American social critic who argues that the traditional idea of a political Left and a Right should be abandoned: '.... the model of ownership, in a society organized around mass consumption, is addiction. The need for novelty and fresh stimulation becomes ever more intense, intervening interludes of boredom increasingly intolerable. It is with good reason that William Burroughs refers to the modern consumer as an "image junkie" .... Drugs are merely the most obvious form of addiction in our society. It is true that drug addiction is one of the things that undermines "traditional values", but need for drugs - that is for commodities that alleviate boredom and satisfy the socially stimulated desire for novelty and excitement - grows out of the very nature of a consumerist economy.' (*New Statesman*, 29 August 1986).

30. *Daily Mirror*, 27 November 1984.

31. For example, *News of the World*, 30 September 1984, *Guardian*, 27 March 1986.

32. *Guardian*, 21 March 1986.

33. *News of the World*, 20 October 1985.

34. For example, 'VICARS SAVE BLONDE RAPED BY WITCHES: Ordeal of drugs and blood lust. A terrified blonde yesterday relived the nightmare of her initiation as a witch. The girl, who fears for her life, told how she was:
MADE to drink cockerel's blood mixed with her own.
RAPED by the coven's high priest in front of 200 people.
HOOKED on heroin handed out by the devil-worshippers to lure innocent youngsters.' (*Daily Mirror*, 16 September 1985.) Heroin is thus associated with secret conspiracies, satanism, violence, enslavement and the corruption of the young.

35. *News of the World*, 29 September 1985.

36. *Daily Mirror*, 7 December 1985.

37. *Daily Mirror*, 6 August 1985.

38. *Daily Mirror*, 31 January 1986.

39. *Guardian*, 31 January 1986.

40. *Daily Mirror*, 1 February 1986.

41. The foregoing material in this paragraph is derived from an outstanding, but unfortunately unpublished, 1984 Cambridge M. Phil. thesis by Tony Borzoni entitled *The Mythology of Heroin and the Press*, plus a *Daily Express* report of 20 September 1984. The *Daily Telegraph* piece appeared on 20 October 1983.

42. *Sun Day*, 2 February 1986.

43. William S. Burroughs, *Junky* (London, Penguin, 1984), p. 143. Originally published in 1953.

44. *Daily Express*, 22 September 1984.

45. The crusading papers displayed a vanguardist attitude towards their place in the struggle that would make the average Trotskyist grouplet seem self-effacing. Reporting a call by trade union officers representing Customs personnel for increased recruitment to improve the interdiction of cocaine, the *Daily Express* ran the banner 'Customs men join *Express* campaign' (11 December 1982). The officers of both sexes who had been stopping the smuggling of illegal drugs as long as they had been in the Customs service would perhaps have liked a little more emphasis on the conflict between their demand and Government public spending policy.

The articles referred to in this paragraph appeared on 14 and 15 April, 1986.

46. *Daily Mirror*, 26 April 1986.

47. *Daily Mirror*, 5 April 1986.

48. 'Rock stars twist the Dragon's tail', *Daily Express*, 20 October 1984. The Boy George quote which follows is from the same source.

49. *Sunday Mirror*, 9 March 1986.

21. The Media Press the Panic Button

Alex Corina

Maybe I'm becoming a little sensitive in my old age, but when I saw the media response to Granada Television's programme "War on Drugs" – you know, the usual shock horror; the bigger the headline, the bigger the outraged response – I felt it couldn't go unchallenged.

The programme and its media aftermath raise three important issues:

1. The way in which Granada Television constructed and orchestrated the media before the programme even went out, and arguably promoted a moral panic and public outrage.

2. A criticism of the programme itself, and the way it could be argued that, on balance, it legitimised a punitive and moralistic approach to drug abuse.

3. The hypocrisy and opportunism of Government ministers, politicians and the like, who express their public outrage at strategies of harm reduction, whilst at the same time giving their private support.

Together, these issues are the reason why so many workers in the firing line: social workers, youth workers, teachers, counsellors and so on, all paid out of the public purse, feel vulnerable and threatened by the McCarthy-like atmosphere generated by the sort of response the programme "War on Drugs" generated.

Firstly:

What do all the people below have in common with each other and with the press cuttings opposite? * (not included in this anthology).

Simon Hardcastle, Alan Billington, David Mellor, Robin Corbett, Martin Goold, Det. Supt. Des Donaloes, Dr. Michael Bush, Kit Williams, Barrie Liss, Ian Wilson, James Hammond and many others:

They all commented on a programme they hadn't seen. The press copy was written before the programme was shown, and they all commented on quotes purported to have been made by Allan Parry, which were not.

A classic case of not checking their facts, assuming that whatever's dished out in a press statement is correct, when it is not. Equally, they were all unprofessional in not being rather more circumspect by insisting on seeing the programme before responding. Arguably worse was one local solvent abuse counsellor, who saw the programme and gave his personal support to Allan Parry, but then wrote to a local newspaper condemning him. With friends like him, who needs enemies?

Alex Corina: The Media Press the Panic Button' from the *MERSEY DRUGS JOURNAL*, (July/August 1987), No. 2, pp. 8-10. Reprinted by permission of the publishers.

As for the press statement itself, issued by Granada on Tuesday 12th May, just before the programme; it casts serious doubt on Granada's journalistic integrity, not least of all because the truth was the first casualty in their attempt to boost viewing figures.

For the record, here is the press statement, together with the transcript of what Allan Parry actually said, so Drugs Journal readers can judge for themselves:

PRESS STATEMENT

GRANADA TELEVISION LIMITED

WAR ON DRUGS

Sniffing glue? Then don't use a big plastic bag to concentrate the fumes. Use a crisp packet.

That is the advice a local authority official gives schoolchildren. Allan Parry, drugs training director of Mersey Health Authority tells school kids that the crisp packet over nose and mouth is safer. A plastic bag over the head may cause black-outs or death. And if a heroin addict comes to him with the veins in his arm dried out and collapsed by drug abuse, but determined to go on injecting, Allan Parry will teach him how to inject heroin in the groin.

These revelations come in Granada Television's series WAR ON DRUGS tonight at 10.30 p.m. on ITV.

Says Parry in the programme:

"If they are determined to use drugs and no matter what we do they still carry on, I don't think we've got any other choice but to try to keep them with all their limbs attached and as healthy as possible."

Conservative Euro-MP Andrew Pearce comments in the programme: "I am shocked even to hear that anybody would say they would give that advice. I think it's awful."

A full transcript of tonight's programme is enclosed. The section dealing with the drugs training officer is on pages 23-36.

WHAT WAS ACTUALLY SAID

The format of the programme was that hypothetical situations were presented by the moderator, in this case Geoffrey Robertson. He asked Allan Parry what he would say to 12-13 year olds about the perils of glue sniffing:

PARRY: I don't think I would start off by saying "I'm going to teach you how to sniff glue safely." I think I would go through the substances that people sniff, explain the problems with different substances.

ROBERTSON: These kids tell you that they put glue in plastic bags, and then they go into toilets and they put the plastic bag over their head and sniff and get a high feeling. Sometimes black out. Is that a dangerous thing to do?

PARRY: Sure, if they are doing that, I would have no hesitation in telling them, if they are determined to do it, not to use a large plastic bag, to use a small one.

ROBERTSON: Use a packet of crisps bag or a small plastic bag?

PARRY: Yes, not to cover their nose and their mouth.

ROBERTSON: You would show them how to sniff glue safely.

PARRY: Less dangerously.

I suppose the English language can mean different things to different people. At best, Granada television was guilty of being highly selective and partial in their reporting. At worst, they were downright dishonest. It was the sort of journalism that deliberately produces a public outcry and the inevitable hate mail, although the overwhelming number of letters and phone calls were in support, with only a couple against. You know the sort of thing: "Allan Parry should be handcuffed to the back of a police car and dragged all round Liverpool till he's dead," (signed Mrs. X).

Secondly:

The programme began refreshingly with the distinguished panel saying things that did not immediately conform to the public image of their roles in society. It didn't last long.

Apparently, it would be OK to minimise the damage to their own social networks, by saying that they wouldn't want to ruin a good party for the sake of someone smoking a joint in the conservatory. When it came to advice about safe solvent or heroin use, the self-appointed guardians of the nation's morals crawled out of the woodwork.

Andrew Pearce, MEP, was "shocked" and "it was awful". And there were others. If Allan Parry had said "Isn't it dreadful taking glue?", and that was that, then they would have been happy, even though it wouldn't prevent a death. Common sense, prevention and harm reduction didn't get a look in.

By the end of the programme, "moral" and "immoral" were translated into "right" and "wrong". "Drugs (i.e. socially unacceptable substances) were not just bad for your health, but downright wrong and deviant. Alcohol and tobacco were OK, of course. Who would even dream of banning them because they cause death in the user or their victims, if taken in excess? Who would dream of a party where you banned alcohol and tobacco? Even the government's own "drink and drive" campaign last Christmas advocated

moderation, not abstinence, if people were **determined** to drink and drive, as a method of preventing road accidents. A classic example of harm reduction. But glue is **wrong**: not unhealthy, or harmful taken this way or that. The logic of harm reduction from a purely health promotion point of view cannot be escaped.

Lastly:

Because it's such a hot potato, drugs is one of the few issues on which politicians can take a personal stance.

Apart from Ireland, it's the only "party line" that cuts right across the political parties. They all just play to the galleries, repeating without question, the knee-jerk moral panic, which is often orchestrated by the press.

On the one hand, Conservative Euro MP Andrew Pearce criticises the common sense approach of harm reduction, although at the same time, his own party's government policy is accompanied by guidelines, that harm from drug abuse is reduced by giving out clean, free syringes.

David Mellor's criticism of the programme similarly flies in the face of the report of his (then) own Department's Advisory Council, of which he was, incidentally, a member. Judge for yourselves.

Advisory Council Report Said:

" .... we decided that we should concentrate on preventive measures which satisfied two basic critieria: a) reducing the risk of an individual engaging in drug misuse; b) reducing the harm associated with drug misuse.

1.12 It is clear that not all preventive measures could be equally effective in terms of both criteria. For example, statutory controls aim to reduce the number of people who misuse drugs by making it more difficult to obtain them. These controls are an essential part of current prevention policy both in this country and internationally. However, the potential risk of such controls is that those who nevertheless misuse drugs may come to greater harm than would otherwise be the case. For example, illegal misuse of drugs in secret in order to avoid police attention or public disapproval may make it harder to obtain early assistance in the event of mishap."

The Problem Today

Although most of the headlines in recent years have concentrated on the new(ish) 'dance drugs' such as ecstasy, and a resurgence of LSD use has also been subject to media concern, we should be careful not to run with the tide of popular fears. Heroin seizures have continued to rise since the mid 1980s, when concern over drug use - mainly heroin - was at its pinnacle. Whereas in 1987 approximately 456 kg of heroin was seized by the police and Customs and Excise, in 1992, 550 kg was seized. The number of registered heroin and methadone addicts in 1987 was 11,339; in 1992 it was 26,975. Apart from the odd glitch, the trend has been an upward one.

Heroin and other opiates have been, and remain, the primary problem drugs in Britain. That is of course not to say that it is the most commonly used illicit drug. In fact substances like cannabis (which account for 80% of all seizures), and amphetamines, which accounts for 15%, and others, such as MDMA (ecstasy) and LSD are used by many more people but present fewer problems to those users in comparison to heroin. Gilman *et al* at this point usefully remind us that drug services, partially because of their workload with opiate users, and also because they are not properly geared up to deal with the new drug users of the 1990s (those using ecstasy and LSD), are not meeting the specific needs of those new users. This should not detract, however, from the continuing needs of opiate users. The heroin 'problem' is now much greater (in numeric terms) than at any time in the 1980s, and yet given the publicity lavished on the currently more fashionable drugs, one could almost be forgiven for thinking that it had actually diminished in size. That public and official concern at any one time may not reflect the real problem, or may exaggerate a particular problem, is explored by Shapiro in *Where Does All the Snow Go?* In 1988 it was forecast, that a crack epidemic was to hit British shores and that once it did it would create problems (due to the 'immediately' addictive nature of the substance) so far unprecedented. The epidemic never came and a police and customs 'crack squad' set up to deal with the impending problem was disbanded after two and a half years of relative (in)operation. In the last few years, however, fears relating to crack and cocaine have resurfaced, almost totally due to the fact that cocaine seizures have gone through the roof. In 1992 over 2,000 kg of cocaine were seized compared to 550 kg of heroin. Conventional interpretations of huge increases in the amount of a drug seized would normally lead to suggestions of accompanying increases in use. Shapiro alerts us to the dangers in taking this too seriously, pointing out that the evidence implies that cocaine, including crack, has not got the foothold in British drug usage that is suggested, and that it is unlikely to get it in the foreseeable future. The 'problem' today, understood in conventional statistical terms, is, as it has long been, one of heroin.

22.   Beyond opiates ... and into the '90s
Mark Gilman

The Lifeline Project in Manchester identified a new group of potential clients among young people attending rave dance venues using a range of drugs including ecstasy, LSD and amphetamine. A cartoon leaflet series was tailor made to attract this group. Experience showed their problems were mainly legal, though later psychological and physical problems emerged. As a group dedicated to lively enjoyment, these young people require a different treatment and educational approach from opiate addicts.

LIFELINE MANCHESTER is sited in shopfront style premises on the street that is the focal point for one of the leading international forces in contemporary youth culture - 'raving', characterised by large numbers of young people dancing till late to loud house music in hot and humid surroundings. It would be wrong to overstate the part that illicit drug use plays in this very popular youth culture - but equally wrong to overlook the fact that large numbers of young people are consuming large amounts of stimulant and hallucinogenic drugs and some are getting into problems. Last year we took a decision to target these young, recreational drug users.

These developments in youth drug use patterns are taking place at a time when drug services are consolidating much of their work within an HIV prevention framework and rightly concentrating their efforts on the 'heavier end' of the market. In our area the type of clients most familiar to drug services are white, unemployed or underemployed men, injecting opiates in a dependent fashion.

Part of the reason why Lifeline decided to target young recreational drug users is precisely because they are being left out as services wrestle with the logistics of accommodating large numbers of opiate dependents.

The task of attracting these 'newer users' fell into four stages. Firstly we had to get a clear idea of who they are - an 'identikit' profile of our target group. This would give us an idea of the key ways they differ from our traditional opiate using clientele, enabling us to review how our service might need to change to attract them.

Secondly, we had to decide how to advertise our service to the target group. Thirdly, we had to develop our service response to their needs as and when they arose. Fourthly, we had to arrange for ongoing monitoring of our contact with this 'new' group as a discreet piece of 'action-research'.

The 'new user' profiled

We built up the identikit profile by contacting young people who were members of the target group. We were able to do this by speaking at length to some young people we knew as a result of some of our staff's interest in following local football teams. Travel

---

to and from away matches and pre- and post-match drinking haunts provided handy arenas for 'testing the water'.

Over the last couple of years there has been a clearly observable overlap between the nightclubbing and terrace cultures - noted at the last football world cup when England supporters took up the now famous chant of "Let's all have a disco!" The practices of 'skinning up' (smoking cannabis), 'having a dab' (of amphetamine sulphate), 'taking a trip' (LSD), and 'doing an 'E'', are making easy transitions from dance floor to terrace.

For many young men the weekend has become a distinct leisure culture that merges mornings, afternoons and nights into one unbroken hedonistic celebration.

Links between football fans and drug use were cemented in the coffee shops of Amsterdam in May 1991 as thousands of Manchester United fans celebrated their club's victorious return to Europe with copious amounts of cannabis. Given that United fans are drawn from across the UK, glorious tales of the joys of cannabis were spread nationwide. Having crossed the line to using cannabis, these young people are now more receptive to experimenting with other drugs.

This first stage produced the following identikit profile of our target group:

- aged 15 to 25, predominantly white and male from working class backgrounds;

- followers of local football teams and local bands, and regular clubgoers;

- officially unemployed or underemployed, but familiar with - and occasionally involved in - the workings of local 'irregular economies';

- having grown up with drugs throughout their formative years, they now view drug use as perfectly normal behaviour.

Hitting the target

We had then to decide how to advertise our service to this target group. As a starting point we built on our experience of producing the harm reduction comic for injecting drug users - Smack in the Eye - by revising two cartoon strips from past issues.

These were reproduced on a single sheet of brightly coloured A4 paper folded in half: Time Tripper is a cartoon strip about the use of hallucinogenic drugs; Call the Cops contains advice for those arrested for drugs offences.

We arranged distribution of these flyers through a limited number of outlets, including record shops and a fashion emporium frequented by the young clubgoers. Both were eagerly received by that target group, whose members began to show an interest in Lifeline.

Following this success we produced another single-sheet flyer featuring a specially invented character, 'Peanut Pete'. Whereas Time Tripper and Call the Cops were drawn from Smack in the Eye. Peanut Pete was designed to speak directly to our target audience.

The first edition of his adventures finds Pete exploring Manchester city centre under the influence of hallucinogenic drugs. Its aim was simply to entertain and tell people what and where Lifeline is. The response was very encouraging. In the three months before the launch of Peanut Pete Lifeline received 23 new referrals where the drug problem concerned either LSD, ecstasy or amphetamine. In the quarter that saw the launch (July to September 1990) new referrals for problems with the same 'recreational' drugs rose to 60.

Legal shock

Having contacted the targets we then had to assess their needs and decide how to address them. We realised that these new users are often in sound physical shape with interesting and active social lives. Their problems arise from the illegality of using their drugs of choice, the psychological effects of 'bingeing' on these drugs, and the social reactions of their families to their drug use. In responding to their requirements, the ability to give quality legal advice fast emerged as of crucial importance. Most of the first wave of new clients at Lifeline were primarily motivated to seek help of a legal nature.

Most opiate users ask us for legal advice because they have been arrested for an acquisitive crime and are citing their drug dependence in mitigation. In contrast, the first members of the target group to approach us had been arrested for serious Misuse of Drugs Act offences involving possession with intent to supply.

They knew quite a lot about the pharmacology of their drugs of choice, what effects to expect, and how to maximise the potential for a positive experience, but we soon realised that they were ignorant in one crucial area - the law on the misuse of drugs.

Commonly, members of our target group purchase a relatively small number of LSD 'trips' or ecstasy tablets (10, 20 or 30) for a discounted wholesale price. Over a weekend these will be sold at a small profit to acquaintances who move in the same social circles. A 'successful' weekend will see the initial investment recouped and the remaining drugs retained for use by the individual and his or her very close friends.

In this setting the vendor is seen as providing an essential service to their social group and enjoys an enhanced standing among them. But the law's attitude is very different: found in possession of over 10 LSD 'trips' or 'Es', a possession with intent to supply charge is a real possibility.

When you have been brought up to regard drug use as non-deviant behaviour, it comes as a great shock to be charged with possessing class A drugs with intent to supply - a charge which carries a maximum penalty of life imprisonment. It was at this stage that we began to ponder some of the wider issues (see panel below).

Mitigation backlash hits user-dealers

Young ecstasy, LSD and amphetamine users may be suffering the legal repercussions of courtroom mitigation tactics. We are getting very good at presenting our opiate using clients to the courts as 'innocent victims', but it follows that someone else must be the 'evil villian'. Those charged with supplying any illicit drugs fit the bill only too well. Members of our target group sell drugs (to consenting others) to finance their own use, and for this are slammed by the courts. Many opiate users are charged with acquisitive crimes like burglary, but by playing the innocent victim are often dealt with relatively leniently. Drug user-dealing may be seen as a 'victimless crime', but by no stretch of the imagination can this be extended to burglary.

Peer group service

Despite the courts' attitudes to them, for members of our target group selling drugs is not primarily a commercial venture. These individuals bear no resemblance either to the stereotype of the 'proselytising junky' or the 'evil drug baron'. They are ordinary young people who subsidise their social life by providing a service in demand by others in their social group. Neither are they the downtrodden resorting to drug-induced oblivion. These youngsters are dedicated consumers too busy enjoying the world as it is - at least on weekends - to engage in ritual chants against their 'oppressors'.

The odd bit of spare cash left on a Monday morning may purchase the latest 'sounds', a new tee shirt, or a pair of trainers. If there was a massive anti-poll tax demonstration in Manchester, these people might buy the accompanying tee shirt, but not *Socialist Worker*.

The irony is that those young people cast in the role of evil villian are often the most enterprising members of their group. They have overcome recession-induced depression, but instead of being heralded as such are facing ridiculously long prison sentences. Non-statutory drugs agencies have a special responsibility to this client group as few statutory services have the time or inclination to provide a service to those without a classic drugs (read opiate) 'habit'. We are seeking to provide a complete legal service to this group that includes pre-court preparation and expert witnessing.

Peanut Pete's paranoia

Young ravers regularly engage in extensive use of powerful hallucinogenic and stimulant drugs. This is requiring our staff to become proficient in recognising and assessing symptoms of mental health disorders that may or may not be drug induced – rediscovering skills dating from the last upsurge in hallucinogenic and stimulant drug use in the late '60s and early '70s. Dealing with bad trips, giving advice on how to avoid them, and how to reduce them are once again becoming bread and butter issues for drugs workers in the '90s.

Ongoing monitoring/research allows us to record and respond to these needs. For example, the second Peanut Pete leaflet dealt specifically with drug-induced paranoia, and we are currently responding to all the attendant physical problems of frequent stimulant use such as weight loss and depression.

A whole series of training issues need to be acted upon. These fall broadly into two categories: training for drugs workers around very specific issues (such as amphetamines and the criminal justice system); and more basic drugs awareness for all those involved with our target group, such as teachers and parents. We are devising a programme of training for education workers and have produced a high quality leaflet for parents in conjunction with a local advertising agency – family work soon becomes important when servicing young drug users.

There must be many workers in non-statutory agencies who are beginning to wonder what unique contribution the voluntary sector can make to drug services. One answer might be that in working with this new client group, workers at Lifeline are now using skills that have lain dormant in work with the typical opiate using client.

This is best summed up by the remarks of one seasoned drugs worker who explained that the most important skill for those working with opiate users is an ability to encourage those in charge of prescription pads to "get scribbling!". In contrast, a typical day's work with this new group might involve giving legal advice to a young, recreational amphetamine user, simultaneously, assessing whether their 'cabbaged' friend is suffering a temporary post-hallucinogenic experience or a truly psychotic episode, while convincing both their families that drug use does not mean social or psychological pathology. Now that is proper drugs work!

23. Where Does All the Snow Go? — The Prevalence and Pattern of Cocaine and Crack Use in Britain

Harry Shapiro

Cocaine or, rather, extracts of coca leaf, were widely available in the nineteenth century as an ingredient of many popular patent medicines and tonics. However, some concern over its addictive potential saw cocaine included in the 1908 Pharmacy Act. Later, via the Defence of the Realm Act, following the First World War scare that prostitutes were giving the drug to soldiers, cocaine passed into the Dangerous Drugs legislation of 1921 (Berridge and Edwards, 1987).

During the 1920s, the drug had a sufficiently high profile in Britain's 'yellow press' for the novelist Dorothy L. Sayers to make cocaine distribution among the 'fast set', the key to her very popular novel *Murder Must Advertise*. However, until very recently, little was heard about the drug apart from occasional media stories about cocaine use mainly among film and pop stars. Even in America, concern about the use of cocaine in the general population is only a phenomenon of the 1980s (Johnson, 1987).

Cocaine's limited prevalence in Britain since the 1950s has probably been determined by at least two main factors. Firstly, the widespread availability of cheap amphetamine, either in pill form diverted from pharmaceutical sources (in the sixties) or illicitly home-produced amphetamine sulphate powder (from the mid-seventies onwards). Secondly, cocaine is an expensive commodity, currently anything up to four times the price per gram of amphetamine for a drug with a much shorter duration of action. In June 1991 the average street price across the UK for 1 gram of amphetamine sulphate was £12-15; for cocaine hydrochloride, £75-100; for crack (about four rocks), £75-100.

Recently, however, cocaine has been making the headlines; first because customs seizures of cocaine hydrochloride powder have been steadily rising and, more specifically, because of concern during 1989 about a predicted 'epidemic' of crack – smokeable form of powdered cocaine.

Information about the prevalence and consequently the patterns of cocaine and crack use in Britain is extremely patchy and incomplete; 'Much has been written in the press about the alleged growth of cocaine consumption. There does not, however, appear to have been any substantial research on the subject at all in the UK' (Wagstaff and Maynard 1988).

So what hard information do we have? Firstly, there are the seizure statistics provided by Customs and Excise and the police. The amount of cocaine seized has been rising since as long ago as 1983, but in 1986, there was a fourfold increase from just over 100 kg to over 400 kg and (with the exception of 1988) it has risen from this baseline ever since to a level in 1991 of over 1000 kg (Figure 1). The major source country has been Colombia, using newly-established trading routes via Spain and Portugal into Europe. Customs have also seized cocaine brought in mainly by women in single-kilo amounts from the Caribbean and Eastern seaboard of the USA.

The reason given by police and customs for the increases in cocaine seizures has been that the American market for the drug has been saturated, prompting the cocaine producers of South America to seek alternative markets. However, it seems more likely that there has been overproduction in the producer countries which has necessitated the search for wider rather than different markets (Royal Canadian Mounted Police, 1986). In 1985 the House of Commons Home Office Committee visited the United States. Commenting on their visit in the subsequent *Misuse Of Hard Drugs (Interim Report)*, they opined, 'We believe from all that we saw and heard, that as the American market becomes saturated the flood of hard drugs will cross the Atlantic' (House of Commons, 1985). Yet despite these and other warnings from politicians, the inevitable taboid press coverage during 1985-86 and the undeniably marked rise in cocaine seizures, we have yet to experience any 'explosion' of cocaine use in the UK. One senior policeman offered the view that better intelligence, greater international cooperation and initiatives such as the Drug Trafficking Offences Act would prove decisive in preventing the UK repeating the US experience (Hewitt, 1987). Nor has the country been deluged in a tidal wave of crack. In 1990 crack seizures were running at about 15 per cent of all seizures of cocaine (Home Office Drugs Inspectorate, 1990) but, while numbers of seizures rose from 12 in 1987 to 352 in 1990, this still amounted to less than one kg of the drug (National Drugs Intelligence Unit, 1991).

Numbers of seizures of all forms of cocaine remained relatively stable until 1989 when the figure rose by 146 per cent from 829 to 2045 (Figure 1.2). In 1990 numbers of seizures dropped by 240 although the weight seized that year rose by 22 per cent from 499 to 611 kg. The total of 1805 seizures in 1990 included over 1000 Metropolitan Police seizures, three-quarters of all police cocaine seizures (Home Office 1991) (Figure 1.3).

Between 1988 and 1989, cannabis seizures by the Metropolitan Police rose sharply by 45 per cent. It is possible that, because of the crack scare, the Metropolitan Police have been targeting those they believe might be potential users and, in the process of increased 'stop and search' activity, have been finding more cannabis. Black communities in London have been increasingly convinced that the advent of crack has given the police a new 'excuse' for harassing black people (*Searchlight*, 1990). A recent study in Lewisham, South London, found that 'whereas 85 per cent of crack users seen by other agencies are white, 95 per cent of crack users arrested by the police are black. It would seem .... that the police have targeted black people and black communities in their operations directed against crack and cocaine misuse' (Mirza *et al.*, 1991). The then-director of the Community Drug Project in south London, Steve Tippell, commented that by concentrating enforcement efforts in the denser areas of black population, the police were fulfilling their own prophecies, 'in a sense what you look for you find - and that doesn't say much about overall patterns of drug use' (Gillman, 1990).

So what do the enforcement statistics actually tell us about the prevalence of cocaine use? The question as to whether it is supply – or demand-side enforcement measures

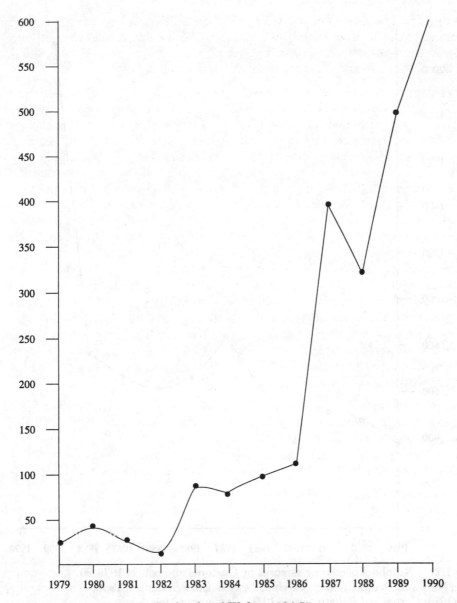

Figure 1.1   Cocaine seizures in England and Wales, 1984-89.
Source: National Drugs Intelligence Unit, *Drug Seizure Statistics*, 1990.

that are the more effective in reducing consumption remains unresolved. Thus, extrapolating from drug seizure figures is always a precarious business. For example, with no national prevalence statistics available, it is impossible to say for sure what increased seizures actually mean in terms of overall consumption. If seizures go up, does this mean we are stopping more of the drug coming into the country through increased vigilance or special targeting, or does it just mean that more is getting

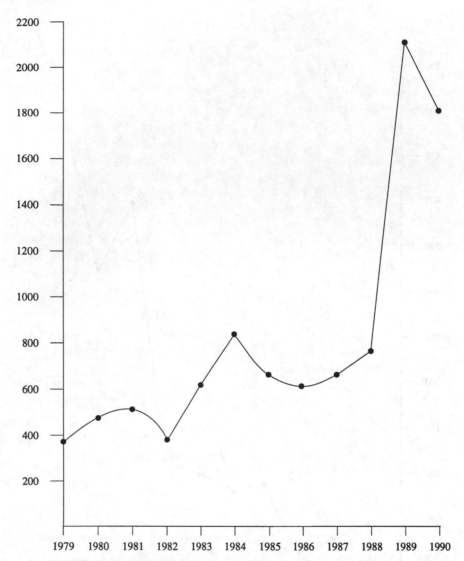

Figure 1.2   Numbers of cocaine seizures by Customs and police, 1979-90.
Source: National Drugs Intelligence Unit, *Drug Seizure Statistics*, 1990.
Home Office Statistical Bulletin, issue 19/91, September 1991.

through, bearing in mind that it is widely believed that only a relatively small percentage of drugs destined for the UK is actually seized? Alternatively, if seizures go down, does this mean that the smugglers have been frightened off by more stringent searching, or are they just more devious at hiding the drugs, or has demand fallen? One possible indicator of what is happening with supply and demand is the price on the streets. During question-time at the 1991 Customs press conference on seizures, it was revealed that the prices of drugs such as cocaine and heroin had remained relatively stable. One obvious conclusion from this is that seizures have had little impact on overall supply. If they had, one would expect the price to have risen sharply, although one might also speculate that the price might be kept artificially high by dealers to maintain the 'status' of the drug among users (particularly the relatively well-off user). However, there is no evidence of this and it could only be ascertained by fieldwork of a kind which has yet to be done. In pointing out the doubtful efficacy of targeting major drug importers, Nicholas Dorn has commented,

> The proportion of the retail ('street') price of illegal drugs that is accounted for by the importation price is very small - around 10% for cocaine in the United States. The greater part of the retail price is accounted for by the price differentials between importers and retailers. It follows that one would have to seize a quite high proportion of imports to shift the price at importation levels up sufficiently to make much difference to retail prices and hence consumption .... The seizure rate would have to rise several hundred per cent in order to raise retail prices enough to dent demand. No known method of interdiction .... can achieve this. (Dorn, 1989)

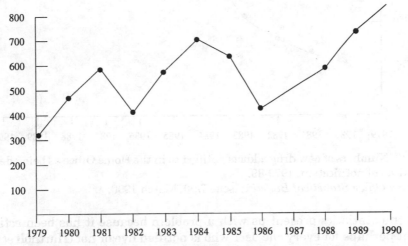

Figure 1.3   Persons found guilty, cautioned or dealt with for cocaine offences, 1979-90. Source: *Home Office Statistical Bulletin*, issue 19/91, September 1991.

How does the amount seized relate to the potential numbers of users? To be able to make any comment on this, we need to start with the numbers of those notified to the Home Office by doctors as being cocaine-dependent. As with all the statistical evidence of cocaine use, the numbers of notified cocaine addicts has been rising steadily. In the ten-year period from 1979 to 1989, the number of new addicts has risen from 126 to 527, while the total figure jumped from 800 in 1987 to over 1000 in 1990 (Figure 1.4). How much cocaine could this group realistically be consuming in a year? One detailed study of a representative sample of cocaine users defined heavy use among the sample as at least 3 g a day (Spotss and Shontz, 1980). One London street agency that sees a number of cocaine users indicates that a typical pattern of heavy cocaine use would be to use the drug on a daily basis for three or four days and then to rest before starting on another 'run' (Community Drug Project, London, 1991). Thus one could calculate that a heavy cocaine user consuming 3 g a day in four-day 'runs' per week could theoretically consume roughly 600 grams a year or just over half a kilo. Thus the 1000 notified users in 1990 could consume around 660 kg a year – about 10 per cent more than the total Customs seizures for the same year.

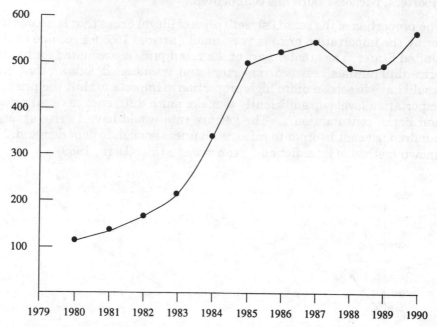

Figure 1.4   Numbers of new drug addicts notified to in the Home Office as being dependent on cocaine at time of notification, 1979-89.
Source: *Home Office Statistical Bulletin*, issue 7/90, March 1990.

However, the statistics present us with a problem because it has been estimated for heroin that perhaps for every one user who is notified five or not (Hartnoll *et al.*, 1985), and there are reasons to believe that those with a cocaine problem are even less likely to come forward (see below). Thus even if one were to multiply the cocaine notification figures only by a factor of five, one has a potential cocaine consumption figure of at least 3000 kilos. Added to that would be an unknown figure for those who use the drug recreationally or occasionally. It should be said that in default of adequate research, the assumption here is that the pattern of cocaine use is similar to that of heroin, in that there is a known heavy-user group, a larger unknown heavy-user group and a much larger recreational group. However, given the widespread availability of amphetamine and the expense of cocaine, it is possible that in Britain the heavy cocaine user group is proportionally much smaller, with the main users of the drug being recreational or occasional consumers.

To try to ascertain the percentage of agency clients actually coming forward with a primary cocaine problem, 70 drug agency reports were surveyed from existing ISDD .

records. These comprised annual reports from individual agencies giving details of client contact and primary drug of use, and also small-area multi-agency studies where information had been collated from a number of different referral sources (for example, drug agencies, probation services, social services, GPs, and so on, on the basis of questionnaires). There are a number of drawbacks to information of this kind, such as the level of compliance from the reporting agencies in returning questionnaires, and double-counting, whereby one client is referred by more than one agency or presents more than once to the same agency. Though they were specifically concerned with the task of ascertaining the extent of cocaine problems, many reports did not differentiate between cocaine and amphetamine, merely listing these under 'stimulants'. In addition, it was often not possible to discern whether the figures related to cocaine mentions with another drug as the primary drug of misuse, and/or whether cocaine was a problem in addition to another main drug, such as opiates. Some agencies reported no referrals at all and very little local prevalence of cocaine use. However, taking all this into account, it was consistently clear that few agencies were seeing clients with a primary cocaine problem, and for those agencies that did see such clients, they represented no more than 1 per cent of the agency caseload. There were exceptions to this pattern; the client caseload for some agencies in the south London area and Manchester included a higher percentage than average of those presenting with a primary cocaine problem than reported in other parts of the country; around 10 per cent in one case. However, in terms of actual numbers of people, this still represented only a handful of individuals in a given year.

Interestingly, comments in those reports which took a broader view of the prevalence of drug use in their area (that is, comments which were not just single-agency based) were clearly aimed at challenging what may have been a distorted local media perspective on cocaine use in that area; for instance 'contrary to media propaganda, the cocaine industry would not appear to have arrived in Salford at present' (Polese, 1987) and from mid-Hampshire, 'there is little evidence to support the belief that cocaine is widely available or used in this area' (Harper, 1987). Other area reports did express some concern that cocaine was increasingly available, albeit from a very low base.

To see whether there had been any changes in the light of recent increases in seizures and notifications, phone-calls were made to ten key drug agencies around the UK, ensuring that there was a representative mix of all environments from rural to inner-city. The picture appears to be similar - some higher rates quoted in London and Manchester, but hardly any clients reporting primary use of cocaine; 'very, very, few' and 'hardly any' were typical remarks. Commenting on the cocaine notification figures for 1989, the Home Office observed,

> The persistently small numbers of cocaine addicts notified (9 per cent) suggest that, despite seizures of cocaine by weight having exceeded those for heroin in 1987 to 1989, misuse of the drug has not so far resulted in significant demands for medical treatment. The only police force area with a high number of new cocaine addicts in 1989 was the Metropolitan Police Division with 270 addicts. No other area had more than 30. (Home Office, 1990)

It might be reasonable to assume that as cocaine is an expensive drug, those with the most problematic use are likely to come from the more financially secure sectors of society. Those from this group who are seeking help are more likely to present first to their own GP who might then refer them on to a private clinic or treatment centre rather than to a 'street agency' in the voluntary sector. To test out this theory, ten private establishments were also included in the telephone survey. Discussions with medical directors revealed that such centres are indeed seeing a higher number of clients with cocaine problems as a proportion of their client/patient group in a year – perhaps 4-10 per cent on average, with the higher figures coming once again from the London area. However, in absolute numbers, relatively few patients are seen with a primary cocaine dependency problem, although apparently there are several for whom cocaine is one drug problem among many (mainly heroin and alcohol).

Thus it could be that there is a far smaller cohort of heavy cocaine users in proportion to those for whom heroin is the major problem drug. However, even if this is correct, there are a number of reasons why those with an acute cocaine problem are less likely to present for treatment than, for example, heroin users. It could be that most people who use cocaine do not actually have a problem with the drug. Or it may be that users do not believe that cocaine is a drug that can cause problems and do not acknowledge as cocaine-related the problems they may be experiencing. But what about the person who is actively seeking advice or treatment? Historically, the drug agencies have been able to offer very little to stimulant users of any description, so there is little incentive for such a user to present for assistance (Standing Conference on Drug Abuse, 1989). Many drug users are understandably reticent about coming forward, for fear that making their drug use known will result in problems with the police, employers, and so on. Given that one of the symptoms of chronic cocaine use can be acute paranoia, one might conjecture that it is hardly surprising that few heavy cocaine users are seen.

What about the prevalence of crack use? Certainly, agencies report seeing even fewer 'crack clients', but interestingly, during the telephone survey, one agency in the Midlands said that although virtually no crack users had presented themselves, agency staff had heard that crack use was 'rife' in certain parts of Birmingham. Seizures of crack have taken place in most of the UK's inner city areas, including London, Liverpool, Manchester, cities in the West Midlands and Cardiff.

One highly contentious issue is the prevalence of cocaine use among the Afro-Caribbean community. Commentators are loath to pursue this point for fear of exacerbating (largely) media portrayals of cocaine use as a 'black drug problem'. Undoubtedly, there *is* cocaine use among sectors of the British Afro-caribbean population. However, it has long been established that irrespective of the drug, black drug users will not readily come forward to primarily white-run street agencies or national health clinics (Awiah *et al.*, 1990) and it is likely that few are able to seek private treatment.

The literature-search for this chapter demonstrates an unknown level of cocaine use by certain sectors of the black community, much as it exists among sectors of the white population. One of the evaluation studies of the Government's anti-heroin campaign noted about cocaine use, among those already using drugs, that 'there were signs of increased trial (especially amongst blacks) and more general interest in trial' and quoted regular injectors from Cardiff as saying, 'There are a load of Rastas round here fixing smack and coke' (Andrew Irving Associates, 1988); while a report from the Sheffield area observed, 'Cocaine is beginning to appear in Afro-Caribbean communities' (Drug Advisory Service, 1989). Young black males who are part of the drug scene in Manchester are financing purchases of expensive cocaine by dealing in other drugs. They also smoke 'crack', but refute the notion by saying that they are using 'washed cocaine', suggesting perhaps that among this group, one's status is demeaned by being dubbed a 'crack' user (North Western Regional Drug Training Unit, 1991). This is not unlike the situation among young people in south London during the craze for smoking heroin or 'chasing the dragon' in the early eighties. It was only a matter of months for the label 'skag head' to be reduced from a heroic salutation to a term of abuse.

However, that cocaine use is far from being only a 'black problem' is shown by the evaluation of the Riverside Community Drug Team in West London conducted by the Centre For Research on Drugs and Health Behaviour. They too stated that 'early research suggested that cocaine use was concentrated within particular ethnic groups'. But later they described the three categories of drug users that they interviewed; one type was designated 'OC' or 'out of contact' with an agency for at least three months. This was the only group of the three that mentioned cocaine and, of 40 respondents, only 3 per cent were 'black British', the rest were either 'white British' or Irish and there were no Afro-Caribbeans (Power *et al.*, 1990).

In fact, there is a longstanding tradition in London of white stimulant use in areas of relatively high-density black population. The majority of illicit amphetamine in circulation during the sixties was diverted from pharmaceutical sources. However, as well as controlling this trade, the Krays and other criminal gangs also oversaw the limited East End production of illicit amphetamine for sale mainly to white youngsters in the West End clubs, many of whom lived in south London (Shapiro, 1989).

What about the prevalence of cocaine-crack use among other groups? There is evidence to show that, for a time, crack was used quite heavily by women working in the sex industries of large cities such as Liverpool and Birmingham (Matthews, 1990; Patel *et al.*, 1989) although heroin remains the primary drug among those within this group for whom drugs are a problem.

Among the general population there is a similar dearth of information. The literature-search included all surveys done of the school population. These are invariably conducted on the basis of self-reported questionnaires which, even when confidential, present the analyst with questions about honesty – the likelihood of 'boasting' or alternatively reticence about personal disclosure. Additionally, there is the problem of truancy; those who are consistently absent from school may (for a number of reasons) be those most liable to come into contact with drugs. However, it is clear from those surveyed that very few young people under 20 are even coming into occasional contact with cocaine. In a 1987 survey of young people in South Sefton, Liverpool, none of the 253 respondents admitted to trying heroin or cocaine or to having a close friend who had even tried these drugs once, while 91 per cent said they had never even been offered those drugs, the highest percentage for that question. Ninety-five per cent said they would never take it (Newcombe and O'Hare, 1988). A similar result was obtained from a survey of Wolverhampton schoolchildren - none of those surveyed had been offered cocaine (Wright, 1990). Higher 'exposure' figures were obtained in West Lothian, where five of 915 13-16-year-olds (0.5 per cent) said they had tried cocaine (West Lothian Drugs Education Project, 1988). School students in England, Scotland and Wales were the subject of a survey conducted by the Health Education Authority's Schools Health Education Unit. Here the highest contact figure was recorded among fifth-form boys, 2.2 per cent of whom said they had been offered cocaine (Balding, 1988). the survey was repeated in 1988 when the figure for this same group had risen to 3.9 per cent (Balding, 1989). Highest of all in terms of actual use to date was a survey in inner London of over 3000 schoolchildren where 1.9 per cent of respondents claimed to have used the drug with varying degrees of frequency from once to daily. 'Cocaine use has been considered negligible among school-age British population. This study shows that 2 per cent of schoolchildren have tried cocaine, more than one third of them repeatedly' (Swadi, 1988). It is conceivable that young people in certain areas of inner London might have a higher-than-average chance of coming into contact with cocaine and other illegal drugs. However, it is doubtful whether such results can be meaningfully extrapolated for the whole of the country.

Certainly, awareness of cocaine and crack has increased among young people. The Wolverhampton survey has been running quinquennially from 1969. In that year 15 per cent mentioned cocaine when asked what drugs are used by addicts. In 1989, that figure had risen to 80 per cent, with 8 per cent also aware of crack at a point early on in the year *before* press coverage of the topic (Wright and Pearl, 1990). The often-claimed notion that cocaine is not regarded as a dangerous drug is belied by the high numbers in the surveys cited above who recognise cocaine as a drug of addiction or who say they would never take it if offered. This is further supported by comments received about cocaine from young people in the 13-20 age range surveyed by another of the market research companies employed to evaluate the impact of the Government's anti-heroin campaign. Awareness of cocaine was almost 100 per cent across the four age groups in the 13-20 band, but only 5 per cent claimed to know anybody who had used it or said they had been offered it themselves and only 1 per cent claimed to have tried it. Cocaine was perceived as lying far closer to heroin than cannabis in terms of dangers; 'unhealthy', 'can kill' and 'don't want to die' were typical of the comments received. The figures for contact with and exposure to heroin were very similar to those for cocaine (Research Bureau Limited, 1988).

Those who are using cocaine from among the wealthier groups in society are unlikely to be the subject of user surveys, so reports are mainly of the anecdotal/confessional type. One reseacher interviewed a woman drug user who had been a legal secretary in the city for some years and had a boyfriend working in the futures market; 'Lots of these characters are cokeheads', she said, 'it gives them confidence and keeps them hyped up and going. They earn so much money that they never get into real trouble with it. And there's always recuperation in a private clinic if they ever need it.' (Power, 1988). In the wake of a 1986 CBI report on drug abuse in industry, the *Daily Telegraph* reported the case of 'John' who had an annual income of £65 000 and allegedly spent £15 000 a year of it on cocaine. 'John' said, 'The City and advertising and television industries are riddled with cocaine. I know of people with responsibility for huge deals who cannot get by without it.' Eventually, 'John' spent two months in a private treatment centre and went on to become actively involved not only in Narcotics Anonymous, but also (because of his drink problem) in Alcoholics Anonymous (Doyle, 1986).

Given how little we know about the prevalence of cocaine and crack use in Britain, it is hardly surprising that there is even less information about the patterns of use and what we have is almost entirely anecdotal. However, we can make a few isolated comments about patterns of use.

In addition to the small area studies located by the literature-search, information was also supplied to the author by the North Western Regional Health Authority Drug Misuse Database (hereafter DMD). This data related to 109 users of cocaine referred during 1989 by a wide range of referral sources, but primarily local community drug teams. As with all 'indicator' information of this kind, it can only provide a window into the total picture of drug use in the wider community of any given area (Donmall, 1990).

Summarising from DMD statistics and other small-area studies, it would appear firstly that cocaine is rarely used with any regularity by those under 20 years of age. Among regular users, it is often used in conjunction with other drugs, especially heroin, and may be injected with heroin (speedballs). Possibly because those who became regular cocaine users were relatively experienced users of other drugs by the time of first use, the progression to injecting cocaine could be rapid. A 1988 survey of the Sefton Probation Drug Team revealed that most of the client group had not tried cocaine before the age of 21 but, when they did, over half were injecting it (Buchanan and Wyte, 1987).

The DMD data shows that of those cited as cocaine users, only 6 per cent of reports gave cocaine as the primary drug of choice; the rest were said to be using heroin as their main drug. Of course, it is possible that cocaine users were presenting as heroin users in order to obtain a prescription for sale, but more likely these figures confirm the thesis that very few primary cocaine users actually present to health and social work agencies.

Cocaine may be used to 'rev' up a user after a bout of heroin or tranquilliser use or, alternatively, these sedative drugs may be used to offset the cocaine 'rush'. Because of the price, cocaine is often regarded as an occasional 'treat' at the weekend by those users most likely to come into contact with agencies. However, it seems that cocaine would be much more popular if it was less expensive. The cocaine 'rush' is perceived as 'smoother' than that experienced with amphetamine and presumably also there is the hope that cocaine would be at a higher purity level than amphetamine which can be cut up to 90 per cent with adulterants. However, this hope may be forlorn; a survey of illicit drug use in the Portsmouth area noted that the price of cocaine was no indicator of purity, much of that currently available being heavily cut with amphetamine. Users knew this and it deterred purchase (Brown and Lawton, 1988).

At present, there is no hard evidence to suggest that crack is consistently attracting a different and/or younger market than cocaine powder, although this drug has been picked up in raids on large parties frequented by young people where cannabis, ecstasy and LSD have also been seized (Strang et al., 1990). While non-users perceive a marked distance between cocaine and cannabis in terms of dangers, among users this does not necessarily seem to be the case. One dealer known to the Lifeline Project in Manchester has been supplying cannabis to middle-class 'professionals' in one of the more affluent parts of the city for over ten years. The dealer told one of the project workers that there had been a recent increase in demand for both cocaine and ecstasy from this cannabis-using group (North Western Regional Drug Training Unit, 1991). Cannabis and cocaine are both seen as social/recreational drugs, typical use of which involves sharing the drug with others in social settings (Murray, 1984).

These middle-class drug users living in Manchester are an example of an unknown number of users who are never the subject of surveys because they neither present for treatment nor come to the attention of the police. One study that did reach beyond agency contacts involved interviews with 92 cocaine users in Scotland contacted by 'snowballing'. This revealed them typically to be polydrug users who used cocaine infrequently: only four had used once a week or more in the past three months, despite previous periods of heavier use. Most were middle class and snorted the drug (Ditton J. et al., 1991). In Toronto, Canada, researchers attempted to construct a profile of the 'typical' cocaine user out in the community. Using personal contacts and an advertising campaign, they interviewed 111 people over 21 who had used cocaine in the past three years and had been in employment for six of the previous twelve months prior to the study. They were surprised that over a third of respondents were women, but concluded that the 'typical' occasional/recreational user was an unmarried male aged 21-25, employed in a white collar occupation, who snorted less than half a gram no more than ten times a year either at home or at a friend's house (Erickson et al., 1987).

To conclude, on the basis of the current research, the overwhelming number of cocaine seizures by the Metropolitan Police and the general distribution of wealth within the UK, the indications are that the greatest concentration of cocaine use in Britain is in London and the South East, although significant use in the wider community is anecdotally reported in other large conurbations such as Manchester and Birmingham. And even if the pattern of heavy cocaine use is not the same as that for heroin, it is likely that there is substantially more cocaine in circulation than is intercepted by the enforcement agencies. Relatively few primary users of cocaine present to agencies, compared with heroin users. Reasons for this may include lack of treatment options for heavy cocaine users and the heightened level of anxiety about making use known, consequent on heavy use of the drug. Epidemiological research in this area may be hampered by the fact that heavy or even frequent recreational use of the drug may be confined to a sector of society unavailable and/or unamenable to research scrutiny.

What of the future for cocaine in Britain? All the statistical evidence available indicates that cocaine use in Britain is on the increase. However, it is still the case that at present, the demand for stimulant drugs in this country is served primarily by home-produced cheap amphetamine sulphate and, more recently, ecstasy. In contrast, cocaine is much more expensive and, in most areas, harder to obtain. For this picture to change dramatically, there would have to be either a significant levelling-out of the price differential between amphetamine and cocaine, or a sustained and ultimately successful enforcement effort at cutting off supplies of amphetamine both internally and from abroad. Alternatively, there would have to be such an overproduction of cocaine in the producer countries that the drug was sold cheaply as a 'loss leader' in Europe to create a market large enough to challenge the current ascendancy of widely-available cheap amphetamine. Even if that did happen, amphetamine manufacturers might respond with new products of their own such as 'Ice' (smokeable methylamphetamine). With the advent of a European free market in 1992, there will be pressure on enforcement agencies to relax border controls. Even so, none of the scenarios for a substantial increase in the overall consumption of cocaine and crack in Britain, likely to impact on drug services nationally, seems probable in the foreseeable future.

Note

The author would like to thank Jasper Woodcock, OBE, Director of the Institute for the Study of Drug Dependence, London and Dr Mike Donmall of the North Western Regional Health Authority Drug Research Unit for comments received during the preparation of this chapter.

References

Andrew Irving Associates (1988) *DHSS: anti-drugs - AIDS campaign. Qualitative evaluation report* (London: Andrew Irving Associates).

Awiah, J., Butt, S., and Dorn, N. (1990) '"The last place I would go:" black people and drug services in Britain', *Druglink*: 5 (5), pp. 14-15.

Balding, J. (1988) *Schoolchildren and Drugs in 1987* (Exeter: Health Education Authority Schools Health Education Unit).

– (1989) *Young People in 1988* (Exeter: Health Education Authority, Health Education Unit).

Berridge, V. and Edwards, G. (1987) *Opium and the People: Opiate use in nineteenth-century England* (New Haven: Yale University Press).

Brown, C. and Lawton, J. (1988) *Illicit Drug Use in Portsmouth and Havant: A local study of a national problem* (London: Policy Studies Institute).

Buchanan, J. and Wyte, G. (1987) *Drug Use and its Implications: A study of the Sefton probation service* (Bootle: Merseyside Probation Service).

Community Drug Project, London. Personal communication 1991.

Ditton, J., Farrow, K. Forsyth, A. *et al* (1991) 'Scottish cocaine users: healthy snorters or delinquent smokers?', *Drug and Alcohol Dependence* 28, pp. 269-76.

Donmall, M. C. (1990) *The Drug Misuse Database: Local monitoring of presenting problem drug use* (London: Department of Health).

Dorn, N. (1989) 'Reflections on Two Rand Reports' (review), *International Journal of Drug Policy*: 1 (3), p. 30.

Doyle, C. (1986) 'High flier downed by drugs', *Daily Telegraph*, 30 September.

Drug Advisory Service (1989) *Report by DAS on Services for Problem Drug Users provided by Sheffield Health Authority ....* (Sutton: DAS).

Erickson, P. G., Adlaf, E. M., Murray, G. F. and Smart, R. G. (1987) *The Steel Drug: Cocaine in perspective* (Massachusetts: Lexington Books).

Gillman, P. (1990) 'Crack for sale', *Sunday Times Magazine*, 1 April, p. 36.

Harper, D. (1987) *Report of a Prevalence Study into the Nature and Extent of Problem Drug Taking in mid-Hampshire* (Winchester: Winchester Health Authority).

Hartnoll, R., Mitcheson, M., Lewis, R., and Bryer, S. (1985) 'Estimating the prevalence of opoids dependence', *The Lancet*: 1 (8422), p. 203.

Hewitt, C. (1987) 'A cocaine explosion?', *Druglink*: 2(2), p. 7.

Home Office (1990) *Statistics of the Misuse of Drugs: Addicts notified to the Home Office, United Kingdom, 1989* (Croydon: Home Office Statistical Division).

Home Office (1991) *Statistics of the Misuse of Drugs: Seizures and offenders dealt with, United Kingdom 1990*. Area tables (Croydon: Home Office Statistical Division).

Home Office Drugs Inspectorate (1990) *Cocaine and crack - update* (London: Home Office Drugs Inspectorate).

House of Commons Home Affairs Committee (1984-5) *Misuse of Drugs (Interim Report)*, HC 1984-1985, no. 399 (London: HMSO).

Johnson, E. M. (1987) 'Cocaine: the American experience', in Allen, D. (ed.), *The Cocaine Crisis* (New York: Plenum Press).

Matthews, L. (1990) 'Female prostitutes in Liverpool', in Plant, M. (ed.), *AIDS, Drugs and Prostitution* (London: Routledge).

Mirza, H. S., Pearson, G. and Phillips, S. (1991) *Drugs, People and Services: Final report of the drug information project to the Lewisham Safer Cities Project* (London: Goldsmiths' College).

Murray, G. F. (1984) 'The Cannabis-Cocaine Connection: A comparative study of use and users', *Journal of Drug Issues*: 14, (4), pp. 665-75.

National Drugs Intelligence Unit (1991) *Drug Seizures 1990* (London: NDIU).

Newcombe, R., and O'Hare, P. (1988) *A Survey of Drug Use among Young People in South Sefton, 1987* (Liverpool: South Sefton Health Authority).

North West Regional Drug Training Unit (1991). Personal communication.

Patel, A., Merrill, J., Vidyasagar, H., and Kahn, A. (1989) 'Cocaine and crack' (letter). *British Medical Journal*: 299, p. 856.

Polese, P. (1987) *Myths or Reality: Drugs problems in Salford* (Salford: Community Drug Team).

Power, R., Jones, S., Dale, A. *et al.* (1990) *The Riverside Community Drug, Alcohol and HIV Team: An evaluation of year one* (London: Centre for Research on Drugs and Health Behaviour).

Power, R. (1988) 'Drug scenes', *New Society*: 83, (1314), p. 17.

Research Bureau Limited (1988) *Heroin Misuse Campaign Evaluation* (London: RBL).

Royal Canadian Mounted Police (1986) *Monthly Digest of Drug Enforcement Statistics*: 6 (8), p. 23.

Searchlight (1990) 'Drugs - why black people suspect the police', *Searchlight*: no. 184, pp. 18-19.

Shapiro, H. (1989) *Waiting for the Man: The story of drugs and popular music* (London: Quartet Books).

Spotts, J. V. and Shontz, F. C. (1980) *Cocaine Users: A representative case approach* (New York: The Free Press).

Standing Conference on Drug Abuse (1989) *Working with Stimulant Users: Report of a SCODA members' conference* (London: SCODA).

Strang, J., Griffiths, P., and Gossop, M. (1990) 'Crack and cocaine use in south London drug addicts 1987-1989', *British Journal of Addiction*: 85, (2), p. 193-6.

Swadi, H. (1988) 'Drugs and substance use among 3,333 London adolescents', *British Journal of Addiction*: 83 (8), pp. 935-42.

Wagstaff, A. and Maynard, A. (1988) *Economic* Aspects *of the Illicit Drug Market and Drug Enforcement Policies in the United Kingdom,* Home Office Research Study No. 95 (London: HMSO).

West Lothian Drugs Education Project (1988) *Annual Report 1986/87* (Livingstone: WLDEP).

Wright, J. D. and Pearl, L. (1990). 'Knowledge and experience of young people regarding drug abuse 1969-1989'. *British Medical Journal:* 300 (6717), pp. 99-103.

Drugs and Crime

Way back in the section on *The Nature of Addiction*, Falk alerted us to the dangers in interpreting certain behaviours as having their aetiology in the use of particular substances. In other words, various cross-cultural investigations permit us to question the link between violence and even alcohol, and PCP (two drugs commonly cited as having strong casual relationship with violence) as a casual one. This is important because we have to be able to see our way through the bio-pharmaceutical mire and identify where drugs may be being scapegoated as the cause of problems, whereas those problems may in fact have deeper social and psychological seatings. Power introduces us to some of the basic issues associated with crime and violence, quickly dealing with some of the complexities and enlightening us about the context of drug related crime and violence. The two following papers take us a little further into the complexities of the relationships. Collins, in summing up the literature on the relationship between drugs and violence, points out some of the most conclusive data to date: 'there is virtually no evidence that the pharmacological effects of drugs (alcohol excepted) account for a substantial proportion of drug related violence'. Where it does occur it is for various structural and contingent reasons, particularly those involved with the illegality of drugs themselves and the criminal justice system which seeks to control them. Violent drug users also often have a history of violence which precedes drug use. Chaiken and Chaiken present us with complementary data which concludes in one section that 'no single sequential or casual relationship is now believed to relate drug use to predatory crime'. That drug users, and especially long-term, high-frequency drug users have a strong relationship to criminality is discussed as are the differences of relationship for different groups of drug users, more or less deviant and more or less involved with the drug distribution system. They further argue that research fails to support 'the hypothesis that use of illicit drugs ultimately results in the user's involvement in predatory crime, *or even that this is the predominant pattern*' (my emphasis). Thus, we are forced to conclude that even outside of cross-cultural formulations, which locate drug related crime and violence within particular populations and cultural influences, the research evidence from within societies (like Britain and the USA which broadly accept the relationship) contradicts many of the common assumptions made about it.

24.   Drugs Crime and Violence
Robert Power

Who, if anyone, needs to worry about drug-related violence? The person on the street, shopkeepers, governments - or drug users themselves? Fieldwork experience in London and a review of the international research literature throws up some unexpected answers.

Any illegal activity, such as the supply and use of illicit drugs, involves varying degrees of criminal behaviour. Concern about associated violence, not in a small part fuelled by sensationalist journalism, is inevitable. In September 1986, the *Daily Express* quoted Metropolitan Police Commissioner Sir Kenneth Newman's prophecy that: "Violence to people on the street could well fall as the need to finance addiction waned. And some of the more perverted crimes such as rape, torture and murder would fall as people breathe a drug-free atmosphere."

To unravel the link between drugs and violence, and to lay to rest some of the myths, three questions need to be addressed.

- Do illicit drugs *in themselves* incite violence, and in particular violent crimes?

- What types of crimes do drug takers commit, and what is the associated level of violence?

- What is the 'arena' of drug-related violence and which groups are its victims?

Do drugs cause violence?

The answer to this question, with one or two qualifications, is no.[1,2] The most common drugs of abuse are strong nervous system depressants valued for their euphoria-inducing and tranquilising effects rather than as aids to aggression (though it's well-known that depressants such as alcohol can release violence through their disinhibitory effects).

Even in the case of hallucinogenic drugs (such as LSD and phencyclidine or PCP), or amphetamines and other stimulants, there is no convincing evidence for a direct link between pharmacological effects and violent crime.

Hallucinogenic drugs do cause bizarre behaviour, which sometimes leads to violence; but this is sporadic and seemingly random, rather than a predictable effect of the drug, and does not result in aggressive crimes, planned and carried out against the person.

• **Amphetamines:** The case regarding stimulants, especially amphetamines - is more complicated. Until the mid-1970s, research tended to conclude amphetamines were a direct cause of violent behaviour.[3] However, this early research has been criticised for concentrating on clinical observations of small numbers of amphetamine users who had exhibited violent behaviour.[4]

Robert Power: 'Drugs Crime and Violence', *DRUGLINK*, (November/December, 1986, pp. 15-16. © Druglink 1986.

Since then, studies have tended to move away from the clinical setting and out on to the streets. The consequence has been to give greater prominence to the mediating effects of personality and context, thereby highlighting the importance of individual differences in reactions to amphetamine.[5] Taking this point of view one step further, it has been stressed that the link between narcotics and violence has largely been generated by political leaders (and one might add the media) rather than by social and biological scientists.

At another level, common wisdom among regular drug users warns against the erratic and aggressive behaviour of 'speed-freaks' and 'barb-heads'. However, such behaviour is unpredictable, often dependent on the situation, and cannot simplistically be attributed to the effects of the drugs themselves.

Are drug users violent?

The short answer to this question is - no more than anyone else. Drug dependence, and the protracted process of procuring expensive illicit drugs, means that for many drug users crime is the only way to gain sufficient income to meet their needs. But most crime committed by regular drug users is non-violent crime against property (predominantly theft), perpetrated in order to support a drug habit.

A whole body of research points to the fact that drug users are more likely to be involved in revenue-raising property crime rather than crime against the person.[6] One US study from the mid-'70s found that drug users, particularly those dependent on heroin, were more inclined to property crimes, whereas non-drug using criminals were not likely to be involved in crimes of violence against the person.

More recently, 75 per cent of crimes (such as shoplifting for resale and burglaries of abandoned buildings) committed by a sample of heroin users in New York were found to have had no clear victims.[7]

Another US study has made a direct link between the price of illicit drugs and the level of property crime, concluding that a one dollar increase in the price of heroin caused the drug user to commit crimes that would net an extra 30 cents.

Not that drugs and crime are never related. It has been said that criminal enterprises in the USA have a tradition of violence; it would be odd if drug-related crime were a total exception. In Britain, where an equivalent culture of violence is not prevalent, the level of violent crime among drug users is low.

• **Home Office statistics** for opiate addicts first notified in 1979 to 1981 show that 42 per cent were first convicted for theft, 19 per cent for drugs, and 18 per cent for burglary.[8] Among the convicted population in general, these figures are 60 per cent, two per cent, and 11 per cent respectively.

The proportion of convictions for burglary and theft (the crimes more likely to be associated with violence) among addicts declined over the period just before, and up to two years after notification. Indeed, the level of violent crime remained lower, at around six per cent of the crimes addicts were convicted of, than the equivalent figure of 12 per cent for the general convicted population. As the Home Office statistics point out: "the involvement of notified addicts in violent crime appeared to be small and stable".[9]

Fieldwork at the Drug Indicators Project among 'addicts' not notified to the Home Office, gives no reason to suspect that the situation is any different for this group, where fraud, shoplifting and theft are the main forms of street-level crime.

It is important to make the point that people dependent on illicit drugs come from all walks of life - not all resort to non-drug crime to support their habits. At one end of the scale celebrities like Boy George can maintain a reported eight gram a day (£640) heroin habit from their legitimate earnings. Others hold down a variety of jobs, live on the dole, and bring up families, without becoming involved in small-scale dealing, or 'serving' to friends, to support their drug dependency.

American research in the 1970s showed that the percentage of dependent drug users resorting to crime as their primary means of support, ranged from a low of about 30 per cent (among white females) to a high of 80 per cent (among black males).[10] Later research confirmed the lower levels of criminal activity among women drug users.

Who suffers?

Again, there is a short answer: violence takes place largely between drug users and drug dealers themselves, though this is not the whole story.

At one level, the violent exploits of internationally organised criminal syndicates in the drug trade, such as the Mafia and the Triads, are legend. The upsurge of cocaine trafficking and the value of the 'narcolire' has meant high stakes are involved. Dramatic machine-gun shoot-outs between importers and distributors on the streets of New York and South Florida, and violent incidents between cocaine dealers in London, have made gripping news.[11]

Such extremes of violence are very much contained within the trafficking world itself, where high rewards and strict codes of conduct mean fierce economic competition, and cursory penalties for misconduct.

At another level, a link can be made with 'terrorist' acts, with both left- and right-wing groups involved in the sale of drugs for revenue to buy arms. The IRA, the Red Brigade, and Basque separatists in ETA, plus a range of neo-nazi groups, have all been implicated in trafficking in heroin or cannabis for arms.

At one end of the political spectrum, drugs and arms trading have created links between European fascists and Lebanese Phalangists. At the other, Turkish left-wing groups were found to be exchanging heroin for guns in the Bulgarian capital, Sofia.

In 1982, Omega 7, the anti-Castro organisation, were responsible for a series of bombings in the USA. After finding 40 pounds of marijuana in the flat of one of its members, the FBI concluded that drug trafficking was helping to finance the group's armoury.[12] In this convoluted way, another chain in the link between drugs and violence can be made.

> Fieldwork experience at the Drug Indicators Project has confirmed that a group of non-drug using criminals have been identifying, threatening, and robbing drug dependent women, who more often than not are living on their own with small children. Out of economic necessity, these women have turned to small-scale dealing to maintain their drug habits and support their families. Pinpointed as particularly vulnerable, they have been systematically threatened by the gang until drugs and money are handed over. Shotguns have been pointed into babies' prams, knives pressed to small children's throats, and bottles of acid held over their heads. That no serious injury has occurred is due to the fact that the women concerned have always given over whatever drugs or money were in their possession.[16]

However, it is between and among drug users themselves that violence more directly related to drugs tends to take place. The daily round of 'scoring' and 'dealing' which fills much of a regular drug user's time, is the arena in which most violence occurs. Adulterated drug deals, 'rip-offs' and robberies, desperation and greed, are all potential scenarios for violence.

A description of the amphetamine scene in San Francisco makes a point that has general application:

"Most of the criminality is directed towards other members of the drug scene ... Most of the violence ... results from an interaction among drug effect, lack of social controls within the subculture, and a variety of economic factors, including the way the market place is sustained by the individual users."[13]

• **Not only do drug users** face violence from fellow users and participants in the illicit drugs market: they are also vulnerable to abuse from other sources. Operating to a large extent outside the protection of the law, isolated and unprotected drug users are easy prey for other criminal groups, who are safe in the knowledge that their activities will not be reported to the police.

Such predatory violence has been common on the London drug scene for some years, but has reached frightening proportions in recent months (see box above for an example). Even when criminals threatening drug users are charged and imprisoned, other groups are all too ready to take their place, so the harassment and violence continues.

In recent years, drug users have been accused of being responsible, not only for the increase in crime and the promotion of drug use among the young, but also for outbreaks of serious unrest, such as the Handsworth riot.

Encouraged by dramatic newspaper headlines and media stereotypes, it is no surprise that public opinion is firmly set against this group of people and 'vigilante' groups have been active on estates in several cities. For example, in Dublin, suspected 'pushers' were threatened with eviction; others were harassed by chanting crowds.[14] More recently, well-publicised anonymous phone lines have given residents in many areas of the UK the chance to identify suspected dealers.

NO ONE WANTS a drugs problem on their own doorstep. Harassment and intimidation, often based on prejudice and misinformation, are no answer. Persecuting drug users and even burning down a rehabilitation centre[15] does nothing to help problems of dependence; neither does it further our understanding of a social issue of serious and worrying proportions.

I have hoped to show that the link between drug users and dealers, violence, crime, drugs and the public, is complex. It is neither clear-cut in terms of causation, nor undirectional in effect.

Summary

- Drugs do not of themselves cause violent criminal behaviour. Drug effects may raise or lower resistance to violent behaviour, but personality, situation and culture remain critical determinants.

- The vast majority of drug-related crime is against property, accomplished to support a dependence upon expensive (and sometimes elusive) illicit drugs.

- Very few regular, dependent, drug users relish petty crime; nor are they proud of it.

- Violent acts are perpetrated by drug users - but so are they by every sector of society. Some will kill for a £10 bag of heroin or a 'line' of cocaine. Others will kill for the price of a taxi fare or on the result of a football match.

- Most violence directly associated with drugs and drug dealing takes place between and among dealers and users themselves.

- However, there is an indirect link between violence and drugs, both with respect to international 'terrorism' and organised syndicated crime.

- People dependent on illicit drugs are sometimes on the receiving end of intimidation and violence from the public they are supposed to threaten.

References

1. McBride D.C. 'Drugs and violence'. *In*: Inciardi J.A. *ed. The drugs-crime connection*. Beverley Hills, Calif.: Sage, 1981, pp. 105-123.

2. Watters J.K., Reinarman C. and Fagan J. 'Causality, context, and contingency: relationships between drug abuse and delinquency'. *Contemp. Drug Probl.*: 1985, pp. 351-373.

3. Grinspoon L. and Hedblom P. *The speed culture: amphetamine use and abuse in America*. Cambridge, Mass.: Harvard University Press, 1975.

4. Greenberg S.W. 'The relationship between crime and amphetamine abuse: an empirical review of the literature'. *Contemp. Drug Probl.*: 1976, 5 (2), pp. 101-130.

5. Watters, *op cit*.

6. Inciardi J.A. and Chambers C.D. 'Unreported criminal involvement of narcotic addicts'. *J. Drug Issues*: 1972, 2 (2), pp. 57-64.

7. Johnson B.D., Goldstein P.J., Preble E., *et al. Taking care of business: the economics of crime by heroin abusers*. Lexington, Mass.: Lexington, 1985.

8.   Home Office. *Criminal convictions of persons first notified as narcotic drug addicts in 1979-81*. Statistical Bulletin, 29 July 1985.

9.   Home Office, *op cit*.

10. Chambers C.D. 'Narcotic addiction and crime: an empirical review'. *In*: Inciardi J.A. and Chambers C.D., *eds. Drugs and the criminal justice system*. Beverley Hills. Calif.: Sage, 1974, pp. 125-142.

11. Schorr M. *Gunfights in the cocaine corral*. New York 11: pp. 48-57.

12. 'The financing of terror'. *Contemporary Affairs Briefing*: 1983, 2 (7).

13. Smith R.C. 'Speed and violence: compulsive methamphetamine abuse and criminality in the Haight-Ashbury district'. *In*: Zarafonetis C.J.D. *ed. Drug abuse: proceedings of the International Conference*. Philadelphia: Lea and Febiger, 1972, pp. 435-448.

14. O'Donohue N. and Richardson S., *eds. Pure murder - a book about drug use*. Dublin: Womens Community Press, 1984.

15. Recently Turning Point's planned rehabilitation centre in West Bromwich was badly damaged in an arson attack following local hostility to the siting of the unit. Suspicions that this hostility was behind the attack are unconfirmed, but is reported that local residents were 'jubilant' at the fire. (Jeremy Laurance. Birmingham's bad Samaritans. *New Society*: 25 April 1986).

16. Power R. 'The other hits'. *City Limit: 260*, 25 Sept-2 Oct 1986.

25.   Summary Thoughts About Drugs and Violence

James J. Collins

Introduction

This final chapter will not repeat in any detail the points made in earlier chapters. Rather, I will make some general statements about the drugs-violence connection, point to the undue influence of popular myths about the drug problem on research and public policy enterprises, and make research recommendations. After early discussion on Goldstein's (1985) tripartite framework, this chapter argues the need for revision of this framework and suggests a more comprehensive conceptual model.

I contend that the most important aspects of the drugs-violence relationship are those associated with violence in the drug distribution system. Because so little is known systematically about this phenomenon, I suggest where attention should be focused to generate scientific and policy-relevant understanding.

Pharmacological, economic compulsive, and systemic violence

In his ground breaking article, Goldstein (1985) proposed three ways that drugs and violence can be related to each other: (1) the *pharmacological* effects of the drug on the user can induce violent behavior, (2) the high cost of drug use often impels users to commit *economic compulsive* violent crime to support continued drug use, and (3) violence is a common feature of the drug distribution system. This last category, which Goldstein calls *systemic* violence, serves a variety of purposes such as protection or expansion of drug distribution market share or retaliation against market participants who violate the rules that govern transactions.

Three chapters in this volume (Fagan, Miller, and Teplin) and the research literature in general indicate that drug-induced pharmacological violence is uncommon. Stated another way, there is virtually no evidence that the pharmacological effects of drugs (alcohol excepted) account for a substantial proportion of drug-related violence. Some qualitative and quantitative data suggest that crack (Honer et al. 1987; Manschreck et al. 1988), PCP (Fauman and Fauman 1982; Simonds and Kashani 1980), amphetamines (Ellinwood 1971; Asnis and Smith 1978; Fink and Hyatt 1978), and barbiturates (Goodman et al. 1986; Tinklenberg and Woodrow 1974; Tinklenberg 1973) have a pharmacologic relationship to violence. These studies are not methodologically strong, however, because they tend to rely on small and specialized samples and tend *not* to control for multiple correlates of violence. The bulk of the evidence suggests a weak or nonexistent relationship, especially when demographic and criminal history factors are included in analyses as control variables. My own research is consistent with

James J. Collins: 'Summary Thoughts About Drugs and Violence' in *DRUGS AND VIOLENCE: CAUSES, CORRELATES AND CONSEQUENCES*, edited by Maria De La Rosa, Elizabeth Lambert and Bernard Gropper (National Institute on Drug Abuse Research Monograph 103, 1990), pp. 265-275. © James J. Collins. Reproduced by permission of the author.

this finding (Collins et al. 1989). Moreover, drug users themselves agree with this conclusion. Drug users typically say that their drug use has no relation to violence (Collins et al. 1989; Fagan, this volume), although the delinquents in the Tinklenberg and Woodrow (1974) study identified barbiturates as the drug most likely to increase aggression.

There is considerable evidence of a relationship between drugs and economic compulsive violence. Robbery typifies economic compulsive violence. The strong correlation between the frequent use of expensive and addictive drugs such as heroin and cocaine and involvement in crimes to generate cash is well known (Ball et al. 1981; Chaiken and Chaiken 1982; Collins et al. 1985; Johnson et al. 1985). Costly drug use is clearly an important correlate of the threatened or actual violence associated with robbery - an offense that generates quick cash that can be spent to purchase drugs.

The most important violence outcomes associated with drug use are those that Golstein refers to as systemic. This violence has been prominently featured in the media in recent years. The death and bloodshed associated with the drug distribution system take a heavy toll on the market participants themselves. Moreover, this violence often spills beyond those involved in illegal drug transactions and affects nonparticipants directly through injury or death and indirectly by disrupting community life. As discussed later, however, systemic drug violence ought not be viewed as a simple function of drug transactions. Complex social and economic factors are also involved.

Research on the violence that characterizes drug distribution settings is scarce. The limited research, journalistic accounts, and anecdotal evidence do permit descriptions of some features of the phenomenon. Drug distribution system violence tends to occur (at least most visibly) in areas that:

- are socially disorganized, that is, in which formal and informal social control is absent or ineffective;

- have traditionally high rates of interpersonal violence; and

- are economically disadvantaged.

These features of the phenomenon have implications for understanding the problem systematically, In his analysis of the future of violent crime, Skogan (1989) identifies several fundamental features of American life that help account for violence. Two of them, economic hardship and family and community social disorganization, appear to be important to the understanding of drug distribution system violence. Drug traffickers appear to come disproportionately from groups and places that are economically disadvantaged - in which selling drugs is an attractive option despite the risks. Reuter et al. (1990) suggest that drug dealing is more financially rewarding than other kinds of crime. In Skogan's (1989) view, the "... theoretical linkage between hardship and violent crime is provided by the structural strain approach to understanding violence. In this view, violence is rooted in structurally induced frustration" (Skogan 1989, p. 242). Understanding drug system violence also will probably require understanding how economic opportunity is linked to involvement in trafficking.

The association of community disorganization and drug distribution violence suggests the need for empirical data to understand *how* these phenomena are related. For example, which comes first? Does community disorganization allow drug markets to become established, or do drug markets in an area precipitate other breakdowns? The association probably is not simple. Drug markets may flourish in areas that are deteriorating and accelerate that deterioration.

Drug distribution system violence can be seen as an economic phenomenon rooted in political and social contexts. Haller (1989) compared it with the violence associated with bootlegging during prohibition. Haller thinks drug distribution violence is more prevalent partly because the heavy criminal penalties associated with heroin and cocaine distribution create a multi-layered distribution system with multiple transactions that are potentially unstable and dangerous. Buyers and sellers fear being ripped off by one another. Haller (1989) further argues that "Ironically enough, one effect of policies ... to deal harshly with drug dealers may have been to increase violence within heroin and cocaine markets and thus to increase the degree to which drug dealing has been controlled by men willing to kill for profit" (Hailer 1989, p. 160). Fagan (this volume) makes a similar point, arguing that individuals unwilling to use violence or to risk exposure to it may avoid drug dealing.

There is a literature in the community and social ecology genre that examines the relationship of formal and informal social control, social change, economic conditions, and other factors to crime in social units such as cities and neighbourhoods (Reiss and Tonry 1986; Sampson 1987; Taylor and Covington 1988). This literature may guide the study of drug distribution system violence. Research on the drug problem has tended to focus on a single or a small number of variables. That approach may not be appropriate to understanding drug distribution system violence, which appears to be grounded in collective conditions such as neighborhood deterioration.

Finally, a point about the current prevalence of drug distribution violence should be made. Journalistic accounts can lead one to conclude that violence associated with drug distribution has increased in the last few years. It is easy to identify cities and neighborhoods where it has emerged recently as a serious problem. I suggest, however, that evidence of a general increase in drug distribution violence is not conclusive for two reasons. First, because drug distribution is geographically mobile, moving from place to place, we may simply be seeing its disappearance in one place and its emergence in a new location. Second, the proliferation of deadly weapons may simply have made drug distribution system violence more lethal and visible. When violence occurs, death and serious injury may be more likely.

Mythical dimensions of the drug problem

The rise of the drug problem on the national agenda has helped focus attention and resources on the problem. Unfortunately, strong concern about the drug problem also encourages public rhetoric that mischaracterizes the problem and that may result in misguided policies and resource commitments. The claims that youth gangs are heavily involved in drug trafficking and violence in an organized way is an example of an apparent myth with the potential to misguide interventions.

273

A recent report to the President characterized gang involvement in drug trafficking as follows:

> ... California is home to one of the most dangerous and menacing developments in drug trafficking, the large scale organized street gang... The Los Angeles gangs are radiating out from the areas where they originated - up the West Coast as far as Seattle and Vancouver, into the heartland as far as Denver, Kansas City, and Chicago, and even to cities on the East Coast... One of the most frightening aspects of California street gangs is their willingness to direct their violence at each other, at the police, at members of the public - at anyone who stands in the way of their operations. (U.S. Attorneys and the Attorney General of the United States 1989, pp. 33-35)

This report clearly suggests that street gangs are making a calculated, organized and ruthless attempt to expand their drug-trafficking activities across the country and to solidify control over drug distribution. There is virtually no systematic evidence to support this characterization. Moore (this volume) points out that sensationalized media and police accounts are almost the sole source of information on gang involvement in crack distribution. She further points out that organized gang involvement in drug distribution is not the norm. Recent research by Fagan on gangs in three cities (1989) also suggests that gangs differ from each other in their involvement in drug sales and violence and, further, that "some incidents no doubt are precipitated by disputes over drug sales or selling territories, but the majority of violent incidents do not appear to involve drug sales" (Fagan 1989, pp. 660-661).

To argue that youth gangs are not typically involved in drug trafficking in an organized way is not to argue that gang members are not involved individually. There is good evidence that juvenile gang members are frequently involved in a wide variety of illegal behaviors - including drug sales. The evidence that youth gangs systematically organize and operate drug markets is poor, and this characterization probably seriously misrepresents reality. The myth of youth gang drug trafficking, to the extent that it results in public action and resource commitment, is counterproductive to dealing with the drug problem constructively.

The above does not argue that drug trafficking lacks formal organization, however. The drug distribution system is quite complex and often involves formal organization. The system is not monolithic - either vertically throughout the distribution levels or geographically. Multiple organizations participate at wholesale and retail levels and in different areas. There is a tendency to ignore this multiplicity and to see fully organized conspiracies where none exist. Exaggerated rhetoric about gang control of drug trafficking is an example.

The U.S. drug problem has proven to be quite intractable - apparently worsening in the face of major attempts to control it. One apparent effect of this intractability and failure to "win the war against drugs" is the identification of bogeymen with concomitant attempts to bring this identified enemy under control. The unfortunate effects are that resources are misallocated, and the failure of misguided policies encourage pessimism and a search for new bogeymen.

The tendency to mischaracterize and sensationalize the drug problem is, in part, a function of the political and public funding processes. Gangs, for example, are a natural focal point for political rhetoric about the "war on drugs." Gangs are not constituencies the politicians need worry about alienating. Belief in the threat of gangs can also be used to argue for law enforcement budget increases to help police to neutralize the threat.

Research provides a real opportunity to neutralize the mythical dimensions of the drug problem. Careful research provides accurate description, and can help, over time, to minimize the damage caused by focusing public attention and resources on phantom problems.

Need to reconceptualize the tripartite framework

Goldstein's (1985) concept of pharmacological, economic compulsive, or systemic violence helped refine thinking about the relation between drug use and violent behavior. Goldstein's influence is clearly apparent in the chapters of this volume and in other work published on the drugs - violence connection. A first step in the next stage of conceptual development is to develop a framework that incorporates the considerable complexity of the drugs-violence connection. The complexity is manifested in two major ways: (1) the three components of the tripartite framework (pharmacological, economic compulsive, systemic) are themselves not simple or mutually exclusive, and (2) factors other than the three concepts also contribute to the occurrence of drug-related violence.

Psychoactive substances have different phamacological effects; they may induce euphoria, act as a stimulant or depressant, result in altered perceptions, and have a variety of other effects. Effects are immediate (minutes, hours), moderate term (hours, days), and long term (months, years). Immediate and longer term effects of the same drug are often different - initial euphoria followed by depression, for example. The behavioral manifestations of drug effects also differ. Goldstein (1989) suggests, for example, that irritability associated with drug withdrawal can increase the likelihood of violence. In a discussion of how alcohol precipitates violence, Pernanen (1981) focuses on cognitive impairment. The point is that the pharmacological concept is complex. Distinctions in drug pharmacology and associated effects on mood and behavior are required to generate better understanding of the drugs – violence connection.

Typical drug-use patterns also underline the complexity of pharmacologic violence. Drug users commonly use multiple drugs together (cocaine and heroin, marijuana and PCP, etc.) or a variety of drugs on different drug-use occasions. Alcohol use is pervasive among many drug users. Thus, interactions between various psychoactive substances are likely to occur. Pharmacologic effects also do not operate independently. Individual psychology, situational factors, and cultural orientation combine with the effects of drugs to shape behavior; Wolfgang and Ferracuti (1967) reviewed and attempted to integrate much of the evidence for a "subculture of violence."

Economic compulsive violence (robbery), even by an addict intent on getting money to feed his or her drug habit, likely has multiple roots. Robbery proceeds may be sought for multiple purposes. The act may be retaliatory as well as acquisitive, for example. Drug distribution system violence should be considered in a multifactoral framework that considers social and economic conditions.

Violence, too, is a complex phenomenon. Violent interactions between individuals have complex etiological roots - typically involving individual, situational, and cultural factors. Violence associated with drug use or distribution is not unique in this regard; it does not evolve simply from the pharmacological, economic compulsive, or distributional influences of drug use. The above discussion suggests that the influence of drugs on violence should be considered in a complex behavioral model.

The categories listed below identify the major factors thought to be associated with violence generally, with special attention given to drugs - violence issues.

Antecedent Influences

Developmental: early injury, abuse, or neglect; socilization experiences
Cultural: norms, values, beliefs

Current Conditions

Drug Pharmacology: cognitive impairment, emotional lability
Social: community disorganization, social control
Economic: opportunity, compulsion
Situational: location, environment

It is suggested that all of the above factors are associated with the propensity to act violently. Considering antecedent influences, there is evidence, for example, that being the victim of child abuse is a risk factor for subsequent violence (Widom 1989). Cultural (or subcultural) factors effect the tendency to act violently. Depending on enculturation experience - the content and internalization of norms, values, and beliefs - individuals are more or less inclined to be violent.

The factors listed under "current conditions" affect the occurrence of drug-related violence in at least two different ways: by drug-induced cognitive impairment, e.g., paranoia, and emotional lability, e.g., irritability.

Social factors such as community disorganization and social control are known to be associated with both drug use and violence. Drug use and drug distribution system violence typically occur in disorganized communities where such things as family stability and effective social control mechanisms are weak. Sampson (1987) and Taylor and Covington (1988) have shown how a variety of economic and social features of neighborhood and family life are associated with violence. The latter study examined the effects of social disorganization and relative deprivation in Baltimore neighborhoods and found declining status to be associated with increases in violence. At an individual level, Goldstein has pointed to the compulsive violence sometimes engaged in to support continued drug use. Drug trafficking can also be viewed as an economic opportunity for those who are blocked from commensurately rewarding legitimate avenues to financial success. The choice of drug trafficking as an occupation may be associated with the willingness to engage in violence. Fagan (this volume) thinks a selection process may operate that attracts individuals to crack distribution who are not averse to violence.

Finally, situational factors will shape the likelihood and type of violence. Selling crack on a street corner for example, may involve a higher risk of violence for a seller than selling in a crack house (Mieczkowski, this volume).

Figure 1 illustrates a scheme for organizing thinking and research about drug-related violence. It incorporates all of the above factors, some of which operate at the level of the individual, others of which operate at a collective level. The arrows indicate hypothesized direct and indirect effects. The model represents the influence of factors temporally. Developmental and cultural effects are suggested to have their influence in early life. Drug pharmacology, social, and economic factors are represented as having contemporary effects. Situational factors are those influences most proximate to the occurrence of the violence.

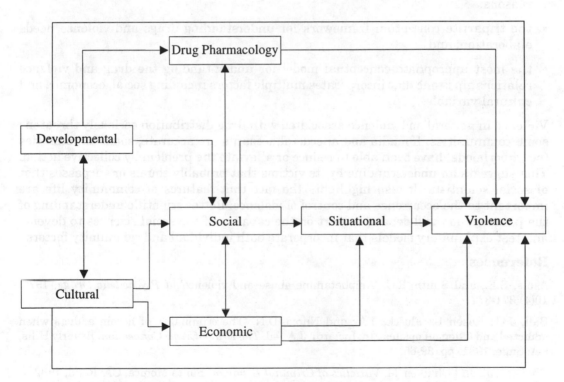

Figure 1   *Conceptual scheme for organizing understanding of the drugs-violence relationship.*

The model needs more formal development but is an initial attempt to interpret some of what is known of past findings and to suggest an approach for organizing future research. The model is ambitious and clearly not fully testable by any single study. It is meant to be a heuristic conceptual device to promote the further development of understanding of violence, especially that associated with drug use and distribution.

Conclusion

Several points have been argued in this chapter:

- the pharmacological effects of drugs (alcohol excepted) are not major factors accounting for interpersonal violence when demographic and other correlates of violence are controlled;

- costly drug use is etiologically important to the occurrence of robbery;

- drug distribution system violence is an important contemporary problem in need of systematic attention from researchers;

- myths have tended to grow up around the drug problem for political and economic reasons;

- the tripartite conceptual framework for understanding drugs and violence needs elaboration; and

- the most appropriate conceptual model for understanding the drug and violence relationship is one that incorporates multiple factors including social, economic, and cultural variables.

Violence in general and violence associated with drug distribution seriously threatens some communities. If media and anecdotal accounts are accurate, some communities (neighborhoods) have been able to reduce or alleviate the problem by collective action. This suggests an understanding by its victims that probably equals or surpasses that of social scientists. It also highlights the fact that features of community life are important to the occurrence and control of violence. Better scientific understanding of the phenomenon will depend in part on the capacity of the social sciences to develop and test explanatory models that incorporate both individual and community factors.

References

Asnis, S.F., and Smith, R.C. 'Amphetamine abuse and violence'. *J Psychedelic Drugs*, 1978, 10(4):371-377.

Ball, J.C.; Rosen L.; Flueck, J.A.; and Nurco, D.N. 'The criminality of heroin addicts when addicted and when off opiates'. In: Inciardi, J.A., ed. *The Drugs-Crime Connection*. Beverly Hills, CA: Sage, 1981. pp. 39-65.

Chaiken, J., and Chaiken, M. *Varieties of Criminal Behavior*. Santa Monica, CA: Rand, 1982.

Collins, J.J.; Hubard, R.L.; and Rachal, J.V. 'Expensive drug use and illegal income: A test of explanatory hypotheses'. *Criminology*, 1985, 24 (4): 743-764.

Collins, J.J.; Powers, L.L.; and Craddock, A. *Recent Drug Use and Violent Arrest Charges in Three Cities*. Research Triangle, NC: Research Triangle Institute, 1989.

Ellinwood, E.H. 'Assault and homicide associated with amphetamine abuse'. *Am J Psychiatry,* 1971, 127(9): 1170-1175.

Fagan, J.' The social organization of drug use and drug dealing among urban gangs'. *Criminology,* 1989, 27 (4): 633-669.

Fauman, B.J., and Fauman, M.A. 'Phencyclidine abuse and crime: A psychiatric perspective'. *Bull Am Acad Psychiatry Law*, 1982, 10(3): 171-176.

Fink, L. and Hyatt, M.P. 'Drug use and criminal behavior'. *J Drug Educ,* 1978, *8(2):* 139-149.

Goldstein, P.J. 'The drugs-violence nexus: A tripartites conceptual framework'. *J Drug Issues,* 1985, 15: 493-506.

Goldstein, P. J. 'Drugs and violent crime'. In: Weiner, N.A., and Wolfgang, M.E., eds. *Pathways to Criminal Violence*. Newbury Park, CA: Sage, 1989. pp. 16-48.

Goodman, R.A.; Merry, J.A.; and Rosenberg, M.L. 'Drug use and interpersonal violence: Barbiturates detected in homicide victims'. *Am J Epidemiology,* 1986, 124 (5): 851-855.

Haller, M.H. Bootlegging: 'The business and politics of violence'. In: Gurr, T.R., ed. *Violence in America*. Vol. 1. Newbury Park, CA: Sage, 1989. pp. 146-162.

Honer, W.G.; Gewirtz, G.; and Turey, M. 'Psychosis and violence in cocaine smokers'. *Lancet* II, 1987, 8556:451.

Johnson, B.D.; Goldstein, P.J.; Preble, E.; Schmeidler, J.; Lipton, D.S.; Spunt, B.; and Miller, T. *Taking Care of Business: The Economics of Crime by Heroin Abusers*. Lexington, MA: Lexington Books, 1985.

Manschreck, T.C.; Allen, D.F.; and Neville, M. 'Freebase psychosis: Cases from a Bahamian epidemic of cocaine abuse'. *Compr Psychiatry,* 1988, 28 (6): 555-564.

Pernanen, K. 'Theoretical aspects of the relationship between alcohol and crime'. In: Collins, J.J.H., ed. *Drinking and Crime: Perspectives on the Relationship Between Alcohol Consumption and Crime Behavior*. New York: Guilford Press, 1981.

Reiss, A.J., and Tonry, M., eds. *Communities and Crime*. Chicago: University of Chicago Press, 1986.

Reuter, P.; Macoun, R.; and Murphy, P. *Money from Crime: A Study of the Economics of Drug Dealing in Washington, D.C.* Santa Monica, CA: Rand Corporation, 1990

Sampson, R. 'Urban black violence: the effect of male joblessness and family disruption'. *Am J Sociol,* 1987, 93:348-382.

Simonds, J.F., and Kashani, J. 'Specific drug use and violence in delinquent boys'. *Am J Drug Alcohol Abuse,* 1980, 7(3,4):305-322.

Skogan, W.G. 'Social change and the future of violent crime'. In: Gurr, T.R., ed. *Violence in America*. Vol. 1. Newbury Park, CA: Sage Publications, 1989. pp. 235-250.

Taylor, R.B., and Covington, J.B. 'Neighborhood changes in ecology and violence'. *Criminology,* 1988, 26(4):553-589.

Tinklenberg, J.R. 'Drugs and crime'. In: *National Commission on Marhuanna and Drug Abuse, Drug Use in America: Problem in Perspective*. Appendix, Vol. 1. Washington, DC: U.S. Govt. Print. Off., 1973. pp. 242-299.

Tinklenberg, J.R., and Woodrow, K.M. 'Drug use among youthful assaultive and sexual offenders'. *Aggression,* 1974, 52:209-224.

U.S. Attorneys and Attorney General of the United States. *Drug Trafficking. A Report to the President of the United States*. Washington, DCL Office of the Attorney General, 1989.

Widom, C.S. 'The intergenerational transmission of violence'. In: Weiner, N.A., and Wolfgang, M.E., eds. *Pathways to Criminal Violence*. Newbury Park, CA: Sage, 1989. pp. 137-201.

Wolfgang, M.E., and Ferracuti, F. *The Subculture of Violence*. London: Tavistock, 1967.

26. Drugs and Predatory Crime
Jan M. Chaiken and Marcia R. Chaiken

Abstract

*Drug abuse and predatory criminality are behavior patterns that coexist in
certain social groups. In other groups, drug abuse often occurs without
predatory criminality. Among populations involved in drug abuse and
predatory crime, a temporal sequence from drug abuse to predatory
criminality is not typical; on the contrary, predatory criminality more
commonly occurs before drug abuse. Drug-abusing offenders who display
increasingly deviant behavior over time eventually cross over a threshold
to heroin addiction or frequent polydrug abuse. The intensity of their
criminal behavior typically escalates substantially. If these high-rate
offenders subsequently decrease the amount of drugs they use, they typically
also lessen their rate of criminal activity. Among offenders who use multiple
types of drugs, individual predatory crime commission frequencies are
typically two or three times higher among offenders when they use multiple
types of drugs than they are for the same offenders when they are in drug
treatment or abstain from drug abuse.*

A strong association has long been surmised between illicit drug use and predatory
crime. Almost twenty years ago, Sutherland and Cressey (1970, p. 164) pointed out that
in the United States "felons are over represented in the addict population, [and] crime
rates are increased considerably by drug addiction." But, although they proposed
several hypotheses to explain the relationship, they summarized the state of knowledge
at the time by saying that "a precise definition of the process by which narcotic drugs
are related to criminal behavior has not been made" (p. 167).

Ten years later, numerous studies of incarcerated or addicted populations had increased
knowledge of the drug/crime nexus; but the information was still complex and
incomplete. Only in regard to heroin addiction did a coherent viewpoint prevail, but it
was not universally accepted. The prevailing view, summarized by Gandossy et al.
(1980), was that drug use propelled income-producing crime primarily because addicts
required money to buy drugs. This view was supported by the following findings: many
serious offenders were drug users and had started using drugs as juveniles; not all drug
users became addicts, but continued drug use frequently led to heroin addiction;
minority group members were proportionately more likely than nonminority group
members to be drug users and to be arrested for crimes; many (although not all) drug
users became addicted before they were involved in criminal pursuits or arrest; among
arrestees and prisoners, drug users were more likely than non drug users to have been
arrested for income-generating crimes rather than crimes of violence; drug users in

treatment were more likely to have been arrested for property crimes than for violent crimes; and the drug users who were most likely to commit numerous crimes were heroin addicts.

At the time, some researchers and many policy makers were convinced from this evidence that a fairly simple causal relation existed between drug use and criminality, especially for minority group members who were disproportionately likely to become involved in drug use: first came some form of drug use as juveniles, then drug use progressed to heroin addiction, and , as heroin addicts, these users committed many nonviolent income-producing crimes to support their habits. But many countervailing facts were already known, such as that a substantial number of casual users of heroin (nonaddicts) existed and were not heavily involved in crime (e.g., Robins, Davi, and Wish 1980).

The picture available from today's research indicates that, while the progression to heroin addiction and income-producing crimes may apply to some drug users, other behavioral sequences also occur often (even *more* often), for example, patterns involving drugs other than heroin, or predatory crime before drug addiction, or violent rather than nonviolent criminality. Some patterns are applicable only in particular subgroups of the population.

In short, no single sequential or casual relationship is now believed to relate drug use to predatory crime. When the behaviors of large groups of people are studied in the aggregate, no coherent general patterns emerge associating drug use per se with participation in predatory crime, age at onset of participation in crime, or persistence in committing crime. Rather, different patterns appear to apply to different types of drug users (Chaiken and Johnson 1988). But research does show that certain types of drug abuse are strongly related to offenders' committing crimes at high *frequencies*– violent crimes as well as other, income producing crimes. The observed relationship applies to various population subgroups, including groups defined by age, race, or sex.

This essay summarizes the known research information – with emphasis on quantitative research - about the association between drug use and *predatory crime*. The association between drug dealing and predatory crime is also discussed, because it is often more pertinent or stronger than the association between drug use and crime.

In discussing predatory crime, we have in mind instrumental offenses committed for material gain. We do not include aggressive crimes such as marital violence, homicide, or assault unrelated to robbery or burglary; public disorder crimes; driving under the influence of alcohol or drugs; or consensual crimes such as prostitution. However, in reviewing the results of published works, some nonpredatory crimes may be included with predatory crimes if they were studied together or summarized together by the original authors.

In summarizing and commenting on the literature on drug use and predatory crime, we use a specialized vocabulary that has been developed in the study of criminal careers (Blumstein et al. 1986). The terms *onset, participation, frequency, desistance,* and *persistence* are drawn from the concept of a criminal career as a sequence of crimes committed by an individual offender (Blumstein et al. 1986). A person's criminal career has its *onset* when he or she commits a crime for the first time, at which time the offender is said to be *participating* in crime. A *participation rate* is the proportion of a group of people who engage in crimes during a specified period. *The frequency* or *rate* of crime commission is the number of crimes committed per year when the offender is free to commit crime (that is, unincarcerated). *Desistance* is the end of the criminal career, and *persistence* refers to a career that lasts a long time between onset and desistance. (Details are in Section III.)

Since this essay focuses on predatory crime and not on assaultive or other destructive behavior resulting from physiological effects of drugs, we do not distinguish among pharmacological classes of drugs such as amphetamines, barbiturates, or hallucinogens. However, as shown in the sections that follow, the types of drugs used by offenders and the frequency with which they use them are important in understanding the connections between drug abuse and predatory crime. Most drug users abuse at least two types of substances; therefore many research studies summarized in this essay categorize types of *drug abuse* rather than types of *drugs* abused. Commonly employed categories of drug abuse, in order of increasing seriousness, are: marijuana and alcohol abuse; use of other nonopiate illicit drugs (possibly in addition to marijuana and alcohol); and opiate or cocaine use, including various derivative form of those substances.

People are generally considered to be involved in a specific category of drug abuse if they have a sustained pattern of involvement. For example, most researchers would not classify as a drug abuser a person who has used marijuana two or three times. Similarly, a person who frequently drinks and also smokes marijuana would be classified by most researchers as involved in marijuana use; this would be the case even if he or she is also known to have used cocaine on one occasion. However, people who have a sustained pattern of relatively serious drug abuse would be classified as involved in that form of drug abuse even though they were more likely to indulge in less serious forms of abuse. For example, people who use heroin every week would be classified as heroin users even if they drank alcohol and smoked marijuana every day.

Almost all the studies discussed in this essay were based on self-reports of drug use and crime. Self-reports are less likely than criminal justice system records or other forms of agency records to underestimate study subjects' involvement in crime, delinquency, or drug use. However, the validity of self-report information about drug abuse and criminality is questionable because respondents may have had difficulty recalling past behavior, may not have understood the questions they were asked, or may either have concealed or exaggerated their illegal activities. Researchers who conduct these studies are aware of these validity issues and use methods that minimize the possible distorting effects on their findings.

The studies most likely to avoid problems of recall are those in which subjects are interviewed at set intervals over a period of time. These studies provide valuable information on the relationships between predatory crime and drug use over the life course. However, many other studies learn about respondents' past behavior retrospectively. When findings from prospective and retrospective studies are similar, they reinforce each other.

The methods used for collecting data about drug use and criminality range from relatively large national surveys to in-depth interviews and observations of small groups. The study subjects include random samples of the nations's youth, groups of school children, addicts in treatment centers, inmates in prisons and jails, defendants whose cases had been just concluded, samples of inner-city youth, probationers, and adult street populations. Aside from studies of addicts in treatment, important data sources drawn on in this essay are the National Youth Survey, a Rand Corporation inmate survey, and interview data from street addicts in New York City. Brief descriptions of these data sources are given here.

1. *National Youth Survey*. The National Youth Survey is a prospective longitudinal study of delinquent behavior, alcohol and drug use, problem-related substance abuse, and mental health problems in a representative sample of American youth (Elliott, Huizinga, and Menard 1989). To date, seven waves of data have been collected on a panel of youths covering the period from 1976 to 1986. (However, published analyses cover only six waves, representing the seven-year period from 1976 to 1983) The random sample was drawn in 1976 and contained 2,360 eligible youths aged eleven to seventeen at the time of the initial interview. Of these 1,735 agreed to participate; by age, sex, and race they were representative of the total eleven- through seventeen-year-old youth population of the United States in 1976. Respondent loss over the six waves of the survey has been 13 per cent. Comparisons of participants across the first six waves indicated that loss by age, sex, ethnicity, class, place of residence, and self-reported delinquency did not substantially influence the underlying distributions on these variables.

Annual involvement in delinquent behavior, use of alcohol and drugs, and mental health problems were self-reported in personal face-to-face interviews, usually in the respondents' homes. Confidentiality was guaranteed, and no information about individuals collected in the National Youth Survey can be released to any person or agency without the respondent's written consent. Delinquent behavior was conceptualized as a parallel measure to official arrest, so that offenses self-reported in the survey can be categorized as Uniform Crime Report (UCR) Index offenses (which are murder and nonnegligent manslaughter, forcible rape, robbery, aggravated assault, burglary, larceny-theft, motor vehicle theft, and arson; murder is not included in the National Youth Survey), UCR Part II offenses (all other criminal offenses), and juvenile status offenses. For each offense, the response set involves an open-ended frequency estimate; respondents who reported ten or more occurrences of a particular offense during the year were also offered a set of categorical responses ranging from "mostly" to "two to three times a day."

Although the delinquency offenses include some drug-related offenses (e.g., selling marijuana), the National Youth Survey includes separate questions about first use, quantity, reasons for using, and sources of alcohol (beer, wine, and hard liquor), marijuana, hallucinogens, amphetamines, heroin, cocaine, and barbiturates. Questions related to mental health capture dimensions of social isolation, depression, and use of mental health services.

The results of the National Youth Survey are extensively reported in papers by the primary data collectors, and the data are also archived and available for secondary data analysis.

2. *Rand Inmate Survey.*[1] In 1978, the Rand Corporation carried out a survey of convicted male offenders housed in prisons and jails in California, Michigan, and Texas. (An earlier anonymous Rand survey of California prisoners obtained only nonspecific information about respondents' drug use and is not cited in this essay.) Self-report data on criminal activity, personal characteristics, and criminal record were obtained from 2,316 inmates by means of a group-administered written questionnaire. In addition, official record data were collected for the prison inmates (and obtained for 1,214 of the 1,380 prison inmates surveyed).

The survey provided detailed information about crimes that respondents had committed during a one- to two-year measurement period immediately prior to their arrest for their current sentenced crime. Inmates reported the date of their arrest and then followed questionnaire instructions to identify the beginning of the measurement period, which was January 1 of the year preceding this arrest. They then answered questions about their activities during the measurement period related to commissions of burglary, robbery, assault, automobile theft, other theft, fraud, drug trafficking, and forgery, check, or credit card offenses. Inmates indicated whether or not they had committed each of these offenses and either the number of commissions (if less than ten) or the number of months during which they committed each crime and their rate of commission in those months. They also answered questions for the same measurement period concerning heavy drinking and use of drugs other than marijuana (subdivided into three categories: heroin/methadone, barbiturates/"reds"/downers, and amphetamines/uppers/"whites"). To obtain data on a retrospective longitudinal basis, the questionnaire also asked briefly about crime commissions and drug use during two two-year reference periods preceding the main measurement period.

The Rand inmate survey was administered at twelve prisons and fourteen county jails. The institutions were selected to yield a broad sample of offenders active in both urban areas and smaller cities within each of the three study states. The prisons included all custody levels within each prison system. The sample was drawn randomly using selection probabilities that resulted in approximating the characteristics of inmates coming into prison or jail during a limited period of time - an "incoming cohort."

The results of the survey and the quality of the self-report data are extensively documented in procedural, methodological, and analytical reports. Also, the data have been archived and are available for secondary analysis.

3. *Street Addicts in New York City.* [2] During 1980-82 the New York State Division of Substance Abuse Services and Narcotic and Drug Research, Inc., collected information from heroin or methadone addicts who lived on the streets in East and Central Harlem and were engaged in some form of criminality. The field workers were exaddict, exoffender staff, who were sent into the streets to locate subjects. They sometimes

approached persons on the street who were unknown to them. More often they found an acquaintance who informally introduced them to potential respondents. The field workers attempted to recruit about one female for every two or three males.

Individuals who were willing to participate in the study were taken by field workers to a research storefront. After obtaining the subjects informed consent, research workers asked them to report the following information about the previous day: types of crimes committed, criminal income, drugs used, purchased, sold, or distributed, cash income from all sources, cash expenditures, involvement in drug treatment, and drugs received at no cost ("in kind"). Respondents were initially interviewed for five consecutive days and then asked to return once a week for the next four weeks. A longitudinal research design was approximated with the East Harlem subjects, by conducting additional cycles of data collection at three-to six-month intervals.

In general, when broad populations are surveyed, as in the National Youth Survey, the results are representative of "typical" behavior. But broad samples often include only small number of people who are serious drug abusers or predatory criminals. Studies that focus on populations of drug abusers, like the New York City street addict studies, or on offender groups, such as the Rand inmate survey, are more valuable for amassing detailed data about seriously deviant behavior. Through a combination of findings from these and other sources described in the remainder of this essay, we can piece together the rich complex of relationships between drug use and predatory crime.

Here is how this essay is organized. Section I summarizes research that indicates the absence of a simple or unified association between drug use and participation in crime. It also discusses the limitations of research based on information about arrested or incarcerated offenders, who are atypical of offenders in general in regard to their drug use. Section II presents evidence showing there is no coherent, general association between drug use and onset or persistence of criminality. Section III reviews the quantitative measures that are used to describe levels of offending activity by discussing and comparing the wide variety of such statistics that appear in the drug literature. Section IV describes the relationships between an offender's drug use and his contemporaneous amount of criminal activity, based partly on a reanalysis of drug abusers' offending frequencies that have been presented in a number of studies. Section V discusses the implications of the observed relationships between drug abuse and predatory crime.

I. Summary of findings from recent research

People who commit predatory crimes over long periods tend also to commit other crimes and to have begun their criminal careers at young ages. Similarly, people who use illicit drugs often or in large quantities tend to use a variety of drugs and to have begun using drugs during adolescence. These seemingly similar groups of persistent offenders and persistent drug users are not necessarily the same people. There appears to be no simple general relation between high rates of drug use and high rates of crime.

A. *Patterns of criminal behavior and drug use*

Research on criminal behavior over the past decade has demonstrated strong interrelationships among age at onset of a criminal career, persistence of criminal activity, rate of committing offenses, and types of offenses committed. In any population of offenders, most commit non-violent offenses and at low rates. Even adult offenders who were incarcerated for violent crimes such as robbery or assault typically committed only one or two of these offenses in the year preceding their incarceration (Chaiken and Chaiken 1982; Visher 1986; Mande and English 1988; Chaiken and Chaiken 1989). However, a relatively small group of offenders commits crimes at very high rates – hundreds of crimes per year when they are free to do so (Chaiken and Chaiken 1982; Ball, Shaffer, and Nurco 1983; Johnson et al. 1985; Ball 1986; Mande and English 1988; Chaiken and Chaiken 1989). Those who frequently commit violent crimes also are very likely to commit other crimes, such as burglary and theft, and to commit one or more of these types of crimes at high rates (Chaiken and Chaiken 1982; Chaiken and Chaiken 1985; Johnson et al. 1985) Moreover, this small group of adult offenders is likely to have started committing crimes as young adolescents - (Chaiken and Chaiken 1982; Hanson et al. 1985; Johnson et al. 1985).

Studies of patterns of drug use have produced parallel findings. Most people who use illicit drugs confine their use to sporadic use of marijuana, while relatively few use other illicit drugs such as barbiturates, amphetamines, cocaine, or heroin (Miller et al. 1983; Johnston, O'Malley, and Bachman 1985, 1986). An even smaller number of people use these drugs frequently (e.g., daily or more often); and those who use any drug in high quantities or at high frequencies are likely to be using also several other types of illicit drugs frequently, often in combination with alcohol (Elliott and Huizinga 1985; Wish and Johnson 1986; Elliott, Huizinga, and Menard 1989). The high-frequency users are also more likely than other users to have started using drugs as adolescents (Newcomb and Bentler 1988).

While these parallel patterns of criminal behavior and drug abuse are strongly interrelated, research does not support the view that they are basically overlapping descriptions of the same people. There are a few severely addicted people who commit no crimes aside from illegal possession of drugs (Collins et al. 1982); and there are criminals who commit numerous serious crimes but are not involved in drug use (Chaiken and Chaiken 1985; Innes 1988). Moreover, for most people, changes over time in individuals' use or nonuse of drugs are not systematically related to changes in their participation or nonparticipation in criminal activity (Kandel, Simcha-Fagan, and Davies 1986; Newcomb and Bentler 1988). One exception, discussed in Section IV, is a repeated finding that, among heroin-using high rate offenders, intensity of offending appears to vary directly with intensity of drug use (e.g., Anglin and Speckart 1986; Nurco et al. 1988).

Research does not support the view that drug abuse necessarily precedes onset of criminal activity, nor does it demonstrate a causal ordering between drug use and criminality. A more coherent interpretation is that drug abuse and participation in crime coexist in some social groups. Rather than having a cause-and-effect relationship, the onset of drug use, the onset of predatory crime, or both, can occur in early puberty as products of similar external factors. Fagan and others have found that both or either of these behaviors can be explained by intervening variables such as destructive factors in the environment (e.g., physical abuse or criminal siblings) or the absence of traditional social controls (e.g., lack of parental attention or participation in rewarding school activities) (White, Pandina, and LaGrange 1987; Fagan and Weis 1990). The more deviant the enrolment, the more likely an adolescent is to perform poorly in school, to use multiple forms of illicit drugs frequently, and to participate frequently in predatory crime (Williams and Kornblum 1985; Simcha-Fagan and Schwartz 1986).

From analysis of self-report surveys of male prison and jail inmates in three states in the late 1970s, we concluded that predatory criminals may be involved in drug use as a part of their nontraditional lifestyle, which in most instances is also evidenced by other factors such as irregular employment and absence of marital ties (Chaiken and Chaiken 1982). However, many long-term offenders in these inmate surveys had never used drugs; in fact, nearly half (47 percent) of inmates who had never used drugs were persistent offenders (they had committed crimes for more than five years prior to their arrest). Generally, older criminals are less likely than younger offenders to use illicit drugs (Wish and Johnson 1986); but even among young delinquents who committed crimes such as robbery, burglary, or serious assaults in inner-city areas, most have been found not to use drugs (Fagan and Weis 1990).

Where then, lies the strong relationship between drug use and criminality? A large body of research, discussed in the remainder of this essay, shows that, among predatory offenders, the ones who are high frequency drug users are also very likely to be *high-rate* predators and to commit many different types of crimes, including violent crimes, and to use many different types of drugs. This finding has been confirmed for adolescents and adults, across states, independent of race, and in many countries. It also is the same for both male sand females with one notable exception: females who use drugs frequently are less likely than males to commit violent crimes (but women drug users are more likely to resort to prostitution, shoplifting, and similar covert, nonviolent crimes at high rates [Sanchez and Johnson 1987]).

The relationship between high-frequency drug use and high-frequency criminality is intensified by long durations of involvement in drug use and predatory crime (Nurco et al. 1988). Adult offenders who commit robbery and burglary at the highest rates typically have been persistent offenders and drug users since they were juveniles, for example, using heroin as juveniles and starting to commit predatory crimes before they were sixteen years old (Chaiken and Chaiken 1982). The earlier the age of onset of cocaine or heroin use, the more likely persistent offenders are to be serious predatory offenders as adults (Chaiken and Chaiken 1985; Collins and Bailey 1987).

B. Drug sellers

In all studies that have examined the issue, the relationship between drug use and criminality has been found to be substantially weaker than the relationship between drug sales and other forms of criminality (Chaiken and Chaiken 1982; Johnson et al. 1985; Chaiken 1986). Most people who sell drugs do so occasionally and privately and are not likely to be involved in predatory crimes. But those who sell drugs publicly, for example in parks, streets, or back alleys, are likely to commit predatory crimes and to commit them at higher rates than people who commit the same type of offenses but do not sell drugs (Johnson et al. 1985; Williams and Kornblum 1985).

Based on surveys of inmates and interviews with other offenders, adult robbers who sell drugs on average report committing many more robberies than robbers who do not sell drugs; these *robbers* also report committing more *burglaries* than many other burglars, especially burglars who do not distribute drugs (Johnson et al. 1985; Chaiken 1986). Among urban youth, drug sales were also found to have a strong association with committing numerous serious crimes, including armed robbery (Fagan and Weis 1990).

While many public drug dealers are themselves frequent users of various types of drugs, others are careful not to mix business with pleasure; they only sporadically use their own illicit merchandise. Yet these nonuser drug dealers still commit predatory crimes, including numerous robberies and burglaries (Chaiken and Chaiken 1982; Williams and Kornblum 1985; Mieczkowski 1986).

Some of the robberies and other assaultive crimes committed by offenders who also sell drugs are systemic aspects of the drug trade (Johnson et al. 1985). Given the highly competitive nature of drug distribution (Kleiman and Smith, in this volume; Moore, in this volume) and the obvious lack of official regulation, violence and robbery are sometimes used to drive competitors out of business or to protect a dealer's money, supplies and connections (Adler 1985; Johnson et al. 1985). Other assaults and predatory crimes committed by drug dealers arise from their need for money for drugs and are opportunistically focused on the first available target (Williams and Kornblum 1985) – although many addicts are able to sustain their use by committing less serious crimes (Goldstein 1985; Hunt, in this volume). However, many predatory crimes are committed by dealers who find vulnerable victims with cash, follow them to a secluded area, threaten or actually injure them and take their money (Chaiken and Chaiken 1985; Hanson et al. 1985).

C. Arrestees are not typical offenders

Researchers' difficulties in sorting out details of the drug/crime nexus can in part be traced to the misleading and unrepresentative nature of information and statistics derived for readily accessible study populations such as arrestees and prisoners. High rate criminals who do not use drugs, or use them only sporadically, are far less likely to be arrested than are their counterparts who use drugs frequently (Chaiken and Chaiken 1985). Most offenders who are arrested for predatory crimes commit few crimes but do exhibit at least low levels of drug use (National Institute of Justice 1988). Among offenders who commit crimes at high rates but are arrested infrequently (so-called "high-rate winners"), many started using illicit drugs as juveniles and continued to use illicit drugs other than marijuana as adults, but only a quarter of them are high-frequency drug users, such as daily users of heroin. Among incarcerated offenders, the ones who are arrested frequently are actually a mix of offenders including two very distinct types of chronic offenders: inept, emotionally disturbed people (as described by Elliott and Huizinga 1985) who do not commit many predatory offenses but are arrested nearly every time they commit a crime (Chaiken and Chaiken 1985); and frequent users of multiple drugs who commit predatory crimes at high rates and are frequently caught because they are opportunistic and do not plan their criminal activities to avoid detection. Over one-third of these high-crime-rate, high-arrest-rate offenders reported onset of heroin use as juveniles and daily heroin use during the period before their last arrest (Chaiken and Chaiken 1985), but they are not characteristic of all offenders who are arrested frequently.

Obviously, a typical group of arrestees or prisoners includes disproportionate numbers of offenders who are arrested frequently and much smaller proportions of offenders who are arrested infrequently. Thus researchers and policymakers alike must be careful not to draw overly broad conclusions about the drug- use patterns of offenders in general by examining information about the drug-use patterns of arrestees or prisoners.

II Chronology of participation in use of illegal drugs and predatory crime

The criminal careers model provides a useful framework for organizing the discussion of research on the relationship between drug use and predatory crime. Similarities and differences between the onset and persistence of these two types of behaviors are discussed in this section. Particular emphasis is given to research on the interrelatedness of the onset and persistence of drug use and predatory crime.

A. *Onset of criminal behavior*

Research does not support the hypothesis that use of illicit drugs ultimately results in the user's involvement in predatory crime, or even that this is a predominant pattern. Studies of youths' drug use and crime that refute this hypothesis have included repeated interviews with over 1,500 youngsters selected as a representative sample for a National Youth Survey (Elliott and Huisinga 1985); in-depth interviews with 100 youngsters in a medium-size upstate city in New York (Carpenter et al. 1988); surveys of over 800 inner-city youths including almost 200 school dropouts (Fagan and Weis 1990); repeated surveys from age fifteen to age twenty-five with a sample of over 1,000 youths selected to be representative of students enrolled in New York State secondary schools (Kandel, Simcha-Fagan, and Davies 1986); and repeated interviews over a period of eight years with a sample of 1,000 youths who originally attended Los Angeles County schools (Newcomb and Bentler 1988).

Virtually all these studies have found that many more youngsters use illicit drugs than are involved in predatory crime. As youthful users of illicit substances approach adulthood, they are likely to continue to use drugs, but they are less likely – not more likely – to commit predatory crimes (Kandel, Simcha-Fagan, and Davies 1986). Moreover, youths who commit serious predatory crimes are more likely to use illicit drugs frequently than are youthful users of illicit drugs to engage in predatory crime (Fagan and Weis 1990).

Research evidence provides little support for the popular conception that most drug-involved offenders begin committing predatory crimes because they want money to buy drugs. In fact, many of them were involved in juvenile delinquency, including minor forms of predatory crime, before they were involved in illicit drug use. The data are more consistent with the commonsensical notion that minor predatory crime is a precursor to serious predatory crime. Prospective longitudinal self-report data from the National Youth Survey (Elliott and Huizinga 1985) and studies based on a sample of New York youngsters (Kandel, Simcha-Fagan, and Davies 1986) demonstrate that, among youngsters who both use drugs and commit nondrug offenses, delinquency is about as likely to begin before as after initial use of illicit drugs.

Table 1: Self-Report of Drug Use and Delinquency, National Youth Survey

Behavior	Percent of Subpopulation	Percent of Total Population
No drug use and no delinquency		46.0
Drug use and no delinquency:		26.5
Alcohol	18.6	
Alcohol and marijuana	7.1	
Alcohol, marijuana, and other drugs	.6	
No drug use but delinquent		8.9
Initial drug use a year or more *before* delinquency involvement:		4.5
Alcohol	3.9	
Alcohol and marijuana	.5	
Alcohol, marijuana, and other drugs	.1	
Initial drug use a year or more *after* delinquency involvement:		8.1
Alcohol	4.7	
Alcohol and marijuana	2.1	
Alcohol, marijuana, and other drugs	1.3	
Initial drug and delinquency involvement occurred in same year:		3.7
Alochol	1.6	
Alcohol and marijuana	2.0	
Alcohol, marijuana, and other drugs	0.1	
Other or not classifiable		4.3

SOURCE - Elliott and Huizinga (1984), table 9.

NOTE - Drugs mentioned refer to those used during the period specified. *Delinquency* is self-reported commission of an Index crime during the reference period (12 months). Percentages do not add to subtotals due to rounding.

For example, table 1, which summarizes data from the National Youth Survey, shows that 16.3 percent of this sample were involved in both drug use and delinquency. Of these, half (8.1 percent) reported initial drug use after delinquency involvement, and the other half reported drug use in the same year as delinquency involvement (3.7 percent) or earlier (4.5 percent). Ethnographic studies, in which researchers spend long periods of time observing and talking to youngsters, have also found that among youths who use drugs and commit predatory crimes, the connection appears to be due more to a style of everyday life than to simply committing predatory crimes to get money for drugs (Williams and Kornblum 1985; Mieczkowski 1986). For example, although youngsters involved in the street drug trade in Detroit used drugs occasionally, they were not addicted and had contempt for the addicts to whom they distributed heroin; as part of being involved in the drug trade they were also involved in more predatory activities involving weapons (Mieczkowski 1986).

These observations, derived from prospective and ethnographic studies of juveniles, find confirmation in retrospective studies of adult offenders. The Rand inmate survey (Chaiken and Chaiken 1982) in three states showed that 12 percent reported committing predatory crimes as adults after using drugs for two or more years; but 15 percent started committing predatory crimes as adults and two or more years later began to use illicit substances (see table 2). When the surveyed inmates were asked about their main reasons for first becoming involved in crime, only 26 percent of those who used illicit drugs cited their drug involvement as a primary motive, and only 20 percent of them cited their drug involvement as their sole reason for getting into crime.

Table 2: Relationship between Drug Use and First Involvement in Crime: Survey of Prison and Jail Inmates in Three States

Response	Subtotals	Percent of Respondents with Usable Data
No drug use during the five- to six-year reference period		42
Began crime during last two calendar years	6	
Began crime during middle two-year period	12	
Began crime during first two-year period	5	
Began crime prior to the entire reference period	19	
Began both crime and drug use prior to entire reference period		26
Began onset of drug use and crime simultaneously during any one of the two-year reporting periods		5
Began crime prior to drug use, during reference period		15
Began drug use prior to crime, during reference period		12

SOURCE - Chaiken and Chaiken (1982), table 5.10.

NOTE - Respondents in 1978-79 provided self-reports on drug use and crime during a thirteen- to twenty-four-month-long measurement period that ended with their arrest on the charge for which they were incarcerated and began on January 1 of the preceding year. This is called the "last two calendar years." Respondents also provided self-reports for the two-year period prior to the measurement period (called the "middle two years") and the two-year period before that (the "first two years"). Missing or unusable data accounted for 12.5 percent of the sample and were excluded from the analysis.

Anglin and Speckart (1987) and Anglin and Hser (1987) have applied sophisticated statistical methods to examine the temporal ordering between addicts' criminality and drug use, using data describing the addicts' behavior in the periods prior to and during their addiction. They find that involvement in property crime activities generally tends to precede the onset of addiction. In particular, approximately half of all first burglaries and more than half of all first thefts proceed addiction. (These studies also illuminate the relationship between addiction and crime frequency, the topic of Section IV below.)

In sum, use of illicit drugs may be a primary cause for initial participation in predatory crime for some offenders; however, for the vast majority of offenders who commit predatory crimes, use of illicit substances appears to be neither a necessary nor a sufficient cause of onset of predatory criminal behavior. Even onset of *narcotic addiction* often does not appear to be casually related to onset of involvement in property crime. Rather, the onset of heroin addiction is often a key point in accelerating an existing criminal career.

B. Persistence of drug use and predatory crime

Studies that have followed the behavior of youngsters over the span of early adolescence to young adulthood indicate that drug use is more likely to persist over this life span than is involvement in predatory crime (Kandel, Simcha-Fagan, and Davies 1986; Newcomb and Betler 1988). Further, continued criminality is more predictive of future drug use than is drug use predictive of criminality. Although over two thirds of youthful users of drugs are likely to continue use as adults, as they approach their late teens and early twenties, half of the juveniles who commit crimes stop (Elliott and Huizinga 1985; Kandel, Simcha-Fagan, and Davies 1986). As they grow older, delinquents are likely to use more addictive drugs - starting with marijuana, progressing to hallucinogens, sedatives and analgesics, and then to cocaine and heroin (Inciardi 1987b). Delinquents most likely to engage in drug use are those who have been sexually abused as children (Dembo et al. 1987). Moreover, almost all persistent serious delinquents are likely eventually to use drugs. Only 18 percent of chronic, serious offenders in the National Youth Survey remained drug free as they aged (Elliott and Huizinga 1985).

A review of cohort studies covering nearly 12,000 boys in Philadelphia, London, Racine (Wisconsin), and Marion County (Oregon) suggests that youngsters are most likely to continue committing serious crimes as adults if they behave badly in school, come from poor families, have other criminals in their immediate family, have a low IQ, and receive inadequate parental attention (Blumstein, Farrington, and Moitra 1985). Retrospective studies of the careers of predatory adult offenders suggest that essentially the same factors are characteristic of persistent offenders who commit the most serious predatory crimes (robbery and burglary) at high rates (Chaiken and Chaiken 1985). While drug abuse may often be concomitant with these predictive factors, it generally has not been shown to have independent value as a predictor of persistent offending.

Although sustained drug use cannot, in general, be considered a cause of predation, involvement in predatory crime increases the probability of serious forms of drug use which in turn enhance continuation and seriousness of a "predatory career." This self-reinforcing relationship has been demonstrated by interviews conducted with patients in methadone treatment about their "addiction careers"; in these studies, Anglin and Speckart (1986) found that theft precedes addiction more frequently than it follows addiction; however, burglary and robbery are more likely to follow than precede addiction; and there is positive covariation between the levels of narcotics use and the numbers and seriousness of crimes committed.

Ethnographic studies of street addicts suggest that these relationships may be explained by involvement in a lifestyle of "taking care of business" in which "the hustle" is any legitimate or illegal activity that can generate income (Hanson et al. 1985). Theft and other minor predatory crimes become a "normal" activity for relatively many elementary school-aged boys raised on inner-city streets. As they approach adolescence, boys in many major cities have the opportunity to participate in the drug trade (Mieczkowski 1986; Hunt, in this volume). Part of the street drug trade often involves keeping a small amount of drugs for personal use and robbing street drug distributors or other community residents of drugs or cash (Johnson et al. 1985). As adults, heroin use may continue as part of this lifestyle, but even regular users of heroin may abstain for relatively long periods in the absence of a safe and lucrative hustle (Hanson et al 1985). Among hustlers, robbery is not generally considered a safe means of obtaining money; however, a relatively small proportion of adult hustlers like to do "stick-ups" (robberies) because they consider the activity adventuresome and exciting (Hanson et al. 1985).

Little is known about the end of hustling lifestyles or the termination of predatory careers among drug-involvement persistent offenders. Recent research suggests that addicted adult offenders often continue to use drugs and commit crimes for twelve or more years in the absence of effective treatment and supervision (Anglin, Piper, and Speckart 1987). There is some evidence that mortality rates are relatively high for this population and that almost half of the deaths are due to drug use (Joe and Simpson 1987). There is also evidence, based on in-depth interviews with over 100 ex-addicts, that the end of a hustling lifestyle can be self-initiated because of a personally negative incident endemic to hustling, such as a threat of bodily harm from another dealer, and can take place in the absence of formal treatment (Biernacki 1986).

Future research is urgently needed on the causes and reasons for desisting from a life of drug use, crime, or both. Most pertinent for policy purposes will be improved information on the manner and extent to which drug addiction extends an addict's criminal career.

III. Measuring and describing the intensity of criminal activity

Moving on from issues related to individuals' *onset* and *termination* of criminal careers, this section and Section IV focus on the *participation rate* in specified types of crimes at various times during the criminal career, and *offending frequencies* (number of crimes per year for individuals who commit a specified type of crime) (Blumstein et al. 1986, pp. 17-20). Information about participation rates and offending frequency has appeared in many guises in the literature on the relationship between drug abuse and criminality, making comparisons across studies quite difficult.

Commonly, and quite consistently, *prevalence* percentages are used in this literature to describe the participation rate of a specified population in some types of criminal activity. But the *offending frequency* lambda (λ), as defined by the National Academy of Sciences Panel on Research on Criminal Careers (Blumstein et al. 1986) – namely the annual rate of committing crimes among those who commit a particular type of crime – is not commonly tabulated or analyzed in the drug-related literature. In our review, we found statistics concerning the values of λ among groups that differ according to their levels and types of drug use only in the appendix of Johnson et al. (1985, table B-13, "Mean Lambdas").

In nearly all cases where an *incidence*, or crime commission, rate is reported in the drug-related literature, it is the aggregate crime rate per capita, which by definition is the offending frequency multiplied by the participation rate d. Whereas the offending frequency λ applies to people who *are* committing the type of crime in question, aggregate crime commission rates apply also to offenders in the group who do not commit the crime (counted as having a zero crime rate) along with those who do commit the crime.

For this reason, aggregate crime rates per capita may differ among study populations, even if the offenders in the populations have similar criminal behavior. For example, if a population of arrestees is divided into subgroups of, say, cocaine users and nonusers, both subgroups can be expected to have higher aggregate robbery rates than the corresponding cocaine users and nonusers in a random sample of the general population. This is because the general population would naturally have a smaller overall participation rate d in robbery, and thus a smaller λd. So it is not possible to learn anything useful about robbers' behavior when using or not using cocaine from these aggregate figures. But comparing the values of the offending frequency (λ) for cocaine users and nonusers in two populations is meaningful and interesting, since λ can be calculated by dividing λd *by* d. For example, in a subgroup 35 percent of whose members commit robbery and whose one-year incidence rate of robbery for the total larger group is 2.3, the mean annual offending frequency λ for those who commit robbery is 6.6 robberies per year (2.3 divided by .35). Researchers (and journal editors) ought to be aware of this benefit of publishing participation rates along with aggregate crime rates, even if one or the other is not particularly pertinent to the analysis in question.

Many different formats have been used for presenting and analyzing aggregate crime-rate information per capita, but these definitional differences have little substantive importance when comparing high-rate with low-rate offenders. This section gives some examples of statistics commonly used for presenting crime-rate information, and the relationships among them. A description of the numerical values of these various statistics, and the conclusions that can be drawn from them, appears in Section IV below.

A. *Group crime rates per unincarcerated year*

Average crime rates per year of street time are rarely calculated for subgroups of offenders defined by their extent of drug use. Chaiken (1986) presents crime rates for subgroups defined by extent of heroin use; these are estimates of the average aggregate number of crimes committed per year of unincarcerated time per person in each subgroup.

B. Annual incidence rates

Annual incidence rates are more common in the literature (e.g., Elliott and Huizinga 1985). These are aggregate crime rates per calendar year (not unincarcerated year). They are also group rates, but they confound the influences of criminal justice system behavior with individuals' crime commission behavior. Individuals who happened to be incarcerated for part of all of the study year could possibly contribute fewer crimes to the average than they would have contributed if they were free, or "on the street." The annualized crime rates reported by Johnson et al. (1985, table 7-2) are definitionally identical to annual incidence rates.

If the incarcerating behavior of the criminal justice system is not pertinent to a study nor expected to change, incidence rates unadjusted for street time are entirely satisfactory for comparing behavior of individuals. However, data concerning crime rates per year of street time are valuable for estimating the specific effects of incarceration on crime rates, especially if one posits possible changes in sentencing policies, or for comparing offending behavior across jurisdictions with different incarceration patterns.

The appropriate crime-rate statistic for any purpose depends on the policy context or research issue under consideration. For example, Marsden, Collins, and Hubbard (1986) point out that publishing average crime rates per unincarcerated year can have a discriminatory policy impact on minority groups whose members are less likely than others to spend an entire year unincarcerated - their crime rates per unincarcerated year can be substantially higher than their annual incidence rates.

A related concern is that offending frequencies that are measured immediately prior to some salient event, such as an arrest or entry into incarceration or drug treatment, are necessarily on average overestimates of "true" offending rates since in some instances the offender's behavior must have contributed to the occurrence of the event in question. Rolph and Chaiken (1987) have shown how to adjust each individual's data about offending frequency so as to estimate a "steady state offending frequency" - that is, the individual's offending rate at a time somewhat remote from the special triggering event. Generally this adjustment was found to be much smaller than a 25 percent reduction (Rolph and Chaiken 1987, app. A).

Some incidence rates are presented for *periods other than a year*, normally the period covered by the data collected in the study. For example, in their study of 175 women in a New York City jail who, in 1983, volunteered to answer questions about their previous drug use and criminal behavior, Sanchez and Johnson (1987) presented six month incidence rates.

C. Crime-day measures

Crime-day measures were first presented by Ball et al. (1982) in their analyses of data obtained in retrospective interviews about past crimes committed by 243 male opiate addicts. These subjects were randomly selected from a population of addicts identified by Baltimore police between 1952 and 1971. These researchers defined a crime-day as "a 24-hour period during which one or more crimes is committed by a given individual.

Each day of the year, then, is either a crime-day or a non-crime day". Crime-days are actually incidence rates which have been capped at a level of no more than one offense per day. Their primary advantage, as compared to crime-rate, is their reliability when self-reports are obtained about frequently occurring crimes – respondents can more reliably report that they committed drug sales on a given day than they can report they committed seventeen drug sales. A disadvantage of crime-day measures is their lack of additivity across types of crimes: two robbery crime-days plus three burglary crime-days may equal three, four, or five total crime days, depending on whether the burglaries were committed on the same days as the robberies or not.

Since most offenders commit most types of predatory crimes at low rates, the differences between a group's average number of crime-days per year and average crime commission rate for predatory crimes are likely to be unimportant for policy purposes. For example, in an analysis for this essay of self-report data from Rand's 1978-79 inmate survey in three states (Chaiken and Chaiken 1982), we found average annual robbery rates to be 1.0 to 1.2 times higher than the number of robbery days per year among various subgroups of the population (that is, average annual crime rates for these groups are at most 20 percent higher than average crime-days per year). We also calculated these ratios from data from Johnson et al. (1985), resulting in exactly the same range for robbery and a range of 1.4–1.8 for theft. By contrast, our calculation for nonpredatory crime showed that drug-sale rates for Rand inmate survey respondents ranged from 3.1 to 5.1 times the number of drug-sale-days per year. (All these ratios reflect the average number of offenses committed per day when the offense is committed.)

Variations among researchers in handling respondents' unclear answers to survey questions contribute a larger uncertainty to estimated annual robbery commission rates than a factor of 1.2, so crime-days per year can be compared with annual crime rates within a smaller degree of error than exists within the crime-rate measure itself. (See Visher [1986] for a discussion of estimating in the face of respondent ambiguity.)

The statistics reported by Ball, Shaffer, and Nurco (1983) and many others who present crime-day measures are crime-days as a percent of total days; thus, if subjects report committing crimes in ten of thirty interview days, the crime-day rate is 33 percent. Such figures can be multiplied by 365 to obtain crime-days per year.

Other variations on crime-day measures include *crime-days per month*(e.g., Anglin and Speckart 1986) and *crime-days per unincarcerated year* (Anglin and Speckart 1987), which are directly comparable with aggregate crime rates per capita for low-rate types of crimes.

D. Pseudo-crime day measures

To facilitate comparisons among studies, some approximations of crime-day measures have been published. These are produced by capping individuals' self-reported crime commissions at thirty crimes per month or 365 crimes per year and averaging the resulting capped rates. (In other words, the day-by-day information is not available to the researcher but is approximated.) For example, Chaiken and Chaiken (1982, p. 161) report capped aggregate crime commission rates for California jail and prison inmates who reported different levels of heroin use. Pseudo-crime-day figures are useful because averages of offense rates are highly sensitive to outliers (e.g., respondents who report thousands of robberies per year). To develop realistic averages, most investigators must cap their data in some way, for example, at the ninetieth percentile, and a cap at 365 crimes per year is as sensible and easy to understand as any other.

Although the literature on criminal behavior of drug users is characterized by a nearly dizzying array of disparate measures of crime frequency, they can be quite easily compared after standardizing them on an annual basis. We do so in the next section.

IV. Magnitudes of differences in crime rates at different levels of drug use

Despite differences among publications in their study populations, types of crimes examined in the study, and definitions of levels of drug use, general consistency emerges in the quantitative picture of the magnitude of crime-rate spread between high-drug-use and low-drug-use populations. This pattern is illustrated in this section by reference to offending frequencies calculated in nine different studies.

Although the source literature does not separate out a category of crime called "predatory crime," many studies that mention particular types of crimes do list statistics for robbery, theft, and burglary, which we include as predatory crime; so, to the extent possible, our summary tabulations here list these crimes separately. Most of the available data showing quantitative levels of offending frequencies are cross-sectional in nature, comparing high-drug-use and low-drug-use offenders during the same period of time, even when the study design is longitudinal (following the same subjects over time).

For example, the figures in table 3, calculated from Elliott and Huizinga's (1984) nationally representative longitudinal sample of youth, demonstrate many of the primary patterns in the relationship between drug abuse and offending frequencies. Contemporaneous drug abuse is very strongly associated with offending frequency. With one exception, the value of λ for multiple drug users is higher than for nonusers. In general, the values of the aggregate crime rate λd for multiple, illicit drug users are ten to twenty times as high as for nonusers (even larger ratios apply for theft). The offending frequency λ is essentially characteristic of groups of offenders categorized by their drug-use levels, while reported participation rates in most types of crimes (especially theft) decline with age. For example, the average individual robbery λ was six for the multiple illicit drug users aged eleven to seventeen and also six for multiple illicit drug users aged fifteen to twenty-one. But the value of the group robbery rate λd for the multiple illicit drug users declined from 1.2 to 0.4, a drop of nearly 70 per cent which is explained by the older group's lower reported participation rate d in robbery. (This decline may be a genuine ageing effect, or it could be that older respondents who are offenders drop out of the survey.)

**Table 3: Crime-Commission Rates per Year among Drug Users
and Nonusers Ages Eleven to Seventeen in 1976 and
Fifteen to Twenty-one in 1980**

| | | Average Crime Rates | | | | | |
| | | Robbery | | Felony Theft | | Total Delinquency* | |
Drug Use	N	Indi-vidual	Group	Indi-vidual	Group	Indi-vidual	Group
Multiple illicit drug use:							
1976	58	6	1.2	16	8.7	92	84.0[+]
1980	187	6	.4	9	2.4	84	71.7[l]
Nonuse (or use of a drug three or fewer times):							
1976	1,244	3	.1	2	.1	16	8.7[+]
1980	483	13	.1	2	.0	11	3.0[l]
Total sample:[++]							
1976	1,719	6	.3	6	7	25	16.1
1980	1,494	6	.3	5	4	30	14.5

SOURCE: - National Youth Survey, reported in Elliott and Huizinga (1984), tables 1 and 2.

NOTE:- "Individual" refers to crimes per calendar year, for those who commit that type of crime. "Group" refers to crimes per calendar year, for all subjects in the category, including those who don't commit the crime. The multiple illicit drug use category includes use of alcohol, marijuana, and other drugs (amphetamines, barbiturates, hallucinogens, cocaine, or heroin) four or more times each.

* The delinquency scale used in this table is the National Youth Survey scale SRD-C. It includes the following offenses: stole motor vehicle, went joy riding, stole something less than £5, stole something £5-£50, stole something greater than £50, bought stolen goods, broke into building/vehicle, carried hidden weapon, aggravated assault, gang fight, hit teacher, hit parent, hit student, prostitution, sold marijuana, sold hard drugs, disorderly conduct, sexual assault, strongarmed students, strongarmed teachers, strongarmed others, panhandled. Robbery includes strongarmed students, strongarmed teachers, strongarmed others. Felony theft includes stole motor vehicle, stole something greater than £50, bought stolen goods, broke into building/vehicle.

[+] The ratio for 1976 of the aggregate crime rate for multiple illicit drug users to the aggregate crime for nonusers is 9.7:1.

[l] The ratio of the 1980 aggregate crime rates is 23.9:1.

[++] The total sample includes two intermediate categories of drug use, not shown separately in the table. These omitted categories are alcohol use (use of alcohol four times or more but no use of any other drug) and alcohol and marijuana use (use of alcohol four times or more and use of marijuana four times or more but no use of other drugs).

In table 3, the subgroups of subjects are not the same people followed longitudinally over the two time periods (except of course for the "total" category); rather, the subgroups are subjects displaying the same form of drug-use behavior in the two time periods. The sample sizes show that the older youths are substantially more likely to be involved in some form of drug abuse than are the younger subjects (over three times as likely to be involved in multiple illicit drug abuse), but the participation rates in criminal activity are lower for the older subjects. Only the individual frequencies (crime commission rates for those who commit the type of crime in question) have been remaining fairly stable among subgroups over the time. These observations may be taken as demonstrating that as drug abuse becomes more widespread among a population, it becomes less indicative of deviance in general and hence of participation in criminal activity.

Among known offender populations, the picture is even clearer. The ratios of crime commission rates between drug users and nonusers in offender populations are comparable to the ratios in general populations, but the rates themselves are substantially higher for offender populations. Chaiken and Chaiken (1982) and Chaiken (1986) present information about preincarceration predatory crime rates derived from the Rand inmate survey's self-reports. Selected figures from these studies, with summaries calculated for this essay, appear in tables 4 and 5.

Table 4: Pseudo-Crime-Days per Year:* Jail and Prison Inmates Surveyed in Three States

Drug Use	N	Robbery	Burglary	Theft other than Auto Theft	All Study Crimes Except Drug Dealing	All Study Crimes[1]
Heroin addiction	357	24.4	51.3	68.7	186.7^2	224.4^3
Heroin use, not addicted	224	9.7	32.2	34.6	100.7	156.2
No drug use	939	4.7	6.8	9.2	35.7^2	48.1^3

SOURCES:- Chaiken and Chaiken (1982), p. 161, for California. Chaiken (1986) for Texas and Michigan. Summary statistics calculated by the authors. Subjects are adult male prison and jail inmates (prison inmates only in Texas).

NOTE:- A fourth drug-use category (use of barbiturates, amphetamines or any drug other than marijuana or prescribed drugs, but no use of heroin) is not shown in this table. Survey respondents are omitted from the tables if their crime-commission rate could not be calculated or their level of heroin use could not be determined from their responses.

* Average crime-commission rates per unincarcerated year, including (with zero crime-days) offenders who do not commit the listed crime, each person's crime rate truncated at 365 per year. The calendar reference period for reporting criminal activity was twelve to twenty-four months long, beginning January of the year before the respondent's arrest. The survey was conducted in 1978 and 1979.

[1] The study crimes are robbery, burglary, auto theft, other theft, forgery and credit card crimes, fraud, assault, and drug dealing.

[2] The ratio in this column of crime-days for heroin addicts to crime-days for nonusers is 5.2:1.

[3] The ratio in this column of crime-days for heroin addicts to crime-days for nonusers is 5.6:1.

Table 5: Pseudo-Crime-Days per Year:
Jail and Prison Inmates Surveyed and Listed by State

Drug Use	N	Robbery	Burglary	Theft other than Auto Theft	All Study Crimes Except Drug Dealing	All Study Crimes
California:						
Heroin addiction	204	33.6	67.6	65.8	214.7*	239.2+
Heroin use	94	13.1	31.4	40.2	100.8	156.0
No drug use	225	2.3	3.4	6.2	23.8*	33.1+
Michigan:						
Heroin addiction	94	16.6	26.3	50.4	130.5	189.9
Heroin use	82	9.2	34.9	23.7	103.1	167.8
No drug use	394	8.3	9.0	12.1	50.6	54.4
Texas prisoner:						
Heroin addiction	59	4.9	34.9	107.7	195.6	228.4
Heroin use	48	3.9	29.2	42.3	96.6	137.0
No drug use	320	2.0	6.6	7.7	25.7	27.6

SOURCES:- Chaiken and Chaiken (1982), p. 161, for California. Chaiken (1986) for Texas and Michigan. Summary statistics calculated by the authors. Subjects are adult male prison and jail inmates (prison inmates only, in Texas).

NOTE:- See table 4 for explanation of the crime-rate measure, drug-use categories, and study crimes.

* The ratio in this column of crime-days for heroin addicts to crime-days for nonusers is 9:1 for California. The similar ratio for Michigan is 2.4:1 and for Texas, 7.6:1.

+ The ratio in this column of crime-days for heroin addicts to crime-days for nonusers is 7.2:1 for California. The similar ratio for Michigan is 3.5:1, and for Texas, 8.3:1.

The prodigious criminal activity levels of offenders who are heavily involved in drug use have been often mentioned but are nonetheless striking when one looks at these tabulated statistics. Table 5 indicates that the *average* heroin addict offender spends more days per year (239 in California, 228 in Texas) working at his chosen (criminal) trade than does the typical factory worker. Since many heroin addicts must commit crimes more frequently than average, they obviously are hard at work on weekends and vacation days as well as weekdays.

Heroin addicts have typically somewhere between five and ten times as many crime-days per year as do offenders in this sample who do not take illicit drugs. (The exception is table 5, for Michigan, is explained by the high levels of auto theft for all incarcerated offenders in Michigan. Auto theft is not shown in the table but is included in the category All Study Crimes.) Considering the generally poor predictability of offenders' crime commission rates that can be obtained by examining their personal characteristics and criminal history (see, e.g., Monahan 1981; Chaiken and Chaiken 1982; Gottfredson and Gottfredson 1986; Farrington 1987; Rolph and Chaiken 1987;

Chaiken and Chaiken 1989), ratios as high as 5:1 to 10:1 represent striking distinctions among offender groups.

Comparable figures for an entirely different incarcerated population examined at a later time period, Sanchez and Johnson's study (1987) of 175 women in jail in New York City, are presented in table 6. Here again, the crime commission rates for property crimes amount to hundreds of offenses per year, and the ratios in crime commission rates between the frequent drug users and the infrequent or nonusers are similar to those presented above for male prison inmates.

Table 6: Crime-Commission Rates:
175 Female Jail Inmates–Riker's Island, New York

Drug Use	N	Property Crimes*		All Study Crimes[+]	
		Individual	Group	Individual	Group
Daily heroin and Cocain use	119	309	226	448	471
No use in past sixty days	25	184	74	186	128

SOURCE:- Sanchez and Johnson (1987), table IX.

NOTE:- "Individual" refers to the offending frequency, that is, crimes per calendar year for those who commit that type of crime. "Group" refers to crimes per calendar year, for all subjects in the category, including those who don't commit the crime. Two categories of drug use are omitted from the table: one to twenty times use of heroin or cocaine in the past sixty days, and twenty-one to fifty-nine times use of heroin or cocaine in past sixty days.

* "Property crimes" including burglary, shoplifting, motor vehicle theft, theft from a motor vehicle, picking pockets, criminal possession of stolen property, and other thefts.

+ "All study crimes" include property crime, drug sales to dealers and users, violent offenses (robbery, aggravated assault, homicide, attempted homicide), fraud offenses (check and credit card forgeries, con games, loan sharking), and prostitution.

The studies discussed in the remainder of this section describe crime frequencies among drug-user populations. The primary observations that we draw from these studies are, first, that it is not drug abuse per se, but the amount of frequency of drug use, that is strongly related to crime commission rates, and, second, that as drug abusers go through some periods of heavy use and other periods of nonuse or lesser drug use, their crime-committing behavior varies over time with their amount of drug use.

Table 7 presents statistics for a street drug-user population. Approximately 200 heroin (or methadone) users provided information about drugs they were using and crimes they had committed in periods between recurrent interviews with researchers; the interviews were conducted in neighbourhood storefronts (Johnson et al. 1985). In contrast with tables 3 and 4, which compared daily heroin or cocaine users with nonusers, table 7 compares daily heroin users with irregular heroin users.

The comparisons in table 7 are cross-sectional; that is, the study subjects were classified once as daily, regular, or irregular heroin users and did not shift among categories. Thus, the irregular users include some people who use heroin frequently on occasion. The table illustrates that even within drug-using populations, the ratio in crime commissions for some types of crime range as high as 5:1 between addicts and irregular users and average 2.4:1 to 2.8:1 for all types of crimes. The offending frequencies in table 7 illustrate that the distinctions in offending behavior between daily heroin users and irregular users are not simply in participation rate. Heroin addicts who commit robbery have an offending frequency of twenty-seven robberies per year, while irregular users who commit robbery have an offending frequency of twelve robberies per year, a ratio of 2.3:1.

Inciardi's (1987a) data for drug-abusing populations in Miami show similar ratios, for example λ=24 robberies per year for narcotics users and fourteen robberies per year for other drug users. Ball et al. (1986, table 631) provide data confirming the same general level of individual crime commission frequencies among addicts in New York, Baltimore and Philadelphia (221 theft crime-days per year for addicts who commit theft in their last addiction period, eighty-nine burglary crime-days per year for those who commit burglary).

Studies of drug addicts who have entered treatment programs give the clearest picture of the extent to which drug abuse is contemporaneously related to crime commission behavior (as opposed to being a persistent characteristic of the particular person). Periods of addiction, or daily drug use, are accompanied by much higher crime commission rates than periods of lesser drug use for the same individual. An illustration is given in table 8, which shows ratios of 6:1 to 8:1 between crime rates in high and low periods of drug use. Anglin and Speckart (1987), commenting on these subjects, indicate that the choice of *initial* drug addiction in this table is particularly pertinent:

> Although most studies examining the narcotics use and crime connection begin with a statement that this is a controversial area of research and that absolute conclusions cannot be drawn, the present authors disagree. Both current and earlier works,... we believe, present strong evidence that there is a strong causal relationship, as least in the United States, between addiction to narcotics and to property crime levels... To a lesser extent nonaddicted narcotics use may also contribute significantly to levels of property crime activities. The largest increase of property crime activities during the addiction career, however, occurs at that point at which daily narcotics use is initiated. It is also clear that the reduction of individual level of addiction, while moderating criminality significantly for most and essentially terminating it for some, does not resolve the problem of property crime behaviors for all. [Anglin and Speckart 1987, p. 33].

Table 7: Crime Commission Rates per Year: Street Drug Users in New York City

Drug use	N	Robbery			Burglary			Theft			All Nondrug Crimes†			All Study Crimes◇	
		Individual	Crime Days	Group	Individual	Crime Days	Group	Individual	Crime Days	Group	Individual	Crime Days	Group	Individual	Group
Heroin use all days	62	27	12	10	60	12	34	131	29	65	216	122*	209	1,447	1,447+
Irregular use	61	12	2	2	14	4	4	69	23	41	133	50*	116	515	515+
Total sample (including regular users)	201	29	21	6	44	6	41	103	18	67	176	88	163	1,074	1,073

SOURCE:- Johnson et al. (1985), tables 7-2, 8-6, 8-13.

NOTE:- "Individual" is the offending frequency, that is, crimes per calendar year for those who commit that type of crime. "Group" is aggregate crimes per calendar year for all subjects in the category, including those who don't commit the crime. "Crime-days" is crime-days per calendar year. The category of regular user is not separately shown in the table but is included in the total.

† Nondrug crimes include robbery, burglary, theft (larceny plus shoplifting for resale only), forgery, con games, prostitution, pimping.

◇ Total study crimes include nondrug crimes plus drug sales, steering, copping, touting, drug thefts, shoplifting for own use, and fare evasion.

* The ratio in this column of crime-days for daily heroin users to crime-days for irregular users is 2.3:1.

+ The ratio in this column of crime-days for daily heroin users to crime-days for irregular users is 2.8:1.

Table 8: Crime-Days per Year: Male Methadone Maintenance Patients

	N	Robbery	Burglary	Theft	All Property Crimes
Year following first daily use:					
Anglos	362	1	31	46	83*
Chicanos	284	2	38	52	94[+]
Year following last daily use:					
Anglos	318	0	3	7	10*
Chicanos	233	0	5	8	15[+]

SOURCE:- Anglin and Speckart (1987), tables 6 and 7.

NOTE:- "All property crimes" include robbery, burglary, theft, and forgery. Anglin and Speckart do not include drug crimes in the study. The figures given here do not entirely agree with published monthly crime commission rates for the same subjects (Anglin and Speckart 1986); however, Anglin (1987) indicates the figures tabulated here are internally consistent, using the definition in Anglin and Speckart (1987).

* The ratio of crime-days for Anglos between first daily use and following last daily use is 8.3:1.

[+] The ratio for Chicanos is 6.3:1.

Similar, but not quite as strong, changes in criminal behavior over time have been reported for other treatment populations. For example, Ball, Shaffer, and Nurco (1983) show aggregate theft rates for male heroin addicts in Baltimore of 125 per year at the start of addiction and thirty-four per year during the first "off" period (under treatment). Marsden, Collins, and Hubbard (1986) show aggregate predatory crime rates for addicts in ten cities entering treatment. Before treatment, clients' crime rates were 12.2 per year, and after treatment, they were 5.4 per year. These represent ratios of two - or three-to-one between crime commission rates before and after treatment, but they do not focus on precisely the same time periods that Anglin and Speckart (1987) found revealed the strongest differences (the period following first addiction versus the period after last addiction).

Another study with parallel findings involved approximately 200 male heroin addicts who were enrolled in methadone maintenance programs in New York and Blatimore, half of whom reported committing no predatory crime before heroin addiction (Nurco et al. 1988). This half differed little from those who committed predatory crime prior to addiction in terms of the types of illicit drugs they used prior to addiction. But the predatory criminals were significantly more likely to have used illicit drugs *frequently* than were the nonpredators during the pre-addiction period.

These respondents, as with other groups of addicts studied, cycled in and out of addictive use of heroin. During periods of nonaddiction, both groups of respondents committed predatory crimes at lower rates than they did during periods of addiction. But the former nonpredators once again committed crimes at lower rates than those who had been predators before addiction (Nurco et al. 1988).

V. Conclusions and implications for the justice system

Use of illicit drugs does not appear to be strongly related to onset and participation in predatory crime; rather, drug use and crime participation are weakly related as contemporaneous products of factors generally antithetical to traditional United States lifestyles. Most of the underlying causative factors, such as irregular employment or weak attachment to school or parents, are not amenable to intervention by the justice system. Moreover, general prevalence figures for drug use do not give much hope that even major reductions in the numbers of people who use illicit drugs could significantly reduce the number of incidents of predatory crime.

More specifically, among adolescents and adults who use illicit drugs, most do not commit predatory crimes. Reducing the number of adolescents who are sporadic users of illicit drugs, especially marijuana, may possibly affect the incidence and prevalence of some types of crime, such as disorderly conduct and driving under the influence of controlled substances, but not predatory crime. In addition, most adults who sporadically use drugs such as hallucinogens, tranquilizers, or cocaine do not commit predatory crimes. Therefore, reducing the number of *adults* who are sporadic users of these types of drugs may also affect the incidence and prevalence of some types of crime, but is unlikely to affect the incidence of predatory crime.

About 50 per cent of delinquent youngsters are delinquent before they start using drugs; about 50 percent start concurrently or after. Reducing the number of adolescents who sporadically use illicit drugs may potentially reduce the incidence and prevalence of minor predatory crime; but these types of crime are more likely to be reduced through comprehensive delinquency prevention measures which do not focus exclusively or particularly on drug abuse.

Persistent use of drugs other than heroin (and perhaps also excluding cocaine) appears to be unrelated to persistence in committing predatory crimes. Among youngsters who use drugs and commit theft or other predatory crimes, most continue to use drugs as adults but stop committing crimes at the end of adolescence. Moreover, almost half of convicted offenders who are persistent offenders never used drugs. Therefore preventing persistent use of drugs other than heroin and cocaine is not likely to reduce the number of persistent predatory offenders.

However, there is strong evidence that predatory offenders who persistently and frequently use large amounts of multiple types of drugs commit crimes at significantly higher rates over longer periods than do less drug-involved offenders, and predatory offenders commit fewer crimes during periods in which they use no heroin.

These findings suggest that criminal justice programs that focus resources on high-rate predatory offenders should include among their selection criteria evidence of persistent, frequent use of multiple types of illicit drugs. In addition, criminal justice system programs that effectively prevent addicted predatory offenders from using heroin appear promising when measured against the goal of reducing the incidence of predatory crime.

References

Adler, Patricia A. *Wheeling and Dealing: An Ethnography of Upper-Level Drug Dealing and Smuggling Communities.* New York: Columbia University Press, 1985.

Anglin, M. Douglas. 'Personal communication with authors', November 30, 1987.

Anglin, M. Douglas, and Yih-Ing Hser. 'Addicted Women and Crime'. *Criminology,* 1987, 25:359-97.

Anglin, M. Douglas, Elizabeth S. Piper, and George Speckart. 'The Effect of Legal Supervision on Addiction and Criminal Behavior'. Paper presented at the thirty-ninth annual meeting of the American Society of Criminology, Montreal, November, 1987.

Anglin, M. Douglas, and George Speckart. 'Narcotics Use, Property Crime, and Dealing: Structural Dynamics across the Addiction Career'. *Journal of Quantitative Criminology,* 1987, 2:355-75.

– 'Narcotics Use and Crime: A Multisample, Multimethod Analysis'. University of California, Los Angeles, Department of Psychology. Mimeographed.

Ball, John C. 'The Hyper-Criminal Opiate Addict'. In *Crime Rates among Drug Abusing Offenders*, edited by Bruce D. Johnson and Eric Wish. Final report to the National Institute of Justice. New York: Narcotic and Drug Research, Inc., 1986.

Ball, John C., Eric Corty, S. Paul Petroski, Henrietta Bond, Anthony Tommasello, and Teri Baker. 'Characteristics of 633 Patients in Methadone Maintenance Treatment in Three United States Cities'. University of Maryland School of Medicine, Department of Epidemiology and Preventive Medicine, Baltimore. Mimeographed, 1986.

Ball, John C., Lawrence Rosen, John A. Flueck, and David N. Nurco. 'Lifetime Criminality of Heroin Addicts in the United States'. *Journal of Drug Issues*, 1982, 3:225-39.

Ball, John C., John W. Shaffer, and David N. Nurco. 'The Day-to-Day Criminality of Heroin Addicts in Baltimore: A study in the Continuity of Offense Rates'. *Drug and Alcohol Dependence,* 1983, 12(1):119-42.

Biernacki, Patrick. *Pathways from Addiction: Recovery without Treatment.* Philadelphia: Temple University Press, 1986..

Blumstein, Alfred, David P. Farrington, and Soumyo Moitra. 'Delinquency Careers: Innocents, Desisters, and Persisters'. In *Crime and Justice: An Annual Review of Research,* 1985, vol. 6, edited by Michael Tonry and Norval Morris. Chicago: University of Chicago Press.

Blumstein, Alfred, Jacqueline Cohen, Jeffrey A. Roth, and Christy A. Visher, eds. *Criminal Careers and "Career Criminals."* Washington, D. C.: National Academy Press, 1986.

Carpenter, Cheryl, Barry Glassner, Bruce D. Johnson, and Julia Loughlin. *Kids, Drugs, Alcohol, and Crime.* Lexington, Mass.: Lexington Books, 1988.

Chaiken, Jan M., and Marcia R. Chaiken. *Varieties of Criminal Behavior.* Santa Monica, Calif.: Rand, 1982.

Chaiken, Marcia R. 'Crime Rates and Substance Abuse among Types of Offenders'. In *Crime Rates among Drug-abusing Offenders*, edited by Bruce D. Johnson and Eric Wish. Final report to the National Institute of Justice. New York: Narcotic and Drug Research, Inc., 1986.

Chaiken, Marcia R., and Jan M. Chaiken. 'Who Gets Caught Doing Crime?' Discussion paper. Washington, D.C.: Bureau of Justice Statistics, 1985.

— *Redefining the Career Criminal: Priority Prosecution of High-Rate Dangerous Offenders.* Washington, D. C.: National Institute of Justice, 1989.

Chaiken, Marcia R., and Bruce D. Johnson. *Characteristics of Different Types of Drug-involved Offenders*. Washington, D.C.: National Institute of Justice, 1988.

Collins James J., and Susan L. Bailey. *Early Drug Use and Criminal Careers*. Research Triangle Park, N.C.P.: Research Triangle Institute. Mimeographed, 1987.

Collins, James J., J. Valley Rachal, Robert L. Hubbard, Elizabeth R. Cavanaugh, S. Gail Craddock, and Patricia L. Kristiansen. *Criminality in a Drug Treatment Sample: Measurement Issues and Initial Findings*. Research Triangle Park, N.C.: Research Triangle Institute, 1982.

Dembo, Richard, Mark Washburn, Eric D. Wish, Horatio Yeung, Aland Getreu, Estrellita Berry, and William R. Blount. 'Heavy Marijuana Use and Crime among Youths Entering a Juvenile Detention Center'. *Journal of Psychoactive Drugs*, 1987, 19:47-56.

Elliott, Delbert S., and David Huizinga. 'The Relationship between Delinquent Behavior and ADM Problems'. Prepared for the Alcohol, Drug Abuse, and Mental Health Administration/Office of Juvenile Justice and Delinquency Prevention State-of-the-Art Conference on Juvenile Offenders with Serious Drug, Alcohol, and Mental Health Problems, April, 1984.

— 'The Relationship between Delinquent Behavior and ADM Problems'. Proceedings of the Alcohol, Drug Abuse, and Mental Health Administration/Office of Juvenile Justice and Delinquency Prevention Research Conference on Juvenile Offenders with Serious Drug, Alcohol, and Mental Health Problems, Washington D.C., 1985.

Elliott, Delbert S., David Huizinga, and Scott Menard. *Multiple Problem Youth: Delinquency, Drugs, and Mental Health Problems*. New York: Springer-Verlag, 1989.

Fagan, Jeffrey, and Joseph G. Weis. *Drug Use and Delinquency among Inner City Youth*. New York: Springer-Verlag (forthcoming), 1990.

Farrington, David P. 'Predicting Individual Crime Rates'. In *Prediction and Classification: Criminal Justice Decision Making,* edited by Don M. Gottfredson and Michael Tonry. Vol. 9 of *Crime and Justice: A Review of Research*, edited by Michael Tonry and Norval Morris. Chicago: University of Chicago Press, 1987.

Gandossy, Robert P., Jay R. Williams, Jo Cohen, and Hendrik J. Harwood. *Drugs and Crime: A Survey and Analysis of the Literature*. Washington D.C.: U.S. Department of Justice, National Institute of Justice, 1980.

Goldstein, Paul J. 'Drugs and Violent Behavoir'. *Journal of Drug Issues* (Fall, 1980), pp. 493-506.

Gottfredson, Stephen D., and Don M Gottfredson. 'Accuracy of Prediction Models'. In *Criminal Careers and "Career Criminals,"* vol 2, edited by Alfred Blumstein, Jacqueline Cohen, Jeffrey A Roth, and Christy A Visher. Washington, D.C.: National Academy Press, 1986.

Hanson, Bill, George Beschner, James M. Walters, and Elliott Bovelle. *Life with Heroin: Voices from the Inner City*. Lexington, Mass.: Lexington Books, 1985.

Hunt, Dana. In this volume. 'Drugs and Consensual Crimes: Drug Dealing and Prostitution'.

Inciardi, James A. 'Exploring the Drugs/Crime Connection'. Newark: University of Delaware, Division of Criminal Justice, Mimeographed, 1987a.

– 'Beyond Cocaine: Basuco, Crack, and Other Coca Products'. Paper presented at the annual meeting of the Criminal Justice Sciences Association, St. Louis, March, 1987.

Innes, Christopher A. *Profile of State Prison Inmates, 1986*. Special report. Washington, D.T.: Bureau of Justice Statistics, 1988.

Joe, George W., and D. Dane Simpson. 'Mortality Rates among Opioid Addicts in a Longitudinal Study'. *American Journal of Public Health*, 1987, 77:347-48.

Johnson, Bruce D., Paul Goldstein, Edward Preble, James Schmeidler, Dougals S. Lipton, Barry Spunt, and Thomas Miller. *Taking Care of Business: The Economics of Crime by Heroin Abusers*. Lexington, Mass.: Lexington Books, 1985.

Johnston, Lloyd D., Patrick M. O'Malley, and Jerald G. Bachman. *Use of Licit and Illicit Drugs by America's High School Students, 1975-84*. Rockville, Md.: National Institute on Drug Abuse, 1985.

– *Drug Use among American High School Students, College Students, and Other Young Adults, National Trends through 1985*. Rockville, Md.: National Institute on Drug Abuse, 1986.

Kandel, Denise B., Ora Simcha-Fagan and Mark Davies. 'Risk Factors for Delinquency and Illicit Drug Use from Adolescence to Young Adulthood'. *Journal of Drug Issues*, 1986, 16:67-90.

Kleiman, Mark A.R., and Kerry D. Smith. In this volume. 'State and Local Drug Enforcement: In Search of a Strategy'.

Mande, Mary J., and Kim English. *Individual Crime Rates of Colorado Prisoners*. Denver: Colorado Department of Public Safety, Division of Criminal Justice, 1988.

Marsden, Mary Ellen, James J. Collins, and Robert L. Hubbard. *Effects of Adjusting Individual Offense Rates for Time at Risk*. Research Triangle Park, N.C.: Research Triangle Institute, 1986.

Mieczkowski, Thomas. 'Geeking Up and Throwing Down: Heroin Street Life in Detroit'. *Criminology*, 1986, 24:645-66.

Miller, Judity D., Ira Cisin, Hilary Gardner-Keaton, Adele Harrell, Philip W. Wirtz, Herbert Abelson, and Patricia Fishburne. *National Survey on Drug Abuse: Main Findings 1982*. Report no. (ADM) 83-1263. Rockville, Md.: National Institute on Drug Abuse, 1983.

Monahan, John, *Predicting Violent Behavior: An Assessment of Clinical Techniques*. Beverly Hills, Calif.: Sage, 1981.

Moore, Mark. In this volume. 'Supply Reduction and Drug Law Enforcement'.

National Institute of Justice. *Drug Use Forecasting (DUF)*. Washington, D.C.: National Institute of Justice, 1988.

Newcomb, Michael D., and Peter M. Bentler. *Consequences of Adolescent Drug Use Impact on the Lives of Young Adults*. Beverly Hills, Calif.: Sage, 1988.

Nurco, David N., Thomas E. Hanlon, Timothy W. Kinlock, and Karen R Duszynski. 'Differential Criminal Patterns of Narcotic Addicts over an Addiction Career'. *Criminology*, 1988, 26:407-23.

Peterson, Mark, Jan Chaiken, Patricia Ebener, and Paul Honig. *Survey of Prison and Jail Inmates: Background and Method*. Santa Monica, Calif.: Rand, 1982.

Robins, Lee N., Darlene H. Davis, and Eric Wish. 'Vietnam Veterans Three Years after Vietnam: How Our Study Changed Our View of Heroin'. In *Yearbook of Substance Abuse*, edited by L. Brill and C. Winick. New York: Human Sciences Press, 1980.

Rolph, John E., and Jan M. Chaiken. *Identifying High-Rate Serious Criminals from Official Records*. Santa Monica, Calif.: Rand, 1987.

Sanchez, Jose E., and Bruce D. Johnson. 'Women and the Drugs-Crime Connection: Crime Rates among Drug-abusing Women at Rikers Island'. *Journal of Psychoactive*, 1987, *Drugs* 19(2):205-16.

Simcha-Fagan, Ora, and Joseph E. Schwartz. 'Neighborhood and Delinquency: An Assessment of Contextual Effects'. *Criminology*, 1986, 24:667-95.

Sutherland, Edwin H., and Donald Cressey. *Criminology*. Philadelphia: Lippincott, 1970.

Visher, Christy. 'The Rand Second Inmate Survey: A Reanalysis'. In *Criminal Careers and "Career Criminals,"* vol. 2, edited by Alfred Blumstein, Jacqueline Cohen, Jeffrey A. Roth, and Christy A. Visher. Washington, D.C.: National Academy Press, 1986.

White, Helene Raskin, Robert J. Pandina, and Randy LaGrange. 'Longitudinal Predictors of Serious Substance Use and Delinquency'. *Criminology*, 1987, 25:715-40.

Williams, Terry M., and William Kornblum. *Growing Up Poor*. Lexington, Mass.: Lexington Books, 1985.

Wish, Eric D., and Bruce D. Johnson. 'The Impact of Substance Abuse on Criminal Careers'. In *Criminal Careers and "Career Criminals,"* vol. 2, edited by Alfred Blumstein, Jacqueline Cohen, Jeffrey A. Roth, and Christy A. Visher. Washington, D.C.: National Academy Press, 1986.

The War on Drugs

Although policy towards drugs and drug users in Britain in recent years has taken the twin-track approach of treatment and punishment (helping drug users and punishing drug dealers and traffickers), for many the momentum is creeping towards greater emphasis on a punitive response. The USA, of course, has tended to run, on the whole, with a primarily penal response since the passing of the Harrison Act in 1914. As has been suggested earlier in this Reader, the symbolic function of a war on drugs may serve a number of purposes to those in power: the reassurance of a worried and anxious population that something is being done (forcefully and with commitment) about a problem they have been told is undermining the essential fabric of their society; the deflection of attention from other problems to one where the rhetoric at least gives hope of its resolution.

Getting tough on drugs is a policy that meets with broad approval both publicaly and across the mainstream political spectrum. The issue, however, in pragmatic terms, relates to the historical success of such wars and the likelihood of their success in the future. Can the war on drugs be won? It is the view of the authors presented here that it cannot. Drug war stalwarts, even those that acknowledge the limitations of the policy to date, would argue that the issue is too important morally to tackle in any other way, that we shouldn't *give in* to evil. This perspective tends to ask for more and more enforcement and more and more resources in order to tackle the business where aggregate profits perhaps supersede that of the oil industry. Stimson suggests that some wars are not winnable and that this is one of them. Customs at the present time fail to impact significantly on smuggling (true also of the United States where expenditure on drug interdiction far exceeds that in Britain) and the problem lies as much outside of British and American shores as within it and many of these problems appear intractable.

Wisotsky elaborates on the problems which would have to be resolved in the producer countries if any impact was to be made on production and supply. Explaining the problems in 'forcing' or cajoling producer countries to eradicate or even reduce supply given the impoverished economic state of the nations and their heavy reliance on products in heavy demand elsewhere he is forced to conclude that significant limitations on the supply of drugs from these regions, short of military occupation, (which would also be likely to fail) is unlikely.

Malyon, in his article, alerts us to some of the dangers of taking a predominately military or war-like stance on dealing with drugs. One effect is to push the debate around drugs into an either/or context. The implication is that if you are not hard on drugs then you are being soft on them. Such a context has made it difficult for any political party to speak out against current policy without courting a label of being soft on the drugs issue, which is potentially political suicide. A further consequence of pushing the debate around drugs towards an either/or context is that it makes it difficult for alternative stances to make themselves heard. Malyon particularly refers us to the experience of Holland, where a more liberal approach to drug use has not produced the expected surge of new drug users that drug warriors warn us against. Written at the height of concern over drugs in the 1980s, the lessons of these papers mid-way through the 1990s remain as relevant as ever.

27.   Can a War on Drugs Succeed?

Gerry Stimson

The government plans new drugs penalties. But well-founded alarm shouldn't stop us questioning current policies. Law enforcement is not enough.

As everyone knows, there has been a huge increase in the successful smuggling of heroin into this country. In the mid-1960s, at the height of the last great scare about hard drugs, there was hardly any smuggled heroin in Britain. Twenty years later, there are few places where you can't find it. Is it really possible to top or slow this supply? What problems face a country trying to control drug smuggling? The government thinks that a tougher approach is the answer: but is it?

No one knows exactly how much heroin is consumed each year in Britain. But the current estimate is that there are upwards of 60,000 regular users, and many more casual ones. So the total is likely to be about three tons a year - ie, more than eight kilograms every day. This heroin is fairly pure. The samples analysed by the British government's forensic science laboratories last winter were 46 per cent pure, on average. This is much higher than the US, where the purity is down at 7 per cent. And heroin in Britain is cheap. It is one of thew few products that have steadily fallen in price in recent years. Between 1980 and 1983, the real price of heroin in Britain (i.e., controlled for inflation) fell by a fifth.

Heroin is now widely available. It sells at about £10 for a tiny packet containing about 60 milligrams of heroin. This is about a quarter of the amount a regular user might take each day.

The question of how to curb the supply might seem to have an easy answer. Being an island, all we need do is strengthen our customs control, or even - as the Commons home affairs select committee has suggested - bring in the navy and the air force to help the customs and the police. The committee described drugs as "the most serious peacetime threat to our national wellbeing."

The tough new approach to drugs was echoed by the Prime Minister's visits to the customs at Heathrow and to the Central Drugs Intelligence Unit at Scotland Yard. She said there was now a war on traffickers and smugglers. "We are after you," she said. "The pursuit will be relentless. We shall make your life not worth living." (Till recently, of course, customs were being pruned back, as part of the government's public expenditure policy.)

But it isn't as simple as that. Let's look at how heroin gets to Britain. The chain of supply starts in some poor country. Most of the heroin now coming to Britain originates in Afghanistan and Pakistan. The rest comes from south east Asian countries like Burma, Thailand and Laos, and the Middle East.

Gerry Stimson: 'Can a War on Drugs Succeed?', *NEW SOCIETY* 15 November, 1985. © New Society 1985. Reprinted with permission of New Statesman and Society.

Heroin is, of course, derived from the opium poppy. Opium growing is a major source of income for many poor farmers. A Pathan farmer may give an acre over to poppies. This will produce about seven kilograms of opium, which will sell (depending on the general success of the crop that year) at between £22 and £100 a kilo. Opium growing needs a lot of labour. The size of the crop is limited by the supply of labour and by the need to put some land over to foodstuffs to feed the workforce. Ten kilos of opium make a kilo of heroin. Opium is converted to heroin in simple local refineries. The local wholesaler in the North West Frontier Province of Pakistan sells it for export at between £3,000 and £4,000 a kilo.

Since the 1970s, there have been many attempts by western countries to persuade producer countries to stop growing opium. This has worked with some former suppliers - Yugoslavia and Turkey, for example. But it has failed in south west and south east Asia.

Two approaches have been tried: crop eradication and crop substitution. Eradication means burning or spraying the growing plants. But this leaves peasant farmers worse off than before. It is, anyway, difficult to carry out. Despite satellite monitoring and sophisticated surveillance, the United States has not eradicated marijuana growing even in its own country. Hence the alternative tack - crop substitution. This means encouraging farmers to grow alternative cash crops, like sugar beet, coffee or flowers. But the difficulty is that the growers are often a long way from the markets for these crops. Transport is hazardous, and the cash returns are much lower. No other crop returns so great a yield per acre as the opium poppy.

What is more, these areas are often beyond the reach of government. In the Golden Triangle of south east Asia, they are controlled by tribal warlords or anti-government rebels. In the North West Frontier region of Afghanistan and Pakistan - the so-called Golden Crescent - they are controlled by fiercely independent tribal groups. In South America, many cocaine-growing areas are controlled by the drug producers themselves. They have private armies that are better equipped than the national armies.

So, these areas are poorly policed, inaccessible, and hostile to government officials and to officials from other countries. The US Drug Enforcement Agency has 20 officials in Pakistan, but they are mostly in the cities, rather than in the growing areas. Visits to growing areas can only be undertaken with heavily armed guards. In Columbia, the six ruling coca families threatened to kill three Drug Enforcement Agency men for each drug producer arrested. In February this year they carried out that threat.

It is no coincidence that the main opium-growing areas have been, and remain, politically unstable. They are often right-wing and anti-communist. They depend on trafficking bands, tribal groups and private armies for border security. Western governments have often supported these people as a buffer against communism.

Quite simply, many people in these countries do not share the western governments' view on the need to control a traditional crop which brings in money. Imagine the response if the Pakistan government sent emissaries here to persuade our distillers to stop producing whisky because whisky drinking was causing a social problem in Pakistan.

Drug production in the third world relies on poverty, a suitable climate and an abundance of labour. It gives poor peasants some extra income. However, this is no place to get romantic. The peasants are exploited, just like most growers of raw materials for export. The big profits are made by the refiners and the exporters. These profits are often taken out of the country, and rarely benefit its economy. Drug production reproduces, in an alarming way, the traditional exploitation of poor countries. Bolivia, a main cocaine producer, is a prime example. Cocaine is now the main dollar-earning export. Its production employs one in ten of the population. Despite pockets of affluence, this has not raised the living conditions for the mass of the people. The history of former drug-producing countries - China, Yugoslavia and perhaps Iran - is that drug production only ceases when there are major economic, political and social changes.

The next stage of the journey taken by the heroin that worries us here is when it is smuggled into Britain. Each year, 36 million passengers arrive from foreign destinations. What are the chances of getting through customs without being searched? The returning holidaymaker may think the search level is high. In fact, very few people are searched by customs, perhaps only one in 100. The person who brings in the heroin could be acting independently, but more likely is paid as a courier, getting anything from £1,000 to £3,000 for the trip. The importer is paying about £6,000 per kilo of heroin, including import costs, and can afford to lose some couriers. If ten couriers are sent through, and one is caught, the loss of heroin is minor, when you set it against the profits. That kilo of heroin will sell for about £20,000 at the next stage of distribution.

The difficulty for the customs men comes not only from passengers, but also from motor vehicles, ships and aircraft. Heroin smugglers are more and more using the cover of commercial freight to bring in large consignments. The customs policy on goods from the EEC is that only 2 per cent are subject to random searches. In 1983 only 6 per cent of all freight brought into the United Kingdom was examined.

Then there are private yachts. On the south coast alone, there are thousands of boats, many capable of sailing to other countries: 6,000 at Chichester harbour, 4,000 on the Hamble, 4,000 at Lymington. The Society of Civil and Public Servants, pressing a claim for more customs staff, reports that on a Sunday night up to 60 yachts on the Hamble may report their arrival from abroad, and a similar number not bother. There are not enough customs officers even to deal with those asking for customs attention.

But contrary to the popular impression, random searches are not the main thrust of the customs effort. Probably less than a fifth of seizures come from random search, and these are likely to hit the one-off independent importer, rather than the large-scale trafficker. Much of the customs work is in intelligence. Drugs are now the largest single part of the operations of the Customs Special Investigation Division. The intelligence men work from both ends of the supply chain – in producer countries (Britain has now stationed a customs official in Pakistan), and in this country. Some of the most spectacular seizures result from this. A recent seizure of 40 kilos of heroin at Felixstowe docks was found in a shipment of brassware from Pakistan.

Despite these successes, the customs would be the first to admit that they have a tough job. The customs have over 200 investigators specially assigned to drugs now. Of these, about 70 work on heroin. The government have plans to create a further 100 new posts during the present financial year, specifically to help prevent drug smuggling.

In 1984, the British customs seized 312 kilos of heroin, and 25 tons of cannabis. But as the Commons select committee acknowledged: "No amount of law enforcement can stop the great bulk of supplies getting through." Seizures have increased. But they probably remain minimal, compared with what is missed. The Chief Investigation Officer for Customs and Excise is reluctant to estimate success rates. But no law enforcement agency anywhere in the world credibly claims more than a 10 per cent interception rate.

After heroin has come into Britain for distribution, control becomes a police responsibility. This is at various levels. All uniformed and plain-clothes officers will deal with any drug offences which arise in the normal course of their duties. Every police force in the country (bar one in Scotland) now has a drugs squad, which, with the CID, will tackle more serious cases. Over and above this there are regional crime squads, which cover cases which cross more than one police authority area. On average, half the activity of the regional crime squads is now concerned with drug offences or drug-related crime. In July the then Home Secretary, Leon Brittan, announced that the squads would be strengthened by "wings" dedicated to drugs work and by an increase of more than 200 officers.

The intelligence men

Intelligence for all these activities is provided at New Scotland Yard by the recently created National Drugs Intelligence Unit. This has replaced the former Central Drugs Intelligence Unit. It is staffed by both police and customs. The seriousness of the Home Office's view of drug distribution is indicated by the fact that the new coordinator heading the national unit is a very senior policeman, Colin Hewett, who has previously headed the Metropolitan Police Special Branch and its anti-terrorist squad.

The police make many more seizures than the customs (2,800 seizures of heroin in 1984). But the seizures are much, much smaller. In terms of quantity, the total police seizures amount to only 10 per cent of those of the customs. Seizing one kilo at import is clearly much cheaper than seizing that kilo when it has been divided up into 1,000 separate one-gram packets at a street level. Despite attempts to move up the chain of supply, most convictions are at the user and user/dealer ends. In 1983, two thirds of police seizures were for less than one gram.

There are more than 1,000 officers in police force drug squads, and in the regional crime squads, with a major commitment to drugs work. Their work resulted in 25,000 convictions or cautions in 1984, for all drugs: and 3,000 for offences concerned with heroin and cocaine. Nearly a half of the people convicted of offences involving heroin or cocaine received immediate custodial sentences. At any one time, there are 1,600 people in prison for drugs offences.

What is the cost of all this work that goes into controlling supplies? No one has totalled up the amount spent on measures to control supply at source, and on customs and policing. But it is unlikely to be less than several hundred million pounds a year. It is certainly several times that spent on prevention, education and treatment.

The government continues to try to tighten the screw. Parole has been removed for major drug traffickers, and the government has increased the maximum penalty for trafficking in Class A drugs (these include heroin and cocaine) from 14 years to life imprisonment. But it is unlikely that even this will deter major importers while the profits remain so high. The structure of drug distribution makes it difficult for police to gain information on such people. Nor will higher penalties be much use in persuading people to inform on those higher up the distribution chain. For them, it may be a choice between a life sentence in prison and a death sentence from a major importer.

Sequestration of assets is another of the government's current proposals. The Queen's Speech last week announced legislation to deprive drug traffickers of their assets – hopefully taking some of the profit out of trafficking. It could be one way of increasing the costs of heroin distribution, which might make heroin a less attractive proposition for criminals. The hurdle here is that a successful policy would require close international cooperation in controlling the flow of capital, and tighter national controls. The government's policies on free exchange control run against this.

What, then, can we make of this labour? Last year, at best, all the time, effort and money put into British customs and police work resulted in the interception of perhaps 10 per cent of imports. If we want to be pessimistic about this, it is a 90 per cent failure rate. And even this had no impact on the price and purity of drugs in Britain. These are sensitive indicators of supply – low price and high purity indicate high supply. With a combination of poor producer countries, and a high demand for heroin at home, all the customs and police efforts cannot stop the import of heroin. At best, they can slow it down a bit. Against this must be set the undoubted (but uncalculated) deterrence effect. Without controls, it is likely that imports would have been much higher.

Could things be done better? There are no easy solutions. What if we put more men and money into policing and customs work: would a doubling of present resources double the seizures? Mrs Thatcher has said that the work of customs must not be hampered by lack of resources and this week Lawson found some extra money. But it is inconceivable that any government – however determined in its fight against drugs – could put enough money in to reduce seriously the amount of heroin coming here. Even a doubling of seizures, would (if nothing else changed) mean that 80 per cent was getting through. And increased seizures are only a small extra cost. The smuggler can counter them by increasing supply (sending through more shipments), reducing quality (selling less pure), or raising the price.

If you don't believe in the free availability of dangerous drugs - and few people seriously entertain that idea - then controls over supply are inevitable. But the question remains: What is the best way?

Let us think again about the first link in the chain, the producer country. Many crop control schemes may have failed, but there is room for a more vigorous and imaginative approach. The British government is spending £200,000 a year for the next five years towards a crop substitution and rural development programme in the North West

Frontier Province and David Mellor, the Home Office minister committed a further £204 million during his recent visit to Pakistan. But this still compares poorly with the money the farmers get for producing the raw material for the three tons of heroin that come to Britain from Pakistan each year. Third world drug production must be seen in the light of the dependent position of these countries in the world economy. As a minimum, western governments could pay farmers a decent price for crop substitution.

An alternative might be for western governments to accept the fact that opium growing will continue so long as these countries remain poor and under-developed, and to purchase opium at source for later destruction. It would cost the British government between £600,000 and £3 million to buy the opium from the Pakistan peasant farmers (or between £9 million and £12 million from the wholesaler). This would guarantee them an income. By analogy with the EEC's Common Agricultural Policy, it would create an opium mountain. And it would interrupt supply at source. It would be a cheap buy, compared with the £100 million a year that London addicts alone are estimated to spend on heroin.

Better still, perhaps, would be to encourage a third world pharmaceutical industry, based on locally grown drugs. This would legitimise controlled production and help economic development.

Education and prevention

And what of the other two links in the chain, importation and distribution within this country? We need some public accountability for resources and effectiveness. The "value for money" calls now made over other state services are equally applicable to law enforcement, as the new Home Secretary, Douglas Hurd, has indicated. What is the best way to control supply through law enforcement? Is there a better return from more money spent on the police; or is the customs better value? The figures on seizures suggest a greater return from customs work.

Law enforcement alone is unlikely to be the answer. We need to find the right balance between public expenditure on education, prevention and treatment - not just on enforcement. The £2 million education and information campaign, and the £11.5 million "pump-priming" for local treatment and rehabilitation projects are welcome. But they begin to look small by comparison with expenditure on enforcement.

28. International Law Enforcement: The Futile Quest for Control of Coca and Cocaine at the Source

Steven Wisotsky

Given the structure of the cocaine industry, the law enforcement system has four principal opportunities to implement its supply reduction strategy. It can target the source of production, shipment to the United States, distribution within the United States, and movement or concealment of the money generated by the cocaine traffic.

With respect to the production phase, the law enforcement system of the United States works against the cultivation of coca and its conversion to cocaine, primarily through (1) on-site law enforcement by South American police agencies who have been trained and equipped largely by the DEA, and (2) crop substitution programs funded by the State Department and operated by the Agency for International Development (AID) in cooperation with agencies of the recipient country. The goals are to prevent excess coca planting in the first instance and, failing that, to seize cocaine before it reaches the United States.

The dramatic expansion during the late 1970s and early 1980s in the size of the black market in cocaine demonstrated the relative powerlessness of U.S. law enforcement agencies to squelch the smuggling of cocaine into the country. Drug enforcement officials themselves soon abandoned the "light at the end of the tunnel" braggadocio that once prevailed, making only modest claims about the effectiveness of drug law enforcement within the borders of the United States. Indeed, the Chief of the Cocaine Investigations Section of the DEA issued a disclaimer about the long-term potency of traditional enforcement methods: "The problem will continue until it is ultimately solved on foreign soil through coca eradication." Accordingly, the DEA argues that crop control must be the "first priority," and the President and Congress agree on the importance of control at the source. As a result, the State Department has responded with expanded or intensified programs intended to suppress cocaine at its source by destroying illegal coca plants and developing substitute crops for the peasant farmers to cultivate. For many good reasons, however, these programs have failed completely in Peru and Bolivia. In fact, the obstacles to suppression of cocaine at the source seem even more insuperable than the barriers to effective drug law enforcement within the United States.

The overseas drug control policy of the United States operates within a framework of international law, United States foreign assistance legislation, and bilateral agreements with coca-producing countries. In the realm of international law, the 1961 Single Convention on Narcotic Drugs obligates signatories, including Peru and Bolivia, to confine cocaine and other scheduled drugs to medical and scientific uses and to participate in "continuous international cooperation and control" toward that end. It establishes a system of production and inventory controls for pharmaceutical cocaine and limits cultivation of coca to the acreage necessary to meet estimated world needs. The production and inventory controls are administered through a statistical return system that reports production of drugs, utilization of drugs for the manufacture of other drugs, imports and exports of drugs, seizures of drugs, and stocks of drugs. Excess production is prohibited by the Single Convention, which regulates the cultivation of coca under the model adopted for the opium poppy. The governments are supposed to confine cultivation to designated areas by licensed growers, who are required to deliver their total crop to a designated governmental agency. These governmental monopolies, in turn, are supposed to prevent diversion of coca to the black market.

The Single Convention requires illegal coca bushes and those growing wild to be destroyed. It outlaws coca leaf chewing and other traditional, native uses in South America after 1986. Additionally, it obliges signatories to assist each other against drug trafficking and to adopt domestic criminal legislation appropriate to that end. Thus, each party is required to adopt penal laws against illicit cultivation, production, manufacture, possession, sale, offering for sale, etc., and to follow the United States legal model in outlawing conspiracy, attempts, and financial operations in connection with such offenses. All drugs, substances, and equipment used in or intended for the commission of any of these offenses are subject to seizure and confiscation.

The flaw in this grand design is its sole reliance on exhortation. The administrative agencies established by the Single Convention do not have enforcement powers. They rely instead upon voluntary compliance, research, international cooperation, and moral suasion. As might be expected, absent powers of investigation, inspection, and sanction, the "controls" established by the Single Convention have been historically ineffective. The 1972 Amendment to the Single Convention made no significant change in these respects, although it did authorize the provision of technical and financial assistance to the government of a noncomplying country as incentives to induce compliance.

Invoking the obligations imposed by international law, and applying the leverage afforded by its own foreign assistance legislation, the United States in recent years has intensified its diplomatic and financial pressures upon the governments of Peru and Bolivia to suppress coca production. The carrot-and-stick inducements include the stationing of DEA agents abroad to provide technical and financial assistance to law enforcement agencies of the host country; according "priority consideration" (under the Foreign Assistance Act of 1961) to programs intended to reduce illicit narcotics cultivation by stimulating broader economic development opportunities; and funding of herbicide projects to destroy narcotics-producing plants.

Additional (dis)incentives sharpen the tools of persuasion. The President of the United States may withhold economic or military assistance from a country that fails "to take adequate steps to prevent narcotic drugs .... from entering the United States unlawfully." In addition to suspension of United States financial aid, under the Rangel Amendment to the Foreign Assistance Act of 1961 the President can block the granting of loans by the International Bank for Reconstruction and Development (IBRD) and the

International Development Association (IDA) to a nation that has not taken adequate steps to prevent the flow of illegal drugs to the United States.

Within this framework of international law and domestic legislation, the bilateral programs of the United States with Peru and Bolivia consist of two basic components: providing technical and financial assistance to the source country's law enforcement agencies, and funding long-term projects to develop crops to replace coca. As to the law enforcement components, the DEA trains, equips, and provides intelligence to South American counterparts. Furthermore, DEA agents stationed in source countries conduct cooperative investigations. For example, "cooperative" cocaine seizures for fiscal year 1979 totaled 10,207 pounds, compared to 1,064 pounds seized within the borders of the United States by the DEA. But there is a limit to the powers of DEA agents abroad. Under the Mansfield Amendment, "no officer or employee of the United States may engage or participate in any direct police arrest action in any foreign country with respect to narcotics control efforts." This limitation is intended "to insure that U.S. personnel do not become involved in sensitive, internal law enforcement operations which could adversely affect U.S. relations with that country."

Training and equipping local drug agents to enforce their own laws is not prohibited by the Mansfield Amendment, and the DEA has been very active in that regard. The DEA claims that interdiction of cocaine at the source is more effective, yielding seizures of larger and purer quantities than occur in the United States. The seizure data bear this out. In 1981, Peruvian authorities seized 5,930 kilograms of coca paste, 44 kilograms of cocaine base, 122 kilograms of cocaine hydrochloride, and 26,807 kilograms of coca leaves. Perhaps the single most dramatic demonstration of the power of enforcement close to the source occurred in 1984, when Colombian authorities effected the largest seizure of cocaine in history - almost 14 *tons* at Tranquilandia, a remote jungle "factory" with a capacity to process about 300 tons a year.

But the practical value of these seizures in achieving supply reduction is elusive. A Congressional subcommittee noted that in spite of massive seizures of cocaine in South America (6.7 tones in FY '79 and 8.4 tones in FY '80) there was no shortage in the United States – "no noticeable reduction in availability or increase in price of cocaine." Apparently, production of cocaine was so great that even seizure of about 16 to 20 percent of the total actually delivered to the United States in that period did not pinch supply enough to raise the black market price. Similarly, the massive 1984 Colombian seizure of 14 tons did not precipitate any general shortage of cocaine or major price increase in the United States.

As a result of its inability to seize enough supplies of cocaine at the source to make a difference, the United States has relied increasingly on pursuit of a long-term "solution" to the cocaine problem: displacement of coca cultivation by policies designed to encourage crop substitution. Since the 1970s, the State Department has been funding pilot projects to encourage peasant farmers to plant cash crops other than coca. Because such projects ignore the laws of the marketplace, they have not worked at all.

In 1981, the United States and Peru jointly undertook a major coca substitution program in the Upper Huallaga Valley (Tingo Maria), the largest illicit coca-growing region of Peru. The project targeted an area of 17,000 hectares of coca out of a national total of 40,000 to 60,000 hectares. The program was funded and administered by the State Department's Bureau of International Narcotics Matters (INM) and the Agency for International Development (AID). AID committed $15 million in loans and $3 million in grant money over a five-year period, augmented by an $8.5 million contribution from the Peruvian government.

The goal of Tingo Maria was to serve as an agricultural development project providing a mix of services needed to improve agricultural productivity in the region. That mix included research, training, road maintenance, marketing, potable water, sanitation, and other services. The intention was to develop, over the long term, viable economic alternatives to the production of coca for the black market, rather than simply to destroy illicit production. In this respect, the Tingo Maria project differed, for example, from Operation Green Sea II (1980), a cooperative enforcement effort with the Peruvian government which eradicated nearly 1,500 acres of coca and destroyed 12 million plants and 57 laboratories without lasting effect. "The long term impact of this one-time effort was primarily psychological." Nevertheless, the Tingo Maria project did include law enforcement funding to destroy illegal plants, an aspect of the program necessary to counteract powerful economic incentives to divert coca to the black market. Market realities dictate that no other crop "over the medium and long term will produce as much income to the farmer as coca."

Under the Peruvian law, all coca production acreage must be registered and the crops sold exclusively to ENACO, the official purchasing agency. In practice, the Peruvian government cannot enforce its monopoly purchasing system because traffickers pay up to five times the government price for the raw coca leaf. Accordingly, a law enforcement component remains necessary, and INM budgeted $17.5 million over a five-year period for enforcement and eradication of illicit plants.

The United States for years pressed the government of Bolivia to adopt a similar program of coca control. Bolivia responded in the early 1970s with a small pilot project to explore the potential for a crop substitution program. Agreements with Bolivia were signed in 1977 whereby the United States funded expanded research into the feasibility of alternative crops and assistance (to the National Directorate for the Control of Dangerous Substances) for a law enforcement program. The Bolivian government registered coca fields for licit production in 1977 and 1981, confining such cultivation to the departments of La Paz and Cochabamba. Plans to implement a crop substitution and development project on the Tingo Maria model were suspended following the "cocaine coup" of July 17, 1980. In response, the United States cut off all aid except food assistance and a small amount of seed money to PRODES. After several more military governments, the civilian government of Hernan Siles Zuazo acceded to power in 1982. That government, friendly to the United States, agreed in principle in 1983 to bring major portions of Bolivia's illicit coca fields under control by eradication and crop substitution. But because of the Zuazo government's tenuous grip on power, the control program remained largely in limbo, although soldiers in the field made some sporadic eradication forays.

The prospects for this two-pronged attack on the illicit cultivation of coca clearly are not promising in either Peru or Bolivia. In a 1978 review of the drug control effort in South America, the General Accounting Office (GAO) concluded that supplies of cocaine to the United States were increasing and that prospects for limiting coca production in South America were "unfavorable." That report could be regarded as old news. One could argue that the income substitution approach represented by the Tingo Maria project had not been tried prior to 1978; that the United States now spends several millions per year more on its South American drug control program; and that AID now has the benefit of experience in this area. But the negative assessment of the 1978 GAO report remains true because it reflects basic, structural factors, not technical problems to be solved by mere programmatic adjustments or even the commitment of more resources. Rather, the unfavorable prospects for displacement of coca are deeply rooted in the political, economic, and cultural life of the Andean nations.

Effective coca control in today's world is implausible for many reasons. First, coca chewing represents a centuries-old revered tradition among the Andean Indians. Coca was a sacrament to the Incas; and there is archeological evidence of coca chewing as early as 300 B.C. Daily coca chewing by the masses probably dates from the Spanish conquest of the Incas in the sixteenth century. Currently, some 4 million of the Indians in Bolivia and Peru, and perhaps 8 million worldwide, regularly chew coca. This represents a majority and near-majority of the two countries. The Bolivian population is 55 percent and 25-30 percent mestizo. Peruvians are 45 percent Indian and 37 percent mestizo.

Coca is thoroughly socialized in Bolivian society. It comes close to serving as a panacea, an all-purpose cure. People chew it or drink it as a tea daily, primarily in the workplace, as a mild stimulant and for the relief of cold, fatigue, and hunger. For this reason the agricultural workday contains several breaks for rest and the chewing of coca. Outside the workplace, "many social activities are solemnized by coca." "Coca fills the role of an all-purpose healing herb .... It might be said to combine the functions of coffee, tobacco, aspirin and bicarbonate of soda in our society." In addition, coca has nutritional value: 183 calories plus some vitamins and minerals in the average daily intake.

For these reasons, even though the Single Convention outlaws coca chewing after 1986, coca forms such an integral part of Indian culture that abolition in this century is out of the question. In fact, many Bolivians resent the pressures for coca eradication and substitution applied by the *Coloso del Norte*. As a result of this hostile reaction, "the American Embassy felt impelled .... to send a spokesman around the country to reassure Bolivians that the United States does not want to eradicate all coca crops." This concession – acceptance of traditional coca cultivation while seeking to ban excess coca grown to make cocaine – almost guarantees defeat of United States policy. Once the licit cultivation of coca is accepted as a fact of life, the economics of the black market dictate the planting or diversion of coca for production of cocaine. Total prohibition would in that respect clarify production ambiguities, although it would generate political controversy and universal defiance. What else should we expect?

Bolivia is the poorest nation in South America, with an annual per capita income in 1979 of $390 and the highest overall death rate in the Western Hemisphere. Life

...ancy for males is 45.7 years, 47.9 for women. Life for the Indians is not only poor ...hort, but hard. They live in remote, inhospitable areas under very primitive, unsanitary conditions. Nutrition is poor. Basic governmental services like hospitals are scarce. Infant morality is 77.3 per 100,000 births. The rate of illiteracy is 65 percent.

Peruvians fare somewhat better on these standard demographic indices, but they confront similar conditions of life. Per capita GNP in Peru in 1979 was $800, ranking it 68th of 145 countries worldwide. The literacy rate was 45 percent. Male life expectancy was 52.59 years, 55.48 for females. The level of hardship appears to be somewhat less onerous than in Bolivia, but Peru is a poor, Third World nation nevertheless.

In both countries, the people who grow and use coca perch on the bottom rung of the social and economic ladder. In meeting the challenge of survival in a subsistence economy, coca is a critical resource, one of the few cash crops that grows well. For many growers, it is the only source of subsistence. Even where there are alternatives, the economics of coca are compelling. In some regions of Bolivia, for example, a hectare crop of coca is worth about $5,000, compared to $500 for a crop of coffee.

Francisco Berbetty Urguieta, a 55-year-old farmer, says that depending on supply and demand, 50 pounds of coca leaves sell at anywhere from about 350,000 pesos to 700,000 pesos, about $175-$350, at the official exchange rate.

"I get three crops a year from these [coca] plants," Berbetty says. His orange trees, he says, "take eight years to develop, then you get only one crop a year. The banana gives good results, but not as good as coca."

Two years earlier, in Coripata, Bolivia, a center of the coca trade in the Yungas (La Paz) region, the author was told by a leader of the *campesinos'* labor organization that coffee, oranges, or other cash crops do not grow well in the relatively poor soil of the Yungas. By contrast, coca fares well, yielding three crops per year. He said, "Coca is our bread; without coca we die." He emphasized an additional dimension in the proliferation of the coca trade. The *campesinos* felt befriended by the traffickers, who gave them cash advances or loans to tide them over between crops. By contrast, they described themselves as victimized or oppressed by the *narcoticos* who had been enforcing government controls (before the Chulumani massacre of October, 1982).

Public sentiment similarly favors Roberto Suarez, the central figure in the Bolivian cocaine trade, and explains in part of his ability to elude his would-be captors. Serving as generous benefactor to his countrymen in the Beni region, he had underwritten education costs for an entire district. As the modern-day Robin Hood of Bolivia, he benefits from the admiration and affection of the populace, who protect him from the government. Carlos Lehder enjoyed similar popularity for a time in Colombia, and the Ochoa family and others continue to do so.

Given these economic and social incentives, the cultivation of coca for the black market has proliferated rapidly, with an estimated 125,000 families in South America earning their livelihood by growing coca. The growth of cultivation in Bolivia has been particularly rapid, estimated by the 1981 NIE at 75 percent from 1977 to 1981. The increase in the vast Chapare region has been even greater, in the range of 183 to 268 percent between 1978 and 1980.

With the first taste of a condition approaching material sufficiency, the *campesinos* of Bolivia have become understandably militant in defense of the coca trade. For example, a mob of 200 coca growers in Chulumani murdered seven Bolivian narcotics agents following a raid by the agents in October, 1982. The government was forced to recall most of its agents from the field because of the danger of further killings. Apart from this violent incident, growers have mounted a general counterattack against government pressures. Thus, in 1982, a small manual and herbicidal eradication project covering 80 to 90 hectares in Yapacani, instigated by the United States, became the subject of extensive criticism in the Bolivian media. A Bolivian television program criticised the eradication project as outside interference with Bolivian concerns. Even the Catholic Church in the city of La Paz denounced the United States "for imposing a policy to liquidate part of our countryside, where the farmer lives exclusively from his products."

Because abuse of cocaine has not (yet) become a serious problem in Bolivian society, the *campesinos* argue that the United States should not force Bolivians to pay the price for solving a Yankee problem. As a result, when the governments of Bolivia and the United States issued a joint communiqué in 1983 announcing an agreement in principle for control of coca by substitution and eradication, a conclave of growers' union representatives denounced the accord. Two years later, hundreds of peasants marched through La Paz to the United States Embassy, shouting, "Long live coca, death to the Yankees." In short, there is no mandate in Bolivian society for the suppression of coca, their "gift from God."

Given these circumstances, how can the Bolivian government possibly fulfill its agreement to wipe out coca production in excess of traditional, legitimate needs within five years through eradication and crop substitution? The government faces intractable problems. First, the thoroughly corrupt enforcement apparatus inherited from the Garcia Meza regime of "Black Eagles" had to be purged and reconstituted, starting with the shutting down of the special narcotics squad because it had "covered up and participated in the cocaine trafficking." Corruption still runs deep, but it almost doesn't matter in light of a more fundamental barrier to enforcement. The simple truth of the matter is that Bolivia depends on coca. The *campesinos* who grow or carry coca, or otherwise find work as drones in the army of cocaine workers, rely on coca to make the difference between subsistence and poverty. The government, for its part, sinking under the weight of an annual inflation rate that ran close to 3,000 percent in 1985 and a staggering foreign debt of almost $5 billion on which it has defaulted, cannot possibly be eager to shut down its primary source of hard currency. In 1984, coca brought in roughly $2 billion in foreign exchange, at least three times the value of Bolivia's leading (official) export, tin.

As a result of this ambivalence, very little coca has been uprooted since the coca substitution and eradication accord between Bolivia and the United States was announced in 1983. In August, 1984, President Zuazo ordered 1,200 troops to destroy coca crops in the Chapare region, where nearly a third of Bolivia's coca is grown. Half that number actually took to the field, and some of them gave local growers advance warning of their raid. One general resigned rather than take action against his countrymen. The elite, 130-man Bolivian army unit known as the Leopards, funded by the United States, has seized bundles of harvested leaves from peasants, and some coca paste, but their "enforcement" has been little more than a gesture. Finally, they were ordered in October, 1984, to make a sweep of the remote Beni region where Suarez and other cocaine "lords" operate huge, feudal-style coca plantations and cocaine-processing plants on a huge scale, up to 100,000 acres. Some have private airstrips. Though they raided several ranches, the Leopards failed to find Suarez; and they seized merely 380 kilos of cocaine.

To fully appreciate Bolivia's enforcement climate, it is necessary to consider its chronic political and economic instability. It brought 199 changes of government from 1825 to the election of President Zuazo, who was kidnapped in 1984 and later released. The delicacy of Bolivian political control obviously limits the power of the government to enforce a law that runs counter to the vital economic interests of large numbers of its own citizens. As a result, in the national elections of 1985, no major candidate spoke out against illicit coca cultivation or promised a crackdown on the cocaine traffic.

BOLIVIAN POLLS SPEAK NO COKE EVIL
WON'T BITE HAND FEEDING RURAL VOTERS IN DRUG AREA

Ucuerena, Bolivia – Fearful of alienating thousands of peasants who earn their living from coca farming, all 18 presidential candidates in Sunday's elections are avoiding debate on the growing problem of cocaine trafficking to the United States.

"Addressing the subject of coca is like walking on the edge of a sword," Victor Paz Estenssoro, the candidate for the Revolutionary National Movement, said in an interview in this village in southwestern Bolivia.

Alberto Diaz Romero, a coca grower from the nearby Chapare lowlands, put it more bluntly: "Any candidate who goes into the Chapare saying he is going to eradicate coca will not come out alive."

In both Peru and Bolivia, the failure of coca control is not a temporary aberration but a function of culture, tradition, and the weakness and poverty of underdevelopment. These basic social conditions render effective enforcement against coca impossible. Widespread corruption in the enforcement agencies, the judiciary, and elsewhere in government is endemic. Indeed, the central governments do not necessarily control major portions of the coca-growing countryside, where traffickers rule like feudal warlords. As the Bolivians avoid going after Suarez in his fiefdom, so the Peruvian police stay out of the "wild border areas" around Lake Titicaca, where government agents were expelled by force.

Even were it to secure control over the remote coca-growing regions, the government would still confront the surprising technical difficulty of eradicating the coca bush. No paraquat-style aerial spraying technique has yet been developed. Because coca is generally grown near or interspersed with other crops in small plots of a hectare or two, chopping the stalk and manually painting the stump with 2-4-D (diesel oil) is necessary to avoid herbicidal damage to other crops. The labor-intensive process also requires that the coca bushes be uprooted manually. But uprooting worsens an already bad erosion problem on the steep slopes in high rainfall areas.

Additionally, the vastness of the illicit coca-growing regions and the abundance of leaves produced in relation to black market needs make the whole idea of crop control seem hopeless, if not actually silly, in view of U.S. inability to kill off a massive domestic marijuana crop. Satellite surveillance revealed approximately 68,000 acres under cultivation just in the Chapare region of Bolivia, with a projected 1982 yield of 82,000 tons of leaves capable of producing in excess of 200 metric tons of cocaine, four times the United States market at that time. Even after a total "scorched-earth" eradication of the Chapare, the productive capacities of the Yungas region of Bolivia and Peru would remain intact.

Ultimately, the economics of coca and cocaine render programs of eradication and crop substitution little more than pie in the sky. Coca enables a poor nation to accrue enormous amounts of foreign exchange. Bolivia's dependence on coca has already been noted. Peru earns $850 million annually. The dilemma that drug-exporting nations face is suggested by the "immediate, wide and generous amnesty" on all illegal income declared in 1982 by the President of Colombia.

Even in Peru, which is politically more stable than Bolivia and less economically dependent upon the cocaine trade, the government backed down in the face of political pressure from the coca growers, repealing its previous commitment to declare illegal and eradicate all coca in the Upper Huallaga Valley. A 1982 law repealed the 1980 decree of a state of emergency in the Upper Huallaga Valley and modified the total illegality of coca cultivation in the region. Turbulence continued in Tingo Maria, however, and the President responded by declaring another state of emergency in 1984. In November, a band of some 50 traffickers "burst into a jungle campsite and opened fire with automatic weapons," killing 19 Peruvians working on a coca control crop.

Even before that dramatic turn of events, a delegation of the House Select Committee headed by Chairman Charles Rangel made an official visit to Tingo Maria in August, 1983, and found that the illicit cultivation of coca had become "a tidal wave." Representatives of the government of Peru told the delegation that severe economic recession and a combination of disastrous droughts and floods had drained the country's resources so greatly that it could not organize and support the forces needed to effectively destroy the illicit cultivation, estimated at 36,000 metric tons, or supress the trafficking in coca paste and cocaine. (The delegation found similar conditions in Bolivia, where cultivation of coca had "dramatically escalated out of control.")

The delegation's suggestion in its report, that "dedicated implementation" of control agreements could "within a few years" bring the coca problem "under control," borders on the fantastic. For the committee to formally recommend that the governments of Peru and Bolivia initiate programs to progressively eliminate the practice of coca leaf chewing by December, 1986, manifests a lack of realism and a disregard of the survival needs of those countries.

Ultimately, the State Department concedes that cultivation of coca "is a social problem that will probably never be solved. Our goal is to make it more manageable." But even that modest goal should be discounted in light of the demonstrated, though unintentional, tendency of agricultural development projects to facilitate expanded cultivation of illicit coca in new areas. For example, United States foreign aid further opened the Chapare region of Bolivia to settlement and development by the building of bridges and roads. With no real markets for other agricultural products, nearly all of the recent settlers in the Chapare grow coca as their main crop. A similar phenomenon occurred in Peru. When an all-weather road from Tingo Maria was built, "it provided easy access to illicit coca plantations for the traffickers."

On the other hand, enforcement in the Tingo Maria area did result in shifting the illicit coca-growing region further into the remote *selva* (jungle). But thousands more square miles of such territory remain available and are rapidly being brought under cultivation. Similarly, brand new acreage in western Brazil has been planted. Thus, new coca cultivation in other countries would undercut whatever success is achieved in Bolivia and Peru. Even if coca were effectively curtailed in *all* of South America, cultivation could shift to other countries, including Indonesia, Madagascar, Guyana, and Sri Lanka (see Figure 4). Coca was in fact grown on a large scale in Java, which until World War II provided much of the coca leaf for the world supply of pharmaceutical cocaine. It doesn't take much, either. A student of mine once calculated that the entire crop of coca leaf necessary to supply the 1980 United States black market would only require about 12 square miles of land. The equivalent figure for 1984 would be about double, not very much considering the vast wilderness areas of the Andes.

Figure 4: Effects of Law Enforcement on Cultivation of Coca Leaf in New Growing Areas

An effective crackdown in Bolivia and Peru would manifest itself in higher prices for coca leaf (P2). At some point, higher prices would make production in less efficient growing areas in these and other countries profitable. The introduction of new sources of supply (SS") would then ease the pressure on price (P3) by increasing total production (Q3).

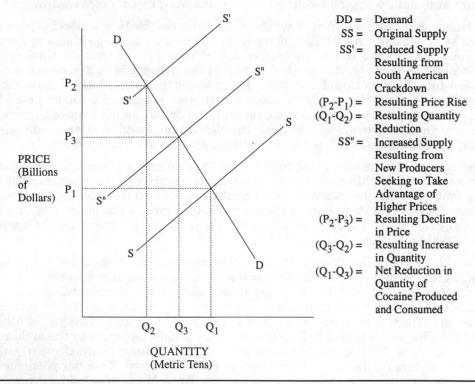

DD =	Demand
SS =	Original Supply
SS' =	Reduced Supply Resulting from South American Crackdown
(P_2-P_1) =	Resulting Price Rise
(Q_1-Q_2) =	Resulting Quantity Reduction
SS" =	Increased Supply Resulting from New Producers Seeking to Take Advantage of Higher Prices
(P_2-P_3) =	Resulting Decline in Price
(Q_3-Q_2) =	Resulting Increase in Quantity
(Q_1-Q_3) =	Net Reduction in Quantity of Cocaine Produced and Consumed

PRICE (Billions of Dollars)

QUANTITY (Metric Tens)

In the very long term, of course, it is possible that the development of a modern socioeconomic infrastructure will transform the conditions of life in Andean Peru and Bolivia and thereby facilitate some measure of control of coca and cocaine production. Short of such a transformation, however, neither the United States nor the source countries can realistically expect to achieve significant limitations on the supply of coca for cocaine without resorting to some radical or violent "fix" such as military occupation of the coca-growing regions. Even then, it is doubtful whether the weak governments involved have the political and economic power to sustain such repression over the long term. Peru, for example, confronts a serious terrorist problem in the Maoist-oriented "Shining Path" insurgency. Bolivia struggles merely to govern itself for more than one year per government. The United States Government exhibits incredibly powerful denial mechanisms in holding out crop control as even a palliative for the "cocaine problem."

29.   Full Tilt Towards a No-Win 'Vietnam' War on Drugs

Tim Maylon

'AMSTERDAM is the cesspit of Europe', huffed Tory MEP Andrew Pierce at a press conference on 1 October. 'The poison from there has spread around. It's like one man with a foul smell in his garden. I believe the Dutch government ought to be looking to their consciences.'

His remarks were the opening shot of a bitter European controversy about methods of managing drug use and abuse. Pierce is a member of the 'European Committee of Enquiry Into The Drugs Problem In The Member States Of The Community' whose report was voted through the European parliament last week under the slogan 'The European Parliament Takes Drugs Seriously.' The report recommends uniform drug enforcement and sentencing approaches throughout the Community - a direct attack on Holland's long-standing liberal drugs policies. Pierce concluded his remarkable concoction of metaphors with a call for fresh pressure on the Netherlands 'to get its stables cleared out.'

Five members of the enquiry committee, a Green, a Communist, and three Socialists including the Labour MEP for London East, Carole Tongue, were so dismayed by the committee's off-hand rejection of drug law liberalisation that they produced a minority report, published simultaneously. This demands further study into the whole question of legalising certain drugs so as to curb the massive illicit market. Pierce's response was characteristic: 'Is that Labour party policy? Is Kinnock going to announce that the Labour party is going soft on drugs?'

Pierce's tone is typical of the present climate in which critics of total war on drugs risk character assassination and accusations of being 'soft on drugs' reminiscent of Senator McCarthy's insults to people he accused of being 'soft on communism'. This witch-hunt is indeed largely an American import. Nancy and Ronald lead the war from their fireside while lesser politicians, both Republican and Democrat, vie to come up with yet more repressive measures in time for the crucial mid-term November elections. As a result, confused children are turning in their sniffing and smoking parents, traffickers are being threatened with the death penalty, a third of all US *Fortune 500* corporations are instituting employee urine tests - some of which will show up brown bread and poppy seed consumption as drug positive - and cannabis is being targeted as 'a gateway drug.' Recidivist users are threatened with incarceration in profit-making, privatised prison camps.

The main institutions so far to have raised objections to this climate are the American military, already ensconced in anti-drugs actions in Bolivia (who fear being involved in

Tim Malyon: 'Full Tilt Towards a No-Win 'Vietnam' War on Drugs', *NEW STATESMAN*, 17 October, 1986. © New Statesman 1986. Reprinted with permission of New Statesman and Society.

a war they are even less likely to win than Vietnam), and the American Civil Liberties Union, who argue that drug testing is a fundamental invasion of privacy. Both the ACLU and employee unions are opposing Reagan's 'jar wars' attempt to urine test about half of all Federal employees.

Current cocaine and 'crack' hysteria stems from the USA. (Crack is a cocaine paste derivative which can be smoked and delivers an intense, short-lived high followed by a depressive 'down'.) For nearly two years, we have been warned that a wave of cocaine powder, heroin's 'twin sister of death' - the phrase is Home Office minister David Mellor's - is about to break on our shores. Massive media and political attention has been concentrated on this substance. Yet under our proverbial noses amphetamines ('speed' or 'whizz') have long been one of the most widely used illicit drugs in the UK. There were five times more amphetamine seizures in the UK in 1985 than cocaine seizures. Amphetamine seizures now exceed heroin seizures and rose by 20 per cent over the previous year, while cocaine busts dropped by a quarter.

The big killers

Amphetamines are of course home produced. Occasional use does not generally cause problems. Damage from chronic abuse, however, has long been appreciated by professionals and neglected by those responsible for providing services, just as there is a disgraceful lack of facilities for tranquiliser abuse, a prescribed drug problem which dwarfs all illegal drugs in sheer numbers of users.

But then, busting bath-tub amphetamine production facilities in Devon and Cornwall, or providing more money for appropriate counselling and prevention services for tranquiliser addicts, does not have the media attraction to compete with David Mellor's recent flights of fantasy over South American jungles. Mellor threw away £1.5 million in grants to South American governments for additional, and certain to be ineffective, law enforcement against a drug which the Americans had persuaded him was important. The headlines looked good and he was promptly promoted on return. The irony of such profligate opportunism has not been lost on the alcohol and tobacco prevention lobbies. Mellor's £1.5 million wasted in South American constitutes over half Britain's entire budget for alcohol education and information.

The Advisory Council On The Misuse Of Drugs estimates that there are 40-70,000 problem drug users in the UK, compared to 750,000-1 million alcohol users at risk and 14.8 million tobacco smokers. There are 5,000-8,000 deaths due to alcohol every year, 100,000 due to tobacco, 200-250 due to illegal drugs and solvents. Youth drinking and smoking are both on the increase. Statistics on car accidents, suicides, violent crime, marital and child abuse, and psychiatric illness due to alcohol are horrifying. The tobacco industry spends over £100 million per annum in the UK on advertising and promotion, and provides the government with £4 billion of revenue. Only £7 million of this is ploughed back into education and information campaigns, despite the DHSS estimate that smoking-related diseases cost £370 million per annum to treat.

This is not to deny the misery and suffering caused by drug addiction, both to users and their friends and families. Nor is it to deny that cocaine and 'crack' may cause problems in the UK. What is important is to bring all drug problems into comparative focus, so that political hyperbole and rhetoric bear some relation to real needs. One of the silliest parts of the European committee of enquiry report, and therefore one of the most illuminating, is its attempted definition of 'drugs' as 'those chemical or plant-derived substances which can cause a user to experience physical, mental or emotional changes and are illegal.'

The crux, of course, is whether David Mellor's jungle warfare is winnable. During my research for this article, speaking with Home Office officials, a senior customs officer, politicians and drug workers in the field, I could find nobody to say that law enforcement could have a significant impact on the illicit market. The European report estimates that 5 per cent of illicit drugs destined for the EEC are seized. Even the report's convenor, Tory MEP Sir Jack Stewart-Clark, reckoned that if the entire armoury of additional law enforcement measures which he is demanding were enacted, 'no more than 20 per cent might be seized - significant reduction, perhaps not; prevention from significant increase, perhaps yes'. David Mellor himself admits that government 'can guarantee to seize but a limited proportion of what comes here.' Even if 20 per cent were seized, it would be unlikely to make a dent on street availability. In producer countries there are already too many illicit crops chasing the consumer market. The US State Department can confirm this. 'Worldwide production of illicit opium, coca leaf and cannabis in 1985,' it stated recently, 'was still many times the amount currently consumed by drug abusers.'

The drug war, however, continues regardless, developing ever newer weapons which inevitably erode precious freedoms. The latest addition to this armoury in the UK is The Drug Trafficking Offences Act which received the royal assent on 8 July. Similar legislation has been enacted in Italy and the USA. The bill received all-party support in parliament despite the fact that it overturns a fundamental cornerstone of British justice, the presumption that a defendant is innocent until proven guilty. Anyone convicted in Crown Court of a drug trafficking offence, however small, is now liable to have all assets acquired during the last six years confiscated, unless they can prove that the assets were legally acquired. This assumption, that assets are illegal unless proven otherwise, is drily described in the *Law Society Gazette*, not an organ prone to overstatement, as 'most unusual in a criminal statute.' The NCCL bitterly opposes it.

The act grants wide powers to police and customs to search suspected traffickers' bank and personal records, and files on them held by government departments. These powers override any secrecy obligations or other statutory restrictions on disclosure of information.

If this is the new weapon, will it succeed? The *Law Society Gazette* has already stated that the act cannot grapple with one fundamental problem - destroying 'the real nerve centre of the operation.' A senior City accountant who has seen the provisions is likewise not optimistic about success. Laundering money is basically a system of passing funds from account to account or through businesses under different names to conceal its origins: 'It's really not difficult if you know how to work the system. The smart people will know the right methods to avoid leaving a trail.' Both the accountant and Jane Goodsir from Release are in agreement that the people most likely to be put on the street by this new law are small-business-person drug users who do some dealing on the side.

It seems extraordinary, in the face of widespread evidence that the drugs war is NOT WINNABLE that so little attention has been paid to alternative strategies.

The key to any fresh approach towards drug use and abuse is acceptance of the fact that humankind has been using a bewildering array of mind-bending substances since the dawn of civilisation and is unlikely to change its ways. A recent Radio 4 documentary, George Monbiot's 'Dreamflower and The Toadstool Spell,' should be compulsory listening for all involved in drug policy formulation. Monbiot demonstrated how massive slices of our culture, folk tradition and religion derive from drug use, from the earliest shamanistic trances to the average sixty thousand pounds of opium consumed every year in 19th century England, to tea, coffee, alcohol and tobacco. 'Our folklore, part of our history, perhaps our religion,' Monbiot concluded, 'are all dependent on chemicals that come from fungi, animals and plants. We are following a tradition of drug dependency.'

Drugs tend to have their most destructive effect on cultures when first introduced, before 'codes of consumption,' to borrow anthropologist Anthony Henman's phrase, have developed. This applies to crack in Miami ghettos; or alcohol abuse in American Indian cultures already adept at coping with a potent array of psychedelic vegetables.

Professor Norman Zinberg MD, from Harvard University, has been researching additive behaviour since the '60s. Widely respected during the Kennedy/Johnson/Carter era of relatively open-thinking on drug issues, he is no longer flavour of the month in Washington. Zinberg has conducted a series of studies in 'controlled' drug use. He cites the example of LSD, a drug which received massive 'shock horror' publicity in the sixties and seventies, and was involved in large numbers of hospital admissions for psychotic behaviour. Its availability and use in the UK and USA has remained remarkably constant over the years. It was my experience, working with Release and other agencies, especially at 'rock' festival emergency facilities, that casualties from LSD use dropped dramatically over the years, even at times when supplies were widely available.

Vim in the veins

Studies in the USA confirm these subjective impressions. 'By the early 1970's,' Zinberg asserts, 'the admission of psychedelic users to mental health facilities for the treatment of acute or even long-term psychotic episodes following drug use, which had occurred frequently in the late sixties and through 1970, had all but disappeared.' Zinberg has recently carried out an important study of 98 heroin users in the Boston area, contacting people through colleges, clinics, friends, and newspaper advertisements. Out of 98 users, he found 61 'controlled' users, who were clearly not addicted and whose lives were not centred around the drug; 30 'compulsive' users; and seven 'marginals'. The controlled users employed an array of strategies, such as not using on consecutive days, only using at weekends, never using before work, not using to counter depression, cleaning up their living area before using, strict budgeting of funds for drugs, not using alone, to cite just a few.

Zinberg concludes that 'emphasis should be shifted from the prevention of all use, to the prevention of dysfunctional use,' comparing good drug education to good sex education. He believes that prohibition actually inhibits the teaching and accumulation of sensible 'codes of consumption'. Recent events underline the sagacity of his words. If some of the British government's drug advertising budget had been spent on putting across the most basic of harm prevention messages, *never to use alcohol in combination with any type of opiate drugs*, Olivia Channon and many others might still be alive today. One third of all illicit drug overdoes in the UK last year occurred in combination with alcohol.

Aids highlights the ethics of harm reduction and prohibition, as it spreads swiftly among injecting addicts who share needles, especially in Scotland where few doctors are prepared to prescribe injectable drugs or needles. Making needles and syringes available with good health education information is a fundamental harm reduction strategy, yet so far, the government has refused to do it. A Scottish Office report now recommends that clean needles and syringes should be made available to addicts. The unpalatable logic of such a move, without any further attempts at harm reduction, is that addicts dying from Vim in their veins is not a legitimate matter for public concern – until they pose a threat to the general population by spreading the Aids virus.

Harm reduction and teaching sensible use patterns has long been the accepted strategy of those concerned with reducing alcohol abuse. The latest Health Education Council booklet *That's The Limit* promotes the slogan 'Why spoil a good thing?' Karin Pappenheim from Alcohol Concern emphasises how health education has abandoned exhortations to stop drinking, 'because that just doesn't work. We are not an anti-drink organisation. People need to learn to be sensible drinkers.' She also believes from a health education standpoint that all drugs should be brought under the same umbrella. 'You can't deal with one drug without looking at the rest. We have to sell all the addictive substances in the same context,' adding that discouraging heroin use may simply lead to increased alcohol abuse, among the young in particular.

Prohibition causes an illicit, uncontrolled market to thrive. The alternative is an orderly introduction of graded controls, which make harmful substances more available and less expensive than more harmful substances. Nobody is suggesting selling heroin across the counter in sweet jars. In fact people who favour abolishing prohibition often take a hard line on the whole area of drug supply, including alcohol and tobacco. They tend, for instance, towards banning advertising. I find it ironic that the most ardent Anglo-American drug warriors are often also the most ardent supporters of the free market and lack of controls on tobacco and alcohol.

There is some evidence that long-term usage does not increase, may even *decrease*, as controls on illicit substances are lifted. All the studies to date have shown no significant difference in usage between decriminalised states and others. New statistics on the USA publicised this 11 October show virtually all illicit drug use to be on the *decrease* – other than cocaine.

The only Western nation still experimenting with quasi-legal supply is Holland, now that the UK has almost given up its heroin prescribing system (*see box*). Trafficking and possession of all common illicit drugs, such as cannabis, heroin and cocaine, are illegal in Holland but Dutch law includes an 'expediency principle' whereby the Public Prosecutions Department can refrain from bringing criminal proceedings 'on grounds deriving from the general good.' Cannabis use and possession are accordingly not usually prosecuted, nor is small-scale supply, particularly in certain quasi-licensed venues.

Since this policy was implemented in 1976, cannabis use in Holland has actually decreased. In 1976, 3 per cent of young people aged 15-16, and 10 per cent of people aged 17-18, had 'occasionally smoked' cannabis. In 1985 these figures were 2 per cent and 6 per cent respectively. In 1983 only 12 per cent of the 14-24 age group in Holland had ever smoked cannabis, as compared to 18 per cent in West Germany (1982). West Germany has no legal supply system for cannabis, and exerts tremendous pressure on the Netherlands government to terminate its own. Cannabis use in West Germany is also rising, in contrast to Holland.

Soft protests of former custodian of 'British System'

H B 'BING SPEAR, a legendary figure in contemporary British drug lore, retired two weeks ago as chief inspector of the Home Office drugs inspectorate where he had worked since 1952. The inspectorate supervises production and distribution of legal supplies of controlled drugs such as heroin, in particular doctors' prescriptions to addicts whom they are treating. As its chief since 1977, Spear had a unique knowledge and experience of the 'British System' of maintaining chronic addicts on legal supplies of opiate drugs, including heroin, which lasted from 1926 to the early eighties. He laments its demise.

Bing is a remarkable figure, a calm besuited Home Office official who 'learned the street', then stayed in touch. He also cares. 'The legend was, he knew all the addicts personally, which was only a slight exaggeration,' remembers Rev Ken Leech, famous for his pioneering work with addicts in the sixties. 'He was very much the sort of person whom addicts would visit and ask for advice. They trusted him, respected him, thought the world of him, which is remarkable. It would only have taken one slip to have lost that.' Although Spear has long enjoyed the respect of addicts and street agencies, successive governments, as well as a powerful clique of senior consultants in the addiction clinics, haven't always appreciated his experience. 'He's been very much a lone fighter,' Leech concludes, 'and I'm not sure people took too much notice of him in the corridors of power.'

Spear particularly regrets the decision, taken by a group of clinic doctors during the late seventies and early eighties, firstly virtually to stop all heroin prescribing, then to stop prescribing injectable drugs, then to deny the validity of long term maintenance prescribing as a treatment mode for chronic addicts. These clinic consultants effectively closed down the 'British System', a unique experiment in harm prevention, without a word of external consultant – at precisely the time that large amounts of illicit Chinese and Iranian heroin were appearing on the street.

'Inevitably it is a matter for the doctors how they treat addicts.' Spear now says to the *NS*, 'What I find difficult to accept is that they have done that in isolation from the problem. There is a relationship between what a doctor does with his prescription pad, how he treats an addict, and what happens to the broader problem. I just wonder what would have happened, whether we could have contained the problem for a while, delayed what we've got now, if those decisions hadn't been taken. It's difficult to say. We would still have a problem, there's no doubt about that. But I think there has been a tendency to place the interests of the medical profession ahead of the interests of the country as a whole.

Spear remembers two Canadian addicts who used to come and see him at the Home Office. 'They used to come in to see me fairly often for a chat. Certainly they could walk in and out of the Home Office and nobody would know they were addicts. Neatly-dressed, well-behaved, reasonable looking, they were on fairly heavy heroin doses, both of them, injecting, had been for yonks. There are stable addicts – the argument is of course is about how many. I'm certainly not arguing that young people who are smoking heroin should be given injectable 'scripts' [Prescriptions]. That's manifestly nonsense.

And what about the distinctions between legal and illegal drugs? 'I heard a lady recently talking about healthy drinking as not harmful. If you say that about drugs, you're in trouble.' He paused and smiled. 'I'd just like to point out the contradiction.'

A problem of supply

Eddy Engelsman is a medical sociologist who is responsible for advising the Dutch government on both alcohol and drug policies. He believes the Dutch will emphatically reject the European committee of enquiry's call for harmonisation of Community sentencing policy, which would destroy Dutch drug philosophy: 'We find it strange, waging drug crusades, giving up fundamental citizens' rights for drugs. The Dutch people form one tight block now, because we are attacked. We do take drug problems seriously, and we have creative, new ideas about them. Now, what we are doing has become unthinkable.'

There are few politicians outside Holland prepared to think the unthinkable. The Labour MP for London East, Carole Tongue, is one. Rare among politicians, she knows what she is talking about in this unpopular field, and is prepared to put her reputation on the line. As a member of the European committee of enquiry she is sufficiently exasperated by the blinkered attitudes of the majority to share in the minority report, whose main recommendation is the establishment of a European study group, and holding of a European conference to look at 'the legislation of drugs in order to eradicate drug trafficking.' After pressure at last week's Strasbourg debate a diluted version of the demand was accepted.

British Labour Party drugs policy remains at core simply a more humane version of Tory policy. Robin Corbett and Frank Dobson, respectively responsible for law enforcement and health, both want more money spent on rehabilitation and prevention. Corbett wants more uniformed customs officers. Dobson supports the provision of needles and syringes to injecting addicts to prevent Aids. They also both want greater restrictions on alcohol, and especially on tobacco advertising. 'Tobacco is the only industry that kills a hundred thousand of its customers every year,' Dobson remarked wryly.

Most politicians with whom I have spoken, left, right or centre, seem to have devoted little original thought to the drug issue, Lords Melchett and Gifford, Peter Archer and Clive Soley being the notable socialist exceptions. The drugs topic, like 'sex' and 'violence', attracts and repels, often inviting rigid, emotionally conditioned defensive reactions from politicians and public alike. The press panders to this.

Labour Party reluctance to face up to fundamental drug policy issues is electorally understandable but could be a grave mistake in the long run. Carole Tongue goes to the heart of the matter in her concluding remark to the *NS*: 'How are we going to face up to the problem of supply of these substances? - because we're not going to get rid of them. The mafia is in *favour* of prohibition. We really should be asking who is benefiting from the present illegal regime.'

We have been told so many times now what massive sums 'the drug barons' earn that we are becoming immune to the implications. Cannabis is now the second largest cash crop in the USA after corn. Of the $30 billion in Eurocurrency deposited in Swiss banks, 20 per cent is estimated to be drug money. Scotland Yard reckons that over £200 million was spent on illicit drugs in 1984 in London alone.

That kind of cash does not just go into yachts, fast cars and high living. The Sicilian mafia owns massive sectors of the legitimate economy, including much of the construction industry, and buys policitians. Money generated by drug trafficking is creating, right now, states within states, in the law enforcement, political and business sectors. People controlling that money have generally been of right wing or far right persuasion. There is also a disturbing, well-documented history of state security services funding operations outside democratic control through the drug traffic.

It is time that the drug warriors like David Mellor realised, not only that their policies are ineffective and increasingly curbing our basic freedoms, but also that they nurture organisations which pose a fundamental threat to our democratic institutions. It is time to start disarming, before it is too late.

The Legalisation of Drugs

The three texts presented in this section outline the main elements in the *debate* on whether currently illicit drugs should be legalised. The previous nine sections however, should have provided the reader with important background information with which to more effectively contextualise and make sense of the dualism which the debate throws up. To try and decide purely by reading or listening to the opposing arguments for and against legalisation without recourse to other information is difficult because you ultimately have to choose who you believe (or want to believe?). In this sense it is recommended that to make the best use of this section it is not read alone but contextualised through the other readings.

Decisions about whether drugs and their use should or should not be permitted need to take into account the relative harm that is caused by them. We have, for example, seen that for the most part the effects of drugs are exaggerated, that our view of them is frequently distorted by the media and the seriousness of the drugs 'problem' is often not a reflection of the number of users but *who* is using them. In addition, sometimes it may also be a useful diversion away from other social problems around which there is less consensus. We have also seen that it is useful to make certain distinctions between understanding various problems normally considered to be caused by the existence of and consequent use of illicit drugs, such as crime and violence, and their correlation with them. For many, much drug related crime is created and/or exacerbated not by the use of particular drugs, but by the illegal context in which they are distributed through the black market. We have seen that traditional methods of resolving the problem through recourse to harsher penalties, increased policing and drug 'education' have failed and continue to fail. Drug use continues to grow, the volume of drugs seized continues to increase as does the number of seizures made. The price of drugs remain low and in many cases continues to fall. True, there must be some point at which the forces of prohibition could overwhelm the forces of supply, but given the extent of failure to date this may have costs for freedom and civil liberties which extend far beyond the problems presented by drug use itself. Indeed, as Szasz indicates, this point has for some already been crossed. That conventional prohibitionist policy has failed (if, as its stated aims it is to prevent the use and growth of drug use remain) needs to be further contextualised by the realisation that (as is now happening in the United States) resources for a war on drugs are likely to be penned back at various times. How can a war be won when its resources are dependent upon the vagaries of the political climate? In this sense, one thing that is certain is that current policies do not appear to have the capability to resolve the problems with which they are commissioned to deal with. The Dutch, as we know, operate a less punitive system, more tolerant of drug *use* and some of the problems encountered by users in other systems are lessened. The half-way house of the Dutch model, however, cannot resolve many of the underlying problems which will remain whilst the market in drugs is an illicit one. Mishan takes us through one legaliser's perspective leaning heavily on an economic model. If the highly profitable black market produces organised and disorganised crime, institutional corruption, substances which are more dangerous because their composition is adulterated and

338

their purity levels inconsistent, high levels of violence related to the dealing and trafficking of drugs, then the argument, simply stated, is that replacing the black market with a legal one would remove the basis upon which these problems are constructed. Wilson presents the case against the legalisation of drugs. He argues that prohibition has had and will continue to have a preventative role and that legalisation would lead to an 'exponential' increase in addiction. He questions the reliability of the legalisers' arguments and suggests that movement away from the existing position is not desirable as such an experiment would in all likelihood be too costly in human terms. Szasz, in a 'classic' article now over twenty years old, revisits some of the basic ground. He is not 'soft' on drugs but suggests that the drug laws prohibiting personal use have no place in a democratic and liberal society. If we are allowed to kill ourselves through ingesting alcohol and smoking tobacco, why not through opium or heroin or cocaine? Ultimately, Szasz revisits a theme which has come up time and again in this Reader: the idea that drug use, and addiction in particular, is actually a moral and political problem, dressed up as a medical and pharmacological problem. Szasz is a clear supporter of the legalisation of drugs and their use not because they will necessarily reduce aggregate harm (although he believes that to be true) but because prohibition has consequences for personal liberty and the incursion of the state which are unreasonable.

The reality of course is that no policy will be fully successful if success is measured in all or nothing terms. Arguing in terms of, 'this will happen if we do this' or 'that will happen if we do that' is resting on an uninformed notion of how policy gets implemented, undermined, distorted and ultimately has to deal with a range of contingent circumstances which make it vulnerable to unintended and unexpected outcomes. The real issue then revolves around which policy which would prove most beneficial, on aggregate, for society as a whole.

30. Narcotics: the problem and the solution

E.J. Mishan

'£60 Million of Cocaine Stowed in Keel of Yacht' runs the newspaper headline, an unnecessary reminder of the war being waged by governments against the clandestine infiltration into their countries of dangerous and addictive drugs.

Media reports of drug smugglers being arrested at sea or at airports, or of consignments of heroin discovered by the police in cellars or on trailers, make for stirring viewing or reading, and are regarded by the public as evidence of the government's unyielding determination to rid the country of this modern scourge. From time to time clarion calls are made by political leaders for sterner measures against drug dealers and the government reaffirms its commitment to stamping out the illegal drugs traffic.

In this respect, at least, we follow the example of the US, and our policies are about as as successful. In 1981 President Reagan pledged himself to wage relentless war on drug traffickers. Since that time, the number of arrests, and the amounts of contraband seized, have more than doubled, as indeed has US expenditure on combating the drug traffic.[1]

To be sure, if the number of arrests made, the number of processing plants destroyed, and the amounts of the drugs captured, could serve as indicators of success in the war against this illicit trade, then the continuing growth over time of public expenditure on enforcement measures would be wholly warranted. But, in fact, this war against drug dealers is not being won in the US, in the UK, or in any Western country. In March of 1988, for instance, the Colombian government, under pressure from the US, launched an army offensive against the drug cartel in Medellin. The results recorded during the first few months were impressive. Over three and a half thousand people were arrested, 30 airplanes captured, 700 processing plants destroyed, and 13,000 kilos of cocaine seized. Again, in August 1989, came another offensive, one involving 20,000 policemen and soldiers. Scores of processing laboratories were destroyed, about 150 planes were confiscated, and 11,000 kilos of cocaine captured. And yet these all-out military campaigns had no perceptible effect on the availability or on the street prices of cocaine.

Nor, of course, did the intensified endeavours of the US. In spite of the utmost vigilance, the mounting exertions, the employment of an array of sophisticated equipment, and the devising of new strategems, narcotics continued and still continue to flow into the country 'with the same ease with which the Viet Cong troops slipped down the Ho Chi Minh trail'.[2] If anything, it is becoming easier to smuggle drugs into the US. In 1980, for example, the wholesale price of a kilo of cocaine in Miami was $60,000. Today it is only $16,000, the purity remaining at a high level.[3]

E.J. Mishan: 'Narcotics:the problem and the solution', *THE POLITICAL QUARTERLY* 61 (1990). pp. 441-462. Reproduced with permission of Basil Blackwell Limited.

The first thing we have to come to terms with is the reason why – by reference to the elaborate and flexible organisation of the international drug market – the chances of our ever winning this kind of war are negligible.

The second thing we have to realise, moreover, is that there are powerful incentives for all employed in the business of monitoring or combating the drug traffic to continue to depict it in almost apocalyptic terms and, therefore, to subscribe to the official view that only the sustained vigilance and the unremitting efforts by the police and other officials have prevented a tidal wave of narcotic drugs breaching the floodgates, swamping the country, and wreaking havoc on society. The public alarm that is propagated by those whose status and prospects have come to depend upon the continuation and intensification of the war on drugs is also fed by wildly exaggerated or wholly fabricated 'horror stories' circulated by the media.[4] In the event, the ordinary citizen, exposed as he frequently is to these dread visions, can no longer think rationally about the problem.

Thirdly, the notion that narcotics pose an insidious threat to our civilisation is untenable. Even were the drugs as dangerous to health as commonly supposed, what grounds are there for the tacit assumption that if prohibition were lifted their consumption would increase so dramatically as to create a social crisis? The citizens of the West do not customarily behave like an unthinking bovine herd, ready to ingest anything placed before them that is cheap and plentiful. After all, alcoholic liquors – regarded by drug specialists as the most dangerous of all drugs – are universally available. Yet the vast majority of citizens are not addicts. Nor is there any expectation that they ever will be. True, many of them indulge in a 'booze up' once in a while, and most people drink occasionally, or even daily, but in moderation. Were the trade in cocaine to be decriminalised, it is reasonable to expect that, after some initial experimenting, the pattern would not be dissimilar to that of alcohol.

Fourthly, there is no clear evidence that collaboration among Western governments to curb the distribution of narcotic drugs tends, on balance, to reduce or to increase either the total amount consumed or the number of addicts. Reasons for suspecting that legal prohibition acts to increase the number of addicts will be mentioned later.

Finally, even if there were grounds for the belief that decriminalisation would tend to raise the number of drug addicts, a sober assessment both of the implications for personal freedom and of the social costs of maintaining prohibition should predispose us to favour legalisation as being the less oppressive option.

The structure of the narcotics market

In appraising the evidence and the arguments, I shall draw for the most part on the American experience of the drug problem, since it is far greater than that of any other Western country and the relevant data it produced are more abundant and accessible.

Compared with the estimate of some one and a half million users of cannabis in this country, and some figure between 75,000 and 150,000 hard drug users, the number of regular consumers of cannabis in the US is put at about 30 million, with the users of cocaine and heroin estimated, respectively, at about 6 million and half a million.[5] A conservative estimate of the annual expenditure on each of these drugs is in the region of $20 billion for cannabis, $30 billion for cocaine, and some $10 billion for heroin.[6]

In response to the methods used in the endeavour to enforce the anti-drug laws, the organisation of the supply side of the market has taken the form of a flexible chain of agents linking grower to consumer. The first link in the chain is obviously the farmer who grows the crop. At present, most of the opium poppies destined to be processed as heroin for the American market are from farms in Asia, while the bulk of the cannabis and practically all the cocaine come from countries in South America.

The second link is that of the exporters who organise the transport, the storage, and the processing, prior to smuggling the finished product into the US. Nearly all the cocaine for the American market comes from Peru, Bolivia, and Colombia, with the really big exporters controlling the trade from the world drug-capital of Medellin, Colombia. In view of their immense wealth and their criminal and political power, members of this Medellin cartel are commonly referred to as the 'drug barons'.

The third, and vital, link in this chain is the group engaged to transport the parcels of drugs by air and by sea from South America to ports and depots in the US. In recognition of the greater risks of capture, the reward for such services is commensurately high. This risk of capturing pilots and consignment is, however, expected to decline with the anticipated introduction of 'drones' (pilotless aircraft), controlled to land in any pre-designated area. It goes without saying that once this pilotless form of transportation is adopted the strategy of the drug exporters will be that of continually changing the landing areas – which will, of course, make capture and arrest that much more difficult.

Forming the fourth link in the chain are the big importers, each of whom sells to a small number of high-level dealers in the principal cities, who in turn sell to a larger number of middle-level dealers in the various towns and cities of the mainland.

The final link is, effectively, an expandable hierarchy that encompasses scores of thousands of operators, full- and part-time. Thus each of the middle-level dealers mentioned above sells to a variable number of lower-level dealers within a town or city, who then sell to street dealers in the different neighbourhoods. In their turn, the street dealers sell small amounts of the drugs to runners, some of whom are mere schoolchildren. In the distribution of all three narcotic drugs this last group numbers hundreds of thousands, and its earnings account for as much as 90 per cent of the retail price of cocaine and heroin.

In view of the extraordinary rewards associated with these illegal ventures it is not surprising to discover that, in addition to the vast army of organised dealers referred to, there are also many smaller groups operating on either side of the Caribbean, not to mention the many 'free-lancers' who, if they are ever successful enough to establish a foothold in this lucrative trade, run the additional risk of attracting the unwelcome attention of the drug barons or the big importers.

Critical implications of the market structure

Since so large a proportion of the final street price of these drugs accrues to the army of domestic distributors that form the final link in the chain of supply, it is not hard to understand why – notwithstanding the frequent and dramatic seizures of large consignments of cannabis, cocaine, and heroin – law-enforcement officials have signally failed to make any lasting impression on the domestic drug traffic. With so dense a network covering every region of the mainland, with nearly all of the multitude of petty dealers easily replaceable, and with bribery operating at every level of enforcement, the occasional success of police efforts to curtail street-level drug sales has little more than media value. Aware of this, the government directs the greater part of enforcement expenditures to the training and equipping of personnel to intercept drug imports.

To the extent that consignments are seized, losses are sustained by the big importers or exporters. But the losses are affordable, and in no case have they succeeded in reducing supplies for very long. In the short run any local short-fall can be made up from inventories, which are substantial. And, given a year or two, crop acreage can be expanded easily enough.

The most one can hope for from interception successes is some rise in the price of drugs. Such a rise would reflect anticipation of future losses of consignment as a proportion of total shipments - plus, perhaps, some additional payment as recompense for the greater risk of arrest of smugglers. This percentage rise in price is, however, to be calculated on the replacement cost of the amount of drugs seized; that is to say, on the *import* price of the drug. But this import price is, as mentioned, only a small fraction of the retail price. In the case of cocaine, for instance, the import price is only about 8 per cent of the retail price; and for heroin it is less than one per cent.[7]

Thus, even if we imagine such fantastic successes that as much as 50 per cent of the cocaine being shipped is captured, the increase in its import price necessary to maintain the drug importers' profits would have the effect of raising the retail price by less than 4 per cent.[8] And a rise in price of this order would, other things being equal, reduce the amount of cocaine consumed by a negligible proportion - by about a quarter of one per cent, if the recent estimates of its price elasticity by the Wharton School economists is accepted.[9]

Needless to remark, a seizure rate that averages 50 per cent would be extremely hard to attain, and harder still to maintain since, with the higher import cost, strenuous efforts would be made to elude capture by transporting drugs in smaller lots, in smaller craft, and by a greater variety of routes. In fact, already faced with growing interception along some of the more direct routes from Colombia, smugglers have begun to trans-ship through Mexico, the cocaine being then flown over the land border.

Nor can the capture of any, or many, of the drug barons themselves do anything to end the drug traffic. If one or more were put out of business, others would expand. The rivalry between drug syndicates is ruthless, as evidenced in recent years by pitched battles in the Miami area for 'territorial rights'. Even if all known executives of the large drug syndicates were arrested, it is virtually certain that the smaller organisations would seize the opportunity to escalate rapidly and then compete ferociously for a larger share of this irresistibly lucrative trade.[10]

This sober assessment of the future prospects of the existing policy of anti-drug enforcement is borne out by the experience of the last few years. The street prices of cannabis and heroin have not increased in 'real' terms, which suggests that smugglers are holding their own notwithstanding the cooperation between governments and the massive increase in resources being directed to drug interception. As for cocaine, it has become easier both to import and to distribute. In consequence its *street* price has fallen, being less than a half in 1988 of that in 1980.[11]

What hope for new strategies?

Although the interception of shipments is apparently the most cost-effective way of seizing illegal drugs, it is to some extent supplemented by other methods. It may be supposed that by switching of expenditure and effort from one method of enforcement to another some optimal mix of strategies might be contrived. In principle this is true. But since no one strategy appears to be very promising, the potential for increased effectiveness is limited, a conclusion that can be confirmed by brief descriptions and appraisals of other methods of surveillance and enforcement.

As indicated earlier, the patrolling of precincts and, therefore, the occasional raid and arrest of domestic drug dealers always have media value. They may even impair temporarily the flow of local supplies. But such police action has apparently no permanent effect in reducing the consumption of narcotics. To be sure, there is always the hope that interrogation of street pushers or local dealers will provide information leading to the arrest of the more powerful figures in the drug ring, and such arrests do occur from time to time – though not frequently enough to result in any permanent reduction in supplies.

One reason for the inefficacy of such attempts at law enforcement is simply that most local dealers fear the wrath of the drug Mafia far more than they fear the police. Despite threats and promises by the police, arrested dealers can seldom be induced to name names. Another reason is that there is widespread corruption both among police officers assigned to drug patrols and among other government officials at higher levels of responsibility, which is not surprising in view of the temptations. In the event, the rational police officer has to balance the risk to himself and his family of incurring the penalties of the law if he is discovered cooperating with, or conniving at, the activities of the drug dealers, against the risk of attracting the displeasure of the latter. And there can be no doubt that the risk and penalties involved in enforcing the law are the greater. Add to these the prospect of substantial perquisites simply for turning a blind eye to the local drug racket, and the sense of public duty strong enough to tilt the balance in favour of dedication to law enforcement is more than can reasonably be expected of the ordinary mortal today, living as he does in a secular and materialistic environment. The real wonder is that there yet remain brave and honest policemen, and that the apprehension and incarceration of top drug criminals do take place from time to time.

Again, apart from the undercover operations of government agencies (such as the setting up of bogus transport and financial concerns with the aim of trapping high level drug distributors), the Drug Enforcement Administration, along with the Internal Revenue Service and the Customs Service, cooperate in investigating the transactions of those suspected of being major dealers, tracing their finances through Currency Transactions Reports. These investigations are facilitated by federal regulations requiring financial institutions to file all currency transactions of $10,000 or more. And if by these means the bank accounts of drug dealers can be identified, federal agencies have the authority to confiscate them.

Such regulations, admittedly, make it more difficult for dealers to 'launder' drug monies, but their net effect only amounts to that of adding a little to the cost and inconvenience of transferring large sums of money to the major suppliers. [12]

Prospects for international strategies

Over the past decade the cooperation of the supplier countries, especially Peru and Bolivia, has been actively sought by the US even though, despite financial pressure and (tacit) threats of trade sanctions, the governments of such countries tend to be reluctant and unable, because of widespread police corruption, to cooperate effectively. [13]

Their reluctance is understandable. The illegal demand by millions of Americans for the products of coca-leaf farmers has become an important source of income to these South American supplier countries. The coca boom is probably a big reason why the Colombian government has been able to avoid re-scheduling its foreign debt. [14] Thus any serious attempt to destroy crops or prevent farmers growing coca plants invariably meets with fierce resistance, and not only from farmers. For this billion dollar trade has brought employment and prosperity to many thousands, from mechanics to pilots, from lawyers to financial advisors.

It is certain that government inspectors travelling through the interior of Peru or Bolivia risk death whenever they are bold enough to condemn coca plantations or processing plants to destruction. The stakes are high, profits from the coca plant being many times as high as those from growing grains or vegetables. Any South American government showing determination to root out the drug trade would also face unyielding opposition, both political and military, from the powerful drug syndicates.

The story is much the same in various countries of Asia. Programmes designed to encourage farmers to switch from opium growing have faltered after some initial success. As with cocaine, the replacement crops officially sponsored are far less profitable than the opium poppy.

Recent attempts to curb the drug barons' output of cocaine by preventing deliveries of acetate and other chemical solvents used in the processing laboratories is a non-starter, if only because of the large number of countries that can supply such solvents. No matter how hard the policy is pressed, the best one can hope for is some rise in cost to the syndicate resulting from an increase in bribes and an increase in terror. Bear in mind also that even a tenfold increase in the cost of such chemicals would raise the street price of cocaine by a negligible amount.

There remains to consider the strategy of spraying coca crops from the air with special herbicides, usually under the guidance of US officials and military personnel. The results have been uninspiring. Less than one per cent of the coca fields in Peru, Bolivia and Colombia were eradicated by these means in 1987, and the loss was more than replaced by new plantings. Indeed, the immediate efficacy of spraying is in doubt. It not only damages other species of flora but, in so far as it can be said to work, it destroys only the leaves of the coca plant and does not affect the roots. According to American newspaper reports, the spraying treatment in fact makes for a sturdier crop in the year following.

For all that, were it possible to discover a more powerful and discriminating herbicide, and were it possible also to find chemical companies and helicopter teams willing to brave the threats of the drug Mafia, the counter-measures that would be taken by the coca farmers are not hard to imagine. The coca plant would be grown intermixed with regular crops, and in smaller lots for better concealment. The additional costs to growers of such camouflage and concealment could be large. But they would make very little difference to the street price of cocaine.

The 'caring' establishment

Though we may go on hoping for the discovery of some 'technical fix' that would make it impossible ever again to grow any of the narcotic plants, we have in the meantime to make a choice between alternative policies, none of which is completely satisfactory. Given the remote prospects of our being able to reduce, or even contain, the spread of narcotic drugs by various strategies and enforcement measures, it is imperative that serious consideration be directed to the one policy option for which, as it happens, there is historic precedent: namely, the removal of prohibition.

Bearing in mind Dr Johnson's observation that people will always find more reasons for rejecting a new proposal than for embracing it, we may as well address ourselves first to the familiar objections that stem from populist 'compassionism' and the institutional support it generates before turning to the more compelling arguments for decriminalising the drug trade.

Notwithstanding the political ascendancy today of what has come to be known as the Radical Right, a paternalistic welfare ideology continues to have a strong hold on the nation's conscience. Too many of our good citizens look for an immediate government response whenever a segment of the population suffers a decline in its welfare arising from some chance event or a change in the law. Indeed, every material setback to a group or occupation occurring in the ordinary course of events, whether temporary or otherwise, tends to be represented as yet another instance of 'social injustice'. And, of course, language accommodates itself to prevailing sentiment. Thus, a few years ago, the rather winsome word 'caring' made its debut into society to become an inseparable companion piece to 'compassionate', itself a blessed word among political spokesmen in the post-war era. Redolent of good Samaritanism, such words have become the standard jingle in all appeals for more government resources.

This 'caring' propensity, which frequently vents itself in deploring the discomforts of prison life, prevails in many other instances in which people are undone by their own greed or folly. It insists that abortion facilities be made readily available on the National Health Service, especially for pregnant teen-aged girls. And if, instead, they elect to bear and rear the child, these husbandless mothers – promoted today to the status of 'single-parent' families – are supported at the expense of the taxpayer. Drug-addicts, too, effectively enjoy compassion-endowed rights to prey on the tax-paying public.

The 'caring' fraternity would, of course, regard it as bad form to point out that the kind of victim whose cause they ardently commend to the public has in fact no one but himself to blame; that it is he who chooses to expose himself to the well-known risks. Rather than acknowledge his culpability, they prefer to believe that he is the hapless victim of circumstances over which he has little control. A more balanced approach to human folly, and one that takes account of extenuating circumstances, follows from the more plausible belief that although people can indeed be influenced by factors outside their control, they are not 'conditioned' by them: there is always scope for the exercise of will. At all events, it should be abundantly clear that the virtual certainty of being cushioned by one state agency or another from the more distressing consequences of surrendering to temptations must operate over time to diminish people's incentive to exercise prudence and restraint.

We may reasonably conclude, then, that the ready availability of facilities for the care and treatment of drug addicts must act to weaken the incentive to resist experimenting with narcotics. Yet the compassion that effectively encourages irresponsibility by shielding people from the full consequences of their foolish actions is not what chiefly concerns us in the context of the drug problem. Far more serious is the fact that this compassion has bred paternalism: the power of the state is now wielded, in a bid to save people suffering the consequences of what is deemed irresponsible behaviour, by depriving us all of any choice in the matter. The far-reaching implications of this reaction of the state, both for individual liberty and for public security, will be broached presently. In the meantime, a few paragraphs on the establishment's interest in maintaining the existing anti-drug policy.

The interests involved in maintaining drug prohibition

Institutional development acts to reinforce 'compassionate paternalism' both as a creed and as a programme. Tending to the needs and treatment of those who get themselves into trouble has become a full-time occupation affording employment to, and conferring status upon, many thousands in the post-war welfare state. Such personnel are not likely to value their services modestly. Indeed, they acquire a professional interest in extending their power by seeking to expand both the range of the services they provide and the numbers they serve. Advertisements in the newspapers, in the buses, in the London Underground, urging us to exercise our rights and to avail ourselves of free advice, free treatment, and a variety of free benefits, have become commonplace. Every extra bit of business is welcome to officials of the welfare agencies, serving as it does to confirm their importance to society and to justify their regular demands for increased funding. What really cause dismay in welfare agencies is evidence of a decline in the number of their clients.

These general observations apply with special force to recent agencies set up and co-opted in the acclaimed war against the drug trade, particularly to those in the US. The seeming importance to the country of these agencies and, therefore, the status and power of their personnel – police officers, coast guards, customs officials, lawyers, research specialists, and so on – continues only so long as an illegal drug traffic continues, and will grow along with the growth of the traffic. It is to be expected that they will seek to justify their power and importance by affirming the view that the narcotics traffic is a modern plague that must be fought by every means and with every resource available. Strong support for anti-drug enforcement will certainly be prevalent among corrupt officials and among police officers in the pay of drug dealers.

As indicated earlier, however, such visions of the calamity that would befall us if all impediments to the import and distribution of narcotic drugs were removed are in the highest degree implausible. In fact, arguments and evidence can be adduced to support the belief that decriminalisation of the drug trade would not make a significant difference to the current trend of drug addiction, and might well act to reduce it. Be this as it may, it is imperative also that we reconsider critically the current prohibition against the trade in the light of libertarian doctrine.

Personal freedom and third-party effects

The familiar dictum that a man is free to act as he chooses provided his actions do not interfere with the freedom of others is at the heart of the libertarian doctrine. An alternative vision, though one in fact which supplements it, is that a man is free to act as he chooses so long as his actions do not weaken the protection of society. Let us restrict ourselves for the present to the former version.[15]

Although it is interference with the *freedom* of others which features in the usual libertarian proviso, the broader interpretation of the dictum would countenance restraint on the freedom of any one whose actions impinge directly on the *welfare* of others. And although treatises will continue to be written about the problem of safeguarding such freedom in modern society, concern with the drug issue impels us to focus only on two or three relevant aspects.

So long as the freedom to choose is that between different varieties of food, clothing, travel, recreation, and voluntary association, there is broad agreement among the political parties in Western democracies, although there can be differences about where exactly to draw lines – bearing in mind that apparel worn in public should not offend the conventions of decency, that language should not be scurrilous, and that the objectives of free association should not include subversive or criminal activity. Yet, whatever allowance is made for margins of uncertainty or dissension, no libertarian would want the state to restrict a man's freedom to choose a course of action solely on the grounds that it might damage his health or reduce his circumstances. Should a man choose to risk his neck by climbing the Matterhorn or swimming the Bosporus, or to risk heart disease by eating fried pork daily, no libertarian would empower the state to interfere.

If, then, under a libertarian dispensation, the law is to be used legitimately to prevent a man's exercising choice in any particular, the action to be restrained has to be one that falls within the familiar provision about its effect on the welfare of others. Only the incidence of 'third-party effects', as we may loosely call them, can justify qualification in the exercise of personal freedom.

These direct third-party effects may be divided into two categories each of which elicits a distinct response from the libertarian: (1) those arising from the use of items specifically designed to injure others, and (2) those arising from the use of goods that are not specifically designed to injure any one, notwithstanding which their production or use may so do.

Weapons devised to kill, wound, or otherwise incapacitate persons obviously fall within the first category, and laws enforced to limit possession of such weapons by ordinary citizens would not be regarded by libertarians as an infringement of basic freedoms. The second category, however, corresponds with the economists' notion of a 'spillover' – defined as those effects of legitimate economic activity that escape the pricing mechanism but which, nonetheless, have incidental and significant effects on the welfare of others.

Neither the economist nor the libertarian would necessarily favour a ban on all spillover-creating activity. In many instances a better solution would be one involving some form of economic reorganisation that would depend upon the costs to the concerned parties, including the state, of avoiding or reducing the damage inflicted. One simple device, much favoured by economists, provided bureaucratic costs are not high, is a tax on the sale of the item in question.[16]

Although the principle of collective action through state agencies in order to remove or reduce the incidence of direct third-party effect, or spillovers, is accepted by libertarians and economists alike, regard must also be paid to practical convenience, to prevailing custom and, in the last resort, to political climate. Everyday life would be intolerably frustrating if various controls were to be placed on the sale and use of hammers, axes, pokers, kitchen knives, and a host of other common utensils – to say nothing of such poisons as weed-killers, herbicides, and pesticides – which can easily be used, and in fact are occasionally used, to kill or injure other people. The bare minimum of everyday freedom cannot be enjoyed without such low-probability risks being incurred. In respect of such items, then, adults are to be treated as responsible beings even though, in the event, a number of them turn out to be homicidal or insane.

The third-party effects of narcotics

A case for singling out narcotic drugs is in some critical way different from items comprehended by our second category is hard to establish. Admittedly, such drugs are not necessary to the good life, but as much may be said for a wide variety of goods consumed daily – including, of course, the consumption of legally permitted drugs. The most commonly used addictive drugs are tobacco and alcoholic beverages, and it is generally recognised that their consumption contributes each year to the death of hundreds of thousands of people. Yet the libertarian goes along with the trend of public opinion in bowing to prevailing custom in respect of such drugs, requiring of the state no more than standard methods of dissuasion – official warnings, taxation, and penalties for particular abuses that may endanger life.

The consistent libertarian cannot therefore argue that narcotic drugs be treated more restrictively than these common drugs unless the risks to third parties – *not* the risks to the drug-user himself – are significantly greater.

In fact they are significantly less. Among those engaged in drug research in the US, there is agreement that it is alcohol which is far and away the most dangerous drug.[17] Since it is legal and everywhere available, the violence associated with its use may properly be attributed to its operation on the brain or nervous system – hence the term 'psychopharmacological violence'. In contrast, of the total violence associated with the drug trade, the proportion that falls within this category is held to be minute. Indeed, nearly all the violence that occurs in connection with the drug trade falls under the two remaining categories, the 'economic compulsive' and the 'systemic'.[18]

In the former, the 'economic compulsive', the motive is simply that of procuring the wherewithal to purchase the narcotic. Thus the common observation that drug addicts steal or assault and rob people is explained by the simple fact that many addicts are also poor and often unemployed or unemployable. Unlike those regular users of narcotics who are well off, such members of the 'underclass' cannot afford to buy their drugs in the amounts they crave at the existing black-market prices. This explanation, obvious enough, is incidentally confirmed by the observation that relatively few women addicts have recourse to robbery or violence, preferring to raise the necessary cash by prostitution.

The third category, the 'systemic' violence is, however, by far the most deadly. It takes place within the dense network of the narcotics supply system and takes form as inter-gang warfare over territory, intra-gang vendettas, and routine intimidation and torture in the endeavour to impose codes of conduct among the lower echelons of drug dealers. Worse yet is the systematic elimination by the cartel of informers, reporters, and incorruptible officers, prosecutors and judges.

It follows that there is no warrant for attributing the third-party effects suffered by innocent members of the public and by law-enforcing personnel to a narcotic-induced predisposition to commit violent acts. Practically all the street violence, all the gang terror and murder, are to be attributed – along with the widespread corruption among enforcement officers – to the policy of criminalising the trade in narcotics. It follows that drug-related crime and violence at all levels would fall away if the existing and in any case unavailing government policies were phased out and the narcotics trade legalised.[19]

Personal freedom and institutionally contrived third-party effects

We have now to address ourselves briefly to those *indirect* third-party effects that arise simply from institutional arrangements, particular regard being paid to the family and the welfare state.

Should a family man turn to alcohol and eventually become incapable of regular employment, his conduct necessarily reduces the material welfare of his wife and children. The comfort and living standard enjoyed by the family are, however, exposed to a variety of risks, some resulting from his choice of occupation, others from his choice of friends, recreations and amusements. Yet recognition of the impact of his decisions in these and other respects on the well-being of his family has never been urged by libertarians as consideration enough to warrant restriction by the state of a man's freedom to drink or smoke or choose his own occupation, recreation, or entertainment.

Regarding the family as the irreducible social cell from which all forms of society are constructed, this freedom to choose is generally conceived by the libertarian as being conferred on the family itself whose individual members arrive at family decisions in their own way, though influenced always by legislation, by prevailing custom, and morality.

To be sure, even in well-ordered societies abuses within the family will occur. The libertarian is not so unworldly as to overlook the possibility of iniquity or irresponsibility among parents. But the remedies he envisages are of the kind that empower direct state intervention only in particular and limited ways, and only where there is already evidence of mistreatment or neglect. The mere risk of abuses occurring in no way justifies abridgments of personal freedom or surrender to the state of powers to regulate or monitor family behaviour.

The welfare state

Turning now to the post-war growth of the welfare state itself, we have to face the pertinent implication that, in consequence of a tax-supported National Health Service, every individual who incurs a risk to his health also imposes a risk, and possibly a pecuniary burden, on the community at large. Anyone who drinks heavily, smokes heavily, or engages in dangerous sports, not only exposes himself to risk but also exposes the taxpayer to a financial risk. Statistically speaking, the greater the proportion of the population engaging in such habits and activities, the larger is the tax burden on the rest of the community.[20] In view of these apparent third-party effects, then, the community would seem to have a legitimate interest in restraining or deterring people from behaving in any way that exposes them to risk.

On the libertarian view, however, this apparent third-party effect may not be used to justify state action to deter individuals from taking personal risks of this sort. These seeming third-party effects cannot, in any case, be classified as spillovers in the accepted economic definition; they are *not*, that is, the *direct* consequence of a person's legitimate economic activity on the welfare of others - as would be, for example, the noxious fumes generated by a plastics factory. Additional taxes borne by the public at large as a result of some people's taking health risks are properly classified as 'pecuniary effects', involving as they do no more than a transfer of income from one group (taxpayers) to another (the recipients of medical treatment). In effect, then, there is a redistribution of income, one which arises simply as a result of institutional arrangements: of the political decision to introduce a National Health Service.[21]

Clearly the tax-burden effect that can arise from maintaining people's freedom to indulge in their vices, sports and recreations is not a *necessary* consequence of any of these activities. For the institutional arrangement in question is entirely an optional one for society. Indeed, if the area of welfare coverage were extended so as to make every person in the community a ward of the state, his every action would result in some gain or loss to the tax-paying public. It would then be quite true to assert that practically every choice made by the citizen affects in some degree the welfare of the wider public. Should it then be concluded that, in the interests of general welfare, the freedom of every one of us has to be regulated or restrained?

Such a conclusion would, of course, be anathema to a free society. Should any Western government that is committed to expand the nation's welfare produce such an argument as grounds for augmenting the existing system of constraints on personal freedom, the response of the electorate would be an unequivocal repudiation. It follows that the tax-burden argument cannot be invoked by a free society to support legislation designed to abridge the freedom to use addictive drugs of any kind, whether caffeine, tobacco, alcohol or narcotics.

The protection of society

Before summing up and concluding, it is pertinent also to consider the alternative libertarian view that would confer all personal freedom consistent with the protection of society. Although 'the protection of society' is a broad and elastic term, including as it does the defence of the realm, our interest here is with the viability and the character of the community.

If, for example, there were good grounds for the belief that the legalisation of narcotics would have repercussions on society far graver than those linked with the consumption of alcohol, in particular if it would beget so widespread and ineradicable an addiction that a substantial proportion of the working population would become incapable of regular employment, then libertarian sentiment would perforce give way to the priority of protecting the community.

Yet such an outcome is in the highest degree implausible. It is common knowledge that opium, or laudanum, was cheap and readily available in England during the nineteenth century – at a time, incidentally, when her rapid economic expansion was the envy of all other countries – and that the use of cocaine by the general public was lawful in the US until 1919. More immediately relevant perhaps are the recent estimates from American data which reveal that the consumption of narcotics does not vary much in response to changes in their prices. A fall of, say, 10 per cent in the street price of heroin is estimated to increase its consumption by about 2 per cent, whereas a 10 per cent fall in the street price of cocaine increase its consumption by only 0.6 per cent.[22] What is more, the variation in the consumption of either drug has strict reference only to the *amount* consumed, not to the numbers of consumers.

Admittedly, these estimates are not conclusive, if only because the range of price variations yielded by the data is limited. But if there is no certainty that a steep fall in narcotics prices would not increase the number of consumers, neither is it very likely that the proportional increase would be substantial. For it is not the high price that keeps the lid on the number of consumers. Those addicts who are in comfortable material circumstances are not deterred by the price. And, apart from the drug dealers themselves, the rest of the market is supported by the under-privileged, most of whom inhabit the black and Hispanic 'ghettoes' of North America.

Thus, although a big fall in street prices would undoubtedly increase the total *amount* of the drugs consumed, especially among the impecunious addicts, there is no reason to believe that it would tend to increase the total *number* of addicts by very much. As indicated earlier, the notion that there is a vast reservoir of potential addicts ready to succumb to the narcotic habit if only street prices were lower and availability were easier is a self-serving myth of the establishment.

Indeed, it is not unreasonable to entertain the conjecture that the scrapping of narcotic controls would tend to reduce the number of addicts or, at least, to slow down the expected rate of increase. And this for the simple fact that the growth of addiction over the last four decades in the US had little to do with price reductions or, for that matter, with the growth of real income. The crucial factor in the spread of the drug habit has been the unrelenting pressure exerted by legions of street pushers in the continuing endeavour to widen the circle of their customers. In other words, *the crucial factor in spreading the drug habit has been the super profits made possible only by governments' illegalisation of the trade*. Such super profits provide an irresistible temptation to all in the drug trade to promote addiction by every possible means – including the distribution of free samples (sometimes mixed into candy) among schoolchildren.

As things stand today, American schoolchildren from the age of nine can earn hundreds of dollars a week by working part-time for street dealers. It should be obvious that only by decriminalising the drug trade, by effectively pulling the rug from under the feet of the drug barons, will this persistent pressure directed to expanding the number of addicts cease to operate.

What is more, one can afford to give hostages to fortune in respect of this numbers game. For it would not matter much if it transpired, after all, that following a repeal of the narcotics' prohibition the number of addicts increased, and increased substantially. In so far as we are concerned primarily with direct third-party effects, in particular organised criminal and street violence, there would almost certainly be an improvement. For once legalised, both 'economic compulsive' and 'systemic' violence are eliminated, leaving only the 'psychopharmacological' violence which is the least important category.

Thus, if we make the pessimistic assumption that as much as 10 per cent of all drug violence is of this sort,[23] it would follow that the total violence in the new narcotics dispensation would decline – unless the number of narcotic addicts increased tenfold, a figure well beyond the most alarming conjecture.

The social cost of maintaining prohibition

Although, in the absence of carefully conducted surveys, the possibility of a significant expansion of drug addiction following the lifting of prohibition cannot be dismissed entirely, this by itself is not the decisive factor. Against even a considerable increase of addiction can be set the classical case for personal freedom already discussed, along with the virtual certainty of a reduction in crime and violence. And this is not all. The mounting costs to society of maintaining prohibitionist policies have now to be thrown into the balance.

A conventional economic valuation of the social cost of illegalising the drug trade restricts itself in the main to three calculable components: (1) expenditures incurred in efforts to suppress the trade; (2) expenditures on the treatment of drug addicts and on education against addiction; and (3) the loss to the nation of resources of capital and labour that are diverted from legitimate economic activity to criminal uses.

Recent estimates in the US have put the first figure at between $10 billion and $12 billion, including as it does federal, state and local outlays on law enforcement.[24] Such figures are underestimates, however, since they omit the costs of the judicial system of penal institutions, and of a large number of counselling and support agencies, public and private. As for the second item (the costs of treatment), apparently no acceptable estimates have yet been made. A rough guess for the third item – what economists would call the 'opportunity cost' of narcotics' crime – would be about $50 billion.[25]

Yet such estimates of the social cost to the US are only the tip of the iceberg. In the economist's idealised world, one in which every person is deemed capable of putting an exact money value on any factor affecting his welfare, the above estimates would be a fraction of the true social cost to the nation of the policy of criminalising the drug traffic. Among the more portentous consequences that elude calculation we have to include the systematic corruption of a disturbing proportion of the police force, customs and other officials, to say nothing of the citizens' awareness of this corruption which tends to reduce their respect for the law. It is supplemented by the more insidious corruption referred to, in which establishment personnel whose remuneration and status have come to depend on the maintenance of drug illegalisation continue supporting and publicising the official and wholly exaggerated views about the power of drugs to subvert the social order.

Worse yet than the corruption, inseparable from an economic activity made inordinately profitable by prohibition, is the enormity of the crime it generates.

A distinction can be made between the street crimes of drug addicts, either on their own account or in the pay of criminals, and those crimes committed by members of drug rings in battles to protect or extend territorial rights. According to a recent survey of police departments in America, about one half of all thefts and burglaries, and about two-thirds of all assaults, can be attributed to persons using or distributing narcotic drugs. According to the same survey, nearly 40 per cent of all the murders committed in areas of more than 100,00 inhabitants are drug-related.[26] It is worse in the large cities. In Washington, DC, for instance, 60 per cent of the murders are believed to be drug-related as compared with 30 per cent in 1980.[27]

Crime and corruption are not, of course, restricted to North America. Since the greater part of the drug-related crime is associated with trade in cocaine, almost all of which is produced in Bolivia, Peru and Colombia, crime and corruption are rife in these South American countries – though most flagrantly in the last-mentioned country where most of the refining facilities are located and which exports the bulk of the cocaine consumed to the US. A year ago the mayor of Bogota, in defending his administration against complaints by American agencies of lack of cooperation, stated that already the bravest of journalists, police and judges had been murdered in the fight to expose, arrest, and bring to justice the drug barons of Colombia.[28]

The demoralising effect over time on the character of the community and the degeneration of the quality of life that has resulted from the surging power of a new criminal underworld are certainly an essential part of the social cost of drug prohibition. And the economist would dearly like to be able to estimate the aggregate of the dollar sums required by each of the total of American families, which sums would be regarded by them as a minimum compensation for having to continue to endure the many untoward consequences of the official policy of drug prohibition. It might well exceed the current figure for Gross National Product.[29]

Concluding observations

Notwithstanding the jubilation which greets the occasional discovery of shipments of narcotics and the arrest of smugglers, there can be no reasonable hope of putting an end to, or even reducing, the drug traffic. In view, then, of the enormous costs to society of vainly trying to protect improvident would-be addicts from themselves by the expedient of criminalising narcotics, there is a powerful case for accepting the small risk of some initial increase in their popularity by de-criminalising them. All the paternalistic rhetoric of members of the 'caring' fraternity cannot conceal the rank injustice of a policy that has subjected the public to a steep escalation of criminal violence and corruption in the futile endeavour to protect reckless individuals from the consequences of their own folly.

Once the case for legalising the narcotics trade is conceded, however, a number of ancillary decisions have to be made. Inasmuch as the health of drug consumers can be severely damaged by substances that are frequently mixed with cocaine and other drugs prior to street sales, legislation should be introduced requiring the testing and labelling of such drugs to ensure their purity. Secondly, a decision has to be taken whether to levy an excise tax on narcotics, as on liquor and tobacco, or whether they should enter the country tax free or even be subsidised. There are arguments for each of these alternatives, but my own preference is for free entry and sale at competitive prices with the usual proviso for minors.[30] I should also favour free and generous rations to impecunious addicts through the National Health Service both in order to stabilise the addiction and to remove all temptation for theft and robbery. The supply of free needles would also reduce the number of AIDS victims that arises from needle-sharing among addicts.

As for treatment and rehabilitation of addicts, desirable though they are, I would, as a libertarian, have reservations about financing them at the expense of the tax-payer. Not only is it inequitable, but awareness of the free availability of such treatment tends to reduce personal responsibility.[31]

Finally, under my preferred proposal, which ensures that no addict be deprived of his daily quantum, many may continue to be vagrants or otherwise make a nuisance of themselves. Rather than keep them under lock and key, especially at a time when prison space is scarce, it would be more expedient and economical to transport persistent offenders to some designated area where they would have the choice of living for the rest of their lives or else of working out their own salvation in a controlled environment encouraged by the prospect of being able to return and resume a normal life.

Some of these tentative suggestions will not go down well with those social workers who find scope for their dedication and skills in the plight of drug addicts. But if our chief concern is, as it should be, with the health and the protection of the nation at large, we must avoid encumbering ourselves with open-ended commitments to provide all the resources needed for the care, the comfort, and the treatment of foolish people who, of their own volition and with foreknowledge of the consequences, elect to take the risk of becoming chronically dependent and incapable.

The proposals in the preceding section are, I repeat, tentative only. They are of secondary importance to the belated reminder that, in respect of the drug problem, society does indeed have a choice, although, as with most political choices, it is one between alternative evils. But the evils are far from being equal. And, as I have sought to establish, governments of the West have thoughtlessly adopted the policy involving the greater social evil.

Thus having, in our paternalistic ardour, rejected the libertarian alternative of permitting all would-be drug consumers to dope themselves at low cost, we now discover that in the process of enforcing the law we have also imposed upon the nation as a whole a staggering burden, one that includes a massive increase in criminal violence and an insidious spread of corruption at all levels of officialdom. And all for what? In spite of continuing arrests of smugglers and seizures of contraband, domestic supplies of drugs are more easily available today than they ever were.

Notes

1. Arrests made among those trading in cocaine and heroin rose from 68,000 in 1981 to 181,000 in 1984 (Uniform Crime Reports, 1981-1984, *Federal Bureau of Investigation*, 1985, Washington, DC). The amount of cocaine seized by Federal Enforcement Agencies rose from 4,800 kilos in 1980 to 12,400 kilos in 1984 (*Organized Crime Enforcement Task Force Program*, Annual Report, 1985, Washington, DC).

    The figures for the UK show comparable growth although the magnitudes are very much smaller. The cocaine seized in 1980 amounted to 40 kilos. By 1986 it was 100 kilos, with provisional estimates for 1987 put at 360 kilos. The amount of heroin captured in 1980 was 90 kilos, rising to 360 kilos in 1985. As for the number of persons sentenced for drug offences, it rose more slowly: from 17,000 in 1980 to about 23,000 in 1985. (*Statistics of the Misuse of Drugs*, UK, 1986, Home Office Statistical Department, London, September 1987.)

2. This apt similitude is from an excellent descriptive article in the *New York Review of Books*, 22 December 1988.

3. The most reliable source on the domestic consumption of drugs in the US is the annual report of the National Narcotics Intelligence Consumers' Committee (NNICC).

4. Newspapers, magazines and television films and documentaries have all shown a strong partiality for horror stories about addicts who gouge out their eyes, pull out their teeth, mutilate and castrate themselves, axe their families, or try to fly from roof tops. The range and popularity of these ghastly stories have been debunked in the professional journals. For some detailed statistics see, for example, Martin Brecher, M.D. *et al.*, 'PCP and Violence: Clinical and Legal Issues', *Journal of Clinical Psychopharmacology*, 1988, Vol. 8, No. 6.

5. The more recent use of 'crack', the high potency cocaine, has been expanding rapidly. In 1985 it represented but 4.6 per cent of the total cocaine consumed (by weight). By 1986 the figure had reached 11.3 per cent.

6. These figures are the cautious 'guestimates' of the economists with whom I spoke when in New York in May 1988. They are very conservative when compared with the figures of Table 2 in a monograph by Peter Reuter and Mark Kleiman, *Risks and Prices: An Economic Analysis of Drug Enforcement*, Chicago, 1986. On BBC 4, an aggregate figure of $120 billion for the year was given by Sally Hardcastle on 19 January 1989. This compares with the figure of $100 billion given by Vice-President Quayle toward the end of February 1989.

7. The traffic in cannabis carries much less risk than either of the other two drugs. Consequently its import price is a larger proportion, being about a quarter of the retail price.

8. Since estimates of past prices are more reliable than those of current prices, we shall adopt the 1980 structure of prices as estimated in the NNICC Report for 1982. The *import* price of cocaine then averaged as much as $50,000 per kilo, allowance having been made for a seizure rate then of some 25 per cent of total shipments. It follows that if there were no seizures at all, the import price would have been three-quarters of that price, or $37,000 per kilo. If now the seizure rate were to become 50 per cent, the shipments necessary to maintain current supplies to the mainland would have to be double those in the hypothetical no-seizure situation. The import price would therefore have to rise to $75,000 per kilo. Compared with the average price of $50,000 in the year 1980 (when 25 per cent of all shipments were being captured) the price would be increased by $25,000 per kilo. But this increase in the import price would raise the retail price of cocaine from $650,000 per kilo to $675,000 per kilo, an increase in the retail price of less than 4 per cent.

9. See *The Anti-Drug Law Enforcement Efforts and Their Impact*, Wharton Report, 1987, pp. 19-21; pp. 114-118.

10. A sophisticated simulation model has been used by a group of American economists in order to trace the potential adaptability of drug smugglers to all the alternative strategies available to the US interdiction agencies. Among the pessimistic conclusions reached by the authors is that, for cocaine, the results are quite unpromising. See P. Reuter *et al.*, *Sealing the Borders*, Rand Corporation, Santa Monica, 1988. Moreover, as the authors point out later, since experienced smugglers have close ties with foreign and US officials, whose cooperation enables them to learn quickly about proposed changes in interception strategies, the simulation model errs on the side of optimism.

11. Indeed, by 1984, cocaine prices were almost half those prevailing in 1980.

12. Through the activity known as 'smurfing' couriers now travel to specific areas of the US in order to pick up millions of dollars from drug sales. They then purchase cashiers' cheques or money orders in denominations of less than $10,000 from many different banks and convey them in packets to persons located in other parts of the country who, in turn, deposit them in bank accounts under fictitious names. See the NNICC Report, 1985-1986.

13. Since 1976, the State Department's Bureau of International Narcotic Matters has attempted to control production in South American countries through diplomatic pressure and economic assistance programmes. The US Drug Enforcement Administration also offers assistance in various forms to governments of supplier countries.

14. See *The Economist*, 8 October 1988.

15. The first is mentioned in Chapter 3 of John Stuart Mill's *Essay on Liberty* and the second in the *Introduction* to that essay.

16. The economic literature on 'spillovers' is immense though, alas, not altogether free from political biases. The reader who is inquisitive about the way economists approach the

problem, and what they conceive to be the key issues, might find it useful to consult Chapter 13 of my *Economic Efficiency and Social Welfare*, London 1981.

17. See Paul Goldstein, 'Drugs and Violent Crime', in M. Wolfgang and N. Weiner (eds), *Violent Crime and Violent Criminals*, New York, 1989. Also see Eric Wish *et al.*, 'Drug Use and Crime in Arrestees in Manhatten', presented at the meeting of the Committee on Problems of Drug Dependence, Baltimore, 11 June 1985.

18. The immoderate consumption of cocaine or heroin, as with the immoderate consumption of alcohol, may also on occasion lead to domestic violence. This is much more common, however, among the poor and shiftless drug addicts – the result frequently of quarrels over the sharing of meagre amounts of drugs or money. Be that as it may, what exercises the public is not so much this in-fighting among couples or families as the street violence suffered by innocent victims.

19. With respect to this third-party aspect we should not omit the auxiliary question of the possible risks to the public arising from a misjudgement by technical personnel in industry acting under the influence of narcotics. Indeed, with the advances being made in technology, there is an increasing variety of circumstances in which the risk to life and limb comes to depend more on the vigilance and judgement of others than our own. Obvious instances are bus and train drivers, airline pilots, and personnel in nuclear and chemical plants or water-purifying plants. It is unnecessary to remark, however, that the minute inspection to which expensive plant and machinery are subject should be, and in fact generally is, also extended to the personnel in charge of their care and operation. Already management requires personnel to undertake physical and psychological tests for positions of responsibility, usually with particular attention to alcoholism and drug addiction, and there is no doubt that governments are disposed to insist on such procedures. Assuming that the vetting of all such personnel continues to be strictly enforced, the legalisation of narcotics of itself poses no additional risks to the public from this cause.

20. There have been allegations (1) that heavy drinkers and smokers so shorten their lives that they actually reduce the burden on the National Health Service, and (2) that, in any case, the excise taxes levied on tobacco and liquor are enough to defray the additional costs to the state of medical resources for their treatment. These allegations were advanced in order to defeat proposals for penalising smokers or drinkers further, or for banning tobacco advertisements. In order to vindicate libertarian principles, however, we need not draw upon such contentions. We may continue to suppose that, on balance, these groups do indeed impose a net burden on the taxpayer.

21. We may note in passing that, as distinct from true spillover effects (as defined by economists), no necessary misallocation of resources results from the prevalence of these 'pecuniary effects'. As mentioned, the latter entail only a redistribution of income. Hence there is no warrant – on economic grounds, at any rate - for prohibiting or restraining any behaviour that involves personal risk in these circumstances.

22. *Wharton Report*, 1987, op. cit.

23. In discussing this aspect of the subject when in the US. I found that even the most knowledgeable of experts were reluctant to put an exact figure on the proportion in the psychopharmacological category, chiefly because as yet no systematic laboratory experiments have been conducted on humans. When I suggested a figure of 10 per cent, however, as I always did, I was assured that the figure was likely to be much less than that.

24. Such expenditures have risen sharply. The Federal drug budget by itself will be close to $9 billion in 1990, and the drug budgets of state and local agencies abut half as much again.

25. The aggregate social cost of the drug traffic for 1980 was put at $60 billion by H.J. Harwood, 'Economic Costs to Society of Alcohol and Drug Abuse and Mental Illness: 1980'. Report submitted to Mental Health Administration, Office of Program Planning and Coordination, Rockville, Maryland, 1984.

26. *Wharton Report*, 1987, *op. cit.* Part V. Survey Results, pp. 90-121.

27. BBC World News, 31 May 1989.

28. According to *Time Magazine*, 4 September 1989, in the fight against the drug cartel 17 journalists, 108 politicians, 157 judges and over 5,000 police and narcotics officers were killed during the period 1982-1988.

29. Of the total police resources in the United States about 25 per cent are currently engaged in drug enforcement and drug-related crime. In this way, persistence with the policy of criminalising narcotics has substantially reduced the police resources available for combatting other crimes.

30. In addition to the usual libertarian proviso about minors, I should enter a recommendation for more government funding of information and of education, especially in schools. And I should certainly urge the banning of all advertising of drugs, including those of alcohol and tobacco.

31. There is, however, nothing to prevent people with strong sympathies for the plight of penurious drug addicts from contributing to private charities created for their treatment and rehabilitation.

31.   Against the Legalization of Drugs

James Q. Wilson

Dr. James Q. Wilson, Collins Professor of Management and Public Policy at UCLA, argues against legalization. Wilson maintains, by appeal to history, that the easier illegal drugs are to obtain, the more widespread is their use. According to his analysis, most Vietnam veterans who regularly used heroin in Southeast Asia gave up the habit in the United States because heroin here is less available and sanctions against its use are more pronounced. He accordingly submits that the worst thing the United States government could do would be to legalize all currently illegal drugs, markedly reducing their price and increasing their availability and use.

Dr. Wilson submits that, while the social costs of criminalization may be high, the social costs of legalization might be higher, especially if there were a great increase in the number of addicts. According to him, legalizing drugs would very likely remove the stigma attached to habits that are damaging to not only physical health but also moral personality. Accordingly, he writes: "Tobacco shortens one's life, cocaine debases it. Nicotine alters one's habits, cocaine alters one's soul."

He argues that legalization would be an extremely risky social experiment whose potential negative consequences might be difficult to reverse, the power of addiction being so great: "there is no way to put the genie back in the bottle, and it is not a kindly genie."

He reasons that the consequences of continuing on our current path of prohibition are, at worst, "heavy costs in law enforcement and some forms of criminality," while the worst consequences of legalization are quite unacceptable: that millions of additional people may have their lives degraded or destroyed.

In 1972, the President appointed me chairman of the National Advisory Council for Drug Abuse Prevention. Created by Congress, the Council was charged with providing guidance on how best to co-ordinate the national war on drugs. (Yes, we called it a war then, too.) In those days, the drug we were chiefly concerned with was heroin. When I took office, heroin use had been increasing dramatically. Everybody was worried that this increase would continue. Such phrases as "heroin epidemic" were commonplace.

That same year, the eminent economist Milton Friedman published an essay in *Newsweek* in which he called for legalizing heroin. His argument was on two grounds: as a matter of ethics, the government has no right to tell people not to use heroin (or to drink or to commit suicide); as a matter of economics, the prohibition of drug use imposes costs on society that far exceed the benefits. Others, such as the psychoanalyst Thomas Szasz, made the same argument.

We did not take Friedman's's advice. (Government commissions rarely do.) I do not recall that we even discussed legalizing heroin, though we did discuss (but did not take

James Q. Wilson: 'Against the Legalization of Drugs', (*COMMENTARY*, February 1990). pp. 21-28. Reproduced by permission of the author and the publisher.

action on) legalizing a drug, cocaine, that many people then argued was benign. Our marching orders were to figure out how to win the war on heroin, not to run up the white flag of surrender.

That was 1972. Today, we have the same number of heroin addicts that we had ten-years ago – half a million, give or take a few thousand. Having that many heroin addicts is no trivial matter; these people deserve our attention. But not having had an increase in that number for over 15 years is also something that deserves our attention. What happened to the 'heroin epidemic' that many people once thought would overwhelm us?

The facts are clear: a more or less stable pool of heroin addicts has been getting older, with relatively few new recruits. In 1976 the average age of heroin users who appeared in hospital emergency rooms was about 27; ten years later it was 32. More than two-thirds of all heroin users appearing in emergency rooms are now over the age of 30. Back in the early 1970s, when heroin got onto the national political agenda, the typical heroin addict was much younger, often a teenager. Household surveys show the same thing – the rate of opiate use (which includes heroin) has been flat for the better part of two decades. More fine-grained studies of inner-city neighborhoods confirm this. John Boyle and Ann Brunswick found that the percentage of young blacks in Harlem who used heroin fell from 8 percent in 1970-71 to about 3 percent in 1975-76.

Why did heroin lose its appeal for young people? When the young blacks in Harlem were asked why they stopped, more than half mentioned "trouble with the law" or "high cost" (and high cost is, of course, directly the result of law enforcement). Two-thirds said that heroin hurt their health; nearly all said they had had a bad experience with it. We need not rely, however, simply on what they said. In New York City in 1973-75, the street price of heroin rose dramatically and its purity sharply declined, probably as a result of the heroin shortage caused by the success of the Turkish government in reducing the supply of opium base and of the French government in closing down heroin-processing laboratories located in and around Marseilles. These were short-lived gains for, just as Friedman had predicted, alternative sources of supply – mostly in Mexico – quickly emerged. But the three-year heroin shortage interrupted the easy recruitment of new users.

Health and related problems were no doubt part of the reason for the reduced flow of recruits. Over the preceding years, Harlem youth had watched as more and more heroin users died of overdoses, were poisoned by adulterated doses, or acquired hepatitis from dirty needles. The word got around: heroin can kill you. By 1974 new hepatitis cases and drug-overdose deaths had dropped to a fraction of what they had been in 1970.

Alas, treatment did not seem to explain much of the cessation in drug use. Treatment programs can and do help heroin addicts, but treatment did not explain the drop in the number of *new* users (who by definition had never been in treatment) nor even much of the reduction in the number of experienced users.

No one knows how much of the decline to attribute to personal observation as opposed to high prices or reduced supply. But other evidence suggests strongly that price and supply played a large role. In 1972 the National Advisory Council was especially worried by the prospect that U.S. servicemen returning to this country from Vietnam would bring their heroin habits with them. Fortunately, a brilliant study by Lee Robins of Washington University in St. Louis put that fear to rest. She measured drug use of Vietnam veterans shortly after they had returned home. Though many had used heroin regularly while in Southeast Asia, most gave up the habit when back in the United States. The reason: here, heroin was less available and sanctions on its use were more pronounced. Of course, if a veteran had been willing to pay enough – which might have meant traveling to another city and would certainly have meant making an illegal contact with a disreputable dealer in a threatening neighborhood in order to acquire a (possibly) dangerous dose – he could have sustained his drug habit. Most veterans were unwilling to pay this price, and so their drug use declined or disappeared.

Reliving the past

Suppose we had taken Friedman's advice in 1972. What would have happened? We cannot be entirely certain, but at a minimum we would have placed the young heroin addicts (and, above all, the prospective addicts) in a very different position from the one in which they actually found themselves. Heroin would have been legal. Its price would have been reduced by 95 percent (minus whatever we chose to recover in taxes). Now that it could be sold by the same people who make aspirin, its quality would have been assured – no poisons, no adulterants. Sterile hypodermic needles would have been readily available at the neighborhood drugstore, probably at the same counter where the heroin was sold. No need to travel to big cities or unfamiliar neighborhoods – heroin could have been purchased anywhere, perhaps by mail order.

There would no longer have been any financial or medical reason to avoid heroin use. Anybody could have afforded it. We might have tried to prevent children from buying it, but as we have learned from our efforts to prevent minors from buying alcohol and tobacco, young people have a way of penetrating markets theoretically reserved for adults. Returning Vietnam veterans would have discovered that Omaha and Raleigh had been converted into the pharmaceutical equivalent of Saigon.

Under these circumstances, can we doubt for a moment that heroin use would have grown exponentially? Or that a vastly larger supply of new users would have been recruited? Professor Friedman is a Nobel prize-winning economist whose understanding of market forces is profound. What did he think would happen to consumption under his legalized regime? Here are his words: "Legalizing drugs might increase the number of addicts, but it is not clear that it would. Forbidden fruit is attractive, particularly to the young."

Really? I suppose that we should expect no increase in Porsche sales if we cut the price by 95 percent, no increase in whiskey sales if we cut the price by a comparable amount – because young people only want fast cars and strong liquor when they are "forbidden". Perhaps Friedman's uncharacteristic lapse from the obvious implications of price theory can be explained by a misunderstanding of how drug users are recruited. In his 1972 essay he said that "drug addicts are deliberately made by pushers, who give likely prospects their first few doses free." If drugs were legal it would not pay anybody to produce addicts, because everybody would buy from the cheapest source. But as every drug expert knows, pushers do not produce addicts. Friends or acquaintances do. In fact, pushers are usually reluctant to deal with non-users because a non-user could be an undercover cop. Drug use spreads in the same way that any fad or fashion spreads: somebody who is already a user urges his friends to try, or simply shows already-eager friends how to do it.

But we need not rely on speculation, however plausible, that lowered prices and more abundant supplies would have increased heroin usage. Great Britain once followed such a policy and with almost exactly those results. Until the mid-1960s, British physicians were allowed to prescribe heroin to certain classes of addicts. (Possessing these drugs without a doctor's prescription remained a criminal offense.) For many years this policy worked well enough because the addict patients were typically middle-class people who had become dependent on opiate painkillers while undergoing hospital treatment. There was no drug culture. The British system worked for many years, not because it prevented drug abuse, but because there was no problem of drug abuse that would test the system.

All that changed in the 1960s. A few unscrupulous doctors began passing out heroin in wholesale amounts. One doctor prescribed almost 600,000 heroin tablets – that is, over 13 pounds – in just one year. A youthful drug culture emerged with a demand for drugs far different from that of the older addicts. As a result, the British government required doctors to refer users to government-run clinics to receive their heroin.

But the shift to clinics did not curtail the growth in heroin use. Throughout the 1960s the number of addicts increased – the late John Kaplan of Stanford estimated by fivefold – in part as a result of the diversion of heroin from clinic patients to new users on the streets. An addict would bargain with the clinic doctor over how big a dose he would receive. The patient wanted as much as he could get, the doctor wanted to give as little as was needed. The patient had an advantage in this conflict because the doctor could not be certain how much was really needed. Many patients would use some of their 'maintenance' dose and sell the remaining part to friends, thereby recruiting new addicts. As the clinics learned of this, they began to shift their treatment away from heroin and toward methadone, an addictive drug that, when taken orally, does not produce a 'high' but will block the withdrawal pains associated with heroin abstinence.

Whether what happened in England in the 1960s was a mini-epidemic or an epidemic depends on whether one looks at numbers or at rates of change. Compared to the United States, the numbers were small. In 1960 there were 68 heroin addicts known to the British government; by 1968 there were 2,000 in treatment and many more who refused treatment. (They would refuse in part because they did not want to get methadone at a clinic if they could get heroin on the street). Richard Hartnoll estimates that the actual number of addicts in England is five times the number officially registered. At a minimum, the number of British addicts increased thirtyfold in ten years; the actual increase may have been much larger.

In the early 1980s the numbers began to rise again, and this time nobody doubted that a real epidemic was at hand. The increase was estimated to be 40 percent a year. By 1982 there were thought to be 20,000 heroin users in London alone. Geoffrey Pearson reports that many cities – Glasgow, Liverpool, Manchester, and Sheffield among them

– were now experiencing a drug problem that once had been largely confined to London. The problem, again, was supply. The country was being flooded with cheap, high-quality heroin, first from Iran and then from Southeast Asia.

The United States began the 1960s with a much larger number of heroin addicts and probably a bigger at-risk population than was the case in Great Britain. Even though it would be foolhardy to suppose that the British system, if installed here, would have worked the same way or with the same results, it would be equally foolhardy to suppose that a combination of heroin available from leaky clinics and from street dealers who faced only minimal law-enforcement risks would not have produced a much greater increase in heroin use than we actually experienced. My guess is that if we had allowed either doctors or clinics to prescribe heroin, we would have had far worse results than were produced in Britain, if for no other reason than the vastly larger number of addicts with which we began. We would have had to find some way to police thousands (not scores) of physicians and hundreds (not dozens) of clinics. If the British civil service found it difficult to keep heroin in the hands of addicts and out of the hands of recruits when it was dealing with a few hundred people, how well would the American civil service have accomplished the same tasks when dealing with tens of thousands of people?

Back to the future

Now cocaine, especially in its potent form, crack, is the focus of attention. Now as in 1972 the government is trying to reduce its rise. Now as then some people are advocating legalization. Is there any more reason to yield to those arguments today than there was almost two decades ago?[1]

I think not. If we had yielded in 1972 we almost certainly would have had today a permanent population of several million, not several hundred thousand, heroin addicts. If we yield now we will have a far more serious problem with cocaine.

Crack is worse than heroin by almost any measure. Heroin produces a pleasant drowsiness and, if hygienically administered, has only the physical side effects of constipation and sexual impotence. Regular heroin use incapacitates many users, especially poor ones, for any productive work or social responsibility. They will sit nodding on a street corner, helpless but at least harmless. By contrast, regular cocaine use leaves the user neither helpless nor harmless. When smoked (as with crack) or injected, cocaine produces instant, intense, and short-lived euphoria. The experience generates a powerful desire to repeat it. If the drug is readily available, repeat use will occur. Those people who progress to "bingeing" on cocaine become devoted to the drug and its effects to the exclusion of almost all other considerations – job, family, children, sleep, food, even sex. Dr. Frank Gawin at Yale and Dr. Everett Ellinwood at Duke report that a substantial percentage of all high-dose, binge users become uninhibited, impulsive, hypersexual, compulsive, irritable, and hyperactive. Their moods vacillate dramatically, leading at times to violence and homicide.

Women are much more likely to use crack than heroin, and if they are pregnant, the effects on their babies are tragic. Douglas Besharov, who has been following the effects of drugs on infants for twenty years, writes that nothing he learned about heroin prepared him for the devastation of cocaine. Cocaine harms the fetus and can lead to physical deformities or neurological damage. Some crack babies have for all practical purposes suffered a disabling stroke while still in the womb. The long-term consequences of this brain damage are lowered cognitive ability and the onset of mood disorders. Besharov estimates that about 30,000 to 50,000 such babies are born every year, about 7,000 in New York City alone. There may be ways to treat such infants, but from everything we now know the treatment will be long, difficult, and expensive. Worse, the mothers who are most likely to produce crack babies are precisely the ones who, because of poverty or temperament, are least able and willing to obtain such treatment. In fact, anecdotal evidence suggests that crack mothers are likely to abuse their infants.

The notion that abusing drugs such as cocaine is a 'victimless crime' is not only absurd but dangerous. Even ignoring the fetal drug syndrome, crack-dependent people are, like heroin addicts, individuals who regularly victimize their children by neglect, their spouses by improvidence, their employers by lethargy, and their co-workers by carelessness. Society is not and could never be a collection of autonomous individuals. We all have a stake in ensuring that each of us displays a minimal level of dignity, responsibility, and empathy. We cannot, of course, coerce people into goodness, but we can and should insist that some standards must be met if society itself – on which the very existence of the human personality depends – is to persist. Drawing the line that defines those standards is difficult and contentious, but if crack and heroin use do not fall below it, what does?

The advocates of legalization will respond by suggesting that my picture is overdrawn. Ethan Nadelmann of Princeton argues that the risk of legalization is less than most people suppose. Over 20 million Americans between the ages of 18 and 25 have tried cocaine (according to a government survey), but only a quarter of a million use it daily. From this Nadelmann concludes that at most 3 percent of all young people who try cocaine develop a problem with it. The implication is clear: make the drug legal and we only have to worry about 3 percent of our youth.

The implication rests on a logical fallacy and a factual error. The fallacy is this: the percentage of occasional cocaine users who become binge users *when the drug is illegal* (and thus expensive and hard to find) tells us nothing about the percentage who will become dependent when the drug is legal (and thus cheap and abundant). Drs. Gawin and Ellinwood report, in common with several other researchers, that controlled or occasional use of cocaine changes to compulsive and frequent use "when access to the drug increases" or when the user switches from snorting to smoking. More cocaine more potently administered alters, perhaps sharply, the proportion of "controlled" users who become heavy users.

The factual error is this: the federal survey Nadelmann quotes was done in 1985, *before* crack had become common. Thus the probability of becoming dependent on cocaine was derived from the responses of users who snorted the drug. The speed and potency of cocaine's action increases dramatically when it is smoked. We do not yet know how greatly the advent of crack increases the risk of dependency, but all the clinical evidence suggests that the increase is likely to be large.

It is possible that some people will not become heavy users even when the drug is readily available in its most potent form. So far there are no scientific grounds for predicting who will and who will not become dependent. Neither socio-economic background nor personality traits differentiate between casual and intensive users. Thus, the only way to settle the question of who is correct about the effect of easy availability on drug use, Nadelmann or Gawin and Ellinwood, is to try it and see. But that social experiment is so risky as to be no experiment at all, for if cocaine is legalized and if the rate of its abusive use increases dramatically, there is no way to put the genie back in the bottle, and it is not a kindly genie.

Have we lost?

Many people who agree that there are risks in legalizing cocaine or heroin still favor it because, they think, we have lost the war on drugs. 'Nothing we have done has worked' and the current federal policy is just 'more of the same'. Whatever the costs of greater drug use, surely they would be less than the costs of our present, failed efforts.

That is exactly what I was told in 1972 – and heroin is not quite as bad a drug as cocaine. We did not surrender and we did not lose. We did not win, either. What the nation accomplished then was what most efforts to save people from themselves accomplish: the problem was contained and the number of victims minimized, all at a considerable cost in law enforcement and increased crime. Was the cost worth it? I think so, but others may disagree. What are the lives of would-be addicts worth? I recall some people saying to me then, "Let them kill themselves." I was appalled. Happily, such views did not prevail.

Have we lost today? Not at all. High-rate cocaine use is not commonplace. The National Institute on Drug Abuse (NIDA) reports that less than 5 percent of high-school seniors had used cocaine within the last 30 days. Of course this survey misses young people who have dropped out of school and miscounts those who lie on the questionnaire, but even if we inflate the NIDA estimate by some plausible percentage, it is still not much above 5 percent. Medical examiners reported in 1987 that about 1,500 died from cocaine use; hospital emergency rooms reported about 30,000 admissions related to cocaine abuse.

These are not small numbers, but neither are they evidence of a nationwide plague that threatens to engulf us all. Moreover, cities vary greatly in the proportion of people who are involved with cocaine. To get city-level data we need to turn to drug tests carried out on arrested persons, who obviously are more likely to be drug users than the average citizen. The National Institute of Justice, through its Drug Use Forecasting (DUF) project, collects urine analysis data on arrestees in 22 cities. As we have already seen, opiate (chiefly heroin) use has been flat or declining in most of these cities over the last decade. Cocaine use has gone up sharply, but with great variation among cities. New York, Philadelphia, and Washington, D.C., all report that two-thirds or more of their arrestees tested positive for cocaine, but in Portland, San Antonio, and Indianapolis the percentage was one-third or less.

In some neighborhoods, of course, matters have reached crisis proportions. Gangs control the streets, shootings terrorize residents, and drug-dealing occurs in plain view.

The police seem barely able to contain matters. But in these neighborhoods – unlike at Palo Alto cocktail parties – the people are not calling for legalization, they are calling for help. And often not much help has come. Many cities are willing to do almost anything about the drug problem except spend more money on it. The federal government cannot change that; only local voters and politicians can. It is not clear that they will.

It took about ten years to contain heroin. We have had experience with crack for only about three or four years. Each year we spend perhaps $11 billion on law enforcement (and some of that goes to deal with marijuana) and perhaps $2 billion on treatment. Large sums, but not sums that should lead anyone to say, 'We just can't afford this any more.'

The illegality of drugs increases crime, partly because some users turn to crime to pay for their habits, partly because some users are stimulated by certain drugs (such as crack or PCP) to act more violently or ruthlessly than they otherwise would, and partly because criminal organizations seeking to control drug supplies use force to manage their markets. These also are serious costs, but no one knows how much they would be reduced if drugs were legalized. Addicts would no longer steal to pay black-market prices for drugs, a real gain. But some, perhaps a great deal, of that gain would be offset by the great increase in the number of addicts. These people, nodding on heroin or living in the delusion-ridden high of cocaine, would hardly be ideal employees. Many would steal simply to support themselves, since snatch-and-grab, opportunistic crime can be managed even by people unable to hold a regular job or plan an elaborate crime. Those British addicts who get their supplies from government clinics are not models of law-abiding decency. Most are in crime, and though their per-capita rate of criminality may be lower thanks to the cheapness of their drugs, the total volume of crime they produce may be quite large. Of course, society could decide to support all unemployable addicts on welfare, but that would mean that gains from lowered rates of crime would have to be offset by large increases in welfare budgets.

Proponents of legalization claim that the costs of having more addicts around would be largely if not entirely offset by having more money available with which to treat and care for them. The money would come from taxes levied on the sale of heroin and cocaine.

To obtain this fiscal dividend, however, legalization's supporters must first solve an economic dilemma. If they want to raise a lot of money to pay for welfare and treatment, the tax rate on the drugs will have to be quite high. Even if they themselves do not want a high rate, the politicians' love of 'sin taxes' would probably guarantee that it would be high anyway. But the higher the tax, the higher the price of the drug, and the higher the price the greater the likelihood that addicts will turn to crime to find the money for it and that criminal organizations will be formed to sell tax-free drugs at below-market rates. If we managed to keep taxes (and thus prices) low, we would get that much less money to pay for welfare and treatment and more people could afford to become addicts. There may be an optimal tax rate for drugs that maximises revenue while minimising crime, bootlegging, and the recruitment of new addicts, but our experience with alcohol does not suggest that we know how to find it.

The benefits of illegality

The advocates of legalization find nothing to be said in favor of the current system except, possibly, that it keeps the number of addicts smaller than it would otherwise be. In fact, the benefits are more substantial than that.

First, treatment. All the talk about providing 'treatment on demand' implies that there is a demand for treatment. That is not quite right. There are some drug-dependent people who genuinely want treatment and will remain in it if offered; they should receive it. But there are far more who want only short-term help after a bad crash; once stabilized and bathed, they are back on the street again, hustling. And even many of the addicts who enroll in a program honestly wanting to help drop out after a short while when they discover that help takes time and commitment. Drug-dependent people have very short time horizons and a weak capacity for commitment. These two groups – those looking for a quick fix and those unable to stick with a long-term fix – are not easily helped. Even if we increase the number of treatment slots – as we should – we would have to do something to make treatment more effective.

One thing that can often make it more effective is compulsion. Douglas Anglin of UCLA, in common with many other researchers, has found that the longer one stays in a treatment program, the better the chances of a reduction in drug dependency. But he, again like most other researchers, has found that drop-out rates are high. He has also found, however, that patients who enter treatment under legal compulsion stay in the program longer than those not subject to such pressure. His research on the California civil-commitment program, for example, found that heroin users involved with its required drug-testing program had over the long term a lower rate of heroin use than similar addicts who were free of such constraints. If for many addicts compulsion is a useful component of treatment, it is not clear how compulsion could be achieved in a society in which purchasing, possessing, and using the drug were legal. It could be managed, I suppose, but I would not want to have to answer the challenge from the American Civil Liberties Union that it is wrong to compel a person to undergo treatment for consuming a legal commodity.

Next, education. We are now investing substantially in drug-education programs in the schools. Though we do not yet know for certain what will work, there are some promising leads. But I wonder how credible such programs would be if they were aimed at dissuading children from doing something perfectly legal. We could, of course, treat drug education like smoking education: inhaling crack and inhaling tobacco are both legal, but you should not do it because it is bad for you. That tobacco is bad for you is easily shown; the Surgeon General has seen to that. But what do we say about crack? It is pleasurable, but devoting yourself to so much pleasure is not a good idea (though perfectly legal)? Unlike tobacco, cocaine will not give you cancer or emphysema, but it will lead you to neglect your duties to family, job, and neighborhood? Everybody is doing cocaine, but you should not?

Again, it might be possible under a legalized regime to have effective drug-prevention programs, but their effectiveness would depend heavily, I think, on first having decided that cocaine use, like tobacco use, is purely a matter of practical consequences; no fundamental moral significance attaches to either. But if we believe – as I do – that dependency on certain mind-altering drugs *is* a moral issue and that their illegality rests in part on their immorality, then legalizing them undercuts, if it does not eliminate altogether, the moral message.

That message is at the root of the distinction we now make between nicotine and cocaine. Both are highly addictive; both have harmful physical effects. But we treat the two drugs differently, not simply because nicotine is so widely used as to be beyond the reach of effective prohibition, but because its use does not destroy the user's essential humanity. Tobacco shortens one's life, cocaine debases it. Nicotine alters one's habits, cocaine alters one's soul. The heavy use of crack, unlike the heavy use of tobacco, corrodes those natural sentiments of sympathy and duty that constitute our human nature and make possible our social life. To say, as does Nadelmann, that distinguishing morally between tobacco and cocaine is "little more than a transient prejudice" is close to saying that morality itself is but a prejudice.

The alcohol problem

Now we have arrived where many arguments about legalizing drugs begin: is there any reason to treat heroin and cocaine differently from the way we treat alcohol?

There is no easy answer to that question because, as with so many human problems, one cannot decide simply on the basis either of moral principles or of individual consequences; one has to temper any policy by a common-sense judgement of what is possible. Alcohol, like heroin, cocaine, PCP, and marijuana, is a drug – that is, a mood-altering substance – and consumed to excess it certainly has harmful consequences: auto accident, bar-room fights, bedroom shootings. It is also, for some people, addictive. We cannot confidently compare the addictive powers of these drugs, but the best evidence suggests that crack and heroin are much more addictive than alcohol.

Many people, Nadelmann included, argue that since the health and financial costs of alcohol abuse are so much higher than those of cocaine or heroin abuse, it is hypocritical folly to devote our efforts to preventing cocaine or drug use. But as Mark Kleiman of Harvard has pointed out, this comparison is quite misleading. What Nadelmann is doing is showing that a *legalized* drug (alcohol) produces greater social harm than *illegal* ones (cocaine and heroin). But of course. Suppose that in the 1920s we had made heroin and cocaine legal and alcohol illegal. Can anyone doubt that Nadelmann would now be writing that it is folly to continue our ban on alcohol because cocaine and heroin are so much more harmful?

And let there be no doubt about it – widespread heroin and cocaine use are associated with all manner of ills. Thomas Bewley found that the mortality rate of British heroin addicts in 1968 was 28 times as high as the death rate of the same age group of non-addicts, even though in England at the time an addict could obtain free or low-cost heroin and clean needles from British clinics. Perform the following mental experiment: suppose we legalized heroin and cocaine in this country. In what proportion of auto fatalities would the state police report that the driver was nodding off on heroin or recklessly driving on a coke high? In what proportion of spouse-assault and child-abuse

369

cases would the local police report that crack was involved? In what proportion of industrial accidents would safety investigators report that the forklift or drill-press operator was in a drug-induced stupor or frenzy? We do not know exactly what the proportion would be, but anyone who asserts that it would not be much higher than it is now would have to believe that these drugs have little appeal except when they are illegal. And that is nonsense.

An advocate of legalization might concede that social harm - perhaps harm equivalent to that already produced by alcohol – would follow from making cocaine and heroin generally available. But at least, he might add, we would have the problem 'out in the open' where it could be treated as a matter of 'public health'. That is well and good, *if* we knew how to treat – that is cure – heroin and cocaine abuse. But we do not know how to do it for all the people who would need such help. We are having only limited success in coping with chronic alcoholics. Addictive behavior is immensely difficult to change, and the best methods for changing it – living in drug-free therapeutic communities, becoming faithful members of Alcoholics Anonymous or Narcotics Anonymous – require great personal commitment, a quality that is, alas, in short supply among the very persons – young people, disadvantaged people – who are often most at risk from addiction.

Suppose that today we had, not 15 million alcohol abusers, but half a million. Suppose that we already knew what we have learned from our long experience with the widespread use of alcohol. Would we make whiskey legal? I do not know, but I suspect there would be a lively debate. The Surgeon General would remind us of the risks alcohol poses to pregnant women. The National Highway Traffic Safety Administration would point to the likelihood of more highway fatalities caused by drunk drivers. The Food and Drug Administration might find that there is a non-trivial increase in cancer associated with alcohol consumption. At the same time the police would report great difficulty in keeping illegal whiskey out of our cities, officers being corrupted by bootleggers, and alcohol addicts often resorting to crime to feed their habit. Libertarians, for their part, would argue that every citizen has a right to drink anything he wishes and that drinking is, in any event, a 'victimless crime'.

However the debate might turn out, the central fact would be that the problem was still, at that point, a small one. The government cannot legislate away the addictive tendencies in all of us, nor can it remove completely even the most dangerous addictive substances. But it can cope with harms when the harms are still manageable.

Science and addiction

One advantage of containing a problem while it is still containable is that it buys time for science to learn more about it and perhaps to discover a cure. Almost unnoticed in the current debate over legalizing drugs is that basic science has made rapid strides in identifying the underlying neurological processes involved in some forms of addiction. Stimulants such as cocaine and amphetamines alter the way certain brain cells communicate with one another. That alteration is complex and not entirely understood, but in simplified form it involves modifying the way in which a neurotransmitter called dopamine sends signals from one cell to another.

370

When dopamine crosses the synapse between two cells, it is in effect carrying a message from the first cell to activate the second one. In certain parts of the brain that message is experienced as pleasure. After the message is delivered, the dopamine returns to the first cell. Cocaine apparently blocks this return, or 'reuptake', so that the excited cell and others nearby continue to send pleasure messages. When the exaggerated high produced by cocaine-influenced dopamine finally ends, the brain cells may (in ways that are still a matter of dispute) suffer from an extreme lack of dopamine, thereby making the individual unable to experience any pleasure at all. This would explain why cocaine users often feel so depressed after enjoying the drug. Stimulants may also affect the way in which other neurotransmitters, such as serotonin and noradrenaline, operate.

Whatever the exact mechanism may be, once it is identified it becomes possible to use drugs to block either the effect of cocaine or its tendency to produce dependency. There have already been experiments using desipramine, imipramine, bromocriptine, carbamazepine, and other chemicals. There are some promising results.

Tragically, we spend very little on such research, and the agencies funding it have not in the past occupied very influential or visible posts in the federal bureaucracy. If there is one aspect of the 'war on drugs' metaphor that I dislike, it is its tendency to focus attention almost exclusively on the troops in the trenches, whether engaged in enforcement or treatment, and away from the research-and-development efforts back on the home front where the war may ultimately be decided.

I believe that the prospects of scientists in controlling addiction will be strongly influenced by the size and character of the problem they face. If the problem is a few hundred thousand chronic, high-dose users of an illegal product, the chances of making a difference at a reasonable cost will be much greater than if the problem is a few million chronic users of legal substances. Once a drug is legal, not only will its use increase but many of those who then use it will prefer the drug to the treatment: they will want the pleasure, whatever the cost to themselves or their families, and they will resist – probably successfully - any effort to wean them away from experiencing the high that comes from inhaling a legal substance.

If I am wrong ...

No one can know what our society would be like if we changed the law to make access to cocaine, heroin, and PCP easier. I believe, for reasons given, that the result would be a sharp increase in use, a more widespread degradation of the human personality, and a greater rate of accidents and violence.

I may be wrong. If I am, then we will needlessly have incurred heavy costs in law enforcement and some forms of criminality. But if I am right, and the legalizers prevail anyway, then we will have consigned millions of people, hundreds of thousands of infants, and hundreds of neighborhoods to a life of oblivion and disease. To the lives and families destroyed by alcohol we will have added countless more destroyed by cocaine, heroin, PCP, and whatever else a basement scientist can invent,

Human character is formed by society; indeed, human character is inconceivable without society, and good character is less likely in a bad society. Will we, in the name of an abstract doctrine of radical individualism, and with the false comfort of suspect predictions, decide to take the chance that somehow individual decency can survive amid a more general level of degradation?

I think not. The American people are too wise for that, whatever the academic essayists and cocktail-party pundits may say. But if Americans today are less wise than I suppose, then Americans at some future time will look back on us now and wonder, what kind of people were they that they could have done such a thing?

Note

1. I do not here take up the question of marijuana. For a variety of reasons – its widespread use and its lesser tendency to addict – it presents a different problem from cocaine or heroin. For a penetrating analysis, see Mark Kleiman, *Marijuana: Costs of Abuse, Costs of Control* (Greenwood Press, 217 pp.).

32. The Ethics of Addiction

Thomas S. Szasz

An argument in favour of letting Americans take any drug they want to take.

To avoid clichés about "drug abuse," let us analyze its official definition. According to the World Health Organization, "Drug addiction is a state of periodic or chronic intoxication detrimental to the individual and to society, produced by the repeated consumption of a drug (natural or synthetic). Its characteristics include: 1) an overpowering desire or need (compulsion) to continue taking the drug and to obtain it by any means, 2) a tendency to increase the dosage, and 3) a psychic (psychological) and sometimes physical dependence on the effects of the drug."

Since the definition hinges on the harm done to both the individual and society, it is clearly an ethical one. Moreover, by not specifying what is "detrimental," it consigns the problem of addiction to psychiatrists who define the patient's "dangerousness to himself and others."

Next, we come to the effort to obtain the addictive substance "by any means." This suggests that the substance must be prohibited, or is very expensive, and is hence difficult for the ordinary person to obtain (rather than that the person who wants it has an inordinate craving for it). If there were an abundant and inexpensive supply of what the "addict" wants, there would be no reason for him to go to "any means" to obtain it. Thus by the WHO'S definition, one can be addicted only to a substance that is illegal or otherwise difficult to obtain. This surely removes the problem of addiction from the realm of medicine and psychiatry, and puts it squarely into that of morals and law.

In short, drug addiction or drug abuse cannot be defined without specifying the proper and improper uses of certain pharmacologically active agents. The regular administration of morphine by a physician to a patient dying of cancer is the paradigm of the proper use of a narcotic; whereas even its occasional self-administration by a physically healthy person for the purpose of "pharmacological pleasure" is the paradigm of drug abuse.

I submit that these judgements have nothing whatever to do with medicine, pharmacology, or psychiatry. They are moral judgements. Indeed, our present views on addiction are astonishingly similar to some of our former views on sex. Until recently, masturbation – or self-abuse, as it was called – was professionally declared, and popularly accepted, as both the cause and the symptom of a variety of illnesses. Even today, homosexuality – called a "sexual perversion" – is regarded as a disease by medical and psychiatric experts as well as by "well-informed" laymen.

To be sure, it is now virtually impossible to cite a contemporary medical authority to support the concept of self-abuse. Medical opinion holds that whether a person masturbates or not is medically irrelevant; and that engaging in the practice or refraining from it is a matter of personal morals or life-style. On the other hand, it is virtually impossible to cite a contemporary medical authority to oppose the concept of drub abuse. Medical opinion holds that drug abuse is a major medical, psychiatric, and public health problem; that drug addiction is a disease similar to diabetes, requiring prolonged (or lifelong) and careful, medically supervised treatment; and that taking or not taking drugs is primarily, if not solely, a matter of medical responsibility.

Thus the man on the street can only believe what he hears from all sides - that drug addiction is a disease, "like any other," which has now reached "epidemic proportions," and whose "medical" containment justifies the limitless expenditure of tax monies and the corresponding aggrandizement and enrichment of noble medical warriors against this "plague."

Propaganda to justify prohibition

Like any social policy, our drug laws may be examined from two entirely different points of view: technical and moral. Our present inclination is either to ignore the moral perspective or to mistake the technical for the moral.

Since most of the propagandists against drug abuse seek to justify certain repressive policies because of the alleged dangerousness of various drugs, they often falsify the facts about the true pharmacological properties of the drugs they seek to prohibit. They do so for two reasons: first, because many substances in daily use are just as harmful as the substances they want to prohibit; second, because they realize that dangerousness alone is never a sufficiently persuasive argument to justify the prohibition of any drug, substance, or artifact. Accordingly, the more they ignore the moral dimensions of the problem, the more they must escalate their fraudulent claims about the dangers of drugs.

To be sure, some drugs are more dangerous than others. It is easier to kill oneself with heroin than with aspirin. But it is also easier to kill oneself by jumping off a high building than a low one. In the case of drugs, we regard their potentiality for self-injury as justification for their prohibition; in the case of buildings, we do not.

Furthermore, we systematically blur and confuse the two quite different ways in which narcotics may cause death: by a deliberate act of suicide or by accidental overdosage.

Every individual is capable of injuring or killing himself. This potentiality is a fundamental expression of human freedom. Self-destructive behavior may be regarded as sinful and penalized by means of informal sanctions. But it should not be regarded as a crime or (mental) disease, justifying or warranting the use of the police powers of the state for its control.

Therefore, it is absurd to deprive an adult of a drug (or of anything else) because he might use it to kill himself. To do so is to treat everyone the way institutional psychiatrists treat the so-called suicidal mental patient: they not only imprison such a person but take everything away from him – shoelaces, belts, razor blades, eating

374

utensils, and so forth – until the "patient" lies naked on a mattress in a padded cell – lest he kill himself. The result is degrading tyrannization.

Death by accidental overdose is an altogether different matter. But can anyone doubt that this danger now looms so large precisely because the sale of narcotics and many other drugs is illegal? Those who buy illicit drugs cannot be sure what drug they are getting or how much of it. Free trade in drugs, with governmental action limited to safeguarding the purity of the product and the veracity of the labeling, would reduce the risk of accidental overdose with "dangerous drugs" to the same levels that prevail, and that we find acceptable, with respect to other chemical agents and physical artifacts that abound in our complex technological society.

This essay is not intended as an exposition on the pharmacological properties of narcotics and other mind-affecting drugs. However, I want to make it clear that in my view, *regardless* of their danger, all drugs should be "legalized" (a mis-leading term I employ reluctantly as a concession to common usage). Although I recognize that some drugs – notably heroin, the amphetamines, and LSD, among those now in vogue – may have undesirable or dangerous consequences, I favor free trade in drugs for the same reason the Founding Fathers favored free trade in ideas. In an open society, it is none of the government's business what idea a man puts into his mind; likewise, it should be none of the government's business what drug he puts into his body.

Withdrawal pains from tradition

It is a fundamental characteristic of human beings that they get used to things: one becomes habituated, or "addicted," not only to narcotics, but to cigarettes, cocktails before dinner, orange juice for breakfast, comic strips, and so forth. It is similarly a fundamental characteristic of living organisms that they acquire increasing tolerance to various chemical agents and physical stimuli: the first cigarette may cause nothing but nausea and headache; a year later, smoking three packs a day may be pure joy. Both alcohol and opiates are "addictive" in the sense that the more regularly they are used, the more the user craves them and the greater his tolerance for them becomes. Yet none of this involves any mysterious process of "getting hooked." It is simply an aspect of the universal biological propensity for *learning*, which is especially well developed in man. The opiate habit, like the cigarette habit or food habit, can be broken – and without any medical assistance – provided the person wants to break it. Often he doesn't. And why, indeed, should he, if he has nothing better to do with his life? Or, as happens to be the case with morphine, if he can live an essentially normal life while under its influence?

Actually, opium is much less toxic than alcohol. Just as it is possible to be an "alcoholic" and work and be productive, so it is (or, rather, it used to be) possible to be an opium addict and work and be productive. According to a definitive study published by the American Medical Association in 1929, ".... morphine addiction is not characterized by physical deterioration or impairment of physical fitness .... There is no evidence of change in the circulatory, hepatic, renal, or endocrine functions. When it is considered that these subjects had been addicted for at least five years, some of them for as long as twenty years, these negative observations are highly significant." In a 1928 study,

Lawrence Kolb, an Assistant Surgeon General of the United States Public Health Service, found that of 199 persons addicted to opiates through medical practice, "90 had good industrial records and only 29 had poor ones ... Judged by the output of labor and their own statements, none of the normal persons had [his] efficiency reduced by opium. Twenty-two of them worked regularly while taking opium for twenty-five years or more; one of them, a woman aged 81 and still alert mentally, had taken 3 grains of morphine daily for 65 years. [The usual therapeutic dose is one-quarter grain, three to four grains being fatal for the nonaddict.] She gave birth to and raised six children, and managed her household affairs with more than average efficiency. A widow, aged 66, had taken 17 grains of morphine daily for most of 37 years. She is alert mentally .... does physical labor every day, and makes her own living."

I am not citing this evidence to recommend the opium habit. The point is that we must, in plain honesty, distinguish between pharmacological effects and personal inclinations. Some people take drugs to help them function and conform to social expectations; others take them for the very opposite reason, to ritualize their refusal to function and conform to social expectations. Much of the "drug abuse" we now witness – perhaps nearly all of it – is of the second type. But instead of acknowledging that "addicts" are unfit or unwilling to work and be "normal", we prefer to believe that they act as they do because certain drugs – especially heroin, LSD, and the amphetamines – make them "sick." If only we could get them "well," so runs this comforting view, they would become "productive" and "useful" citizens. To believe this is like believing that if an illiterate cigarette smoker would only stop smoking, he would become an Einstein. With a falsehood like this, one can go far. No wonder that politicians and psychiatrists love it.

The concept of free trade in drugs runs counter to our cherished notion that everyone must work and idleness is acceptable only under special conditions. In general, the obligation to work is greatest for healthy, adult, white men. We tolerate idleness on the part of children, women, Negroes, the aged, and the sick, and even accept the responsibility to support them. But the new wave of drug abuse affects mainly young adults, often white males, who are, in principle at least, capable of working and supporting themselves. But they refuse: they "drop out"; and in doing so, they challenge the most basic values of our society.

The fear that free trade in narcotics would result in vast masses of our population spending their days and nights smoking opium or mainlining heroin, rather than working and taking care of their responsibilities, is a bugaboo that does not deserve to be taken seriously. Habits of work and idleness are deep-seated cultural patterns. Free trade in abortions has not made an industrious people like the Japanese give up work for fornication. Nor would free trade in drugs convert such a people from hustlers to hippies. Indeed, I think the opposite might be the case: it is questionable whether, or for how long, a responsible people can tolerate being treated as totally irresponsible with respect to drugs and drug-taking. In other words, how long can we live with the inconsistency of being expected to be responsible for operating cars and computers, but not for operating our own bodies?

Although my argument about drug-taking is moral and political, and does not depend upon showing that free trade in drugs would also have fiscal advantages over our present policies, let me indicate briefly some of its economic implications.

The war on addiction is not only astronomically expensive; it is also counterproductive. On April 1, 1967, New York State's narcotics addiction control program, hailed as "the most massive ever tried in the nation," went into effect. "The program, which may cost up to $400 million in three years," reported the *New York Times*, "was hailed by Governor Rockefeller as 'the start of an unending war.'" Three years later, it was conservatively estimated that the number of addicts in the state had tripled or quadrupled. New York State Senator John Hughes reports that the cost of caring for each addict during this time was $12,000 per year (as against $4,000 per year for patients in state mental hospitals). It's been a great time, though, for some of the ex-addicts. In New York City's Addiction Services Agency, one ex-addict started at $6,500 a year in 1967, and was making $16,000 seven months later. Another started at $6,500 and soon rose to $18,000. The salaries of the medical bureaucrats in charge of these programs are similarly attractive. In short, the detection and rehabilitation of addicts is good business. We now know that the spread of witchcraft in the late Middle Ages was due more to the work of witchmongers than to the lure of witchcraft. Is it not possible that the spread of addiction in our day is due more to the work of addictmongers than to the lure of narcotics?

Let us see how far some of the monies spent on the war on addiction could go in supporting people who prefer to drop put of society and drug themselves. Their "habit" itself would cost next to nothing; free trade would bring the price of narcotics down to a negligible amount. During the 1969-70 fiscal year, the New York State Narcotics Addiction Control Commission had a budget of nearly $50 million, excluding capital construction. Using these figures as a tentative base for calculation, here is what we come to: $100 million will support 30,000 drug addicts at $3,300 per year. Since the population of New York State is roughly one-tenth that of the nation, if we multiply its operating budget for addiction control by ten, we arrive at a figure of $500 million, enough to support 150,000 addicts.

I am not advocating that we spend our hard-earned money in this way. I am only trying to show that free trade in narcotics would be more economical for those of us who work, even if we had to support legions of addicts, than is our present program of trying to "cure" them. Moreover, I have not even made use, in my economic estimates, of the incalculable sums we would save by reducing crimes now engendered by the illegal traffic in drugs.

The right of self-medication

Clearly, the argument that marijuana – or heroin, methadone, or morphine – is prohibited because it is addictive or dangerous cannot be supported by facts. For one thing, there are many drugs, from insulin to penicillin, that are neither addictive nor dangerous but are nevertheless also prohibited; they can be obtained only through a physician's prescription. For another, there are many things, from dynamite to guns, that are much more dangerous than narcotics (especially to others) but are not prohibited. As everyone knows, it is still possible in the United States to walk into a store and walk out with a shotgun. We enjoy this right not because we believe that guns are safe but because we believe even more strongly that civil liberties are precious. At the same time, it is not possible in the United States to walk into a store and walk out with a bottle of barbiturates, codeine, or other drugs.

I believe that just as we regard freedom of speech and religion as fundamental rights, so we should also regard freedom of self-medication as a fundamental right. Like most rights, the right of self-medication should apply only to adults; and it should not be an unqualified right. Since these are important qualifications, it is necessary to specify their precise range.

John Stuart Mill said (approximately) that a person's right to swing his arm ends where his neighbor's nose begins. And Oliver Wendell Holmes said that no one has a right to shout "Fire!" in a crowded theater. Similarly, the limiting condition with respect to self-medication should be the inflicting of actual (as against symbolic) harm on others.

Our present practices with respect to alcohol embody and reflect this individualistic ethic. We have the right to buy, possess, and consume alcoholic beverages. Regardless of how offensive drunkenness might be to a person, he cannot interfere with another person's "right" to become inebriated so long as that person drinks in the privacy of his own home or at some other appropriate location, and so long as he conducts himself in an otherwise law-abiding manner. In short, we have a right to be intoxicated – in private. Public intoxication is considered an offense to others and is therefore a violation of the criminal law. It makes sense that what is a "right" in one place may become, by virtue of its disruptive or disturbing effect on others, an offense somewhere else.

The right to self-medication should be hedged in by similar limits. Public intoxication, not only with alcohol but with any drug, should be an offense punishable by the criminal law. Furthermore, acts that may injure others – such as driving a car – should, when carried out in a drug-intoxicated state, be punished especially strictly and severely. The right to self-medication must thus entail unqualified responsibility for the effects of one's drug-intoxicated behavior on others. For unless we are willing to hold ourselves responsible for our own behavior, and hold others responsible for theirs, the liberty to use drugs (or to engage in other acts) degenerates into a license to hurt others.

Such, then, would be the situation of adults, if we regarded the freedom to take drugs as a fundamental right similar to the freedom to read and worship. What would be the situation of children? Since many people who are now said to be drug addicts or drug abusers are minors, it is especially important that we think clearly about this aspect of the problem.

I do not believe, and I do not advocate, that children should have a right to ingest, inject, or otherwise use any drug or substance they want. Children do not have the right to drive, drink, vote, marry, or make binding contracts. They acquire these rights at various ages, coming into their full possession at maturity, usually between the ages of eighteen and twenty-one. The right to self-medication should similarly be withheld until maturity.

In short, I suggest that "dangerous" drugs be treated, more or less, as alcohol is treated now. Neither the use of narcotics, nor their possession, should be prohibited, but only their sale to minors. Of course, this would result in the ready availability of all kinds of drugs among minors – though perhaps their availability would be no greater than it is now, but would only be more visible and hence more easily subject to proper controls. This arrangement would place responsibility for the use of all drugs by children where it belongs: on parents and their children. This is where the major responsibility rests for the use of alcohol. It is a tragic symptom of our refusal to take personal liberty and responsibility seriously that there appears to be no public desire to assume a similar stance toward other "dangerous" drugs.

Consider what would happen should a child bring a bottle of gin to school and get drunk there. Would the school authorities blame the local liquor stores as pushers? Or would they blame the parents and the child himself? There is liquor in practically every home in America and yet children rarely bring liquor to school. Whereas marijuana, Dexedrine, and heroin – substances children usually do not find at home and whose very possession is a criminal offense – frequently find their way into the school.

Our attitude toward sexual activity provides another model for our attitude toward drugs. Although we generally discourage children below a certain age from engaging in sexual activities with others, we do not prohibit such activities by law. What we do prohibit by law is the sexual seduction of children by adults. The "pharmacological seduction" of children by adults should be similarly punishable. In other words, adults who give or sell drugs to children should be regarded as offenders. Such a specific and limited prohibition – as against the kinds of generalized prohibitions that we had under the Volstead Act or have now with respect to countless drugs – would be relatively easy to enforce. Moreover, it would probably be rarely violated, for there would be little psychological interest and no economic profit in doing so.

The true faith: scientific medicine

What I am suggesting is that while addiction is ostensibly a medical and pharmacological problem, actually it is a moral and political problem. We ought to know that there is no necessary connection between facts and values, between what is and what ought to be. Thus, objectively quite harmful acts, objects, or persons may be accepted and tolerated – by minimizing their dangerousness. Conversely, objectively quite harmless acts, objects, or persons may be prohibited and persecuted – by exaggerating their dangerousness. It is always necessary to distinguish – and especially so when dealing with social policy – between description and prescription, fact and rhetoric, truth and falsehood.

In our society, there are two principal methods of legitimizing policy: social tradition and scientific judgement. More than anything else, time is the supreme ethical arbiter. Whatever a social practice might be, if people engage in it, generation after generation, that practice becomes acceptable.

Many opponents of illegal drugs admit that nicotine may be more harmful to health than marijuana; nevertheless, they urge that smoking cigarettes should be legal but smoking marijuana should not be, because the former habit is socially accepted while the latter is not. This is a perfectly reasonable argument. But let us understand it for what it is – a plea for legitimizing old and accepted practices, and for illegitimizing novel and unaccepted ones. It is a justification that rests on precedent, not evidence.

The other method of legitimizing policy, ever more important in the modern world, is through the authority of science. In matters of health, a vast and increasingly elastic category, physicians play important roles as legitimizers and illegitimizers. This, in short, is why we regard being medicated by a doctor as drug use, and self-medication (especially with certain classes of drugs) as drug abuse.

This, too, is a perfectly reasonable arrangement. But we must understand that it is a plea for legitimizing what doctors do, because they do it with "good therapeutic" intent; and for illegitimizing what laymen do, because they do it with bad self-abusive ("masturbatory" or mind-altering) intent. This justification rests on the principles of professionalism, not of pharmacology. Hence we applaud the systematic medical use of methadone and call it "treatment for heroin addiction," but decry the occasional non-medical use of marijuana and call it "dangerous drug abuse."

Our present concept of drug abuse articulates and symbolizes a fundamental policy of scientific medicine – namely, that a layman should not medicate his own body but should place its medical care under the supervision of a duly accredited physician. Before the Reformation, the practice of True Christianity rested on a similar policy – namely, that a layman should not himself commune with God but should place his spiritual care under the supervision of a duly accredited priest. The self-interests of the church and of medicine in such policies are obvious enough. What might be less obvious is the interest of the laity: by delegating responsibility for the spiritual and medical welfare of the people to a class of authoritatively accredited specialists, these policies – and the practices they ensure – relieve individuals from assuming the burdens of responsibility for themselves. As I see it, our present problems with drug use and drug abuse are just one of the consequences of our pervasive ambivalence about personal autonomy and responsibility.

I propose a medical reformation analogous to the Protestant Reformation: specifically, a "protest" against the systematic mystification of man's relationship to his body and his professionalized separation from it. The immediate aim of this reform would be to remove the physician as intermediary between man and his body and to give the layman direct access to the language and contents of the pharmacopoeia. If man had unencumbered access to his own body and the means of chemically altering it, it would spell the end of medicine, at least as we now know it. This is why, with faith in scientific medicine so strong, there is little interest in this kind of medical reform. Physicians fear the loss of their privileges; laymen, the loss of their protections.

Finally, since luckily we still do not live in the utopian perfection of "one world", our technical approach to the "drug problem" has led, and will undoubtedly continue to lead, to some curious attempts to combat it.

Here is one such attempt: the American government is now pressuring Turkey to restrict its farmers from growing poppies (the source of morphine and heroin). If turnabout is fair play, perhaps we should expect the Turkish government to pressure the United States to restrict its farmers from growing corn and wheat. Or should we assume that Muslims have enough self-control to leave alcohol alone, but Christians need all the controls that politicians, policemen, and physicians can bring to bear on them to enable them to leave opiates alone?

Life, liberty, and the pursuit of highs

Sooner or later we shall have to confront the basic moral dilemma underlying this problem: does a person have the right to take a drug, any drug – not because he needs it to cure an illness, but because he wants to take it?

The Declaration of Independence speaks of our inalienable right to "life, liberty, and the pursuit of happiness." How are we to interpret this? By asserting that we ought to be free to pursue happiness by playing golf or watching television, but not by drinking alcohol, or smoking marijuana, or ingesting pep pills?

The Constitution and the Bill of Rights are silent on the subject of drugs. This would seem to imply that the adult citizen has, or ought to have, the right to medicate his own body as he sees fit. Were this the case, why should there have been a need for a Constitutional Amendment to outlaw drinking? But if ingesting alcohol was, and is now again, a Constitutional right, is ingesting opium, or heroin, or barbiturates, or anything else, not also such a right? If it is, then the Harrison Narcotic Act is not only a bad law but is unconstitutional as well, because it prescribes in a legislative act what ought to be promulgated in a Constitutional Amendment.

The questions remain: as American citizens, should we have the right to take narcotics or other drugs? If we take drugs and conduct ourselves as responsible and law-abiding citizens, should we have a right to remain unmolested by the government? Lastly, if we take drugs and break the law, should we have a right to be treated as persons accused of crime, rather than as patients accused of mental illness?

These are fundamental questions that are conspicuous by their absence from all contemporary discussions of problems of drug addiction and drug abuse. The result is that instead of debating the use of drugs in moral and political terms, we define our task as the ostensibly narrow technical problem of protecting people from poisoning themselves with substances for whose use they cannot possibly assume responsibility. This, I think, best explains the frightening national consensus against personal responsibility for taking drugs and for one's conduct while under their influence. In 1965, for example, when President Johnson sought a bill imposing tight federal controls over pep pills and goof balls, the bill cleared the House by a unanimous vote, 402 to 0.

The failure of such measures to curb the "drug menace" has only served to inflame our legislators' enthusiasm for them. In October 1970 the Senate passed, again by a unanimous vote (54 to 0) "a major narcotics crackdown bill."

To me, unanimity on an issue as basic and complex as this means a complete evasion of the actual problem and an attempt to master it by attacking and overpowering a scapegoat – "dangerous drugs" and "drug abusers." There is an ominous resemblance between the unanimity with which all "reasonable" men – and especially policitians, physicians, and priests – formerly supported the protective measures of society against witches and Jews, and that with which they now support them against drug addicts and drug abusers.

After all is said and done, the issue comes down to whether we accept or reject the ethical principle John Stuart Mill so clearly enunciated: "The only purpose [he wrote in *On Liberty*] for which power can be rightfully exercised over any member of a civilized community, against his will, is to prevent harm to others. His own good, either physical or moral, is not a sufficient warrant. He cannot rightfully be compelled to do or forbear because it will make him happier, because in the opinions of others, to do so would be wise, or even right .... In the part [of his conduct] which merely concerns himself, his independence is, of right, absolute. Over himself, over his own body and mind, the individual is sovereign."

By recognizing the problem of drug abuse for what it is – a moral and political question rather than a medical or therapeutic one – we can choose to maximise the sphere of action of the state at the expense of the individual, or of the individual at the expense of the state. In other words, we could commit ourselves to the view that the state, the representative of many, is more important than the individual; that it therefore has the right, indeed the duty, to regulate the life of the individual in the best interests of the group. Or we could commit ourselves to the view that individual dignity and liberty are the supreme values of life, and that the foremost duty of the state is to protect and promote these values.

In short, we must choose between the ethic of collectivism and individualism, and pay the price of either – or of both.

Drugs in Sport: Moral Dilemmas

Many of the issues in the sporting world relating to drug use are becoming increasingly similar to those in the non-sporting world. This is especially true since the inclusion of anabolic steroids in 1990 into the US Controlled Substances Act effectively brought the distribution, possession, or prescription of anabolic steroids under control and made the intent to distribute without a valid prescription a felony, and recent pressure here in Britain to incorporate steroids into the Misuse of Drugs Act (1971) means that the two worlds are increasingly intertwined. One of the problems however is that few in authority in the world of sport, particularly those in Olympic sports (which have tended to take a lead in this issue), demonstrate much knowledge about drug use in society and tend to an insular view of the problem of drugs in sport. They believe it presents a different set of problems and that prohibition would be based on perhaps less problematic criteria: that the use of performance enhancing drugs is unfair and that the athletes must be protected against the serious health care risks that they present. The main problem here is that policy makers in the sporting world are possibly re-inventing the [square] wheel when it comes to legislating against drugs, with many of the adopted policies proven to be ineffective in the non-sporting world. On this basis the two papers in this section try to re-contextualise the nature of the problem of drug use in sport. Coomber illustrates the pitfalls of exacerbating the war on drugs in sport to achieve drug free competition, both as an unattainable goal, and as an (unintended) consequence, as a policy perhaps increasing the overall level of drug-related harm as opposed to preventing it. Cashmore similarly questions a number of assumptions about the nature of prohibitory legislation against performance enhancing drugs, pursuing the argument that the ideal of a level playing field in sport is undermined by all manner of inequities, many of which are contributed to by the laws of various sports or sporting authorities themselves.

33. Drugs in Sport: Rhetoric or Pragmatism

Ross Coomber

Ross Coomber looks at the latest battleground in the 'War on Drugs', the sporting arena, and contends that an effective policy on drugs in sport should be based on pragmatism because the means to detect and prevent their use do not exist.

The message from sports' governing bodies for some time now has suggested that sport is largely drug free and that appropriate detection methods are available and being employed to ensure it stays that way in the name of fair play and health protection. If at times the problem appears to be getting out of hand, all that is needed is an injection of more of the same, i.e. spend increasingly greater sums of money to enhance detection and therefore reduce demand by making the activity too precarious to warrant continued involvement. On the surface, evidence appears to support this supposition, and as a consequence validates the existing policy stance which severely punishes those who attempt to gain advantage through the use of performance enhancing drugs. The policy of prohibition, combined with the policy of testing for drugs and the consequent castigation and public shame if caught, seems to act as sufficient deterrent and thus as successful policy. There are, however, a number of reasons why current policy regarding performance-enhancing drugs is both inadequate and misinformed. This will be examined with particular reference to harm reduction as an alternative basis for policy on drugs in sport.

How many?

Sporting authorities such as the International Olympic Committee (IOC), the International Amateur Athletics Foundation (IAAF) and the British Amateur Athletics Board (BAAB) point to small numbers of competitors found to have banned substances in their urine at major sporting events such as the Olympic Games, the World Championships and at national competitions. In the 1988 Seoul Olympic Games, for example, only 10 competitors, including Ben Johnson, were disqualified for the use of performance-enhancing drugs. Out of roughly 13,000 athletes who competed in Seoul this represents 0.08% and suggests that the idea of widespread drug use has little foundation. This picture, however contrasts significantly with that portrayed by athletes* themselves and a number of officials who have, on occasion, been willing to talk out. Anecdotal reports of the extent of drug use are startling. Some (like the ex-British Olympic runner David Jenkins, a self confessed user convicted of trafficking and supplying drugs to athletes) suggest that as many as 50% of the Olympic competitors and up to two-thirds of medal winners took drugs in Seoul (Ward and Rice,

---

* Although many of the examples given refer directly to athletes, the term 'athlete' should be taken to mean those participants involved in competitive sporting activities which may conceivably benefit from enhanced performance.

Ross Coomber: 'Drugs in Sport: Rhetoric or Pragmatism', *THE INTERNATIONAL JOURNAL OF DRUG POLICY* (1993), Vol. 4, No. 4, pp. 169-178.© Ross Coomber.

1989). Such accusations are not only made by 'shamed' athletes such as Jenkins. Other famous British athletes such as Tessa Sanderson and Daley Thompson have argued publicly that between 60% and 80%, respectively, of British athletes are on drugs (Sanders, 1986; Coni et al., 1988) and in the USA reports of widespread use of performance-enhancing drugs are also commonplace. Some high-placed officials such as Prince Alexandre de Merode, the head of the IOC's medical Commission, has suggested that 10% or more of the competitors at the 1992 Barcelona Olympics had used them (Hubbard, 1993) and Dr James Puffer, chief physician of the US Olympic team, has, even more pessimistically, estimated that the figure of top athletes was around 50% (Doust et al., 1988). Essentially, however, apart from a few high profile officials occasionally talking more candidly (perhaps just before or after the implementation of new legislation), we have a situation where most of the governing bodies officially declare that the problem of drug use is minimal and has been effectively contained, whereas competitors willing to speak out, those who use, have used and do not use, claim that drug use is actually common if not prevalent. Even if we argue that the estimates of Daley Thompson (80%) and Tessa Sanderson (60%) are a tenfold exaggeration (an arbitrary (under?) estimate on my part) that would still mean that between 780 and 1040 of the 13 000 competitors at the Seoul Olympics had used drugs. As I mentioned above, only 10 were found guilty and disqualified. In the wake of the Ben Johnson affair in Seoul, the Canadian Government set up an official enquiry, The Commission of Inquiry into the Use of Drugs and Banned Practices Intended to Increase Athletic Performance, headed by one of their senior judges, Charles Dubin. Citing Sir Arthur Gold, chairman of the British Olympic Committee, that, 'only the careless and ill-advised get caught' and after hearing a great deal of evidence, much of it citing prevalence levels in excess of 50%, the report concludes in respect to prevalence that 'many, many more athletes than those actually testing positive have taken advantage of banned substances and practices (Dubin, 1990, p. 349). A similar enquiry carried out by the Australian Senate also heard evidence which suggested that '70 per cent of the athletes in Australia's international pool took, or had taken, ergogenic [performance enhancing] aids and that 25 per cent of the 29 athletes in Australia's 1988 Olympic track and field squad had taken, or were taking, ergogenic aids in their preparation for Seoul' and accepted that drug taking in Australian sport was 'widespread' (Black, 1989, p. 62).

It seems then the 'War on Drugs' is also being lost in the sporting arena. If we accept that far more athletes use performance-enhancing drugs than is officially accepted and recorded, what we need to explore is how is it possible to have such a wide disjuncture between the pronouncements of sporting authorities and those closer to the ground. There appears to be two primary reasons for such a difference. First, current procedures are inadequate as a means of detecting the great majority of the use of performance-enhancing drugs. Second, it has been argued that sporting authorities have not been and are unlikely to be entirely candid about the extent of drug use in sport because of the perceived damage a more realistic appraisal may have on the multi-million pound industry (Dubin 1990; Voy 1991; Simson and Jennings, 1992). If the use of performance-enhancing drugs is common rather than anomalous, policy designed to deal with it should reflect this situation, not ignore, deny or underplay it.

If the use of performance-enhancing drugs was uncommon then the existing policy of prohibition and punishment could be considered effective; as it is, it can only be considered ineffective and inappropriate.

Will athletes stop using performance-enhancing drugs?

As in the non-sporting world, demand for prohibited drugs is likely to continue- albeit for different reasons; the problem, however, has its similarities. Those using drugs are unlikely to respond to or trust sporting authority indictments of various substances as either unethical or unhealthy or to listen to their pleas for abstention – the 'Don't be a Dope' campaign by the British Athletic Federation being the latest equivalent to the much criticised 'Just Say No' campaign waged against heroin use in Britain in the 1980s. Athletes are and will continue to take drugs. It would be wrong to try to suggest deterministic factors which make athletes use drugs because the pressures and motivations are undoubtedly manifold. However, some evidence is revealing and perhaps indicative of why athletes use performance-enhancing drugs. One survey of over 100 top American athletes in the late 1970s revealed that nearly 55% of them reported that they would be willing to take a drug which would kill them within a year if it could assure them of an Olympic gold medal (cited in Donohoe and Johnson, 1986); a follow-up to this study in 1984, using similar methodology, found that, of 198 world class athletes, 52% said they would take a 'wonder drug' that would probably kill them after 5 years if it guaranteed success (Goldman 1984). Recent studies of anabolic steroid users in gymnasiums have also indicated that the motivation to use steroids came from the perceived benefits obtained from their use and that knowledge of the purported risks did little if anything to deter them from use (Tricker et al., 1989); in fact users are often unconvinced of the credibility of the research, citing cigarettes and alcohol as carrying greater risk (Korkia and Stimson, 1993). This study also reported that 87% of the 94 interviewees who responded to the question said that they would continue to use steroids if they became illegal. Clearly, dissuasion from regular use to abstinence is difficult to achieve on the basis of proselytising about either health or the ethics of fairness. The expected benefits from performance-enhancing drugs at present appear to heavily outweigh the fear of the potential risk. For some, the accolade of a gold medal may provide the motivation to use them; for others, it may well be the benefits that accrue with sporting success. As Weis has said:

> 'the more sport becomes professionalised, the more winning as opposed to the means by which it is achieved, is emphasised as the goal of sports aspirations and, finally, the more significant the economic or other consequences of victory are, the greater is the probability that the rules of sport will be violated in favor of other interests... Wherever victory and success are the highest goals, the end will legitimize illegitimate means.'
>
> Weis, 1976 quoted in Johansson 1987, p. 95

Whatever the reasons, and they are varied (desire to win or succeed at any cost; desire not to be at a disadvantage to those already taking the drugs; the pressure to gain or keep sponsorship either to continue participating or to provide a comfortable income; the fame, wealth and glory which accompanies success; the desire to 'fill out' [for cosmetic or competitive purposes]; the 'encouragement' from other athletes, coaches or even family; a lack of confidence in scientific 'risk' evidence) drug use is deemed to be legitimate for many in practice if not as an ideal. What we have to accept is that there is nothing intrinsic to modern competitive sport which encourages athletes to care for the 'taking part' over the winning. Sport at the top is effectively a career not a microcosm or model of how we should behave morally and socially. For these reasons and more it is difficult to see the use of performance-enhancing drugs declining voluntarily.

Can athletes be prevented from using performance-enhancing drugs:more of the same?

If athletes are unlikely to stop of their own volition, can we reasonably expect sporting authorities to succeed in preventing drug use? A historically informed answer would suggest not. Detection techniques and facilities have improved significantly in recent years, especially at the major sporting events, but levels of detection have not risen consistently or significantly. We find, for example, that, in the 1976 Montreal Olympic Games, 2.9% of the 275 tests were positive for anabolic steroids; in Moscow in 1980 there were no positive returns from 1500 tests; in Los Angeles (1984) 1.1% of the 1510 were positive; in Seoul (1988) 2% of the 1500 tested were positive (Yesalis, 1993). Athletes, of course, are fully aware that testing will take place at the Olympics and other major sporting events, and have ample opportunity to clear their system of tell-tale traces of drug use and/or 'hide' possible traces with so-called masking agents. This average of 2% or thereabouts for positive testing of anabolic steroids in the Olympics has even been superior in certain major sporting events in the USA, such as the 1987 US Olympic Festival in Greensboro where only 1.0% of 628 tested were positive, and the 1988 and the 1989 Olympic Committee-sponsored events were 0.2% recorded positive from 5000 tests in both cases (Yesalis, 1993). When the US Olympic Committee carried out tests at a number of events unannounced, i.e. where the athletes did not expect testing to take place, the picture looked completely different. Rather than 2% or less testing positive for anabolic steroids, the figure was in fact closer to 50% (Simson and Jennings, 1992). Athletes clearly have the ability, on the whole, to avoid the detection of their use of drugs such as anabolic steroids from current technology. Moreover, the idea that detection methods are effectively reigning in and reducing demand by keeping ahead of the users' ability to avoid detection is in reality somewhat problematic (Donohoe and Johnson, 1986; Feerstle, 1993). Rather than technology keeping drug use at bay, it has and is in fact tending to help users stay ahead of the means to detect the use of performance-enhancing drugs. Even those involved in the detection of their use have revealed the concern of the sporting authorities by pointing out that one of the main problems for the future is the use of artificially manufactured substances such as somatotropin and erythropoietin. Somatotropin is a synthetic growth hormone reputedly more effective than anabolic steroids, with fewer unwanted (side) effects,* and mimicking a naturally occurring substance in humans, for the sake of determining foul play, is to date beyond the capabilities of the testers. Likewise erythropoietin, again a naturally occurring substance in humans, permits red blood cells to carry more oxygen and thus reproduce the effects expected from the previous

* The efficacy of human growth hormone as a performance-enhancing drug is highly questionable as are its claims to be less harmful than anabolic steroids. It is, however, taken by athletes on this broadly assumed basis.

practice of blood-doping, and increase endurance. Although these substances are detectable, erythropoietin and growth hormone occur differentially in individuals, some having high and some low levels, and there is at present no way of knowing what an individual's 'natural' level should be. Added to the way that 'progress' is permitting athletes to avoid detection should be added the long list of techniques that have been and are being used by athletes to successfully provide false samples (the use of catheters and other means to supply clean urine; 'masking agents' such as diuretics which hide or flush out residues of the banned drug; and/or the use of 'other' ergogenic compounds which are not on the banned list) and, of late, the questioning in court, by Butch Reynolds, Katrin Krabbe, Jason Livingston and others of the reliability of the testing procedures themselves. The infallibility of the tests has also been questioned (Ferstle, 1993) and, in relation to non-IOC accredited laboratories, found seriously wanting (Uzych, 1991). If detection procedures are lacking (and even random, out of competition testing will not resolve the problem of the use of naturally occurring substances), and they clearly appear to be, the way forward is not to push for more artillery, as in the wider 'War on Drugs', because the evidence suggests that new ways to avoid detection will be employed.

As if the technical problems of detecting the use of performance-enhancing drugs in athletes was not sufficient to undermine attempts to reduce demand, the logistics of producing a uniform, consistent (across sports governing bodies, within nations and through-out the world) and therefore effective anti-doping policy have, to date, proved difficult to achieve, and possible future developments, where governing bodies are increasingly controlled by the athletes taking part, may make the process ever more unlikely (Houlihan, 1991), if indeed at all possible.

Prevention through attempting to cut back demand has, to date, largely failed. Prevention of supply is likely to be similarly unsuccessful as it has been historically for illicit drugs such as cocaine, heroin and marijuana in the world outside of sport, where enforcement resources are much more plentiful. Athletes have commonly testified to the ease of access to and the availability of performance-enhancing drugs (Davies, 1984; Goldman, 1984; Sanderson, 1986) and the likelihood of this availability being stemmed while demand remains high is slim indeed.

Sport in the twentieth century – a commercial undertaking:effects on policy

The greatest level of anti-doping detective work takes place in athletics. To a large extent this is because athletics and its primary showpiece – the Olympics- have over the years been attributed with a set of ideals which are as much a part and parcel of the sporting activities as the competing itself. In fact notions such as 'taking part' being the *raison de'être* of participation in sport, rather than the winning, have always rested uneasily with the glories and motivations supplied by Gold, Silver or Bronze received on an Olympic podium. Contemporary sport is also qualitatively different to the era in which more idealised notions of sport were reconstructed in the late nineteenth century, and this tends to undermine that already fragile tension: the fact that amateur sport as we know it is all but dead. When Baron Pierre de Coubertin – the founder of the modern Olympics – stated that 'The important thing in life is not the triumph but the struggle. The essential thing is not to have conquered but to have fought well', he could have barely imagined the context in which sporting events take place today. Top 'amateur' athletes receive what are effectively large payments for participating and continuing to compete (appearance money, sponsorships, scholarships, prizes, employment which is often little more than a well-paid sinecure) just about any time they perform and even the sacred cow of 'olympicdom' now permits professional (multi-millionaire) basketball and tennis players to compete legitimately for its own prizes, as long as the receive no direct payment for being Olympians. The 1993 World Championships, for example, presented each of its gold medal winners with a £20,000 Mercedes Benz (Bierley, 1993) and the payment of appearance money to ensure the top names are in attendance to help maintain the status and credibility of the event was resisted this time, but is unlikely to hold out much longer. Major events need to continue to succeed or they will decline.

Second string events such as the World Cup, which followed in the wake of the 1992 Olympics, suffered from such a failure of credibility as many of the world's top athletes chose not to take part in it – the effect was to destabilise the event even further. Athletics is now a multi-billion pound commercial undertaking. If athletic events decline, the bottom begins to fall out of the now lucrative industry. This has led to suggestions that it is not in the interests of bodies, such as the IOC, the IAAF or in fact any body attempting to maintain a high profile for its sporting activity, either to disclose the true level of doping infringements (reports of positive tests going unreported) or to put in place prevention policies which would make the use of performance-enhancing drugs very much more difficult. The damage – or at least the perceived damage – that may be done to an event such as the Olympics, if the public feel themselves not to be watching great athletes but artificially induced achievements, is seen to be far reaching and potentially fatal, in a commercial sense.

The IOC and other sporting authorities have, on the one hand, to be seen to be doing something about drugs, but, on the other, exercise damage limitation for the 'good' of the sport as a whole. If too many Ben Jonsons are consistently found, in the name of keeping sport clean, this too may detract from public confidence, for sport would be self evidently dirty. The sincerity of policy designed to mitigate against drug use in sport has therefore been questioned by a number of commentators and enquiries (Gold, 1989; Dubin, 1990; Simson and Jennings 1992). Although I have suggested so far that the technology and the application are not available to detect the use of drugs successfully to act as an effective deterrent, Simson and Jennings (1992) cynically but forcefully argue that, even where it has caught competitors out, at times these positives have been selectively covered up; this is because some of the names involved are so prominent that it would not have been in the long-term interests of athletics to expose them. Voy (1991), moreover, frustrated in his attempts to help clean up athletics in the USA, also suggests that sporting authorities are complicit in the cover up and not in the eradication of drug use. Although it is true that the US Olympic Committee set up unannounced tests before the Los Angeles games which they described as an 'educational, non-punitive, drug-testing programme', Simson and Jennings suggest that the real reason for its existence was to ensure that US Olympians did not embarrass the host nation during the games themselves. The chances of the USA hosting the games for the second time in a space of 12 years would surely not have borne fruit if American athletes were seen to be less drug free than other nations. Simson and Jennings argue that the 'education programme' was 'a transparent joke;... It was a godsend to the dopers. They flocked to use the lab, to discover more precisely how fast their bodies cleared of tell-tale steroid traces ... No Americans were caught at the LA Games. Fourteen foreign competitors were' (Simson and Jennings, 1992, p. 190). Robert Voy, the former Chief Medical Officer and Director of Sports Medicine and Science for the US Olympic Committee between 1984 and 1989, has said that 'Allowing national governing bodies... such as the United States Olympic Committee to govern the testing process to ensure fair play in sport is terribly ineffective. In a sense, it is like having the fox guard the hen house' (Voy, 1991, p.101). The commitment to providing 'drug-free' sporting events therefore is not necessarily the same as a commitment to preventing athletes from taking drugs.

It may be argued then that current policy is sometimes more symbolic in nature than it is a sincere and concerted effort to ensure that drug use in sport is effectively curtailed.

Reasons and justification for the prohibition of performance-enhancing drugs

The main justifications for the banning of performance-enhancing drugs are that they do provide an unfair advantage to athletes over those who do not take them, and their use is likely to cause harm to the athlete involved. These two essentially ethical justifications (Fraleigh, 1985), one based on the moral responsibility of governing bodies to protect athletes from unreasonable injurious practices and the other on the assumption that drugs introduced unfair advantage, are despite initial appearances far from being self-evidently straightforward or unproblematic.

Regarding unfair practice, there are policy inconsistencies, for example, surrounding what counts as banned substances and practices regarding the enhancement of performance. Erythropoietin, used to reproduce the effects of altitude training, is banned whereas the practice of training at altitude is, quite reasonably, permitted. The use of anabolic steroids to get stronger and to enhance training is banned (if performance is enhanced through anabolic steroid use it is only in conjunction with hard, specialised training and diet) whereas an otherwise debilitated athlete is permitted to use (under medical supervision) cortico-steroid pain killers to enable him or her to compete almost immediately to satisfactory levels – Peter Elliot in the Seoul Olympics won Silver after undergoing a series of cortisone injections – when they would not otherwise be able to. At the time of writing a new 'food supplement' (used incidentally by world champions Linford Christie, Sally Gunnel and Colin Jackson) has been much vaunted as able to produce up to a 5-7% enhancement of performance (Brown, 1993) – the sort of improvement attributed to some drugs. One, however, is permissible, the other not.

For the purposes of this article and the policy prescription which will be outlined, it is not, however, entirely relevant whether the so-called performance-enhancing drugs actually do improve a competitor's performance significantly. The important factor relevant to policy analysis and prescription is that many (most?) athletes believe that they do. This belief is unlikely to be countered by the now long espoused denials by medical authorities that performance-enhancing drugs do not work – mainly because they tend to be used by athletes in ways which are unlikely for ethical reasons, to be duplicated (and therefore verified) in humans for the purpose of research, e.g. polypharmacy and 'stacking', or the use of a number of different anabolic steroids and substances at the same time in doses that are in excess of what would normally be considered safe. Also, in relation to drugs such as anabolic steroids, athletes can see that changes have occurred (increase in bulk), giving, rightly or wrongly, the impression that this will aid performance.* As regards the stimulants (and over a longer period, the anabolic steroids), a feeling of well-being may be experienced, leading to the belief, if not the actuality, that performance has been or is being enhanced. If athletes believe performance-enhancing drugs work, then policy makers have to be pragmatic and accept that traditional health education† approaches which encourage abstinence through attempts to scare off the user through stories of what exaggerated horrors might happen to them ('heroin screws you up' style) if they 'misuse' or 'abuse' drugs are apparently as unsuccessful in the world of sport as they have been in the non-sporting environment (compare Segal, 1976; De Haes, 1987; Goldberg et al., 1991) and may in fact have the deleterious effect of arousing interest where it previously did not exist (Advisory Council in the Misuse of Drugs 1984; Cashmore, 1990; Yesalis, 1990).

On the second issue (the use of performance-enhancing drugs is likely to cause physical or psychological harm), the extent of that harm needs to be questioned. Implicit, at least in there denunciation of anabolic steroids in particular, is the notion that severe long-term effects, if not fatal illness, is the probable outcome of non-medically supervised use. This is once again a mirror of how illicit drugs in the non-sporting world are often represented and once again a less than useful piece of alarmist exaggeration. Many of the unwanted effects from anabolic steroids, such as testicular atrophy, high blood pressure, acne, abnormal liver functioning and aggressiveness have been shown to be largely short-term reversible effects, with a return to normal functioning following either abstention from steroid use or, in the case of abnormal liver functioning, after a few weeks even if use is continued (Windsor and Dumitru, 1988). As regards long-term and more severe problems, the jury is still out. However if drugs such as anabolic steroids are used extensively, and have been for some time, the level of serious problems often ascribed to such use, especially given the practice of stacking over many years, should lead us to expect a large number of serious casualties becoming increasingly visible. This is not the case. Just as in the non-sporting environment, the level of actual casualties (death and serious long-term health problems) which can be directly attributed to the substance in question⚧ (be it heroin, cocaine or steroids) is far below that widely presumed or suggested. On occasion a highly publicised 'public interest

* Of course in some sports such as body building, or for those looking for purely cosmetic improvements, the objective of using a variety of substances would include the bulking effect, perhaps in preference to any gains in strength.
† Ironically, as Cashmore (1990) points out, belief in the efficacy of drugs is heightened by the millions of pounds spent on attempts to prevent the use of performance-enhancing drugs at the expense of the sporting authorities. If the drugs don't work, why prevent their use? In this sense the traditional education campaign is effectively running counter to itself.
⚧ In fact, most of the deaths commonly attributed to the use of performance-enhancing drugs have been stimulant, not steroid, related and even in these cases the numbers remain low with famous examples such as Len Bias in the USA and Tommy Simpson in the UK being brought up time and time again to maintain impact.

story' may allow an individual to ascribe current health problems to past use of performance-enhancing drugs, but these occur rarely and it is far from clear how many of these individuals would have contracted their particular problem even if they were not taking drugs. At the very least, a review of the literature suggests (as regards anabolic steroids) that the real level of risk is in fact far less than is commonly assumed, rhetorically and publicly stated: 'Although anabolic steroids have been used in the United states for about 30 years, no study has demonstrated an increased risk for cardiovascular or peripheral vascular disease in athletes who have used steroids' (Windsor and Dumitru, 1992, P. 48). Even when the 'much discussed and *little observed* phenomenon' (Windsor and Dumitru, 1988, p. 42. my emphasis) of liver tumours is discussed, the relationship is strong with a particular group of oral anabolic agents isolated around the C17 a-alkylated derivatives of testosterone (Windsor and Dumitru, 1988; Friedl, 1993) and can for the most part be avoided. In fact Friedl (1993, p. 135) is forced to concede that 'From the evidence of studies of androgen administration, it is not readily apparent that we can attribute significant adverse health effects to androgens as a general class'. When we consider how many steroid users there are (up to 500,000 adolescent users in the USA alone (Buckley et al., 1993) and millions world wide), the way that steroids have been used (stacking and in conjunction with other compounds), the length of time they have been used (around 30 years) and the many research projects set up just to show how dangerous steroids are, I would suggest that there is a shortfall of evidence for the purported and consequently extrapolated risks. The corticosteroids mentioned earlier as a legitimate performance-enhancing drug present contradiction also in policy regarding health concerns of athletes. The corticosteroids themselves have risks attached which include (after prolonged administration) some of those consistent with the use of anabolic steroids, e.g. acne, and in women problems relating to menstruation and excess hair growth. Other risks include problems with adrenal insufficiency mimicking that produced by Addison's disease if the athlete is not withdrawn slowly (Donohoe and Johnson, 1986) and posssibly changes to mood. However, and perhaps more seriously, by enabling an athlete to compete on an existing injury, long-term problems which would have been avoided through abstinence from competition may be produced.

What we find then is that the argument to ban these drugs on the basis of health risks is seriously undermined by making corticosteroids available to athletes despite the well-known hazards attached to them Moreover, if the use of substances, such as cortisone, which permits athletes to perform when they would not otherwise have been able to – perhaps causing more damage in the process – is considered legitimate, then the concepts of 'performance enhancing' and health protection that are being employed are clearly very narrow ones. These are concepts that I would argue are contradictory to the ethical justification for the banning of performance-enhancing drugs in the first place.

Although the risks attached to these drugs seem to be somewhat exaggerated they do nevertheless raise questions of policy efficacy.

Effects of prohibition: more harm than good?

Given that prohibition appears not to be effective in reality in the prevention of the use of drugs in sport and that at times it reveals itself to be inconsistently applied, we need to consider whether a policy of prohibition ironically produces unintentional effects which work against the stated desire to protect the health of the athlete.

At present athletes who use performance-enhancing drugs have no recourse to reliable help or advice. Their activities are forced underground leaving them more vulnerable to the vagaries of drug use. The problem is worse where prohibition in sport is combined with criminalisation by law. In the USA, where use of anabolic steroids is arguably more prevalent than elsewhere and more widespread across a broader range of ages than elsewhere, the problems and consequences of the criminalisation of steroids may already be being felt. Whereas previously they were being provided largely by other athletes and the quality of the produce was consistent, with criminalisation there appears to be a shift in the distribution network towards the sellers of street drugs (Yesalis, 1993). With production becoming more difficult and expensive, laboratories are forced further underground, with the possible effect of a less reliable (safe) product. The potential for adulteration is further increased when the distribution network increasingly includes sellers of other illicit drugs, whereby the standard practice to optimise profit is to adulterate their goods. This is a common problem for users of street drugs but for the users of anabolic steroids it is new. Because athletes are unsure of the quality of the drugs they are buying, or because normal supply routes are less reliable than they used to be, there seems to be growing evidence that other compounds are being used as performance-enhancing drugs (Yesalis, 1990). If the use of drugs in sport appears to get worse in Britain – who likes to take a lead in these affairs – the recent call for prohibition may well be repeated and eventually successful, leading us even further from a policy of resolution.

It is my contention that, in recognition of the continuing use of and experimentation with performance-enhancing drugs by athletes, and the large numbers involved, prohibition should be lifted.* This would enable athletes to seek the kind of assistance for their drug use that they receive for other aspects of their training regime – such as nutrition. At the very least, policy should entail: the provision of harm-minimisation literature available at all athletics meeting (and where appropriate); how to use various drugs safely; which compounds absolutely should not be mixed; that injectable androgens appear safer than oral ones; and how to reduce risk associated especially with injections given the broader context of HIV/AIDS. Such literature should not recommend doses or practices so that the literature will be disregarded. It should recognise stacking and polypharmacy, and relate to athletes how to reduce harm associated with this. One foreseeable advantage of harm-reduction programmes of this kind may be that they will also facilitate access to athletes willing, under an anonymous and non-punitive setting, to be involved in meaningful research of the effects of this type of behavior, improving our knowledge of the consequences of drug use – on both health and performance – and making it more credible in the eyes of what constitutes a comparatively research hungry group of drug users.

* Of course, in the USA this would also mean decriminalisation.

Conclusion

Policy on drugs in sport needs to be pragmatically approached on the basis that athletes do and will continue to use performance-enhancing drugs and that the effective means to prevent use are unavailable and unlikely to be so. Given this, appeals to more idealistic notions of sport and fair play tend to ignore the context in which sport is played out and to prevent appropriate policy from being enacted to do just what most governing bodies profess as an objective: to protect the health of the athlete.

References

Advisory Council on the Misuse of Drugs, *Prevention*. London: HMSO, 1984.

Bierley, S. 'All sweetness and insight', *The Guardian,* August 23, London, 1993.

Black, *Drugs in Sport: An Interim Report of the Senate Standing Committee on Environment Recreation and the Arts*. Australia Government Publishing Service, Canberra, 1989.

Brown, M. 'Performance Enhancement', *Coaching Focus,* No. 23, Summer 1993, National Coaching Federation, 1993.

Buckley, W.E. Yesalis, C.E. and Bennell, D.L. 'A study of anabolic steroid use at the secondary school level: recommendations for prevention'. In Yesalis, C.E. (ed.), *Anabolic Steroids in Sport and Exercise* Leeds: Human Kinetics, 1993.

Cashmore, E. *Making Sense of Sport*. London: Routledge, 1990, 1994.

Coni, P., Kellan and, G. and Davies, D. *Drug Abuse Enquiry Report*. Amateur Athletics Association, 1988.

Davies, S. with Severs, M. *Against the Tide*. London: Willow Books, 1984.

De Haes, W.F.M. 'Looking for effective drug education programmes: fifteen years of exploration of the effects of different drug education programmes'. In *Health*, 1987, 2, 433-438.

Donohue, T. and Johnson, N.I. *'Foul Play: Drug Abuse in Sports'*. Oxford: Basil Blackwell, 1986.

Doust, D. Hughes, R. and Freman, S. 'Fallen Heroes', *The Sunday Times,* 2nd October, 1988.

Dubin, C.L. *Commission of Inquiry into the Use of drugs and Banned Practices Intended to Increase Athletic Performance*. Minister of Supply and Services, Ottawa, Canada, 1990.

Ferstel, J. 'Evolution and politics of drug testing'. In Yesalis, C.E. (ed.) *Anabolic Steroids in Sport and Exercise.* Leeds: Human Kinetics, 1993.

Fraleigh, W.P. 'Performance-enhancing drugs in sport: the ethical issue'. *Journal of the Philosophy of Sport,* 1985, *XI,* 23-29

Friedl, K. 'Effects of anabolic steroids on physical health'. In Yesalis, C.E. (ed.), *Anabolic Steroids in Sprot and Exercise*. Leeds: Human Kinetics, 1993.

Gold, A. Interview in *Athletics Today* **3 (52),** 28 December, 1989, 10-11.

Goldberg, L. Bents, R. Bosworth, E. Trevisan, L. and Elliot, D.L. *Pediatrics,* 1991, 87, 283-286.

Goldman, B. with Bush, P. and Klatz, R. *Death in the Locker Room* London: Century Publishing, 1984.

Houlihan, B. *The Government and Politics of Sport*. London: Routledge, 1991.

Hubbard, A. Brotherhood of the Needle. *The Observer I,* 7 March, 1993.

Johanson, M. 'Doping as a threat against sport and society: the case of Sweden'. *International Review of the Sociology of Sport*, 1987, 22, 83-96.

Korkia, P. And Stimson, G.V. *Anabolic Steroid Use in Great Britain: An Exploratory Investigation* The Centre for Research on Drugs and Health Behaviour, London, 1993.

Sanderson, T. with Hickman, L. *Tessa: My Life in Athletics.* London: Willow Books, 1986.

Segal, M. 'Drug education versus drug abuse education'. In Miller, L. and Einstein, S. (eds) *Drugs and Society: Contemporary Social Issues*. Jerusalem: Jerusalem Academic Press, 1976.

Simson, V. and Jennings, A. *The Lord of the Rings: Power, Money and Drugs in the Modern Olympics*. London: Simon & Schuster, 1992.

Tricker, R. O'Neill, M.R. and Cook, D. The incidence of anabolic steroid use among competitive bodybuilders. *Journal of Drug Education*, 1989, 19, 313-325.

Uzych, L. 'Drug testing of athletes'. *British Journal of Addiction*, 1989, 86, 25-31.

Voy, R. with Deeter, K.D. *Drugs, Sport and Politics*, Champaign IL: Leisure Press, 1991.

Yesalis, C.E. 'Winning and performance-enhancing drugs – our dual addiction'. *The Physician and Sports Medicine*, 1990, 18, 3.

Yesalis, C.E. (ed.) 'Incidence of anabolic steroid use: a discussion of methodological issues'. In: Anabolic Steroids in Sport and Exercise. Leeds: Human Kinetics, 1993.

Ward, M. and Rice, B. *Taking Drugs or Taking Part*. Salford: Tacade, 1989.

Windsor, R.E. and Dumitru, D. 'Anabolic steroid use by athletes: How serious are the health hazards?'. *Postgraduate Medicine*, 1988, 84,37-49.

34.　　　　　　A Question of Drugs

Ellis Cashmore

The other athletic's revolution

Years hence, people will tell their children about the Olympic games of 1988. They may recall the sprint treble victory of Florence Griffith Joyner, Surinam's first-ever medallist, Anthony Nesty, or perhaps the upset Soviet defeat of the US basketball team which had won eighty-four out of eight-eight previous games in six decades of Olympic play. But the event that will be stamped in people's memories will not be a sporting achievement, but rather, Ben Johnson's positive dope test and its aftermath. This included his being stripped of the gold medal he had won for his 100-metre sprint win, the expunging of his time from the record books, and the most exhaustive ever international media coverage of a sports story. The vast majority of the millions who watched Johnson stride imperiously to victory in 9.79 seconds on 24 September might have confused the name Stanozolol with others, like Shanavozov, the Soviet boxer, or Butuzova, the archer. By 26 September, only recluses wouldn't have realized that this was the brand name of the anabolic steroid detected in Johnson's urine sample.

Modern sport has taken on an almost Manichaean character in which good coexists with evil; the evil is represented increasingly by the spread of the use of drugs amongst athletes eager to improve their performance and willing to risk all manner of chemical side-effects, or even direct effects in the attempt to build muscle, steady the hand, flush out body fluid, speed up the metabolism, or spark more aggression. There are drugs available that can assist in all these, but woe for any athlete caught taking them. Johnson was quickly demythologized from the fastest man in the world, to the 'world's greatest cheat', cloven hoofs and horns virtually replacing his Diadora spikes and gold medal. While he was the thirty-first competitor to be disqualified for drug use since the International Olympic Committee (IOC) instituted full-scale testing in 1972, Johnson's stature in world sport ensured that his case would make news everywhere and that he as an individual would carry the sins of everybody. As well as his medal and record, he instantly lost at least $2 million in performance-related product endorsements.

Johnson was extraordinary in that he was discovered with traces of steroid in his system and roundly shamed because of it. The vast majority of the twenty-two athletes tested daily at the Olympic games yielded negative results. But the suspicion was, and is, that Johnson was quite ordinary in another respect: he was simply one of countless others who systemically used drugs to enhance performance and who either 'came off' them early enough to escape detection, or masked their presence with an additional drug, such as probenecid (sometimes used to treat gout), though this too was banned in 1988. In 1987 (not an Olympic year) IOC tests brought to light 521 infringements using anabolic steroids, 37 of them involving the use of stanozolol, but this almost certainly conceals the true extent of drug use among athletes. Prior to the Olympics of 1988, it

Ellis Cashmore: 'A Question of Drugs' from *MAKING SENSE OF SPORT*, (Routledge 1990; new impression 1994), pp. 107-129. © Ellis Cashmore, 1990.

was estimated that one in ten British athletes regularly used drugs, an estimate that contrasted markedly with that of former Olympic silver medallist and convicted trader in steroids, David Jenkins; he guessed that as many as 50 per cent of athletes had used drugs at some time. The discrepancy suggests a 'dark figure', the true proportions of which are destined to remain unknown.

Track and field events have no monopoly on drugs, of course, and scandals of lesser proportions have affected American football (stimulant use) and, to a much lesser extent, boxing (stimulants and narcotic analgesics; diuretics use is overlooked). Weightlifters and body builders compete in sports in which steroids confer obvious advantages. It's quite probable that drug use in sport dates back to ancient times. Greeks are said to have used hallucinogenic extracts from mushrooms to aid their performance. Chemically active derivatives of plants have had many applications. The opium extract morphine has been used extensively for the relief of pain, colchicine from the autumn crocus is a well-known treatment for gout, and the heart drug digitalis comes from foxglove. There are countless other examples in history and, today, natural derivatives are quite commonly used to treat ailments and often to enhance performance; the Asian root ginseng is thought to have all manner of beneficial properties. Natural stimulants to alter body functions have been used extensively, particularly as a prelude to fighting. In sport we know little of the systematic application of stimulants, though after 1879 when 6-day cycle races began in Europe, riders favoured ether and caffeine to delay the onset of fatigue sensations. Sprint cyclists used nitroglycerine, a chemical later used in conjunction with heroin, cocaine, strychnine, and others to make 'speedballs' which were given to race horses before races in the 1930s. The highly poisonous stimulant strychnine was also used by the winners of the 1904 Olympic marathon.

Cycling perhaps more than any other sport drew world attention in the 1960s to both the extent of drug taking in sport and its perils when two competitors actually died after taking doses of amphetamines. Knut Jensen collapsed and died at the 1960 Olympics after taking nonicol, a blood dilatory, and seven years later, Tommy Simpson died during the Tour de France. In the same decade, stories escaped from American baseball and football clubs that told of the extensive use of amphetamines and narcotic analgesics. Paul Hoch, in *Rip Off the Big Game*, drew together a number of accounts from the 1960s to conclude 'that the biggest drug dealers in the sports world are none other than team trainers' (1972: 122). Coaches were administering amphetamines to 'pep' players up, and analgesics to help them play painlessly while carrying injuries before a game *and* 'tranquilized to get their eyeballs back in their head – to even get a night's sleep' after. Hoch cites two players who filed law suits against their clubs for administering drugs 'deceptively and without consent' (1972: 123), and which eventually proved detrimental to their health. Various exposees led to a California state legislative subcommittee on drug use in alcoholism to extend the tight regulations on drug abuse in horse racing to human sport! The movie *North Dallas Forty* graphically shows football players trotting onto the field as virtual zombies after taking copious amounts of dope.

Law and drugs

Many of the drugs used by sports performers are available often without prescription, in EC countries and the USA. But, in 1989, an amendment to the British Misuse of Drugs Act 1971, made the illegal possession of anabolic steroids a criminal offence. This was the first time that sport's own rules for banning the use of drugs were given the force of law, making sport's own sanctions (e.g. bans) largely irrelevant. Possession of drugs, which if used excessively can promote cancers, carried a maximum of a fine and a two-year gaol sentence. Producers, importers, and suppliers faced unlimited fines and gaol sentences of up to five years.

The drugs we now tend to associate with sport are anabolic steroids and cocaine. Sketchy evidence suggests that some NFL players were experimenting in the 1960s. Jack Scott in *The Athletic Revolution* (1971) reported that over a quarter of one college team had used steroids. In the same book, Scott covered the 1968 Olympics, at which competitors talked freely not about the morality of taking drugs but of the practicality: which drugs were most effective? While estimates about the extent of steroid use are always hopelessly flawed, it's at least suggestive that less than twenty years after Scott's information, an article in *Sports Illustrated* stated that NFL steroid users accounted for between 40 and 90 per cent of all players (13 May 1983). The Players' Association rejected this. In 1984, Robert Goldman, the director of sports medicine research at the Chicago Osteopathic Medicine Centre, attributed the death of six sports performers to steroid use. In the UK, body builder, Keith Singh, died with liver tumours after a period of using steroids. In 1987, the IOC recorded 521 cases which tested positive for steroid use; and this was sixteen years after the International Amateur Athletic Federation (IAAF) had introduced antidrug legislation.

Cocaine

This drug's striking effects on the CNS have made it appealing to many sports performers. The first site of action is the cortex and the effects of the stimulant can manifest themselves as exhilaration, euphoria, or laughter. There is some evidence that cocaine increased perceptual awareness and thinking abilities. It also reduces fatigue sensations. In low doses, there is no impairment in body movement co-ordination to offset the increase in activity levels. Higher doses may lead to excessive stimulation of the lower brain centres, prompting convulsive movements. Long-term effects are severely detrimental. Used topically, cocaine can work as a local anaesthetic. Contrary to popular belief, it has little in common with opiates such as heroin or morphine and is not physically addictive in the same way as these, though it often leads to a powerful psychological dependence.

While anabolic steroids have specific functions and are confined mainly to sports, cocaine is used recreationally by a variety of groups. In the 1980, its status as a yuppie drug enhanced its appeal. Tales of cocaine use by football, baseball, and basketball players are legion. Richard Lapchick (1986) refers to an 'epidemic in American sport' and highlights some of the sports stars who are still either in gaol or fighting addictions.

Seven New England Patriots were identified as having a 'serious drug problem' on the day following their appearance in the 1986 SuperBowl. In the same year, a pro footballer and a college basketball player died from cocaine poisoning, fifty-seven top senior collegiate prospects for the NFL draft tested positively, twenty-one major league baseball players were penalized, and Michael Ray Richardson was banned by the National Basketball Association after his fourth failed test for cocaine. Many world class boxers, including Hector Camacho and Gilberto Roman (former holders of world titles) were penalized in the 1980s. Atlanta Falcons' Dave Croudip was, at the time of writing, the most recent victim of a cocaine overdose.

Trying to quantify the amount of drug use in sport is as futile as trying to assess the extent of drug taking in society generally: the truth will never be known. Yet there is enough illustrative evidence, anecdotes, 'insider accounts', and publicized cases to infer that drug use in sport has been growing steadily since the 1940s and more rapidly since the crucial decade of the 1960s, when drug use generally became widespread. Questions arise out of this. What are the drugs and what are they supposed to do? Why are more and more sports performers prepared to use them? How do governing bodies react to drug use and how will this reaction affect sport?

Banned substances

The IOC's banned list includes 4,000 substances which are grouped into five categories of drugs. They are anabolic steroids, stimulants, narcotic analgesics, beta blockers, and diuretics. I will deal with them in that order.

Johnson's case led to a general awareness of the 'danger' of anabolic steroids, but little appreciation of the actual purpose they can serve in the human body. The idea behind using an anabolic steroid is to mirror the chemical action of the male hormone testosterone in the body and facilitate muscle growth; 'anabolic' means build up. The basic function of testosterone is to control the natural production of sperm cells and this, in turn, affects the male's masculine appearance. A feedback control system is at work involving the hypothalumus; this secretes a hormone called LHR which stimulates the pituitary gland to secrete luteinizing hormone (LH) and this, in turn, stimulates the testes to produce the testosterone. A high concentration of testosterone inhibits the secretion of LHR by the hypothalamus which causes a stop in the level of testosterone, triggering the hypothalamus to release more LHR, LH, and ultimately testosterone in a smoothly regulated system.

Once in the bloodstream the molecules of the hormone discharged by the testes can affect other parts of the body. It is the task of endocrinology to study the processes and effects of molecules produced by glands and secreted directly into the blood. Experiments are complicated by the obvious fact that organs that are suspected of producing hormones always have important functions and their removal is followed by death. There are alternatives to surgical removal and combinations of methods have established what the main hormones are, the endocrine glands, or organs, that produce them, and their major effects. Other effects are less well established, but still strongly suspected and the muscle building spin-off of testosterone is one of them. Sceptics still harbour alternative suspicions and suggest a placebo might be at work; believers in the power of testosterone convince themselves even in the absence of physical change.

Placebo

A pharmacologically inert substance is given to patients usually to humour them rather than affect any cure. Yet the substance often works as effectively (if not more so) as an active substance because the patient believes it will. The substance is called a placebo and its result is known as the *placebo effect*. This has many applications outside the clinical setting. Weightlifters have been told they were receiving an anabolic steroid while, in fact, only some of them received it – the others were given a placebo. Both groups improved leg presses, the first group by 135 lbs, the other (receiving the placebo) by 132 lbs. The sheer expectation of benefit seems to have been the crucial factor. A similar process can work in reverse. For example, subjects may be given active drugs together with information that they will have no effect: consequently the drugs may not have any effect. In other words, the direct effect of drugs alone may not be any more powerful than the administrator's or experimenter's suggestions alone.

As long ago as the 1930s, a synthesized version of testosterone was produced and used to help castrated males. Its clinical use was seen as limited, being confined to individuals with rare blood disorders, including some anaemias (having too little haemoglobin) and for wasting conditions in the elderly. But this testosterone appeared to encourage the proliferation of cells in muscle and to induce more aggression in the user – known as 'roid rage'. This alerted coaches to the benefits: first, in rapid muscle faculty for more intense training; second, in encouraging a more positive and aggressive approach to both training and competition.

While anabolic steroids are the most widely used drug in track and field events, stimulants are the second most common and probably the most popular in sport as a whole. Amphetamine use has been widespread for at least three decades. The basic effect of stimulants is to get messages to a complex pathway of neurons in the brainstem called the arousal system, or reticular activating system (RAS). This system is ultimately responsible for maintaining consciousness and determining our state of awareness. So, if the RAS bombards the cerebral cortex with stimuli, we feel very alert and able to think clearly. Amphetamines are thought to cause chemical neurotransmitters, such as dopamine, to increase, so enhancing the flow of nervous impulses in the RAS and stimulating the entire CNS. The sympathetic nervous system is stimulated, speeding up heartrate, raising blood pressure, and dilating pupils. In sports terms, the performer is fired up and resistant to the sensation of fatigue, particularly the muscular pain associated with lactic acid.

One problem facing users active in sport, who need nutrition for the release of energy is that amphetamines depress appetites. They used to be prescribed to dieters, though less so nowadays because dieters became dependent on the drug. This came about because the body quickly develops a tolerance, probably through the readiness of the liver to break down the drug rapidly. An obvious temptation is to increase the dose to achieve the same effect. So, with increased use of the drug, the user becomes dependent. Weight loss and dependence are the more obvious effects; others include irritability (probably due to irregular sleep) and even a tendency towards paranoia. Cyclists Jensen and Simpson demonstrated that the effects can be terminal.

There is another class of stimulants called sympathomimetic amine drugs, such as ephedrine, which, as the name suggests, acts not on the brain but directly on the nerves affecting the organs. (This produces effects in the sympathetic part of the autonomic nervous system: it speeds up the action of the heart, and constricts the arteries and increases lung inflation). Ephedrine is used commonly as a decongestant and is often prescribed for asthma suffers.

At the 1988 Olympics, a pentathlete, Alexander Watson, of Australia, was disqualified for having an excessive level of caffeine in this system. To have reached such a level he would have needed to have drunk forty regular-sized cups of coffee; other methods include the use of a suppository or the chewing of small nuts of caffeine.

Narcotic analgesics are used in all walks of life, but especially in sports where injuries are commonplace and a tolerance to pain is essential. Soccer and US football are examples of games involving the 'walking wounded'. Derivatives of the opium poppy were probably used by ancient Mesopotamians around 3000 BC; they left instructions for use on wax tablets. There are now methods of producing such derivatives synthetically. Opium, heroin, codeine, and morphine, along with the newer 'designer' drugs, are all classified as narcotics which relieve pain and depress the CNS, producing a state of stupor. Reflexes slow down, the skeleton is relaxed, and tension is reduced. The negative effects are much the same as those of amphetamines, with the additional one of specific neurons becoming dependent on the drug and so providing a basis for addiction.

The immediate effects of stimulants or narcotic analgesics would be of little or no service to sports performers who rely on fineness of judgement, sensitivity of touch, acuity of sight, and steadiness of hand. Success in sports like darts, archery, snooker, shooting, or show jumping is based on calmness and an imperviousness to 'pressure'. The Canadian snooker player Bill Werbeniuk was famed for his customary ten pints of beer to help him relax before a game. His CNS would become duller and tensions presumably disappeared. How he managed to co-ordinate hand and eye movements, stay awake, or even just stay upright is a mystery! Alcohol has serious drawbacks, which include nausea and impaired judgement.

Werbeniuk

While Vancouver-based professional snooker player Bill Werbeniuk was known for his consumption of large quantities of lager, he was also a habitual user of inderal, a beta blocker which helped counteract the effects of an hereditary nervous disorder. After criticism from the British Minister for Sport, the World Professional Billiards and Snooker Association (WPBSA) reviewed its drug policy and included inderal on its list of banned substances. Unable to find an alternative, Werbeniuk admitted to the WPBSA that he intended to continue using the drug and was eventually banned from tournaments.

Beta blockers are a newer alternative. Originally used by patients with irregular heartbeats, these relieve anxiety by controlling the release of adrenaline and by lowering the heartrate; they are used by edgy showbusiness performers.

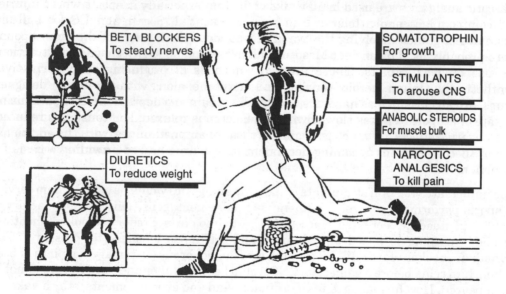

Weightlifters and other sport performers who compete in categories based on body weight have to calibrate their diet and preparation carefully. A couple of pounds, even ounces, over the limit can destroy months of conditioning if the performer is made to take off the excess at the weigh-in. Skipping, saunas, and other methods of instant weight reduction can be debilitating. Competitors in weight-controlled sports always check-weigh during the days preceding an event and, should their weight seem excessive, may take diuretics. These substances -widely used therapeutically for reducing fluid levels – excite the kidneys to produce more urea and, basically, speed up a perfectly natural waste disposal process. Diuretics are found in alcoholic drinks and coffee (in the caffeine), which explains why a visit to the toilet is necessary shortly after imbibing any of these liquids. Diuretics inhibit the secretion of the antidiuretic hormone which serves as a chemical messenger, carrying information from the pituitary gland at the base of the brain to parts of the kidneys, making them more permeable and allowing water to be reabsorbed into the body (thus conserving fluid). Hormones, of course, are carried in the blood. If the messages don't get through, the kidneys move the water out of the body. Continued use of diuretics can damage the kidneys. In recent years, the suspicion has grown that competitors have not only been using diuretics to reduce weight, but to flush out other substances, in particular the above-mentioned drugs. It follows that competitors found to have diuretic in their urine immediately have their motives questioned. Kerrith Brown, of Great Britain, lost his Olympic bronze medal for judo despite pleading that the diuretic, furosemide, found in his urine was introduced into his system by a medical officer who gave him an anti-inflammatory substance containing the chemical to reduce a knee swelling.

Another athlete to be disqualified, though at an earlier Olympics, was Martti Vainio who lost his silver medal for the 10,000 metres at Los Angeles after steroid traces were discovered in his urine. The Finn had been careful enough to cease using the drug well before competition to escape detection, but had blundered by having himself injected with blood that had been removed from his body early in 1984 when training at altitude. In chapter 2 we noted the importance of protein molecule haemoglobin, which is found in red blood cells. It has a remarkable ability to form loose associations with oxygen. As most oxygen in the blood is combined with haemoglobin rather than simply dissolved in plasma, the more haemoglobin present in a red blood cell, the more oxygen it can transport to the muscles. Obviously then, performers can benefit from having a plentiful supply of oxygen to react with glucose and release energy stored in food. The advantage of training at altitude, where the oxygen in the atmosphere is scarce, is that the body naturally compensates by producing more haemoglobin. The performer descends to sea level carrying with him or her a plentiful supply of haemoglobin in the blood, which gradually readjusts (over a period of weeks). Each day spent at lower altitudes diminishes the benefit of altitude training: proliferation of haemoglobin ceases in the presence of available atmospheric oxygen. One way to 'capture' the benefits is to remove a quantity of highly oxygenated blood during intense altitude training, store it, and reintroduce it into the circulatory system immediately prior to competition, which is what Vainio and probably many others did. He neglected to take account of the fact that he had been on steroids during the time spent at altitude and that the stored blood contained evidence of this.

The 'doping' in this process doesn't refer to the administration of drugs, but to the more correct use of the term, pertaining to a thick liquid used as a food or lubricant. There is, however, a synthetic drug that can achieve much the same effect. Erythropreotin (EPO) facilitates the production of extra red blood cells, which absorb oxygen, and leaves the user with no tell-tale needle tracks. As EPO does not show up in urinalysis, inspection is possibly only by blood tests, before and after competition, to take red blood cell counts. As well as being more convenient than a transfusion, EPO has the advantage of being undetectable in competitors who object to invasive techniques on religious or ethical grounds. 'Blood doping' or 'blood boosting' and EPO, in a sense, copy the body's natural processes and, at the moment, their long-term effects seem to be broadly the same as those of living at high altitudes.

Another, more controversial, method of mimicking nature is by extracting the naturally occurring growth hormone somatotropin, which is produced and released by the pituitary gland, as discussed in chapter 2. This hormone controls the human rate of growth by regulating the amount of nutrients taken into the body's cells and by stimulating protein synthesis. Overproduction of the hormone may cause a child to grow to giant proportions (a condition referred to as gigantism), whereas too little can lead to dwarfism. The growth hormone also affects fat and carbohydrate metabolism in adults, promoting a mobilization of fat which becomes available for use as fuel, and sparing the utilization of protein. The potential of this mechanism for promoting growth has not been lost on field athletes, weightlifters, body builders, and others requiring muscle build. Illicit markets in growth hormone extracted from foetuses have been uncovered, though a synthetically manufactured version, somatonorm, may make this redundant. Eventually, skeletal and muscular abnormalities may result. These outward physical signs are some of the few reliable ways of determining whether performers have been taking the hormone, in either form, or whether they have an abnormally high level. Nor would pure EPO be detectable through existing techniques. This has led some to believe that drug users can always stay one step ahead of those wishing to identify them: the line between what is 'natural' and 'unnatural' for the human body is not so clear-cut as testers would like and science finds ways of replicating nature. Others believe that drug-testing methods are keeping pace and hold up the Johnson case as an example of how not even the elite can escape detection, given a vigilant team of toxicologists and a sophisticated laboratory. The system at Seoul was a costly state-of-the-art set-up and easily the most effective drug detection centre to date. Before moving on, we should briefly take note of its apparatus and methods.

Hewlett-Packard, the multinational computer specialists, charged the IOC $3 million to set up the scientific testing equipment at the Korean Advanced Institute of Science and Technology. The system of gas chromatography and mass spectroscopy could, according to its makers, 'detect concentrations [of banned substances] as low as one part per billion; roughly the equivalent to detecting traces from a teaspoonful of sugar after it has been dissolved in an Olympic swimming pool'. A further claim was that it could check a compound found in urine against 70,000 held in a computer's database in 'less than a minute'.

The entire testing process has four phases. 1) Within an hour of the finish of an event, two samples of a performer's urine are taken, one is tested for acidity and specific gravity so that testers can get a broad indication of any illegal compounds. 2) The sample is then split into smaller batches to test for certain classes of drugs, such as anabolic steroids, stimulants, etc. Testers make the urine alkaline and mix it with solvents, like ether, causing any drugs to dissolve into the solvent layer, which is more easily analysed than urine itself. 3) This solvent is then passed through a tube (up to 25 metres long) of gas (or liquid chromatogram) and the molecules of the solvent separate and pass through at different rates, depending on their size and other properties (such as whether they are more likely to adhere to the material of the tube itself). More than 200 drugs are searched for in this period, which lasts about 15 minutes. 4) Any drugs found are then analysed with a mass spectrometer, which bombards them with high energy ions, or electrons, creating unique chemical fingerprints, which can be rapidly checked against the database. Should any banned substances show up, the second sample is tested in the presence of the performer. (Another method is radioimmunoassay, in which antibodies to known substances are used like keys that will only fit one lock; the lock is the banned substance which is found by the key that fits it.)

Encouraged by the Seoul experience, the IOC stated its intention to implement all-year-round testing and while it is by far the most stringent sports body, others have followed its example. Efforts to stamp out drugs are obviously related to the degree of drug use in sport and, as I indicated earlier, there seems to have been a fairly sharp increase over the past twenty to thirty years. The reasons for that increase are discussed below.

Bodies under control

Sport is a human enterprise, as are the many sciences and technologies that have assisted or augmented it. Readers of this book may be engaged in a scientific endeavour to explore the application of academic study to sport. Some explorations, especially in the field of medicine, have yielded striking results. Injuries are better tended, pains are anaesthetized, and recoveries are accelerated. Nutrition has aided both training and performance. Psychology has helped strengthen commitment and develop beneficial attitudes. Biomechanics has identified more efficient methods of locomotion.

Pharmacology's specific contribution is more ambiguous. Sports performers can legally benefit from some drugs, for example painkillers, but not from others, such as those that add speed and power to an athlete's performance. Despite this ambiguity, many sports competitors seem willing to assist their performances by using both prescribed and proscribed drugs. Changes over the past fifty years have ensured that drugs are now part of sport. To authorities, sport has a 'drug problem'; to competitors, drugs are simply available for use should they be required. The first point to remember when trying to uncover the reasons for the apparent rise in drug use is that sport is not a solitary endeavour. Romantic visions of lone trainers are rife, of course, but, in practice, the pursuit of excellence in sport is a team effort. And, over the decade, teams have grown larger and have been augmented with a widening network of 'back-ups', including medical personnel and the whole range of technologies they employ. The scientifically designed and assisted preparation of Balboa's Soviet opponent in *Rocky IV* was a fiction that strayed only marginally from fact. High-tech training equipment, monitoring systems, and specialized personnel all combine to assist a competitor and, ultimately, improve performance. In the process, the individual's body practically becomes the property of scientists. Drugs are but one element in an elaborate technology of control, which has led to the hysterical view that modern sport is contested by scientists more than actual performers.

As we saw in chapter 4, the historical trend that Norbert Elias calls the civilizing process has fostered a dual approach to the human being in which the physical body is subordinated to the rational mind. Scientific advances have made it possible to 'rescue' the body from its natural state and reshape it in accordance with the mind's imperatives. We find in works of literature diverse treatments of much the same theme. Shelley's *Frankenstein* and Stevenson's *Dr Jekyll and Mr Hyde* show attempts by scientists either to reconstruct or remould humans, in both cases with hideous, unanticipated consequences. Many found the Press sisters, Irine and Tamara, rather hideous products of Soviet sports science. They dominated their events (hurdling and pentathlon; shot and discuss, respectively) in the 1960s and retired – fortuitously, perhaps – before sex testing was introduced in 1962. But their appearances were freakishly muscular; their flat chests and heavy jaws had the hallmarks of steroid users. Mutterings suggested the sisters' bodies had undergone fundamental chromosomal changes during their preparations.

All sport demands changes in the body and bodily processes. Even though physical input varies from sport to sport, all involve some degree of mastery over technique and this by extension means adjusting the body, whether it be adding strength or sensitivity of touch. The higher the level of achievement, the higher the level of bodily control required. Every activity demands physical control; sport demands an exaggerated level of control that only discipline and surveillance will achieve. Control over the body has always been integral to sport. Yet recently, the degree of control technically possible has been raised considerably by the whole panoply of sport-related science. The claim made in the preamble to the old tv series, *The Six Million Dollar Man*, namely, that 'we have the technology ....', had a little too much truth concealed inside it to be totally dismissed!

The civilizing process itself implicates individuals in some form of control over their bodies; Elias focuses mainly on the restraint in using physical violence, but notes the simultaneous trend for people to subdue spontaneous bodily functions and control their physical being. Sport, in this sense, is regarded as a cathartic release from the stressful tensions generated by the trend towards control. But, of course, sporting activity has also been controlled externally by governing organizations and internally by individual participants who needed to transform and canalize 'their drives and feelings' as Elias puts it, rather than remain in the 'grip' of their impulses. Success of any kind in a competitive activity means comforting and this, in turn, means internal disciplining – control. So, control over the functioning and even appearance of the human body has been important to all societies where, as Elias puts it, 'fairly high civilizing standards are safeguarded'.

In the late twentieth century the body is open for big business. Health foods, fitness clubs, sports goods, diets, rowing machines; all these and many more money-spinning goods and services cater for people eager to reproportion their bodies according to socially desirable standards. Consider also some of the traumatic experiences to which bodies are subject, such as Aids, smoking, pollution, rape, and child abuse. These form layers of a rich soil, as John Hargreaves would have it, 'the compost in which moral panic flourishes and on which the forces of law and order thrive' (1987: 141).

Not only have we been encouraged to take control over our bodies; we have become acutely aware of the power at our disposal for doing so. Drugs are one such source of power. We can alter the most basic of bodily functions, like eating, sleeping, and defecating with the appropriate drugs. Pain can be removed, rest can be restored, even moods can be heightened or depressed depending on the 'need'. Nothing is more rational than the desire to have consummate mastery over the body. Only a short step away is the irrational, of course, and dependence surrenders mastery to the drug itself, taking away responsibility, and eventually resolve, from the user and subverting the control once held over the body.

Sports performers are meant to stop short of the irrational. Success is contingent on organizing physical and mental facilities in accordance with structural rules and imperatives, so control over the body is absolutely necessary. Careful use of artifacts to attain such a control has been generously endorsed in sport, but drugs have acquired a notoriety that has not affected exercise equipment, from stop watches to multigyms, esoteric diets based on everything from vitamins to recycled urine and monitoring that can produce elaborate physical and psychological profiles. What were once take-them-or-leave-them facilities became essential equipment for some sports. It seems quite illogical to suggest that drugs would be ignored in a world awash with devices to keep the body under control. Medications to alleviate pain or accelerate healing processes became parts of performers' baggage to be carried in kitbags. Many experimented with the alleged benefits of hypnotherapy, autogenics and other 'positive thinking' techniques. Vitamins, phosphate, and cortisone (steroid) injections became commonplace. Sedatives calmed nerves.

Set in a wider context, trends in sport reflect what goes on in life generally. The past twenty odd years have witnessed the rise of new spirits. Young people have welcomed the use of stimulants, hallucinogens, and all manner of narcotics to alter behaviour and perception. But recent generations have edged towards drug dependence: tranquillizers have led a seemingly endless list of prescriptives to counter the stress-inducing effects of modern life. The 'drug culture' is worldwide and transgenerational, embracing those who wish to open new doors to perception, those who merely want to make it to the next day, and many more besides. Whether they like it or not, sports performers are part of a universal culture in which drugs of one form or another play an important role.

The science-assisted effort to pursue athletic excellence and the enveloping swirl of drug dependence: take the two together and one has a compelling mixture. Sport, if only because of its competitive nature, has urged its competitors to exploit the gifts of science, and our habits as a population have been transformed by the availability of drugs. Some might wish to add a further factor to this combination – an exaggeration of the importance of winning. Commercialism is the malefactor here; as sport has slid further from the corinthian ideal, its passage lubricated by business interests, so the joy of competing for its own sake has been superseded by an unprincipled win-at-all-costs approach; winning is what matters in modern sports. Exactly *how* one wins is largely irrelevant. Few people would doubt that victory in any sport is currently very important. Whether this is anything new or just a continuation of old traditions is open to question. Those to whom the cherishing and upholding of ideals are so important, often ignore the fact that sport, by definition, is competitive and competition is meaningless unless some individual or group is actually doing their level best to win. Commercialization has certainly increased the tangible rewards for winning. Olympic winners of ten years ago went home with a gold medal; today they take with them a portfolio of contracts worth six figure sums. A victorious world championship boxer can look forward to a purse worth dozens of thousands of dollars – if not millions – while his vanquished opponent may be relegated straight to low-budget promotions.

It was but a few years ago that snooker and darts were down-to-earth sports enjoyed by those who liked a drink at the local pub; quite unlike the modern players for whom a major professional title means a substantial premium on their earnings. Clearly, there is more at stake nowadays, in terms of both material gains and status. And this has fostered more aggressive competitors, prepared to train more and even risk more to realize their ambitions. If science can help the realization, then common sense dictates that sports performers use it; if drugs can assist, one can be sure many competitors will give only a sideways glance to moral signposts reading 'road to corruption'. Sport is too profound, too serious, and too lucrative for simplistic slogans. The crucial edge which drugs can provide may be the difference between a fortune and ignominy. Competition has come to occupy such a central place, not only in sport but in modern society, that it would be a virtual betrayal of sporting ideals to neglect the potential of drugs in maximizing performance. Three trends together help explain why sports performers have been prepared to use drugs: advances in science; growth of drug culture; and intensification of competitiveness. But, equally important as changes in actual use are the changes in reactions to drugs and, more pertinently, the reasons for the changes.

By accident or choice?

The reasons why the IOC and other sports' governing bodies are prepared to go to quite extraordinary lengths in their efforts to solve the supposed drug problem may be self-evident to many. But we will evaluate each reason on its own merits, beginning with the most obvious.

Drugs are not fair. They confer artificially induced advantages on the user and competing with such advantages in tantamount to cheating. Fairness is a rather troublesome concept to define, but we can assume, with Peter McIntosh, who wrote the book *Fair Play*, that: 'Fairness is related to justice' and 'breaking the rules with intent to avoid the penalties' as a definition of 'cheating' is too simple (1979: 2 and 182). He favours the definition of Gunther Lüschen who believes that the 'principle of chance beyond differences in skill and strategy are violated' when the conditions agreed upon for winning a contest 'are changed in favour of one side' (1976: 67). Drugs change the conditions for winning. But, then again, so do many other things.

Take the example of blood doping for which athletes may draw penalties, including bans. In a strict sense, this is cheating. But, how about athletes born in Kenya or Ethiopia, both several hundred feet above sea level? Such athletes may be fortunate enough to be brought up in an atmosphere that encourages haemoglobin production in the body and they may find the transition to sea level really quite comfortable as a result. Witness as evidence the dominance of Kenyan middle and long distance runners over the past twenty years. Equipped with naturally conferred advantages, Kenyans capitalized on the track and cross country circuits, leaving weary European and American athletes in their wake.

Another 'accident of birth' meant that the 5-year-old Boris Becker was given every available coaching and equipment facility to help him develop his tennis skills. His parents, being wealthy, could afford to indulge their child and, as things turned out, their money was a shrewd investment, for Becker became the youngest ever Wimbledon champion and, in so doing, unlocked a multi-million dollar treasure chest. Let's imagine that tennis produced its equivalent of former boxing champion, James Toney, an archetypal ghetto child from Detroit, who had the added disadvantage of being black. Were this imaginery figure to play Becker, would it be a fair match? When they came face-to-face in matchup, the conditions may appear fair, but one would hardly say they were 'fair' in a deeper sense. One player has benefited from *social* advantages in a similar way to Kenyan runners, who have benefited *naturally* from being born at high altitudes. Sporting competition has inbuilt inequalities that militate against fairness. What fairness, for instance, is there when Zola Budd, a female runner of little athletic distinction and with only one major international title, could command £90,000 for a single race, while many of her competitors (some of whom beat her) ran for expenses only? Budd's worth was based yet again on birthplace, in her case South Africa. It would be a naive person indeed who believed all is fair in sport in the modern world and that background, whether social or natural, is irrelevant to eventual success or failure.

Drugs are taken by choice. There is a difference between the advantages bestowed by social background or place of origin and those that are enjoyed by the taker of drugs. Sports performers can, as the slogan goes, 'say "no" to drugs' in much the same way as many say 'yes'. Swallowing tablets or allowing oneself to be injected are voluntary activities over which individuals have a high degree of control; one presumes – and only *presumes* – that they realize the potential costs as well as benefits and they exercise volition when doing or agreeing to the action. Obviously, the same performers have no say in where they were born or the state of their parents' bank account. By contrast, using drugs involves procuring an advantage quite voluntarily.

Yet there is more to this: first, because there are many other forms of advantage that are actively sought out and, second, because some are better placed than others either to seek out or eschew them. Were you a Briton following home Dominic Kirui in a 5,000-metre race, you might wish you were born in Kenya. Impossible, of course, so you might think about going to high altitudes and engaging in a spot of blood doping. Quite possible, but illegal. Another possibility is just to train in some part of the world high enough to give you some advantage, or at least to neutralize Kirui's advantage. Perfectly possible and legal. The probable result is an advantage quite legitimately obtained through voluntary effort. But an advantage is gained all the same.

Not that everyone is able to exercise choice in such matters: a dedication to competition, a determination to win, and an unflinching resolve to withstand pain are needed and these qualities are easier to come if the alternative is a one-way ticket back to the ghetto. If your alternatives look unpromisingly bleak, then choices can be rather illusory. Ben Johnson was born in Jamaica and migrated to Canada in 1980 at the age of 19, his ambition being the same as any migrant, namely, to improve his material life. Lacking education, but possessing naturally quick reflexes (which couldn't be changed) and fast ground speed (which could), he made the best of what he had, so that, within four years, he was in the Canadian Olympic team. Sport is full of stories like Johnson's: bad news – poor origins, little education, few occupational prospects; good news – physical potential and the opportunity to realize it. There's no realistic choice, here. Countless young people with some form of sporting prowess when faced with the 'once-and-for-all' decision of whether or not to sink their entire efforts in the one area in which they just might achieve success don't want to contemplate the alternatives. Given the chance, they'll go for it. And this means maximizing every possible advantages in an intensely competitive world. It's doubtful whether any athlete with a similarly deprived childhood would have any compunction about gaining an edge by any means. The choices they have are often too stark to need much mulling over.

Asking whether choice was exercised in trying to determine whether cheating took place is not adequate. Even if we were to dismiss the claims of a performer (who tested positive for a given drug) that his or her drink was spiked (or similar), the question of whether that person *freely* exercised choice remains. Returning to Becker, let's suppose he was found guilty of something untoward; it's feasible to argue that his choice was less restricted than a Turkish migrant worker's son in West Germany whose one chance for some material success is through sport. All this isn't intended to exonerate those from deprived backgrounds who have sought an advantage through 'foul' means rather than 'fair'. It merely cast doubts on the hard-and-fast distinction between fair play and cheating. If we want to sustain the distinction, we have to ignore the manifold advantages or disadvantages that derive from a person's physical and social background and which are beyond his or her power to change. We can attempt to get round this by isolating the element of choice and defining cheating only when a person has consciously and deliberately taken some action to gain advantage. This works up to a point if we cast aside doubts about the circumstances in which the decision was made. Again, backgrounds are important in influencing the decision. So the pedestal on which sport stands when it tries to display itself as a model of fair play is not quite as secure as it might at first seem. Not only are advantages dispensed virtually at birth, but they operate either to limit or liberate a person's ability to make choices.

Drugs are harmful to health. Sport's central philosophical point seems to be that, whatever people's backgrounds, if they are given the chance to gain advantages over others, they may fairly do so as long as they stop short of knowingly using chemical substances (at least *some* chemical substances). Most drugs used to enable or assist performance rather than gain advantage by enhancement are acceptable. So it was perfectly possible for British runner Peter Elliott to earn his 800 metres silver medal while being treated with a painkilling drug to alleviate a groin strain, while ten other competitors at the same Olympics were disqualified, two for using the diuretic pseudofurosemide (which *may* have been used to conceal anabolic steroids).

Some might counter the argument that supports ⁺his by saying that the ability to achieve anything at all in sport is limited by the body's natural early warning system – pain – and interfering with this is artificial and unnatural. 'But unlikely to cause any long-term damage in the user of certain painkillers' might be the riposte. To which the answer might be that there are other types of conditioning that do not include drugs, but which are detrimental to a performer's health. A good example of this might be the former gymnast, Olga Korbut, who in her early teens was a lovable urchin who charmed the world's tv viewers by her spellbinding displays, but who in her twenties was a haggard, arthritic anorexic. The effect on health of a great many banned drugs is negligible by comparison. Intensive training, controlled dieting, hypnotherapy, and 'psyching' techniques, as well as many more practices used by modern competitors may yet prove to have long-term consequences. Looking at monstrously distorted wrestlers, weightlifters, and body builders, whose training includes massive protein ingestion, one wonders what state of health many will have twenty years from now.

This has led some observers to believe that the use of drugs is no better or worse than some other aids to performance. They are certainly no worse than many of the drugs commonly available outside the world of sport and, obviously, tobacco and alcohol come into the reckoning as major factors in cancer and heart disease. Most sports frown on smoking and drinking too, though some, like motor racing and cricket, have been grateful for sponsorship from tobacco companies while others, like soccer, have been uncertain what position to take towards alcohol. Even everyday drugs, such as aspirin and antihistamine, which we presume to be innocuous, are not completely without potentially harmful consequences. Caffeine found in coffee and tea is mildly harmful, but who would dream of banning its general use? The argument that some drugs are more harmful than others has an *Animal Farm* logic to it and, as such, is fraught with inconsistencies. Even if some drugs were found to be dangerous (and steroids in particular are thought to be responsible for cancers and deaths) it would be something of an intrusion into the lives of responsible individuals to tell them not to take them.

Medical bodies are not averse to doing this as the campaigns, or more properly, the crusades of the British and American Medical Associations against boxing have shown. Prolonged involvement in boxing exposes the boxer to the risk of brain damage and many other less severe injuries, is the claim of the anti-boxing lobbyists. So boxers have to be protected, if necessary from themselves, in exactly the same way as any other sports competitors contemplating actions that may result in harm to their health. The effect on health of many banned drugs is small compared to that of boxing. But to make boxing illegal because of this presumes that all the young and physically healthy young men (and a few women in some parts of the world) are oblivious to the hazards of the sport when they enter. It assumes they are not rational, deliberating agents with some grasp of the implications of boxing – a grasp sufficient for them to do a cost-benefit calculation and weigh up the probable rewards against the probable losses.

Were information about the long-term consequences of boxing or drug use concealed, then the 'protectors' would have a very strong case. But the results of scientific tests are available and to assume that competitors are so witless as to know nothing of this is insulting and patronizing. If young people with a chance to capitalize on the sporting potential are informed of the dangers involved in their decision to pursue a line of action, then it is difficult to support a case for prohibiting this, at least in societies not prone to totalitarianism. Boxers may well judge the brain damage they risk in their sport preferable to the different kind of 'brain damage' they will almost certainly sustain in a repetitive industrial job over a 40-year period, or in an unbearably long spell put of work. Other sports performers with few prospects outside sport may evaluate their own positions similarly and, when the mephisophelean bargain presents itself, the decision of whether or not to box should be theirs. Unless, of course, one believes that superordinate moral agents should guide our thoughts and behaviour.

But the crudity and patronage of one argument doesn't license disingenuousness in the attack on it; which means that we should acknowledge that sports performers of whatever level do not reach decisions unaided. We have noted previously that all manner of influence bear on an individual's decision and, quite apart from those deriving from background, we have to isolate coaches and trainers. Bearing in mind the case of American football in the 1960s when coaches were assuming virtual medical status in dispensing drugs, we should remind ourselves of the important roles still played by these people in all sports. We must also realize that sport is populated by many 'Dr Feelgoods' who are only too happy to boost performance without necessarily informing the competitor of all the possible implications. It's quite probable that many competitors are doing things, taking things, even thinking things that may jeopardize their health. But do they know it? Perhaps sports authorities might attempt to satisfy themselves formally that all competitors in sports which do hold dangers are totally aware of them and comfortable about their involvement. This would remove the educational task from coaches and trainers and shift the onus onto governing organizations.

Drugs *are* harmful to health – as are many other things. Sports authorities quite properly communicate this, though the distinctions that are often made between harmful substances and activities and apparently innocuous ones are frequently arbitrary and difficult to support with compelling evidence. Further, the assumptions carried by governing bodies in their efforts to regulate the use of drugs can be seen in some lights as demeaning, suggesting that performers themselves are incapable of making assessments and decisions unassisted.

Sports performers are role models for the young. It follows that if athletes are known and seen to use drugs of any kind, then young people may be encouraged to follow. There is adequate evidence to support this and, while the substances which competitors use to enhance performance are often different to the ones that cause long-term distress at street-level, the very act of using drugs may work as a powerful example. But the argument can't be confined to sport: many rock musicians as well as writers and artists use drugs for relief or stimulus. Rock stars arguably wield more influence over young acolytes than the sports elite. The shaming of a sports performer found to have used drugs and the nullifying of his or her performance is a deterrent or a warning to the young: 'Do this and you will suffer the same fate.' But Pearl Jam isn't disgraced and the band's albums aren't taken from the charts if it's discovered that they recorded it while using coke. No one considers asking Pavarotti for a urine sample after one of his concerts. The music of Charlie Parker, a heroin addict, the acting of Cary Grant, who used LSD, the writing of Dylan Thomas, an alcoholic, all have not been obliterated; nor has the idolatry afforded them. Sports performers are different in the sense that they operate in and therefore symbolize a sphere where all is meant to be wholesome and pure. But this puts competitors under sometimes intolerable pressure to keep their haloes straight and maintain the pretence of being saints. Clearly, they are not, nor, given the competitive nature of sport, will they ever be. Gone are the days portrayed in

Chariots of Fire when winners were heroes to be glorified and losers were 'good sports' for competing.

Nowadays, hard cash has spoiled the purity. A yearning for money has introduced a limitless capacity for compromise and previously 'amateur' or 'shamateur' sports organizations, including the IOC, have led the way by embracing commercialism rather than spurning it. Competitors too are creatures of a competitive world and probably more preoccupied with struggling to win than with keeping a clean image.

These then are the main reasons why governing bodies have sought to eliminate drugs from sport and discredit those found using them. Yet the opposing school of thought has advanced its argument quite simply on two grounds. The first ground is practical and involves recognizing that drugs are part of modern sport and whatever attempts are made to extirpate them, ways and means will be found. In a decade's time, it is possible that there will be no way of preventing competitors from taking drugs which does not involve prison-like supervision in training as well as competition: inspection, invigilation, regulation, and punishment would become features of sport.

The second ground is a moral one and involves bringing into the debate the people who are least frequently consulted – the performers. Peter Corrigan of *The Observer*, writing on the positive test of 1988 Tour de France winner, Pedro Delgado, observed that none of the other 180 competitors had protested at Delgado's infringement or showed any disinclination to continue to race with him. Corrigan suggested that the demands of the race itself were so great that drugs were essential and that cyclists should be allowed to make up their own minds on whether or not to use them. This harkens back to my previous point about the appropriate assumptions organizations hold about performers. Were they to be seen as able, reasoning, and aware humans equipped with up-to-date information on drugs, then it's possible that we could safely leave the big decisions to them, as Corrigan suggested.

It's quite possible that many would object to drugs, but it is also possible that many would object to those elite performers who can afford to employ a staff of doctors and nutritionists and use only permitted drugs. It's possible that some might object to the use of blatant pace-makers in track events, for they are only of service to specific athletes. Maybe they wouldn't see steroid-pumped sprinters as mere projectiles fuelled by drugs, but as athletes so utterly committed to pursuing excellence that they are prepared to rip apart the limits of their own frame to run faster than others. It would be useful to know what competitors thought. This is not an argument designed to satisfy purists, but it is certainly a cogent one and one wonders why sports organizations, in particular the IOC, haven't paused to consider it. Instead they have gone headlong down the road of regulation and punishment, spending millions of dollars on test centres all over the world in a campaign that borders on the obsessive. In the process, the mystique of drugs is enlarged, convincing sports performers that drugs do enhance performance, when, in fact they only *may*. Richard Nicholson, editor of the *Institute of Medical Ethics Bulletin*, has for a long time, through his journal, suggested that the main benefit of drugs is a placebo effect – that psychologically competitors expect an improvement in performance and produce it. In other words, inert substances can affect improvements if only the user believes in their efficacy. Banning drugs makes them appear more useful than they probably are and so makes them more attractive and ultimately more effective.

Why then has sport committed inordinate amounts of money to the control of drugs? We have considered the more conventional and predictable reasons for the hard line against drugs. We have also exposed some of the ambiguities and even contradictions in these. Against these reasons, there is what seems a practical and morally-sound case for legitimizing drugs in sport. It seems insufficient to argue that sport benefits from purging itself of drugs; this may be so in an ideal world, but in reality, the concept is vague and unspecific. Exactly who or what in sport benefits? Were we to approach the question cynically, we might cast eyes outside sport and isolate beneficiaries who have no formal position on drugs in sport, but stand to profit very handsomely from the current attack on drugs. The companies supplying the equipment used for testing clearly have vested interests in the attempts of the IOC and other organizations. They have the technology without which those attempts are worthless. For the campaign on drugs to be in any degree successful, detective technologies will have to keep pace with ingenious chemists. This is an expensive business. The 1988 laboratory cost the IOC $3 million from Hewlett-Packard. Future centres are to cost more. Drug testing in sport is set to become a virtual industry in itself. The cost of drug testing represents a multimillion dollars outflow from sport into private industry. Clearly, someone is profiting. Perhaps it is sport – if it can successfully instigate a return to its glorious past. This is unlikely. But while it tries, big business will stand by and applaud its stance, pausing only to prepare its next colossal invoice.

This is but one facet of an alliance between sport and business that has developed over the past several decades. Many nowadays go further than calling it an alliance: sport *is* big business, they would argue. Next, we'll consider the argument.

Further reading

Living with Drugs *by Michael Glossop (Temple Smith, 1982; Ashgate, 1994) is a calm and detached analysis of drugs and their misuse in modern society by a psychologist who is clearly not convinced that the effects of drugs are solely due to the substances themselves. In other words, Glossop looks at the influences on drug taking, not only the placebo effect, but the range of other factors that surround drugs and make them attractive.*

Drugs in Sport *edited by D. Mottram (E. & F. N. Spon, 1988) is, as its title suggests, a specialist text designed for those seeking a detailed account of drug use in sport. It is a useful source book.*

'Becoming a marijuana user' *by Howard Becker (in* American Journal of Sociology, *vol. 59, 1953) has become something of a classic article on drug use. In a sociological perspective, the article describes the cultural aspects of drug use: how one actually learns the methods of taking drugs, interprets their effects and generally experiences drug taking. Its relevance to sport is in highlighting how cultural contexts (e.g. in athletics) can commission drug taking and provide a frame of reference for understanding the results.*

'Sports and drugs' by Martyn Lucking (in Sport, Culture and Ideology, *edited by J. Hargreaves, Routledge & Kegan Paul, 1982) provides the recent background to drug use in sport and the effects of drugs on athletic performance. The article is useful on a factual level but concludes embarrasingly: 'I anticipate that the 1980s may well see a virtual elimination of the current widespread use'!*